Pass the PMP Exa

A Practical Guide to Project Management Principles: Training for Success

Dr. Jack D. Harpool PMP
S. Spagnola MPW

Jack D. Harpool

PhD, PMP

Author and Course Lecturer

Pass the PMP Exam Manual – A Practical Guide to Project Management Principles: Training for Success

Dr Jack D. Harpool, PMP, is the Founder and CEO of Global Project Management Information Systems Services, which has been in business for over a decade, and a certified Project Management Professional (PMP).

In 2005, Dr. Harpool, a Senior Program Manager and other associates were responsible for implementing Hospital and Long-Term Care Management Information Systems in New York and in Ohio, with project work valued at $20 to $25 + million dollars.

Dr. Harpool is also a certified Construction Project Manager (bonded with contractor license) and Chief Executive Officer, owner and developer of Greensburg Opportunity Park Self Storage (www.greenselfstorage.com) located in North Canton Ohio.

Dr. Harpool has served as a consultant both to the Federal Government and to commercial businesses, Ashland University and worked as a Senior Plans and Operations Information Technology (IT) Consultant to the Pentagon with a Top Level Secret Security Clearance and for the Under - Secretary of the US Army, Department of Defense on numerous, special classified IT projects.

Dr. Harpool taught at Ashland University (2008-2015) in the MBA area of *Project Management* and is the author of six (6) publications, which include *Systems Analysis and Design Projects* (Times Mirror/Mosby Collette Publishing), and *Business Data Systems: A Practical Guide* (Wm. C. Brown Publishers and Company), used at over 350 United States and international universities. While at Ashland University, he designed, developed and instructed the *MBA Project Management Distance Learning* (internet) core specialization curricula. These courses were quality assured, by the University of Maryland in their Quality Matters Program and were taught in the classroom, online and in a hybrid version. The Project Management Institute (PMI) evaluated these courses and the courseware. As a result, Ashland University received an award of most coveted status as a Global Registered Education Provider (REP) for your Project Management Professional, PMP training.

A graduate of the University of Akron with an earned PhD and a graduate of the US Army Command and General Staff College, Dr. Harpool retired as an Army Reserve Officer at the rank of Lieutenant Colonel.

Sheri Spagnola
MPW

Pass the PMP Exam Manual –
A Practical Guide to Project Management Principles: Training for Success

Sheri graduated in 2013, with a Master in Professional Writing, MPW. She has been a freelance Technical Writer for the past five years and has written articles, grants, patronage letters, a business math course and RFP's, as well as designing editing and creating promotional literature for Le Radici, Petrosino Wellbeing Foundation, Firestone, Diamond Elite Sports, SBN, Kent State Stark Writing Center and others. She also served one year as Co-Editor of the *Writing Center Review* at Kent State Stark University. At the same time, she compiled, marketed and lectured on topics for writing workshops at Stark State College of Technology as well as conducting speaking engagements at 2nd April Art Gallery.

This is her second collaboration with the highly talented team at Global Project Management Information System Services and her second co-authorship with Jack Harpool PhD, Project Management Professional PMP.

Favorite Quote: "The more I learn, the more I realize I don't know" – Albert Einstein

Start:

Before you take the PMI Exam: Click on the following link:

Anytime you see this camera symbol it depicts useful links (URL)'s to information related to the specific subject matter

Check out the infographic located at the following link:
http://links.pmi.mkt6308.com/servlet/MailView?ms=MzQyMzkyNjYS1&r=MzA3MzI1NDY0OTI3S0&j=MTQwMzI4MTMwMAS2&mt=2&rj=MTQwMzI4MTI5OQS2&rt=0

Scroll down within the infographic and click on and review the articles under the two buttons labeled *Roadmap for Rookies and Ready to Accelerate.*

Study for the PMP Exam by reviewing the following link:
https://globalproject.management/lesson/how-to-prepare-for-the-pmp-exam/

Grow:

Preface

A Practical Guide to Project Management Principles: Training for Success is intended as a companion text to the Global Project Management Information System Services (GPMISS) online lecture series,

GLOBAL PROJECT.MANAGEMENT www.globalproject.management

The purpose of this guide/manual is to help decode the principles of the (*PMBOK® Guide*) – Sixth Edition, Project Management Institute Inc., 2017. This manual can also be purchased in an e-book form. This text can also be used in colleges and universities at the graduate level. Please contact Ben at ben.rinehart@globalproject.management for licensing fee rates.

For those intending to sit for any of the PMI exams, what makes this manual different from others is the explicit information detailed with outlines, charts, graphs, etc., contained within. Page numbering takes place throughout and is meant to make the data easier to look up and highlight if necessary, regardless of the platform being used.

This manual is set up so that you, as the reader, are able to skip to whatever chapter needs reinforcement as it parallels the layout and format of the (*PMBOK® Guide*) – Sixth Edition.

Details of each chapter include a legend to verify any/all attributions and Student Learning objectives that are included at the beginning of each chapter. After reading each chapter, there is a corresponding summary at the end of the chapter that explains and answers each facet of the Student Learning Outcomes.

Part II, the Standard for Project Management is also included in this text.

In this manual, each chapter is divided into sections as follows:

Introduction Overview
Student Learning Objectives
Chapter Keywords
PMBOK Details Section
Answers to Student Learning Objectives
Chapter Questions that may be on the PMI Exam

<u>Example for Chapter 5:</u>

Chapter 5, Project Scope Management, Introduction Overview
Chapter 5, Project Scope Management, Student Learning Objectives
Chapter 5, Project Scope Management, Chapter Keywords
Chapter 5, Project Scope Management, Answers to Student Learning Objectives
Chapter 5, Project Scope Management, Questions that may be on the PMI Exam

Go:

PMP® Exam Prep Self-Guided

Project Management Syllabus Index:

Global Project Management Information System Services

Project Management Syllabus
Pass the PMP® Exam
Pass the CAPM® Exam

Project Management
Course Code: GPMISS101
Contact Hours: 40

Instructor: Jack D. Harpool, Ph.D., PMP

Identification of Training Needs:

According to PMI®, there is a dynamic and growing need for Certified Project Managers throughout the world. These needs are exemplified by companies that need professional instruction and training so that their personnel can be certified. The *PMBOK® Guide* 6th Edition is PMI®'s guide to Initiating, Planning, Executing, Monitoring and Controlling, and Closing project work. Global Project Management (www.globalproject.management) is offering the PMBOK101 course to satisfy this training need.

According to PMI's Pulse of the Nation between 2010 and 2020, 15.7 million new project management roles will be created globally, across seven project-intensive industries including Manufacturing, Finance & Insurance, Information Services, Utilities, Business Services, Oil & Gas and Construction (Project Management Institute) all while reaching an economic impact of over $18 trillion. Training needs are identified by meeting PMI®'s "Project Management Professional" (PMP®) standards. This is found in the Content Outline showing how to pass the PMP® exam, which will be discussed in this syllabus.

The PMI Talent Triangle shown below highlights the numerous skills that employers value the most. They are: Leadership, Technical Management, and Strategic and Business Management. PMI®'s Continuing Certification Requirements (CCR) will emphasize these skills. Our program of study includes many highlights of these skill areas. These areas are stressed in and through our on line "Pass the PMP® Exam" program of instruction.

PMI Talent Triangle™

Obtaining, Continuing Certification Requirements (CCR), called, PDU's, (Professional Development Units), begins after the PMP® exam has been passed. After you pass your PMP® exam, you will need to earn 60 PDU (Professional Development Units) every 3 years to maintain your PMP® credentials. More information is available regarding this in a separate document.

Explanation of PMI® Talent Triangle:

Skill Area	Definition
Technical	Knowledge, skills and behaviors related to specific domains of project, program and portfolio management. The technical aspects of performing one's job/role.
Leadership	Knowledge, skills, and behaviors involved in the ability to guide, motivate and/or direct other to achieve a goal.
Strategic and Business Management	Knowledge of and expertise in the industry/organization, helping you align your team in a way that enhances performance and better delivers business outcomes.

Who should Attend: Pass the PMP® Exam?

- Project Managers
- Team Members
- Project Leaders
- Project and Design Engineers
- Program Managers

- Operations Managers
- Functional Managers

Download: PMI PMP® Exam Content Outline
The PMP® exam outline, found in the link on next page, emphasizes the project management domains, tasks, knowledge and skill areas that are to be tested. It further identifies the exam content which shows the proportion of exam questions that will appear on the PMP® exam. These domains include process areas called:

- Initiating (13%)
- Planning (24%)
- Executing (31%)
- Monitoring and Controlling (25%)
- Closing (7%)
- Total 100%

Additionally, the PMP® exam content details and outlines:

- performance domain 1 Initiating
- performance domain 2 Planning
- performance domain 3 Executing
- performance domain 4 Monitoring and Controlling
- performance domain 5 Closing

Download Examination Content Outline:

Click Here to Download (External Link from PMI)

Dr. Jack Harpool's On Line PMP Prep course video lectures emphasize these areas and should be reviewed before studying the actual PMBOK 6th edition videos. Please refer to the necessary continuing education requirements, located at https://globalproject.management/lesson/continuing-education-requirements/

Course Materials (Required/Optional Text and Materials):

1. A Guide to the Project Management Body of Knowledge, 6th Edition (*PMBOK®Guide*), Project Management Institute **(required text)** ISBN: 978-1-62825-184-5
   - *PMBOK Guide*®, Sixth Edition (PDF) is available for download to all PMI® Members for free. You need to login to the PMI® website with your PMI® user ID/Password, to download the PDF. The file is password protected. When you try

to open the file, it will prompt you for a password. In order to open the file, you need to enter your PMI® (www.pmi.org) password.

- Be sure to purchase a hard copy at www.amazon.com or www.PMI.org. You will be recording your notes as you listen to Dr. Harpool's PMBOK® 6th Edition on line PMP Prep videos.

2. Q & As for the *PMBOK® Guide* 6th edition. **(required text):** Contributors: Alton, Anbari, Holdcraft, Hseih, Johnson, Wu and Souza). Go to www.PMI.org. This text can also be found online. These are sample PMP® Exam Questions to assist in your preparation for each section (i.e., chapter) of the PMBOK Guide.

3. Project Management for Information, Technology, Business and Certification: Gopal K. Kapur- **(optional text).** This is a Pearson Prentice Hall Publication. Go to www.amazon.com to purchase this optional text. This is a classic text consisting of numerous Project Management ideas, concepts and applications. It can be used as a reference book.

4. Dr. Jack Harpool videos that emphasize Passing the PMP® Exam are located at www.globalproject.management . Instructions will be provided on this website.

5. *Pass the PMP Manual-A Practical Guide to Project Management Principles: Training for Success student manual* **(optimal text)** at www.globalproject.management. This manual may be purchased at www.amazon.com and is authored by Dr. Jack Harpool along with Sheri Spagnola. It is organized with each manual chapter found in the same structure as the *PMBOK® Guide 6th Edition.* There is also an **e-version to be available**.

   Each chapter begins with **student learning objectives** (in the form of Questions) followed by a chapter overview, key words and then the chapter details follow. The chapter ends with a chapter summary. The summary provides **answers to the very helpful student learning objectives** (questions)

6. What are the eligibility requirements for PMP® certification? These requirements can be found at www.PMI.org.

   a. The PMP® certification requirements for both college graduates and non-graduates are cited in the table below:

Educational Qualifications	Project Management Experience	Project Management Education
Non-College Graduates	5 years/7500 hours	35 hours
College Graduates	3 years/4500 hours	35 hours

Downloads to Review

7. **CAPM® Certification Handbook**

If you are working towards the CAPM® certification, you may use the **Pass your PMP Exam** educational material as well. The Certified Associate Project Management, document covers

1. How to use the CAPM® Certification handbook
2. About PMI®'s Certification Program
3. Overview of CAPM® Credentials
4. CAPM® Certification application and payment
5. PMI® Audit Process
6. CAPM® recertification
7. CAPM® Examination Policies and Procedures
8. Certification Policies and Procedures
9. PMI® Code of Ethics and Professional Conduct
10. PMI® Certification Application/Renewal Agreement

8. **Continuing Certification Requirements Handbook**

This material should be reviewed to maintain your PMP® credentials after you pass your PMP exam. Recall you need 60 PDUs every 3 years. CCR Certification Requirements Handbook covers;

1. How to us the Continuing Certification Requirements (CCR) Handbook
2. CCR Program Overview
3. CCR Requirements
4. CCR Process
5. Explanation of Professional Development Units
6. Certification renewal fees and policies
7. How to maintain multiple PMI® certifications
8. Certification Status
9. Transition to the updated CCR Program

9. **Project Management Professional (PMP®) Examination Content Outline**

   This document explains the content of the PMP® certification exam cited above. Project Management Professional (PMP®) Examination Content Outline stresses;

   1. Introduction to the document
   2. Exam content outline
   3. Domains, Tasks, and Knowledge and Skill Statements
   4. Initiating, Planning, Executing, Monitoring & Controlling and Closing
   5. Cross Cutting Knowledge and Skills
   6. Role Delineation Study (RDS) Process

   Please refer to the necessary continuing education requirements, located at https://globalproject.management/lesson/continuing-education-requirements/. The online prep course provides a video explanation of the PMP Exam content outline.

10. **IMPORTANT NOTICE: These are errata sheets i.e. corrections to the PMBOK® Guide 6th Edition- Errata 3rd printing.**

    You should print out these errata sheets, as there is a need to refer to these errata sheets **before viewing** the Pass the PMP Exam on line videos. These are minor editorial changes that PMI made to the text and figures after the initial text publication. You may update (pen and pencil) your **manual** and with the errata sheets information. The videos do not reflect these corrections. You should not worry about the editorial details, as you view Dr. Harpool's videos. Thank you for this consideration!

    https://www.pmi.org/pmbok-guide-standards/foundational/pmbok/errata-sheets

11. **These free Center of Disease Control templates** are standard Project Management documents, used in many business as is or modified. They are useful for doing Project Management work. They are provided as guidance and may be referenced in your **Pass the PMP® Exam videos**. Please consider printing these sample templates and having them available before reviewing Dr. Jack Harpool's videos.

12. **Understand and apply PMI®'s Code of Ethics and Professional Conduct** located at https://www.pmi.org/learning/library/project-managers-code-of-ethics-10343.

Course Description:

Based upon the Project Management Institute's (PMI®) standards and resource material, this online course PMBOK101 stresses professional development activities, coupled with academic principles in the practice and Passing of the PMP® Exam.

This course provides an overview of the Knowledge Areas and Processes Groupings of modern Project Management. These processes were cited earlier. The Knowledge Areas emphasized includes: Project Integration Management, Project Scope Management, Project Time Management, Project Cost Management, Project Quality Management, Project Human Resource Management, Project Communications Management, Project Risk Management, Project Procurement Management, Project Stakeholder Management.

The PMI® Process groups (i.e. Initiating Process Group, Planning Process Group, Execute Process Group, Monitoring and Controlling Process Group and Closing Process Group) are emphasized.

The course will also cover common project management tools like precedence diagramming, work break down structures, risk analysis and earned value analysis, etc. Additionally, managing projects from start to finish will be professionally emphasized in a real-world environment.

Course Content:

This course discusses a broad area of topics and factors necessary for understanding the (*PMBOK® Guide* 6th edition).

Characteristics and barriers of effective and ineffective teams will be stressed in handling conflict, problem resolution and effective time management etc. Project Communication and Documentation will include Status Reporting, handling of Project Meetings etc.

Various topics include: project management key concepts, trends and emerging practices, tailoring considerations, considerations for **Agile/Adaptive** environments, business case development, defining the project, significance of a project charter, communication plans, and other subsidiary plans are discussed.

The project manager's role in leadership, team development, project organization structures, project planning, scheduling and executing, control and maintaining costs and business value will also be emphasized.

Student Learning Outcomes:

Students will learn the specialized body of knowledge presented in the *PMBOK® Guide* 6th edition.

At the conclusion of this on-line course, the student should be able to pass all online prep exams for each PMBOK® chapter by scoring a minimum of 80% found within the video framework: This course is unique and totally unlike other PMP prep courses in that Dr. Harpool has designed this course with an integrated practical PMP and (*Pass the PMP Exam®* Manual) prep course, coupled with (Dr. Harpool's videos) academic track. You learn how to pass the PMP Exam with video chapter exam alerts. And you learn how to run projects from the start to the end of the project

- Define and understand the Project and Product Life Cycles and compare it to the Project Management Process Groups.
- Define 5 Process Groups and 10 Knowledge Areas: See *PMBOK® Guide* Table 1-4 page 25.

Project Management Framework: PMBOK 6th Ed. Chapter 1-3

- Describe project management terminology and definitions by listening to the online video of **Definitions-Glossary Terms** PMBOK 6th edition P 698 – 726. There are over **400 definitions** that will aid you in using project management terms, jargon and buzz words.
- Differentiate between project, program, portfolio and operations management
- Describe various life cycle approaches
- Describe EEFs (Enterprise Environmental Factors) and OPAs (Organizational Process Assets)
- Define and describe Project Manager leadership skills, techniques and other competencies

Project Integration Management – PMBOK 6th Ed. Chapter 4

- Define Project and Program Boundaries - Statement of Work (SOW), Project Charter and various Deliverables etc.
- Develop and understand the sections of a standard Project Charter by applying various tools and techniques.

Sample Project Charter is provided. Refer to ABC Project Charter sample videos by Dr. Harpool. located at *ABC Academy Daycare Center,* (14:39 minutes) https://globalproject.management/lesson/abc-daycare-project-charter-example/

Project Stakeholder Management- Project Scope Management- Project Schedule Management- Project Cost Management – Project Resource Management – Project Quality Management – Project Risk Management – Project Communications Management – Project Procurement Management – PMBOK 6th Edition Chapters 5 - 13

- Describe the importance of a Project Management Plan and select the subsidiary plan(s) needed for a specific project
- Manage all project knowledge areas and process groups (initiate, plan, direct, manage, monitor, control and close project work or phase)
- Describe the importance of Customer requirements and how they are met as the project evolves from its start to its completion. This is called progressive elaboration.
- Be able to explain the significance and value of a Project Charter, Project Management Plan, Project Subsidiary Plans, Work Breakdown Structures (WBS), Network Diagram, Risk Register, Project Communication Plan, Formulas for Earned Value Systems etc.
- Select the proper tool(s) and technique(s) and process(es) to plan and create outputs for Integration, Stakeholder, Scope, Schedule, Costs, Resources, Risk, Communications, Risk and Procurement Management work See Chapters 5 - 13.
- Know how to estimate time, resource utilization and cost factors when undertaking a Project.
- Define levels of Project Risks, evaluate Risk response alternatives and control mitigation techniques
- Describe the responsibilities and skills of an effective Project Manager in motivating the Project Team.
- Identify the components of Communicating Project Status and Documentation at all management levels.
  Embedded online PMP like Exams—See Student Assessment Criteria
- If you have not achieved a passing grade of 80% in this material, please review any of the educational material so that you are prepared to take your PMP® exam.

Student Assessment Criteria:

In order to, Pass the PMP® Exam, there will be simulated exams and quizzes, embedded throughout the educational material and available to the online student.

Each student is responsible for all assigned readings in the (*PMBOK® Guide,* 6th Edition), (GPMISS) *Pass the PMP Exam®* Manual, and Q&A for the *PMBOK® Guide* 6th Edition and to listen to all the Pass **the PMP Exam videos**.

The specific Student Learning Outcomes identified above will be assessed throughout the PMP® type exam questions and video instruction. To pass the sample PMP® exam questions and quizzes a student must maintain an 80% exam grade average. If the student does not attain an 80% grade he/she will not be allowed to continue listening to the next PMBOK® chapter video until the grade is remediated. This is done by reviewing the material again. Repetition is learning.

Teaching Methodology:

This course is a critical thinking course. Therefore, a substantial portion of the video session material and exam grade scores will be based upon **project management thinking** that causes the student to do more than rote memorization. The student will learn how to look beyond the obvious and understand the underlying principles. This is especially within the ITTO (Inputs, Tools and Techniques and Outputs) sections found within the Knowledge Areas.

Schedule: Passing the PMP Exam material in 6 to 12 weeks

If you are willing to adhere to a 6 to 12-week schedule, we suggest that you study and complete all of our online materials. This includes reading the complete *PMBOK® Guide* 6th Edition, (*Pass the PMP Exam*® Manual), viewing all of Dr. Harpool's videos and taking all suggested exams and quizzes.

You must follow this schedule by completing each weekly assignment.

Please download the schedule file as shown in the syllabus. Click on camera icon below.

The file is located in this syllabus under Schedule: Passing the PMP Exam

Assignments (Videos, PMP Prep Exams, etc.):

Each student is responsible for all assigned *PMBOK® Guide* 6th Edition exams, video content and manual.

Certificate of Completion

Participation and completing the entire course with an 80% pass rate is required to receive a **Certificate of Completion**. This certificate of completion should assure the student that he/she will pass the PMP® Exam. A weekend WebEx session(s) may be periodically held to answer student questions and help you pass the PMP® exam.

Applying for a PMI® Membership:

Each student enrolled in the PMBOK101 course material should apply for PMI® membership **before taking** our "Pass the PMP Exam" material.
Visit www.pmi.org to find the membership application:
The following steps are to be followed when applying for PMI® Membership.

PMI Membership Application Steps

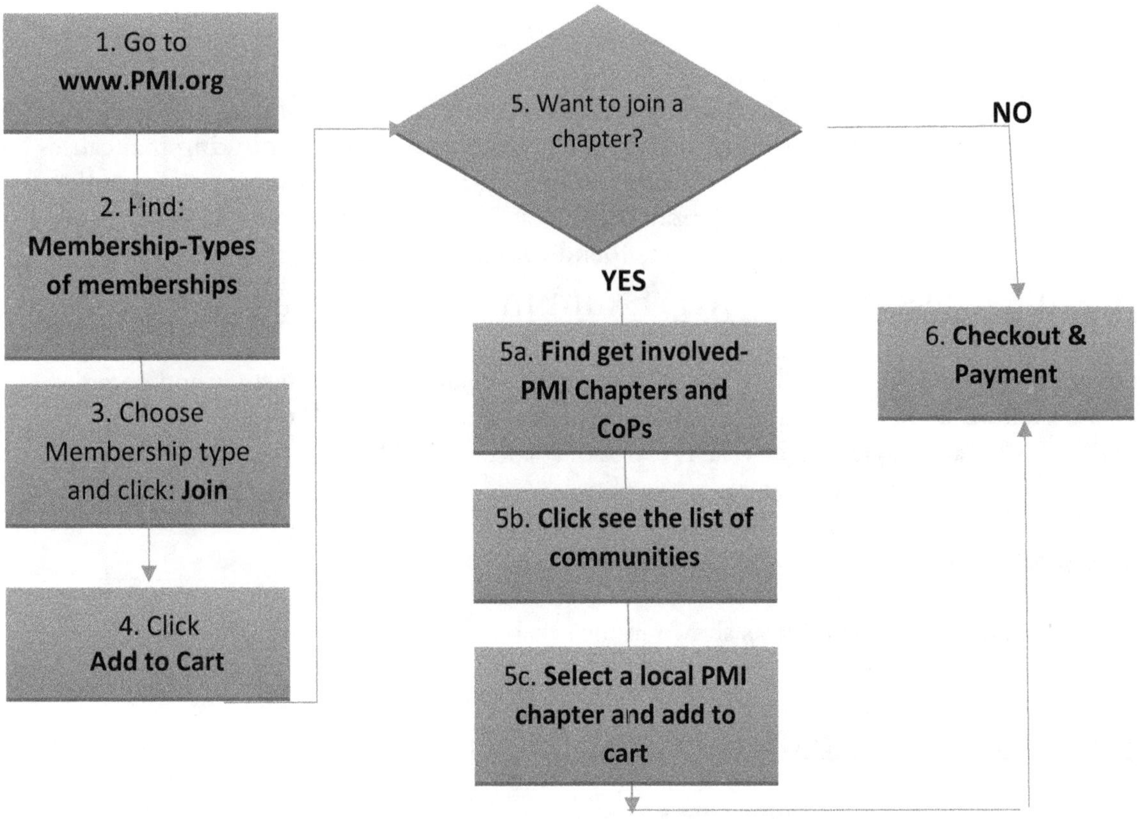

<u>Types of Memberships and Costs:</u>

Individual Membership:	$129 to join (plus $10 application fee) $129 renewal
Student Membership:	$32 to join $32 to renew
Retiree Membership:	$65 to renew

You are now ready to enroll in the **Pass the PMP Exam**.

Please visit www.globalproject.management and login to access your online course.

Thank You and Contact Information

Thank you for choosing to sign up for our course. We take your feedback seriously. If you have any questions, comments, or questions during your time taking this course, please reach out to the below contacts. Please specify your issue or questions in as much detail as possible. Also, please also remember to cite your name, your country, the name of this course (GPMISS 101) in the subject and/or body of your email.

For questions related to this course, please contact:

Enrollment and Course Guidance

Jackie Misja (jackie.misja@globalproject.management)

Issues/Questions Related to Course Material

Jack Harpool (jack.harpool@globalproject.management)

Global Project Management Information System Services (GPMISS) HAS PARTNERED WITH TESTUDAAN, which is located at www.testudaan.com. Our gratitude is extended to them for the use of their more than 3600 PMP-like exam questions found at their website.

Testudaan is the **PMP Exam Simulator** with a large question bank of simulated, knowledge areas and process groups' tests, updated regularly to align with the latest PMBOK. These questions were created to make sure that the questions align to the latest pattern of real life PMP exam questions.

The six (6) areas shown below can be found at the www.testudaan.com site.

1. **PROCESS GROUP**

   Exams for all Process Groups (Initiating, Planning, Executing, Monitoring and Controlling and Closing).

2. **RESULT ANALYSIS**

   Provides an in-depth review of your test results in the practice exam, so you know your areas in which you need improvement.

3. **PREPARE REALISTIC**

   Exams that provide you with a real feel of the actual PMP Exam and prepare you for the actual exam environment.

4. **MARK FOR REVIEW**

   The **mark for review** button is a feature that marks a question for later review.

5. **EMAIL REPORT**

   You can send a summary of your exam report to your email for your own personal record keeping.

6. **PAUSE EXAM**

   Students can also pause the exam and re-start at a later time. This option is not available in the real PMP exam.

Be focused!

The 5/25 Rule

If you want to pass the PMP, focus your priorities and the execution of tasks without distraction. See *Warren Buffet's 5/25 Rule will help you focus on what Matters*, (6:25 minutes) at https://youtu.be/gkhtYs22bLI

Also see, *Five (5) Quick Steps to becoming a PMP*, can be found at https://globalproject.management/lesson/5-quick-steps-for-becoming-a-pmp/

None of the information contained in this manual reduces the need to read the (*PMBOK® Guide)* – Sixth Edition, Project Management Institute Inc., 2017.

A helpful PMP preparation schedule shown on the next page is useful for exam planning purposes.

Start - Grow - Go

You may complete the instructional material in as little as six (6) weeks. You can devise your own flexible schedule for success around your own personal preference or professional responsibilities.

You may complete the instructional material in as little as six (6) weeks. You can devise your own flexible schedule for success around your own personal preference or professional responsibilities.

Link to Sample Video shown below:
https://globalproject.management/course/pmp-exam-prep-self-guided-6th-edition/

- RECOMMENDED SCHEDULE FOR SUCCESS -

SIX (6) EFFECTIVE STUDY TIPS TO HELP PASS THE PMP EXAM PREP

6 Week Schedule	12 Week Schedule	Reading/ Videos	Assignments
WEEK 1	WEEK 1		1. **Signup** – For the PMP 2. **Signup** – As a PMI Member 3. **Read** – 2 x 3 – PMBOK Guide 6th Edition 4. **Read** – Table of Contents – PMBOK Guide 6th Edition 5. **Signup** – For the TestUdaan Test Simulator
WEEK 2	WEEK 2	**Read** – PMBOK Chapter 1 **Watch** – Harpool GPM Chapter 1 **Read** – "Pass the PMP Manual" Chapter 1	Complete Prep Course Chapter 1
	WEEK 3	**Read** – PMBOK Chapter 2 – 3 **Watch** – Harpool Videos Chapter 2 – 3 **Read** – "Pass the PMP Manual" Chapter 2 – 3	Complete Prep Course Chapter 2 – 3
WEEK 3	WEEK 4	**Read** – PMBOK Chapter 4 **Watch** – Harpool GPM Chapter 4 **Read** – "Pass the PMP Manual" Chapter 4	Complete Prep Course Chapter 4
	WEEK 5	**Read** – PMBOK Chapter 5 – 6 **Watch** – Harpool GPM Chapter 5 – 6 **Read** – "Pass the PMP Manual" Chapter 5 – 6	Complete Prep Course Chapter 5 – 6
WEEK 4	WEEK 6	**Read** – PMBOK Chapter 7 **Watch** – Harpool GPM Chapter 7 **Read** – "Pass the PMP Manual" Chapter 7	Complete Prep Course Chapter 7
	WEEK 7	**Read** – PMBOK Chapter 8 – 9 **Watch** – Harpool GPM Chapter 8 – 9 **Read** – "Pass the PMP Manual" Chapter 8 – 9	Complete Prep Course Chapter 8 – 9
WEEK 5	WEEK 8	**Read** – PMBOK Chapter 10 **Watch** – Harpool GPM Chapter 10 **Read** – "Pass the PMP Manual" Chapter 10	Complete Prep Course Chapter 10
	WEEK 9	**Read** – PMBOK Chapter 11 – 12 **Watch** – Harpool GPM Chapter 11 – 12 **Read** – "Pass the PMP Manual" Chapter 11 – 12	Complete Prep Course Chapter 11 – 12
	WEEK 10	**Read** – PMBOK Chapter 13 **Watch** – Harpool GPM Chapter 13 **Read** – "Pass the PMP Manual" Chapter 13	Complete Prep Course Chapter 13 Annex A1
WEEK 6	WEEK 11	**Review** – All Material (videos, manual, exam questions, and PMBOK Guide 6th Edition	
	WEEK 12	**Review** – All material again **Rest** – For a few days **Signup** – To Take the PMP Exam with PMI	

COURSE

When preparing for any of the PMP certifications, **Study Tips** are an all important factor. There are many **study tips** for you to use. Other useful materials can be found on our website: www.globalproject.management.

1. **GET COMFORTABLE**: Only you know what makes you comfortable. Experiment with different locations. Do you need complete quiet, or do you prefer music in the background? What about scenery? Is outdoors best, or does indoors provide a respite from unpredictable weather conditions? Perhaps a little of each type on occasion helps to relieve pressure. Whatever you choose, get comfortable.

2. **ASSIGN YOUR TIME**: Keep to a schedule as best you can. Do you study better in the morning for half an hour after a cup of tea or coffee? What about small bites of time on your lunch break? Do longer stretches. Try 30 minutes to an hour in the evening so you can sleep on the information.

3. **REPETITION IS KEY**: Read all the study materials; then read them again. On the third try, skim the information; then, mentally test yourself on small details. Or, reverse this process, skim first, then, go for the details. Try dividing your study time in increments by assigning each section a set amount of time. When you have gone over each section in detail, start at the beginning and work your way through again. Chances are you will learn something new each time.

4. **KNOW YOUR TERMINOLOGY**: All definitions can be found in *(PMBOK® Guide)* – Sixth Edition), Glossary 695-726. These can make great flashcards. Terminology and definitions are explained on Dr. Harpool's online videos, *Pass the PMP Exam Prep Course* located at www.globalproject.management

5. **FOCUS ONLY ON WHAT YOU NEED TO KNOW:** Prepare for the exam by learning what will be on the exam and that which requires your utmost attention. Then focus on your weakest areas by using the pre-test on www.globalproject.management. The exam simulator in our course can be used for this assessment.

6. **EQUATIONS and PLAN TITLES**: As with terminology, **you need to study and memorize each section title and any related documents**. Equations are a bit trickier. You will not be asked to memorize all of them, but you will need to know some of them. You may look up the most common ones and start from there. Either way, there will be PMI Exam questions related to equations found in (A Guide to the Project Management Body of Knowledge (*PMBOK® Guide*) – Sixth Edition). See Table 7-1, P 267, *Earned Value Calculations Summary.*

The authors of this manual have included information links, so you are able to really appreciate the practical job context within which you may be doing **real project management work.** These information links are intended to make the PMBOK more realistic and interesting as you study the main manual material. This is your professional development track.

NOTE: This linked material will not be found in the PMP exam that you are preparing to take and you are not compelled to open the information links. But, they will enrich your reading of this manual and can make the subject matter come alive. Additionally, there may be points made in the link that can trigger your recall of PMBOK facts to better sensitize you when you take the real PMP exam.

Good luck in your studies! Think Success! Think Success! Think Success!

You may want to check out the article, *Photos: The 10 Best Places to Get Work Done Outside of the Office,* by Macey Bayern.
https://www.techrepublic.com/pictures/photos-the-10-best-places-to-get-work-done-outside-of-the-office/

Remember, everyone learns best in their own way. See the next page for six different types of learning styles and see what works for you. It could be a combination of several learning styles. See the next page.

SIX (6) TYPES OF LEARNING STYLES

TO HELP PASS THE PMP EXAM PREP COURSE

7. **VISUAL LEARNERS**: Use our online video lectures and visual study aids, such as charts, diagrams and online glossary or key terminology.

8. **AUDITORY LEARNERS**: Use our online video lectures or record your own key concepts and listen as you do other tasks.

9. **TACTILE LEARNERS**: Must feel the process. Some suggestions are to use flashcards, or a touch phone to access our lectures and other materials, which can be found at our site, www.globalproject.management.

10. **SOCIAL LEARNERS**: Form a study group. Be engaged with like-minded others while you study and discuss PMBOK chapter material.

1. **SEQUENTIAL LEARNERS**: Learn as you go. Retain the information in detail. Then move on.

2. **BIG PICTURE LEARNERS**: Needs to know the overall outcome, the lay of the land first, and then focus on the details.

See the next page for some helpful mnemonic study aids.

TEN (10) MNEMONICS STUDY AIDS TO HELP PASS THE PMP EXAM PREP COURSE

Most people will find that a mixture of learning styles work best. Listed below are some categories that may help different learning styles using mnemonics. Mnemonics is a tool used for associating and coding information to help memory recollection and retention. This list is by no means exhaustive. Suggestions follow each type of learning style. This list of terms has been taken from *The Learning Center Exchange.* Possible learning style suggestions follow each term.

1. Music Mnemonics: Auditory Learners, Visual Learners
2. Name Mnemonics: Auditory Learners
3. Expression or Word Mnemonics: Auditory Learners
4. Model Mnemonics: Visual Learners
5. Ode or Rhyme Mnemonics
6. Note Organization Mnemonics: Tactile Learners, Visual Learners
7. Outlines: Sequential Learners
8. Image Mnemonics: Visual Learners
9. Connection Mnemonics: Social Learners, Big Picture Learners
10. Spelling Mnemonics: Auditory Learners, Visual Learners

https://www.learningassistance.com/2006/january/mnemonics.html.

EXAMPLE: By using just the first letters of all processing groups, a helpful sentence can be created to more easily remember the processing groups.

INITIATE, PLAN, EXECUTE, MONITOR & CONTROL, CLOSING, could become:

In **P**hysical **Ed**ucation **M**ary **C**ries **C**onstantly.

Disclaimer: All direct quotes in this text are attributed as (A Guide to the Project Management Body of Knowledge, (*PMBOK® Guide)* – Sixth Edition) Project Management Institute Inc., 2017, Page #, after each section and any/all paraphrased or original wording is attributed as (P #), before or after each section. All Graphs, Charts, Tables and Figures are attributed as: (*PMBOK® Guide,* Fig. #-# or #/#, P #, *Title of Graph, Chart, Table or Figure*).

Table of Contents

PMI, PMP, CAPM, PMI-ACP, PMI-RMP, PMI-SP and *PMBOK® Guide* are registered marks of the Project Management Institute

Contents

For questions related to this course, please contact:

Enrollment and Course Guidance

Jackie Misja (jackie.misja@globalproject.management)
USA Cell: (330) 418-3399

Technical Issues

Ben Rinehart (ben.rinehart@globalproject.management)

Issues/Questions Related to Course Material

Jack Harpool (jack.harpool@globalproject.management)
USA Cell: (330) 819-5579

Chapter 1: INTRODUCTION

PMI, PMP, CAPM, PMI-ACP, PMI-RMP, PMI-SP and *PMBOK® Guide* are registered marks of the Project Management Institute, 2017 and all references, from this point on, are from the Project Management Institute, (A Guide to the Project Management Body of Knowledge, *(PMBOK® Guide)* – Sixth Edition).

In this manual, you will find that the overview material can become somewhat redundant. This has purposely been designed to reinforce the subject matter and your thoughts about the importance of the material that will occur as questions and answers on and in the Project Management Professional, PMP exam take place.

This does not replace the need to read: (A Guide to the Project Management Body of Knowledge, *(PMBOK® Guide)* – Sixth Edition), Project Management Institute 2017.

"Begin at the beginning…and go on until you come to the end, then stop." Lewis Carroll

Student Learning Outcomes

1. There are 12 enterprise-wide projects listed in the PMBOK 6th Edition. Does the design of a small web-based library qualify? What factors influence a small, medium or large enterprise wide project? See Chapter 2, P 38-40. Why not? See P 1.

2. What does good practice mean to project managers? Are good skills and techniques good practice? Are skill and knowledge good practice? Are techniques and skills good practice?
3. What is a **Standard** (P 2-3)? Is a Standard a document established by an authority? Is a Standard a document established by a customer? Is a Standard a document established by general consent?
4. There are two (2) types of Code of Ethics and Professional Conduct (P 3). Are they **Aspirational, Desired, Compulsory** or **Mandatory**, or a combination?
5. What are the major characteristics/attributes of a project (P 4-7):
6. What are the five (5) Process Management Process Groups? Put them into the correct order of operation (P 23).
    - Planning Process Group
    - Initiating Process Group
    - Executing Process Group
    - Closing Process Group
    - Monitoring and Controlling Process Group
7. Is the **Project** Life Cycle the same as the ***Product*** Life Cycle? Explain.
8. Which PMBOK 6th Edition Knowledge Area is missing (P 25)?
    - Stakeholder
    - Integration
    - Schedule
    - Cost
    - Risk
    - Quality
    - Resource
    - Communications
    - Procurement
9. What is the sequence and order of importance of the three (3) Business Documents often referenced in the Project Charter? See Fig. 1-8, P 30, *Interrelationship of Needs Assessment and Critical Business Documents.*
10. Projects always need to be successful. What are the three (3) questions the stakeholders and project manager must answer to assure project success? See 1.2.6.4 P 34, **Project Success**. Are these the correct questions you need to ask for project success?
    - What does business success look like for this project?
    - Is it important for success to have metrics?
    - What external factors may/may not limit success?

CHAPTER ONE: INTRODUCTION

INTRODUCTION: CHAPTER 1 OVERVIEW: PMBOK® 6th Edition P 1-29

The overview and purpose of (A Guide to the Project Management Body of Knowledge, (*PMBOK® Guide)* – Sixth Edition), Project Management Institute 2017, is to show the student that the project manager needs to apply project management practices, principles, processes, tools and techniques to have successful project outcomes.

Please see the article, *How to become a PMP*, located at https://www.snhu.edu/about-us/news-and-events/2018/09/how-to-become-a-project-manager

The *PMBOK® Guide* begins with some examples of enterprise-wide projects including Pyramids of Giza, Olympic Games, the Great Wall of China, the building of the Taj Mahal, etc. The text continues with a discussion of what is good practice. The area of project management standards is described. Standards may be descriptive, or they may be prescriptive. 2.) The chapter describes the value of using project management lexicons (i.e. vocabulary). This includes the Project Management Process Groupings: Initiating, Planning, Executing, Monitoring, Controlling and Closing project management work. There are numerous lexicon (vocabulary) words that are commonly used in the profession of a project manager. It is imperative that the project manager demonstrate a high level of ethics called the ***Code of Ethics and Professional Conduct*, which** can be found at the following link:

https://search.pmi.org/default.aspx?q=code+of+ethics, and the PM must be able to conduct themselves in a manner that demonstrates true professionalism.

The PM always needs to ask the question: Is what we are doing considered a project? In terms of projects, there are some basic elements of what a project is. A project is a temporary endeavor that is undertaken to create a unique product, result or service. Unique, means profoundly different from other projects. There are many examples of projects, such as:

- Developing a new pharmaceutical compound
- Expanding a tour guide service
- Merging of multiple organizations together, etc.

CHAPTER 1 INTRODUCTION OVERVIEW

A project can last for months, a half year, a full year, two years, three years, or four years or more. There is a beginning and an end to all projects. Eventually, a true project will come to a conclusion. When the project or phase is complete, it is closed.

Projects must drive change. Corporations have strategic initiatives that are based on a three to five year period, more or less. The Project Manager helps the corporation move into a new reality. The project manager or project manager business analyst used in this context, takes the current state (as is), or the existing system, and determines how to create the future state (to be) of the system or company. Value for the organization reflects project success in meeting the company's strategic goals.

Projects interface with programs, portfolios and operations management. In using the *PMBOK® Guide*, it is important that we recognize that the project and development life cycles are not one in the same. A project life cycle is usually a series of phases that a project passes through, from the start of the project, to the end of the project. It is basically the framework for managing the project. The phases may be sequential. They may be integrated. They may overlap. There are various phases that are described initially as part of Chapter 1 Introduction. Project Lifecycles may consist of:

- Predictive Lifecycle
- Interactive Lifecycle
- Incremental Lifecycle
- Adaptive Lifecycle
- Hybrid Lifecycle

In any project phase there are going to be times of stops, reviews or pauses, where decisions need to be made. Do we stop the project at that phase, or do we postpone or delay the project, or go on to the next phase? That is called **Phase Gate Review**.

There are five (5) major project process groups. All projects should go through these process groupings. The groupings are outlined below:

1. The **Initiating Process Group** begins the project
2. The **Planning Process Group** establishes the scope of the project work to be done and refines the project objectives
3. The **Executing Process Group** requires the project team to perform the work.
4. The **Monitoring and Control Process Group** requires the project manager to track, review and regulate the work being performed
5. The **Closing Process Group** closes or ends the project or phase.

CHAPTER 1 INTRODUCTION OVERVIEW

The Project Manager needs to manage project knowledge.

There are ten (10) Project Management Knowledge Areas. Every project manager needs to manage the processes as identified by the various process groups, shown above. There also has to be a broad and deep knowledge base, such as managing scope, cost or schedule aspects. The Knowledge Areas are:

1. Project Integration Management – Chapter 4
2. Project Scope Management – Chapter 5
3. Project Schedule Management – Chapter 6
4. Project Cost Management – Chapter 7
5. Project Quality Management – Chapter 8
6. Project Resource Management – Chapter 9
7. Project Communications Management – Chapter 10
8. Project Risk Management – Chapter 11
9. Project Procurement Management – Chapter 12
10. Project Stakeholder Management – Chapter 13

These knowledge areas need to be utilized from the time that the project is started and throughout the project work until the project or phase is closed. The textbook is structured and based on principles shown in Table -4, P 25, *Project Management Process Group and Knowledge Area Mapping*. Be sure to refer to that as you proceed through the various chapters in this text. The text also emphasizes data and project management information. It is important that project managers tailor the application of the process groups to the uniqueness of the project management methodology that is required by the participating company in doing the project management work.

Table 1.4, P 25, *Project Management Process Group and Knowledge Area Mapping,* on the next page.

Knowledge Areas	Project Management Process Groups				
	Initiating Process Group	**Planning Process Group**	**Executing Process Group**	**Monitoring and Controlling Process Group**	**Closing Process Group**
4. Project Integration Management	4.1 Develop Project Charter	4.2 Develop Project Management Plan	4.3 Direct and Manage Project Work 4.4 Manage Project Knowledge	4.5 Monitor and Control Project Work 4.6 Perform Integrated Change Control	4.7 Close Project or Phase
5. Project Scope Management		5.1 Plan Scope Management 5.2 Collect Requirements 5.3 Define Scope 5.4 Create WBS		5.5 Validate Scope 5.6 Control Scope	
6. Project Schedule Management		6.1 Plan Schedule Management 6.2 Define Activities 6.3 Sequence Activities 6.4 Estimate Activity Durations 6.5 Develop Schedule		6.6 Control Schedule	
7. Project Cost Management		7.1 Plan Cost Management 7.2 Estimate Costs 7.3 Determine Budget		7.4 Control Costs	
8. Project Quality Management		8.1 Plan Quality Management	8.2 Manage Quality	8.3 Control Quality	
9. Project Resource Management		9.1 Plan Resource Management 9.2 Estimate Activity Resources	9.3 Acquire Resources 9.4 Develop Team 9.5 Manage Team	9.6 Control Resources	
10. Project Communications Management		10.1 Plan Communications Management	10.2 Manage Communications	10.3 Monitor Communications	
11. Project Risk Management		11.1 Plan Risk Management 11.2 Identify Risks 11.3 Perform Qualitative Risk Analysis 11.4 Perform Quantitative Risk Analysis 11.5 Plan Risk Responses	11.6 Implement Risk Responses	11.7 Monitor Risks	
12. Project Procurement Management		12.1 Plan Procurement Management	12.2 Conduct Procurements	12.3 Control Procurements	
13. Project Stakeholder Management	13.1 Identify Stakeholders	13.2 Plan Stakeholder Engagement	13.3 Manage Stakeholder Engagement	13.4 Monitor Stakeholder Engagement	

Table 1-4 (Guide). Project Management Process Group and Knowledge Area Mapping

Before the project actually begins, the project manager is likely to be involved in the creation of two (2) business documents referred to as:

1. **Business Case:** This is an economic feasibility study. It could also be a technical study or operational study. The Business Case will list the objectives and reasons to initiate the project.
2. **Benefits Management Plan:** This describes how and where the benefits of the project will be delivered and how they will be measured.

These two business documents coupled with the needs assessment, precedes the starting of the project and the creation of the Project Charter.

Fig. 1.8, P 30, *Interrelationship of Needs Assessment and Critical Business/Project Documents*

It is vital that the project manager and the project sponsors define and create a document called the **Project Charter.** The Project Charter authorizes the beginning of the project. It is a document that will be signed off by the project sponsor(s), stakeholder(s) and all interested parties. It authorizes the existence of the project and promises to provide authority and funds so that the project manager can run the project. The **Project Management Plan** is a document that strategizes how the project will be done and how the work will be performed. It describes how the work is to be initiated, planned, executed, monitored, controlled and closed. To ensure project success, it is important to answer various questions about the project. We measure the quality of the answers to each of the following questions, such as:

- What does success look like for the project?
- How will the success of the project be measured?
- What factors may affect success?

It is extremely important that the Project Manager, along with the Sponsor(s) and company leadership guarantees the project is aligned with major corporate strategic goals and objectives. This requires project integration into the company program or portfolio.

KEY WORDS: CHAPTER 1

- PMBOK® 6th Edition
- Project Management Body of Knowledge
- PMBOK
- Project Management Practices
- PMP Exam Prep Course
- PMBOK Guide
- Code of Ethics and Professional Conduct
- Definition of a Project
    - Unique product, service or result
    - Temporary endeavor
    - Project drive change
    - Project enable business value creation
- Professional Conduct
- Factors that led to the creation of a project
    - Project and developmental life cycles
    - Project phases
    - Phase gate
- Business Value
- Project Management Importance
- Program Portfolios
- Operations Management
- OPM3
- Project and Development Lifecycles
    - Predictive Lifecycle
    - Iterative Lifecycle
    - Incremental Lifecycle
    - Adaptive Lifecycle
    - Hybrid Lifecycle
- Project Management Processes
- Initiating Process Group
    - Planning Process Group
    - Executing Process Group
    - Monitoring and Controlling Process Group
    - Closing Process Group
- Project Management Knowledge Areas
    - Project Integration Management
    - Project Scope Management
    - Project Schedule Management
    - Project Cost Management
    - Project Quality Management
    - Project Resource Management
    - Project Communication Management
    - Project Risk Management
    - Project Procurement Management
    - Project Stakeholder Management
    - Project Management Tailoring
- Project Management Business Documents
- Project Business Case
- Project Management Benefits Plan
- Project Success
- Project management data
- Project management information
- Tailoring
- Project management business documents

CHAPTER 1 INTRODUCTION OVERVIEW

- Project Charter
- Project Management Process Groups
    - Business case
    - Business management plan
    - Benefits management plan
    - Needs assessment
- Project success measure

CHAPTER 1 PMBOK INTRODUCTION DETAILS

1.1 OVERVIEW AND PURPOSE OF THIS MANUAL

Project Management is about how to manage a project. While it is not a new concept, there are Standards provided by the Project Management Institute (PMI), cultivated by leaders and managers collectively applying researched and sound practices to create the PMBOK. If you follow these Standards in *A Guide to the Project Management Body of Knowledge, (PMBOK® Guide)* – Sixth Edition, Project Management Institute Inc., 2017, and read our manual as a companion source, you can greatly increase your chance of passing the PMP Exam on your first attempt.

Note: Any references found in this manual for Figs, Tables and Charts, etc. may be found in the above referenced guide, unless otherwise stated.

Some project examples taken from the PMBOK Guide are shown below:

1. Pyramids of Giza
2. Olympic Games
3. Great wall of China
4. Taj Mahal
5. Publication of a children's book
6. Panama Canal
7. Development of commercial jet airplanes
8. Polio Vaccine
9. Human begins landing on the moon
10. Commercial Software Applications
11. Portable Devices to use the Global Positioning System (GPS)
12. Placement of the International Space Station into Earth's orbit

The PMBOK is needed to clarify "… proven traditional practices that are widely applied as well as innovative practices that are emerging in the profession" *A Guide to the Project Management Body of Knowledge, (PMBOK® Guide)* – Sixth Edition, Project Management Institute Inc., 2017, P 1."

Generally Recognized and **Good Practice** are recommendations that the Project Manager should take into account on any project (P2).

The *PMBOK® Guide* is a foundation to build methodologies, policies, procedures, tools and techniques and the cycle phases of the practice of project management. A Methodology is "…a system of practices, techniques, procedures and rules used by those who work in a discipline"

CHAPTER 1 PMBOK INTRODUCTION DETAILS

A Guide to the Project Management Body of Knowledge, (PMBOK® Guide) – Sixth Edition, Project Management Institute Inc., 2017, P 2.

1.1.1 The Standard for Project Management

Project Management requires a set of established guidelines and rules, known as Standards, to achieve a common objective or result. Since every project is different, needs and approaches will vary, which leads to and is known as Project Tailoring. Because of this, **descriptive practices** are used instead of **prescriptive practices**. Descriptive practices allow for a more creative management structure, while prescriptive methodologies detail and define expectations.

1.1.2 Common Vocabulary

"A **Common Vocabulary** is an essential element of a professional discipline. The *PMI Lexicon of Project Management Terms* provides the foundational professional vocabulary that can be consistently used by organizations, portfolio, program, and project managers and other project stakeholders" *A Guide to the Project Management Body of Knowledge, (PMBOK® Guide)* – Sixth Edition, Project Management Institute Inc., 2017 (P 3). The document that can be referenced for this vocabulary is The *PMI Lexicon of Project Management Terms.* See glossary, P 695-726 *(PMBOK® Guide)* – Sixth Edition), Project Management Institute 2017.

1.1.3 Code of Ethics and Professional Conduct

The Project Management Institute (PMI) created a *Code of Ethics and Professional Conduct*, which lays out parameters related to responsibility, respect, fairness and honesty, defining these four values as its foundation (P 5).

There are two (2) other types of Standards to keep in mind:

1. **Aspirational Standards**: The conduct that practitioners who are also PMI members, certification holders or volunteers strive to uphold
2. **Mandatory Standards**: Establish firm requirements and, in some cases, limit or prohibit practitioner behavior

Note: "Practitioners who are also PMI members, certification holders or volunteers and who do not conduct themselves in accordance with these standards will be subject to disciplinary procedures before PMI's Ethics Review Committee" *A Guide to the Project Management Body of Knowledge, (PMBOK® Guide)* – Sixth Edition, Project Management Institute Inc., 2017, P 3.

1.2 FOUNDATIONAL ELEMENTS

Foundational Elements must be understood when practicing Project Management concepts and can be found in this section.

1.2.1 Projects

"A Project is a temporary endeavor undertaken to create a unique product, service or result" *A Guide to the Project Management Body of Knowledge, (PMBOK® Guide)* – Sixth Edition, Project Management Institute Inc., 2017 (P 4).

The four (4) **Foundational Elements** are (P 4):

1. **Unique Product**: Can either be a component of another item, an enhancement or a correction to an item or a new item
2. **Service**: An ability to perform a service
3. **Result**: An outcome or document
4. **Combination**: One or more services, products or results

A Project is temporary in nature, meaning it has a definite start and end date. However, the Project end is only attained when certain criteria are met.

Note: While it is true that Projects are temporary, **deliverables** can extend beyond the Closing of the Project.

The expected end result of a Project is to drive change, thereby producing **Business Value** by transitioning the participating company, from one state, the (as is) **Current State** to achieve the desired results, known as the (to be) **Future State** (P 6).

Fig. 1-1, P 6, *Organizational Transition via a Project*).

Some projects may provide both **Tangible** and **Intangible** elements (P 7).

Projects are initiated in response to four (4) fundamental categories that act upon organizations. They are as follows (P 4):

1. Meet Regulatory, Legal or Social Requirements
2. Satisfy Stakeholder Requests or Needs
3. Create, Improve or Fix Products, Processes or Services
4. Implement or Change Business or Technological Strategies

These form the context from which projects are initiated *(PMBOK® Guide,* (PMBOK® Guide, Fig. 1-2, P 8, *Project Initiation Context* and Table 1-1, P 9, *Examples of Factors that Lead to a Creation of a Project*).

- **Temporary Endeavor** (P 5): Projects have a definite start and end, but projects can range from a short duration to many years. The end is reached when one or more of the criteria below are satisfied (P 5):
    - Project's objectives have been met
    - Project's objectives cannot or will not be met
    - Funding is exhausted or no longer available for allocation to the project
    - The need for the project no longer exists
    - Human or physical resources are no longer available
    - Project is terminated for legal cause, or convenience

- **Projects Drive Change**: Projects are set up to move the organization from one state to another. *(PMBOK® Guide,* (PMBOK® Guide, Fig. 1-1, P 6, *Organizational State Transition via a Project*).
- **Projects enable Business Value Creation**: Business Value is the net quantifiable benefit from a business endeavor.

You can refer the following article for more clarification: *The Business Value of Design* at https://www.mckinsey.com/business-functions/mckinsey-design/our-insights/the-business-value-of-design

The benefit from a project can be tangible, or intangible, or both.
Tangible examples are listed below (P 7):

- Monetary Assets
- Stockholder Equity
- Utility
- Fixtures
- Tools
- Market Share

Intangible examples are listed below (P 7):

- Goodwill
- Brand Recognition
- Public Benefit
- Trademarks
- Strategic Alignment
- Reputation

- **Project Initiation Context**: There are four (4) fundamental categories for this focus (P 7):
    - Meet regulatory, legal or social requirements
    - Satisfy Stakeholder requests or needs
    - Implement or change business or technological strategies
    - Create, improve or fix products, processes or services

Fig. 1-2, P 8, *Project Initiation Context*
Table 1-1, P 9, *Examples of Factors that lead to the Creation of a Project*

1.2.2 The Importance of Project Management

Project Management is a temporary state defined by a project. In order to effectively manage a project, the Project Manager (PM) needs to be effective in the following way when a PM is present and doing their work successfully (P 10):

Effective Project Management:

- Meet business objectives
- Satisfy stakeholder expectations
- Be more predictable
- Increase chances of success
- Deliver the right products at the right time
- Resolve problems and issues

- Respond to risks in a timely manner
- Optimize the use of organizational resources
- Identify, recover or terminate failing projects
- Manage constraints
- Balance the influence of constraints
- Manage change wisely

Ineffective Project Management: In the absence of a PM, or projects that do not follow recommendations or standards can result in:

- Missed Deadlines
- Cost Overruns
- Poor Quality
- Rework
- Uncontrolled Expansion of the Project
- Loss of Reputation for the Organization
- Unsatisfied Stakeholders
- Failures in achieving Objectives for which the project was undertaken

1.2.3.1 Overview

A project can be handled in one of three (3) ways (P 11):

1. **Project**: Stands on its own, outside of a portfolio or program.
2. **Program**: May be grouped within a program portfolio. If a project is within a program or portfolio, a PM may interact. Programs can run for years.
3. **Portfolio:** Projects, Programs, Subsidiary Portfolios and Operations managed as a group.

Program Management and Portfolio Management will differ from Project Management based on:

- Life Cycles
- Activities
- Objectives
- Focus
- Benefits

Portfolios, programs, project and operations may use the same resources and engage with the same stakeholders. All are ruled by coordinated governance. *(PMBOK® Guide,* (PMBOK® Guide, Fig. 1-3, P 12, *Portfolio, Programs, Projects and Operations).*

In Program and Project Management, the focus is on doing programs and projects correctly, i.e. **Right way**, while Portfolio Management emphasizes doing the **Right** programs and projects.

1.2.3.2 Program Management

Program Management: A **Program** is a collection of related projects. The goal in managing these Projects is to achieve a common outcome by obtaining benefits and control not possible if all the components were to be handled individually. This task can be accomplished by (P 14):

- Aligning with the organizational or strategic direction that affects program and project goals and objectives
- Allocating the program scope into program components
- Managing interdependencies among the components of the program
- Managing program risks that may impact multiple projects
- Resolving constraints and conflicts that affect multiple projects
- Resolving issues between the component project and the program level
- Managing change requests within a shared governance framework
- Allocating budgets across multiple projects within the program
- Assuring benefits realization from the program and component projects

Table 1-2, P 13, *Comparative Overview of Project, Portfolio and Program Management.*

1.2.3.3 Portfolio Management

A **Portfolio** contains Projects, Programs, Subsidiary Portfolios and Operations. The purpose of Portfolio Management is listed below (P 15):

- Guide organizational investment decisions
- Select a mix of programs and projects
- Provide decision-making transparency
- Prioritize team and physical resource allocation
- Increase the likelihood of realizing the desired return on investment (ROI)
- Centralize the management of the aggregate risk profile

1.2.3.4 Operations Management

Operations management certifies that ongoing business operations will flow smoothly by choosing the most efficient resources needed to meet customer requirements.

1.2.3.5 Operations and Project Management

Although ongoing **operations** are outside of the scope of a project, there may be intersecting points where two areas cross, such as (p 16):

- Projects can intersect with operations at various points during the product life cycle
- Ongoing operations can intersect while improving operations or the product development process
- Ongoing operations can intersect with the end of the product life cycle
- Ongoing operations can intersect at each closeout phase

1.2.3.6 Organizational Project Management (OPM) and Strategies

Organizational Project Management (OPM) and Strategies: Organizational Project Management is a more structured way of treating programs, project and portfolios as inter-related parts of a whole. Success will depend on choosing organizational practices needed to achieve a successful outcome.

- **Portfolio Management**: The consolidation and management of projects or programs
- **Program Management:** The management of one or more inter-related programs as a group to achieve the desired results.
- **Project Management** uses knowledge, tools and skills for the achievement of organizational goals and objectives

Also, refer to *(PMBOK® Guide,* (PMBOK® Guide, Fig. 1-4, P 17, *Organizational Project Management).*

1.2.4 Components of the Guide

When Projects are managed effectively, they result in a successful completion. Please refer to and study the following tables and figures that are found in the above referenced guide.

Table 1-3, P 18, *Description of PMBOK® Guide Key Components* and Fig. 1.5, P 22, *Interrelationship of PMBOK® Guide Key Components in Projects.*

1.2.4.1 Project and Development Life Cycles

A **Project Life Cycle** provides the framework for a series (types) of phases that can be (P 19):

1. Sequential
2. Interactive
3. Overlapping

Within the **Project Life Cycle**, there may be a series of phases adapted to the development of the product services, or result. These are known as **Development Life Cycles** and are referred to as (P 19):

1. **Predictive**: The project scope, time and cost are determined early in the phases of the lifecycle
2. **Iterative**: The project scope is determined early in the project lifecycle, but time and cost estimates are routinely modified as the project team's understanding of the product increases
3. **Incremental**: The deliverable is produced through a series of iterations that successfully add functionality within a predetermined time frame
4. **Adaptive**: They can be agile at the start of an iteration

See *Agile vs. Waterfall: The three most Impactful Differences*, by Ashley Hunt (9:24 minutes), located at https://www.youtube.com/watch?v=ygVXGSn2DIQ

5. **Hybrid**: A combination of predictive and adaptive lifecycles

The PM decides the life cycle for each project, while recognizing the project needs to be tailored to accommodate any determining factors that may affect project success. This life cycle flexibility may be undertaken using the following (P 19):

1. Identifying the Process or Processes needed to be performed in each Phase
2. Performing the process or processes identified in the appropriate Phase
3. Adjusting the attributes of a Phase

Project Life Cycles are independent of **Product Life Cycles**. A project life cycle is a series of phases that a project goes through from start to finish (P 19). A product life cycle is a series of phases that represent the evolution of a product from concept through delivery, growth and maturity to retirement (P 19).

1.2.4.2 Project Phase

Project Phases are collections of logically arranged steps/activities that result in the completion of one or more deliverables. All attributes are unique to a specific phase. Some of the attributes of naming a Project Phase include (P 20):

- Name
- Number
- Duration
- Resource Requirements
- Entrance Criteria
- Exit Criteria

Some types of Phase names for a Project Phase are listed below:

- Concept Development
- Feasibility Study
- Customer Requirements
- Solution Development
- Design
- Prototype
- Build
- Test
- Transition
- Commissioning
- Milestone Review
- Lessons Learned

Various factors can influence Project Phases (P 21):

- Management Needs
- Nature of the Project
- Unique Characteristics of the Industry, Organization or Technology

- Project Elements
- Decision Points

1.2.4.3 Phase Gate

Phase Gate: A Phase Gate (Synonyms: Phase Review, Stage Gate, Kill Point, Phase Entrance, Phase Exit) is held at the end of a Phase. Select Phase Gates names are appropriate to the project are (P 21):

- Phase Review
- Stage Gate
- Kill Point
- Phase Entrance
- Phase Exit

The project's performance and progress are compared to some of the following project and business documents (P 21):

- Project Business Case
- Project Charter
- Project Management Plan
- Benefits Management Plan

A decision, or no decision, will be made as a result of the quality/timeliness of the project's progress (P 21):

- Continue to the next phase
- Continue to the next phase with modification
- End the project
- Remain in the phase
- Repeat the phase or elements of it

1.2.4.4 Project Management Processes

Project Management Activities (Project Management Processes) are executed from the start to the end of a Project Life Cycle. This concept can be explained by knowing that every project management process will create one or more inputs and outputs. This is accomplished by using appropriate management **Tools and Techniques**. These **inputs or outputs** may be in the form of a Deliverable, or an Outcome, which is the end result of a process. All Processes take place, no matter the organization or industry.

As a general rule, Project Management Processes produce Outputs, which will most likely result in (P 22):

- An Input to another Process or a Deliverable
- A Deliverable of the Project or Project Phase

(*PMBOK® Guide,* (PMBOK® Guide, Fig. 1-6, P 22, *Example Processes: Inputs, Tools and Techniques and Outputs*).

Processes usually fit into one of the following categories such as (P 22):

- Used once or a predefined points in the project
- Performed periodically as needed
- Performed continuously throughout the project

1.2.4.5 Project Management Process Groups

A Project Management Process Group is designed to achieve specific project objectives and may be grouped into the following five Project Management Process Groups (P 23):

1. **Initiating Process Group**: Processes used to define a new project or a new phase
2. **Planning Process Group**: Processes required to establish the scope of the project, refine the objectives and define a course of action
3. **Executing Process Group:** Processes performed to complete the work defined in the Project Management Plan
4. **Monitoring and Controlling Process Group**: Processes performed to track, review and regulate the progress and performance of the project
5. **Closing Process Group**: Processes performed to formally complete or

close the project, phase or contract

Note: Process Groups are not the same as Project Phases.

1.2.4.6 Project Management Knowledge Areas

In addition to Process Groups, processes are also categorized by Knowledge Areas. A Knowledge Area is described in terms of its Component Processes, Practices, Inputs, Outputs, Tools and Techniques. Knowledge areas are used as the PM does project work during the life of the project. Table 1-4, P 25, *Project Management Process Group and Knowledge Area Mapping.*

The ten (10) Knowledge Areas are (P 23-24):

1. **Project Integration Management:** Uses processes and activities to identify, define, combine, unify and coordinate various project management activities
2. **Project Scope Management:** The processes required to ensure the project includes all the work required and only the work required
3. **Project Schedule Management:** The processes required to ensure the timely completion of the project
4. **Project Cost Management:** Includes the processes involved in planning, estimating, budgeting, financing, funding and controlling costs
5. **Project Quality Management:** Includes the processes for incorporating the organization's quality policy regarding planning, managing and controlling the project and product quality requirements
6. **Project Resource Management:** Includes the processes to identify, acquire and manage needed resources
7. **Project Communications Management:** Includes the processes required to ensure timely and appropriate planning, collection, creation, distribution, storage, retrieval, management, control, monitoring and ultimate disposition of a project
8. **Project Risk Management:** Includes the processes of conducting risk management planning, identification, analysis, response planning, response implementation and monitoring risk on a project
9. **Project Procurement Management:** Includes the processes necessary to purchase or acquire products, services, or results needed from outside the

project team

10. **Project Stakeholder Management:** Includes the processes required to identify the people, groups or organizations that could affect or be affected by the project, to analyze stakeholder expectations and their impact on the project, and to develop appropriate management strategies for effectively engaging stakeholders in project decisions and executions

The Knowledge Areas numbers refer to the PMBOK, 6th Edition chapters where that information is described.

Ex.'s

Project Integration Management can be found in Chapter 4
Project Scope Management can be found in Chapter 5
Project Schedule Management can be found in Chapter 6
Project Cost Management can be found in Chapter 7, etc.

See (and Study) Table 1-4, P 25, *Project Management Process Groups and Knowledge Areas* shown on next page:

Please listen to the following video, *Elaboration of the Process Flow of the PMBOK® Guide, 6th Edition* (53:22 minutes), by Ricard Vargas, https://www.youtube.com/watch?v=GC7pN8Mjot8, as you refer to Table 1-4, on the following page.

Knowledge Areas	Project Management Process Groups				
	Initiating Process Group	**Planning Process Group**	**Executing Process Group**	**Monitoring and Controlling Process Group**	**Closing Process Group**
4. Project Integration Management	4.1 Develop Project Charter	4.2 Develop Project Management Plan	4.3 Direct and Manage Project Work 4.4 Manage Project Knowledge	4.5 Monitor and Control Project Work 4.6 Perform Integrated Change Control	4.7 Close Project or Phase
5. Project Scope Management		5.1 Plan Scope Management 5.2 Collect Requirements 5.3 Define Scope 5.4 Create WBS		5.5 Validate Scope 5.6 Control Scope	
6. Project Schedule Management		6.1 Plan Schedule Management 6.2 Define Activities 6.3 Sequence Activities 6.4 Estimate Activity Durations 6.5 Develop Schedule		6.6 Control Schedule	
7. Project Cost Management		7.1 Plan Cost Management 7.2 Estimate Costs 7.3 Determine Budget		7.4 Control Costs	
8. Project Quality Management		8.1 Plan Quality Management	8.2 Manage Quality	8.3 Control Quality	
9. Project Resource Management		9.1 Plan Resource Management 9.2 Estimate Activity Resources	9.3 Acquire Resources 9.4 Develop Team 9.5 Manage Team	9.6 Control Resources	
10. Project Communications Management		10.1 Plan Communications Management	10.2 Manage Communications	10.3 Monitor Communications	
11. Project Risk Management		11.1 Plan Risk Management 11.2 Identify Risks 11.3 Perform Qualitative Risk Analysis 11.4 Perform Quantitative Risk Analysis 11.5 Plan Risk Responses	11.6 Implement Risk Responses	11.7 Monitor Risks	
12. Project Procurement Management		12.1 Plan Procurement Management	12.2 Conduct Procurements	12.3 Control Procurements	
13. Project Stakeholder Management	13.1 Identify Stakeholders	13.2 Plan Stakeholder Engagement	13.3 Manage Stakeholder Engagement	13.4 Monitor Stakeholder Engagement	

Table 1-4 (Guide). Project Management Process Group and Knowledge Area Mapping

1.2.4.7 Project Management Data and Information

In the course of running a project, Project Data is collected and analyzed in context, aggregated and transformed in context to become project information. This needs to be accomplished throughout the project life cycle. This information may be stored and distributed into different formats. There are three (3) categories of Project Management data and information shown below (P 26):

- **Work Performance Data:** Information identified during activities that specifies which activities have started, which ones have completed and any of the activities in progress in order to carry out the project work
- **Work Performance Information**: Collected during project execution through the Controlling Process. This information is compared to and contrasted with other data, such as costs, budget, work performed, resources and funding schedules to determine if the project is within budget goals or if there is a variance from the original plan. This information will determine if corrective or preventative action is necessary.
- **Work Performance Reports**: A physical or electronic representation of Work Performance Information compiled in project documents and necessary to the Perform Change Control Process

Fig. 1-7, P 27, *Project Data, Information and Report Flow).*

Project Data is collected on a continual basis throughout the Project life cycle and it is important to remember the definitions shown above regarding this aspect (P 26):

1.2.5 Tailoring

In **Tailoring**, PM's apply a project management methodology to their work, a system of practices, techniques, procedures and rules used by those who work in a discipline. Project Management Methodologies may be (P 28):

1. Developed by experts within the organization
2. Purchased from Vendors

3. Obtained from Professional Associations
4. Acquired from Government Agencies

Tailoring may be necessary when the organization may require specific project management methodologies. Since every project is unique, not all processes, tools and techniques, inputs or outputs will be needed. The project manager will therefore tailor each project differently, taking into consideration whether the customer is internal or external to the organization.

1.2.6 Project Management Business Documents

Project Management Business Documents, such as the project business case and project benefits management plan captures the essence of why a project is undertaken.

Table 1.5, P 29, *Project Business Documents*

Project Sponsor: Generally accountable for the development and maintenance of the project business case document.

Project Manager: Responsible for providing any/all recommendations and oversight to keep the project business case, project management plan, project charter, and project benefits management plan success measurements in alignment with one another and with the goals and objectives of the organization.

Project Managers should appropriately tailor their Project Management Documents. PM's need to work with the appropriate program managers to ensure the project management documents are aligned with the program documents.

Also, see and study (*PMBOK® Guide,* (PMBOK® Guide, Fig. 1-8, P 30, *Interrelationship of Needs Assessment and Critical Business/Project Documents).*

1.2.6.1 Project Business Case

The **Project Business Case** is a document used throughout the Project Life Cycle and may be used before the project starts and can result in a Go/No-Go Decision for the project (P 30-32).

A Business Case should include the following format elements, but there may be other factors involved. The general organization of the business case is business needs, analysis of the situation and recommendations (P 31).

CHAPTER 1 PMBOK INTRODUCTION DETAILS

1. **Business Needs:**

- Determine what is prompting the need for action
- Situational Statement
- Stakeholder Identification
- Identification of the Scope

2. Analysis of the Situation:

- Identify Organizational Strategies, Goals and Objectives
- Identify Root Cause of the Problem or Opportunity
- Perform Gap Analysis
- Identify Known Risks
- Identify Critical Success Factors
- Identify Decision Criteria

Some examples of criteria categories used in the analysis of a situation:

- **Required:** Action Required to address the problem or opportunity
- **Desired:** Action Desired to address the problem or opportunity
- **Optional:** Not essential

Some options (examples) for addressing the Business Problem:

- **Do Nothing**: Business as Usual option
- **Do the minimum work required**: The minimum amount of work require to address the problem or opportunity
- **Do more than the work required**: Meets the minimum requirements and some or all of the other documented criteria

3. Recommendation (P 32):

- Statement of Recommended Option
- Items to include in the Statement:
    - Analysis Result of Options
    - Constraints, Assumptions, Risks and Dependencies
    - Success Measures

- When using an Implementation Approach, the following may apply:
    - Milestones
    - Dependencies
    - Roles and Responsibilities
- Evaluation:
    - Statement for measuring potential benefits

1.2.6.2 Project Benefits Management Plan

The **Project Benefits Management Plan** describes how and when the benefits of the project will be delivered. Project Benefits are defined as an outcome of action such as providing benefits to the sponsoring organization and intended Stakeholders. The Project Benefits Management Plan begins early in the project life cycle. The **Project Charter** provides the PM the authority to apply organizational resources to project activities. The **Project Management Plan** is a document defining how the project will be executed, monitored and controlled, may be issued by the project sponsor formally authorizing the existence of a project (P 33).

The **Project Benefits Management Plan** may include the following key elements (P 33):

- Target Benefits
- Strategic Alignment
- Timeframe For Realizing Benefits
- Benefits Owner
- Metrics
- Assumptions
- Risks

The Benefits Management Plan makes use of the data and information documented in the Business Case and Needs Assessment (Report) and is an iterative activity.

1.2.6.3 Project Charter and Project Management Plan

The **Project Charter** authorizes the PM to formally apply resources to a project and the **Project Management Plan** defines how the project will be executed, monitored and controlled (P 34).

1.2.6.4 Project Success Measures

Project Success Measures: It may sometimes seem impossible to agree on project success when dealing with Stakeholders whose view on project success may differ from the organization's standpoint. However, it is also possible for a project to be successful from a scope/schedule/budget viewpoint, and yet still be unsuccessful from a business viewpoint. A Project's success may include such factors (P 34):

- Completing the Project Benefits Management Plan
- Meeting the agreed-upon financial measures documented in the business case. These financial measures may include:
    - Net present value (NPV)
    - Return on investment (ROI)
    - Internal rate of return (IRR)
    - Payback period (PBP)
    - Benefit-cost ration (BCR)
    - Meeting business case non-financial objectives
    - Completing movement of an organization from its current state to the desired future state
    - Fulfilling contract term and conditions
    - Meeting organizational strategy, goals and objectives
    - Achieving stakeholder satisfaction
    - Acceptable customer/end-user adoption
    - Integration of deliverable into the organization's operating environment
    - Achieving agreed-upon quality of delivery
    - Meeting governance criteria

    - Achieving other agreed-upon success measures or criteria

In addition to the above, there are three (3) questions the PM must always ask themselves (P 34):

- What does success look like for this project?
- How will success be measured?
- What factors may affect the success of the project?

Summary: Answers to Student Learning Outcomes

1. The example of a web-based library does not fit into what is considered an enterprise project, because of its small size. However there are some examples of Enterprise Environmental Factors (EEF's) and Organizational Process Assets (OPA's) that can influence a certain size project listed below:

   Internal Enterprise Environmental Factors P 38

   - Organizational Culture
   - Organizational Structure
   - Organizational Governance
   - Employee Capability

   External Environmental Factors P 39

   - Marketplace Conditions
   - Social, and Cultural Influences and Issues
   - Legal Restrictions
   - Physical and Environmental Elements

   Organizational Process Assets P 39-40

   - Process Policies and Procedures
   - Organizational Knowledge Bases

2. Principles of Good Practice include all of the following (P 2):

   - Skills
   - Knowledge
   - Techniques

3. A **Standard** is established by any of the following (P 3):

   - An authority
   - General consent

- A need
- An example

4. There are two (2) types of **Code of Ethics and Professional Conduct** (P 3):

   - Aspirational
   - Mandatory

5. The characteristics/attributes of a project are (P 6-7):

   - Unique product, service or result undertaken to fulfill objectives
   - Temporary endeavor that has a definite beginning and end
   - Projects drive changes in organizations
   - Projects enable business value creation

6. The five (5) Project Management Process Groups in order of operation are:

   - Initiating
   - Planning
   - Executing
   - Monitor and Controlling
   - Closing

   See Fig. 1-5, P 18, *Interrelationship of PMBOK® Guide Key Components in Projects.* This couples with the ten (10) Knowledge Areas. See Table 1-4, P 25, *Project Management Process Groups and Knowledge Area Mapping.*

7. The **Project Life Cycle** and the **Product Life Cycle** are not the same. The Project Life Cycle is a series of phases that a project goes through from start to finish and measures work that takes place during a project. The **Product Life Cycle** is an evolution of the product from the idea stage through retirement of the project (P 19).

8. Project Scope (P 23-24).

9. The three (3) Business Documents in order are:

   - **Needs Assessment** (strategies or tactical)
   - **Business Case** (feasibility study to validate needs probability of project, usually

financial in nature)

- **Business Benefit Plan** (Documented Explanation for creating, maximizing and sustaining the benefits of the project management plan)

10. Three (3) questions that must always be answered by Stakeholders or Project Managers are (P 34):

- What does success look like for the project?
- How will success be measured?
- What factors may affect success?

Similar Questions that may be on the PMI Exam related to Chapter 1

1. Project management process groups are _____.

    A. Initiating, planning, expediting, and control
    B. Plan, organize, develop, and control
    C. Plan, do, observe, and commit
    D. Initiating, planning and executing, monitoring and controlling, and closing

    Correct answer is D: Initiating, planning and executing, monitoring and controlling, and closing are project management process groups.

2. Joe is an excellent programmer, who was promoted to a role of Project Manager because he understands technology better than anyone else in the company. Unfortunately, he is having trouble doing the project management job and his projects are failing. What is this an example of?

    A. Gold plating
    B. Halo effect
    C. Pre-assignment
    D. Ground rules

    Correct answer is B: The halo effect is when you put someone in a position who is not qualified for that position. Just because Joe is a great programmer, does not mean he will make a good project manager.

3. Which Statement best describes the relationship between project life cycle phases and project management processes?

    A. Project management processes correspond one to one with project life cycle phases
    B. Project life cycle phases can repeat within a project management process
    C. Project management processes can repeat within a project life cycle

D. Project management processes are completely independent of project life cycle phases

Correct answer is C: The Project management processes should be implemented for each project life cycle phase. Option A is incorrect as process groups are not synonymous with project phases. Each phase may be carried out by altogether different function or organization. Option B is incorrect because it is the opposite of the correct option. Option D is incorrect because a relationship can exist between the initiating, planning and closing processes and traditional project life cycle phases such as design coding, testing, integration and closure.

4. ATEL is preparing to host its first annual 6K half marathon in Delhi. You have worked on a similar project for the organization two years ago, when it co-hosted the 10k walk through Mumbai Pune expressway. Which of the organizational process assets might be helpful to you for your new project?

   A. The project SOW, which describes the high-level details of the run/walk program
   B. The strategic plan, because you'll want to make sure the project reflects the overall strategic direction of the organization
   C. Historical information on the 10K run project
   D. The organization's PMIS system

   Correct answer is C: Historical information on projects of a similar nature can be helpful while initiating new projects. They can help in formulating project deliverables and identifying constraints and assumptions and also later in the project planning processes as well.

5. The Manavalanagar Company has authorized your company to generate electricity from bio-gas at various wastewater treatment plants. It intends to set up eight co-generation plants and three hydroelectric generation plants with a combined capacity of over 13 megawatts. You are the project manager for setting up one such plant. Since, it is the first plant to be set up, you are also expected to tailor the organization's standard policies/procedures with respect to this project. You decide to reach out to the PMO and gain access to organizational process assets. Which of the following documents you are least likely to find under the processes and procedures category?

A. Templates
B. Performance Measurement Baselines
C. Financial Control Procedures
D. Change Control Procedures

Correct answer is B: As per the, *A Guide to PMBOK*, project files from previous projects, like scope, cost, schedule, performance measurement baselines, etc., are part of the Corporate Knowledge Base and not Processes and Procedures category under Organizational Process Assets.

You **may now move on to Chapter Two: The Environment in which Projects Operate**

Chapter 2: The Environment in which Projects Operate: Achieve Success through Project Design and Environment

"If you can't explain it simply, you don't understand it well enough." Albert Einstein

Student Learning Outcomes

CHAPTER 2 INTRODUCTION OVERVIEW: THE ENVIRONMENT IN WHICH PROJECTS OPERATE

START

1. The environment in which the Project Manager works affects the success of the projects and plays a significant role in the life cycle of the project. These include Enterprise Environmental Factors (EEF's) and Organizational Process Assets (OPM's). Do they also include all of the following factors?:

Internal Enterprise Environmental Factors P 38

- Organizational Culture and Structure
- Organizational Business
- Organizational Governance
- Employee Capability

External Environmental Factors P 39

- Marketplace Conditions
- Social, and Cultural Influences and Issues
- No Legal Restrictions
- Physical and Environmental Elements

Organizational Process Assets P 39

- Process Policies and Procedures
- Organizational Knowledge Environments

2. A system is a collection of various components working separately or together. Are all of the following statements correct? Which one is incorrect (P 42)?

- Systems can be dynamic
- Systems can be optimized
- Systems are linear in responsiveness

3. Organizations will vary in structure. Influences of Organizational Structures on Projects, Table 2-1, P 47, *Influences of Organizational Structures on Projects*, identifies ten (10) different structure types. Each reflects various project characteristics when a project manager is working in a particular structured environment. Which Organizational Structure Type is missing?

- Organic or Simple

- Functional (centralized)
- Matrix-Strong
- Matrix-Weak
- Matrix-Balanced
- Project Oriented (Composite Hybrid)
- Virtual
- Hybrid
- PMO

4. There are three (3) types of PMO's that standardizes project related governance processes and practices. The common sharing of resources, methodology, tools and techniques will vary in control and influence of project. Which three (3) are correct?

   - Supportive
   - Controlling
   - Dictatorship
   - Laisse faire
   - Directive

START

THE ENVIRONMENT IN WHICH PROJECTS OPERATE: CHAPTER 2

OVERVIEW: PMBOK® 6TH Edition P 37-45

There are numerous factors which insure success of a new project. These factors are internal and external to the organization. They are called, **Enterprise Environmental Factors (EEF's), and are internal or external to the organization. Use of these factors or the knowledge of the available** elements will help fortify and support the goals and objectives of the project.

There are also **Organizational Process Assets (OPA's)** that need to be used that will influence the management of the project. These include policies and procedures that are followed and must be adhered to, based upon the rules and regulations for the industrial standards that dictate such policies. These, too, are followed to assure success of the project.

Organizational knowledge repositories should also be used by the PM. These are computerized databases of information that will help the project manager develop metrics for the project, aide in gathering historical information of similar projects that were completed in the past, and may include scope, cost, schedule and other baseline examples that are useful in the lessons-learned area of running a project.

All projects are part of an **organizational system**. The organizational system determines the powers and influences the interests and competence of the people that are interfacing with you as a project manager and with your project team.

There are various organizational structure types in which the project manager may work. They are identified as:

1. Organic or Simple
2. Functional
3. Multi-divisional
4. Matrix Strong
5. Matrix Weak
6. Matrix Balanced
7. Project Oriented (Composite IT size)
8. Virtual Hybrid
9. Hybrid
10. PMO (Project Management Office)

Refer to Table 2.1, P 47, *Influences of Organizational Structures on Projects*

The Project Management Office (PMO) is an organizational structure that standardizes the project related governess processes. The PMO also facilitates the sharing of resources and methodologies to assist the project manager's success. The Project Management Office (PMO) may make recommendations, assist in knowledge transfer, terminate projects or take other actions. The primary function of the PMO is to manage shared resources, and identify various methodologies that the project manager should follow in coaching, mentoring and training.

CHAPTER 2 INTRODUCTION OVERVIEW: THE ENVIRONMENT IN WHICH PROJECTS OPERATE

KEY WORDS CHAPTER 2: The Environment in which Projects Operate

- Enterprise environmental Factors (EEF)
- Organizational Process Assets (OPA)
- Organizational Systems
- Organizational Structure Types:
  - Organic or Simple
  - Functional (Centralized)
  - Multi-Divisional
  - Matrix-Strong
  - Matrix-Weak
  - Matrix-Balanced
  - Project-Oriented (Composite Hybrid)
  - Virtual
  - Hybrid
  - PMO
- Work groups arranged by:
  - Project Manager Authority
  - Project Manager Role
  - Resource Availability
  - Project Budget
  - Project Management Administrative Staff (Coaching/Mentoring)
- Project Management Office (PMO)
- Organizational Knowledge Repositories
- Organizational Governance Framework

START

LEGEND

The following Legend shows how to correctly read the *PMBOK® Guide* references and attributions correctly for Chapter 2: The Environment in which Project's Operate PMBOK Details.

Legend:

Chapter Section	Chapter Section Title	Page Number

Example from Chapter Six shown below:

6.5.1.4	Enterprise Environmental Factors (P 209)

All direct quotes are attributed as (A Guide to the Project Management Body of Knowledge, *(PMBOK® Guide)* – Sixth Edition) Project Management Institute Inc., 2017, Page #, after each section and any/all paraphrased or original wording is attributed as (P #), before or after each section. All Graphs, Charts, Tables and Figures are attributed as: *(PMBOK® Guide,* (PMBOK® Guide, Fig. #-# or #/#, P #, *Title of Graph, Chart, Table or Figure*).

START

2.1 OVERVIEW

Factors affecting a project's outcome are shown below (P 37):

- Enterprise Environmental Factors (EEFs): Outside the organization or enterprise
- Organizational Process Assets (OPAs): Within the organization

Although these are not the only factors affecting a project, either one of these may have a negative/positive impact on a project's success.

Fig. 2-1, P 37, *Project Influences.* Diagram shown below:

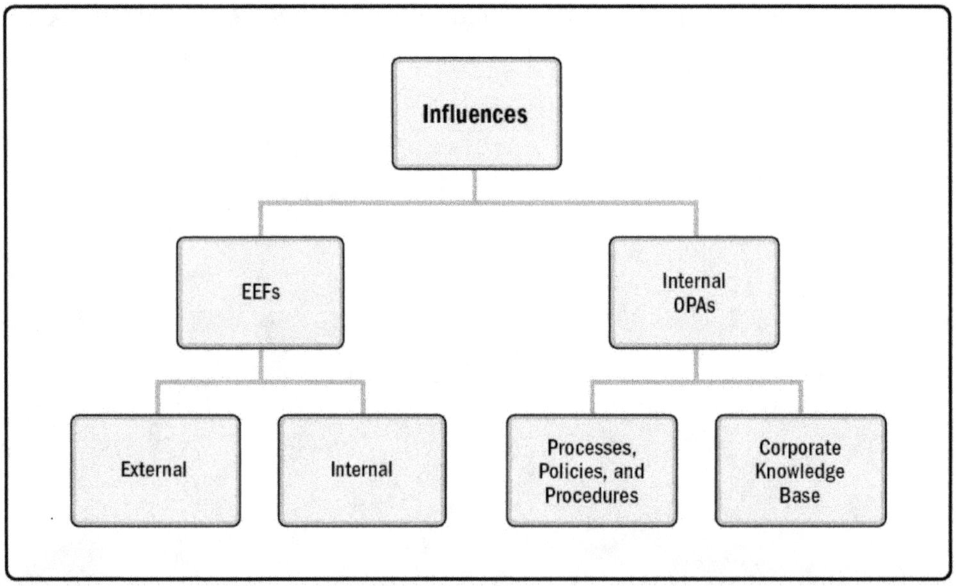

Figure 2-1 (Guide). Project Influences

2.2 ENTERPRISE ENVIRONMENTAL FACTORS (EEF)

Outside factors, known as **Enterprise Environmental Factors,** consist of circumstances or conditions (internal or external) where the project team must deal with conditions outside the scope of the project itself. These circumstances, whether they are positive or negative, may compromise management options and must be seriously taken into account for every project. These are not under the control of the project team.

2.2.1 EEFs Internal to the Organization

Internal Factors in an organization (P 38):

- **Organizational Culture, Structure and Governance.**

Please refer to the following article link, *Gather Round*, by Karen Smits, located at http://www.pmnetworkdigital.com/pmnetwork/october_2018/MobilePagedArticle.action?articleId=1427374#articleId1427374

- **Geographic Distribution Of Facilities And Resources**
- **Infrastructure**
- **Information Technology Software**
- **Resources Availability**
- **Employee Capability**

2.2.2 External to the Organization

External Factors in an Organization (P 39):

- **Marketplace Conditions**
- **Social and Cultural Influences and Issues**

START

- **Legal Restrictions**
- **Commercial Databases**
- **Academic Research**
- **Government or Industry Standards**
- **Financial Considerations**
- **Physical Environmental Elements**

2.3 ORGANIZATIONAL PROCESS ASSETS

Organizational Process Assets (OPA)'s are Internal to the organization, which means they may be updated by team members, and become Inputs to other processes.

Organizational Process Assets are grouped by category (P 39):

- Processes, policies, and procedures: Not updated and is generally established by PMO (P 40)
- Organizational knowledge bases: Updated throughout the project (P 40)

2.3.1 Processes, Policies and Procedures

Please note that the process groups are combined in this example. See Table 1-4, P 25, *Process Management Process Groups and Knowledge Area Mapping.* They are traditionally identified as:

1. Initiating
2. Planning
3. Executing
4. Monitoring and controlling
5. Closing

The processes, policies and procedures followed by an organization shown below are not inclusive (P 40-41):

Initiating and Planning Process Groups (P 40):

- Guidelines and Criteria for Tailoring the Organization's set of standard Processes and Procedures

- Specific Organizational Standards
- Product and Project Life Cycles, and Methods and Procedures
- Templates
- Preapproved Supplier Lists and various types of Contractual Agreements

Executing, Monitoring and Controlling Process Groups (P 40-41):

- Change Control Procedures
- Traceability Matrices
- Financial Controls Procedures
- Issues and Defect Management Procedures
- Resources Availability control and Assignment Management
- Organizational Communication Requirements
- Procedures for Prioritizing, Approving and Issuing Work Authorizations
- Templates
- Standardized Guidelines, Work Instructions, Proposal Evaluation Criteria and Performance Measurement Criteria
- Product, Service or Result Verification and Validation Procedures

Closing Process Groups (P 41):

- Project Closure Guidelines or Requirements

2.3.2 Organizational Knowledge Repositories

Organizational Knowledge Repositories are used for storing and retrieval of information. They are not limited to the list below (P 41):

- Configuration Management Knowledge Repositories
- Financial Data Repositories
- Historical Information and Lessons Learned Knowledge Repositories
- Issue And Defect Management Data Repositories
- Data Repositories for Metrics
- Project Files from Previous Projects

START

2.4 ORGANIZATIONAL SYSTEMS

2.4.1 Overview

A Project Manager (PM) must carry out a project using specific criteria determined by the organization. In order to do this effectively, the PM must be aware of any/all limitations and wield their power, influence, competence, leadership and political astuteness in the best way possible to achieve project success. Simply put, this means the PM should be able to identify who does what and when. **System Factors** such as accountability, responsibility and authority must also be acknowledged and managed according to the standards of the organization (P 42).

System Factors that affect a project may include the following (P 42):

- Management Elements
- Governance Frameworks
- Organizational Structure Types

A **System** is a collection of companies that together may produce results not obtainable by individual components alone (P 42).

In order for a project to have a successful outcome, there must be a **System**, meaning, all of the information/data required to execute the project must be communicated, organized and understood by all of the parties involved.

A **Component** is and identifiable element within the project or organization (P 42):

A distinguishable part contained within an organization/project. Interactions of these **Components** with other **Systems,** produces organizational cultures and their competencies.

System Principles means:

- **Systems** are Dynamic
- **Systems** can be Optimized
- **System Components** can be Optimized
- **Systems** and their components cannot be Optimized at the same time
- **Systems** are Nonlinear in Responsiveness

Systems may change internally when interactions between components change. They may also change when relationships and dependencies change. Usually, Systems are controlled by the organization's management. The management then decides what action to take based on transactions between the system and the components. The end result is the action(s) taken by the PM who must take into account the governance of the organization (P 42-43).

2.4.2 Organizational Governance Framework

Organizational Governance Framework is a predetermined set of conditions and criteria within the levels of participation by the organization, which are used to facilitate and carry out any requirements necessary for a successful project outcome, while taking into consideration (P 43):

- People, Roles, Structures and Policies
- Direction and Oversight through Data Analysis and Feedback

2.4.2.1 Governance Framework

Governance Framework is a framework which allows authority and decisions to be exercised in the organization and may include (P 43):

- Rules
- Policies
- Procedures
- Norms
- Relationships
- Systems
- Processes

Governance Framework influences how:

START

- Objectives of the Organization are set, i.e. defined and described, and achieved
- Risk is monitored and assessed
- Performance is optimized

2.4.2.2 Governance of Portfolios, Programs and Projects

Portfolios, Programs and **Projects** must be governed. Below you will see all four (4) Governance Domains (P 44).

Four (4) Governance Domains:

- Alignment
- Risk
- Performance
- Communications

All four (4) domains have the following functions which are:

- Oversight
- Control Integration
- Decision Making

All of these functions support the **Governance Framework** within a portfolio or program environment. There is no one-size-fits all, meaning governance framework is tailored to each individual Project as needed to produce the best overall outcome to the organizational culture, type of products produced and the unique needs of the organization.

2.4.3 Management Elements

"**Management Elements** are the components that comprise the key functions or principles of general management in the organization. The general management elements are allocated within the organization according to its governance framework and the organizational structure type selected" (Project Management Institute, *A Guide to the Project Management Body of Knowledge, (PMBOK® Guide)* – Sixth Edition, Project Management Institute Inc., 2017, Page 44).

Some of the **Key Functions** or **Principles of Management** are shown below (P 44):

- Division of Work using specialized skills and availability to perform work
- Authority given to perform work
- Responsibility to perform work appropriately assigned based on such attributes as skill and experience
- Discipline of Action
- Unity of Command
- Unity of Direction
- General Goals of the Organization take precedence
- Paid fairly for work performed
- Optimal use of Resources
- Clear Communication Channels
- Right Materials to the Right Person for the Right Job at the Right Time
- Fair and equal treatment of people in the workplace
- Clear Security of Work Positions
- Safety of People in the Workplace
- Open Contribution to Planning and Execution by each person
- Optimal Morale

Only certain individuals within an organization are authorized to implement **Management Elements** in a project according to the corresponding organizational structure.

2.4.4 Organizational Structures Types

Organizational Structure Type is the organized flow of management, authority and the tradeoffs of variables (P 45).

Two key (2) types of Variables:

- Organizational Structures and types available
- Optimization of Organizational Structures

<u>There is not a one-size fits all structure.</u>

Another type of structure is one unique to an individual organization. However, there is one other organizational structure common in project management, which will be discussed later in this manual.

2.4.4.1 Organizational Structure Types

Organizational Structures Types take many forms.

Table 2-1, P 47, *Influences of Organizational Structure on Projects.*

2.4.4.2 Factors in Organization Structure Selection

Factors in Organization Structure Selection: Many factors need to be considered when selecting an **Organizational Structure** since each **Factor** may rank higher or lower in importance.

Table 2-1, P 47, *Influences of Organizational Structures on Projects.* You must study this table very closely. Numerous PMI Exam questions are based on this content.

Some **Organizational Structure** options are shown below (P 46):

- Degree of alignment with Organizational Objectives
- Specialization Capabilities
- Span Of Control Efficiency and Effectiveness
- Clear Path for escalation of Decisions
- Clear Line and Scope of Authority
- Delegation of Capabilities
- Accountability Assignment
- Responsibility Assignment
- Adaptability of Design
- Simplicity of Design
- Efficiency of Performance
- Cost Considerations
- Physical Locations
- Clear Communication

2.4.4.3 Project Management Office

"A **Project Management Office (PMO)** is an organizational structure that standardizes the project-related governance processes and facilitates the sharing of resources, methodologies, tools, and techniques" (Project Management Institute, *A Guide to the Project Management Body of Knowledge, (PMBOK® Guide)* – Sixth Edition, Project Management Institute Inc., 2017, Page 48).

Shown below are three (3) types of **PMO**'s with definitions and how each type influences the project (P 48):

- **Supportive:** Provide a consultative role to project managers by supplying templates, best practices, training, access to information, and lessons learned from other projects. The degree of control provided by the PMO is **low**.
- **Controlling:** Provides support and require compliance through various means. The degree of control provided by the PMO is moderate and compliance may involve:
    - Adoption of **Project Management Frameworks** or **Methodologies**
    - Use of specific **templates, forms** and **tools**
    - Conformance to **Governance Frameworks**

- **Directive:** Control of the projects is taken by directly managing the projects. Project Managers are assigned by and report to the PMO. The degree of control provided by the PMO is **high.**

The projects within a **Project Management Office** do not necessarily have to be related. These projects may simply be managed as a group. Whatever form or function, the organizational needs must take precedence (P 48).

The PMO can if needed, become a stakeholder and make key decisions, such as (P 49):

- Make Recommendations
- Lead Knowledge Transfer
- Terminate Projects
- Take other Actions

Some of the ways a **PMO** should support the **PM**:

- Managing Shared Resources
- Identifying and Developing Project Management Methodology, Best Practices and Standards
- Coaching, Mentoring, Training and Oversight
- Monitoring Compliance with Project Management Standards, Policies, Procedures and Templates
- Developing And Managing Project Policies, Procedures, Templates and other shared documentation
- Coordinate Communication across Projects

Summary: Answers to Student Learning Outcomes

1. The following are **NOT** examples of Enterprise Environmental Factors (EEF's) and Organizational Process Assets (OPA's):

Internal Enterprise Environmental Factors P 38

- Organizational Business

External Environmental Factors P 39

- No Legal Restrictions

Organizational Process Assets P 39

- Organizational Knowledge Environments

2. The correct statement is:

- Systems are non-linear in responsiveness

3. The Missing Organizational Structure Type in a projects is:

- Multidivisional

4. The three (3) types of PMO's that are correct are:

- Supportive
- Controlling
- Directive

The two (2) incorrect PMO types are:

- Dictatorship
- Laisse faire

Similar Questions that may be on the PMI Exam related to Chapter 2

1. In order to contain the power losses and increase the energy efficiency factor, the State Electricity Board has undertaken a major step to fully automate the power utilities infrastructure and also process the power distribution information online. You, as a project manager have to deal with a large number of employees at all locations, who have been working for years in a particular way. This change will bring up a lot of uncertainty. It has now been decided to involve employee union representatives. You are in the process of collecting information to develop the project charter. The more or less fixed terms of the employee unions are considered as _____

   A. Constraints
   B. Assumptions
   C. Requirements
   D. Collective Bargaining Agreements

   Correct answer is A: In a Project like this, which is going to affect internal and external stakeholders and fundamentally change the way of working Union agreements have to be factored in for the overall success. It is highly inadvisable to ignore employee concerns/interests whenever we undertake major change in an organization. These concerns are always treated like constraints during project planning.

2. The policies, methodologies and templates for managing projects within the organization should be supplied by the _____.

   A. Project Sponsor.
   B. Functional Department
   C. Project Management Office (PMO)
   D. Project Manager

   Correct answer is C: This is a role of the project management office.

3. Paul has just received his PMP certification and is working with his sponsor to make an effort to establish a Project Management Office (PMO) in his company for the first time. He seems to have good clarity about projects, programs and portfolios. What is not a true goal for a program?

A. Resolving resource constraints
B. Aligning organizational/strategic direction that affects project and program goals and objectives
C. Resolving issues and change management within a shared governance structure
D. Setting up, maintaining, and carrying out communications among stakeholders that are active, effective, and collaborative in nature

Correct answer is D: All the options relate to programs, except choice D which is more related with project management.

4. Some project stakeholders approach you about the details of a newly introduced enterprise project management methodology. They are a bit apprehensive, but do not totally negate the methodology. They came to you because you have worked for many years together, but they are unsure about the impact of this new policy. How should you handle this situation as a project manager?

A. Inform the stakeholders that they will always be in the communication loop
B. Provide them a documentation of the new policy
C. Inform the project management office (PMO) and ask them to resolve the queries of the stakeholders
D. Tell the stakeholders that this policy is important and cannot be changed

Correct answer is D: The PMO handles the new policies of the organization related to Project Management. The Project manager should direct the stakeholders to the correct person in the PMO, who in turn would be best equipped to provide the right guidance.

5. The purpose of the review of deliverables and the project performance at the conclusion of a project phase is to ______.

A. Determine how many resources are required to complete the project according to the project baseline.
B. Adjust the schedule and cost baselines based on past performance.
C. Obtain customer acceptance of project deliverables.
D. Determine whether the project continues to be aligned with

business case and project objectives.

Correct answer is D: The phase end review is also called Kill points, or Stage gates. The primary purpose is to ensure that the purpose for which the project was started remains intact and the business case holds.

You may now move on to Chapter Three: The Role of the Project Manager (PM)

Chapter 3: The Role of the Project Manager: Control the WBS

PMI, PMP, CAPM, PMI-ACP, PMI-RMP, PMI-SP and *PMBOK® Guide* are registered marks of the Project Management Institute, 2017 and all references, from this point on, are from the Project Management Institute, (A Guide to the Project Management Body of Knowledge, *(PMBOK® Guide)* – Sixth Edition).

"…Plan your day to achieve your goals … [then] keep to your plan." Dale Carneige

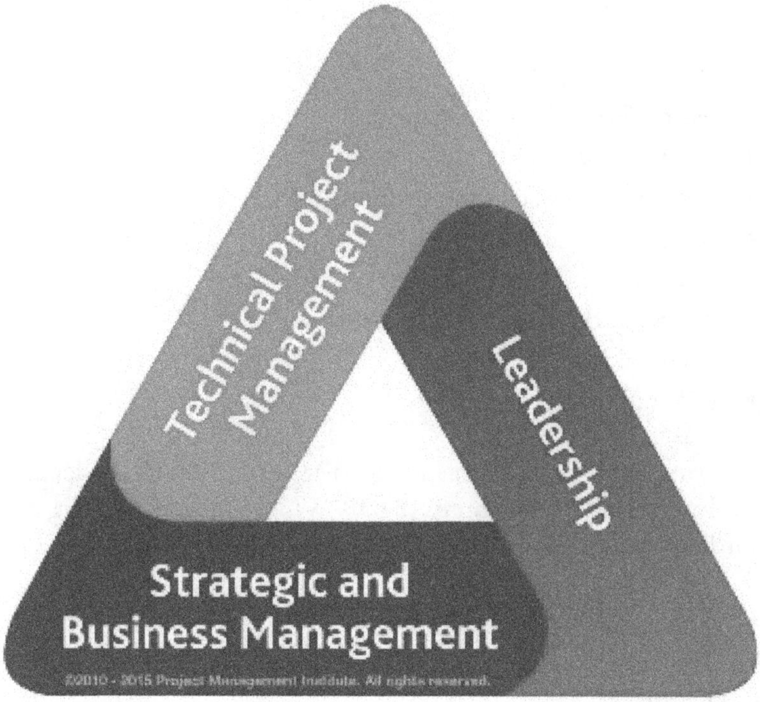

Student Learning Outcomes

1. There are major differences in the roles of the Project Manager, Functional or Business Manager, or Operations Manager. Are the following correct (P 52)?

    - The Project Manager, assigned by performing organization, leads the project team to achieve the project objectives
    - The functional or business unit manager does not provide oversight for a functional or business unit
    - The operations manager ensures that business units are efficient

2. There are three (3) PMI Talent Triangle Competencies (P 57). Which three (3) are correct?

    - Non-Technical Management
    - Tactical Business Management
    - Enterprise-Wide Business management
    - Technical Management
    - Leadership
    - Strategic Business Management
    - General Management
    - Marketing Management

3. Power is often supported by another individual's perception of the leader (P 63) and is demonstrated by the leader's attributes (P 63). Which of the following perceptions are correct, according to the PMBOK, 6th Edition?

    - Positional
    - Informational
    - Controlling
    - Tolerant
    - Political
    - Situational
    - Understanding
    - Personal or Charismatic
    - Intolerant
    - General

- Relational
- Communicator

4. A Project Manager leads in various ways, based on real or adopted styles. What are the six (6) Leadership Styles (P 65)? Choose the correct ones from the list below:

    - Laissez-Faire
    - Change Agent
    - Transactional
    - Servant Leader
    - Autocratic
    - Hybrid Leadership
    - Transformational
    - Charismatic
    - Process-Minded
    - Relational
    - Interactional

5. Personality differences vary from leader to leader. These individual differences may be characteristics that include patterns of thinking, feeling and behaviors (P 66). What are some personality characteristics or traits? Use the list below to assess the correct answers:

    - Authentic
    - Detached
    - Friendly
    - Imaginative
    - Courteous
    - Creative
    - Disingenuous
    - Worldly
    - Emotional
    - Cultural
    - Emotional

6. Integration is important for the project manager whose job is to assure the alignment of project objectives and strategic results with the goals of the portfolio, program and business areas. What are the three (3) Levels of Integration? (P 66-67) Choose from the list below:

    - Process Level
    - Cognitive Level
    - Context Level
    - Process-Led
    - Cognitive-Led

CHAPTER THREE INTRODUCTION: THE ROLE OF THE PROJECT MANAGER

THE ROLE OF THE PROJECT MANAGER: CHAPTER 3 OVERVIEW: PMBOK® 6TH Edition P 51-68

The Project Manager (PM) plays a critical role in the leadership of their project team and working with project sponsors. There are various skills and knowledge areas that need to be mastered. The project manager is very similar to a conductor that leads an orchestra. He or she may not be able to play every instrument, but should be able to perform various roles in ensuring the orchestra is playing according to tune, maintaining a rhythm and giving a superb orchestral performance.

The Project Manager has an influence and impact upon the success of any project.

Fig. 3-1. P 53, *Example of Project Manager's Sphere of Influence.*

Influence takes place in group settings and one-on-one settings. The PM influences the project team, resource managers, interfaces with governing bodies, sponsors, steering committee, project management offices (PMO)'s and deals with stakeholders, suppliers, customers and end users.

The project manager needs to exhibit competency. It is one thing to be academically competent and vocationally qualified. It is another thing to be truly competent. There are three (3) areas according to the **PMI Talent Triangle** that the project manager must excel in. They are (P 56-60):

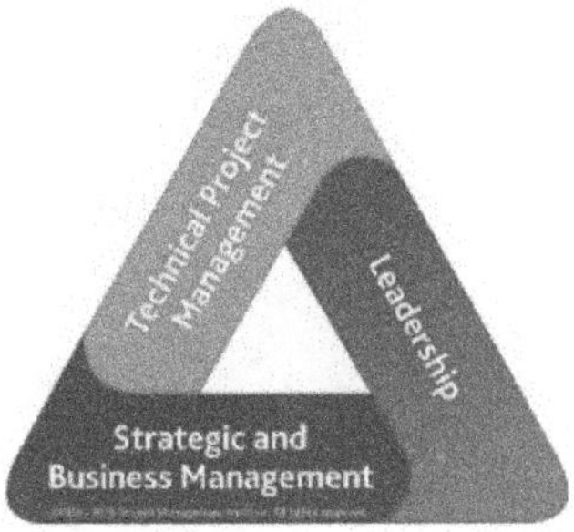

1. Technical Project Management
2. Leadership
3. Strategic and Business Management

Fig. 3-2, P 57, *The PMI Talent Triangle®*

CHAPTER 3 INTRODUCTION OVERVIEW: THE ROLE OF THE PROJECT MANAGER

Project managers are leaders. A leader is a visionary; a leader is optimistic and positive, and is able to collaborate with others. A leader successfully manages relationships, and communicates with top-level managers, sponsors and stakeholders. Leaders are respectful of others, and exhibit personal and professional integrity. Leaders are culturally sensitive and are lifelong learners (P 61). The PM leader needs to understand politics, power and getting things done. See section (3.4.4.3). The PM leader also needs to understand the various forms of power and that leadership and management are not synonymous.

See section (3.4.5), and Table 3-1, P 64, *Team Management and Team Leadership Compared.*

There are six types of leadership styles. These types may be used individually, collectively, or as a hybrid.

1. Laissez-faire leadership allows the team to make their own decisions. The term laissez-faire means to leave alone.
2. Transactional leadership focuses on the goals and accomplishments to achieve various rewards.
3. Servant leadership commits to serve and put other persons first.
4. Transformational leadership empowers followers through idealized attributes and behaviors.
5. Charismatic leadership inspires and exhibits a high level of energy and enthusiasm.
6. Interactional leadership combines transactional, transformational and charismatic leadership styles.

Study Leadership Styles. Section 3.4.5.1, P 65 (A Guide to the Project Management Body of Knowledge, *(PMBOK® Guide)* – Sixth Edition), Project Management Institute 2017.

The Project Manager (PM) needs to understand how integration management works. See Section 3.5, Performing Integration, P 66-68). Chapter 4 goes into great detail. It is outlined below (P 67-68):

1. Performing Integration at the Process Level
2. Performing Integration at the Cognitive Level
3. Integration at the Context Level
4. Integration and complexity

KEY WORDS CHAPTER 3: The Role of the Project Manager

- Project Manager Sphere of Influence
- Tacit Knowledge
- Business Knowledge
- Holistic View
- Competing Restraints
- Industry Trends
- Explicit Knowledge
- PMI Talent triangle
    - Technical Project Management Skills
    - Strategic and Business Management Skills
    - Leadership Styles
        - Laissez-Faire
        - Transactional
        - Servant
        - Transformational
        - Charismatic
        - Interactional
- Quality Skills of a Leader
- Referent Power
- Integration
- Pressure-Based
- Guilt-Based
- Integration
- Power Politics
- Power
- Leadership
- Management

LEGEND

The following Legend shows how to correctly read the *PMBOK® Guide* references and attributions correctly for Chapter 3: The Role of the Project Manager PMBOK Details.

Legend:

Chapter Section	Chapter Section Title	Page Number

Example from Chapter Six shown below:

6.5.1.4	Enterprise Environmental Factors	(P 209)

All direct quotes are attributed as (A Guide to the Project Management Body of Knowledge, (*PMBOK® Guide)* – Sixth Edition) Project Management Institute Inc., 2017, Page #, after each section and any/all paraphrased or original wording is attributed as (P #), before or after each section. All Graphs, Charts, Tables and Figures are attributed as: (*PMBOK® Guide,* Fig. #-# or #/#, P #, *Title of Graph, Chart, Table or Figure*).

3.1 OVERVIEW

Project Managers (PM)'s typically get involved in a project from the beginning to the closing. They can also become involved before the project's actual start up (initiating) process and before the scope of their duties will most likely vary from one organization to another. The PM's roles in the project are tailored to fit the organization and the project itself. A PM must understand the Membership Roles and Responsibilities of all team members. They must take responsibility for the team they manage. PM's are expected to have the knowledge and skills to lead their team to project success (P 91).

3.2 DEFINITION OF A PROJECT MANAGER

The **Project Manager** is a person assigned to the organization's project to lead the project team and to successfully carrying out the project's objectives (P 52).

3.3 THE PROJECT MANAGER'S SPHERE OF INFLUENCE

3.3.1 Overview

Project Managers have many **obligations.** They must have the capabilities and skills to perform the required duties within their **Sphere of Influence** (P 52).

Fig. 3-1, P 53, *Example of Project Manager's Sphere of Influence*

3.3.2 The Project

The PM balances the needs/requirements of the team with those of the **Project Objectives** expectations for, as well as balancing the competing constraints and maximizing available resources.

The PM must communicate with all members of the team, the project sponsor and other stakeholders. The PM accomplishes this by using **soft skills**. These skills include interpersonal skills and the ability to manage people (P 53).

The ability to communicate across multiple aspects of the project and across all organization levels is vital to project success, decision making and problem resolution. Shown below are some ways to accomplish this (P 53):

- Developing finely tuned skills using multiple methods (verbal, written, non-verbal)
- Creating, maintaining and adhering to communications plans and schedules
- Communicating predictable and consistently
- Seeking to understand the project stakeholder's communication needs
- Making communications concise, clear, complete, simple, relevant and tailored
- Relay important positive/negative news
- Incorporate feedback channels

- Relationship skills in networking

3.3.3 The Organization

The **Project Manager (PM)** must be pro-active in interacting with others in the **Organization**. This includes communicating progress with other managers and the **Project Sponsor** while the project is ongoing. Along with these duties, the Project Manager must (P 54):

- Demonstrate the value of **Project Management**
- Increase acceptance of **Project Management** practices in the organization
- Advance the efficiency of the **PMO** when one exists in the organization

The PM's roles may consist of reporting to a **Functional Manager** or other PM's who may report to a PMO, Portfolio Manager or Program Manager. At times, the PM may need to solicit advice from a **SME** (Subject Matter Expert), depending on organizational needs.

3.3.4 The Industry

The PM must be aware of how and when current industry trends may affect the assigned project. Such trends include those, but are not limited to those shown below (P 55):

- Product and Technology Development

Forget the most popular programming languages, here's what developers actually use, (2:13 minutes) located at https://www.techrepublic.com/article/forget-the-most-popular-programming-languages-heres-what-developers-actually-use/ by Alison DeNisco Rayome.

- New and Changing Market Niches
- Standards
- Technical Support Tools
- Economic Forces that impact the immediate project
- Influences affecting the Project Management Discipline
- Process Improvement and Sustainability Strategies

3.3.5 Professional Discipline

Professional Discipline: The PM must always undergo professional developmental and training. The PM must maintain and enhance their skills in project management theory and practice. This includes **Knowledge Transfer** and **Integration** of new subject matter and practices. This includes the following (P 56):

- Contribution of knowledge and expertise at the national and global levels
- Participation in training, continuing education and development
  - In the project management profession
  - In a related profession
  - In other professions

All organizations need to be **learning organizations**.

3.3.6 Across Disciplines

Across Disciplines: A PM should always be available to inform and educate other professionals on matters of using project management approaches, tools and techniques and in advancing the profession of project management (P 56).

3.4 PROJECT MANAGER COMPETENCIES

3.4.1 Overview

The **Project Management Competency Development (PMDC) Framework** identifies the skills needed by the PM to be successful in their project work.

Fig. 3-2, P 57, *The PMI Talent Triangle*™.

The **PMI Talent Triangle** focuses on the PM's need to develop the three (3) **Key Skill Sets** (P 56):

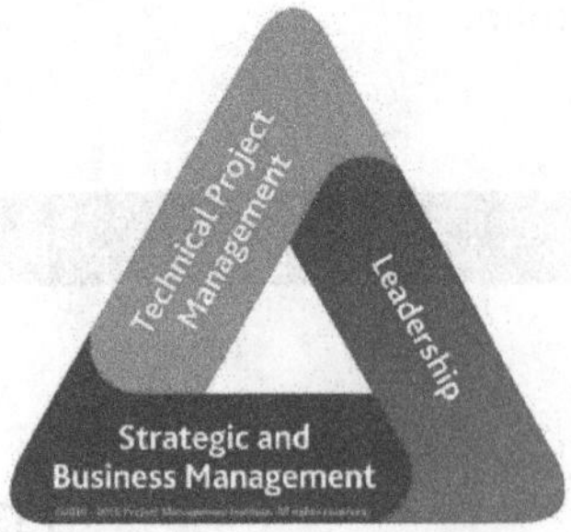

- **Technical Project Management:** Knowledge, skills and behaviors related to the technical aspects of performing one's role
- **Leadership:** Knowledge, skills and behaviors needed to guide, motivate and direct a team and to help an organization achieve its business goals

- **Strategic and Business Management:** Knowledge of and expertise in the industry and organization

Project Managers need to have a balance of all three (3) key skill sets in order to be truly effective and successful in running projects (P 56).

Please watch, *The PMI Talent Triangle* (8:29 minutes), video explanation located at the following address: https://www.youtube.com/watch?v=qlhGgp04zgQandauthuser=0

3.4.2 Technical Project Management Skills

Technical Project Management Skills are skills that effectively apply project management knowledge to deliver desired project outcomes.

Project Managers should consistently demonstrate proficiency in the following key skills shown below (P 58):

- Focus on the critical top technical project management elements for each project they manage, such as:
  - Critical success factors for the project
  - Schedule,
  - Selected financial reports
  - Issue log
- Tailor both traditional and agile tools, techniques, and methods for each project
- Make time to plan thoroughly and prioritize diligently
- Manage project elements to meet project schedule deadlines, bring projects under budget, efficiently utilize resources and minimize risks

3.4.3 Strategic and Business Management Skills

Strategic and Business Management Skills involve the ability to see the macro level overview of the organization and to effectively negotiate/implement actions that support strategic company alignment and innovation.

Project Managers should be familiar with the business process and to be able to negotiate and implement decisions that (P 58):

- Explain to others the essential business aspects of the project
- Work with the project sponsor, team, and subject matter experts to develop an appropriate project delivery strategy for the organization
- Implement strategies in a way that maximizes the business value of the project

In order to make the best decisions, the PM may need to seek outside expertise. The PM should educate themselves as much as possible about how the project's goals and expectations fit the company's strategic goals. At the very least, the PM should know enough about the organization and how to create approaches that aligns with the following:

- Strategy
- Mission

The Project Manager is seldom ever asked to write a Vision or Mission Statement for the company. That typically is the province of the company's Executive team, Owners and/or Board of Directors. However, the Project Manager needs to be able to interpret and explain to others in the project team, the organizational aspects to include among others: Strategy, Mission, Goals and Objectives of the company etc.

Additionally, the project manager needs to have leadership skills while being a visionary that helps describe and translate the company's products, goals and objectives into the project initiatives.

When a project is conceptualized/idealized, the Project Manager is then required to devise the Project Charter, which authorizes the existence of a project with the authority to apply organizational resources to the project.

See the following link, *Nonprofit Mission Statements vs. Vision Statements*, (7 minutes) by George Weiner, at https://www.wholewhale.com/tips/nonprofit-mission-statements-vs-vision-statements/

- Goals and objectives
- Products and services;
- Operations
- The market and the market condition
- Competition

In order to understand how the interrelationship with business and strategic factors may affect a project, the Project Manager (PM) must first understand the following factors (P 59):

- Risks
- Issues
- Financial Implications
- Cost vs. Benefits Analysis
- Business Value
- Benefits Realization Expectations and Strategies
- Scope
- Budget
- Schedule
- Quality

Only when the PM has thoroughly studied the organization, will they be able to make sound decisions and recommendations for a project. The PM must always be on the lookout for changes, making sure to keep the business and project strategies aligned on a continuous basis.

3.4.4 Leadership Skills

Leadership Skills are essential to success, meaning the PM must be able to (P 60):

- Guide People
- Motivate People
- Direct a Team of People

This skillset includes:

- Negotiation Abilities

- Resilience
- Communication
- Problem Solving
- Critical Thinking
- Interpersonal Skills

> *"...the leader must be ready when the opportunity presents itself."*
> Doris Kearns Goodwin

A project consists of people working together towards a common outcome. Now, more than ever, leadership skills are becoming increasingly more demanding in the ever-changing landscape of Project Management.

Article: *Leadership in the Storm: How Four U.S. Presidents Handled Turmoil,* by Doris Kearns Goodwin, link located at the following link (2018): http://knowledge.wharton.upenn.edu/article/leadership-in-turbulent-times/?utm_source=kw_newsletter&utm_medium=email&utm_campaign=2018-10-04

Also, check out the article, *Become a Better Delegator with these Tech Project Management Tips*, by Forbes Technology Council, located at: https://www.forbes.com/sites/forbestechcouncil/2018/09/27/become-a-better-delegator-with-these-tech-project-management-tips/

3.4.4.1 Dealing with People

The PM must interact with people on a consistent basis, because the majority of their time is spent dealing with people. The PM must apply their leadership skillsets at all times and with a variety of people who normally are involved in the outcome of the project. These include (P 60):

- Project Stakeholders
- Project Team
- Steering Team
- Project Sponsors

3.4.4.2 Qualities and Skills of a Leader

Research shows that the **Qualities** and **Skills** of a **Leader** include (P 61):

- Being a Visionary
- Being Optimistic/Positive
- Being Collaborative, etc.

Leaders manage relationships and conflicts by:

- Building Trust
- Satisfying Concerns
- Seeking Consensus
- Balancing Competing and Opposing Goals
- Applying Persuasion, Negotiation, Compromise and Conflict Resolution Skills
- Developing and Nurturing Personal and Professional Networks
- Taking a long-term view that Relationships are just as important as the Project
- Continuously Developing and applying Political Acumen

An effective leader communicates by:

- Managing Expectations
- Accepting Feedback
- Giving Feedback
- Asking and Listening
- Being respectful
- Exhibiting integrity by being culturally sensitive, courageous, a problem solver and decisive
- Giving credit to others where due
- Being a life-long learner who is results-and action-oriented
- Focusing on the important things, including:
    - Continuously prioritizing work

- Finding and using a prioritizing method
- Differentiating high-level strategic priorities
- Maintaining vigilance on primary project constraints
- Remaining flexible on tactical priorities
- Being able to sift through massive amounts of information to obtain the most important information
- Having a holistic and systemic view of the project, taking into account internal and external factors equally
- Being able to apply critical thinking
- Being able to build effective teams, be service-oriented and have fun and share humor effectively with team members

3.4.4.3 Politics, Power and Getting Things Done

Politics, Power and Getting Things Done: Getting things done efficiently, correctly and on time is the ultimate goal of the PM. Acquiring leadership skillsets and developing the ability to deal with politics is never-ending, and translates to influence, negotiation, autonomy and ultimately power.

Power and Politics are not exclusively good or bad or positive or negative. What is most important is how the PM manages the project. The PM must understand organizational strategies while observing relationships, collecting data and sensing the environment within the organization. The PM must negotiate and select the appropriate actions and team to carry out the project's needed activities. Communication and relationship building with other people helps to ensure project activities are completed on time to produce successful outcomes (P 42).

Power, by its very nature can be complex and must be handled accordingly. There are many varied forms of power that can be used by the PM which are shown below (P 63):

- Positional
- Informational
- Referent
- Situational
- Personal/Charismatic
- Relational
- Expert
- Reward Oriented
- Punitive or Coercive
- Ingratiating
- Pressure-Based
- Guilt-Based
- Persuasive
- Avoiding

Study the list on P 63, 6th Ed. An effective and successful PM must be proactive, while still working within the organizational boundaries and at the same time exercising focused **forms of power**.

3.4.5 Comparison of Leadership and Management

Leadership and management are not synonymous. Please see below (P 64):

- **Management**: Directing a person how to get from one point to another using a prescribed set of behaviors

- **Leadership**: Working with others through discussion or debate methods to guide them from one point to another

Table 3-1, P 64, *Team Management and Team Leadership Compared.*

Leadership style shows up when the PM balances leadership techniques with management approaches.

3.4.5.1 Leadership Styles

A PM's particular **Leadership Style** may be demonstrated in many creative ways. The particular style is based on what the PM's personal preference is and what is needed as appropriate for the project. Some factors to consider in making style choices are shown below (P 65):

- Leader Characteristics
- Team Member Characteristics
- Organizational Characteristics
- Environmental Characteristics

Some common examples of a **Leadership Style** (read and study) that a PM can adapt are (P 65):

- Laissez-Faire
- Transactional

- Servant Leader
- Transformational
- Charismatic
- Interactional

3.4.5.2 Personality

Personality is how one thinks, feels and behaves. Please study each personality characteristics and traits shown below (P 66):

- Authentic
- Courteous
- Creative
- Cultural
- Emotional
- Intellectual
- Managerial
- Political
- Service-Oriented
- Social
- Systemic

A PM should use all of these traits to some degree. However, some may be stressed more depending on the organization or project needs. The PM should use the best-approved behavior for different situations.

3.5 PERFORMING INTEGRATION

Performing Integration (P 66):

- Project Managers play a key role in working with the project sponsor to understand the strategic objectives and to ensure that the alignment of the project objectives and results fit those of the portfolio, program and business areas.

- Project Managers are responsible for guiding the team to work together and to focus on what is essential at the project, program or portfolio level.

3.5.1 Performing Integration at the Process Level

Performing Integration at the Process Level: Project management is about a set of processes and activities that may or may not overlap or interact with each other during the life of the project (P 67).

The PM must integrate the project processes and the Knowledge Areas as the team interacts with each other to produce a successful project outcome.

3.5.2 Integration at the Cognitive Level

Integration at the Cognitive Level: The methods used to manage a project are many and varied. The PM should learn about the company's culture, the complexity of the project and how best to motivate the stakeholders and team participants. All **Knowledge Areas** must be thoroughly integrated into the process groups (P 67).

3.5.3 Integration at the Context Level

Integration at the Context Level: Many changes have taken place in the management of projects and the PM needs to be aware of these changes and how to use them to the best advantage, by using social networking platforms and virtual teams, while considering cultural norms. These actions will facilitate project success (P 67).

3.5.4 Integration and Complexity

Integration and Complexity: Let us first address what is considered **Complexity.** All projects have some aspect of complexity. Projects considered very complex can become very difficult to manage (P 67).

Integration: The PM must take into consideration any or all components both inside and outside of the project. Any complexity found, may be defined as (P 68):

- Containing multiple parts
- Possessing a number of connections between the parts
- Exhibiting dynamic interactions between the parts
- Exhibiting behavior produced as a result of interactions that cannot be explained as the simple sum of the parts

Being able to identify key elements that determine complexity at the beginning of a project can determine success or failure.

Summary: Answers to Student Learning Outcomes

1. The following is incorrect regarding the major role differences of a Project Manager, Functional Business Unit Manager or Operations Manager (P 52)?

   - The functional or business unit manager does not provide oversight for a functional or business unit

2. Identify the three (3) PMI Talent Triangle components (P 57).

   - Technical Management
   - Leadership
   - Strategic Business Management

3. What are the various attributes that are demonstrated by leader's power (P 63)?

   - Positional
   - Informational
   - Tolerant
   - Situational
   - Personal or Charismatic
   - Relational

4. These are the six (6) leadership styles (P 65):

   - Laissez-Faire
   - Transactional
   - Servant Leader
   - Transformational
   - Charismatic
   - Interactional

5. What are the personality traits that may vary from leader to leader?

   - Authentic
   - Courteous
   - Creative

- Cultural
- Emotional

6. What are the three (3) levels of integration (P 66-67)?

- Process Level
- Cognitive Level
- Context Level

Similar Questions that may be on the PMI Exam related to Chapter 3

1. Jenny is the project manager at a biotech company, where she is leading a cross-functional team to develop a treatment for leukemia. The organization has a balanced matrix structure, where all of her project team members report to different functional managers, but none of the team members report to her directly. Her project has extremely high visibility in the company and there is a lot of pressure on her to deliver the cancer treatment on time and within budget. However, she is concerned whether she will have the necessary authority and power to complete the project deliverables. Which of the following types of powers will be most effective in her situation?

   A. Expert power
   B. Legitimate power
   C. Coercive power
   D. Referent power

   Correct answer is A: Expert power is generally regarded as the best form of power, particularly in this situation. The Project is technical and the Project manager does not enjoy full authority on resources or budget. People follow her more for her expertise.

2. You are the project manager and your project has reached the end. Your project has been successful in terms of requirements, scope, schedule and cost. The functional manager, under whom various team members used to work, is upset because many of his staff quit while working on the project. This is because of the long hours of the project and lack of management support. Which of the following is the most correct statement about this project?

   A. The project manager did not obtain adequate resources and did not set a realistic deadline based on resources available.
   B. The project was within budget and time and achieved its objectives. Upper management is responsible for providing adequate resources, and the project manager managed the project well with available resources.
   C. The project should be measured against how successfully it met its charter. This was not done during this project.
   D. The functional manager is responsible for his staff and obtaining adequate resources to meet the schedule once it has

been set. The project and project manager achieved all of its goals set forth in the charter.

Correct answer is A: The Project Manager is responsible for proper planning and seeking adequate resources for the project from senior management/project sponsor and not the functional manager. It is very clear from the question that there was no realistic planning in place, which led to overworked resources, low morale and loss of employees. This situation could have been avoided if resource requirements were estimated correctly and management provided adequate support to the project manager.

3. Michael just joined ABC enterprises. He finds that his role in the organization is to keep track of status and make some of the minor decisions on the project without having to run them by the functional manager. He is working as a _____.

   A. Project Manager
   B. Project Coordinator
   C. Project Expediter
   D. Team Member

Correct answer is B: A project coordinator has no powers to decide on project budget, schedule or other performance parameters. Members do not report to the functional manager. A Project Coordinator can make certain minor decisions without having to ask the functional manager.

4. Robert worked in the Oil and Gas industry for many years and most of that time he was the Project Manager. He is now laid off and looking for a new job. He is now interviewing with a Functional Organization. What is the role of the project manager in a Functional Organizational Structure on Projects?

   A. Part-time: May or may not be a designated job role like coordinator
   B. Full-time: Designated job role
   C. Part-time: Done as part of another job and not a designated job role like coordinator
   D. Part-time: Embedded in the functions as a skill and may not be a designated job role like coordinator

Correct answer is D: In the Functional organization, the project manager is part-time and may or may not have a designated job role like coordinator.

5. Mahesh is authoring a document which details the vision of an exercise which requires few resources from his team. He decided to give the go ahead by allocating resources to the exercise and defining the output expected in the authored document. What could be the possible role of Mahesh?

    A. The project manager
    B. Member of Quality Group
    C. Project Sponsor / Portfolio Manager.
    D. Member of PMO

    Correct answer is C: Project initiation is done by the Sponsor/Portfolio Manager. The PM at times provides support in making the Project Charter.

6. The president and the vice president of marketing department of a software development organization hold a meeting to discuss a change to a key task in the design phase of a project. After the discussion, they tell the project manager to make the appropriate changes. What role is being played by the project manager in this scenario?

    A. Proactive senior management
    B. A project-based organization
    C. A project coordinator role
    D. Effective decision making

    Correct answer is D: This is the best response. A project coordinator's authority and decision-making ability are limited to minor decisions. Senior management makes the significant decisions that will impact the scope and success of the project. There is not enough information given to determine whether Answer A or C are correct.

You may now move on to Chapter Four: Project Integration Management

Chapter 4: Project Integration Management: All Projects must Produce Business Value

"It's amazing how much you can accomplish when it doesn't matter who gets the credit." Unknown

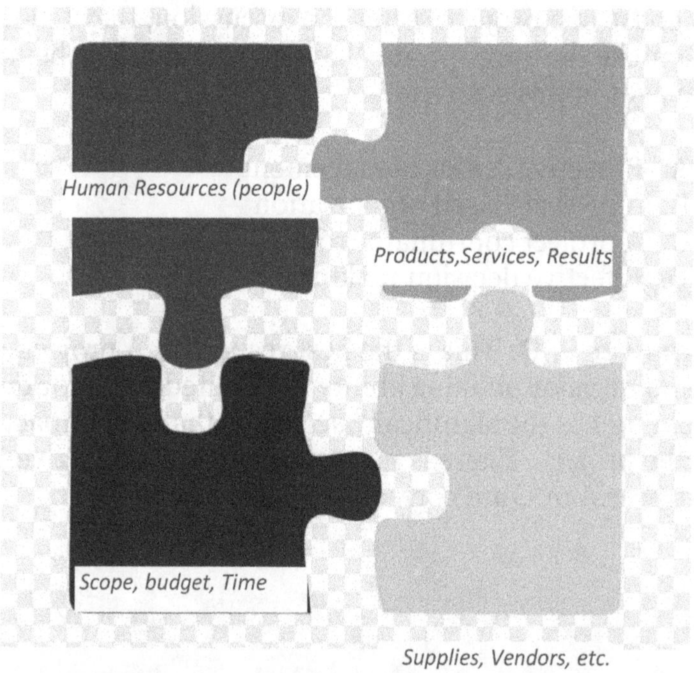

Student Learning Outcomes

1. What is meant by **Integration Management** (P69)?
2. The Project Manager needs to make **choices** regarding **Project Integration**

Management. List five (5) of those choices (P 69).

3. List all seven (7) processes (steps) in **Project Integration Management** and describe each area (P 70).
4. Project Integration is performed by the Project Manager with the help of the project team (P 72). Many of the processes in **Project Integration Management** are often iterative. There are many **New Concepts** for Project Integration Management. What are these new concepts?
5. When combining results from all of the knowledge areas, the Project Manager may consider the use of various **Emerging Practices** (P 73). List them.
6. The Project Manager may wish to **tailor** the **Project Integration Management** process (P 74). List the eight (8) considerations.
7. What is **Develop Project Charter** and what is its **key benefit** (P 75)?
8. What are **Business Documents** (P77)?
9. What is an **Agreement** as it serves as an input to **Develop Project Charter**? (P 78)?
10. In **Develop Project Charter**, what four tools and techniques (P 79-80) may be used to produce its two (2) output documents: Project Charter and the Assumption Log?
11. What is **Develop Project Management Plan** (P 82) and its **key benefit**?
12. The output of **Develop Project Management Plan** (P 86) consists of only one output. It is called the Project Management Plan. List the three base lines of the Project Management Plan (P 87).
13. What is meant by **Direct and Manage Project Work** (P 90) and its benefits?
14. What is a **Change Request** (P 96)? What are the four (4) types?
15. What is meant by **Manage Project Knowledge** and what are its **key benefits** (P 98)?
16. One of the many tools and techniques that may be used in **Manage Project Knowledge** (P 104) is **Interpersonal and Team Skills**. List five (5) of these skills.
17. What is **Monitor and Control Project Work** and its benefits (P 105)?
18. List the inputs to **Monitor and Control Project Work** (P 106).
19. List the **data analysis tools and techniques** that may be used in Monitor and Control Project Work (P 111).
20. There are three (3) types of **Change Requests** that may be used in Monitor and Control Project Work (P 112). List all three (3).
21. What is **Perform Integrated Change Control** and its benefits (P 113)?
22. What is a **Change Control** Board (CCB) (P 115)?
23. There are numerous **tools and techniques** that may be used in **Perform Integrated Change Control** (P 119). Decision-making is one of these. List the three (3) **decision-making techniques** that may be used.
24. What is meant by **Close Project or Phase** and what is its **key benefit** (P 121)?
25. What is meant by **Final Product, Service or Result Transition** (P 127) in Close Project or Phase: Outputs?
26. What is the **Final Report** (P 127)?

CHAPTER FOUR INTRODUCTION: ALL PROJECT MUST PRODUCE BUSINESS VALUE

PROJECT INTEGRATION MANAGEMENT: CHAPTER 4 OVERVIEW: PMBOK® 6TH Edition P 69-127

Background: Project Integration includes making choices about (P 69):

- Resource allocation
- Balancing competing demands
- Examining any alternative approaches
- Tailoring the processes to meet the project objectives
- Managing the interdependencies among the Project Management Knowledge Areas

Fig. 3-1, P 53, *Example of Project Manager's Sphere of Influence*
Fig. 1-5, P 555, *Example of Process Group Interactions within a Project or Phase*
Fig. 3-3, P 120 this book, *Project Management Process Interactions*

Project Integration Management is a process. It is a complex process to identify, define, combine and unify various processes. There are seven (7) project integration management processes as outlined below. They are (P 359):

1. The Project Manager needs to **Develop a Project Charter** (Section 4.1) which authorizes the project
2. The Project Manager needs to **Develop a Project Management Plan** (Section 4.2)
3. The Project Manager needs to **Direct and Manage Project Work** (Section 4.3) efforts
4. The Project Manager needs to be able to **Manage Project Knowledge** (Section 4.4)
5. The Project Manager needs to **Monitor and Control Project Work** (Section 4.5)
6. Upon changes to the project, the Project Manager needs to **Perform Integrated Change Control** (Section 4.6)
7. The Project Manager must officially **Close Project or Phase** (Section 4.7)

Project Integration Management is a collaborative effort requiring the integration of PMBOK knowledge areas and the overlapping of project process groups and product work. See Fig. A, P 118, this book.

Process Groups are interrelated activities used to create a product, service or result. These project processes are divided into one or two major categories, project managed sources and product oriented processes.

See Fig. 3.1, P 87, *Project Management Process Groups*, which can be found in the (*PMBOK® Guide*) – Fifth Edition: **Not found in PMBOK 6th Edition. See Diagram on next page.**

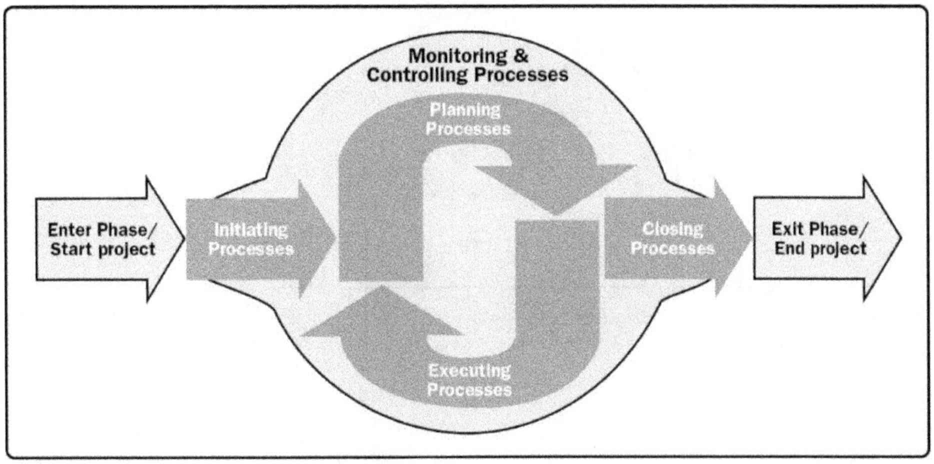

Figure 3-1. Project Management Process Groups

Project Integration Management is the first knowledge area to be emphasized in the PMBOK 6th Edition, and the other nine (9) knowledge areas all interact with the project integration management areas.

Table 1-4, P 25, *Project Management Process Group and Knowledge Area Mapping.*

Fig. 1-5, P 555, *Example of Process Group Interactions within a Project or Phase*, shown below.

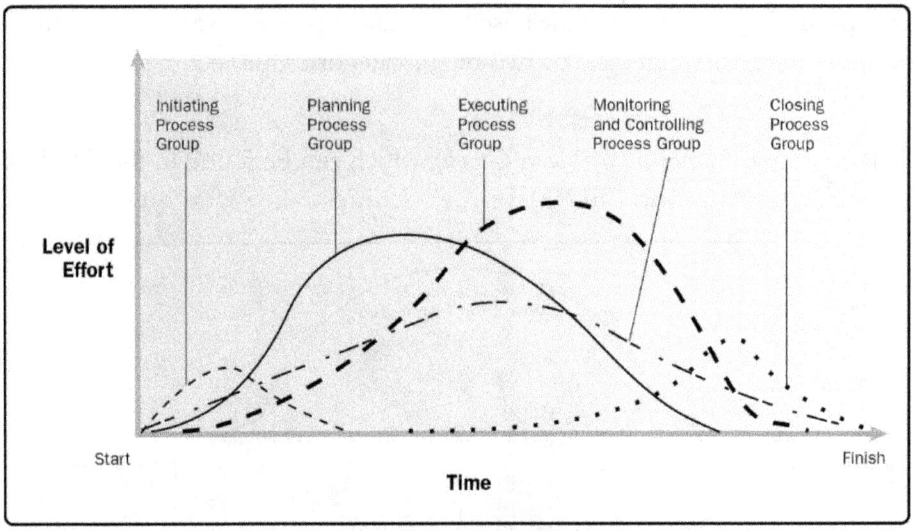

Figure 1-5 (Standard). Example of Process Group Interactions Within a Project or Phase

Study Fig. 3-3, *Process Management Interactions,* which can be found in the (*PMBOK® Guide*) – Fifth Edition (shown on the next page). **Not found in PMBOK 6th Edition.**

Be sure to study the Fig. 3-3, as it graphically details the specific **Inputs and Outputs** of each of the five (5) process groupings shown below:

1. Initiating Process Group
2. Planning Process Group
3. Executing Process Group
4. Monitoring and Controlling Process Group
5. Closing Process Group

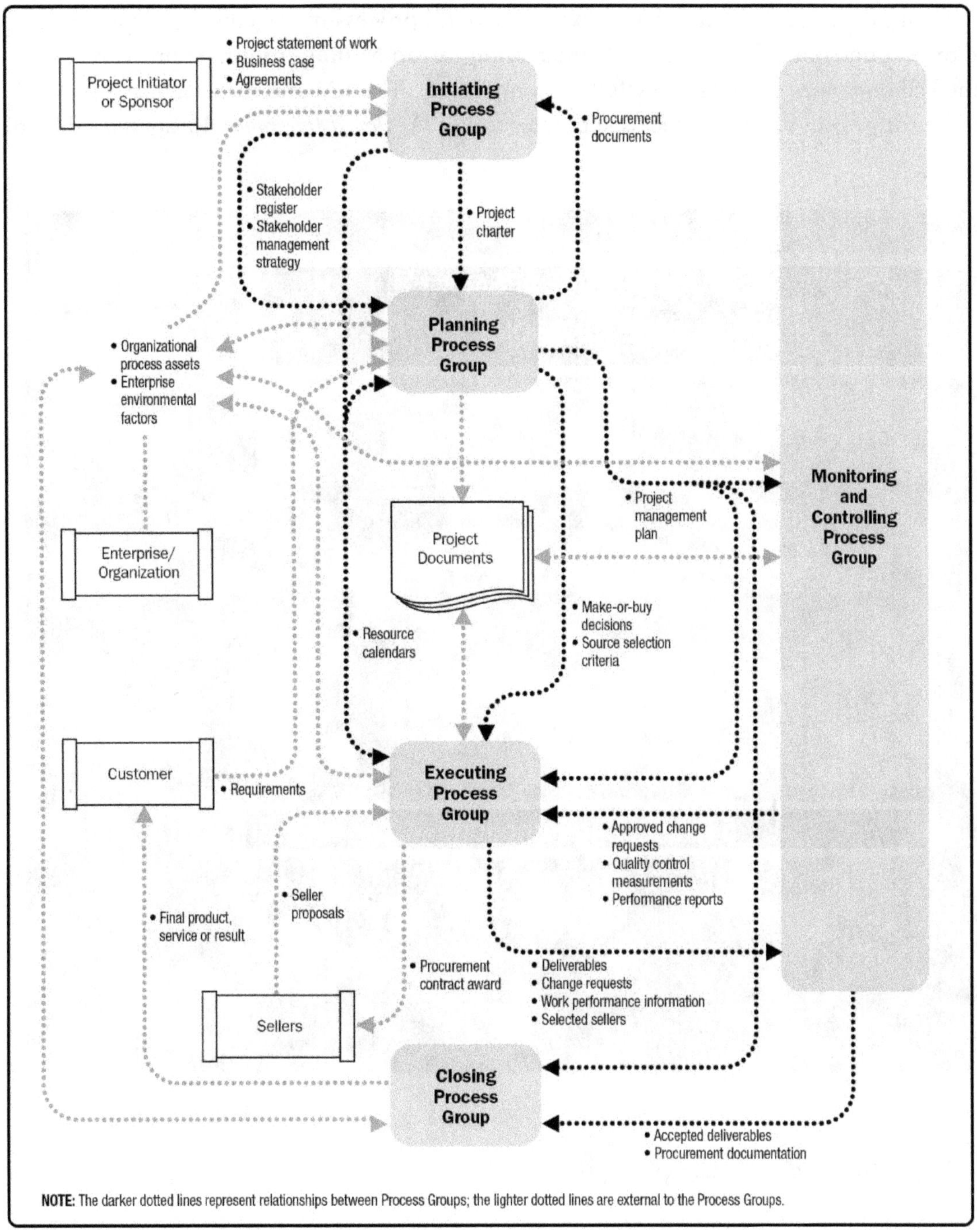

Figure 3-3. Project Management Process Interactions

A Guide to the Project Management Body of Knowledge (PMBOK® Guide) – Fifth Edition.

Various processes and activities are needed to tie together the many tasks of unifying and integrating all the project knowledge areas with all five (5) process management groups for a specific project outcome. This is called **Project Integration Management**. If properly performed all outcomes can be successfully accomplished. The PM and their team is responsible for project success. Once again, refer to Fig. A, *Project Integration Management*, shown below.

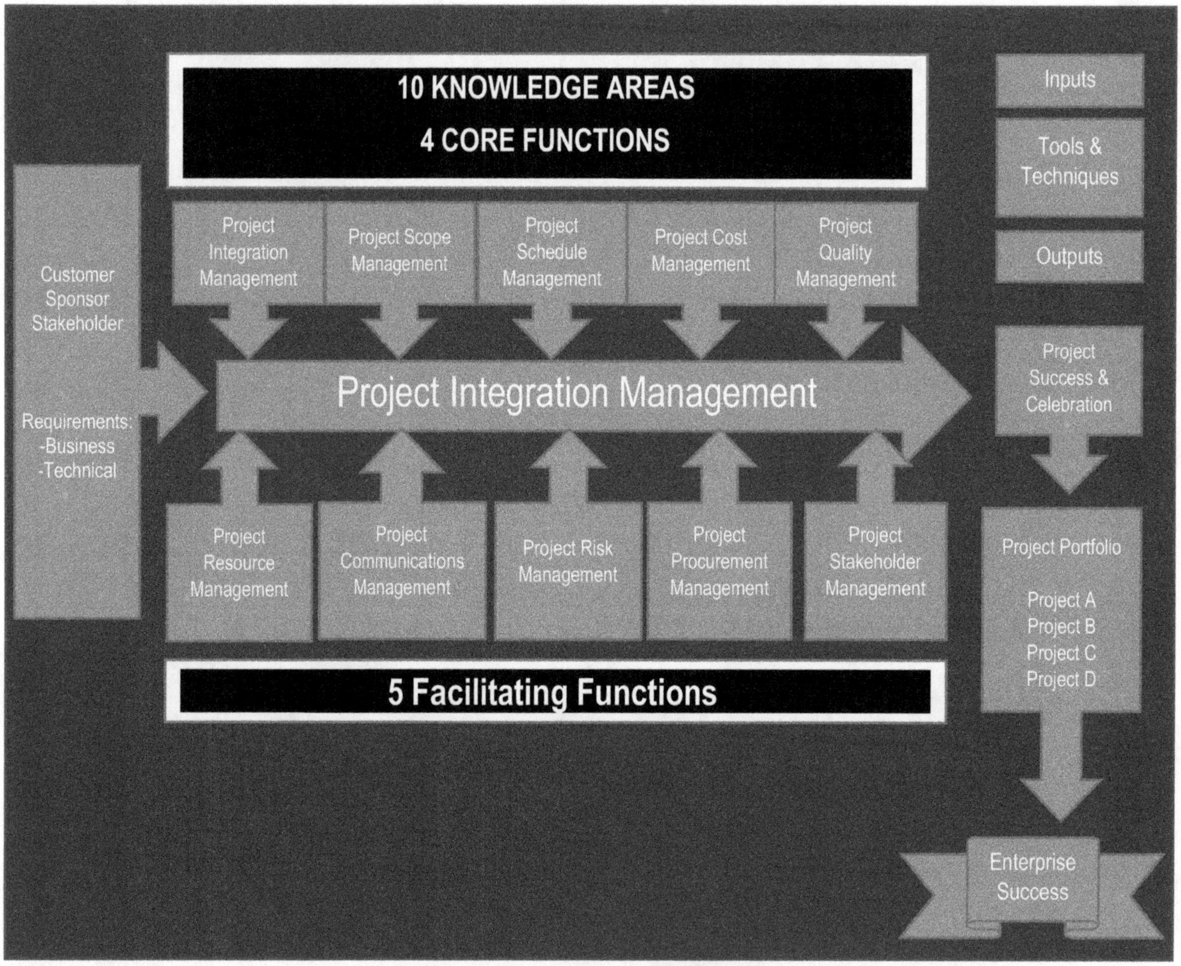

Fig. A Project Integration Management

Project Integration Management includes the following seven (7) specific processes (P 70):

(4.1) **Develop Project Charter**: The process of developing a document that formally authorizes the existence of a project and provides the project manager with the authority to apply organizational resources to project activities.
(4.2) **Develop Project Management Plan**: The process of defining, preparing and coordinating all plan components and consolidating them into an integrated project management plan.
(4.3) **Direct and Manage Project Work**: The process of leading and performing the work defined in the project management plan, and implementing approved changes to achieve the project's objective.
(4.4) **Manage Project Knowledge**: The process of using existing knowledge and crating new knowledge to achieve the project's objectives and contribute to organizational learning.
(4.5) **Monitor and Control Project Work**: The process of tracking, reviewing and reporting overall progress to meet the performance objectives defined in the project management plan.
(4.6) **Perform Integrated Change Control**: The process of reviewing all change requests; approving a changes, and managing changes to deliverables, organizational process assets, project documents and the project management plan; and communicating the decisions.
(4.7) **Close Project or Phase**: The process of finalizing all activities for the project, phase or contract.

The most seasoned and experienced PM knows that all projects are unique and will be managed in unique ways. The integration of process groupings and application of the 10 knowledge areas will also vary. All of the process groups will consist of Inputs, Tools and Techniques and Outputs (ITTO)'s and knowledge areas, which are the processing means by which the Input values (information) **is transformed** by the Tools and Techniques to produce certain Outputs.

Fig. 4-1, P 71, *Project Management Integration Overview*

Key Concepts for Project Integration Management: There are tailoring considerations such as tailoring the project life cycle, the development life cycle and the management approach, knowledge management, change, governance, lessons learned and benefits (P 74).

Trends and Emerging practices in Integration Management:

There are various concepts and trends and emerging practices in project that are taking place in project integration management. Innumerable automated tools are being used. The use of **visual management tools**, the **parsing of project knowledge management**, the **expanding of the manager's responsibility a**nd the use of various approaches of running a project, such as the use of **hybrid approaches**, specifically the use of agile and other interactive practices are becoming **common**. It is vital that the Project Manager tailors their project work in a way that will lend itself to project success.

Tailoring Considerations: These are not limited to the following:

Project Life Cycle: What is an appropriate project lifecycle? What phases should comprise the project lifecycle?

Developmental Life Cycle: What developmental lifecycle and approaches are appropriate for the product, service or result? Is a Predictive or Adaptive approach appropriate? If adaptive, should the product be developed incrementally or iteratively? Is a hybrid approach the best?

Management Approaches: What management processes are most effective based on the organizational culture and complexity of the project?

Knowledge Management: How will knowledge be managed in the project to foster a collaborative working environment?

Change: How will change be managed in the project?

Governance: What control boards, committees and other stakeholders are parts of the project? What are the project status reporting requirements?

Lessons Learned: What information should be collected throughout and at the end of the project? How will historical information and lessons learned be made available to future projects?

Benefits: When and how should benefits be reported; at the end of the project or at the end of each iteration or phase?

Considerations for Agile/Adaptive Environments:

Iterative and Adaptive environments promote the engagement of the team members. They in turn determine how plans and components should be integrated. Expectations of the PM are not altered, but the team members control the details of product planning and delivery. The team must be able to respond to changes and build a collaborative decision-making environment.

Develop Project Charter:

The Project Manager develops the document called the Project Charter. The Project Charter authorizes the project's existence, provides the manager with the authority to obtain resources and provides the understanding of the project's goals and objectives.

The Project Charter highlights the scope of the project, the risks associated with the project, the cost of the project, the timeline of the project, the schedule of the project and reflects a formal record of the project.

The **key benefit** of this process is that it provides a direct link between the project and the strategic objectives of the organization and creates a formal record of the project and shows an organizational commitment to the project.

Please refer to the chart on the next page: DEVELOP PROJECT CHARTER (SECTION 4.1)

Chapter Four: Project Integration Management

4.1 DEVELOP PROJECT CHARTER

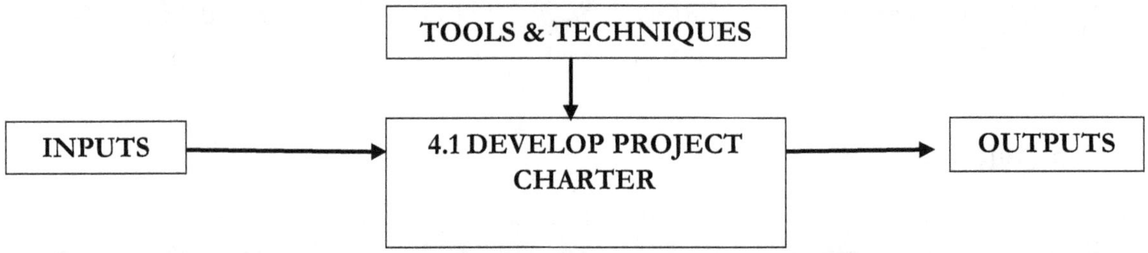

4.1 DEVELOP PROJECT CHARTER: Overview

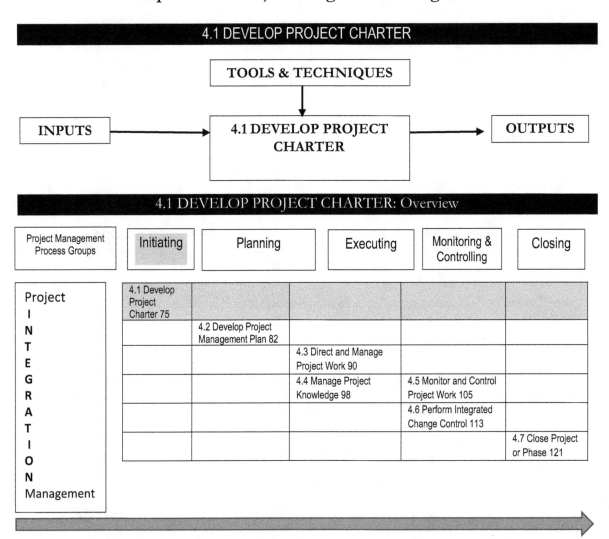

Project Management Process Groups	Initiating	Planning	Executing	Monitoring & Controlling	Closing
Project INTEGRATION Management	4.1 Develop Project Charter 75				
		4.2 Develop Project Management Plan 82			
			4.3 Direct and Manage Project Work 90		
			4.4 Manage Project Knowledge 98	4.5 Monitor and Control Project Work 105	
				4.6 Perform Integrated Change Control 113	
					4.7 Close Project or Phase 121

4.1 DEVELOP PROJECT CHARTER: ITTO Processes

.1 Inputs	.2 Tools and Techniques	.3 Outputs
.1 Business Documents 77 • Business Case 77 • Benefits Management Plan 77 .2 Agreements 78 .3 Enterprise Environmental Factors 78 .4 Organizational Process Assets 79	.1 Expert Judgment 79 .2 Data Gathering 80 • Brainstorming 80 • Focus Groups 80 • Interviewing 80 .3 Interpersonal and Team Skills 80 • Conflict Management 80 • Facilitation 80 • Meeting Management 80 .4 Meetings 80	.1 Project Charter 81 .2 Assumption Log 81

Fig. 4-2, P 75, *Develop Project Charter: Inputs, Tools and Techniques and Outputs*
Fig. 4-3, P 76, *Develop Project Charter: Data Flow Diagram*

The **Project Management Plan** is a document used to define, prepare and coordinate activities and resources into an integrated project management plan (P 82). All plan components are called **Subsidiary Plans**. They are components of the integrated Project Management Plan. The **key benefit** of this process is the production of a comprehensive document that defines the basis of all project work and how the work will be performed. The Project Manager leads and directs the work that is defined in the Project Management Plan. The Project Management Plan will change as new knowledge about the project requirements evolve. In the area of managing project knowledge, the Project Manager uses existing knowledge to create new knowledge to achieve the project's objectives, while at the same time, contributing to the organizational success of the company.

The **Project Management Plan** defines how the project is executed, monitored and controlled and closed (P 83). I t may be developed at the summary of detailed level. It needs to be robust to reflect the ever-changing project environment. It needs to be baselined along the lines of scope, time and cost. The baseline will be used to measure progress advances or hindrances. Changes to the baseline can only be accomplished through the **Perform Integrated Change Control** process.

All projects produce **deliverables**. A **deliverable** is any unique, verifiable product, result, or capability acquired as a result of completing a particular process or phase. They are typically tangible components.

The project manager, while performing the project work, concurrently controls and monitors the project work. This means the Project Manager tracks the work, reviews the work and reports the overall progress to the stakeholders and to the sponsors. Successful work should show what is being achieved in meeting goals and objectives of the project. Status reporting is done throughout the project.

Please refer to the chart below: **DEVELOP PROJECT MANAGEMENT PLAN (SECTION 4.2)**

Chapter Four: Project Integration Management

4.2 DEVELOP PROJECT MANAGEMENT PLAN

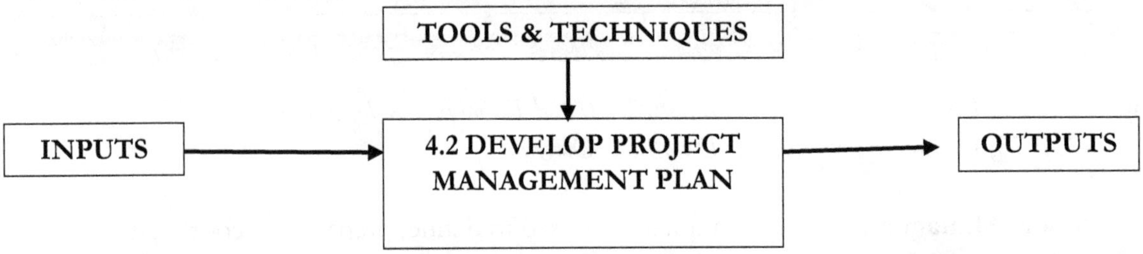

4.2 DEVELOP PROJECT MANAGEMENT PLAN: Overview

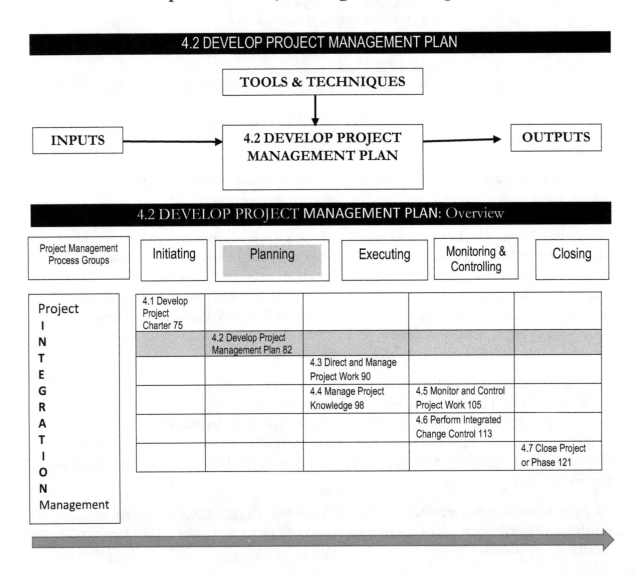

Project Management Process Groups	Initiating	Planning	Executing	Monitoring & Controlling	Closing
Project INTEGRATION Management	4.1 Develop Project Charter 75				
		4.2 Develop Project Management Plan 82			
			4.3 Direct and Manage Project Work 90		
			4.4 Manage Project Knowledge 98	4.5 Monitor and Control Project Work 105	
				4.6 Perform Integrated Change Control 113	
					4.7 Close Project or Phase 121

4.2 DEVELOP PROJECT MANAGEMENT PLAN: ITTO Processes

.1 Inputs	.2 Tools and Techniques	.3 Outputs
.1 Project Charter 83 .2 Outputs From Other Processes 83 .3 Enterprise Environmental Factors 84 .4 Organizational Process Assets 84	.1 Expert Judgment 85 .2 Data Gathering 85 • Brainstorm 85 • Checklists 85 • Focus Groups 85 • Interviews 85 .3 Interpersonal and Team Skills 86 • Conflict Management 86 • Facilitation 86 • Meeting Management 86 .4 Meetings 86	.1 Project Management Plan 86

Fig. 4-4, P 82, *Develop Project Management Plan: Inputs, Tools and Techniques and Outputs*
Fig. 4-5, P 82, *Develop Project Management Plan: Data Flow Diagram*

<u>**Direct and Manage Project** work</u>:

This is the process of leading and performing the work defined in the Project Management Plan and implementing approved changes to achieve the project's objectives (P 90). The **key benefit** is that it provides overall management of the project work and deliverables, thus improving the probability of project success. This process is performed throughout the project life cycle.

See chart on next page: DIRECT AND MANAGE PROJECT WORK (SECTION 4.3)

Chapter Four: Project Integration Management

4.3 DIRECT AND MANAGE PROJECT WORK

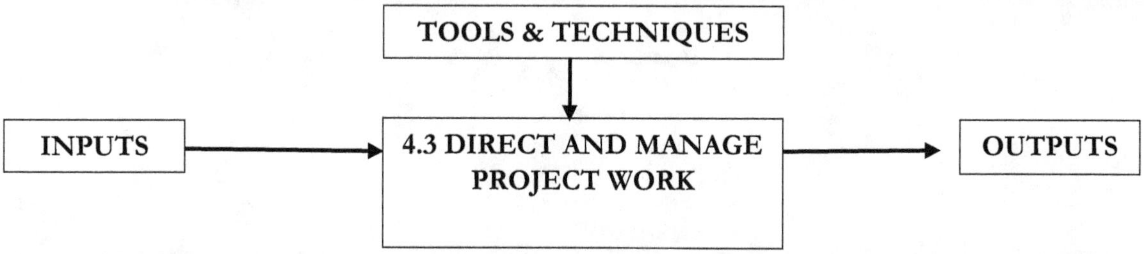

4.3 DIRECT AND MANAGE PROJECT WORK: Overview

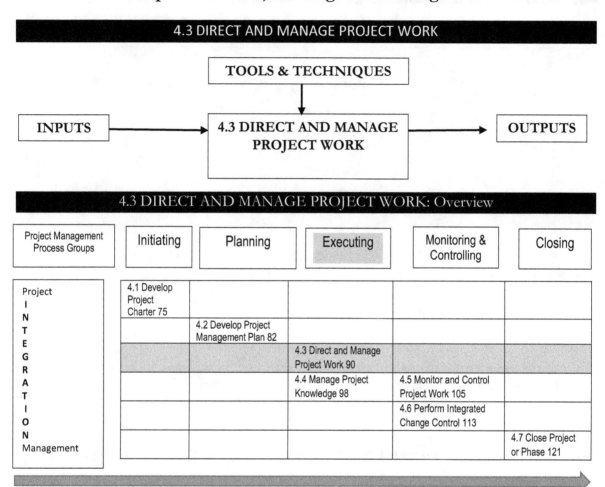

Project Management Process Groups	Initiating	Planning	Executing	Monitoring & Controlling	Closing
Project INTEGRATION Management	4.1 Develop Project Charter 75				
		4.2 Develop Project Management Plan 82			
			4.3 Direct and Manage Project Work 90		
			4.4 Manage Project Knowledge 98	4.5 Monitor and Control Project Work 105	
				4.6 Perform Integrated Change Control 113	
					4.7 Close Project or Phase 121

4.3 DIRECT AND MANGE PROJECT WORK: ITTO Processes

.1 Inputs	.2 Tools and Techniques	.3 Outputs
.1 Project Management Plan 92 • Any Components 92 .2 Project Documents 92 • Change Log 92 • Lessons Learned Register 92 • Milestone List 92 • Project Communications 92 • Project Schedule 93 • Requirements Traceability Matrix 93 • Risk Register 93 • Risk Report 93 .2 Approved Change Requests 93 .3 Enterprise Environmental Factors 93 .4 Organizational Process Assets 94	.1 Expert Judgement 94 .2 Project Management Information Systems 95 .3 Meetings 95	.1 Deliverables 95 .2 Work Performance Data 95 .3 Issue Log 96 .4 Change Requests 96 .5 Project Management Plan Updates 97 • Any Component 97 .6 Project Documents Updates 97 • Activity List 97 • Assumption Log 97 • Lessons Learned Register 97 • Requirements Documents 97 • Risk Register 97 • Stakeholder Register 97 .7 Organizational Process Assets Updates 97

Fig. 4-6, P 90, *Direct and Manage Project Work: Inputs, Tools and Techniques and Outputs*
Fig. 4-7, P 91, *Direct and Manage Project Work: Data Flow Diagram*

Manage Project Knowledge:

This is the process of using existing knowledge and creating new knowledge to achieve the project's objectives and contribute to organizational learning. The **key benefit** is that prior organizational knowledge is leveraged to produce or improve the project outcomes and knowledge created that will be available to support organizational operations and future projects or phases. This process is performed throughout the project life cycle.

See chart on next page: MANAGE PROJECT KNOWLEDGE (SECTION 4.4)

Chapter Four: Project Integration Management

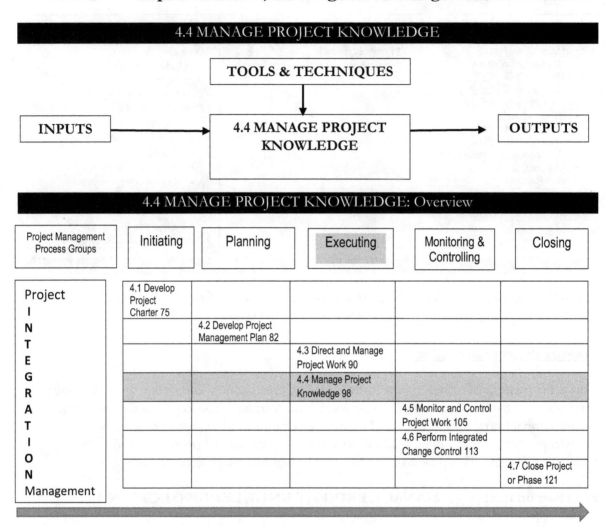

4.4 MANAGE PROJECT KNOWLEDGE

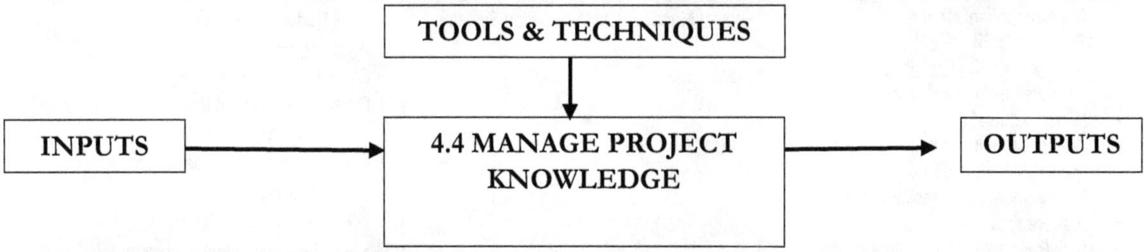

4.4 MANAGE PROJECT KNOWLEDGE: Overview

Project Management Process Groups	Initiating	Planning	Executing	Monitoring & Controlling	Closing
Project INTEGRATION Management	4.1 Develop Project Charter 75				
		4.2 Develop Project Management Plan 82			
			4.3 Direct and Manage Project Work 90		
			4.4 Manage Project Knowledge 98		
				4.5 Monitor and Control Project Work 105	
				4.6 Perform Integrated Change Control 113	
					4.7 Close Project or Phase 121

4.4 MANAGE PROJECT KNOWLEDGE: ITTO Processes

.1 Inputs	.2 Tools and Techniques	.3 Outputs
.1 Project Management Plan 100 • Any Components 100 .2 Project Documents 101 • Lessons Learned Register 101 • Project Team Assignments 101 • Resource Breakdown Structure 101 • Source Selection Criteria 101 • Stakeholder Register 101 .3 Deliverables 101 .4 Enterprise Environmental Factors 101 .5 Organizational Process Assets 102	.1 Expert Judgement 102 .2 Knowledge Management 102 .3 Information Management 103 .4 Interpersonal and Team Skills 104 • Active Listening 104 • Facilitation 104 • Leadership 104 • Networking 104	.1 Lessons Learned 104 .2 Project Management Plan Updates 105 • Any Component 105 .3 Organizational Process Assets Updates 105

Fig. 4-8, P 98, *Manage Project Knowledge: Inputs, Tools and Techniques and Outputs*
Fig. 4-8, P 99, *Manage Project Knowledge: Data Flow Diagram*

Monitor and Control Project Work:

This is the process of tracking, reviewing and reporting the overall the progress to meet the performance objectives defined in the project management plan (P 105). The **key benefit** is that it allows stakeholders to understand the current state of the project, to recognize the actions taken to address any performance issues and to have visibility into the future project status with cost and schedule forecasts. This process is performed throughout the project.

See chart on next page: MONITOR AND CONTROL PROJECT WORK (SECTION 4.5)

Chapter Four: Project Integration Management

4.5 MONITOR AND CONTROL PROJECT WORK

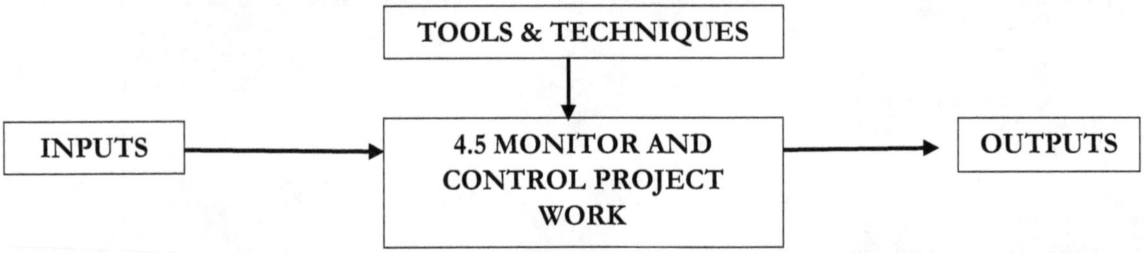

4.5 MONITOR AND CONTROL PROJECT WORK: Overview

Project Management Process Groups	Initiating	Planning	Executing	Monitoring & Controlling	Closing
Project INTEGRATION Management	4.1 Develop Project Charter 75				
		4.2 Develop Project Management Plan 82			
			4.3 Direct and Manage Project Work 90		
			4.4 Manage Project Knowledge 98		
				4.5 Monitor and Control Project Work 105	
				4.6 Perform Integrated Change Control 113	
					4.7 Close Project or Phase 121

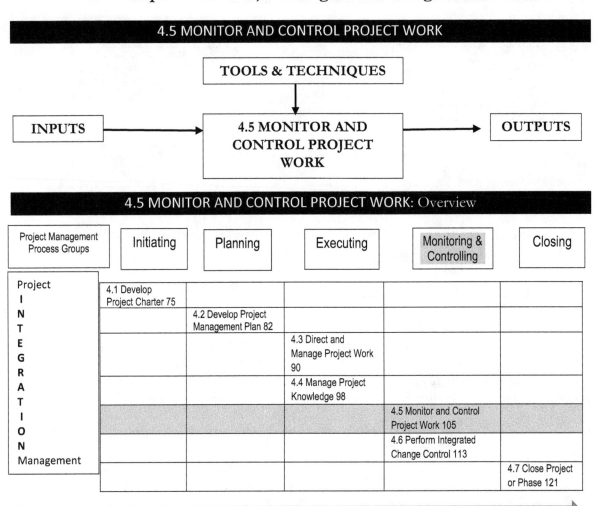

4.5 MONITOR AND CONTROL PROJECT WORK: ITTO Processes

.1 Inputs	.2 Tools and Techniques	.3 Outputs
.1 Project Management Plan 107 • Any Components 107 .2 Project Documents 108 • Assumption Log 108 • Basis of Estimates 108 • Costs Forecasts 108 • Issue Log 108 • Lessons Learned Register 108 • Milestone List 108 • Quality Reports 108 • Risk Register 108 • Risk Report 108 • Schedule Forecasts 109 .3 Work Performance Information 109 .4 Agreements 109 .5 Enterprise Environmental Factors 109 .6 Organizational Process Assets 110	.1 Expert Judgement 110 .2 Data Analysis 111 • Alternative Analysis 110 • Cost Benefit Analysis 111 • Earned Value Analysis 111 • Root Cause Analysis 111 • Trend Analysis 111 • Variance Analysis 111 .3 Decision Making 111 .4 Meetings 111	.1 Work Performance Reports 112 .2 Change Requests 112 .3 Project Management Plan Updates 112 • Any Component 112 .4 Project Documents Updates 113 • Cost Forecasts 113 • Issue Log 113 • Lessons Learned Register 113 • Risk Register 113 • Schedule Forecasts 113

Fig. 4-10, P 105, *Monitor and Control Project Work: Inputs, Tools and Techniques and Outputs*
Fig. 4-11, P 106, *Monitor and Control Project Work: Data Flow Diagram*

Perform Integrated Change Control:

All projects will have changes. Change is life. All project change requires evaluation. Changes need to be approved, not approved or postponed. Perform integrated change control is the process of reviewing all change requests, approving changes and managing changes to deliverables, project documents and the project management plan. Communication decisions to stakeholders and sponsors are paramount. The **key benefit** of this process is that it allows for documented changes within the project and all changes need to go through **Perform Integrated Change Control Processes**. This process is performed throughout the project life cycle. Please refer to the chart on the next page, Perform Integration Change Control.

See chart on next page: PERFORM INTEGRATED CHANGE CONTROL (SECTION 4.6)

4.6 PERFORM INTEGRATED CHANGE CONTROL

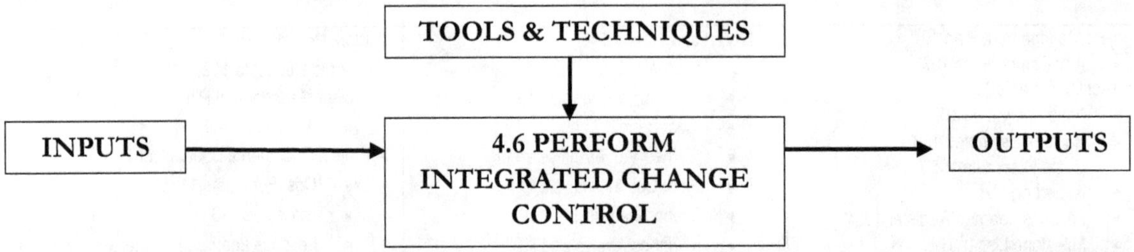

4.6 PERFORM INTEGRATED CHANGE CONTROL: Overview

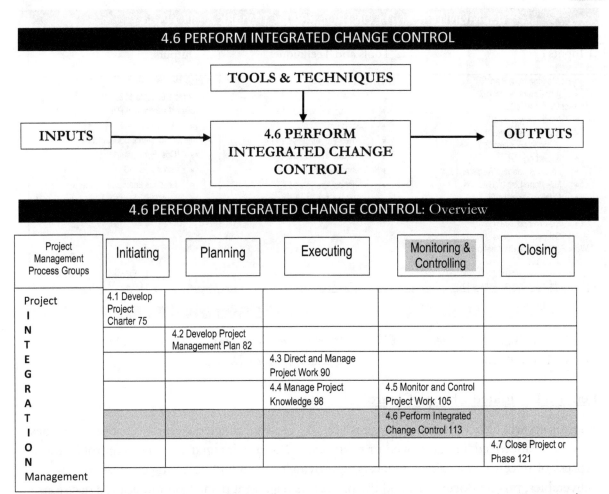

Project Management Process Groups	Initiating	Planning	Executing	Monitoring & Controlling	Closing
Project INTEGRATION Management	4.1 Develop Project Charter 75				
		4.2 Develop Project Management Plan 82			
			4.3 Direct and Manage Project Work 90		
			4.4 Manage Project Knowledge 98	4.5 Monitor and Control Project Work 105	
				4.6 Perform Integrated Change Control 113	
					4.7 Close Project or Phase 121

4.6 PERFORM INTEGRATED CHANGE CONTROL: ITTO Processes

.1 Inputs	.2 Tools and Techniques	.3 Outputs
.1 Project Management Plan 116 • Change Management Plan 116 • Configuration Management Plan 116 • Scope Baseline 116 • Schedule Baseline 116 • Cost Baseline 116 .2 Project Documents 116 • Basis of Estimates 116 • Requirements Traceability Matrix 116 • Risk Report 116 .3 Work Performance Reports 116 .4 Change Requests 117 .5 Enterprise Environmental Factors 117 .6 Organizational Process Assets 117	.1 Expert Judgment 118 .2 Change Control Tools 118 .3 Data Analysis 119 • Alternative Analysis 119 • Cost Benefits Analysis 119 .4 Decision Making 119 • Voting 119 • Autocratic Decision Making 119 • Multicriteria Decision Analysis 119 .5 Meetings 120	.1 Approved Change Requests 120 .2 Project Management Updates 120 • Any Component 120 .4 Project Documents Updates 120 • Change Log 120

Fig. 4-12, P 113, *Perform Integrated Change Control: Inputs, Tools and Techniques and Outputs*
Fig. 4-13, P 114, *Perform Integrated Change Control: Data Flow Diagram*

Close Project or Phase:

This is the process of finalizing all activities of the project, phase or contract. The **key benefit** of this process is that the information is archived. The planned work completed and the organizational team resources are released to pursue new endeavors.

There are legal, administrative and financial closing steps that need to take place in the closing of a project or phase. This process is performed once, or at predefined point in the project.

Please refer to the chart on the next page: CLOSE PROJECT OR PHASE (SECTION 4.7)

Chapter Four: Project Integration Management

4.7 CLOSE PROJECT OR PHASE

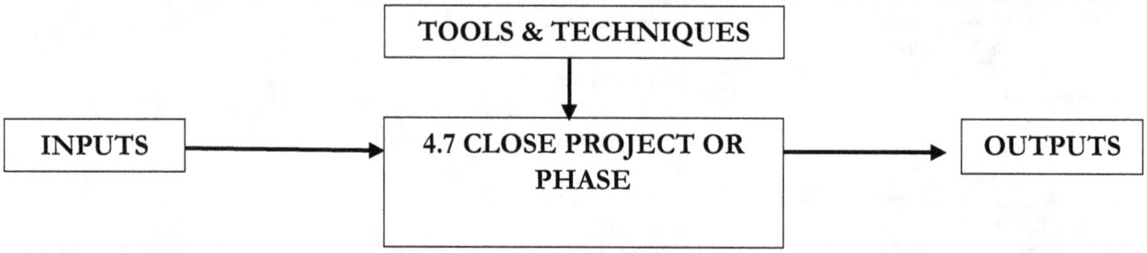

4.7 CLOSE PROJECT OR PHASE: Overview

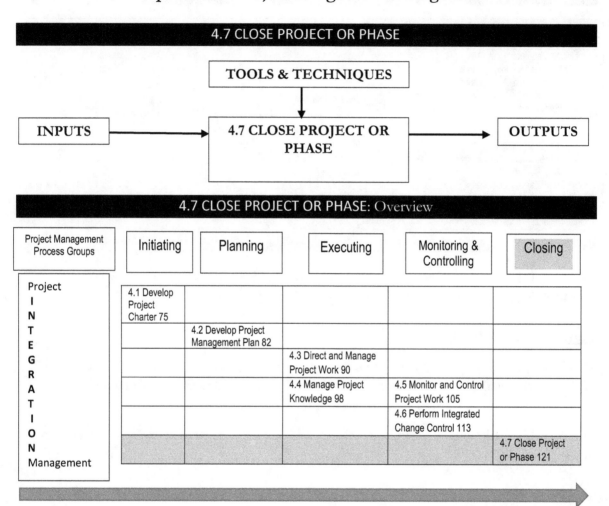

Project Management Process Groups	Initiating	Planning	Executing	Monitoring & Controlling	Closing
Project INTEGRATION Management	4.1 Develop Project Charter 75				
		4.2 Develop Project Management Plan 82			
			4.3 Direct and Manage Project Work 90		
			4.4 Manage Project Knowledge 98	4.5 Monitor and Control Project Work 105	
				4.6 Perform Integrated Change Control 113	
					4.7 Close Project or Phase 121

Cont. on next page

4.7 CLOSE PROJECT OR PHASE: ITTO Processes

.1 Inputs	.2 Tools and Techniques	.3 Outputs
.1 Project Charter 124 .2 Project Management Plan 124 • All Components 124 .3 Project Documents 124 • Assumption Log 124 • Basis of Estimates 124 • Change Log 124 • Issue Log 124 • Lessons Learned Register 124 • Milestone List 124 • Project Communications 124 • Quality Control Measures 124 • Quality Reports 124 • Requirements Documentations 124 • Risk Register 125 • Risk Report 125 .4 Accepted Deliverables 125 .5 Business Documents 125 • Business Case 125 • Benefits Management Plan 125 .6 Agreements 125 .7 Procurement Documentation 125 .8 Organizational Process Assets 126	.1 Expert Judgment 126 .2 Data Analysis 126 • Document Analysis 126 • Regression Analysis 126 • Trend Analysis 126 • Variance Analysis 126 .3 Meetings 127	.1 Project Documents Updates 127 • Lessons Learned Register 127 .2 Final Product, Service or Result Transition 127 .3 Final Report 127 .4 Organizational Process Assets Updates 128

Fig. 4-14, P 121, *Close Project or Phase: Inputs, Tools and Techniques and Outputs*
Fig. 4-15, P 122, *Close Project or Phase: Dara Flow Diagram*

KEY WORDS: CHAPTER 4: All Projects must produce Business Value

Project Integration Management
Resource Allocation
Tailoring
Project Charter
Project Management Plan
Direct and Manage Project Work
Manage Project Knowledge
Monitor and Control Project Work
Perform Integrated Change Control
Close Project/Phase
Automated tools
Visual Management Tools
Hybrid Methodologies
Governance
Lessons Learned
Agile/Adaptive Environments
Business Case
Agreements
Brainstorming
Focus Groups
Conflict Management
Facilitation
Assumption Log
Expert Judgment
Brainstorming
Check Lists
Focus Groups
Interviews
Subsidiary Management Plans
Base Lines

- Scope Base Line
- Schedule Base Line
- Cost Base Line
- Performance Measurement Base Line

Change Management Plan
Configuration Management Plan
Project Life Cycle
Development Approach
Management Reviews
Milestone List
Requirements Traceability Matrix
Risk Report
Approved Change Request
Change Requests

- Corrective Action
- Preventive Action
- Defect Repair
- Updates

Deliverables
Work Performance Data
Issue Log
Activity Lists
Requirements Documentation
Risk Register
Stakeholder Register
Explicit Knowledge
Tacit Knowledge
Resource Breakdown Structure
Legal Requirements
Regulatory Requirements
Active Listening
Cost Forecasts
Schedule Forecasts
Agreements
Alternative Analysis
Cost Benefit Analysis
Earned Value Analysis
Root Cause Analysis
Trend Analysis
Variance Analysis

LEGEND

The following Legend shows how to correctly read the *PMBOK® Guide* references and attributions correctly for Chapter 4: Project Integration Management PMBOK Details.

Legend:

Chapter Section	Chapter Section Title	Page Number

Example from Chapter Six shown below:

6.5.1.4	Enterprise Environmental Factors	(P 209)

All direct quotes are attributed as (A Guide to the Project Management Body of Knowledge, *(PMBOK® Guide)* – Sixth Edition) Project Management Institute Inc., 2017, Page #, after each section and any/all paraphrased or original wording is attributed as (P #), before or after each section. All Graphs, Charts, Tables and Figures are attributed as: (*PMBOK® Guide,* Fig. #-# or #/#, P #, *Title of Graph, Chart, Table or Figure*).

4. PROJECT INTEGRATION MANAGEMENT

Project Integration Management is a process whose purpose is to identify, define, unify and coordinate project management within (work) each of the process management groups. It incorporates processes and activities and should consider the following choices (P 69):

- **Resource Allocation**: people, equipment, material, etc.
- **Balancing Competing Demands**: time, scope, cost and quality
- **Examining Alternative Approaches**: predictive vs. agile vs. hybrid
- **Tailoring the processes to meet Project Objectives**
- **Managing Interdependencies among Project Management Knowledge Areas**

The Project Integration processes are:

- **Develop Project Charter** (Section 4.1)
- **Develop Project Management Plan** (Section 4.2)
- **Direct and manage Project Work** (Section 4.3)
- **Manage Project Knowledge** (Section 4.4)
- **Monitor and Control Project Work** (Section 4.5)
- **Perform Integrated Change Control** (Section 4.6)
- **Close Project or Phase** (Section 4.7)

Table, 1-4, P 25, *Project Management Process Group and Knowledge Area Mapping.*
Fig. 4-1, P 71, *Project integration Management Overview*

Key Concepts for Integration Management are (P 72):

- Ensure the deliverable due dates of the product, service or result and project lifecycle and the Benefits Management Plan are aligned
- Provide a Project Management Plan that will achieve the project's objectives
- Ensure the creation and use of the appropriate knowledge
- Manage the performance and changes of the activities in the Project Management Plan

- Make integrated decisions regarding key changes that may affect the project
- Measure and monitor the project's progress and take appropriate action to meet project objectives
- Collect data on results achieved, analyze the data to obtain information and then communicate the information to the relevant stakeholders
- Complete all project work and formally close each phase, contract for each project as a whole
- Manage phase transitions when necessary

Trends and Emerging Practices in Project Integration Management (P 73):

- **Use of Automated Tools**: It is necessary to use a project management information system (PMIS) to manage the volume of data incurred by a project
- **Use of Visual Management Tools**: Visual management tools are sometimes used to provide real-time overviews when transmitting vast amounts of information to team members
- **Product Knowledge Management**: It is important to transfer knowledge to the target audience and transitory work force
- **Expansion of the Project Manager's Responsibilities**: The project manager's role is now encompassing other roles, such as project business case development, benefits management, identification and engagement of stakeholders and managing interfaces with other departments and senior management personnel
- **Hybrid Methodologies**: Some of the new practices, such as agile, iterative (repetitive) business analysis techniques for requirements management and tools for identifying complex elements in a project, etc. are being incorporated into the organization

Tailoring considerations are used to adapt/modify the standard way that project integration management is applied (P 74):

- **Project Lifecycle**: What is an appropriate lifecycle and what phases should compromise the project lifecycle?
- **Developmental Lifecycle**: What developmental lifecycle and approach are appropriate for the product, service or result? Is a predictive or adaptive

approach appropriate? If adaptive, should the product be developed incrementally or iteratively? Is a hybrid approach best?

- **Management Approaches**: What management processes are most effective?
- **Knowledge Management**: How will knowledge be managed effectively?
- **Change**: how will change be managed?
- **Governance**: What control Boards, Committees and other Stakeholders are part of the Project?
- **Lessons Learned**: What information should be collected? How will historical and lessons learned be archived?
- **Benefits**: When and how should benefits be reported?

Considerations for Agile/Adaptive Environments:

These approaches engage team members and promote them as local domain experts (P 74). In turn, these team members determine the integration of plan and components. Project Manager (PM) expectations do not change, but the PM does delegate detailed planning and delivery. The PM's goal is to promote a collaborative approach and will work well when team members have a broader range of skills.

5 

Tips for Facilitators of Agile Meetings, by Dominika Bula at https://opensource.com/article/18/10/agile-culture-5-tips-meeting-facilitators

The New Frontier: Agile Automation at Scale, by Federico Berruti, Geet Chandratre and Zaid Rab, located at: https://www.mckinsey.com/business-functions/operations/our-insights/the-new-frontier-agile-automation-at-scale

4.1 DEVELOP PROJECT CHARTER.

The **Develop Project Charter** process allows the PM the formal authority to apply organizational resources to the project activities. The **key benefit** is to provide a direct link between the strategic objectives and also creates a formal record of the project.

Fig. 4-2, P 75, *Develop Project Charter: Inputs, Tools and Techniques and Outputs*
Fig. 4-3, P 76, *Develop Project Charter: Data Flow Diagram*

The Project Charter establishes a formal relationship between the performing and requesting organizations, but in the case of external projects, a Formal Contract is the preferred way to establish an agreement. The Project Manager should be assigned as early as possible in the project, usually while the Project Charter is being developed and always before a project is undertaken. A Project Charter is not a contract as there is no consideration or money involved or exchanged.

See video *ABC Daycare* Project Charter Example,
at https://globalproject.management/lesson/abc-daycare-project-charter-example/

Guide, Fig. 4-2, P 75, *Develop Project Charter: Inputs, Tools and Techniques, and Outputs* and *(PMBOK® Guide,* Fig. 4-3, P 76, *Develop Project Charter: Data Flow Diagram).*

This signed Project Charter authorizes the work to begin, while an authorized person takes on the role of a PM. The PM will be assigned their role before any planning takes place. The **Project Charter** may be developed with help from the sponsors or Subject Matter Experts (SME)'s, etc.

4.1.1 Develop Project Charter: Inputs

4.1.1.1 Business Documents

The **Business Case** provides information for decision-making. The business case coupled with the benefits analysis determines whether the needs of the project justify the cost and any potential beneficial outcomes. The **Business Case** will be produced by one of the following (P 78):

- **Market Demand**
- **Organizational Need**
- **Customer Request**
- **Technological Advance**
- **Legal Requirement**
- **Ecological Impacts**
- **Social Need**

The **Project Charter** will use information taken from the **Business Case**.

How to write a Business Case — 4 Steps to a Perfect Business Case Template, by guest blogger Martin Webster, located at https://www.workfront.com/blog/how-to-write-a-business-case-4-steps-to-a-perfect-business-case-template

Fig. 1-8, P 30, *Interrelationship of Needs Assessment and Critical Business/Project Documents.*

4.1.1.2 Agreements

Agreements: Contracts are used when a project is carried out for an external customer. Agreements are also used to document project intentions and may be in the form of (P 78):

- Contracts
- Memorandums of Understanding (MOU)'s
- Service Level Agreements (SLA)'s
- Letter of Agreement
- Letter of Intent
- Verbal Agreement
- E-mail, etc.

See Section 12.1.1.6 Organizational Process Assets, (P 471-472) (Contract Types) for additional information about contracts (A Guide to the Project Management Body of Knowledge, *(PMBOK® Guide)* – Sixth Edition) Project Management Institute Inc., 2017.

4.1.1.3 Enterprise Environmental Factors

Enterprise Environmental Factors show below can influence the **Develop Project Charter** process (P 78):

- Government or Industry Standards
- Legal and Regulatory Requirements and/or Constraints
- Marketplace Conditions
- Organizational Culture and Political Climate
- Organizational Governance
- Stakeholder Expectations and Risk Thresholds

4.1.1.4 Organizational Process Assets

Organizational Process Assets shown below can influence the Develop Project Charter process (P 79):

- Organizational Standard Policies, Processes and Procedures
- Portfolio, Program and Project Governance Framework
- Monitoring and Reporting Methods
- Templates
- Historical Information and Lessons Learned Repository

4.1.2 Develop Project Charter: Tools and Techniques

4.1.2.1 Expert Judgement

Expert Judgement is known as expertise in a defined application area, such as a Subject Matter Expert (SME) and this group or person(s) will make appropriate judgments for any activities. Expertise should be taken into consideration on the following topics (P 79):

- Organizational Strategy
- Benefits Management
- Technical Knowledge of the Industry and Focus Area of the Project
- Duration and Budget Estimation
- Risk Identification

4.1.2.2 Data Gathering

Some of the many **Data-Gathering Techniques** are shown below (P 80):

- **Brainstorming**: Identifies a list of ideas in a short time span
- **Focus Groups**: Stakeholders and SME's convene together to learn about perceived risks and success criteria
- **Interviews**: Used to gather information about high-level requirements, assumptions, constraints, approval criteria, etc. from Stakeholders by talking face-to-face

4.1.2.3 Interpersonal and Team Skills

Some of the various **Interpersonal and Team Skills** that may be used include (P 80):

- **Conflict Management**: Used to bring Stakeholders into alignment with project objectives, success criteria, high-level requirements, project description, summary milestones and other elements of the Charter
- **Facilitation**: Guiding a group to a successful decision, solution or conclusion
- **Meeting Management**: Preparing an agenda to ensure a representative for each key stakeholder group is represented and the meeting requires advance notice, agenda outline future actions (steps) and follow up as required

4.1.2.4 Meetings

Meetings with key stakeholders are held to refine project objective, establish success criteria, determine key deliverables, agree on high-level requirements and other needed data.

***8 Tips for running more Successful Meetings*, by 'The Distilled Man' (8:51 minutes) at**
https://www.youtube.com/watch?v=ypxH_2qdePc

Preparation tips:

1. Each group member should have a folder or notebook that is dedicated to the team's meetings
2. Agendas should be sent out prior to the meeting
3. People making presentations/reports should send information out prior to the meeting
4. Each group member should accept personal responsibility for being prepared and at the meeting on time

<u>Meeting structure</u>: A good meeting structure creates focus, energy and follow through. Tips for creating structure:

1. Make sure the outcomes are clear for every meeting
2. Eliminate meetings that don't require the group to provide feedback, make plans or decisions
3. Make sure the right people are at the meeting
4. Start and end meetings on time
5. Document all decisions and actions

- **Outcome-based agenda**
    a. Agenda should begin with a short list of meeting outcomes (feedback, decisions or plans)
    b. List of meeting content items
    c. Brief description of the meeting process that will be used to achieve a meeting outcome
- **Action minutes**
    a. Records the group's decisions and action items
    b. Identify who is responsible
    c. Identify when the item will be completed
    d. Distribute after the meeting (24 hours or less)
    e. Action item progress is reviewed at the next meeting

<u>Accountability</u> – Honesty, healthy confrontation, support and a commitment to performance builds teamwork. Tips for creating an accountability culture:

1. Ensure there is an accounting for all commitments made
2. Agree on a process to manage performance breakdowns
3. Confront fellow group members openly. Eliminate both blame and excuses.
4. As appropriate, offer support to help all group members succeed.

<u>Facilitation</u> – Effective facilitation creates synergy and helps groups make good decisions. Tips for improving facilitation:

1. Train all group members how to facilitate meetings
2. Rotate the formal facilitation role from meeting to meeting
3. Without blame, regularly assess the quality of interaction within your group
4. Consider an outside facilitator when meeting stakes are high and/or for longer meetings

4.1.3 Develop Project Charter: Outputs

4.1.3.1 Project Charter

The **Project Charter** documents high-level information on the project, product, service or result. The project should be undertaken to satisfy the intended results, such as (P 81):

- Project Purpose
- Measurable Project Objectives
- High-Level Requirements
- High-Level Project Description, Boundaries and Key Deliverables
- Overall Project Risk
- Summary Milestone Schedule
- Preapproved Financial Resources
- Key Stakeholder List
- Project Approval Requirements
- Project Exit Criteria
- Assigned Project Manager
- Name and Authority of the Sponsor or other person(s) authorizing the Project Charter

Refer to ABC Project Charter sample videos by Dr. Harpool. See the video located at *ABC Academy Daycare Center,* https://globalproject.management/lesson/abc-daycare-project-charter-example/

4.1.3.2 Assumption Log

The **Assumption Log** contains both **High-level Assumptions** and lower level activities and tasks produced by any ongoing project operations (updates occur during the project lifecycle(s). These assumptions can be found in the Business Case before any work is done on the project and will emerge in the write up of the Project Charter (P 81).

4.2 DEVELOP PROJECT MANAGEMENT PLAN

Develop Project Management Plan defines the subsidiary plan components and consolidates them into an **Integrated Project Management Plan** (P 82). The subsidiary plan includes coverage of project scope, schedule, cost quality, resource, communications, risk, procurement and stakeholder agendas.

The **key benefit** of this process is a comprehensive document that defines the basis of all of the project work to be done and how it will be performed.

The Inputs, Tools and Techniques, and Outputs of this process can be referenced in the following:
Fig. 4-4, P 82, *Develop Project Management Plan: Inputs, Tools and Techniques, and Outputs*
Fig. 4-5, P 82, *Develop Project Management Plan: Data Flow Diagram.*

The **Project Management Plan** can be at the summary level or highly detailed, but should always be applied as an agile process that reflects and ever-changing project environment. The plan should be baselined for scope, time and cost, and updated as required and only be changed through the Integrated Change Process. In this way, the Project Management Plan is progressively elaborated.

If a project is contained within a program or portfolio, any steps taken should stay be consistent within the Program or Portfolio Management Plan requirements.

4.2.1 Develop Project Management Plan: Inputs

4.2.1.1 Project Charter

The **Project Charter** is used by the project team for initial project planning. High-Level information should be provisionally defined at this time (P 83).

4.2.1.2 Outputs from Other Processes

Outputs from Other Processes are incorporated into the Project Management Plan. This includes Sections 5-13 of the 6th Edition PMBOK.

4.2.1.3 Enterprise Environmental Factors

Some of the **Enterprise Environmental Factors** that may have an effect on the **Develop Project Management Plan** can consist of (P 84):

- Government or Industry Standards
- Legal and Regulatory Requirements and/or Constraints
- Project management body of knowledge for vertical markets, etc.
- Organizational structure, culture, management practices, and sustainability
- Organizational governance framework
- Infrastructure

4.2.1.4 Organizational Process Assets

Organizational Process Assets affecting the **Develop Project Management Plan** includes those shown below (P 84):

- Organizational Standard Policies, Processes and Procedures
- Project Management Plan Template Including:
    - Guidelines and Criteria for Tailoring the Organization's Set of Standard Processes
    - Project Closure Guidelines or Requirements
- Change Control Procedures
- Monitoring/Reporting Methods
- Project Information from previous similar Projects
- Historical Information
- Lessons Learned

4.2.2 Develop Project Management Plan: Tools and Techniques

4.2.2.1 Expert Judgment

The following list is a guide to obtaining expertise when needed from any person(s) or groups (P 85):

- Tailoring the project management process to meet project needs
- Developing additional components of the project management plan as needed
- Determining the Tools and Techniques to be used
- Developing technical and management details
- Determining resources and needed skill levels
- Defining the level of configuration management to apply
- Determining which project documents will be subject to the formal change control process
- Prioritizing the work according to project needs

4.2.2.2 Data Gathering

Some of the many Data Gathering Techniques are shown below (P 84):

- **Brainstorming**: Used to collect ideas and solutions about the project approach
- **Checklists**: Used to guide the PM to develop the plan or help verify al the required information is included in the Project Management Plan
- **Focus Groups**: Brings Stakeholders together to discuss the project management approach
- **Interviews**: Brings Stakeholders and SME's together to obtain specific information to develop the Project Management Plan

4.2.2.3 Interpersonal and Team Skills

Interpersonal Team Skills include (P 86):

- **Conflict Management**: This may be necessary to bring diverse Stakeholders into alignment on all aspects of the Project Management Plan
- **Facilitation**: Ensures effective participation and that participants achieve a mutual understanding, all contributions are considered and all results have a full buy-in, according to the decision process established for the project
- **Meeting Management**: Ensures all meetings are run properly

4.2.2.4 Meetings

The purpose of **Meetings** are to discuss strategies, approaches and the execution process as to how the project will be conducted, monitored and controlled (P 86).

- **Small Projects**: One team performs the planning and execution and as a result, the initiation process starts earlier.

- **Large Projects**: A project management team does most of the planning. After initiation, the rest of the team is brought up-to-date.

The Project Manager should hold a kick-off meeting at the start of each phase of a multi-phase project.

4.2.3 Develop Project Management Plan: Outputs

4.2.3.1 Project Management Plan

The **Project Management Plan** explains how a project will be executed, monitored and controlled and closed out. It contains all the necessary data needed to complete these processes. There are ten (10) plans that reflect the ten (10) Project Management Knowledge Areas.

Table 1-4, P 25, *Project Management Process Group and Knowledge Area Mapping.*

Some of the components (called subsidiary plans) are necessary to complete these process (P 87):

- **Scope Management Plan**
- **Requirements Management Plan**
- **Schedule Management Plan**
- **Cost Management Plan**
- **Quality Management Plan**
- **Resource Management Plan**
- **Communications Management Plan**
- **Risk Management Plan**
- **Procurement Management Plan**
- **Stakeholder Engagement Plan**

Baselines: The three (3) Baselines are the approved versions that are compared to actual results (P 87):

- Scope Baseline: Scope Statement, WBS and WBS Dictionary
- Schedule Baseline: Of the Schedule Model
- Cost Baseline: Of the time-phased project budget

Additional Components: Some components are produced as Outputs of another process and some are produced during other processes. Others will be dependent on the project. Some of these components may include the following (P 88):

- Change Management Plan
- Configuration Management Plan
- Performance Measurement Baseline
- Project Lifecycle
- Development Approach
- Management Reviews

Other documents necessary to manage the project can be found in (PMBOK® Guide, Table 4-1, P 89, *Project Management Plan and Project Documents).*

Fig. 3-3, P 120, Chapter 4 Introduction of this manual, *Project Management Process Interactions.*

4.3 DIRECT AND MANAGE PROJECT WORK

Direct and Manage Project Work means to lead and perform the approved work and implement changes in the Project Management Plan that is being used throughout the project. The **key benefit** of this process is that it provides overall management of the project work and deliverables, thereby achieving greater probability of success. This process is performed throughout the project life cycle.

Fig. 4-6, P 90, *Direct and Manage Project Work: Inputs, Tools and Techniques and Outputs*
Fig. 4-7, P 91, *Direct and Manage Project Work: Data Flow Diagram*

4.3.1 Direct and Manage Project Work: Inputs

4.3.1.1 Project Management Plan

The **Project Management Plan** may contain any component that may be an input to another process.

4.3.1.2 Project Documents

Project Documents: Inputs to **Direct and Manage Project Work** may consist of the following (P 92):

- **Change Log**: Contains the status of all Change Requests
- **Lessons Learned Register**: Identifies where to set rules or guidelines for team activities
- **Milestone List**: Shows scheduled dates for specific milestones
- **Project Communications**: Includes Performance Reports, Deliverable Status and other information generated by the Project
- **Project Schedule**: Includes at least the list of Work Activities, their durations, resources and planned and start and finish dates
- **Requirements Traceability Matrix**: Links product requirements to the deliverables
- **Risk Register**: Provides information on threats and opportunities
- **Risk Report**: Provides information on sources of overall project risk along with summary information on identified individual project risks

4.3.1.3 Approved Change Requests

Approved Change Requests: Is an **Output of Perform Integrated Change Control**, which is executed by the project team and may/may not have an effect on the project or Project Management Plan documents, or other project documents (P 93).

4.3.1.4 Enterprise Environmental Factors

Enterprise Environmental Factors: Direct and Manage Project Work may be affected by the following (P 93):

- Organizational Structure, Culture, Management Practices and Sustainability
- Infrastructure
- Stakeholder Risk Thresholds

4.3.1.5 Organizational Process Assets

Organizational Process Assets: Direct and Manage Project Work may be affected by the following (P 94):

- Organizational standard policies, processes and procedures
- Issue and defect management procedures
- Issue and defect management databases
- Performance measurement database
- Change control and risk control procedures
- Project information from previous projects

4.3.2 Direct and Manage Project Work

4.3.2.1 Expert Judgment

Expert Judgment: Groups or individuals with specialized knowledge or training or extensive knowledge should be consulted in the areas shown below (P 94):

- Technical knowledge of the specific project's industry
- Cost/budget management

- Legal procurement
- Legislation/regulations
- Organizational governance

4.3.2.2 Project Management Information System (PMIS)

A **Project Management Information System (PMIS)** provides tools, such as (P 95):

- Scheduling Software
- Work Authorization Systems
- Configuration Management Systems
- Information and Collection Systems
- Interfaces to other Online Systems
- Automated Gathering and Reporting on Key Performance Indicators (KPI)

4.3.2.3 Meetings

Types of **Meetings** may include (P 95):

- Kick Off
- Technical
- Sprint/Iteration Planning
- Scrum Daily Standups
- Steering Group
- Problem Solving
- Progress Update
- Retrospective Meetings

4.3.3 Direct and Manage Project Work: Outputs

4.3.3.1 Deliverables

Deliverables are any unique and verifiable product, service, ability to perform a service and are usually the outcome of a project (P 95).

4.3.3.2 Work Performance Data

Work Performance Data are the raw observations and measurements identified during activities being performed to carry out the project work and can include (P 95):

- Work Completed
- Key Performance Indicators (KPI)
- Technical Performance Measures
- Actual Start and Finish Dates of Schedule Activities
- Story Points Completed
- Deliverables Status
- Schedule Progress
- Number of Change Requests
- Number of Defects
- Actual Costs incurred
- Actual Durations, etc.

4.3.3.3 Issue Log

An **Issue Log** documents all issues where they are recorded and tracked. Issue may happen throughout the project. The issue log is updated as a result of monitoring and controlling activities caused by project problems, inconsistencies or conflicts that do not impact project performance. This data may include (P 96):

- Issue Types
- Person's name who raised Issue
- Description
- Priority
- Person assigned to Issue
- Target Resolution Date
- Status
- Final Solution

4.3.3.4 Change Requests

Change Requests can be initiated from inside or outside the project. This is a formal process consisting of a proposal to modify or change project policies or procedures and must include the following (P 96):

- **Corrective Action**: Realigns performance of project work
- **Preventative Action**: Assures work is aligned with the Project Management Plan
- **Defect Repair**: Modification of a nonconforming product or component
- **Updates**: Changes to formally controlled project documents

Be sure to study this area.

4.3.3.5 Project Management Plan Updates

Project Management Plan Updates: All changes to be made to the Project Management Plan must go through the Change Control Process via a change request.

4.3.3.6 Project Documents Updates

Project Documents Updates: Documents that may be updated when implementing Change Requests include (P 97):

- **Activity List**: May be updated with additional or modified activities
- **Assumption Log:** Contains a record of all the assumptions and constraints and may be updated or closed out
- **Lessons Learned Register**: Lessons Learned will be finalized before being entered into the Repository and updates will occur as needed to improve future performance
- **Requirements Documentation**: New requirements may be identified during this process
- **Risk Register**: Provides information on all known risks
- **Stakeholder Register**: Additional information on new or existing stakeholders are gathered and recorded

4.3.3.7 Organizational Process Assets Updates

Any **Organizational Process Assets** may be updated when Change Requests are executed (P 97).

4.4 MANAGE PROJECT KNOWLEDGE

Manage Project Knowledge means to use prior knowledge with newer knowledge to create a system that functions with greater efficiency and improves project outcomes. The **key benefits** are:

- The leveraging of prior organizational knowledge to improve project outcomes
- Making project knowledge available to support organizational operations, future projects or phases

Fig. 4-8, P 98, *Manage Project Knowledge: Inputs, Tools and Techniques and Outputs*
Fig. 4-9, P 99, *Manage Project Knowledge: Data Flow Diagram*

4.4.1 Manage Project Knowledge: Inputs

4.4.1.1 Project Management Plan

Inputs to the **Project Management Plan** are involved with all of the subsidiary components.

4.4.1.2 Project Documents

Some of the **Project Documents** that may be considered Inputs are (P 101):

- Lessons learned register
- Project team assignments
- Resource breakdown structure
- Stakeholder register

4.4.1.3 Deliverables

A **Deliverable** is any unique and verifiable product, result or capability to perform a service that is required and produced to complete a process, phase, or project (P 101). **Deliverables** are any tangible components designed and completed to meet project objectives and can be a part of the project management plan.

4.4.1.4 Enterprise Environmental Factors

Enterprise Environmental Factors that could affect the Manage Project Knowledge process may be comprised of the following (P 101):

- **Organizational, Stakeholder and Customer Culture**: a trusting working relationship and no-blame culture is essential to managing knowledge
- **Geographic Distribution of Facilities and Resources**: Methods may be tailored to determine knowledge gaining and sharing
- **Organizational Knowledge Experts**: Experts may be provided by an organization specializing in knowledge management
- **Legal and Regulatory Requirements and/or Constraints**: Includes confidentiality agreements

Fig. 2.1, P 37, *Project Influences*

4.4.1.5 Organizational Process Assets

Organizational Process Assets that may affect the Manage Project Knowledge process are (P 102):

- **Organizational standard policies, processes and procedures**: may include confidentiality to information, security and data protection
- **Personnel Administration**: includes employee development and training records
- **Organizational communication requirements**: includes formal rigid communication requirements
- **Formal knowledge-sharing and information-sharing procedures**: includes learning reviews before, during and after projects and project phases

Fig. 2.1, P 37, *Project Influences*

4.4.2 Manage Project Knowledge: Tools and Techniques

4.4.2.1 Expert Judgment

Expert Judgment: Groups or Individuals with specialized knowledge or training or extensive knowledge should be consulted in the areas shown below (P 102):

- Knowledge Management
- Information Management
- Organizational Learning
- Knowledge and Information Management Tools
- Relevant Information from other Projects

4.4.2.2 Knowledge Management

Knowledge Management is about connecting with others to produce new knowledge using the following Tools and Techniques, which are not inclusive and may be added to at some point (P 102):

- Networking
- Communities of practice
- Meetings
- Work shadowing
- Reverse shadowing
- Discussion forums: focus groups
- Knowledge-sharing events
- Workshops
- Storytelling
- Creativity and idea management
- Knowledge fairs and cafes
- Training and interaction among learners

All of the above Tools and Techniques are most effective when used in face-to-face meetings. Starting out with face-to-face meetings, can be followed up with virtual meetings. Once a professional relationship has been established.

4.4.2.3 Information Management

Tools and Techniques used in **Information Management** include the following, but are not necessarily the only methods available (P 103):

- Methods for codifying explicit knowledge
- Lessons learned register
- Library services
- Information gathering
- Project management information system (PMIS)

4.4.2.4 Interpersonal and Team Skills

Some of the **Interpersonal and Team Skills** shown below may be used (P 104):

- **Active Listening**: Reduces misunderstanding and communication sharing
- **Facilitation**: Guides groups to a successful decision, solution or conclusion
- **Leadership**: communicates vision and inspires the project team to focus on the appropriate knowledge and knowledge objectives
- **Networking**: Allows informal connections and relations among project Stakeholders
- **Political Awareness**: Helps the project manager to plan communications based on the project environment

4.4.3 Manage Project Knowledge: Outputs

4.4.3.1 Lessons Learned Register

The **Lessons Learned Register** is an output of **Manage Project Knowledge**. It is created to register categories and descriptions of any impacts, recommendations and proposed actions that are connected with a particular situation affecting the project (P 104).

4.4.3.2 Project Management Plan Updates

Project Management Plan Updates must go through the Change Control Process via a Change Request (P 105).

4.4.3.3 Organizational Process Assets Updates

Since all projects will create new knowledge, all **Organizational Process Assets** must be updated (P 105).

4.5 MONITOR AND CONTROL PROJECT WORK

Monitor and Control Project Work means to track, review and report overall progress, which is performed throughout the project to meet the performance objectives defined in the Project Management Plan (P 105). The **key benefit** is to allow stakeholders to understand the current project state (as is), the activities needed to address performance issues and to predict future cost and schedule forecasts for the future (to be) project status.

Fig. 4-10, P 105, *Monitor and Control Project Work: Inputs, Tools and Techniques and Outputs*
Fig. 4-11, P 106, *Monitor and Control Project Work: Data Flow Diagram*

Monitoring involves the processes of gathering information, gauging measurements and evaluating the project on a continuous basis with the intention to assess measurement and trends to affect process improvements. **Controlling** is the process of governing actions concerned with preventative or corrective measures and the resulting decisions of such actions. Control includes determining the corrective or preventative actions, or re-planning the action to resolve performance issues. The processes of Monitor and Control project work will include (P 107):

- Compare actual project performance against the Project Management Plan
- Assess performance on a regular basis to make determinations for corrective or preventative actions and make recommendations
- Check the status of individual risks
- Maintain accurate and timely information concerning the project's products
- Provide information to support Status Reporting, Progress Measurement and Forecasting
- Provide Forecasts to update current Cost and Schedule Information

- Monitor implementation of Approved Changes as they occur
- Provide approved appropriate reporting on project status to Program Management
- Ensure the Project stays aligned with the Business Needs

4.5.1 Monitor and Control Project Work: Inputs

4.5.1.1 Project Management Plan

The **Project Management Plan** is involved with Monitoring and Controlling the project work and any component of the Project Management Plan may be considered as an input (P 107).

4.5.1.2 Project Documents

Some of the **Project Documents** that may be considered Inputs to the Project Management Plan are listed below (P 108):

- **Assumption Log**: Contains information about assumptions and constraints
- **Basis of Estimate**: Indicates how the various estimates were derived
- **Cost Forecasts**: Used to determine if the project is within defined tolerance ranges for budget
- **Issue Log**: Used to document and monitor who is responsible for resolving specific issues by a target date
- **Lessons Learned Register**: May contain information on effective responses for variances and corrective and preventative actions
- **Milestone List**: shows scheduled dates for specific Milestones
- **Quality Reports**: Includes Quality Management issues
- **Risk Register**: Provides information on threats and opportunities
- **Risk Report**: Provides information on the overall Project risk as well as individual risks
- **Schedule Forecasts**: Used to determine if the project is within defined tolerance ranges for schedule

4.5.1.3 Work Performance Information

Work Performance Information is amassed during the project execution and forwarded to the Controlling process. This information is compared to and contrasted with other data, such as costs, budget, work performed, resources and funding schedules to determine if the project is within budget goals or if there is a variance from the original plan. This information will determine if corrective or preventative action is necessary (P 109).

4.5.1.4 Agreements

Agreements: A procurement agreement is a document that outlines the terms and conditions of buyer and seller decisions as to what each will provide the other, in terms of products and/or what services will be performed (P 109).

4.5.1.5 Enterprise Environmental Factors

Some of the **Enterprise Environmental Factors** that can affect the **Monitor and Control** Project Work are (P 109):

- Project Management Information Systems
- Infrastructure
- Stakeholder Expectations and Risk Thresholds
- Government or Industry Standards

4.5.1.6 Organizational Process Assets

Some of the **Organizational Process Assets** that can affect the **Monitor and Control** Project Work are (P 110):

- Organizational Standard Policies, Processes and Procedures
- Financial Control Procedures
- Monitoring and Reporting Methods
- Issue Management Procedures
- Defect Management Procedures
- Organizational Knowledge Base

4.5.2 Monitor and Control Project Work: Tools and Techniques

4.5.2.1 Expert Judgment

Expert Judgment: Groups or individuals with specialized knowledge or training or extensive knowledge should be consulted in the areas shown below (P 110):

- Earned Value Analysis
- Interpretation and Contextualization of Data
- Techniques to Estimate Duration and Costs
- Trend Analysis
- Technical Knowledge within the Industry and Focus Area of the Project
- Risk Management
- Contract Management

4.5.2.2 Data Analysis

Some of the **Data Analysis Techniques** that may be used in the Monitoring and Controlling processes are (P 111):

- **Alternative Analysis:** A form of deciding on several alternatives and analyzing each one before making a decision
- **Cost-Benefit Analysis:** Determines the best cost corrective action to assess project deviations
- **Earned Value Analysis**: Compares performance measurement baselines to the actual schedule or cost performance and monitors three (3) key measurements for each work package, such as scope, schedule and cost
- **Root Cause Analysis**: The process of identifying a problem at its core and taking action to prevent or correct the risk
- **Trend Analysis**: Used to validate models used in the organization to forecast future performance based on past results
- **Variance Analysis**: Used to improve the metrics of the organization and may be conducted in each knowledge area used to review the difference or variances between planned and actual performance

4.5.2.3 Decision Making

A **Decision Making** technique that may be used in the Monitoring and Controlling process is (P 111):

- Voting: This can include decisions based on unanimity, majority or plurality

4.5.2.4 Meetings

Types of **Meetings** may include the following (P 111):

- Face-to-Face
- Virtual
- Formal
- Informal
- User Groups
- Review Meetings

4.5.3 Monitor and Control Project Work

4.5.3.1 Work Performance Reports

A **Work Performance Report** is concerned with the accumulation of physical or electronic data meant to prompt actions, decisions or awareness on the part of the Stakeholders. A Work Performance Report may be defined as a Status Report or a Progress Report. These Report can contain information such as (P 112):

- Status Reports
- Progress Reports
- Earned Value Graphs and Information
- Trend Lines
- Forecasts
- Reserve Burndown Charts
- Defect Histograms
- Contract Performance Information

- Risk Summaries, Etc.

A Work Performance Report may be presented in the form of:

- Dashboards
- Heat Reports
- Stop Light Charts, Etc.

4.5.3.2 Change Requests

A Change Request is the actions taken to compare actual results with planned results and must go through the **Perform Integrated Change Control Process**. Some of the changes might include (P 112):

- **Corrective Action**: An intentional activity that realigns the performance of the Project Work with the Project Management Plan
- **Preventative Action**: An intentional activity to ensure the future performance of the Project Work is aligned with the Project Management Plan
- **Defect Repair**: An intentional activity that modifies a nonconforming product or product component

4.5.3.3 Project Management Plan Updates

Project Management Plan Updates are any changes to the Project Management Plan and must be processed by way of a Change Request. Changes made during the Monitor and Control processes may influence the project's outcome (P 112-113).

4.5.3.4 Project Documents Updates

Some of the **Project Documents Updates** may include the following (P 113):

- **Cost Forecasts**: Changes in Cost Forecasts resulting from this process are recorded using Cost management Processes
- **Issue Log**: New issues raised as a result of this process are recorded in the Issue Log
- **Lessons Learned Register**: Effective responses for variances and corrective and preventative actions are recorded in the Lessons Learned Register

- **Risk Register**: New risks identified during this process are recorded in the Risk Register
- **Schedule Forecasts**: Changes in Schedule Forecasts resulting from this process are recorded using Schedule Management Processes

4.6 PERFORM INTEGRATED CHANGE CONTROL

Perform Integrated Change Control is the process of reviewing all change requests, approving changes and managing changes to deliverables, project documents and the project management plan, then communicating decisions (P 113). The Perform Integrated Change Control Process is the responsibility of the Project Manager. Documented changes are then integrated while keeping in mind overall project risk factors. The **key benefit** of this process is to allow documented changes to take place in an integrated manner while considering overall project risk.

Fig. 4-12, P 113, *Perform Integrated Change Control: Inputs, Tools and Techniques and Outputs*
Fig. 4-13, P 114, *Perform Integrated Change Control: Data Flow Diagram*

A Stakeholder(s) Change Request, preferably in written form, can influence the Project Scope and Product Scope factors. These changes can be instituted at any time during the project lifecycle. However, changes must be formally introduced once the baseline is established. A **Change Control Board** (CCB), to formally review, evaluate, approve, defer, or reject changes will be instituted when required/needed.

4.6.1 Perform Integrated Change Control: Inputs

4.6.1.1 Project Management Plan

Some elements included in the **Project Management Plan** may include the following (P 116):

- **Change Management Plan**: This plan defines the process for managing change on the project and documents the roles and responsibilities of the Change Control Board (CCB)
- **Configuration Management Plan**: This plan defines those items that are configurable, those items that require formal change control, and the process for controlling change to those items
- **Scope Baseline**: The Scope Baseline is compared to actual results to determine

if a change, corrective action or preventative action is needed and provide the definition of the project and the product

- **Schedule Baseline:** Comparison with actual results is made to determine if a change or correction is needed and assess the impact of changes in the Schedule Baseline
- **Cost Baseline:** Used to assess the impact of changes to the Project cost and may be updated to reflect approved change requests or changes caused by compression techniques

4.6.1.2 Project Documents

Some **Project Documents** that may be considered inputs to the **Perform Integrated Change Control process** are (P 116):

- **Basis of estimates:** Indicates how the duration, costs and resource estimates were derived and can be used to calculate the impact of the change in time, budget and resources
- **Requirements traceability matrix:** Assesses the impact of change on the Project Scope
- **Risk report:** Presents information on sources of overall and individual project risk

4.6.1.3 Work Performance Reports

Work Performance Reports are a necessary part of the **Perform Change Control Process** because they may or may not affect resource availability, schedule and cost data, earned value reports and burnup or burndown charts (P 116-117).

4.6.1.4 Change Requests

Change Requests include **Corrective Action, Preventative Action** and **Defect Repair,** along with any updates. These changes could influence project baselines and are normally decided by the PM (P 117).

4.6.1.5 Enterprise Environmental Factors

Some of the **Enterprise Environmental Factors** that may affect the **Perform Integrated Change Control** process are (P 117):

- Legal Restrictions
- Government or Industry Standards
- Legal/Regulatory Requirements or Constraints
- Organizational Governance or Framework
- Contracting and Purchasing Constraints

4.6.1.6 Organizational Process Assets

Some of the **Organizational Process Assets** that may affect the Perform Integrated Change Control process are (P 117):

- Change Control Procedures
- Procedures for approving and issuing Change Authorizations
- Configuration Management Knowledge

4.6.2 Perform Integrated Change Control: Tools and Techniques

4.6.2.1 Expert Judgment

Expert Judgment: Groups or Individuals with specialized knowledge or training or extensive knowledge/experience should be consulted in the areas shown below (P 118):

- Technical Knowledge within the Industry and Focus Area of the Project
- Legislation and Regulation
- Legal and procurement
- Configurations Management
- Risk Management

4.6.2.2 Change Control Tools

Change Control Tools are used to manage **Change Requests** and are based on project needs and must support **Configuration Management** activities (P 118):

- **Identify configuration item**: Identification and selection of a Configuration Item to provide the basis for which the product configuration is defined and verified, products and documents are labeled, changes are managed and accountability is maintained
- **Record and report configuration item status**: Information recording and reporting about each **Configuration Item**
- **Perform configuration item verification and audit**: Ensures that the composition of a Project's **Configuration Item** is correct and that corresponding changes are registered, assessed, approved, tracked and correctly implemented
- **Identify changes**: Identify and select a **Change Item** for process or project documents
- **Document changes**: Documents the change into a proper **Change Request**
- **Decide on Changes**: Review the changes: Approving, deferring, rejecting or making any other decisions about changes to the project documents, deliverables or baselines
- **Track changes**: Verify the changes are registered, assessed, approved and tracked and final results are communicated to the stakeholders

Managing change requests/decisions should be distributed to the appropriate Stakeholders and the Change Control Board.

4.6.2.3 Data Analysis

Some of the **Data Analysis Techniques** that may affect the **Perform Integrated Change Control** process are (P 119):

- **Alternative analysis**: Used to assess requested changes and decide which are accepted, rejected or need to be modified
- **Cost-benefit analysis**: Helps to determine if the requested change is worth the cost

4.6.2.4 Decision Making

Some of the **Decision Making** techniques that may affect the **Perform Integrated Change Control** process are (P 119):

- **Voting**: Can take the form of unanimity, majority or plurality for decisions
- **Autocratic decision making**: One individual takes on the responsibility of making decisions for the entire group
- **Multicriteria decision-making**: Uses a Decision Matrix to provide a systematic analytical approach to evaluate the requested changes according to a set of predefined changes

4.6.2.5 Meetings

The Change Control Board (CCB) will hold **Meetings** to decide on approving, rejecting or deferring any change requests and these changes will create an impact on time, cost, resource or risk and communicated appropriately.

4.6.3 Perform Integrated Change Control: Outputs

4.6.3.1 Approved Change Requests

Approved Change Requests take place according to the change management plan. Approved change requests are implemented through the direct and manage project work process (P 120).

4.6.3.2 Project Management Plan Updates

Project Management Plan Updates may include changes and impacts that occur as a result of the Perform Integrated Change Control Process. Only changes from the last Baseline forward should be made.

4.6.3.3 Project Documents Updates

Project Documents Updates may include changes that occur as a result of the **Perform Integrated Change Control Process** (P 120).

4.7 CLOSE PROJECT OR PHASE

Close Project or Phase means to close out all activities for the individual phase or the entire project or contract. Team resources are free to be used if needed elsewhere. Information will be archived and all planned work is completed until the next phase or project occurs. The **key benefit** of this process is to archive project phase information, assure that the planned work is completed and the organizational team is released.

Fig. 4-14, P 121, *Close Project or Phase: Inputs, Tools and Techniques and Outputs*
Fig. 4-5, P 122, *Close Project or Phase: Data Flow Diagram*

The Project Manager (PM) reviews the **Project Management Plan** to make sure all deliverables are accepted, all activities have been completed and objectives have been satisfied. The activities shown below must be undertaken for administrative closure, but there may also be other types of activities related to specific projects not mentioned here (P 123):

Actions necessary to complete **Exit Criteria** for the phase or project includes:

- All documents and deliverables must be up-to-date
- Confirm delivery and formal acceptance of deliverables by customer(s)
- Ensure all costs are charged to project
- Close project accounts
- Reassign with any excess project material
- Reallocate project facilities, equipment and other resources
- Elaborate the final project's reports

Actions related to completion of **Contractual Agreements** applicable to project or phase includes:

- Confirm formal acceptance of seller's work
- Finalize open claims
- Update records to reflect final results
- Archive all information for future use

Activities needed to:

- Collect project or phase records
- Audit project or success failure
- Manage knowledge sharing and transfer
- Identify lessons learned
- Archive project information

Any Activities necessary to transfer project's products, services or results to the next phase or to production or operations and collect suggestions for improvement needs to be done during close project or phase. Updating policies and procedures and the measurements of stakeholder satisfaction should be undertaken. There are also procedures or activities that need to be implemented if a project is prematurely terminated before its planned completion.

4.7.1 Close Project or Phase: Inputs

4.7.1.1 Project Charter

The **Project Charter** documents information on the project, product, service or result, such as project success criteria and approval requirements. A review of eh Project Charter and its contents should be received at the time of the project close out (P 124).

4.7.1.2 Project Management Plan

The **Project Management Plan** components are inputs to Close Project or Phase.

4.7.1.3 Project Documents

Some **Project Documents** that might be Inputs to **Close Project or phase** (P 124):

- **Assumption Log**: Contains both High-level Assumptions and lower level activities and tasks produced by any ongoing project operations (updates occur during the project lifecycle(s). These assumptions can be found in the Business Case before any work is done on the project and will emerge in the Project

Charter

- **Basis of Estimates**: Used to evaluate how the estimation of durations, costs, resources and cost control compare to actual results
- **Change Log**: Contains the status of all Change Requests
- **Issue Log**: Used to check that there are no open issues
- **Lessons Learned Register**: Lessons Learned will be finalized before being entered into the Repository
- **Milestone List**: Shows final dates on which project milestones are accomplished
- **Project Communications**: Includes any and all communications
- **Quality Control Measurements**: Documents results of Quality Control activities
- **Quality Reports**: Includes all Quality Assurance Issues
- **Requirements Documentation**: Used to demonstrate compliance with the Project Scope
- **Risk Register**: Provides information on all known risks
- **Risk Report**: Provides information on risk status

4.7.1.4 Accepted Deliverables

Accepted Deliverables in **Close Project or phase** may include (P 125):

- Product Specifications
- Delivery Receipts
- Work Performance Documents
- Partial or Interim Deliverables for phased or cancelled Projects

4.7.1.5 Business Documents

Some of the **Business Documents** in Close Project or Phase include (P 125):

- **Business Case:** Used to determine if the expected outcomes match the actual outcome
- **Benefits Management Plan:** Outlines the target benefits of the project

4.7.1.6 Agreements

Agreements are terms and conditions as specified in the Procurement Management Plan. A multifaceted project may require the management or sequencing of many contracts.

4.7.1.7 Procurement Documentation

All **Procurement Documentation** must be collected, indexed and filed. The information below shows what must be done to close the project or phase (P 125):

- Contract Schedule Information
- Information Regarding Scope
- Information Regarding Quality
- Information Regarding Cost Performance
- All Contract Change Documentation
- Payment Records
- Catalogued Inspections

The above information may be used for the Lessons Learned Register.

4.7.1.8 Organizational Process Assets

Some of the **Organizational Process Assets** in Close Project or Phase include (P 126):

- Project or Phase Closure Guidelines or Requirements
- Configuration Management Knowledge Base containing versions and Baselines of all Official Organizational Standards, Policies, Procedures and any/all Project Documents

4.7.2 Close Project or Phase: Tools and Techniques

4.7.2.1 Expert Judgement

Expert Judgment: Groups or Individuals with specialized knowledge or training or extensive knowledge should be consulted in the areas shown below and later received or reassigned (P 126):

- Management Control
- Audit
- Legal and Procurement
- Legislation and Regulations

4.7.2.2 Data Analysis

Some **Data Analysis** techniques of Close Project or Phase include (P 126):

- **Document analysis**: Assesses available documentation to allow lessons learned and knowledge sharing
- **Regression Analysis**: analyzes interrelationships between different project variables
- **Trend analysis**: Used to validate models used in the organization
- **Variance analysis**: Used to improve the metrics of the organization

4.7.2.3 Meetings

Meetings for Close Project or Phase are held to (P 127):

- Confirm Deliverables are Accepted
- Validate Acceptance Criteria has been met
- Evaluate Satisfaction of Stakeholders
- Gather Lessons Learned
- Transfer Knowledge and Information from the Project to the Archives
- Celebrate Success

These meetings may be face-to-face, virtual, formal or informal.

4.7.3 Close Project or Phase: Outputs

4.7.3.1 Project Documents Updates

Project Documents Updates are the Lessons Learned Register, which includes the final data on project or phase closure and may contain Benefits Management, the Business Case, Risk Management, Issue Management, Stakeholder Engagement, etc. (P 127).

4.7.3.2 Final Product, Service or Result Transition

Final Product, Service or Result: Once this criteria is met, the Final Product, Service or Result may be **handed over**, operated by and become the responsibility of another group or organization at the end of the project's lifecycle or phase.

4.7.3.3 Final Report

A final report should be written and presented by the PM to the project stakeholders. This is a formal presentation. Some factors in the **Final Report** of Close Project or Phase include (P 127):

- **Summary Level Description** of project or phase
- **Scope Objectives**
- **Quality Objectives**
- **Cost Objectives**
- **Summary of the Validation Information** for the final product, service or result
- **Schedule Objectives**
- **Summary of how the Final Product, Service or Result** is achieve**d** and the business needs identified in the business plan
- **Summary of any Risks or Issues** and any resolutions associated with them

4.7.3.4 Organizational Process Assets Updates

Some of the **Organizational Process Assets** in Close Project or Phase include (P 128):

- **Project documents**: Documentation resulting from project activities
- **Operational and support documents**: Required for an organization to maintain, operate and support any product or service provided by the project
- **Project or phase closure documents**: Consists of formal documentation that indicates completion of the project or phase
- **Lessons learned repository**: Contains information from previous projects that have been experienced and any process improvement recommendations will be filed for future use

Summary: Answers to Student Learning Outcomes

1. **Project Integration Management** is the knowledge area that is integral to successfully execute the entire project life cycle from start to finish (P69).

2. The **Project Manager** needs to be able to make **choices** regarding the following (P 69):

    1. Resource allocation
    2. Balancing competing demands
    3. Examining any alternative approaches
    4. Tailoring the processes
    5. Managing interdependencies among project management knowledge areas

3. The seven (7) **Project Integration Management Processes** are (P 70):

    1. **Develop Project Charter**: This document formally authorizes the existing of the project and provides a project manager authority to apply organizational resources.
    2. **Develop Project Management Plan**: This process defines, prepares and coordinates all plan components and subsidiary plans and consolidates them into an integrated project plan.
    3. **Direct and Manage Project Work**: This process is one of leadership. Project manager must perform the project work required in the project management plan as well as implement approved changes.
    4. **Manage Project Knowledge**: This process uses existing knowledge and creates new knowledge to achieve project objectives and contributes to organizational learning.
    5. **Monitor and Control Project Work**: This is a process of tracking and recording overall progress to meet performance objectives. It is defined in the Project Management Plan.
    6. **Perform Integrated Change Control**: This is a process of reviewing all change request; approving and managing changes to deliverables.
    7. **Close Project or Phase**: This process is one of finalizing all activities for the project phase or contract.

Fig. 4-1, P 71, *Project Integration Management Overview*

4. New concepts for **Project Integration Management** are listed below (P 72):
    - Assuring that deliverables/due dates, etc., are aligned with the Benefits Management Plan.
    - Achieving project objectives as defined in the Project Management Plan.
    - Creation and use of knowledge within and outside the project boundaries.
    - Managing performance and change activities in the Project Management Plan.
    - Making integrated decisions.
    - Measuring and monitoring project progress.
    - Collecting, analyzing and communicating data and information to stakeholders.
    - Completing all project work, closing each completed phase, contract and the project as appropriate.
    - Managing phase transitions.

5. The following five (5) tools are **emerging practices** that should be useful to the Project Manager in context with the principles of Project Integration Management (P 72):
    - Automated tools.
    - Visual management tools.
    - Project knowledge management.
    - Expanding the Project Manager's responsibility.
    - Hybrid methodologies for example: agile, business analysis, technologies, etc.

6. The Project Integration Management process may be **tailored** to the unique needs of the project. Tailoring considerations can include (P 74):

    - Project Life Cycle
    - Development Life Cycle
    - Management Approaches
    - Knowledge Management
    - Managing Change
    - Governance
    - Lessons Learned
    - Benefits Reporting

7. The Project Manager is responsible to **Develop the Project Charter** (PC). The Project Charter is a document that formally authorizes the existence of a project. It provides the authority to apply organizational resources to project activities. The Project Charter's **key benefits** are as follows:

    - Provides a direct link between the project and the strategic objectives of the organization.
    - Creates a formal project record.
    - Shows organizational commitment to the project.

    The project charter development process is performed once or at predefined points on the project time line.

    Fig. 4-2, P 75, *Develop Project Charter: ITTO's*
    Fig. 4-3, P 76, *Develop Project Charter: Data Flow Diagrams*

8. **Business Documents** are inputs to Develop Project Charter. They consist of the Business Case and the Benefits Management Plan. Both documents are developed prior to the Project Charter (P 77).

    Fig. 1-8, P 30, *The Pre-Project Work Time Line*

9. **Agreements** are used to define initial project intentions. They may take the form of a Contract, Memorandums of Understanding(s) (MOU's), Service Level Agreements (SLA), Letters of Agreement (LOA), Letters of Intent (LOI), Verbal Agreements, E-Mail, or any other written or verbal agreements. A contract is used when a project is performed for an external customer (P 78).

10. The following four (4) tools and techniques that may be used to create the **Project Charter and the Assumption Log** (P 79-80.)

    1. Expert Judgment
    2. Data Gathering (Brain storming, focus groups, and interviews)
    3. Interpersonal and Team skills (conflict management, facilitation, and meeting management)
    4. Meetings

11. **Develop Project Management Plan** is the process of defining, preparing, and coordinating all plan components and consolidating them into an integrated Project Management Plan. The Project Plan can consist of selective subsidiary plans as noted below (P 82):
    1. Scope Management Plan
    2. Requirements Management Plan
    3. Schedule Management Plan
    4. Cost Management Plan
    5. Quality Management Plan
    6. Resource Management Plan
    7. Communications Management Plan
    8. Risk Management Plan
    9. Procurement Management Plan
    10. Stakeholder Engagement Plan

    The **key benefit** of Develop Project Management Plan is to produce a comprehensive document that defines:

    - The basis of all the project work, and
    - How the work will be performed.

    Fig. 4-4, P 82, *Develop Project Management Plan: ITTO's*
    Fig. 4-5, P 82, *Develop Project Management Plan: Data Flow Diagram*

12. The **Project Management Plan** consists of ten (10) subsidiary management plans and three base lines (P 87). The subsidiary management plans are outlined above.
    The three base lines are:
    1. Scope Baseline
    2. Schedule Baseline
    3. Cost Baseline

13. **Direct and Manage Project Work** is the process of leading the project team to perform the work defined in the Project Management Plan and implementing approved changes so that the project objectives are achieved (P 90). The **key benefit** is the provision of overall management of the project's work and its deliverables to improve project success.

    Fig. 4-6, P 90, *Direct and Manage Project Work: ITTO's*
    Fig. 4-7, P 91, *Direct and Manage Project Work: Data Flow Diagram*

14. **Change Request** is an output of Direct and Manage Project Work (P 96). Change requests may include:
    - Corrective Action
    - Preventative Action
    - Defect Repair
    - Updates (to formally controlled project documents)

Note:* STUDY *and read their descriptions.

15. **Manage Project Knowledge** is the process of using existing knowledge and creating new knowledge to achieve project objectives and add to organizational learning (P 98). The **key benefit** is to leverage prior organizational knowledge to produce or improve project outcomes and future knowledge to support operations and future projects or phases.

    Fig. 4-8, P 98, *Manage Project Knowledge: ITTO's*
    Fig. 4-9, P 99, *Manage Project Knowledge: Data Flow Diagram*

16. **Interpersonal and Team Skills** (P 104) in Manage Project Knowledge may include:
    - Active Listening
    - Facilitation
    - Leadership
    - Networking
    - Political Awareness

17. **Monitor and Control Project Work** is the process of tracking, reviewing, and reporting the overall project progress to meet the performance objectives defined in the Project Management Plan (P 105). Its **key benefit** is to:
    - Assure the stakeholders understand the current state of the project.
    - Recognize needed action to address performance issues.
    - Future project status must include cost and schedule forecasts.

    Fig. 4-10, P 105, *Monitor and Control Project Work: ITTO's*
    Fig. 4-11, P 106, *Monitor and Control Project Work: Data Flow Diagram*

18. The following are inputs to **Monitor and Control Project Work** (P 106):

    - Project Management Plan (any subsidiary component)
    - Project Documents
    - Assumption Log
    - Basis of Estimates
    - Cost Forecasts
    - Issue Log
    - Lessons Learned Register
    - Milestone List
    - Quality Reports
    - Risk Register
    - Risk Report
    - Schedule Forecast
    - Work Performance Information
    - Agreements
    - Enterprise Environmental Factors
    - Organizational Process Assets

19. **Data Analysis** tools and techniques (P 111) that may be used in Monitor and Control Project Work include:

    - Alternative Analysis
    - Cost Benefit Analysis
    - Earned Value Analysis
    - Root Cause Analysis
    - Trend Analysis
    - Variance Analysis

    Definition to these terms (P 111).

20. Three (3) **Change Requests** (P 112) may be used in Monitor and Control Project Work. They are:
    - Corrective Action
    - Preventive Action

- Defect Repair

21. **Perform Integrated Change Control** (P 113) is the:

    1. Process of reviewing all change requests.
    2. Approving Changes.
    3. Managing changes to deliverables, project documents, and the project plan, and
    4. Communicating the decisions.

The **key benefit** is that it allows for documented change to take place in the project; and to address changes in an integrated fashion, while c8onsidering overall project risk, etc.

22. The **Change Control Board (CCB)** (P 115) is a formally ***chartered*** *group* that is responsible for:
    1. Reviewing
    2. Evaluating
    3. Approving
    4. Deferring and
    5. Rejecting changes to the project.

The CCB records and communicates these decisions to the project stakeholders.

23. The three (3) decision making tools and techniques (P 119) that may be used in **Perform Integrated Change** control are:

- Voting
- Autocratic Decision Making
- Multi-criteria Decision Analysis

STUDY **and read their descriptions** (P 119).

24. **Close Project or Phase** is the process of finalizing all activities for the project, phase or contract (P 121). The **key benefit** is to archive all project/phase information regarding the completed project work and releasing the project resources.

Fig. 4-14, P 122, *Close Project or Phase: ITTO's*
Fig. 4-15, P 123, *Close Project or Phase: Data Flow Diagram*

See detailed actions and activities to satisfy completion of phase/project exit criteria/contractual agreements, etc. (P 123).

25. At the completion of delivering (P 127) the project's **Final Product, Service or Result Transition**, the Project Manager will need to hand over to a different group or organization the final project results. This group or organization is then responsible to operate, maintain and/or support it throughout its life cycle (P 127).

26. The **Final Report** is a formal summary and presentation of the project performance (P 127). It is commonly prepared by the Project Manager. It will include:

- Summary level description of the project or phase.
- Scope objectives, etc., and evidence that the completion criteria was met
- Quality objective criteria and verification of acceptance
- Cost objectives, etc. and reason for variances
- Summary of validation for the final product, service or result

Similar Questions that may be on the PMI Exam related to Chapter 4

1. What is the process for comparing actual to baseline schedules, examining the statement of work, understanding cost overruns and assessing risk?

   A. CCB Meetings
   B. Monitor and Control Project Work
   C. Manage and Direct Team
   D. Contract negotiation

   Correct Answer is B: The Monitor and Control Project Work process is concerned with comparing actual project performance against the project management plan and assessing performance to determine whether any corrective or preventive actions are indicated. Also, to identify new risks and identifying, analyzing, tracking and monitoring existing project risks to make sure the risks are identified, their status is reported and that appropriate risk response plans are being executed.

2. Which of the following processes is not always part of the closing process group?

   A. Deliverable signoff
   B. Updating archives
   C. Releasing the Team
   D. Control procurement

   Correct answer is A: Deliverable signoff is a part of the validate scope process. As per the PMBOK, all other processes constitute the closing process group.

3. While conducting project closure activities, a relatively new project manager of a software production company found that some of the procedures followed in the organization are different from previous companies he had worked for. He became confused. What should he refer to, in order to get clarity on the procedures to verify that the exit criteria have been met?

A. Close Project or Phase
B. Control Procurements
C. Expert Judgment
D. Administrative Closure Procedure

Correct Answer is D: The administrative closure procedure lists the actions to verify that the project deliverables have been accepted and that the exit criteria have been met.

4. John has successfully completed a wide area network (WAN) project for an MNC. There were many issues during the execution of the project. Although the customer accepted the completed project scope, the team is still documenting and archiving the lessons learned. What is the status of the project?

    A. Complete
    B. Incomplete
    C. Closed
    D. Under Execution

Correct Answer is B: The project requires formal closing and stands incomplete, until lessons learned are documented, and all records archived.

5. You are working on a construction project. Your team and senior manager believes that the work is complete. However, one the stakeholders disagrees. He feels that one of the deliverables is not acceptable. What is the best way to handle the conflict?

    A. Renegotiate the contract
    B. Consult the contract and follow its claims administration procedure (CAP)
    C. File a lawsuit and force the stakeholder to accept the deliverable
    D. Follow the administrative and contract closure procedure

Correct Answer is B: Most contracts have precise clauses explaining how claims should be resolved. Since it is in the contract, it is legally binding, and both the buyer and seller need to follow it. Hence, claims administration procedure (CAP) in the contract should be consulted. Usually it is not feasible to renegotiate a contract, especially at the time of project closure. Also, lawsuits should only be filed if there are absolutely no other alternatives. Administrative and contract closure procedures helps resolve the closing process of project. However, the project cannot be closed until claims are resolved. A dispute between a buyer and a seller is called a claim.

6. Donald Pumps, a NYSE listed multinational manufacturing company, has presence in 30 countries worldwide. Your company is selected to implement an enterprise resource planning (ERP) system to streamline their operations. This implementation is expected to improve/enhance company's manufacturing, procurement, sales, supply chain and payment systems. You are the project manager for the same. Most of your staff is not PMP certified and you are nearing project completion. In one of the team meetings, your team's project leader was questioned about the right approach to work, with respect to controlling quality and closing the project. Which of the following processes and activities are correct?

   A. Control quality, close project or phase and control procurements
   B. Validate scope, control quality, close project or phase and control procurements
   C. Control quality, validate scope and close project or phase
   D. Validate scope, control quality and control procurements

   Correct answer is C: First, the product or project deliverable is inspected by the performing organization under control quality process. Second, it is taken to the client for formal acceptance under validate scope process. Third, on acceptance the phase or project is closed.

7. A PMP certified project manager joins a telecom company for a project referred to as Easy Communicate. After joining the company, he analyzed and determined the project is no longer a project and has evolved into an ongoing, operational activity. Because of the lack of appropriate knowledge, no one in the company was aware of this fact. Now, the project manager finds it important to formally document the status of the project and report it to the management. Under what status shall the project manager categorize this project?

   A. Close project or phase
   B. Planning
   C. Initiation
   D. Monitor and Control

   Correct answer is A: The project should be moved to close project or phase as it has evolved into an ongoing operation and is no longer a project. Users might have already started using the product/service on regular basis without formal closure of project by PM.

8. Your project just completed and one of your subcontractors has sent you floor seats to the next big hockey game to thank you for your business. What is the best way to respond?

    A. Thank the subcontractor, but do not give him preference in the next RFP
    B. Thank the subcontractor, but politely refuse the gift
    C. Ask for tickets for the entire team, so that it is fair to everyone
    D. Report the subcontractor to PMI

Correct answer is B: The PMP Code of Professional Conduct says that you are not allowed to accept any kind of gift, not even after the project has finished. That would be the same thing as taking a bribe.

9. A leading manufacturer of consumer electronics, personal computers and peripherals has decided to drive growth and profit by implementing an online CRM (customer relationship management) solution. Industry benchmarks suggest the CRM solution should generate $100M-$300M in bottom the benefits. The project timeline is very aggressive and there is a lot at stake with this project. Your company has been awarded the project and you are the project manager. The project began on a good note but is getting increasingly difficult day by day due to its sheer complexity. Stakeholders are getting jittery and want you set things in order soon. You discovered that there was another similar project implemented by your company last year and you could really benefit from the information. What should be your next step?

    A. Contact the concerned project manager and ask for assistance
    B. Obtain lessons learned and guidance from the PMO
    C. Increase project resources particularly subject matter experts
    D. Raise a change request and push to get some more time for project execution from project sponsors

Correct answer is B: PMO is the custodian for all previously executed projects. Hence, the best approach will be to reach out to the PMO and seek assistance. Similar projects have been done in past, so the best way is to look for organization process assets from PMO. Option C and D are not the best approach as the information provided in the question is not sufficient. Option A is incorrect as you can never be sure about the success of the previous project manager in the company and whether he/she would be willing to help you.

10. John is implementing a WAN network project for a retail chain spread across 1000 locations across the country. The project is of 1-year duration and has a budget of $100M. There are 25 key stakeholders and a sponsor. Who is responsible for undertaking project integration?

    A. Customer
    B. Team Members
    C. Stakeholders
    D. Project Manager

Correct answer is D: It is John's responsibility to see that the project work is coordinated well and the project always give a unified and consolidated view.

You may now move on to Chapter Five: Project Scope Management

Chapter 5: Project Scope Management: Work within Project Boundaries

"A project is complete when it starts working for you, rather than you working for it." Scott Allen

Student Learning Outcomes:

1. What is **Project Scope Management** and list the six (6) **Project Scope Management** Processes (P 129)?
2. In key concepts for **Project Scope Management**, scope can be a term described within a project's context. What is the difference between **Product Scope** and **Project Scope** (P 131)?
3. In an **adaptive** or **agile life cycle**, which two (2) processes are repeated for each iteration (P 131)?
4. The **Scope Baseline** (P 131) for a project is the approved version of (1) the **Project Scope Statement, (2) The Work Breakdown Structure (WBS), and (3) WBS Dictionary.** In what type of **life cycle** would the project manager be working?
5. Which **type of life cycle** does the project manager use **backlogs** to reflect current user requirements (P 131)?
6. When the **Project Manager collaborates** with business analysis professionals, what are some **activities** that **require collaboration** (P 132)? This is a Trend and Emerging Practice in Project Scope Management.
7. Which **method**, either Agile or Predictive, deliberately requires less time in defining and agreeing upon **Scope Requirements** (P 133)?
8. **What is Plan Scope Management and its benefits?** In the Plan Scope Management Process, there are two (2) outputs (P 135). What are they?
9. Which plan is a **component** of the **Project Management Plan** that describes **how** the project and product requirements will be analyzed, documented, and managed (P 137)?
10. **What is meant by Collect Requirements and its key benefit (P 138)?**
11. The following are **Data Gathering Techniques** used in **Collect Requirements** (P 138):

    1. **Brainstorming**,
    2. **Interviews**,
    3. **Focus groups**,
    4. **Questionnaires and Surveys**, and
    5. **Benchmarking**.

    Which technique is commonly used to **compare with comparable companies and organizations to identify best practices and provide a basis for measuring performance** (P 143)?

12. Which **Interpersonal and Team Skill** emphasizes brainstorming with a voting process to prioritize useful ideas (P 144)?
13. The **Context Diagram** usually depicts **Product Scope** by showing the business system

and how other active systems interact within the context diagram components. Which process group is used in this work (P 146)?

14. What is the name of the **document_that links product requirements from their origin to their deliverables that satisfy them (P 148)?**
15. **What is Define Scope and its benefits?** The **Project Scope Statement** is an output of **Define Scope** (P 154). Why is this document so important?
16. **What is meant by Create WBS and what is its key benefit? (P 156)?**
17. What is meant by **decomposition** and what are **some activities followed in creating a WBS** (P 152-161)?
18. What is a **WBS Dictionary** (P 162)?
19. **What is meant by Validate Scope and what are its key benefits (P 163)?**
20. Which **process group** brings objectivity and increases the possibility of final product, service or result to the **acceptance process** by **validating end deliverables** (P 163)?
21. **What is meant by Control Scope and what are its key benefits (P 167)?**
22. Which **process group** is known for **monitoring project status** and **product scope and manages changes to the Scope Baseline** (P 171)?

CHAPTER FIVE INTRODUCTION: WORK WITHIN PROJECT BOUNDARIES

PROJECT SCOPE MANAGEMENT: CHAPTER 5 OVERVIEW: PMBOK® 6th Edition P 129-172

Project Scope Management identifies the boundaries and the depth of the project work to be performed (P 129). This area is a process that includes the work required and only the work required to complete the project successfully. Project Scope Management is primarily concerned with defining and controlling what is and what is not going to be completed in the project.
There are six (6) Project Scope Management processes that the project manager needs to carefully and consistently follow (P 129). They are:

(5.1) **Plan Scope Management** is a process of creating the scope management plan that requires documentation. This documentation tells us how the project and product scope is going to be defined and how it is going to be validated and controlled.

(5.2) **Collect Requirements** is the second process. This process collects requirements from the beneficiaries, stakeholders, sponsors, the users for the 'to be' system. Collect requirements must determine, document, and manage stakeholder needs and their requirements to meet project objectives. Collect requirements is done by interviews, by questionnaires, by sampling of reports, or using other various elicitation models, tools, and techniques.

(5.3) **Define Scope** is a process which requires detailed analysis and detailed write-ups of the scope description for the project and for the product. Upon completing the detailed project description and product, the work is divided into work packages that are assigned to the project team or management stakeholders.

(5.4) **Create Work Breakdown Structures (WBS)** is breaking the work down into work packages and deliverables to the lowest level of work that is going to be assigned to the project team. This is a process of sub-dividing project deliverables and project work into smaller, more manageable components.

Please refer to the following links: *Demystifying the WBS*, (article) by Jim Lombardi, located at https://www.linkedin.com/pulse/demystifying-wbs-jim-lombardi/.

Also, see *Work Management*, (4:57 minutes), by Dallas Flett-Wapash, Garrett Gilroy, Jennifer Joubert, and Selena Harrison: https://youtu.be/mpVcGpTvDvo.

(5.5) **Validate Scope** is a formalization process. It is one of making certain that the completed project deliverables are accepted by the recipients, users or stakeholders of the project. There are going to be changes to the product scope or product. This may change the project approach.

(5.6) **Control Scope** is the final process of monitoring the status of the project and the product scope and managing changes that will go through an Integrated Change Control (ICC) process. The changes to the scope will add or subtract work to (from) the project scope baseline.

Fig. 5-1, P 130, *Project Scope Management Overview*

Key concepts for Project Scope Management:

There are a number of key concepts regarding Project Scope Management. Scope can refer to either product scope or project scope (P 131). The **product scope** actually deals with features and functions that characterize a product, service or result. The **project scope** is performed to deliver a specific product service or result with the specified features and functions. This term, project scope, is often viewed as including the product scope.

The Project life cycle can range from predictive approaches at one end, to adaptive or agile approaches at the other end of the life cycle continuum. In the predictive life cycle, the project deliverables are defined at the beginning of the project and any changes to the scope are progressively made. In an adaptive or agile life cycle, the deliverables are developed over multiple iterations where detailed scope is defined and approved for each iteration.

Trends and Emerging Practices in Project Scope Management:

There are numerous Trends and Emerging Practices that are taking place in project scope management (P 132). Business analysis deals with defining, managing, controlling requirements and understanding work. Today, the project manager may serve as a business analyst as well as the project manager. In order to determine scope requirements, the project manager/business analyst must determine

1. The problems
2. Identify the business needs and recommend viable solutions
3. Elicit documents and stakeholder requirements
4. Facilitate successful implementation of the product, service or result

Tailoring Considerations:

It is quite common that the project manager and the project team will tailor the approach that the project scope management processes should take. This can include (P 133):

- Knowledge and requirements management
- Validation and control
- Development approach
- Stability requirements
- Governance

Considerations for Agile/Adaptive Environments:

If the project manager, the sponsor or the company considers Agile, then it is important to realize that scope is often not understood at the beginning of the project even while the project is evolving. In agile methods, one deliberately spends less time trying to define and agree on the scope in the early stages of the project, but spends more time in the process (P 133). Discovery and refinement will unlock the design needed. The release version will refine the requirements.

Plan Scope Management:

The process of Plan Scope Management is create a scope management plan. This plan documents how the project and product(s) will be defined, validated and controlled throughout the project life cycle.

The **key benefit** of Plan Scope Management is that it provides guidance and direction on how scope will be managed from the beginning throughout the end of the project (P 134). There are a number of inputs, tools, techniques and outputs that are used in plan scope management.

https://globalproject.management/lesson/how-to-prepare-for-the-pmp-exam/

See chart on next page: **PLAN SCOPE MANAGEMENT (Section 5.1)**

Chapter Five: Project Scope Management

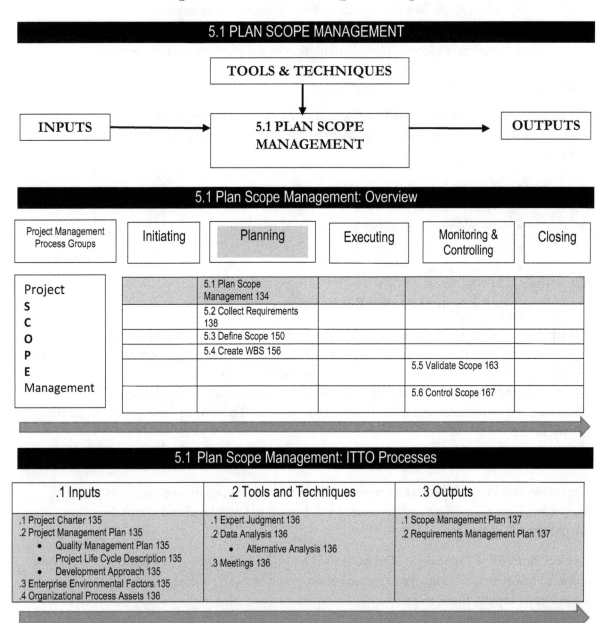

5.1 PLAN SCOPE MANAGEMENT

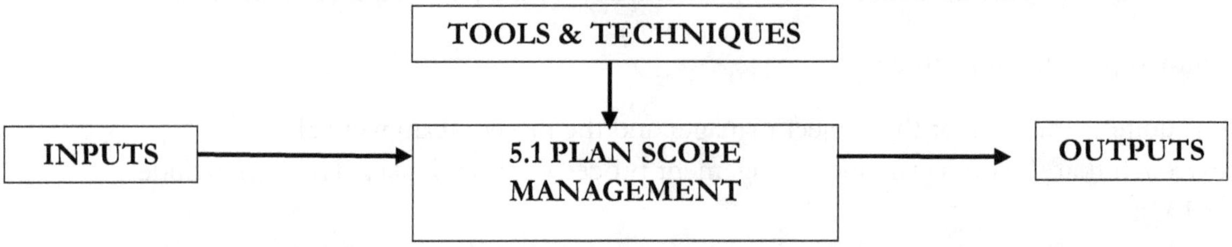

5.1 Plan Scope Management: Overview

Project Management Process Groups	Initiating	Planning	Executing	Monitoring & Controlling	Closing
Project SCOPE Management		5.1 Plan Scope Management 134			
		5.2 Collect Requirements 138			
		5.3 Define Scope 150			
		5.4 Create WBS 156			
				5.5 Validate Scope 163	
				5.6 Control Scope 167	

5.1 Plan Scope Management: ITTO Processes

.1 Inputs	.2 Tools and Techniques	.3 Outputs
.1 Project Charter 135 .2 Project Management Plan 135 • Quality Management Plan 135 • Project Life Cycle Description 135 • Development Approach 135 .3 Enterprise Environmental Factors 135 .4 Organizational Process Assets 136	.1 Expert Judgment 136 .2 Data Analysis 136 • Alternative Analysis 136 .3 Meetings 136	.1 Scope Management Plan 137 .2 Requirements Management Plan 137

Fig. 5-2, P 134, *Plan Scope Management: Inputs, Tools and Techniques and Outputs*
Fig. 5-3, P 134, *Plan Scope Management: Data Flow Diagram*

Collect Requirements:

Collect Requirements is the process of determining, documenting and managing stakeholder needs to meet objectives and requirements (P 138). The **primary benefit** of collect requirements is that it provides the basis for defining the product scope and the project scope. There are a number of inputs, tools, techniques and outputs in collect requirements.

Fig. 5-4, P 138, *Collect Requirements: Inputs, Tools and Tools and Techniques and Outputs*
Fig. 5-5, P 138 and 139, *Collect Requirements: Data Flow Diagram.*

See chart on next page: **COLLECT REQUIREMENTS (Section 5.2)**

Chapter Five: Project Scope Management

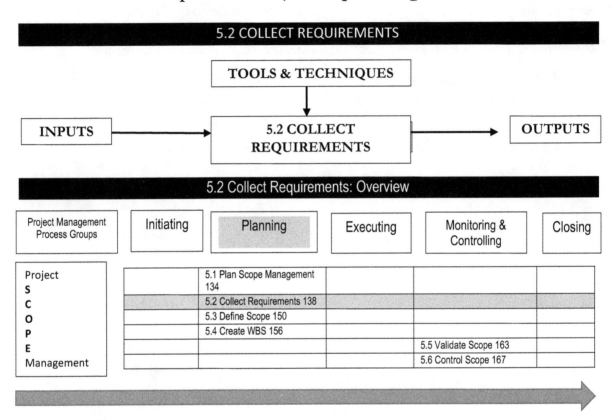

5.2 COLLECT REQUIREMENTS

TOOLS & TECHNIQUES

INPUTS → 5.2 COLLECT REQUIREMENTS → OUTPUTS

5.2 Collect Requirements: Overview

Project Management Process Groups	Initiating	Planning	Executing	Monitoring & Controlling	Closing
Project **S** **C** **O** **P** **E** Management		5.1 Plan Scope Management 134			
		5.2 Collect Requirements 138			
		5.3 Define Scope 150			
		5.4 Create WBS 156			
				5.5 Validate Scope 163	
				5.6 Control Scope 167	

5.2 Collect Requirements: ITTO Processes

INPUTS	TOOLS and TECHNIQUES	OUTPUTS
.1 Project Charter 140 .2 Project Management Plan 140 • Scope Management Plan140 • Requirements Management Plan 140 • Stakeholder Engagement Plan 140 .3 Project Documents 141 • Assumption Log 141 • Lessons Learned Register 141 • Stakeholder Register 141 .4 Business Documents 141 • Business Case 141 .5 Agreements 141 .6 Enterprise Environmental Factors 141 .7 Organizational Process Assets 141	.1 Expert Judgment 142 .2 Data Gathering 142 • Brainstorming 142 • Interviews 142 • Focus Groups 142 • Questionnaires and Surveys 143 • Benchmarking 143 .3 Data Analysis 143 • Document Analysis 143 .4 Decision Making 144 • Voting 144 • Multicriteria Decision Analysis 144 .5 Data Representation 144 • Affinity Diagrams 144 • Mind Mapping 144 .6 Interpersonal And Team Skills 144 • Nominal Group Technique 144 • Observation/Conversation 145 • Facilitation 145 .7 Context Diagram 146 .8 Prototypes 147	.1 Requirements Documentation 147 .2 Requirements Traceability Matrix 148

Define Scope:

The process of Defining Scope is developing a detailed description of the project and products. The **key benefit** of this process is that it describes the product, service or result boundaries and acceptance criteria.

See chart below: **DEFINE SCOPE (Section 5.3)**

Chapter Five: Project Scope Management

5.3 DEFINE SCOPE

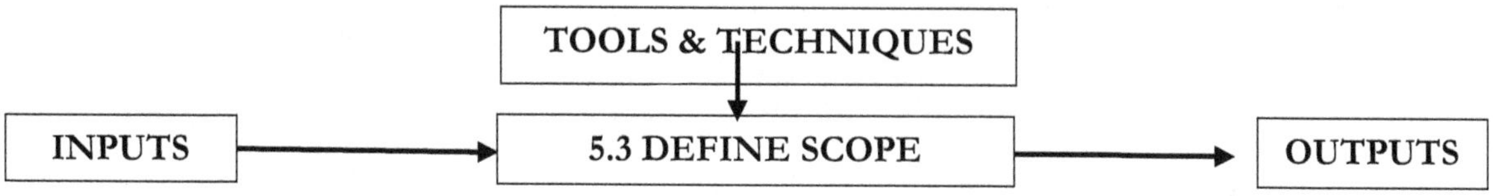

5.3 Define Scope: Overview

Project Management Process Groups	Initiating	Planning	Executing	Monitoring & Controlling	Closing
Project SCOPE Management		5.1 Plan Scope Management 134			
		5.2 Collect Requirements 138			
		5.3 Define Scope 150			
		5.4 Create WBS 156			
				5.5 Validate Scope 163	
				5.6 Control Scope 167	

5.3 Define Scope: ITTO Processes

INPUTS	TOOLS and TECHNIQUES	OUTPUTS
.1 Project Charter 152 .2 Project Management Plan 152 • Scope Management Plan152 .3 Project Documents 152 • Assumption Log 152 • Requirements Documentation 152 • Risk Register 152 .4 Enterprise Environmental Factors .5 Organizational Process Assets 152	.1 Expert Judgment 153 .2 Data Analysis 153 Alternative Analysis 153 .3 Decision Making • Multicriteria Decisions Analysis 153 .4 Interpersonal and Team Skills 153 .5 Product Analysis 153	.1 Project Scope Statement 154 .2 Project Documents Updates 155 • Assumption Log 155 • Requirements Documentation 155 • Requirements Traceability Matrix 155 • Stakeholder Register 155

Fig. 5-8, P 150, *Define Scope: Inputs, Tools and Techniques and Outputs*
Fig. 5-9, P 150, *Define Scope: Data Flow Diagram*

Create WBS (Work Breakdown Structure):

Create WBS is the process of subdividing project deliverables and project work into smaller, more manageable components, called work packages. The **key benefit** of this process is that it provides a framework of what is to be delivered (P 156). This process is performed one time or multiple times where predefined points are required in the project.

See chart on next page: **CREATE WBS (Section 5.4)**

Chapter Five: Project Scope Management

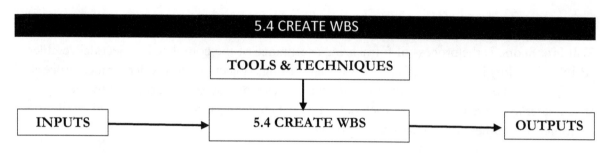

5.4 CREATE WBS

TOOLS & TECHNIQUES

INPUTS → **5.4 CREATE WBS** → **OUTPUTS**

5.4 Create WBS: Overview

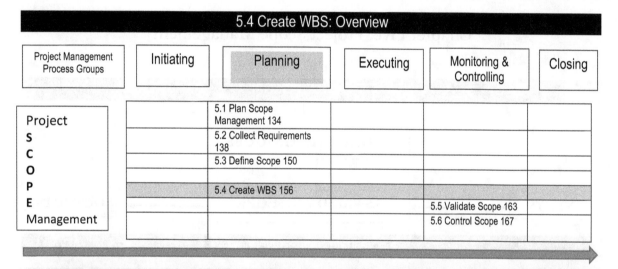

Project Management Process Groups	Initiating	Planning	Executing	Monitoring & Controlling	Closing
Project SCOPE Management		5.1 Plan Scope Management 134			
		5.2 Collect Requirements 138			
		5.3 Define Scope 150			
		5.4 Create WBS 156			
				5.5 Validate Scope 163	
				5.6 Control Scope 167	

5.4 Create WBS: ITTO Processes

INPUTS	TOOLS and TECHNIQUES	OUTPUTS
.1 Project Management Plan 157 • Scope Management Plan 157 .2 Project Documents 157 • Project Scope Statement 157 • Requirements Documentation 157 .3 Enterprise Environmental Factors 157 .4 Organizational Process Assets 157	.1 Expert Judgment 158 .2 Decomposition 158	.1 Scope Baseline 161 .2 Project Documents Updates 162 • Assumption Log 162 • Requirements Documentation 162

Fig. 5-10, P 156, *Create WBS: Inputs, Tools and Techniques and Outputs*
Fig. 5-11, P 156, *Create WBS: Data Flow Diagram*
Fig. 5-12, P 158, *Sample WBS Decomposed Down through Work Packages*
Fig. 5-13, P 159, *Sample WBS Organized by Phase*

Fig. 5-14, P 160, *Sample WBS with Major Deliverables*

Validate Scope:

Validate Scope is the process of formalizing acceptance of the completed project deliverables (P 163). The **key benefit** of this process is that it brings objectivity to the acceptance process and increases the probability of the final product, service or result to be accepted by the stakeholder(s) where they validate each deliverable. Generally, a sign-off is required by the customer that authenticates customer approval.

See chart below: **VALIDATE SCOPE (Section 5.5)**

Chapter Five: Project Scope Management

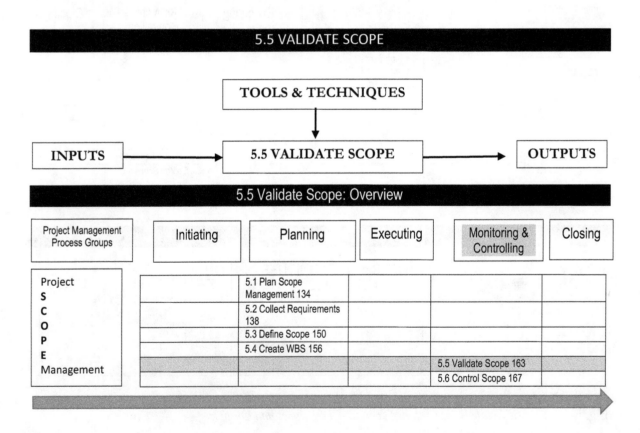

5.5 VALIDATE SCOPE

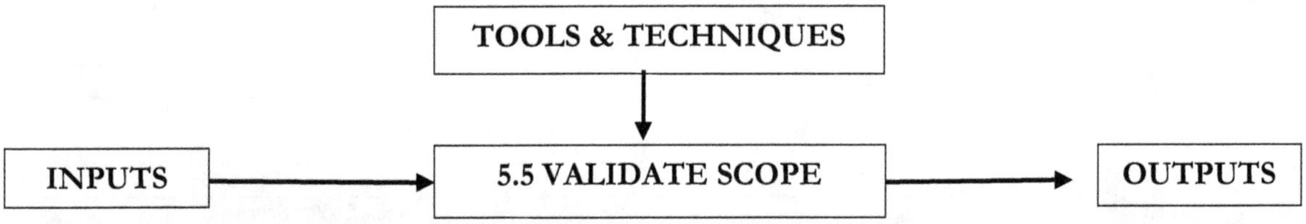

5.5 Validate Scope: Overview

Project Management Process Groups	Initiating	Planning	Executing	Monitoring & Controlling	Closing
Project SCOPE Management		5.1 Plan Scope Management 134			
		5.2 Collect Requirements 138			
		5.3 Define Scope 150			
		5.4 Create WBS 156			
				5.5 Validate Scope 163	
				5.6 Control Scope 167	

5.5 Validate Scope: ITTO Processes

INPUTS	TOOLS and TECHNIQUES	OUTPUTS
.1 Project Management Plan 165 • Scope Management Plan 165 • Requirements Management Plan 165 • Scope Baseline 165 .2 Project Documents 165 • Lessons Learned Register 165 • Quality Reports 165 • Requirements Traceability Matrix 165 .3 Verified Deliverables 165 .4 Work Performance Data 165	.1 Inspection 166 .2 Decision Making 166 • Voting 166	.1 Accepted Deliverables 166 .2 Work Performance Information 166 .3 Change Requests 166 .4 Project Documents Updates 167 • Learned Lessons Register 167 • Requirements Documentation 167 • Requirements Traceability Matrix 167

Fig. 5-15, P 163, *Validate Scope: Inputs, Tools and Techniques and Outputs*
Fig. 5-16, P 164, *Validate Scope Data Flow Diagram*

Control Scope:

Control Scope is the process of monitoring the status of the project and product scope and managing changes to the baseline (P 167). The **key benefit** of this process, control scope, is that the scope baseline is maintained throughout the project. Control scope is performed throughout the project end, and is the process of monitoring project status and changes to the project scope baseline is maintained.

See chart on next page: **CONTROL SCOPE (Section 5.6)**

Chapter Five: Project Scope Management

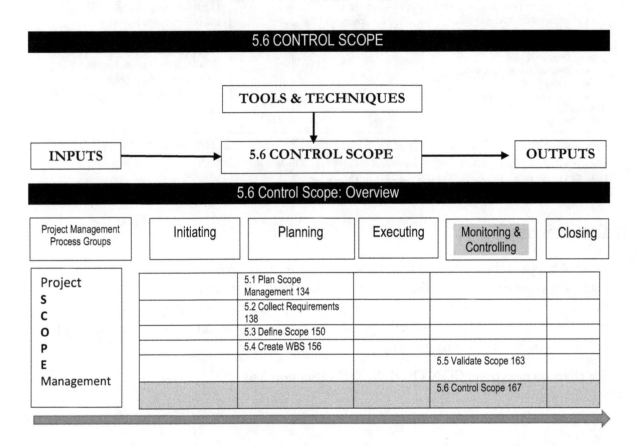

5.6 CONTROL SCOPE

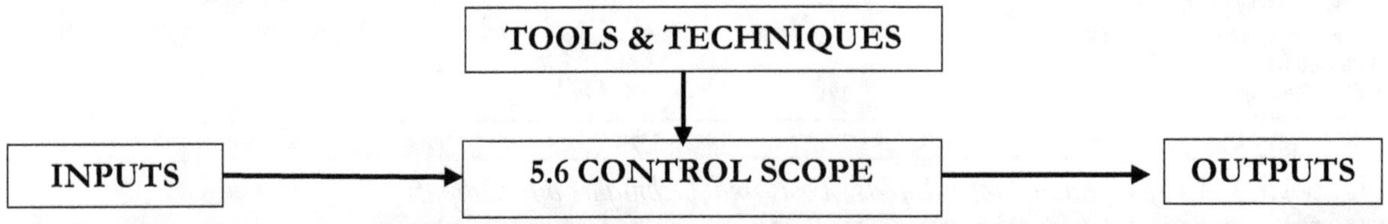

5.6 Control Scope: Overview

Project Management Process Groups	Initiating	Planning	Executing	Monitoring & Controlling	Closing
Project SCOPE Management		5.1 Plan Scope Management 134			
		5.2 Collect Requirements 138			
		5.3 Define Scope 150			
		5.4 Create WBS 156			
				5.5 Validate Scope 163	
				5.6 Control Scope 167	

5.6 Control Scope: ITTO Processes

INPUTS	TOOLS and TECHNIQUES	OUTPUTS
.1 Project Management Plan 169 • Scope Management Plan 169 • Requirements Management Plan 169 • Change Management Plan 169 • Configuration Management Plan 169 • Scope Baseline 169 • Performance Measurement Baseline 169 .2 Project Documents 169 • Lessons Learned Register 169 • Requirements Documentation 169 • Requirements Traceability Matrix 169 .3 Work Performance Data 169 .4 Organizational Process Assets 170	.1 Data Analysis 170 • Variance Analysis 170 • Trend Analysis 170	.1 Work Performance Information 170 .2 Change Requests 170 .3 Project Management Plan Updates 171 • Scope Management Plan 171 • Scope Baseline 171 • Schedule Baseline 171 • Cost Baseline 171 • Performance Measurement Baseline 171 .4 Project Documents Updates 171 • Lessons Learned Register 171 • Requirements Documentation 171 • Requirements Traceability Matrix 171

Fig. 5-17, P 167, *Control Scope: Inputs, Tools and Techniques and Outputs*
Fig. 5-18, P 168, *Control Scope: Data Flow Diagram*

KEY WORDS: CHAPTER 5

Scope Management Plan
Requirements Management Plan
Plan Scope
Collect Requirements
Define Scope
Create WBS
Validate Scope
Scope Management Plan
Requirement Management Plan
Project Charter
Business Documents
Expert Judgment
Brainstorming
Interviews
Focus Groups
Questionnaires and Surveys
Benchmarking
Data Analysis
Decision Making

- Voting
- Multi-Criteria Decision Making
- Autocratic Decision Making

Affinity Diagrams
Mind Mapping
Nominal Group Technique
Facilitation
JAD Sessions QFD
User Stories
Context Diagram
Prototypes
Solution Requirements
Requirements Traceability Matrix
Requirements Documentation
Assumption Log
Product Analysis
Project Scope Statement
WBS
WBS Dictionary
Decomposition
Work Package
Planning Package
Risk Register
Interpersonal and Team Skills
Product Scope Description
Scope Baseline
Deliverables
Acceptance Criteria
Stakeholder Register
Decomposition
WBS Dictionary
Requirements Management Plan
Requirements Traceability Matrix
Inspection
Change Request
Lessons Learned Register
Change Management Plan
Configuration Management Plan
Scope Baseline
Performance Measurement Baseline
Work Performance Data Analysis
Variance Analysis
Trend Analysis;
Schedule Baseline
Cost Baseline

LEGEND

The following Legend shows how to correctly read the *PMBOK® Guide* references and attributions correctly for Chapter 5: Project Scope Management PMBOK Details.

Legend:

Chapter Section	Chapter Section Title	Page Number

Example from Chapter Six shown below:

6.5.1.4	Enterprise Environmental Factors	(P 209)

All direct quotes are attributed as (A Guide to the Project Management Body of Knowledge, *(PMBOK® Guide)* – Sixth Edition) Project Management Institute Inc., 2017, Page #, after each section and any/all paraphrased or original wording is attributed as (P #), before or after each section. All Graphs, Charts, Tables and Figures are attributed as: (*PMBOK® Guide,* Fig. #-# or #/#, P #, *Title of Graph, Chart, Table or Figure*).

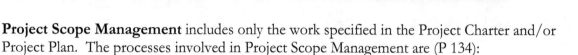

5. PROJECT SCOPE MANAGEMENT

Project Scope Management includes only the work specified in the Project Charter and/or Project Plan. The processes involved in Project Scope Management are (P 134):

- **Plan Scope Management**
- **Collect Requirements**
- **Define Scope**
- **Create WBS**
- **Validate Scope**
- **Control Scope**

Some of the **Key Concepts for Project Scope Management**:

- **Product Scope**: Features and functions that characterize a product, service or result
- **Project Scope**: Work performed to deliver a product, service or result with the specified features and functions, sometimes viewed as including Product Scope.

Predictive approaches and Agile approaches to a project are separate entities, with the Predictive approach defining the deliverables at the beginning of the project and the Adaptive/Agile approach having deliverables defined over a period of time (multiple iterations) and the detailed scope is defined and approved for each iteration when it begins.

Adaptive Lifecycles are meant to respond with high levels of change and require ongoing Stakeholder engagement. When using an Adaptive/Agile Lifecycle, sponsor and customer representative should be engaged and provide feedback on the project on deliverables as they ae created and make sure the product backlog reflects their current needs.

Two processes, Validate Scope and Control Scope are repeated for each iteration, however, in a predictive environment, validate scope happens with each deliverable or phase review as an ongoing process. Validate scope is also the process of formalizing acceptance of the completed project deliverables. Verified deliverables are an input to the validate scope process. Accepted deliverables are an output of the validate scope process.

In Predictive Projects, the Scope Baseline is the approved version of the Project Scope Statement, WBS and the associated WBS dictionary. In Adaptive Lifecycles, Backlogs and User Stories are used to reflect current needs.

The completion of Project Scope is measured against the Project Management Plan. Product Scope is measured against Product Requirements.

Trends and Emerging Practices for Project Scope Management:

Requirements Activities need to be defined, managed and controlled and some of the emerging trends for Project Scope Management will include the following (P132):

- Determine Problems and Identify Business Needs
- Identify and Recommend viable solutions
- Elicit, document and manage Stakeholder Requirements
- Facilitate the successful implementation of the product, service or result

This process ends with the Requirement Closure, which transitions the product, service or result to the recipient. Also, the PM is ultimately responsible for ensuring all activities are accounted for in the Project Management Plan. As an ongoing process the PM and Business Analyst must communicate in order to create a successful outcome.

Tailoring Considerations:

Some considerations to take into account when Tailoring include (P 133):

- **Knowledge and Requirements Management:**
    - Does the organization have existing formal or informal knowledge and requirements management systems?
- **Validation and Control:**
    - Does the organization have existing formal or informal validation and control-related policies, procedures or guidelines?
- **Development Approach:**
    - Does the organization use Agile Approaches in managing projects?
    - Is the Development Approach Iterative or Incremental?
    - Is a predictive Approach used?
    - Will a Hybrid Approach be productive?
- **Stability of Requirements:**
    - Are there areas of the project with unstable requirements?
    - Do unstable requirements necessitate the use of Lean, Agile or other Adaptive techniques until they are stable or well defined?
- **Governance:**
    - Does the organization have formal or informal audit and governance policies, procedures and guidelines?

Consideration for Agile/Adaptive Environments:

At times Scope is not understood at the beginning of a project and/or it evolves during the project life cycle. When using an Agile method, less time is taken to define and agree on the scope and more time is taken for establishing ongoing discovery and refinement. In the Agile Approach, the requirements become the Backlog.

5.1 PLAN SCOPE MANAGEMENT

In Project Management, Scope can be referred to as the project scope, or the product scope. The terminology, **Plan Scope Management**, refers to a specific set of characteristics or deliverables necessary to complete a project. The **key benefit** of this process is that it provides guidance and direction on how a project will be managed throughout the project.

Fig. 5-2, P 134, *Plan Scope Management: Inputs, Tools and Techniques and Outputs*
Fig. 5-3, P 134, *Plan Scope Management: Data Flow Diagram*

5.1.1 Plan Scope Management: Inputs

5.1.1.1 Project Charter

The **Project Charter** is the authorization of a project, which gives the project manager (PM) the ability to apply organizational resources to project activities. It is an Input to the Project Management Plan and provides the foundation for the Scope Management process. The Project Charter documents all aspects, assumptions, constraints, etc. and gives a specific, detailed account about the product, service or result of the product. The Project Charter also provides high-level project descriptions and product characteristics.

5.1.1.2 Project Management Plan

Some of the possible **Project Management Plan** components are (P 135):

- **Quality Management Plan**: The organization's Quality Policy, Methodologies and Standards may affect the way the Project and the Product Scope will be managed
- **Project Lifecycle Description**: Determines the series of phases that a project passes through during the project's timeline
- **Development Approach**: Defines whether Waterfall, Iterative, Adaptive, Agile

or a Hybrid approach will be used

5.1.1.3 Enterprise Environmental Factors

Some **EEF** that may/may not influence the Plan Scope Management: (P 135):

- Organization's Culture
- Infrastructure
- Personnel Administration
- Marketplace Conditions

5.1.1.4 Organizational Process Assets

Organizational Process Assets that may/may not influence the Plan Scope Management: (P 136):

- Policies and procedures
- Historical Information and Lessons Learned Knowledge Base

5.1.2 Plan Scope Management: Tools and Techniques

5.1.2.1 Expert Judgment

Input(s) provided by **Subject Matter Experts (SME)'s** with specific skill sets are often invited to attend meetings. Their expertise contributes to the creation of the Scope Management Plan.

5.1.2.2 Data Analysis

Data Analysis is a technique, although it is not limited to Alternative Analysis (P 136).

5.1.2.3 Meetings

Project Team **Meetings** include the project manager, sponsor, stakeholders, team members, etc. The idea is to develop the Scope Management Plan using strategies and methods by anyone with the responsibility for the Scope Management Process.

5.1.3 Plan Scope Management: Outputs

5.1.3.1 Scope Management Plan

The **Scope Management Plan** is a component of the Project Management Plan. The Scope Management Plan describes how the scope will be defined, developed, monitored and controlled, and validated. Factors involved in the Scope Management Plan include (P 137):

- Process for preparing a detailed Project Scope Statement
- Process that enable the creation of the WBS from the detailed project scope statement
- Process that establishes how the WBS will be maintained and approved
- Process that specifies how formal acceptance of the completed project deliverables will be obtained
- Process to control how changes to detailed Project Scope Statement will be processed (4.5)

5.1.3.2 Requirements Management Plan

The **Requirements Managements Plan** is a component of the Project Management Plan that describes how the project and product will be analyzed, documented and managed. This may/may not include the following (P 137):

- How requirements will be planned, tracked and reported
- Configuration management activities such as:
    - How changes to the project will be initiated
    - How impacts will be analyzed
    - How impacts will be tracked and reported
    - Authorization levels require to approve these levels
- Requirements prioritization process
- Product metrics that will be used along with the rationale for using them

- Traceability structure to reflect which requirement attributes will be captured on the traceability matrix

5.2 COLLECT REQUIREMENTS

These are the requirements necessary to document and plan stakeholder needs along with the requirements to meet the project objectives. The **key benefit** is that it provides the basis for defining the product scope and project scope.

Fig. 5-4, P 138, *Collect Requirements: Inputs, Tools and Techniques and Outputs*
Fig. 5-5, P 139, *Collect Requirements: Data Flow Diagram*

Requirements can be grouped into classifications such as:

- **Business Requirements**: Describes the higher-level needs of the organization as a whole
- **Stakeholder Requirements**: Describes the needs of a stakeholder or stakeholder group
- **Solution Requirements**: Describes features, functions and characteristics of the product, service, or result that will the business and stakeholder requirements
- **Transition Requirements**: Describes temporary capabilities, such as data conversion and training requirements need to transform from the as-is state to the future to-be state
- **Project Requirements**: Describes the actions, processes, or other conditions the project needs to meet
- **Quality Requirements**: Will capture any condition or criteria needed to validate the successful completion of a project deliverable or fulfilment of other project requirements

5.2.1 Collect Requirements: Inputs

5.2.1.1 Project Charter

The **Project Charter** gives a specific, high-level or detailed account about the product, service or result being created by the project. In this way, details can be developed later.

5.2.1.2 Project Management Plan

Some components contained in the Project Management Plan are (P 140):

- **Scope Management Plan**: Contains information on how the Scope Management Plan will be defined and developed
- **Requirements Management Plan:** Contains information on how project requirements will be collected, analyzed and documented
- **Stakeholder Engagement Plan:** Used to understand Stakeholder communication requirements and the level of Stakeholder engagement in order to assess and adapt to the level of Stakeholder participation in requirements activities

5.2.1.3 Project Documents

Project Documents that may be updated and considered as Inputs are (P 141):

- **Assumption Log**: Identifies assumptions about the product, environment, stakeholders and other factors that may affect requirements
- **Lessons Learned Register**: Provides data on effective requirements collection techniques
- **Stakeholder Register**: Used to identify Stakeholders who can provide data on requirements

5.2.1.4 Business Documents

The **Business Case Document** can affect the Collect Requirements process. The criteria contained in the Business Case can be required for meeting the business needs. See P 77-78, Business Case details.

5.2.1.5 Agreements

Any information connected to products, services or results. Refer to section 12.2.3.2, P 489.

5.2.1.6 Enterprise Environmental Factors

Some of the **Enterprise Environmental Factors** can affect the Collect Requirements process are (P 141):

- Organizational Culture
- Infrastructure
- Personnel Administration
- Marketplace Conditions

5.2.1.7 Organizational Process Assets

Some of the **Organizational Process Assets** that can affect the Collect Requirements process are (P 141):

- Policies and Procedures
- Historical Information
- Lessons Learned Repository

5.2.2 Collect Requirements: Tools and Techniques

5.2.2.1 Expert Judgment

Expert Judgment is guided by historical information and can provide environmental insight and information if the PM examines similar projects. When necessary, individuals or groups who have unique skills or training should be sought out in the fields shown below: (P 142):

- Business Analysis
- Requirements Elicitation
- Requirements Analysis
- Requirements Documentation
- Project Requirements in previous Projects
- Diagramming Techniques
- Facilitation
- Conflict Management

5.2.2.2 Data Gathering

Some types of **Data Gathering** Techniques are shown below (P 142):

- **Brainstorming**: A comprehensive compilation listing potential and actual project risks, good for generating ideas.
- **Interviews**: A comprehensive compilation listing potential and actual project risks
- **Focus Groups**: Consists of project stakeholders and Subject Matter Experts (SME)'s who have a vested interest and want to learn about the project's expectations. A facilitator will guide the group until a consensus is reached.
- **Questionnaires and Surveys**: Techniques for compiling information quickly. A target group is asked explicit questions related to a project's needs and/or requirements.
- **Benchmarking**: Comparing one business model to another of similar origin and deciding which practices are best performed, or to identify needed improvements. This is then used a basis for measuring performance

5.2.2.3 Data Analysis

Some examples of **Data Analysis** documents are shown below (P 143):

- Agreements
- Business Plans
- Business Processes and/or Interface Documentation
- Business Rules Repositories
- Current Process Flows
- Marketing Literature
- Problem/Issue Logs
- Policies and Procedures
- Regulatory Documentation
- Requests for Proposals
- Use Cases

5.2.2.4 Decision Making

Some **Decision Making** techniques that may be used in the Collect Requirements Process (P144):

- **Voting**: A collective decision-making technique with some examples shown below:
  - Unanimity: Everyone agrees on a single course of action
  - Majority: Support for a decision is reached by more than 50% of those involved
  - Plurality: The largest block in a group decides even if a majority is not achieved
- **Autocratic Decision Making**: One individual makes the decisions for all involved
- **Multicriteria Decision Analysis**: Uses a Decision Matrix to provide a systematic analytical approach for the establishment of criteria

5.2.2.5 Data Representation

Some **Data Representation** techniques that may be used in this process are (P 144):

- **Affinity Diagrams**: Allows large numbers of ideas to be classified into groups for review and analysis
- **Mind Mapping**: Consolidates ideas created through individual brainstorming sessions into a single map to reflect commonality and differences in understanding and to generate new ideas

5.2.2.6 Interpersonal and Team Skills

Some **Interpersonal and Team Skills** that may be used in this process are (P 144):

- **Nominal Group Technique**: Ideas brainstormed by small groups, then those ideas are reviewed by larger groups
- **Observation/Conversation**: Observing the team members and engaging them in conversations. This takes place in order to assess the work progress toward the project deliverables and attitudes of the team members themselves regarding their role in the project
- **Facilitation**: Foster the development of a **Project Charter** and **Project Management Plan**

5.2.2.7 Context Diagram

A **Context Diagrams** is an example of a Scope Model. They are useful when illustrations are needed to show a business system. A Context Diagram usually shows Inputs and Actors to the business system, provided that the Inputs and System Actors receive Outputs from the business system.

Fig. 5-6, P 145, *Context Diagram*

5.2.2.8 Prototypes

Prototypes: A working model of the product/processes to obtain feedback on requirements. Prototypes utilize the concept of Progressive Elaboration and feedback generation of the product or process. Storyboarding is when an example is used to show navigation through webpages, screens or user interfaces.

5.2.3 Collect Requirements: Outputs

5.2.3.1 Requirements Documentation

Requirements Documentation describes how individual requirements meet the business needs for the project. These documents can be high-level or progressively detailed. Some Requirements Documentation might involve the following (P 147):

Business Requirements, such as:

- Business and Project Objectives for Traceability
- Business Rules for the Performing Organization
- Guiding Principles of the Organization

Stakeholder Requirements, Such As:

- Impact to other Organizational Areas
- Impacts to other Entities Inside/Outside the Performing Organization
- Stakeholder Communications and Reporting Requirements

Solution Requirements, such as:

- Functional/Nonfunctional Requirements
- Technology and Standard Compliance Requirements
- Support and Training Requirements
- Quality Requirements
- Reporting Requirements

Transition Requirements

- Temporary Capabilities
    - Data Conversion
    - Training Measurements
- Quality requirements

Project Requirements, such as:

- Levels of Service, Performance Safety, Compliance, etc.
- Acceptance to Criteria

5.2.3.2 Requirements Traceability Matrix

Requirements Traceability Matrix: "A Requirements Traceability Matrix is grid that links product requirements from their origin to the deliverables that satisfy them" (Project Management Institute, *A Guide to the Project Management Body of Knowledge, (PMBOK® Guide)* – Sixth Edition, Project Management Institute Inc., 2017, Page 148.

Tracing may consist of:

- Business Needs, Opportunities, Goals and Objectives
- Project Objectives
- Project Scope/WBS Deliverables
- Product Design
- Product Development
- Test Strategy and Test Scenarios
- High-Level Requirements to more detailed Requirements

Fig. 5-7, P 149, *Example of a Requirements Traceability Matrix*

5.3 DEFINE SCOPE

The **Define Scope** Process concerns the detailed development of the project and the product. The **key benefit** of this process is that it describes the product, service or result boundaries and acceptance criteria.

Fig. 5-8, P 150, *Define Scope: Inputs, Tools and Techniques and Outputs*
Fig. 5-9, P 151, *Define Scope: Data Flow Diagram*

5.3.1 Define Scope: Inputs

5.3.1.1 Project Charter

The **Project Charter** is the formal authorization of a project giving the project manager the ability to apply organizational resources to project activities. The Project Charter documents all aspects, assumptions, constraints, etc. The Project Charter also provides high-level project description and product characteristics and approves requirements (P 152).

5.3.1.2 Project Management Plan

The **Project Management Plan** is a detailed description of the project and product. The Project Management Plan documents how the project scope will be refined, validated and controlled.

Fig. 5-8, P 150, *Define Scope: Inputs, Tools and Techniques and Outputs*
Fig. 5-9, P 151, *Define Scope: Data Flow Diagram*

The define scope process chooses which elements to be used during the Collect Requirements process.

5.3.1.3 Project Documents

Some **Project Documents** that can be considered as Inputs for Define Scope are (P 152):

- **Assumption Log**: Identifies Assumptions and Constraints about the Project, Product, Environments, Stakeholders, etc.
- **Requirements Documentation**: Identifies requirements that will be incorporated into the Scope
- **Risk Register**: Contains Response Strategies that can affect the Project Scope

5.3.1.4 Enterprise Environmental Factors

Some of the **Enterprise Environmental Factors** that can affect the Define Scope process are (P 152):

- Organization's Culture
- Infrastructure
- Personnel Administration
- Marketplace Conditions

5.3.1.5 Organizational Process Assets

Examples of how **Organizational Process Assets** can affect a project (P 122):

- Policies, Procedures and Templates for a Project Scope Statement
- Project Files from Previous Projects
- Lessons Learned from previous Phases or Projects

5.3.2 Define Scope: Tools and Techniques

5.3.2.1 Expert Judgment

Expert Judgment analyzes data for developing the Project Scope Statement. This data may be procured from many sources, such as:

- Other Units within the Organization
- Consultants
- Stakeholders (can be customers or sponsors)
- Professional Associations
- Technical Associations
- Industry Groups
- Subject Matter Experts (SME)'s

5.3.2.2 Data Analysis

Some examples of **Data Analysis** include (P 153):

- Alternatives Analysis: Evaluates various ways to meet the requirements of the Project Charter

5.3.2.3 Decision Making

Decision Making is a technique used in the Define Scope process that may include Multicriteria Decision Analysis, which uses a Decision Matrix.

5.3.2.4 Interpersonal and Team Skills

Interpersonal and Team Skills: Facilitation is an example of a **Team Skill**, used in Workshops. By working in tandem with key Stakeholders, the goal is to reach a consensus via cross-functional and common understanding of the project deliverables and project and product boundaries (P 153).

5.3.2.5 Product Analysis

Shown below are some examples of Product Analysis techniques (P 153):

- Product Breakdown
- Requirements Analysis
- Systems Analysis
- Systems
- Engineering
- Value Analysis
- Value Engineering

5.3.3 Define Scope: Outputs

5.3.3.1 Project Scope Statement:

The **Project Scope Statement** " … is a description of the project scope, major deliverables, assumptions and constraints" (Project Management Institute, *A Guide to the Project Management*

Body of Knowledge, (PMBOK® Guide) – Sixth Edition, Project Management Institute Inc., 2017, Page 154).

A detailed Project Scope Statement will include:

- **Product Scope Description**: Progressively elaborates the characteristics of the product, service, or result described in the Project Charter and requirements documentation
- **Deliverable**: any unique and verifiable product, result or capability to perform a service required to be produced to complete a process, phase or project
- **Acceptance Criteria**: A set of conditions required to be met before deliverables are accepted
- **Project Exclusions**: Generally identifies what is excluded from the project

Table 5-1, P 155, *Elements of the Project Charter and the Project Scope Statement*

5.3.3.2 Project Documents Updates

Project Documents that may be updated (P 155):

- **Assumption Log**: Updated with additional assumptions or constraints
- **Requirements Documentation**: Updated with additional or changed requirements
- **Requirements Traceability Matrix**: Reflects updates in requirements documentation
- **Stakeholder Register**: Additional information on existing or new Stakeholders is gathered as a result of this process and recorded in the Stakeholder Register

5.4 CREATE WBS

The **WBS** is a process that breaks down and subdivides project deliverables into manageable steps to make the work easier to complete each component. The **key benefit** of this process it that it provides a framework of what has to be delivered.

Please refer to the YouTube Video, *Work Breakdown Structure Demonstration,* (8:57), at https://youtu.be/FklYonNknRs.

Fig. 5-11, P 156, *Create WBS: Inputs, Tools and Techniques and Outputs*
Fig. 5-11, P 156, *Create WBS: Data Flow Diagram*

5.4.1 Create WBS: Inputs

5.4.1.1 Project Management Plan

The **Project Management Plan** describes how the WBS requirements will be analyzed, documented and managed from the Project Scope Statement.

5.4.1.2 Project Documents

Some **Project Documents** can be Inputs for this process are shown below (P 157):

- **Project Scope Statement**: Describes work being performed and the work that is excluded
- **Requirements Documentation**: Describes how individual requirements meet the business needs for the project

5.4.1.3 Enterprise Environmental Factors

Enterprise Environmental Factors may be used as outside sources, such as industry specific standards, to aid in the development of the WBS (P 157).

5.4.1.4 Organizational Process Assets

Organizational Process Assets with the potential to affect the WBS (P 157):

- Policies, Procedures and Templates for the WBS
- Project Files from previous projects
- Lessons learned from previous projects

5.4.2 Create WBS: Tools and Techniques

5.4.2.1 Expert Judgment

Expert Judgment analyzes data for developing the Project Scope Statement and should be used when considering individuals and groups with specific knowledge or experience on similar projects (P 158).

5.4.2.2 Decomposition

Decomposition is used for dividing and subdividing the project scope and project deliverables into smaller and more manageable parts (work).

Fig. 5-12, P 158, *Sample WBS Decomposed Down Through Work Packages*
Fig. 5-13, P 159, *Sample WBS Organized by Phase*

Decomposition will usually involve (P 158):

- Identify and analyze the Deliverables and related work
- Structure and organize the WBS
- Decompose the upper WBS levels into lower-level detailed components
- Verify the degree of Decomposition of the deliverables is appropriate

The WBS structure can be represented by (P 159):

- Using phases of the Project Lifecycle as the second level of Decomposition and the third level represented by the project and products
- Using Major Deliverables as the second level of Decomposition and
- Incorporating subcomponents

Fig. 5-12, P 158, *Sample WBS Decomposed Down through Work Packages*
Fig. 5-13, P 159, *Sample WBS organized by Phase*
Fig. 5-14, P 160, *Sample WBS with Major Deliverables*
Fig. 5-15, P 163, *Validate Scope: Inputs, Tools and Techniques and Outputs*

5.4.3 Create WBS: Outputs

5.4.3.1 Scope Baseline

Scope Baseline is a component of the Project Management Plan and includes the final Scope Statement (approved version) and the **WBS** and its associated **WBS Dictionary**. It can only be changed through formal Change Control procedures.

Components of the **Scope Baseline** include (P 161):

- **Project Scope Statement**: Includes the description of the Project Scope, Major Deliverables, Assumptions and Constraints
- **WBS**: A hierarchal description of the total scope of work to be carried out by the Project Team to accomplish the Project Objectives and create the required Deliverables
- **Work Package:** The lowest level of the WBS and each is part of a Control Account
- **Planning Package:** A Control Account may contain one or more Planning Packages, which is a work breakdown structure below the control account and above the Work Package, but does not include detailed schedule activities

WBS details (P 162).

5.4.3.2 Project Documents Updates

Project Documents that may be updated (P 162):

- **Assumption Log**: Updated with additional assumptions and constraints that were identified during the create the WBS process
- **Requirements Documentation**: Updated to include approved changes resulting from the WBS process

5.5 VALIDATE SCOPE

"Validate Scope is the process of formalizing acceptance of the completed project deliverables" (Project Management Institute, *A Guide to the Project Management Body of Knowledge, (PMBOK® Guide)* – Sixth Edition, Project Management Institute Inc., 2017, Page 163). The **key benefit** of this process is that it brings objectivity to the acceptance process and increases the probability of final product, service or result acceptance by validating each deliverable.

Fig. 5-15, P 163, *Validate Scope: Inputs, Tools and Techniques and Outputs* and
Fig. 5-16, P 164, *Validate Scope: Data Flow Diagram.*

5.5.1 Validate Scope: Inputs

5.5.1.1 Project Management Plan

The **Project Management Plan** includes:

- **Scope Management Plan**
- **Requirements Management Plan**
- **Scope Baseline**, which contains approved version of scope statement, WBS and associated dictionary

5.5.1.2 Project Documents

Some **Project Documents** that can be Inputs to this process are shown below (P 165):

- **Lessons Learned Register:** Lessons learned earlier in the project can be applied to later phases in the project to improve the efficiency and effectiveness of validating deliverables
- **Quality Reports:** May include all quality assurance issues managed or escalated by the team, recommendations for improvement and the summary of findings form the Quality Control process
- **Requirements Documentation:** Requirements are compared to the actual results to determine if a change, corrective action or preventative action is deemed necessary
- **Requirements Traceability Matrix:** Contains information about requirements, including how they will be validated

5.5.1.3 Verified Deliverables

Verified Deliverables are completed Project Deliverables verified through the Quality Control Process.

5.5.1.4 Work Performance Data

Work Performance Data might include such factors as (P 135):

- Degree of Compliance With Requirements
- Number of Non-Conformities
- Severity of the Non-Conformities

5.5.2 Validate Scope: Tools and Techniques

5.5.2.1 Inspection

Inspection(s) are sometimes known as (P 166):

- Reviews
- Product Reviews
- Walkthroughs

In particular cases, different terms may apply and have different meanings.

5.5.2.2 Decision Making

An example of **Decision Making** is Voting and is used by Stakeholders and Project Team members to reach a conclusion by majority (P 166).

5.5.3 Validate Scope: Outputs

5.5.3.1 Accepted Deliverables

Accepted Deliverables that meet established acceptance criteria are formally signed off by customer or sponsor (P 166).

5.5.3.2 Work Performance Information

Work Performance Information relates information regarding project progress (P 166).

5.5.3.3 Change Requests

Change Requests are unaccepted deliverables needing a defect repair process, which requires reason(s) for the change(s). The Change Requests are processed for review and disposition through perform integrated change control processes (P 166).

5.5.3.4 Project Documents Updates

Any documents requiring updating as a result of the Validate Scope Process may include (P 136):

- **Lessons Learned Register:** : Can be updated with more efficient techniques for a particular process that will be finalized before being entered into the Repository
- **Requirements Documentation:** May be updated with actual results of validation activity and any requirements the project or product should adhere to regarding Stakeholder needs or expectations are recorded
- **Requirements Traceability Matrix:** Updated with the results of the validation, including the method used and the outcome

5.6 CONTROL SCOPE

"Control Scope is the process of monitoring the status of the project and product scope and managing changes to the Scope Baseline" (Project Management Institute, *A Guide to the Project Management Body of Knowledge, (PMBOK® Guide)* – Sixth Edition, Project Management Institute Inc., 2017, Page 167). The **key benefit** of this process is that the scope baseline is maintained throughout the project.

Fig. 5-17, *Control Scope: Inputs, Tools and Techniques and Outputs* and
Fig. 5-18, P 168, *Control Scope: Data Flow Diagram.*

5.6.1 Control Scope: Inputs

5.6.1.1 Project Management Plan

Information shown below is utilized to Control Scope in the **Project Management Plan** (P 169):

- **Scope Management Plan**: Sections from this plan describe how the Project Scope will be monitored and controlled
- **Requirements Management Plan**: this plan is a component of the Project Management Plan and describes how the project requirements will be analyzed, documented and managed
- **Change Management Plan**: This plan defines the process for managing change on the project
- **Configuration Management Plan:** This plan defines those items that are configurable, those items that require formal change control, and the process for controlling change to those items
- **Scope Baseline**: The Scope Baseline is compared to actual results to determine if a change, corrective action or preventative action is needed
- **Performance Measurement Baseline:** When using Earned Value Analysis, the Performance Measurement Baseline is compared to the actual results

5.6.1.2 Project Documents

Project Documents that may be considered as Inputs for the Control Scope process (P 169):

- **Lessons Learned Register:** Lessons Learned from previous projects can be applied to later phases in the project to improve Scope control
- **Requirements Documentation:** Used to detect any deviation in the agree-upon Scope for the project or product
- **Requirements Traceability Matrix:** Helps to detect the impact of any change or deviation from the Scope Baseline on the project objectives

5.6.1.3 Work Performance Data

Work Performance Data includes factors, such as (P 169):

- Number of Change Requests
- Number of requests accepted
- Number of deliverables completed, etc.

5.6.1.4 Organizational Process Assets

Organizational Assets may affect the Control Scope Process (P 139), such as:

- Existing Formal/Informal Scope
- Control-Related Policies, Procedures And Guidelines
- Monitoring and Reporting Methods
- Templates Used

5.6.2 Control Scope: Tools and Techniques

5.6.2.1 Data Analysis

Data Analysis Techniques that may be used in the Control Scope Process (P 170):

- **Variance Analysis (Used in EVM):** Compares the Baseline to the actual results
- **Trend Analysis**: Examines project performance over time to determine

whether performance is improving or deteriorating

5.6.3 Control Scope: Outputs

5.6.3.1 Work Performance Information

Work Performance Information includes (P170):

- Correlated and Contextualized Information on Project's Progress
- Categories of Changes Received
- Identified Scope Variances and Causes
- How Identified Scope Variances and Causes impact Schedule or Cost
- Forecasts of Future Scope Performance

5.6.3.2 Change Requests

Change Requests are documents stating a needed change(s). Changes may be preventative, corrective, defect repair processes, or enhancement requests

5.6.3.3 Project Management Plan Updates

Project Management Plan Updates may contain (P 171):

- **Scope Management Plan:** The scope management plan may be updated to reflect a change in how scope is managed.
- **Scope Baseline**: If the approved change requests have an effect on the project scope, then the scope statement, the WBS and the WBS Dictionary are revised and reissued to reflect the approved changes through Perform Integrated Change Control process.
- **Schedule Baseline**: Changes to the schedule baseline are incorporated in response to approved changes in scope, resources or schedule estimates. In some cases, schedule variances can be so severe that a revised schedule is needed to provide a realistic basis for performance measurement.
- **Cost Baseline:** Changes to the cost baseline are incorporated in response to approved changes in scope, resources or cost estimates. In some cases, cost variances are so severe that a revised cost baseline is needed to provide a realistic basis for performance measurement.
- **Performance Measurement Baseline**: If the approved change requests

have an effect on the project besides the project scope, then the corresponding cost baseline and schedule baselines are revised and reissued to reflect the approved changes

5.6.3.4 Project Document Updates

Project Document Updates may contain (P171):

- **Lessons Learned Register**: Updated with techniques that are efficient and effective in controlling Scope
- **Requirements Documentation**: Updated with additional or changed requirements
- **Requirements Traceability Matrix**: Reflects updates in Requirement Documentation

Summary: Answers to Student Learning Outcomes

1. **Project Scope Management** is the process required to ensure that the project includes all the work required and only the work required to complete the project successfully. The processes are as follows (P 129):

    - **Plan Scope Management**- The process of creating a scope management plan that documents how the project and product scope will be defined, validated and controlled.
    - **Collect Requirements** – The process of determining, documenting, and managing, stakeholder needs and requirements to meet project objectives.
    - **Define Scope** – The process of developing a detailed description of the project and product.
    - **Create WBS** – The process of subdividing project deliverables and project work into smaller, more manageable components.
    - **Validate Scope** – The process of formalizing acceptance of the completed project deliverables.
    - **Control Scope** – The process of monitoring the status of the project and product scope and managing changes to the scope baseline.

    Fig. 5-1, P 130, *Project Scope Management Overview*

2. **Product Scope** describes the features and functions that characterize a product, service or result. Project Scope is the work performed to deliver a product, service or result, with the specified features and functions. Project Scope may include product scope descriptions (P 131).

3. **Validate Scope** and **Control Scope** are repeated for each iteration in an **adaptive or agile** life cycle (P 131). **Collect Requirements, Define Scope,** and **create WBS** are repeated for each iteration as well as in the beginning of each iteration.

4. **Predictive Projects** use the **Project Scope Statement, the WBS and the WBS Dictionary** (P 131).

5. **Adaptive Life Cycles** uses **backlogs** to reflect current user requirements (P 131).

6. **Trends and Emerging Practices** indicate that **collaboration** may take place between the Business Analyst and the Project Manager (P 131). The following activities are samples of the joint work between the Business Analyst and Project Manager.

    - Determine problems and business needs.
    - Identify and suggest solutions.
    - Elicit, document, manage stakeholder requirements to meet business needs and objectives.
    - Facilitate implementation of the product, service or end result of the project or program.

7. **Agile Methods** (P 133) ***uses less* time** in defining and agreeing on Scope Requirements than the **Predictive Approach**.

8. Plan Scope Management is the process of creating a scope management plan that documents how the project and product will be defined, validated and controlled. The **key benefit** is that it provides guidance and direction on how scope will be managed throughout the project. In the **Plan Scope Management Process,** (P 135) the two outputs are:

    1. **Scope Management Plan**
    2. **Requirements Management Plan**.

9. The **Requirements Management Plan** describes the project and the product requirements. The Requirements Management Plan is a **component** of the Project Management Plan that describes how project and product requirements will be analyzed documented and managed (P 137).

10. The **key benefit** of **Collect Requirements** is that it provides the basis for *defining* the **Product Scope** and **Project Scope** (P 138). It is the process of determining, documenting, and managing stakeholder needs and requirements to meet the project objectives.

    Fig. 5-4, P 138, *Collect Requirements: ITTO's*
    Fig. 5-5, P 139, *Collect Requirements: Data Flow Diagram*

11. **Benchmarking Technique** (P 143) is used to provide a **basis for measuring performance.** It involves comparing actual or planned products, processes and

practices with others of comparable organizations.

12. **Nominal Group Technique** uses a ***voting process*** to prioritize ideas (P 144).

13. The **Collect Requirements** process group includes the use of **context diagrams** that show how business systems interact (P 138).

14. **Requirements Traceability** is a means to trace the development of the approved requirements throughout the **start (origin)** to the **end of the project work/product**. This is done until the project work/product is closed, completed or signed off. It is a matrix/grid linking requirements and the deliverables that satisfy the user's level of acceptance. This certifies that the actual requirements throughout the project lifecycle add business value and links the products to the business and project objectives (P 148-149).

15. Define scope is the process of developing a detailed description of the project and product. The **key benefit** is that it describes the product, service or result boundaries and acceptance criteria. The **Project Scope Statement** describes the work that will be performed (in scope) and the work that is excluded (out of scope) and is an **output of Define Scope** and documents completing the **Project Scope and Product Scope** (P 154). It includes the project scope description, major deliverables, assumptions and constraints. It enables the project team to perform more detailed planning and new project work. The **key benefit** is that it provides the baseline for evaluating requests for change that are within or outside the project boundaries.

16. The Project Manager and their team will need to **sub-divide project deliverables** and project work into manageable components so that the work can be more easily assigned to an available team or stakeholder resources. The **key benefit** of this process is that it provides a framework of what work has to be delivered. The **Work Breakdown Structure (WBS)** is used in organizing and structuring the work as defined in the scope of the project. The **WBS components,** called **Work Packages** are used to control the work being performed, as they are the lowest level of the work components (P 158-161).

Fig. 5-10, P 156, *Create WBS: ITTO's*
Fig. 5-11, P 156, *Create WBS: Data Flow Diagram*

17. **Decomposition** is a technique used in the **creation of the WBS**. The level of decomposition is principled on the need of the Project Manager to manage assign work to the project team and control the project (P 158-161). Here are some **activities** that need to be considered:

    - **Identify** all the deliverables needed and related work to do the assigned work.
    - **Analyze** the deliverables.
    - **Structure** the WBS.
    - Take the largest WBS levels and break them down into do-able components called **Work Packages**.
    - **Assign ID Codes** to the components.
    - **Verify** with your team and/or stakeholders that the degree of structure is appropriate.

    Fig. 5-12, P 158, *Sample WBS Decomposed Down Through Work Packages*
    Fig. 5-13, P 159, *Sample WBS Organized by Phase*
    Fig. 5-14, P 160, *Sample WBS with Major Deliverables*

18. The **WBS Dictionary** supports the WBS and includes document information about each component of the **WBS**. It lists **detailed deliverables, activity and scheduling information about each work breakdown package, and the WBS Dictionary**. It can also provide information. See Work Packages (P 162).

19. The **Validate Scope** is the process of **formalizing acceptance** of the completed project deliverables (P 163). The **key benefit** allows objectivity to the acceptance process and increases the probability of final product, service or result acceptance by validating that the deliverables meet the specified requirements.

20. **Validate Scope** brings objectivity to the process and ensures stakeholder acceptance of the product, service or result (P 163).

21. **Control Scope** is the process of monitoring the status of the **project and product scope** while **also managing changes to the key baseline.** The **key benefit** is that the scope baseline is maintained throughout the project life cycle (P 167).

    Fig. 5-17, P 167, *Control Scope: ITTO's*

Fig. 5-18, P 168, *Control Scope: Data Flow Diagram*

22. **Scope Baseline** (P 171). When the performance measurement baseline has a severe variance, a **change request** must be submitted to the **change control board** to alter the Scope Baseline. This will provide a realistic basis for performance measurement.

Similar Questions that may be on the PMI Exam related to Chapter 5

1. You have joined a new company in the capacity of a project manager, since the old manager quit the company. The project WBS is already made. In order to have clarity you want to see the detailed description of work packages. You can find these descriptions in ______.

   A. Project Charter
   B. Statements of Work
   C. Requests for Tenders
   D. WBS Dictionaries

   Correct answer is D: A WBS dictionary's purpose is to let the concerned person know what is in the scope of the corresponding work package and what is out of scope. It mentions resource requirement, estimated cost, duration, assumptions and constraints for the work package.

2. You have been hired by a large consulting firm to lead an accounting project. You have reviewed the work done by the previous project manager. You determine the needs of the project and divide the work into work packages so that you can show how all of it fits into categories. What are you creating?

   A. A WBS
   B. A Schedule
   C. A Project Scope Statement
   D. A Contract

   Correct answer is A: A Work Breakdown Structure (WBS) is the best way to visualize all of the work that will be done on your project. It divides all of the work into work packages and shows how it fits into higher-level categories. By looking at the WBS, you can communicate to other people just how much work is involved in your project.

3. Martha has replaced a project manager who has moved on to another project. She wants to identify if there have been any changes in scope since the initiation phase and whether they have been accounted for, as this might

affect the project. Which is the best document she should refer to?

A. Stakeholder register
B. Project Management plan
C. Change log
D. Issue log

Correct answer is C: A change log is used to document changes that occur during a project.

4. Many projects are undertaken to produce a service that generally does not have physical characteristics and attributes that can be measured and quantified to ensure conformance to the requirement and specifications. When the end product of a project is service ______.

   A. Measurements cannot be applied to a service, the criteria is either pass or fail
   B. Measurements are not factual and just a rough estimation and thereby they do not show the correct status of progress
   C. Measurements can be determined based on client's expectations and the responsibility assigned to individuals
   D. Measurements are not necessary if the project is internal

Correct answer is C: Whether service, product or result (end deliverable of a project), measurement has to be established based on client's expectations and the responsibility assigned to individuals.

5. Jack has created the project cost estimate and submitted the same to the sponsor for approval. His sponsor calls him up for a meeting. His sponsor shows his displeasure in the meeting and says that the cost estimates should be lower at least by 20% if not more. What should be Jack's best approach to this situation?

   A. As the project progresses, there are several activities which can be looked into for cost reduction
   B. Reduce at least 15% from the estimates straightaway
   C. Discuss with the sponsor any activities to be removed and their impact on project objectives.
   D. Hire additional resources with lower pay rates

Correct answer is C: It is the best answer in this scenario. The PM should analyze the impact of any change. A reduction in cost means reduction in activities which in turn might add to risk, reduce quality etc. All these have to be discussed with the sponsor before any changes are implemented.

6. What is the purpose of reviewing deliverables and performance at the conclusion phase of a project?

   A. Determine how many resources are required to complete the project according to the project baseline
   B. Adjust the schedule and cost baselines based on past performance
   C. Obtain customer acceptance of project deliverables
   D. Determine whether the project continues to be aligned with the business case and project objectives

Correct answer is D: Phase Exit review is also known as Kill Points, or Stage Gates. This is to ensure that the purpose for which the project was initiated remains intact and the business cases hold its place.

7. Which of the following addresses the purpose of the Validate Scope process?

   A. Validate Scope results in changes to scope
   B. Validate Scope results in accepted deliverables by client
   C. Validate Scope results in accepted requirements by client
   D. Validate Scope results in verified deliverables

Correct Option is B: Validate Scope is a process where the customer performs inspection on deliverables and provides a sign off if the deliverables are acceptable. Choice D - Verified deliverables are an output from Control Quality.

8. How does a WBS help a project stakeholder?

   A. Stakeholders do not use a WBS, only the project team references the WBS
   B. Stakeholders use a WBS to enforce contractual agreements
   C. These elements assist stakeholders in developing a clear vision of the product and the overall steps to produce it
   D. The WBS functions as the organizational breakdown structure (OBS) for stakeholders

   Correct Option is C: The WBS helps to focus communication and accountability at a level of detail required to manage a project. Option A is incorrect because stakeholders do use a WBS. Option B is incorrect but tempting because a WBS does define scope. However, it is not used to enforce a contractual agreement only a law can do that. Option D is incorrect because an OBS is an organizational breakdown structure, and is not related to project elements.

9. Amit is the manager of a software project. His client has agreed on a Project Scope Statement at the beginning of the project, but whenever the client verifies deliverables, he comes up with features that he would like to add into the product. Amit is working with the client to find what requirements were missed in the planning stages of the project and how to plan better in the future. What is the best description of his project's current situation?

   A. Gold Plating
   B. Scope Creep
   C. Alternatives Analysis
   D. Schedule Variance

   Correct Answer is B: The project scope is changing every time the client is asked to verify the product — this is scope creep. The best way to avoid that is to be sure that the Project Scope Statement that is written in the planning stages of the project is understood and agreed to by everyone on the project. Scope changes should never come up late in the project because that is when they cost the most and will jeopardize the team's ability to deliver.

10. Dave is the project manager for a construction project that is building a gazebo. When the project first started, he met with the stakeholders to define the scope. The sponsors mentioned that the gazebo is a really important part of their daughter's wedding ceremony that was planned seven months ahead. In fact, they said that if the gazebo could not be completed in seven months, it would not be worth it for them to even start the project. Dave wrote down the seven-month deadline to put in his Project Scope Statement. In which section of the document did the deadline appear?

    A. Project Deliverables
    B. Project Objectives
    C. Project Constraints
    D. Project Assumptions

Correct answer is C: Since the project absolutely must be completed in seven months for it to be worth doing, the deadline is a constraint. It must be met for the project to be considered successful.

You may now move on to Chapter Six: Project Schedule Management

Chapter 6: Project Schedule Management: Delegate Time Wisely

"Planning without action is futile, action without planning is fatal."
Cornelius Fitchner

Student Learning Outcomes

1. What are the seven (7) **Project Schedule Management** Processes? List and describe each one (P173).
2. What is a **Schedule Model** (P175)?
3. What is **Iterative Scheduling** with a backlog (P177)?
4. Does **On-Demand Scheduling**, as we used in a **Kanban System**, utilize the concept of products being developed incrementally (P 177)? Yes or No? Explain.
5. The Project Manager is often required to **tailor** the **Project Schedule Management Processes.** List four (4) tailoring considerations (P 178)?
6. In an **Agile or Adaptive Environment**, does the Project Manager's role Change (P 178)?
7. **What does Plan Schedule Management mean and what are the key benefits of this process (P 179)?**
8. What are the established elements in the **Schedule Management Plan** (P 182)?
9. **What is meant by Define Activities and what is the key benefit (P 183)?**
10. What is **Rolling Wave Planning** (P 185)?
11. What is **Cost Base Line** (P 186)?
12. **What is meant by Sequence Activities and what is the key benefit (P 187)?**
13. What is the **PDM Method** and list and describe the **four activity relationships** (P 189-190)?
14. What are the differences between and define the following **PDM Dependencies: Mandatory, Discretionary, External and Internal** (P 191-192)?
15. Define **Lead Time** and define **Lag Time** (P 192-193).
16. What is **a Project Schedule Network Diagram** and how is it illustrated (P 193)?
17. **What is meant by Estimate Activity Durations and its key benefits (P 195)?**
18. There are eight (8) ways **to Estimate Activity Durations.** Define four out of the eight ways (P 200-203).
19. **What does Develop Schedule mean and what is its key benefit (P 205)?**
20. What does **Critical Path Method** mean (P 210)?
21. What is meant by **Resource Leveling, Crashing and Fast Tracking** (P 211)?
22. What is a **Bar Chart** and what is its use (P217)?
23. **What does Control Schedule mean and what is its key benefit (P 222)?**
24. Describe the purpose of **Control Schedule** and list five (5) **Data Analysis Techniques used in Project Schedule Management** (P 222).

CHAPTER SIX INTRODUCTION: DELEGATE TIME WISELY

PROJECT SCHEDULE MANAGEMENT: CHAPTER 6 OVERVIEW: PMBOK® 6th Edition P 173-230

Project Schedule Management includes the processes that a project manager follows to manage the team's timely completion of the project. The Project Schedule Management processes are divided into six (6) process groupings:

(6.1) **Planned Schedule Management:** This process establishes policies and procedures and documentation for a number of activities to include planning, developing, managing, executing and controlling the project schedule.

(6.2) **Define Activities:** This process identifies and documents the specific actions or tasks the project manager needs to perform to produce approved project deliverables.

(6.3) **Sequence Activities:** This process identifies and documents the relationships among the project activities.

(6.4) **Estimate Activity Durations:** This process estimates the number of work periods such as days, months, weeks, or years needed to complete individual activities coupled with the estimated resources to complete the activities.

(6.5) **Develop Schedule:** This process requires the project manager and the project team to analyze activity sequences, durations, resource requirements and schedule constraints to create a project schedule model. The project schedule model is a prototype model that will be refined and later used for project execution, monitoring, and controlling the project work.

(6.6) **Control Schedule:** This process is one that requires the project manager to monitor the status of the project, to update the project schedule, and also manage changes to the schedule baseline.

Fig. 6-1, P 174, *Project Schedule Management Overview*

Key Concepts for Project Schedule Management

The project management team selects the scheduling method, such as critical path or agile approach. Software scheduling tools may be used to create the schedule model for the project. The detailed project schedule should be flexible throughout the project, and easily adjusted upon increased understanding of risk and value-added impacts. The detailed schedule needs to be flexible to respond to increased project knowledge awareness, risk issues, and exploiting opportunities for value added activities.

See Fig. 6-2, 176, *Scheduling Overview*

See the blog link, *What is the difference between Schedule Model and Project Schedule?,* https://www.pmhangout.com/discussion/170/what-is-the-difference-between-schedule-model-and-project-schedule

Trends and Emerging Practices in Project Schedule Management

In today's fast-paced, highly competitive global market, it is vital that product work create value which may be released to the customer even ahead of schedule. There are emerging practices for project scheduling. **Iterative scheduling with the backlog** is a form of rolling-wave planning. It is based on adaptive life cycles. Agile approaches may also be considered. Here, user stories are prioritized and refined prior to product construction. The benefit of the agile approach is less documentation. It welcomes changes throughout the development lifecycle in a very easy fashion. **On-demand scheduling** is typically used in a Kaban system, which is based upon a theory of constraints and pool-based scheduling concepts from lean manufacturing. This often is used for projects that evolve the product incrementally. Here, tasks may be bundled for projects that have similar scope characteristics.

Tailoring Considerations

The project manager will need to tailor the way the project schedule management processes are applied. This may be done by considering:

- Lifecycle Approach
- Resource Availability
- Project Dimensions
- Technology Support

Considerations For Agile/Adaptive Environments

Adaptive approaches use short lifecycles to undertake project work. Adaptation is used quickly and is necessary. Adaptive approaches manifest iterative scheduling and on-demand pool-based scheduling. To address the full delivery lifecycle for scheduling for large based systems, a predictive approach, adaptive approach, or both may be considered or adopted.

Plan Schedule Management:

The key benefit of planned schedule management is that it provides guidance and directions on how the project schedule will be managed throughout the project lifecycle (P 179).

See chart on next page: **PROJECT SCHEDULE MANAGEMENT (Section 6.1).**

Chapter Six: Project Schedule Management

6.1 PLAN SCHEDULE MANAGEMENT

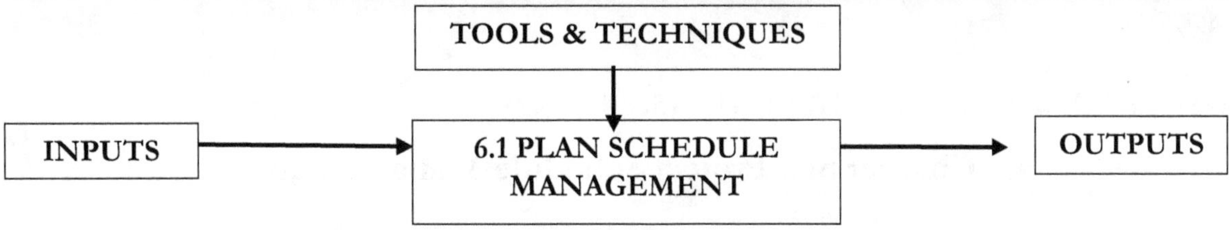

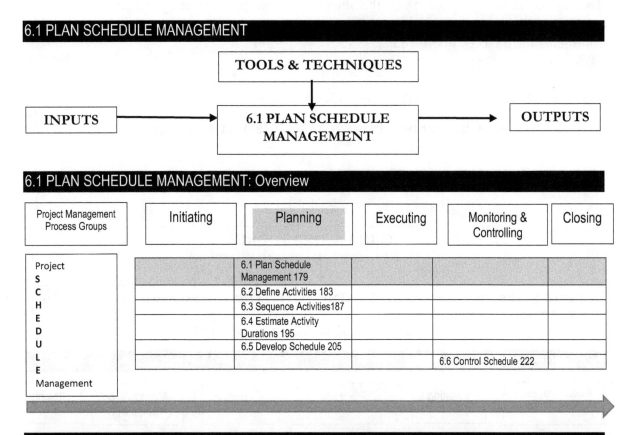

6.1 PLAN SCHEDULE MANAGEMENT: Overview

Project Management Process Groups	Initiating	Planning	Executing	Monitoring & Controlling	Closing
Project SCHEDULE Management		6.1 Plan Schedule Management 179			
		6.2 Define Activities 183			
		6.3 Sequence Activities 187			
		6.4 Estimate Activity Durations 195			
		6.5 Develop Schedule 205			
				6.6 Control Schedule 222	

6.1 PLAN SCHEDULE MANAGEMENT: ITTO Processes

INPUTS	TOOLS and TECHNIQUES	OUTPUTS
.1 Project Charter 180 .2 Project Management Plan 180 • Scope Management Plan 180 • Development Approach 180 .3 Enterprise Environmental Factors 180 .4 Organizational Process Assets 180	.1 Expert Judgment 181 .2 Data Analysis 181 .3 Meetings 181	.1 Schedule Management Plan 181

Fig. 6-3, P 179, *Plan Schedule Management: Inputs, Tools and Techniques*
Fig. 6-4, P 179, *Plan Schedule Management: Data Flow Diagram*

Define Activities:

The key benefit of define activities is that the process decomposes work packages into scheduled activities, or provides a basis for estimating, scheduling, executing, monitoring, and controlling the project work (P 183).

See chart below: **DEFINE ACTIVITIES (Section 6.2).**

Chapter Six: Project Schedule Management

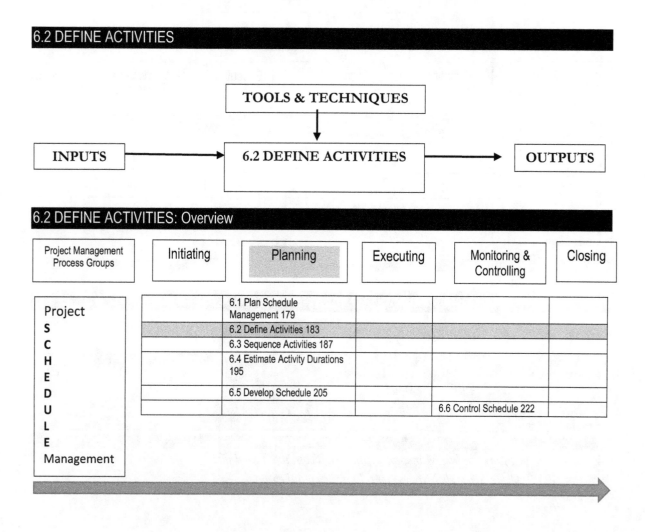

6.2 DEFINE ACTIVITIES

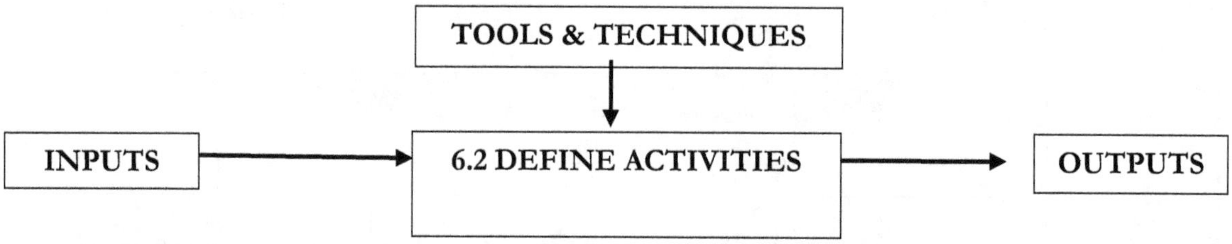

6.2 DEFINE ACTIVITIES: Overview

Project Management Process Groups	Initiating	Planning	Executing	Monitoring & Controlling	Closing
Project SCHEDULE Management		6.1 Plan Schedule Management 179			
		6.2 Define Activities 183			
		6.3 Sequence Activities 187			
		6.4 Estimate Activity Durations 195			
		6.5 Develop Schedule 205			
				6.6 Control Schedule 222	

6.2 DEFINE ACTIVITIES: ITTO Processes

INPUTS	TOOLS and TECHNIQUES	OUTPUTS
.1 Project Management Plan 184 • Schedule Management Plan 184 • Scope Baseline 184 .2 Enterprise Environmental Factors 184 .3 Organizational Process Assets 184	.1 Expert Judgment 184 .2 Decomposition 185 .3 Rolling Wave Planning 185 .4 Meetings 185	.1 Activity List 185 .2 Activity Attributes 186 .3 Milestone List 186 .4 Change Requests 186 .5 Project Management Plan Updates 186 • Schedule Baseline 186 • Cost Baseline 186

Fig. 6-5, P 183, *Define Activities: Inputs, Tools and Techniques*
Fig. 6-6, P 183, *Define Activities: Data Flow Diagram*

Sequence Activities:

The key benefit of sequence activities is that it defines the logical sequence of work to obtain the efficiencies, given all project constraints (P 187).

See chart on next page: **SEQUENCE ACTIVITIES (Section 6.3)**

Chapter Six: Project Schedule Management

6.3 SEQUENCE ACTIVITIES

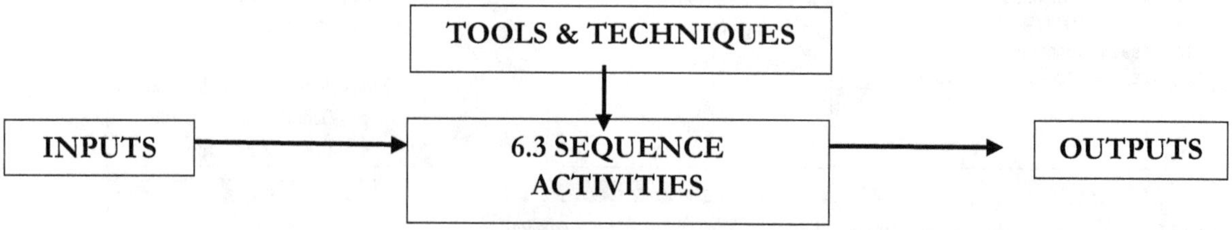

6.3 SEQUENCE ACTIVITIES: Overview

Project Management Process Groups	Initiating	Planning	Executing	Monitoring & Controlling	Closing
Project SCHEDULE Management		6.1 Plan Schedule Management 179			
		6.2 Define Activities 183			
		6.3 Sequence Activities 187			
		6.4 Estimate Activity Resources 195			
		6.5 Develop Schedule 205			
				6.6 Control Schedule 222	

6.3 SEQUENCE ACTIVITIES: ITTO Processes

INPUTS	TOOLS and TECHNIQUES	OUTPUTS
.1 Project Management Plan 188 • Schedule Management Plan 188 • Scope Baseline 188 .2 Project Documents 188 • Activity Attributes 188 • Activity List 188 • Assumption Log 188 • Milestone List 188 .3 Enterprise Environmental Factors 189 .4 Organizational Process Assets 189	.1 Precedence Diagramming Method (PDM) 189 .2 Dependency Determination and Integration 191 .3 Leads and Lags 192 .4 Project Management Information System 193	.1 Project Schedule Network Diagrams 194 .2 Project Documents Updates 194 • Activity Attributes 194 • Activity List 194 • Assumption Log 194 • Milestone List 194

Fig. 6-7, P 187, *Sequence Activities: Inputs, Tools, Techniques and Outputs*
Fig. 6-8, P 187, *Sequence Activities: Data Flow*

Chapter Six: Project Schedule Management

6.4 ESTIMATE ACTIVITY DURATIONS

TOOLS & TECHNIQUES

INPUTS → 6.4 ESTIMATE ACTIVITY DURATIONS → OUTPUTS

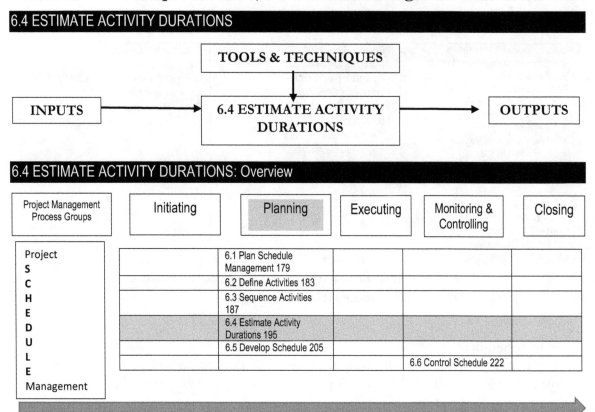

6.4 ESTIMATE ACTIVITY DURATIONS: Overview

Project Management Process Groups	Initiating	Planning	Executing	Monitoring & Controlling	Closing
Project SCHEDULE Management		6.1 Plan Schedule Management 179			
		6.2 Define Activities 183			
		6.3 Sequence Activities 187			
		6.4 Estimate Activity Durations 195			
		6.5 Develop Schedule 205			
				6.6 Control Schedule 222	

6.4 ESTIMATE ACTIVITY DURATIONS: ITTO Processes

INPUTS	TOOLS and TECHNIQUES	OUTPUTS
.1 Project Management Plan 198 • Schedule Management Plan 198 • Scope Baseline 198 .2 Project Documents 198 • Activity attributes 198 • Activity List 198 • Assumption Log 198 • Lessons Learned Register 198 • Milestone List 198 • Project Team Assignments 198 • Resource Breakdown Structure 198 • Resource Calendars 199 • Resource Requirements 199 • Risk Register 199 .3 Enterprise Environmental Factors 199 .4 Organizational Process Assets 199	.1 Expert Judgment 200 .2 Analogous Estimating 200 .3 Parametric Estimating 200 .4 Three-Point Estimating 201 .5 Bottom Up Estimating 202 .6 Data Analysis 202 • Alternative Analysis 202 • Reserve Analysis 202 .7 Decision Making 203 .8 Meetings 203	.1 Duration Estimates 203 .2 Basis of Estimates 204 .3 Project Documents Updates 204 • Activity Attributes 204 • Assumption Log 204 • Lessons Learned Register 204

Fig. 6-12, P 195, *Estimate Activity Durations: Inputs, Tools, Techniques* and *Outputs*
Fig. 6-13, P 196, *Estimate Activity Durations: Data Flow Diagram*

Develop Schedule:

The **key benefit** of this process is that it generates a schedule model with planned dates for completing project activities (P 205). It is performed throughout the project lifecycle.

Fig. 6-2, P 176, *Scheduling Overview*

See chart on next page: **DEVELOP SCHEDULE (Section 6.5)**

Chapter Six: Project Schedule Management

6.5 DEVELOP SCHEDULE

TOOLS & TECHNIQUES

INPUTS → 6.5 DEVELOP SCHEDULE → OUTPUTS

6.5 DEVELOP SCHEDULE: Overview

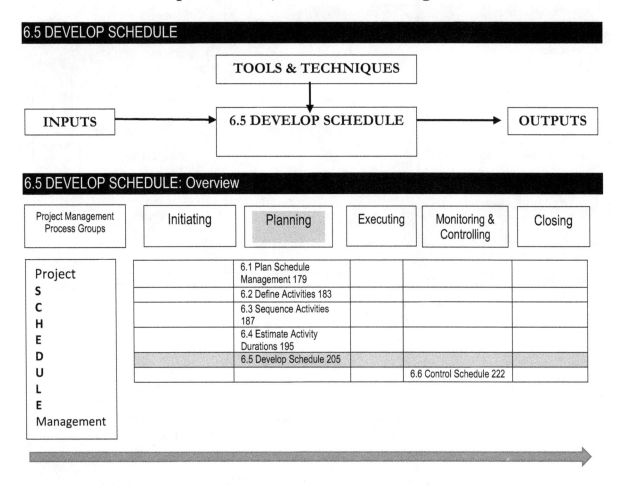

Project Management Process Groups	Initiating	Planning	Executing	Monitoring & Controlling	Closing
Project SCHEDULE Management		6.1 Plan Schedule Management 179			
		6.2 Define Activities 183			
		6.3 Sequence Activities 187			
		6.4 Estimate Activity Durations 195			
		6.5 Develop Schedule 205			
				6.6 Control Schedule 222	

6.5 DEVELOP SCHEDULE: ITTO Processes

INPUTS	TOOLS and TECHNIQUES	OUTPUTS
.1 Project Management Plan 207 • Schedule Management Plan 207 • Scope Baseline 207 .2 Project Documents 207 • Activity Attributes 207 • Activity List 207 • Assumption Log 207 • Basis of Estimates 208 • Duration Estimates 208 • Lessons Learned Register 208 • Milestone List 208 • Project Schedule Network Diagram 208 • Project Team Assignments 208 • Resource Calendars 208 • Resource Requirements 208 • Risk Register 208 .3 Agreements 208 .4 Enterprise Environmental Factors 209 .5 Organizational Process Assets 209	.1 Schedule Network Analysis 209 .2 Critical Path Method 210 .3 Resource Optimization 211 .4 Data Analysis 213 • What-If Scenarios 213 • Simulation 213 .5 Leads and Lags 214 .6 Schedule Compression 215 .7 Project Management Information System 216 .8 Agile Release Planning 216	.1 Schedule Baseline 217 .2 Project Schedule 217 .3 Schedule Data 220 .4 Project Calendars 220 .5 Change Requests 220 .6 Project Management Plan Updates 221 • Schedule Management Plan 221 • Cost Baseline 221 .7 Project Document Updates 221 • Activity Attributes 221 • Assumption Log 221 • Duration Estimates 221 • Lessons Learned Register 221 • Resource Requirements 221 • Risk Register 221

Fig. 6-14, P 205, *Develop Schedule: Inputs, Tools, Techniques and Outputs*
Fig. 6-15 P 206, *Develop Schedule: Data Flow Diagram*

Control Schedule:

The **key benefit** of the control schedule process is that the schedule baseline is maintained throughout the project (P 222). This process is performed throughout the project lifecycle.

See chart on next page: **PROJECT SCHEDULE MANAGEMENT (Section 6.6)**

Chapter Six: Project Schedule Management

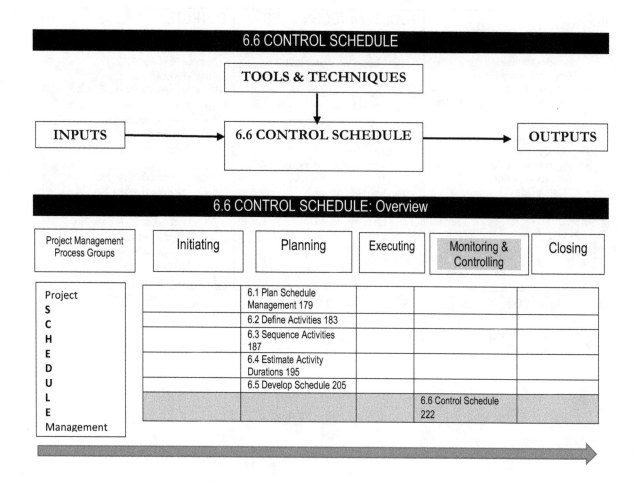

6.6 CONTROL SCHEDULE

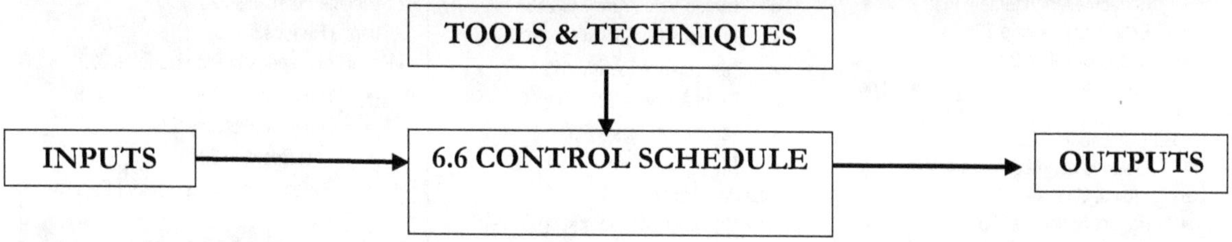

6.6 CONTROL SCHEDULE: Overview

Project Management Process Groups	Initiating	Planning	Executing	Monitoring & Controlling	Closing
Project SCHEDULE Management		6.1 Plan Schedule Management 179			
		6.2 Define Activities 183			
		6.3 Sequence Activities 187			
		6.4 Estimate Activity Durations 195			
		6.5 Develop Schedule 205			
				6.6 Control Schedule 222	

6.6 CONTROL SCHEDULE: ITTO Processes

INPUTS	TOOLS and TECHNIQUES	OUTPUTS
.1 Project Management Plan 224 • Schedule Management Plan 224 • Schedule Baseline 224 • Scope Baseline 224 • Performance Measurement Baseline 224 .2 Project Documents 225 • Lessons Learned Register 225 • Project Calendars 225 • Project Schedule 225 • Resource Calendars 225 • Schedule Data 225 .3 Work Performance Data 225 .4 Organizational Process Assets 25	.1 Data Analysis 226 • Earned Value Analysis 226 • Iterations Burndown Chart 226 • Performance Reviews 227 • Trend Analysis 227 • Variance Analysis 227 • What-If Scenario analysis 227 .2 Critical Path Method 227 .3 Project Management Information System PMIS) 227 .4 Resource Optimization 227 .5 Lead and Lags 228 .6 Schedule Compression 228	.1 Work Performance Information 228 .2 Schedule Forecasts 228 .3 Change Requests 229 .4 Project Management Plan Updates 229 • Schedule Management Plan 229 • Schedule Baseline 229 • Cost Baseline 229 • Performance Measurement Baseline 229 .5 Project Documents Updates 230 • Assumption Log 230 • Basis of Estimates 230 • Lessons Learned Register 230 • Project Schedule 230 • Resource Calendars 230 • Risk Register 230 • Schedule Data 230

Fig. 6-22, P 222, *Control Schedule; Inputs, Tools and Techniques and Outputs*
Fig. 6-23, P 223, *Control Schedule: Data Flow Diagram*

KEY WORDS: CHAPTER 6

- Trends And Emerging Practices
- Tailoring Considerations
- Agile/Adaptive Environments
- Agile Approach
- Development Approach
- Expert Judgment
- Data Analysis
- Scope Baseline
- Release And Iteration Links
- Level Of Accuracy
- New Measure
- Organizational Procedure Links Control Thresholds
- Earned Value Management Decomposition
- Rolling Wave
- Meetings
- Activity Attributes
- Milestone List
- Change Request
- Schedule Baseline
- Cost Baseline
- Cost Performance Index
- Scope Baseline
- Activity Attributes
- Activity List
- Assumption Log
- Data Analysis
- Earned Schedule (ES)
- Earned Value Analysis
    - Planned Value
    - Earned Value
    - Actual Cost
- Earned Value Management (EVM)
- Financing Cost Baseline
- Funding Limit Reconciliation
- Management Reserve
- Performance Measurement Baseline
- Plan Cost
- Project Cost Management
    - Estimate Cost
    - Control Cost
    - Determine Budget
- Milestone List
- Precedence Diagramming Method (PDM)
- Predecessor Activity
- Successor Activity
- Finish To Start (FS)
- Finish To Finish (FF)
- Start To Start (SS)
- Start To Finish (SF)
- Mandatory Dependency
- Discretionary Dependency
- External Dependency
- Internal Dependency
- Leads And Lags
- Project Management Information Systems (PMIS)
- Project Schedule Network Diagram
- Assumption Log
- Long Diminishing Returns
- Advances In Technology
- Motivation Of Staff
- Lessons Learned Register Resource
- Breakdown Structure
- Resource Calendars
- Resource Environments Risk Register
- Expert Judgment
- Analogous Estimating
- Parametric Estimating

- Three Point Estimating
  - Triangular Distribution
  - Beta Distribution
- Bottom-Up Estimating
- Reserve Analysis
- Data Analysis
- Reserve Analysis
- Decision-Making
- Duration Estimates
- Basis Of Estimates
- Duration Of Estimates
- Risks Register
- Risk Management Plan
- Schedule Management Plan
- Critical Path Method
- Resource Optimization
- Resource Leveling
- Resource Smoothing
- Data Analysis
- What-If Scenario Analysis
- Simulation
- Monte Carlo
- Probability Distribution
- Leads And Lags
- Schedule Compression
- Crashing
- Fast Tracking
- Agile Release Planning
- Product Vision
- Product Roadmap
- Release Plans
- Iterations
- Iteration Plans
- Features
- User Stories
- Tasks
- Bar Chart
- Control Schedule
- Earned Value Analysis
- Iteration Burn Down Chart
- Performance Reviews
- Trend Analysis
- Charts
- Forecasting
- Variance Analysis
  - Schedule Variance
  - Cost Variance
  - Schedule Performance Index
- What-If Scenario Analysis

LEGEND

The following Legend shows how to correctly read the *PMBOK® Guide* references and attributions correctly for Chapter 6: Project Schedule Management PMBOK Details.

Legend:

Chapter Section	Chapter Section Title	Page Number

Example from Chapter Six shown below:

6.5.1.4	Enterprise Environmental Factors	(P 209)

All direct quotes are attributed as (A Guide to the Project Management Body of Knowledge, (*PMBOK® Guide)* – Sixth Edition) Project Management Institute Inc., 2017, Page #, after each section and any/all paraphrased or original wording is attributed as (P #), before or after each section. All Graphs, Charts, Tables and Figures are attributed as: (*PMBOK® Guide,* Fig. #-# or #/#, P #, *Title of Graph, Chart, Table or Figure*).

6. PROJECT SCHEDULE MANAGEMENT

Project Schedule Management provides the framework and the Schedule Baseline for measuring progress throughout the project. Plan Schedule Management includes the processes required to manage the timely completion of the project. The activities listed below are generally done in sequence, but there may be occasions when not all of them are done repetitively.

- **Plan Schedule Management**
- **Define Activities**
- **Sequence Activities**
- **Estimate Activity Durations**
- **Develop Schedule**
- **Control Schedule**

Fig. 6-1, P 174, *Plan Schedule Management Overview*

Key Concepts for Project Schedule Management:

A detailed plan for Schedule Management will show how and when the project will provide the services and results define in the Project Scope (P 175). A Scheduling Method will be chosen by the Project Team such as a Critical Path Method, or Agile Approach and the project schedule should remain flexible throughout the project.

Trends and Emerging Practices in project Schedule Management:

Shown below are some of the emerging practices for Scheduling Methods (P 177):

- **Iterative Scheduling with a backlog**: A form of Rolling Wave Planning based on Adaptive Lifecycles. Requirements are documented in User Stories.
- **On-Demand Scheduling**: Normally used in a Kanban System, based on constraints and pull-based scheduling concepts from Lean manufacturing. It does not rely on a schedule, but pulls work from a backlog and used a resources become available.

Tailoring Considerations:

Some of the considerations to be taken into account are (P 178):

- **Lifecycle Approach**:
    - What is the most appropriate approach?
- **Resource Availability**:
    - What are the factors influencing durations?
- **Project Dimensions**:
    - How will the problems of project complexity, technological uncertainty, product novelty, pace or progress tracking impact the desired level of control?
- **Technology Support**:
    - Is technology used to develop, record, transmit, receive and store project schedule model information, and is it readily accessible?

Considerations for Agile/Adaptive Environments:

Adaptive Approaches use short cycles, review the work results, provide rapid feedback on approaches and sustainability of deliverables, and adapt as necessary to the organizational environment (P 178). However, in a large organizations, there may be ongoing small and large projects taking place concurrently and the PM must know how to incorporate each element effectively based on the particular requirements of each program using Scaling Factors, such as team size, geographical distribution, regulatory compliance, organizational complexity and technical complexity.

6.1 PLAN SCHEDULE MANAGEMENT

In order to **Plan Schedule Management Plan**, the Project Manager must establish policies, procedures and documentation in order to execute a project successfully. The PM must also plan, develop, execute and control the project according to the Schedule Management Plan. The **key benefit** of this process is to provide guidance and direction on how the project will be managed.

Fig. 6-3, P 179, *Plan Schedule Management: Inputs, Tools and Techniques and Outputs*
Fig. 6-4, P 179, *Plan Schedule Management: Data Flow Diagram*

6.1.1 Plan Schedule Management: Inputs

6.1.1.1 Project Charter

The **Project Charter** contains the summary milestone schedule and project approval requirements (P 160).

6.1.1.2 Project Management Plan

The **Project Management Plan** may contain the following (P 180):

- **Scope Management Plan**
- **Development Plan**

6.1.1.3 Enterprise Environmental factors

Enterprise Environmental Factors that can influence the Plan Schedule Management Process (P 180):

- Organizational Culture and Structure
- Team Resource Availability and Skills
- Scheduling Management Software
- Guidelines and Criteria for Tailoring the Organization's set of Processes and Procedures
- Commercial Databases

6.1.1.4 Organizational Process Assets

Some of the **Organizational Process Assets** influencing Plan Schedule Management are (P 180):

- Historical Information
- Existing Formal and Informal Schedule Development
- Templates and Forms
  Monitoring and Reporting Tools

6.1.2.1 Expert Judgment

Expert Judgment is guided by historical information and provides environmental insight and information if the PM examines similar projects. The PM should consider the following (P 181):

- Schedule Development, Management and Control
- Scheduling Methodologies
- Scheduling Software
- The Specific Industry for which the Project is developed

6.1.2.2 Data Analysis

Data Analysis is a technique, although it is not limited to Alternative Analysis.

6.1.2.3 Meetings

Meetings are held in order to Develop the Schedule Management Plan and may be formal or informal (181).

6.1.3 Plan Schedule Management: Outputs

6.1.3.1 Schedule Management Plan

The **Schedule Management Plan,** a subsidiary plan, and is a part of the **Project Management Plan** which contains activities for developing, monitoring and controlling the schedule and may set the groundwork for the following (P 181-182):

- **Project Schedule Model Development**: Used in the development of the Project Schedule Model
- **Release and Iteration length**: When using an Adaptive Lifecycle, the time-boxed periods for Releases, Waves and Iterations are specified
- **Level of Accuracy**: Specifies an acceptable range used to determine realistic activity duration estimates
- **Unit of Measure**: All units of measure are defined for each resource
- **Organizational Procedures Links**: The WBS structure provides the framework for the Schedule management Plan
- **Project Schedule Model Maintenance**: uses to update status and record progress of the project in the Schedule Model
- **Control Thresholds**: Variance Thresholds may be specified to indicate an agreed-upon amount of variation
- **Rule of Performance Measurement**: EVM rules or other physical measurement are set, for example:
    - Rules for establishing percent complete
    - EVM Techniques
    - Schedule Performance Measurements
- **Reporting Formats:** formats and frequency for the various Schedule Reports are defined

6.2 DEFINE ACTIVITIES

In order to produce product deliverables, you must identify and record any specific actions that need to be executed, such as planning and defining any schedule activities in advance of doing the work.

Fig. 6-5, P 183, *Define Activities Data Flow Diagram*
Fig. 6-6, P 183, *Define Activities: Data Flow Diagram*

The **key benefit** of Define Activities is to breakdown the project work into Work Packages and then into schedule activities that will be used as a basis for estimating, scheduling, executing and monitoring and controlling the project work.

6.2.1 Define Activities: Inputs

6.2.1.1 Project Management Plan

The **Project Management Plan** is an Input, which contains specific information needed to carry out the project work. The level of detail must be structured in a way to communicate what needs to be done to manage the work. The components of this plan include (P 184):

- **Schedule Management Plan**
- **Scope Baseline**

6.2.1.2 Enterprise Environmental Factors

Enterprise Environmental Factors influencing the Define Activities Process may be (P 184):

- Organizational Cultures and Structure
- Published Commercial Information
- Project Management Information Systems (PMIS)

6.2.1.3 Organizational Process Assets

Organizational Process Assets influencing the Define Activities Process (P 184) may be:

- Lessons Learned Repository
- Standardized Processes
- Templates
- Existing Formal/Informal Activity Planning-Related Policies

6.2.2 Define Activities: Tools and Techniques

6.2.2.1 Expert Judgment

Expert Judgment is about SME's who may provide input for defining activities

6.2.2.2 Decomposition

Decomposition is a process that divides and subdivides project scope and project deliverables into smaller more manageable components (P 185).

6.2.2.3 Rolling Wave Planning

Rolling Wave Planning (a form of Progressive Elaboration) means current tasks are detailed, but future tasks are defined at a higher level (185).

6.2.2.4 Meetings

Meetings are held face-to-face, virtually, or informally with Team Members or SME's.

6.2.3 Define Activities: Outputs

6.2.3.1 Activity List

The **Activity List** is comprised of all schedule activities necessary to complete the project.

6.2.3.2 Activity Attributes

Activity Attributes: All Activities contain set periods, where all work is executed and may have resources and costs associated with such work.

6.2.3.3 Milestone List

A **Milestone List** specifies milestones (short-lived timeframes) which are mandatory and which are optional (P 186).

6.2.3.4 Change Requests

Change Requests are put into place once the project has been baselined if it has been determined the changes are necessary.

6.2.3.5 Project Management Plan Updates

Some of the **Project Management Plan Updates** may be identified as (P 186):

- **Schedule Baseline**: Defines when project costs will be incurred
- **Cost Baseline**: Changes to the Cost Baseline are in direct response to approved schedule activities

6.3 SEQUENCE ACTIVITIES

Sequence Activities identifies and documents relationships among project activities (P187).

Fig. 6-7, P 187, *Sequence Activities: Inputs, Tools and Techniques and Outputs*
Fig. 6-8, P 187, *Sequence Activities Data Flow Diagram*

The **key benefit** of Sequence Activities is that this process defines the logical sequence of work given the impact of project constraints.

6.3.1 Sequence Activities: Inputs

6.3.1.1 Project Management Plan

The **Project Management Plan** determines the scheduling method and tool being used for the project and may include the following (P 188):

- **Schedule Management Plan**
- **Scope Baseline**

6.3.1.2 Project Documents

Some **Project Documents** that may be considered as Inputs to this process are (P 188):

- **Activity Attributes**: All Activities contain set periods, where all work is executed and may have resources and costs associated with such work.
- **Activity List**: Contains all Schedule Activities
- **Assumption Log**: Assumptions and Constraints may affect the way activities are sequenced, relationships between activities and the need for Leads and Lags
- **Milestone List**: Contains specific dates for Milestones

6.3.1.3 Enterprise Environmental Factors

Some **Enterprise Environmental Factors** that might impact the Sequence Activities Process are (P 189):

- Government or Industry Standards
- Project Management Information Systems (PMIS)
- Scheduling Tools
- Company Work Authorization Systems

6.3.1.4 Organizational Process Assets

Some of the **Organizational Process Assets** that may influence Sequence Activities Processes (P 189):

- Portfolio and Program Plans and Project Dependencies and Relationships
- Existing Formal/Informal Activity Planning-Related Policies, Procedures and Guidelines
- Templates
- Lessons Learned Repository

6.3.2 Sequence Activities: Tools and Techniques

6.3.2.1 Precedence Diagramming Method

The **Precedence Diagramming Method (PDM)** is "…used for constructing a schedule model in which activities are represented by nodes…" and "includes four types of dependencies or logical relationships to show the sequence in which the activities are to be performed." Such relationships are described as follows:

- **Finish-to-Start (FS)**: A logical relationship in which a successor activity cannot start until a predecessor activity has finished
- **Finish-to-Finish (FF)**: A logical relationship in which a successor activity cannot finish until a predecessor activity has finished
- **Start-to-Start (SS):** A logical relationship in which a successor activity cannot start until a predecessor activity has started
- **Start-to-Finish (SF):** A logical relationship in which a successor activity cannot finish until a predecessor activity has started

Project Management Institute, (A Guide to the Project Management Body of Knowledge, *(PMBOK® Guide)* – Sixth Edition), Project Management Institute Inc., 2017, Page 189.

Fig. 6-9, P 190, *Precedence Diagramming Method (PDM) Relationship Types*

6.3.2.2 Dependency Determination and Integration

Dependencies may consist of (P 191):

- **Mandatory Dependencies**: These dependencies that are legally or contractually required or inherent in the nature of the work
- **Discretionary Dependencies**: These dependencies are sometimes referred to as preferred logic, preferential logic, or soft logic
- **Internal Dependencies**: Involve a relationship between project activities and non –project activities
- **External Dependencies**: Involve a precedence relationship between project activities and are generally inside the project team's control

6.3.2.3 Leads and Lags

Leads and Lags: "A Lead is an amount of time whereby a successor activity can be advanced with respect to a predecessor activity," while, "A Lag is the amount of time whereby a successor activity will be delayed with respect to a predecessor activity" Project Management Institute, (A Guide to the Project Management Body of Knowledge, *(PMBOK® Guide)* – Sixth Edition), Project Management Institute Inc., 2017, Page 192.

Fig. 6-10, P 158, *Examples of Lead and Lag*
Fig. 6-11, P 193, *Project Schedule Network Diagram*

6.3.2.4 Project Management Information Systems (PMIS)

Project Management Information Systems contains scheduling software to make it easier to plan, organize and adjust activity sequences, lead and lag values, etc.

6.3.3 Sequence Activities: Outputs

6.3.3.1 Project Schedule Network Diagrams

A **Project Schedule Network Diagram** visually displays logical relationships (dependencies) between project activities (P 194).

6.3.3.2 Project Documents Update

Some **Project Documents** that might be updated are (P 194):

- **Activity Attributes:** May describe a sequence of events or defined predecessor or successor relationships
- **Activity List**: Contains all Schedule Activities and may be affected by any changes in relationships during sequencing activities
- **Assumption Log:** Assumptions and Constraints may affect the way activities are sequenced, relationships between activities and the need for Leads and Lags
- **Milestone List**: : Specifies which milestones (short-lived timeframes) are mandatory and which are optional and contains specific dates for Milestones

6.4 ESTIMATE ACTIVITY DURATIONS

Estimate Activity Resources is estimating what resources and the number of work persons, and how much of those resources are needed to complete the project. The **key benefit** is that this processes provides the amount of time each activity will take to complete.

Fig. 6-13, P 195, *Estimate Activity Durations: Inputs, Tools and Techniques and Outputs*
Fig. 6-13, P 196, *Estimate Activity Resources Data Flow Diagram*

6.4.1 Estimate Activity Durations: Inputs

6.4.1.1 Project Management Plan

Some of the **Project Management Plan** components are (P 198):

- **Schedule Management Plan**: Defines the Schedule methodology used to accomplish the project goals as well as level of accuracy required to estimate activity durations
- **Scope Baseline**: Contains the WBS Dictionary, which includes technical details that may affect effort and duration estimates

6.4.1.2 Project Documents

Some of the Project Documents to be considered as Inputs to this process are (P 198):

- **Activity Attributes:** Items on the Activity List stipulate what data (attributes) are used to estimate resources according to each activity
- **Activity List:** Contains a record of any activities needing any resources
- **Assumption Log:** Identifies risks based on assumptions
- **Lessons Learned Register:** Contains information from previous projects that has been experienced and any process improvement recommendations will be filed for future use
- **Milestone List:** specifies which milestones (short-lived timeframes) are mandatory and which are optional and may have scheduled dates (P 153).
- **Project Team Assignments:**
- **Resource Breakdown Structure: Resource Breakdown Structure:** A means of breaking down resources into smaller categorized sections and labeled according to the type of resource and where that resource is in regard to a set hierarchy
- **Resource Calendars:** Specify when and how resources are available during a prescribed activity
- **Resource Requirements:**
- **Risk Register:** Identifies risks and any pertinent data belonging to a particular risk. The Risk Register is updated when the need arises

6.4.1.3 Enterprise Environmental Factors

Some **Enterprise Environmental Factors** that might influence the Estimate Activity Durations Process are (P 199):

- Duration Estimating Databases and other Reference Data
- Productivity Metrics
- Published Commercial Information
- Location of Team Members

6.4.1.4 Organizational Process Assets

Some of the **Organizational Process Assets** that may influence the Estimate Activity Durations are (P 199):

- Historical Duration Information
- Project Calendars
- Estimating Policies
- Scheduling Methodology
- Lessons Learned Repository

6.4.2 Estimate Activity Durations: Tools and Techniques

6.4.2.1 Expert Judgment

Expert Judgment: This tool can estimate or prescribe actions based on experience from previous projects.

6.4.2.2 Analogous Estimating

Another tool for, Estimate Activity Durations is **Analogous Estimating**, which uses historical data from a similar activity or project (P 200). This particular tool can also estimate or prescribe actions for cost or duration times, based on experience from previous projects. This technique is less costly and less time consuming, but also less accurate. It may be used for the entire project scope or just parts of the project.

6.4.2.3 Parametric Estimating

Parametric Estimating is a more accurate technique than Analogous Estimating and can also be used for the entire project scope or just parts of the project. Analogous Estimating uses a statistical relationship between historical data and other variables.

6.4.3 Estimate Activity Durations: Outputs

6.4.2.4 Three-Point Estimating

Three-Point Estimating is a tool that uses three estimates to help pinpoint an approximate time range for the duration of an activity. The outcomes of using this tool range as follows (P 201):

- **Most likely** (tM): Based on the duration of the activity
- **Optimistic** (t0): Based on analysis of the best-case scenario
- **Pessimistic** (tP): Based on analysis of the worst-case scenario

See P 201 for detailed definitions of the **Three-Point Estimating Tool** and to learn about two commonly used formulas:

- Triangular Distribution
- Beta Distribution

One formula that is used is $tE=(t0+tM+tP)/3$.

6.4.2.5 Bottom-Up Estimating

Bottom-Up Estimating is "… a method of estimating project duration or cost by aggregating the estimates of the lower-level components of the WBS" Project Management Institute, A Guide to the Project Management Body of Knowledge, *(PMBOK® Guide)* – Sixth Edition), Project Management Institute Inc., 2017, Page 202.

6.4.2.6 Data Analysis

Some of the techniques used for Data Analysis are (P203):

- **Alternative Analysis**: A form of deciding on several alternatives and analyzing each one before making a decision.
- **Reserve Analysis**: The process of assembling specific contingency reserves into the project schedule

6.4.2.7 Decision Making

Decision Making is the ability to negotiate and influence the organization and the project management teams (P 203). One method is voting, commonly used in an Agile environment.

6.4.2.8 Meetings

Meetings are used to estimate Activity Durations (P 203). Agile approaches will use Sprint or Iteration planning meetings, generally held on the first day of the Iteration.

6.4.3 Estimate Activity Durations: Outputs

6.4.3.1 Duration Estimates

Duration Estimates is a quantitative assessment of necessary time frames/periods needed to complete a project and do not include Lags. They may however include a range of possible results, for example (P 203):

- A range of two (2) weeks ± 2 days, indicating the activity will take at the very least eight (8) days, but not more than twelve (12) days (assuming a five (5) day work week)
- A 15% probability of exceeding three (3) weeks (high probability - 85% - that the activity will take three (3) weeks or less

6.4.3.2 Basis of Estimates

The **Basis of Estimates** supports the Duration Estimate and any documents derived from this process must be detailed and clear as to how the data was compiled. Shown below is some of the information that should be used to support these estimates (P 204):

- Documentation of how the Estimate was developed
- Documentation of any Assumptions that were made
- Documentation of any Known Constraints
- Indication of range of Possible Estimates
- Indication of the confidence level of the Final Estimates
- Documentation of Individual Project Risks

6.4.3.3 Project Documents Updates

Some **Project Documents Updates** are (P 204):

- **Activity Attributes:** These are updated to include any revised resource requirements and any other revisions generated by the Develop Schedule process
- **Assumption Log:** Any changes in Assumptions regarding duration, resource utilization, sequencing or other data
- **Lessons Learned Register:** Can be updated with more efficient techniques for a particular process that will be finalized before being entered into the Repository

6.5 DEVELOP SCHEDULE

Develop Schedule is necessary to create the Project Schedule Model. It is about analyzing "… activity sequences, durations, resource requirements and schedule constraints" (*PMBOK® Guide,* P 205). The **key benefit** of this process is that it generates a schedule model with planned dates for completing project activities.

Fig. 6-14, P 205, *Develop Schedule: Inputs, Tools and Techniques and Outputs*
Fig. 6-15, P 206, *Develop Schedule: Data Flow Diagram*

6.5.1 Develop Schedule: Inputs

6.5.1.1 Project Management Plan

Some of the **Project Management Plan** components are (P 207):

- **Schedule Management Plan:** Identifies Scheduling method and tools used to create the Schedule
- **Scope Baseline:** Contains the Scope Statement, WBS and WBS Dictionary with details about the project deliverables

6.5.1.2 Project Documents

Some of the **Project Documents** that can be considered as updates for the Develop Schedule process are (P 207):

- **Activity Attributes:** Specifies the necessary details that will be used as basis to produce the Schedule Model.
- **Activity List:** Lists activities that will be included in the Schedule Model
- **Assumption Log:** Contains any Assumptions and Constraints that may impact the Schedule Model
- **Basis of Estimates:** All Estimates should be clear and concise and how the duration estimates were derived
- **Duration Estimates:** Number of assessed work timeframes needed to finish all activities
- **Lessons Learned:** Any data gathered regarding Develop Schedule Model earlier in the project may be applied to make improvements later on in the project
- **Milestone List:** A list of specific dates for any scheduled Milestones
- **Project Schedule Network Diagram:** A diagram containing all the logical relationships of predecessors and successors
- **Project Team Assignments:** The specification of which resources are assigned to each category (activity)
- **Resource Calendars:** Specifies availability of resources
- **Resource Requirements:** Identifies the type and quantities of resources needed for the project activities
- **Risk Register:** Affects the Schedule Model and provides details of Identified Risks

6.5.1.3 Agreements

Agreements may provide Vendors with possible Inputs to the Project Schedule.

6.5.1.4 Enterprise Environmental Factors

Some of the Enterprise Environmental Factors that may affect the Develop Schedule Process are (P 209):

- Government or Industry Standards
- Communication Channels

6.5.1.5 Organizational Process Assets

Some of the Organizational Process Assets that may affect the Develop Schedule Process are (P 209):

- Scheduling and Methodology containing the policies governing Schedule Model Development and Maintenance
- Project Calendars

6.5.2 Develop Schedule: Tools and Techniques

6.5.2.1 Schedule Network Analysis

The **Schedule Network Analysis** (an iterative process) is a technique that produces the Schedule Model and uses many different analytical techniques, such as the Critical Path Method, Resource Optimization Techniques and Modeling Techniques, but may also contain other techniques as shown below (P 209):

- Assessing the need to aggregate Schedule Reserves
- Reviewing the Network to see if the Critical Path Method has high-risk activities, or long lead times

6.5.2.2 Critical Path Method

The **Critical Path Method** compares the amount of buffer remaining to the amount of buffer needed to protect the delivery date and can help determine Schedule Status. Be sure to read and study section 6.5.2.2, Critical Path Method, (P 210).

Article: *Critical Path Method: A Project Management Essential,* by Andrew Slate at *https://www.wrike.com/blog/critical-path-is-easy-as-123/*

6.5.2.3 Resource Optimization:

Examples of **Resource Optimization Techniques**:

- **Resource Leveling**: A technique in which start and finish dates are adjusted based on resource constraints with the goal of balancing demand for resources with the available supply.
- **Resource Smoothing**: A technique that adjusts the activities of a schedule model such that the requirements for resources on the project do not exceed certain pre-defined resource limits

Fig. 6-17, P 212, *Resource Leveling*

6.5.2.4 Data Analysis

Some of the Data Analysis Techniques that may be used in the Develop Schedule Process are (P 213):

- **What-If Scenario Analysis:** This technique is the process of evaluating scenarios in order to predict their effect, positively or negatively, on project objectives
- **Simulation:** Involves calculating multiple project durations with different sets of activity assumptions, usually using probability distributions constructed from the three-point estimates to account for uncertainty

6.5.2.5 Leads and Lags

Lead and Lags are used during Network Analysis for the purpose of creating a sustainable Schedule.

6.5.2.6 Schedule Compression

Schedule Compression techniques might be (P 215):

- **Crashing:** A technique used to shorten the duration for the least incremental cost by adding resources
- **Fast Tracking**: A schedule compression technique in which certain

activities or phases normally done in sequence are performed in parallel for at least a portion of their duration

Fig. 6-19, P 215, *Schedule Compression Comparison*

6.5.2.7 Project Management Information Systems (PMIS)

Project Management Information Systems (PMIS) contains scheduling software to speed the process of building a schedule.

6.5.2.8 Agile Release Planning

Agile Release Planning is adaptive and change-driven (P 216). Be sure to read and study Fig. 6-20, P 216, *Relationship Between Product Vison, Release Planning and Iteration Planning.*

6.5.3 Develop Schedule: Outputs

6.5.3.1 Schedule Baseline

An approved version of a schedule model that can be changed only through formal Change Control procedures and is used as a basis for comparison to actual results (P 217).

6.5.3.2 Project Schedule

An Output of a Schedule Model is the **Project Schedule** and is often represented in one of the formats shown below (P 217):

- **Bar Charts** (also known as Gantt Charts): represent schedule information where activities are listed on the vertical axis, dates are shown on the horizontal axis and activity durations are shown as horizontal bars placed according to start and finish dates
- **Milestone Charts**: Similar to bar charts, but only identify the start or competition of major deliverables and key external influences

Please refer to the following, *External Influence*, http://www.pmnetworkdigital.com/pmnetwork/october_2018/MobilePagedArticle.action?articleId=1427371#articleId1427371.

- **Project Schedule Network Diagrams:** Commonly presented in the activity-on-node diagram format showing activities and relationships without a time scale, sometimes referred to as pure logic diagram

Fig. 6-21, P 219, *Project Schedule Presentations — Examples*

6.5.3.3 Schedule Data

Schedule Data: A collection of data used for defining and controlling the Schedule, such as (P 220):

- Resource Requirements
- Alternative Schedules
- Applied Schedule Reserves

6.5.3.4 Project Calendars

A **Project Calendar** is used to track time, duties and cost, by categorizing and showing available time slots for various activities, durations of those activities, and budget for resources.

6.5.3.5 Change Requests

Change Requests can be the result of modifications to the Project Management Plan or other components (P 220).

6.5.3.6 Project Management Plan Updates

Some of the components that may be changed in the Project Management Plan Updates are (P 221):

- **Schedule Management Plan**: May be updated to reflect changes in the Schedule
- **Cost Baseline:** Changes to the Cost Baseline are in direct response to approved schedule activities

6.3.5.7 Project Documents Updates

Some of the components that may be changed in the Project Documents Updates are (P 221):

- **Activity Attributes**: These are updated to include any revised resource requirements and any other revisions generated by the Develop Schedule process
- **Assumption Log**: Any changes in Assumptions regarding duration, resource utilization, sequencing or other data
- **Duration Estimates**: The number and availability of Resources may change and need to be updated as requires
- **Lessons Learned Register**: May be updated with techniques used in the Develop Schedule Model
- **Resource Requirements**: Resource leveling can impact preliminary estimates for the type and quantities of resources required
- **Risk Register**: This may need updated to reflect opportunities or threats perceived through scheduling assumptions

6.6 CONTROL SCHEDULE

Control Schedule is monitored at all times during the project with the main purpose being to update the Project Schedule and manage changes to the Schedule Baseline. The **key benefit** of this process is that the schedule baseline in monitored throughout the project.

Fig. 6-22, P 222, *Control Schedule: Inputs, Tools and Techniques and Outputs*
Fig. 6-23, P 223, *Control Schedule: Data Flow Diagram*

6.6.1 Control Schedule: Inputs

6.6.1.1 Project Management Plan

Some of the components in the Project Management Plan may include (P 224):

- **Schedule Management Plan**: This plan may be updated to reflect a change in the way the schedule is managed
- **Schedule Baseline**: Comparison with actual results is made to determine if a

change or correction is needed

- **Scope Baseline**: The project WBS, deliverables, constraints and assumptions documented in the Scope Baseline are considered when monitoring and controlling the schedule baseline
- **Performance Measurement Baseline**: When using Earned Value Analysis, the Performance Measurement Baseline is compared to the actual results

6.6.1.2 Project Documents

Some of the components in the Project Documents that can be considered as Inputs for Control Schedule are (P 225):

- **Lessons Learned Register**: Lessons learned, what has been experienced and process improvement recommendations should be filed for future use
- **Project Calendars**: More than one calendar may be required to calculate schedule forecasts
- **Project Schedule**: Refers to most recent versions with notations for updates, activities, completed activities and started activities
- **Resource Calendars**: Shows the availability of team and physical resources
- **Schedule Data**: Will be reviewed and updated in the Schedule process

6.6.1.3 Work Performance Data

Work Performance Data is information that specifies which activities have started, which ones have completed and any of the activities in progress, such as (P 225):

- Actual duration
- Remaining duration
- Physical percent complete, etc.

6.6.1.4 Organizational Process Assets

Organizational Process Assets that influence Control Schedule processes (P 188):

- Existing Formal/Informal Schedule Control-Related Policies, Procedures And Guidelines
- Schedule Control Tools
- Monitoring and Reporting Methods to be used

6.6.2 Control Schedule: Tools and Techniques

6.6.2.1 Data Analysis

Some of the Data Analysis Techniques that can be used in the Control Schedule are (P 226):

- **Earned Value Analysis**: Schedule performance measurements, such as, schedule variance (SV) and schedule performance Index (SPI) are used to assess the magnitude of variation to the original schedule baseline
- **Iteration Burndown Charts**
- **Performance Reviews**: Compares, measures and analyzes Schedule Performance
- **Trend Analysis**: Examines project performance over time to determine whether performance is improving or deteriorating
- **Variance Analysis**
- **What-If Scenario Analysis**

Fig. 6-24, P 226, *Iteration Burndown Chart*

6.6.2.2 Critical Path Method

The **Critical Path Method** compares the amount of buffer remaining to the amount of buffer needed to protect the delivery date and can help determine Schedule Status.

How to Calculate Critical Path: Project Management professional (PMP)® Exam Prep (12:07 minutes), located at: https://youtu.be/0Lo4zsB-bjE.

6.6.2.3 Project Management Information System

The **Project Management Information System** allows the PM to track planned dates vs. actual dates, report variances and forecast any changes to the project schedule model.

6.6.2.4 Resource Optimization

Resource Optimization Techniques is the scheduling of activities and resources required by those activities.

6.6.2.5 Leads and Lags

Leads and Lags are adjusted, if necessary, during Network Analysis to bring project activities back into alignment with the plan (P 228).

6.6.2.6 Schedule Compression

Schedule Compression is about finding ways, if necessary, to bring project activities back into alignment with the plan by Fast Tracking or Crashing Schedule remaining work to be done (P 228).

6.6.3 Control Schedule: Outputs

6.6.3.2 Schedule Forecasts

Schedule Forecasts estimates or predicts outcomes of conditions or events (P 229). All forecasts are based on what is known at the time of the forecast, the projects past performance and the expected future performance and are updated as necessary.

6.6.3.3 Change Requests

Schedule variances may result in **Change Requests** and will be processed through the Perform Integrated Change Control Process.

6.6.3.4 Project Management Plan Updates

Examples of **Project Management Plan Updates**:

- **Schedule Management Plan**: This plan may be updated to reflect a change in the way the schedule is managed
- **Schedule Baseline**: Changes to the Schedule Baseline are incorporated in response to approved change requests, related to project scope changes, activity resources, or activity duration estimates
- **Cost Baseline:** This may be updated to reflect approved change requests or changes caused by compression techniques
- **Performance Measurement Baseline**: Any changes to Scope, Schedule Performance or Cost Estimates will change the Performance Measurement Baseline and must be adjusted accordingly

6.6.3.5 Projects Documents Updates

Some of the **Projects Documents** that can be updated are (P 230):

- **Assumption Log**: Schedule performance may indicate the need for revisions
- **Basis Of Estimates:** Schedule performance may indicate the need to revise the way durations estimates were developed
- **Lessons Learned Register:** Can be updated with more effective techniques
- **Project Schedule**: The Schedule Model can be updated and populated with current Schedule changes
- **Resource Calendars:** Can be updated to reflect changes
- **Risk Register**: May be updated due to Schedule Compression techniques
- **Schedule Data**: New Project Schedule Network Diagrams may be developed to display approved remaining durations and modifications to the Schedule

Summary: Answers to Student Learning Outcomes

1. **Project Schedule Management** includes processes to manage all of the project activities, tasks and processes within the constraints of the schedule. The task of managing time is challenging and daunting; thus, the Project Manager needs to know what activities need to be done (start date and end dates), by whom, the resources required, and their time frame, which include Lead and Lag (slack) times for each activity. The Critical Path (CP) is the quickest way to finish the project without taking other measures. It needs to be identified as the project activities evolve. The components and brief overview description of each of the six (6) Schedule Management Processes are shown on and listed below (P 173):

    1. **Plan Schedule Management** is a process of **establishing policies, procedures and documentation.** The Project Manager and their team need to devise a plan to create the project schedule. General start and end dates for the entire project or phase must be established to include developing, managing, executing and controlling the project schedule. This plan will vary as the project evolves and other project information becomes available.

    2. **Define Activities** is a process of using all of the **project deliverables** that have been identified, and then **documenting which activities/tasks are needed to produce the project deliverables**.

    3. **Sequence Activities** is a process of using the identified activities cited above and **documenting relationship**(s) **among the project activities**.

    4. **Estimate Activity Durations** is a process of **estimating the number of work periods (days, weeks, months, etc.) to complete individual activities** with the estimated resources.

    5. **Develop Schedule** is a process of analyzing activity sequences, durations, resource requirements and schedule constraints to create a schedule model. This **Schedule Model Diagram** will form a network of activities dependent upon one another. This process includes: end of activity sequences, duration times, resource requirements and schedule constraints. This will ultimately be called the Project Schedule Model that will be used for project execution, monitoring, and controlling the project work.

6. **Control Schedule** is a process that is used to **manage and monitor the status of the project and update the project schedule to reflect changes to the schedule baseline.**

Fig. 6-18, P 174 *Overview Project Schedule Management*

2. The **Schedule Model** is used as a **representation of the plan for executing, initiating, monitoring and controlling project work.** It should include estimations of activity durations, planned dates, resources, dependencies, constraints, and other information to aid in creating the project schedule (P 175).

3. There are **Trends and Emerging Practices in Project Schedule Management** (P 177). They are **Iterative Scheduling with Backlog Activities and On-Demand Scheduling work.** Iterative Scheduling with a Backlog is a form of Rolling Wave Planning that is based upon adaptive life cycles, such as agile approach for product development. The requirements are documented in user stories that are prioritized prior to construction. The product features are developed in periods of work called **Time Boxes**. This approach is often used to deliver incremental value to the customer.

4. **On Demand Scheduling** is used in **operational** or **sustainment** environments for **product development** on an **incremental basis**. Here, tasks are bundled into similar size and scope work (P 177).

   Four (4) **tailoring considerations** in **Project Schedule Management** are (P 178):

   1. Life cycle Approach
   2. Resource Availability
   3. Project Dimensions
   4. Technology Support

5. In an **agile or adaptive environment** the Project Manager's role does not change. The Project manager needs to be familiar with a variety of tools and techniques to understand their use and applicability to the environment (P 178).

6. **Plan Schedule Management** is the **process** of establishing the policies, procedures and documentation for planning, developing, managing, executing and controlling the project schedule (P 179). The key benefit of this process is to provide guidance and directions for managing the schedule as project work evolves and deliverables/milestones are met.

   Fig. 6-4, P 179, *Plan Schedule Management: ITTO's*
   Fig. 6-5, P 180, *Plan Schedule Management: Data Flow Diagram*

7. The **Schedule Management Plan** is output of Plan Schedule Management and consists of the following established elements (P 182):

    - **Project Schedule Model Development, Release and Iteration Lengths**
    - **Level of Accuracy**
    - **Units of Measure**
    - **Organization Procedure Links**
    - **Project Schedule Model Maintenance**
    - **Control Thresholds**
    - **Rules of Performance Measurement**
    - **Reporting Formats**

8. **Define Activities** is the process of identifying and documenting the specific action to be performed to produce the project deliverables. The key benefit of **Define Activities** is it decomposes work packages into scheduled activities that provide a basis for estimating, scheduling, executing, monitoring and controlling project work throughout the project lifecycle (P183).

    Fig. 6-6, P 183, *Define Activities: ITTO's*
    Fig. 6-7, P 183, *Define Activities: Data Flow Diagram*

9. **Rolling Wave Planning** is a Tool and Technique of **Define Activities**. It is an iterative planning technique (P 185). It is a form of **progressive elaboration** that is applicable to

    - Work packages
    - Planning packages
    - Release planning; when using an agile or waterfall approach

10. The **Cost Baseline** is an output of **Define Activities,** and is used as a basis for cost comparison to actual cost (P 186). When approved changes to the schedule occur, changes to the cost baseline must be made through the Change Control Procedures (P 703). The Cost Baseline is the approved version of the Time-Phased Project Budget, excluding any Management Reserves.

11. **Sequence Activities** is the process of identifying and documenting relationships among the project activities (P 187). The key benefit of this process is that it defines the **logical sequence of work**, given all project constraints.

    Fig. 6-7, P 187, *Sequence Activities: ITTO's*
    Fig. 6-8, P 188, *Sequence Activities: Data Flow Diagram*

12. The **Precedence Diagramming Method (PDM)** is a technique used in **Sequence Activities** (P 189). A **schedule model** graphically shows activity sequences and illustrates four (4) types of time related relationships (P 190):

    1. **Finish to Start (FS)**
    2. **Finish to Finish (FF)**
    3. **Start to Start (SS)**
    4. **Start to Finish (SF)**

    Fig. 6-9, P 190, *Precedence Diagramming Method (PDM) Relationship Terms*

    Be sure to **READ** and **STUDY** the four types of dependencies or logical relationships

13. There are four (4) Time Dependencies in the PDM (Precedence Diagramming Method) (P 191-192):

    1. **Mandatory**: Legally or contractually required.
    2. **Discretionary**: Established based on knowledge of best practices.
    3. **External**: Involve relationships between project activities and non-project activities.
    4. **Internal**: Involve a precedent relationship between project activities and are generally within the project team's control.

14. A **Lead** is the amount of time (say in days, weeks, months, etc.) when a successor activity can be advanced (moved forward in the calendar of dates) with respect to a predecessor activity (P 192). A Predecessor Activity is a task or series of tasks that must be completed before a successor task starts. A **Lag** is the amount of time whereby a successor activity can be delayed when a predecessor activity starts.

    Fig. 6-10, P 192 *Examples of Lead and Lags*

15. A **Project Schedule Network Diagram** is a graphic representation showing the schedule in a schematic form (P 193). It is the output result of **Sequence Activities.** It shows the logical activity relationships and the various activity dependencies.

    Fig. 6-11, P 193 *Project Schedule Network Diagram*

16. **Estimate Activity Durations** is a **process of estimating the number of work periods** (Days, Weeks, Months, Years) needed **to complete individual activities** with estimated resources (P 195). The key benefit is that it provides the amount of time each activity will take to complete.

    Fig. 6-12, P 195, *Estimate Activity Durations: ITTO's*
    Fig. 6-13, P 196, *Estimate Activity Durations: Data Flow Diagram*

17. Four (4) of the eight (8) ways to **Estimate Activity Durations** (P 200-203) are:

    1. **Analogous Estimating** is a technique in using **historical** data (duration or cost data) from similar projects or activities. This analogous data is useful in estimating project durations, or cost for projects that are similar, yet have limited current data about the assigned project.

    2. **Parametric Estimating** uses an **algorithm** or **statistical relationship** between historical data and the variable to calculate activity parameters such as cost, budget and duration.

    3. **3-Point Estimating** uses a **formula** to compute estimation times for activities. The formula for **Triangular Distribution** is

$$tE = (t0 + tM + tP)/3$$

tE = Time Estimated

tM= Most Likely Time

t0= Optimistic Time

tP= Pessimistic Time

4. **Bottom-Up Estimating** is a method of **summing, aggregating** the project duration or cost, when an activity cannot be estimated within a reasonable degree of confidence. It is done by summing up the lower level components of the Work Breakdown Structure (WBS.)

The other ways to estimate activity durations are: **Expert Judgment; Data Analysis; Decision Making; and Meetings.**

18. **Develop Schedule** (P 205) is a process of analyzing activity sequences, durations, resource requirements and schedule constraints to create a schedule model. This schedule model will be used for project execution/monitoring/controlling. The key benefit is that it generates a **Schedule Model** with **planned dates** for completing project activities.

Fig. 6-14, P 205, *Develop Schedule: ITTO's*
Fig. 6-15, P 206, *Develop Schedule: Data Flow Diagram*

19. **Critical Path Method (CPM)** is a method used to **estimate the minimum project time from start to finish of a project** (P 210.)

Fig. 6-16, P 211 *Example of Critical Path Method*

20. In **Resource Leveling,** start and finish dates are adjusted to balance resource needs with available supplies (P 211). **Crashing,** is when extra resources are supplied to shorten the schedule duration for the least-incremental cost by adding resources. **Fast Tracking** is when activities or phases are done alongside each other to speed up the process (P 215). It is a schedule compression technique.

Fig. 6-17, P 212 *Resource Leveling*
Fig. 6-19, P 215 *Schedule Compression Comparisons*

21. **A Bar Chart** is a diagram representing schedule related data necessary for completion of the project. Also known as a **Gantt Chart**, in which activities, dates, and activity durations are mapped out by way of start and end-dates.

Fig. 6-21, P 211, *Project Schedule Presentation - Examples*

22. **Control Schedule** is a process of ***monitoring project status activities and progress.*** It also includes managing changes to the schedule baseline. In performance reviews, six (6) Data Analysis Techniques can be used, which are (P 222):

    - **Earned Value Analysis** (P 226)
    - **Iteration Burndown Chart** (P 226)
    - **Performance Reviews** (P 227)
    - **Trend Analysis** (P 227)
    - **Variance Analysis** (P 227)
    - **What-If Scenario Analysis** (P 227)

    Fig. 6-22, P 226, *Control Schedule: ITTO's*
    Fig. 6-23, P 227, *Control Schedule: Data Flow Diagram*
    Fig. 6-24, P 226, *Iteration Burndown Chart*

    Be sure to Study/Review the **Data Analysis Techniques** and descriptions.

23. **Control Schedule** (P 226-227) is a process of monitoring project status activities and progress. It also includes managing changes to the schedule baseline. In performance reviews, six (6) Data Analysis Techniques can be used, which are:

    - **Earned Value Analysis** (P 226)
    - **Iteration Burndown Chart** (P 226)
    - **Performance Reviews** (P 227)
    - **Trend Analysis** (P 227)
    - **Variance Analysis** (P 227)
    - **What-If Scenario Analysis** (P 227)

    Fig. 6-24, P 226, *Iteration Burndown Chart*

    Be sure to Study/Review the Data Analysis Techniques and descriptions.

Similar Questions that may be on the PMI Exam related to Chapter 6

1. To determine staffing requirements, the Project Manager first needs a/an ______.

   A. Organization Breakdown Structure
   B. Responsibility Assignment Matrix
   C. Resource Breakdown Structure
   D. Work Breakdown Structure

   Correct Answer is D: On decomposition of work package, activities are defined and resources are estimated for each activity, therefore the WBS is essentially required to come up with the needed staffing requirements.

2. You are a project manager for a major project that has 10 subcontractors. To ensure the best control, you direct the project control section leader to develop a schedule that ______.

   A. Compresses yours and the subcontractors activity durations by ten percent, which will be used as a reserve
   B. Includes the detailed activities of the subcontractors in addition to the details of your work
   C. Excludes any subcontractor schedule because the subcontractors are paid to manage and meet the critical interface dates
   D. Includes interface points for subcontractors and you let the subcontractors develop their detailed schedules for the individual management of time

   Correct Option is B: Any schedule that is developed has to have a realistic schedule. This schedule should include the detailed activities of the subcontractors and the details of your work which can be used for tracking purposes.

3. Mac is executing his Business Process Re-engineering Project when he realizes the resources that were promised at the start of the project are not available presently. What should he do?

   A. Tell management how the resources were originally promised to his project
   B. Re-plan the project without resources
   C. Evaluate and explain the impact if the resources that were promised are not made available
   D. Crash the critical path

Correct option is C: Mac should evaluate the impact and explain the same to those concerned.

4. Which of the following is the best method for briefing project progress (schedule vs. calendar) to management?
   A. Histogram to show percent of work on the project that has been completed
   B. Bar chart of all activities on the summary schedule
   C. Combination of the full (detail) network and the summary network
   D. Network of all activities on the summary schedule

   Correct option is B: Whenever a PM reports project progress, such as an updated schedule to the management, a bar chart of all activities on the summary schedule is used and actual complete shadings and vertical lines represent the actual date.

5. Kathy is a project manager in a Retail company. In her project, she came across a situation where a critical task was delayed by a few days. As the next step, she changed the activities to be done in parallel. Which of the following techniques is used here?

   A. Fast tracking
   B. Crashing
   C. Optimizing schedule
   D. Monitoring and Controlling

   Correct Option is A: Fast tracking is doing work in parallel.

6. You are a certified project management professional working as a project manager at Fly High Airlines. You know that the schedule can often be impacted to the extent that work activity must be accelerated by the increase of people and equipment. The most frequent reason for acceleration is ______.

   A. The project manager believes that the original schedule was not valid and that acceleration is needed to meet the planned end date
   B. An opportunity to place a system in service at an early date forces the owner to impose a new completion date
   C. The progress of work activities was poor in the beginning of the project
   D. An increase or change in the scope of work that must be completed within the original time frame

   Correct answer is D: Whenever there is an increase or change in the scope of work and if it has to be completed within the original time frame, activity duration has to be shortened by increase in resources.

7. John is implementing a CRM project for a telecom service provider to increase customer responsiveness. In between, due to large number of unnecessary changes, the project scope has increased. However, the end date is fixed and cannot be further negotiated. This change in scope may result in which of the following?

   A. Negative slack for the project
   B. Zero slack for the project
   C. Positive slack for the project
   D. Delayed slack for the project

   Correct answer is A: Once the end date is fixed but scope has substantially changed, it can result into negative float for critical activities.

8. Hazel is a project manager in an IT project which is running late. She is considering crashing and fast-tracking, as options to bring the project back on track. Which of the following statements is not true?

   A. She should look for effort-driven activities as those are the only activities that can be crashed
   B. She should be bothered about the risks that can be added due to fast-tracking because if there are any errors, changes, or omissions in the overlapping activities, both activities might be affected.
   C. She should also think of cost, as crashing might add labor and other resources thereby adding to the cost
   D. She should not be bothered with effort-driven activities, as neither crashing, nor fast-tracking is affected by effort-driven activities

   Correct answer is D: Crashing is only valid for activities that are effort-driven activities, adding to the cost and fast tracking leads to risk of rework.

9. Stella is a project manager for a Customer Relationship Management Deployment Project. Her project is running behind the schedule and she needs to crash certain activities to bring the project back on schedule.

   Details of the activities are shown below: Task A, B, and D is on critical path, task C and E are in the near-critical path.

   Task A: Regular time is three weeks, crash time is three weeks, regular cost is

$12,000, and crash cost is $14,000
Task B: Regular time is five weeks, crash time is three weeks, regular cost is $15,000, and crash cost is $25,000
Task C: Regular time is four weeks, crash time is two weeks, regular cost is $16,000, and crash cost is $18,000
Task D: Regular time is six weeks, crash time is three weeks, regular cost is $14,000, and crash cost is $20,000
Task E: Regular time is four weeks, crash time is two weeks, regular cost is $11,000, and crash cost is $12,000

Which of the following lists the tasks in the correct crashing order?

A. Tasks C, B, D
B. Tasks A, D, B
C. Tasks A, B, D
D. Tasks C, E, A

Correct answer is B: Tasks A, B, D are on critical path, crashing them would compress the schedule. In this case, the extra crashing cost per saved week has not been given. Therefore, you need to compute that amount. Because only task A, B, and D are in the critical path, you need to compute crashing cost for these activities alone.

Here is how you can compute the extra crashing cost per saved week

Compute number of saved weeks = regular time – crash time
Find cost difference = regular cost – crash cost
Divide the difference in cost by number of saved weeks

Task A: Regular Weeks = 5, Crash Weeks = 3,
Number of Saved Weeks = 5 – 3 = 2

Regular Cost = 12,000, Crash Cost = 14,000,
Difference in Cost = $14,000 – $12,000 = $2,000
Extra Crashing Cost Per Saved Week (in $) = 2,000 ÷ 2 = 1,000 per week

Task B: Number of Saved Weeks = 2
Difference in Cost = $10,000
Extra Crashing Cost Per Saved Week (in $) = 10,000 ÷ 2 = 5,000 per week

Task D: Number of Saved Weeks = 3
Difference in Cost = 6,000
Extra Crashing Cost Per Saved Week ($) = 6,000 ÷ 3 = 2,000 per week

10. Your project's precedence diagram shows the following activities on two critical paths, D-E-J-K-L and D-E-F-L. Each activity consumes at least four days. If management asks you to reduce the project by two days, which of the activities are most likely to change?

    A. L and D
    B. E and J
    C. K and L
    D. D and E

    Correct answer is D: If we draw the network diagram, we will find that D and E are common activities on the two critical paths.

You may now move on to Chapter Seven: Project Cost Management

Chapter 7: Project Cost Management: Time is Money

"Beware of little expenses. A little leak will sink a great ship." Benjamin Franklin

Student Learning Outcomes

1. List and describe the order of the four (4) process descriptions of **Project Cost Management** (P 231) and explain why project cost management is so very important.
2. What three **(3) general key concepts for Project Cost Management** should the project manager understand (P 233)?
3. New **Trends and Emerging Practices** in project cost management are occurring. What **term** is used to measure the efficiency with which work is being accomplished (P 233)?
4. The project manager may need to **tailor** the manner in which **Project Cost Management (**P 234) processes are applied. List **five (5) Tailoring Cost** considerations.
5. What is the importance of a **Cost Baseline** (P 233)? Identify three **(3) general financial management techniques** useful in **Project Cost Management.**
6. **What is Plan Cost Management and its key benefits (P 235)?**
7. List the eight **(8) elements of the Cost Management Plan** (P 238-239) and the items that can be included as infrastructure details for planning, structuring and controlling costs.
8. **What is Estimate Costs and its key benefit (P 240)? In estimating of costs, Rough Order of Magnitude (ROM) is used (P 241-242). What is ROM and what is its value?**
9. What are the **three (3) components of Scope Baseline** (P 242)?
10. Three Point Estimating is a tool-technique used in **Estimate Costs**. In **Three-Point Estimating** of costs, list three (3) estimates that can be useful to define the approximate ranges for computing an activities cost (P 244)? What two formulas are used in **Triangular and Beta Distributions** (P 245)?
11. Describe what **Determine Budget** means and its key benefits (P 248).
12. What are six **(6) Tools and Techniques** that may be used by the Project Manager in the **Determine Budget Process** (P 252-253)?
13. What are the various **components of the Project Budget and Cost Baseline** and what is **Reserve Analysis** (P 254-255)?
14. **What does it mean to Control Cost and what is the key benefit (257)?**
15. In Control Cost, what are the five **(5) tools and techniques** the Project Manager may find useful (P 260-265)?
16. **Earned Value Analysis (EVA)** is a data analysis methodology that combines scope, schedule and resource measurements to evaluate project progress and performance. What are the four (4) variances that may be computed to help **monitor variations** from the approved cost baseline (P 262-263)?
17. In **Cost Forecasting**, what are the three (3) cost performance methods that are useful when using **EVA** (P 264-265)?
18. What are the **formulas** for **Earned Value Analysis (EVA)?**
    Fig. 7-1, P 267 *Earned Value Calculations Summary*

CHAPTER SEVEN INTRODUCTION: TIME IS MONEY

PROJECT COST MANAGEMENT: CHAPTER 7 OVERVIEW: PMBOK® 6th Edition P 231-270

Project Cost Management is a process. It includes four (4) processes, which are Planning, Estimating, Budgeting, Financing, Managing and Controlling Cost.

(7.1) **Plan Cost Management:** This process defines how the project costs will be documented for estimating, budgeting, managing, monitoring and controlling all project costs.

(7.2) **Estimate Costs:** This process requires the approximation of the monetary resources that are needed to complete all project work that has been defined in the scope statement to complete the project work.

(7.3) **Determine Budget:** This process represents a summation or aggregation of the estimated cost of work packages, or individual activities in order to establish an authorized cost baseline.

(7.4) **Control Cost:** This process requires the project manager and team and selected stakeholders to monitor the status of the project and especially project costs that will be updated as they occur. Any project changes will be managed to the cost baseline.

Fig. 7-1, P 232, *Overview of the Project Cost Management Process*

Key Concepts for Project Cost Management

It is important that project cost management considers all stakeholder requirements. Different stakeholders measure project costs in a variety of ways. Costs are primarily concerned with the cost of resources needed to complete the project. These include all resources such as, material, labor and services that are part and parcel to the project work. Project Cost Management may deal with cost prediction and analysis, and also the use of financial management techniques to calculate return on investment, discounted cash flow and investment payback analysis is important for the project manager to understand (P 233).

Trends and Emerging Practices in Project Cost Management

Earned Value Management (EVM), the concept of **Earned Schedule Theory (ES)** must be understood and applied in the role of the project manager. A popular trend includes the use of **Earned Value Management Systems (EVMS). Earned Schedule Value (ESV)** is an extension of the theory and practice of earned value management. It is important to recognize the project manager needs to certify that the project is handled effectively and efficiently in dealing with cost. There are Earned Value formulas and calculations that are used for forecasting, project completion dates, etc. (P 233).

Fig. 7-1 P 267, *Earned Value Calculations Summary Table*

Study these Formulas:

PV, EV, AC, BAC, CV, SV, VAC, CPI, SPI, EAC (4 Formulas), ETC, and TCPI

Tailoring Considerations (P 234)

The project manager may be required to tailor the way the project cost management processes are applied (P 235). Such considerations include knowledge management, estimating and budgeting, earned value management, use of agile approach, governance, etc. There are two types of environments that a project manager may find he or she will be working in: **Predictive** or **Agile/Adaptive**. Cost estimations will vary based upon the environment of either one or the other.

Plan Cost Management:

Plan Cost Management is the process of defining **how** the project costs will be estimated, budgeted, managed, monitored and controlled. It is very difficult to assess detailed costs in an agile/adaptive environment because of frequent project changes (P 234). In projects that experience rapid changes (i.e. high-variability projects), and that are subject to strict/tight budgets, the scope and the schedule are adjusted more than the cost baseline.

The **key benefit** of this process is that it provides guidance and direction on how the project cost will be managed throughout the project.

See chart on next page: **PLAN COST MANAGEMENT (Section 7.1)**

Chapter Seven: Project Cost Management

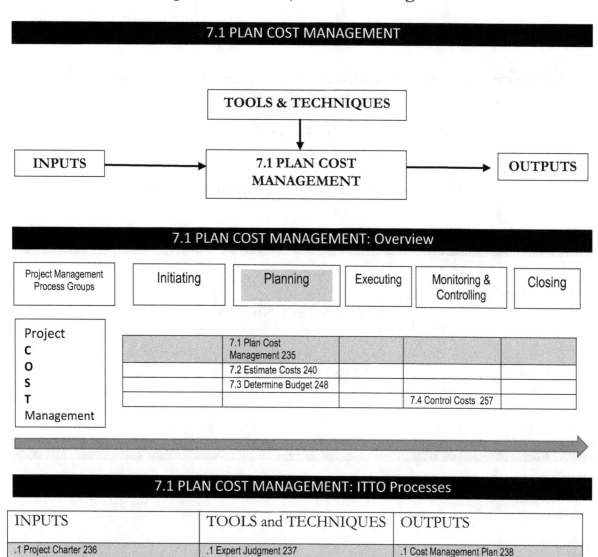

7.1 PLAN COST MANAGEMENT

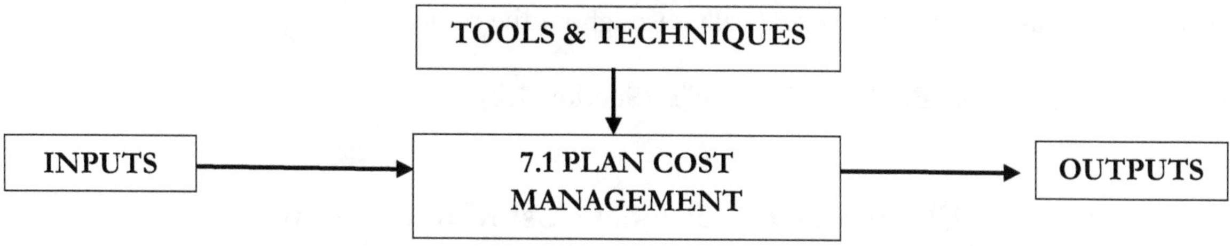

7.1 PLAN COST MANAGEMENT: Overview

Project Management Process Groups	Initiating	Planning	Executing	Monitoring & Controlling	Closing
Project COST Management		7.1 Plan Cost Management 235			
		7.2 Estimate Costs 240			
		7.3 Determine Budget 248			
				7.4 Control Costs 257	

7.1 PLAN COST MANAGEMENT: ITTO Processes

INPUTS	TOOLS and TECHNIQUES	OUTPUTS
.1 Project Charter 236 .2 Project Management Plan 236 • Schedule Management Plan 236 • Risk management Plan 236 .3 Enterprise Environmental Factors 236 .4 Organizational Process Assets 237	.1 Expert Judgment 237 .2 Data Analysis 238 .3 Meetings 238	.1 Cost Management Plan 238

Fig. 7-2, P 235, *Plan Cost Management: Inputs, Tools and Techniques and Outputs*
Fig. 7-3, P 235, *Plan Cost Management: Data Flow Diagram*

<u>Estimate Cost:</u>

Estimate Cost is a process that requires estimating, or making an approximation of the costs of total resources needed to complete the work (P 240).

The **key benefit** of this process is it determines the monetary resources that are required for the project. This is performed periodically throughout the project.

See chart on next page: **ESTIMATE COST (Section 7.2)**

Chapter Seven: Project Cost Management

7.2 ESTIMATE COST

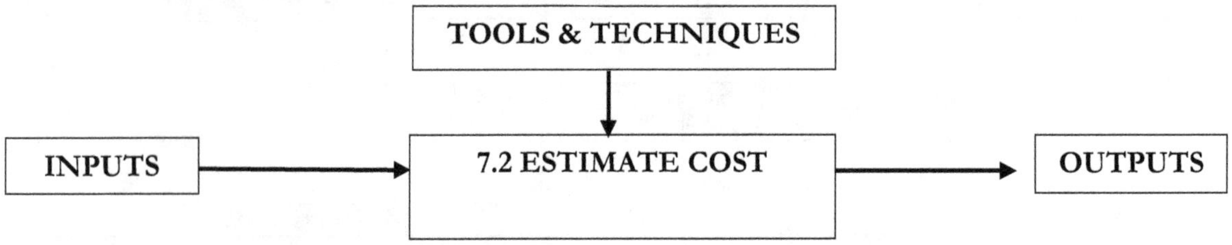

7.2 ESTIMATE COST: Overview

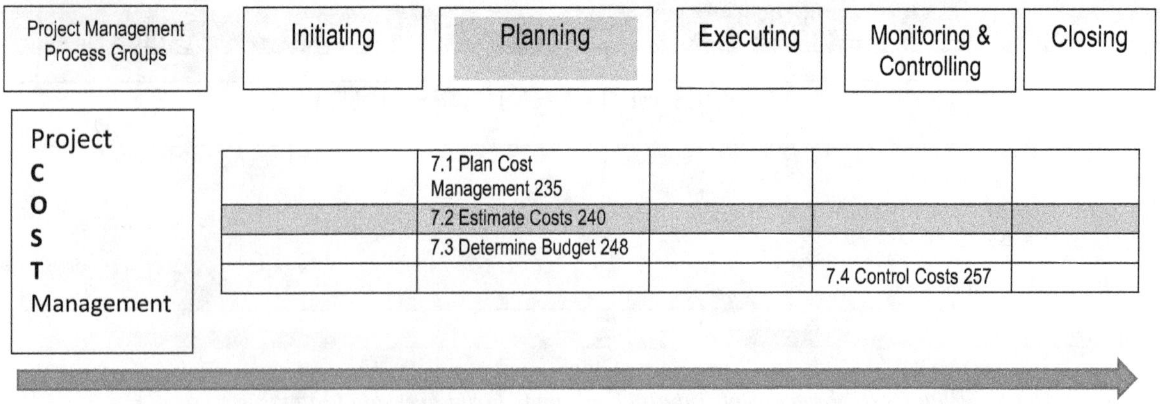

7.2 ESTIMATE COST: ITTO Processes

INPUTS	TOOLS and TECHNIQUES	OUTPUTS
.1 Project Management Plan 241 • Cost Management Plan 241 • Quality Management Plan 241 • Scope Baseline 242 .2 Project Documents 242 • Lessons Learned Register 242 • Project Schedule 242 • Resources Requirements 242 • Risk Register 242 .3 Enterprise Environmental Factors 243 .4 Organizational Process Assets 243	.1 Expert Judgment 243 .2 Analogous Estimating 244 .3 Parametric Estimating 244 .4 Bottom-Up Estimating 244 .5 Three-Point Estimating 244 .6 Data Analysis 245 • Alternative Analysis 245 • Reserve Analysis 245 • Cost of Quality 245 .7 Project Management Information System 246 .8 Decision Making 246 • Voting 246	.1 Cost Estimates 246 .2 Basis of Estimates 247 .3 Project Document Updates 247 • Assumption Log 247 • Lessons Learned Register 247 • Risk Register 247

Fig. 7-4, P 240, *Estimate Cost: Inputs, Tools, Techniques and Outputs*
Fig. 7-5, P 240, *Estimate Cost: Data Flow Diagram*

A cost estimate is a quantitative assessment. It includes the identification and clarification of costing alternatives. In this process, **make vs. buy — buy vs. lease**, and the **sharing of resources** may be evaluated. Cost may have a **Rough Order of Magnitude (ROM).** The ROM of the project initiation phase may have an estimate that may range from -25 to +75%. The definitive estimate of cost in later project stages will have a greater accuracy--the definitive estimate ranges from -5% to +10% of the estimate cost.

Determine Budget:

Determine Budget is the process of summarizing (aggregating) the estimated costs of individual activities on work packages to establish a cost baseline.

The **key benefit** of this process is to determine the cost baseline against which project performance will be monitored and controlled (P 248). Determine Budget is performed once or at predetermined points throughout the project. A project budget includes all authorized funds to execute the project.

See chart on next page: **DETERMINE BUDGET (Section 7.3)**

Chapter Seven: Project Cost Management

7.3 DETERMINE BUDGET

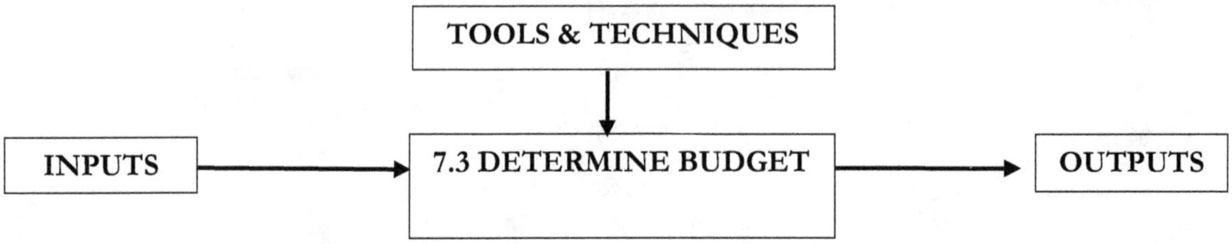

7.3 DETERMINE BUDGET: Overview

Project Management Process Groups	Initiating	Planning	Executing	Monitoring & Controlling	Closing
Project **C O S T** Management		7.1 Plan Cost Management 235			
		7.2 Estimate 240			
		7.3 Determine Budget 248			
				7.4 Control Schedule 257	

7.3 DETERMINE BUDGET: ITTO Processes

INPUTS	TOOLS and TECHNIQUES	OUTPUTS
.1 Project Management Plan 250 • Cost Management Plan 250 • Resource Management Plan 250 • Scope Baseline 250 .2 Project Documents 250 • Basis of Estimates 250 • Cost Estimates 250 • Project Schedule 250 • Risk Register 250 .3 Business Documents 251 • Business Case 251 • Benefits Management Plan 251 .4 Agreements 251 .5 Enterprise Environmental Factors 251 .9 Organizational Process Assets 251	.1 Expert Judgment 252 .2 Cost Aggregation 252 .3 Data Analysis 252 • Reserve Analysis 252 .4 Historical Information Review 253 .5 Funding Limit Reconciliation 253 .6 Financing 253	.1 Cost Baseline 254 .2 Project Funding Requirements 255 .3 Project Documents Updates 255 • Cost Estimates 255 • Project Schedule 255 • Risk Register 255

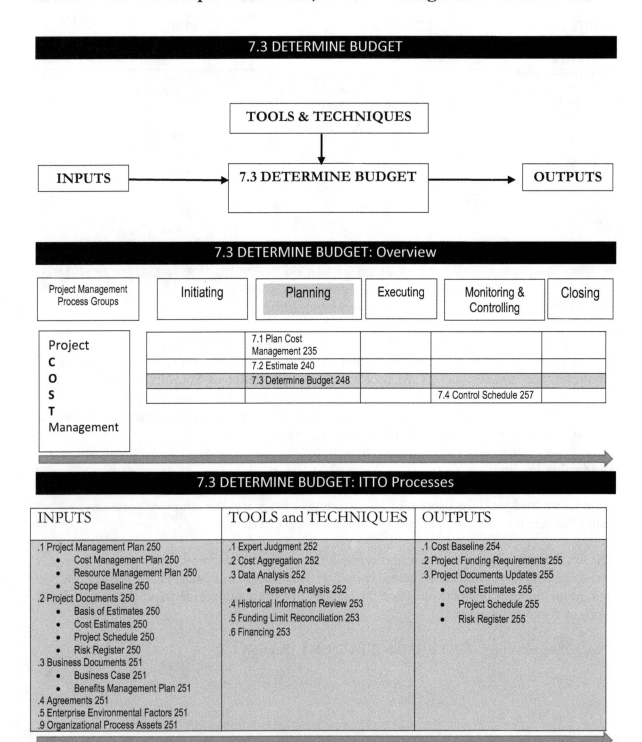

Fig. 7-6, P 248, *Determine Budget: Inputs, Tools, Techniques and Outputs*
Fig. 7-7, P 249, *Determine Budget: Data Flow Diagram*

Control Costs:

Control Costs is the process of monitoring the project status in order to update the project costs and manage changes to the cost baseline.

The **key benefit** of **Control Costs** is that the cost baseline is maintained throughout the project life cycle (P 257).

See chart on this page: **CONTROL COSTS (Section 7.4)**

Chapter Seven: Project Cost Management

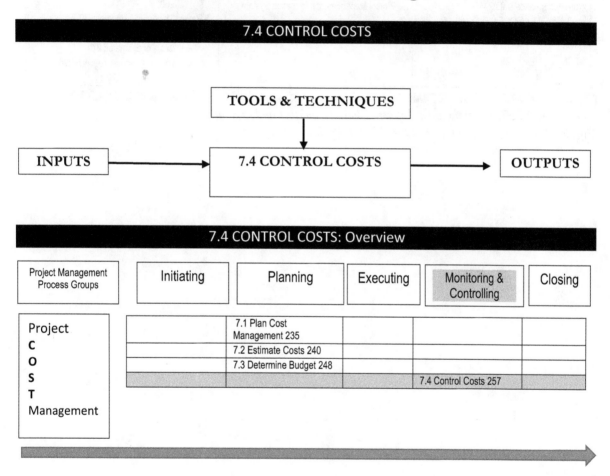

7.4 CONTROL COSTS

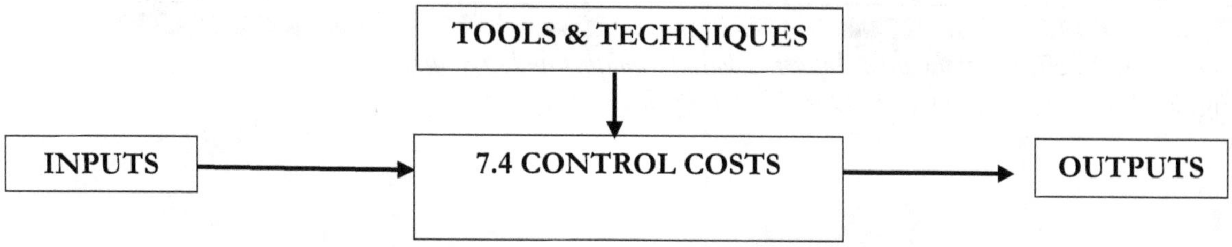

7.4 CONTROL COSTS: Overview

Project Management Process Groups	Initiating	Planning	Executing	Monitoring & Controlling	Closing
Project COST Management		7.1 Plan Cost Management 235			
		7.2 Estimate Costs 240			
		7.3 Determine Budget 248			
				7.4 Control Costs 257	

7.4 CONTROL COSTS: ITTO Processes

INPUTS	TOOLS and TECHNIQUES	OUTPUTS
.1 Project Management Plan 259 • Cost Management Plan 259 • Cost Baseline 259 • Performance Measurement Baseline 259 .2 Project Documents 260 • Lessons Learned Register 244 .3 Project Funding Requirements 244 .4 Work Performance Data 244 .5 Organizational Process Assets 245	.1 Expert Judgment 260 .2 Data Analysis 261 • Earned Value Management 261 • Variance Analysis 262 • Trend Analysis 263 • Reserve Analysis 265 .3 To-Complete Performance Index (TCPI) 266 .4 Project Management Information System 268	.1 Work Performance Information 268 .2 Costs Forecasts 269 .3 Change Requests 269 .4 Project Management Plan Updates 269 • Cost Management Plan 269 • Cost Baseline 269 • Performance Measurement Baseline 269 .5 Project Documents Updates 270 • Assumption Log 270 • Basis of Estimates 270 • Lessons Learned Register 270 • Risk Register 270

Fig. 7-10, P 257, *Control Costs: Inputs, Tools, Techniques and Outputs*
Fig. 7-11 P 258, *Control Costs: Data Flow Diagram*

KEY WORDS: CHAPTER 7

- Planned Cost management
- Estimate Cost Determined
- Budget Control Cost
- Earned Value Management (EVM)
- Schedule Management Plan
- Risk Management Plan
- Sell Funding
- Funding with Equity
- Funding with Debt
- Make vs. Buy
- Purchasing, Leasing, Renting
- Unit of Measure
- Level of Precision
- Level of Accuracy
- Measurement Reporting Format
- Procedure Links
- Control Thresholds
- Rules of Performance Measurement
- Reporting Formats Quantitative Assessment
- Cost Management Plan
- Quality Management Plan
- Scope Baseline
- Lessons Learned Register
- Risk Register
- Published Commercial Information
- Exchange Rates
- Inflation
- Expert Judgment
- Analogous Estimating
- Parametric Estimating
- Bottom-Up Estimating
- Three point Estimating
- Triangular distribution
- Beta Distribution
- Alternative Analysis
- Reserve Analysis
- Cost of Quality

- Project Management Information Systems (PMIS)
- Assumptions Log
- Authorized Cost Baseline
- Project Schedule
- Risk Register
- Business Case
- Benefits Management Plan
- Cost Aggregation
- Funding Limit Reconciliation
- Financing
- Management Reserves
- Control Account
- Work Performance data
- Variance Analysis
- Earned Value Analysis (EVA)
    - Planned Value
    - Earned Value
    - Actual Cost
- Forecasting
- Financial Analysis
- Variance Analysis
    - Schedule Variance
    - Cost Variance
    - Schedule Performance Index
    - Cost Performance Index
- Trends Analysis
    - Charts
    - Forecasting
    - EAC Forecast
    - ETC i.e. work performed at

the budget rate
    - EAC forecast for ETC work
    - Performed at the present (CPI)
    - EAC Forecast for ETC Work Considering both SPI and CPI
- Reserve Analysis-Complete Performance Index
- Table 7-1 Earned Value Management (EVM)

LEGEND

The following Legend shows how to correctly read the *PMBOK® Guide* references and attributions correctly for Chapter 7: Project Cost Management PMBOK Details.

Legend:

Chapter Section	Chapter Section Title	Page Number

Example from Chapter Six shown below:

6.5.1.4	Enterprise Environmental Factors	(P 209)

All direct quotes are attributed as (A Guide to the Project Management Body of Knowledge, *(PMBOK® Guide)* – Sixth Edition) Project Management Institute Inc., 2017, Page #, after each section and any/all paraphrased or original wording is attributed as (P #), before or after each section. All Graphs, Charts, Tables and Figures are attributed as: (*PMBOK® Guide,* Fig. #-# or #/#, P #, *Title of Graph, Chart, Table or Figure*).

7. PROJECT COST MANAGEMENT

Project Cost Management includes all of the approved project work, described in the Project Charter and/or the Project Plan or other associated documents. The processes involved in Project Cost Management are:

- **Plan Cost Management**
- **Estimate Costs**
- **Determine Budget**
- **Control Costs**

Fig. 7-1, P 232, *Plan Cost Management Overview*

Key Concepts for Project Cost Management:

The cost of resources needed to complete project activities is the focus of Project Cost Management (P 233). This means that any project decisions regarding recurring costs of using, maintaining and supporting the product, service or results may have an effect on the overall costs. The PM should also keep in mind that Stakeholders may measure cost efficiency in different ways and at different times.

Trends and Emerging Practices in Project Cost Management:

Emerging Trends include the expansion of Earned Value Management (EVM) and the concept of Earned Schedule (ES), which is an extension to the theory and practice of EVM (P 233). The ES replaces the Schedule Variance measures used in the traditional EVM (earned value – planned value) with ES and actual time (AT). Examples (P 233).

Tailoring Considerations:

Some of the considerations for Tailoring are (P 234):

- **Knowledge Management:**
  - Does the organizational have a formal Knowledge Management and Financial Database Repository that a PM is required to use, and is it readily accessible?
- **Estimating and Budgeting:**
  - Does the organization have an existing formal or informal cost estimating and budgeting-related policies, procedures and guidelines?
- **Earned Value Management:**
  - Does the organization use Earned Value Management in managing

projects?

- **Use of Agile Approach**:
  - Does the organization use Agile Methodologies in managing project?
  - How does this impact cost estimating?
- **Governance**: Does the organization have formal or informal audit and governance policies, procedures and guideline?

Considerations for Agile/Adaptive Environments:

Lightweight estimation methods may be used to calculate fast, high-level forecasts which can be adjusted as changes arise in projects with high levels of uncertainty but in projects with strict budgets, scope and schedule factors are often adjusted to stay within any cost constraints.

7.1 PLAN COST MANAGEMENT

The **Cost Management Plan** is about defining how project costs will be estimated and budgeted (P 235).

The **key benefit** of **Plan Cost Management** is to provide guidance and direction for managing costs.

Fig. 7-2, P 235, *Plan Cost Management: Inputs, Tools and Techniques and Outputs*
Fig. 7-3, P 235, *Plan Cost Management: and Data Flow Diagram*

The **key benefit** of **Plan Cost Management** is to provide guidance and direction for managing costs.

7.1.1 Plan Cost Management: Inputs

7.1.1.1 Project Charter

The summary budget is included in the **Project Charter** which is then used to create detailed project costs (P 236).

7.1.1.2 Project Management Plan

The Project Management Plan may contain some of the following components (P 236):

- **Schedule Management Plan**:
- **Risk Management Plan**:

7.1.1.3 Enterprise Environmental Factors

Enterprise Environmental Factors that affect Plan Cost Management are (P 236):

- Organizational Culture and Structure
- Market conditions describe what products, services and results are available in the regional/global market
- Currency exchange rates from any/all countries connected to the project
- Published management information system
- Productivity differences in different parts of the world

7.1.1.4 Organizational Process Assets

Some **Organizational Assets** that affect Plan Cost Management are (P 237):

- Financial Controls Procedures
- Historical Information
- Financial Databases
- Existing Formal/Informal Cost Estimating and Budgeting-Related Policies, Procedures and Guidelines

7.1.2 Plan Cost Management: Tools and Techniques

7.1.2.1 Expert Judgment

Expert Judgment is a process of gathering historical information, which can provide essential data for the Cost Management plan (P 237).

7.1.2.2 Data Analysis

Data Analysis is a technique, although it is not limited to Alternative Analysis (P 238).

7.1.2.3 Meetings

Meetings may be held to determine what is involved in the Cost management Plan.

7.1.3 Plan Cost Management: Outputs

7.1.3.1 Cost Management Plan

Cost Management Tools and Techniques are included in the **Cost Management Plan** and can provide a basis for the following (P 238):

- **Units of Measure**: Each unit used in measurements is defined for each of the resources
- **Level of Precision**: The degree to which cost estimates will be rounded up or down, based on scope of activities and magnitude of project
- **Level of Accuracy**: The acceptable range used in determining realistic costs estimates
- **Organizational Procedure Links**: The Work Breakdown Structure (WBS) provides the framework for the Cost Management Plan
- **Control Thresholds**: Variance threshold for monitoring cost performance
- **Rules of Performance Measurement**: Earned Value Management (EVM) rules of performance measurement are set, such as those shown below:
    - Define which measurement of control accounts will be permitted
    - Establish the EVM techniques
    - Specify tracking methodologies and the EVM computation equations
- **Reporting Formats**: Formats and frequency for various cost factors are defined
- **Additional Details**: Some of the additional cost management activities are listed below (P 239):
    - Description of strategic funding choices
    - Procedure to account for fluctuations in currency exchange rates
    - Procedure for project cost recording

7.2 ESTIMATE COSTS

7.2 Estimate Costs: Inputs

Estimate Costs is a process to approximate the cost to do the project work.

The **key benefit** is to determine how much money is needed for the entire project.

Fig. 7-4, P 240, *Estimate Costs: Inputs, Tools and Techniques and Outputs*
Fig. 7-5, P 240, *Estimate Costs: Data Flow Diagram*

7.2.1 Estimate Costs: Inputs

7.2.1.1 Project Management Plan

The **Project Management Plan** may contain some of the following components (P 241):

- **Cost Management Plan**: Describes the estimating methods that may be used
- **Quality Management Plan**: Describes the activities and resources needed for the project Management Plan
- **Scope Baseline**: Includes the Project Scope Statement, WBS and WBS Dictionary:
    - **Project Scope Statement**: Reflects funding constraints
    - **Work Breakdown Structure (WBS)**: Provides relationships among all product deliverables
    - **WBS Dictionary** and related detailed **Statements of Work (SOW):** Provides an identification of the Deliverables and a description of the work in each WBS deliverable component

7.2.1.2 Project Documents

Some of the Project Documents that can be considered for the Estimate Costs Process are (P242):

- **Lessons Learned Register**: When creating Cost Estimates, previous Lessons Learned can be applied to improve the accuracy and precision of the Cost Estimates

- **Project Schedule**: Generally created at a high level showing somewhat arbitrary start to end dates and as the project evolves, the schedule becomes detailed to precise and includes the type, activity and amount of time that the team and physical resources will be active on the project.
- **Resource Requirements**: Identify the types and quantities of each resource required for each work package or activity
- **Risk Register**: Contains details of individual project risks and foresees events to manage negative/threats vs. positive/opportunities and other information used to Estimate Costs

7.2.1.3 Enterprise Environmental Factors

Some **Enterprise Environmental Factors** that may reflect on the Estimate Costs processes (P 243):

- **Market Conditions**: A description of what products, services and results are available from the market and under what terms and conditions
- **Published Commercial Information**: resource cost rate information is often available from commercial databases that track skills and human resources costs, while providing standard costs for material and equipment
- **Exchange Rates and Information**: Large scale projects that continue for multiple years with multiple currencies must take into consideration inflation and fluctuations and built into the Estimate Costs process

7.2.1.4 Organizational Process Assets

Some **Organizational Process Assets** that may affect the **Estimate Costs** processes includes (P 243):

- **Cost Estimating Policies**
- **Cost Estimating Templates**
- **Historical Information** and **Lessons Learned Repository**

7.2 Estimate Costs: Tools and Techniques

7.2.2.1 Expert Judgment

Expert Judgement may help to decide which methods to use, or what combinations of methods may work best for the particular project.

7.2.2.2 Analogous Estimating

Analogous Estimating are values such as those shown below can be used as a basis to estimate the parameter or measurement for the current project (P 244):

- Scope
- Budget Cost

Or, these values can be combined with estimating using **Duration or Measures of Scale** like those shown below:

- Size
- Weight
- Complexity

7.2.2.3 Parametric Estimating

Parametric Estimating is a cost estimate is formed by using **Historical Data, combined with other variables,** calculating estimates and then applying this information to the entire project, or just parts of a project (P 244).

7.2.2.4 Bottom-Up-Estimating

Bottom-Up Estimating is used when reporting and tracking specific details and then applied to particular areas of a project, so it can then be summarized to higher levels (P 244).

7.2.2.5 Three-Point Estimating

Three-Point Estimating is "The accuracy of single-point activity may be improved by considering estimation uncertainty and risk using three estimates to define an approximate range for an activity's cost" shown below:

- **Most Likely (cM):** Cost of Activity, based on realistic effort assessment for required work and predicted expenses
- **Optimistic (cO):** Activity cost based on analysis of the best-case scenario for the activity
- **Pessimistic (cP):** Activity cost based on analysis of the worst-case scenario for the activity
- **Triangular Distribution** $\mathbf{cE = (c0 + cM = cP)/3}$
- **Beta Distribution** (from a traditional PERT Analysis). $cE = (c0 + 4cM +$

cP)/6

7.2.2.6 Data Analysis

Some of the **Data Analysis** techniques that can be used in Estimate Costs process are (P 245):

- **Alternative Analysis:** A form of deciding on several alternatives and analyzing each one before making a decision
- **Reserve Analysis:** The process of assembling specific contingency reserves into the project schedule
- **Cost of Quality:** Assumptions about the cost of Quality can be used to prepare estimates

7.2.2.7 Project Management Information System (PMIS)

The **Project Management Information System** may consist of (P 246):

- Spreadsheets
- Simulation Software
- Statistical Analysis Tools

7.2.2.8 Decision Making

Decision-Making Techniques involve an assessment process by the group to arrive at multiple alternatives for future use. Voting may be one of these assessment processes.

7.2.3 Estimate Costs: Outputs

7.2.3.1 Cost Estimates

Quantitative assessments of the probable costs required to complete project work.

7.2.3.2 Basis of Estimates

Basis of Estimates: Some cost estimates may include the following documentation (P 247):

- **Basis of the Estimate**
- **Assumptions** (all)
- **Known Constraints**
- **Range of Possible Estimates**
- **Confidence level of Final Estimate**

7.2.3.3 Project Documents Updates

Project Documents Updates: Updates will most likely will be made to the **Risk Register**, but other documents that may also be updated are shown below (P 247):

- **Assumption Log**: During the Cost Estimates process, new assumptions may be made, new constraints identified, and existing assumptions or constraints may be revisited and changed
- **Lessons Learned Register**: Can be updated with techniques that were efficient and effective in developing cost estimates
- **Risk Register**: May be updated when appropriate risk responses are chosen and agreed upon during the Estimate Cost process

7.3 DETERMINE BUDGET

Determine Budget is "… aggregating the estimated costs of individual activities or work packages to establish and authorize" the cost baseline. Project Management Institute, (A Guide to the Project Management Body of Knowledge, *(PMBOK® Guide)* – Sixth Edition), Project Management Institute Inc., 2017, Page 248. The **key benefit** of this process is that it determines the cost baseline against which project performance can be monitored and controlled.

Fig. 7-6, P 248, *Determine Budget: Inputs, Tools and Techniques and Outputs*
Fig. 7-7, P 249, *Determine Budget: Data Flow Diagram*

7.3.1 Determine Budget: Inputs

7.3.1.1 Project Management Plan

Some of the factors involved in the **Project Management Plan** are (P 250:

- **Cost Management Plan**: Describes how the Project costs will be implemented into the budget
- **Resource Management Plan**: Provides data regarding rates, travel costs, etc. to estimate overall budget
- **Scope Baseline**: Includes Project Scope Statement, WBS and WBS Dictionary details for cost estimation and management

7.3.1.2 Project Documents

Some examples of **Project Documents** used in the Determine Budget process that may be used as Outputs are (P 250):

- **Basis of Estimates:** Used to evaluate how the estimation of durations, costs, resources and cost control compare to actual results
- **Cost Estimates**: Cost estimates for each activity within a work package is aggregated to obtain a cost estimate
- **Project Schedule:** Includes planned start and finish dates for all activities
- **Risk Register**: Updates to the Risk Register are included with Project Document updates

7.3.1.3 Business Documents

Some Outputs of the Determine Budget process are **Business Documents** and are shown below (P 251):

- **Business Case**: Identifies critical success factors for the project
- **Benefits Management Plan**: Includes target benefits

7.3.1.4 Agreements

Agreements: Any costs or information connected to products, services or results will/may be used when determining the budget.

7.3.1.5 Enterprise Environmental Factors

Exchange Rates can be affected by **Enterprise Environmental Factors** and must be understood and built into the Determine Budget process.

7.3.1.6 Organizational Process Assets

Some of the **Organizational Process Assets** that may affect the Determine Budget Process are (P 251):

- Existing formal/informal cost budgeting-related policies, procedures and guidelines
- Historical Information and Lessons Learned Repository
- Cost Budgeting Tools
- Reporting Methods

7.3.2 Determine Budget: Tools and Techniques

7.3.2.1 Expert Judgment

Expert Judgment helps in determining the budget and may include (P 252):

- Previous Similar Projects
- Information in the Industry
- Financial Principles and
- Funding Requirements and Sources

7.3.2.2 Cost Aggregation

Cost Aggregation occurs when work packages are aggregated for higher-level factors in the WBS.

7.3.2.3 Data Analysis

Data Analysis may use **Reserve Analysis** as one technique that may be used in the Determine Budget Process to establish management reserves. If there are changes to the Cost Baseline, management reserves are used.

7.3.2.4 Historical Information Review

Historical Relationships that **result in parametric or analogous estimates** varies and are most likely to be reliable when the following is true (P 253):

- Historical Information used to develop the model is accurate
- Parameters used in the model are readily quantifiable
- Models are scalable

7.3.2.5 Funding Limit Reconciliation

Funding Limit Reconciliation should take place when there is a variance among planned and actual funding limits. This sometimes requires rescheduling to even out expenditures

7.3.2.6 Financing

External **Financing** requires criteria be met by the project needs and an Agreement drawn up between the two parties (P 253). In addition, the funding party may have their own conditions that need to be met before providing resources. This will most likely take place in long-term projects.

7.3.3 Determine Budget: Outputs

7.3.3.1 Cost Baseline

The **Cost Baseline** will be compared to actual cost and is a result of approved budgets for any activities.

Fig. 7-8, P 255, *Project Budget Components*
Fig. 7-9, P 255, *Cost Baseline, Expenditures and Funding Requirements*

7.3.3.2 Project Funding Requirements

Project Funding Requirements, such as total funding and periodic funding requirements are taken from the **Cost Baseline.**

Fig. 7-9, P 214, *Cost Baseline, Expenditures and Funding Requirements*

7.3.3.3 Project Documents Updates

Some of the **Project Documents** that may be updated could include those shown below (P 256):

- **Cost Estimates**: Updated to record any additional data
- **Project Schedule**: Estimated costs for individual activity can be recorded
- **Risk Register**: New Risk identified will be recorded and managed accordingly

7.4 CONTROL COSTS

Control Costs is the process of monitoring the status of the project to update the project costs and managing changes to the cost baseline. This process concerns monitoring the cost burn rate and the status of costs overruns and underages to the estimated budget. The **key benefit** is the cost baseline is maintained.

Fig. 7-10, P 257, *Control Costs: Inputs, Tools and Techniques and Outputs*
Fig. 7-11, P 258, *Control Costs: Data Flow Diagram*

Project Cost Control includes the following (P 259):

- Influencing the factors that create changes to the authorized cost baseline
- Ensure that all change requests are acted on in a timely manner
- Managing the actual changes when and as they occur
- Ensures that cost expenditures do not exceed authorized funding
- Monitor cost performance to isolate and understand variances from the approved cost baseline
- Monitor work performance against funds expended
- Preventing unapproved changes

- Informing appropriate stakeholders of all approved changes and associated costs
- Bringing expected cost overruns within acceptable limits

7.4.1 Control Costs: Inputs

7.4.1.1 Project Management Plan

Controlling Costs in the **Project Management Plan** consists of (P 259):

- **Cost Management Plan**: This describes how the project costs will be managed and controlled
- **Cost Baseline**: This is compared with actual results to determine if a change, corrective action or preventative action is necessary
- **Performance Measurement Baseline**: The Performance Measurement Baseline is compared to actual results

7.4.1.2 Project Documents

One **Project Document** that may be considered as an Input for the Control Costs Process could be the (P 260):

- Lessons Learned Register

7.4.1.3 Project Funding Requirements

Project Funding Requirements are requirements that include projected expenses and liabilities.

7.4.1.4 Work Performance Data

Some of the **Work Performance Data** includes data concerning project progress, such as which cost have been (P 260):

- Authorized
- Incurred
- Invoiced
- Paid

7.4.1.5 Organizational Process Assets

Some of the **Organizational Process Assets** that may affect the **Control Costs** process are (P 260):

- Existing formal/informal cost control-related policies, procedures and guidelines
- Cost Control Tools
- Monitoring and reporting methods to be used

7.4.2 Control Costs: Tools and Techniques

7.4.2.1 Expert Judgment

Some of the Expert Judgments used during the Control Costs Process are shown below (P 260):

- Variance Analysis
- Earned Value Analysis (EVA)
- Forecasting
- Financial Analysis

7.4.2.2 Data Analysis

Some of the **Data Analysis** techniques that can be used to control costs are (P 261):

- **Earned Value Analysis (EVA)**: Compares performance measurement baselines to the actual schedule or cost performance and monitors three (3) key measurements for each work package (P 261):
    - **Planned Value**: An authorized budget assigned to scheduled work
    - **Earned Value**: A measure of work performed
    - **Actual Cost**: The realized cost incurred for the work performed on an activity during a specific time period

- **Variance Analysis**: Used to improve the metrics of the organization by using explanations, impacts and corrective actions for cost and the variance at completion and can include the following (P 262):
    - **Schedule Variance**: A measure of schedule performance

between earned value and planned value

- **Cost Variance**: The amount of budget deficit or surplus at a given point in time expressed as the difference between the earned value and the actual cost
- **Schedule Performance Index**: A measure of schedule efficiency expresses as the ratio of earned value to planned value
- **Cost Performance Index**: A measure of the cost efficiency of budgeted resources expressed as a ration of earned value to actual cost

- **Trend Analysis**: Examines Project performance over time as a way of determining improvement or deterioration using one of the Trend Analysis Techniques known as Forecasting that follows (P 264):
    - **Forecasting**: A Forecast may be developed for the Estimate at Completion that may differ from the Budget at Completion based on project performance, but only three (3) methods are generally used to calculate EAC values (P265):
        - **EAC Forecast for ETC work performed at budgeted rate:**
          Equation: $EAC = AC + (BAC - EV)$
        - **EAC Forecast for ETC work performed at the present CPI:**
          Equation: $EAC = BAC / CPI$
        - **EAC Forecast for ETC work considering both SPI and CPI factors:**
          Equation: $EAC = AC + [(BAC - EV) / (CPI \times SPI)]$

Fig. 7-12, P 264, *Earned Value, Planned Value and Actual Costs*

- **Reserve Analysis**: Used to monitor the **status of contingency** and management reserves for the project to determine if the reserves are still needed or if more are required.

7.4.2.3 To-Complete Performance Index

The **To-Complete Performance Index** is a measure of **Cost Performance**. **The TCPI (Calculated Cost Performance Index)** is completed on remaining work to meet the project's goals, which may be the BAC, or the EAC.

Fig. 7-13, P 268, *To-Complete Performance Index (TCPI)*
Table 7-1, P 267, *Earned Value Calculations Summary Table)*

Study and read carefully P 261-265. This is a very difficult area to comprehend and prepare for the PMI PMP Exam. Numerous formulas need to be memorized, taken from Table 7-1 on the following page.

If you're looking for more clarification, please see *Project Cost Management*, by Emily Berry, MBA, PMP, CAPM, at: https://www.youtube.com/watch?v=gY1RNbOVRrU (18 minutes) based upon the PMBOK 5th edition, though the concept and application are compatible with the PMBOK 6th edition.

Earned Value Analysis

Abbreviation	Name	Lexicon Definition	How Used	Equation	Interpretation of Result
PV	Planned Value	The authorized budget assigned to scheduled work.	The value of the work planned to be completed to a point in time, usually the data date, or project completion.		
EV	Earned Value	The measure of work performed expressed in terms of the budget authorized for that work.	The planned value of all the work completed (earned) to a point in time, usually the data date, without reference to actual costs.	EV = sum of the planned value of completed work	
AC	Actual Cost	The realized cost incurred for the work performed on an activity during a specific time period.	The actual cost of all the work completed to a point in time, usually the data date.		
BAC	Budget at Completion	The sum of all budgets established for the work to be performed.	The value of total planned work, the project cost baseline.		
CV	Cost Variance	The amount of budget deficit or surplus at a given point in time, expressed as the difference between the earned value and the actual cost.	The difference between the value of work completed to a point in time, usually the data date, and the actual costs to the same point in time.	CV = EV - AC	Positive = Under planned cost Neutral = On planned cost Negative = Over planned cost
SV	Schedule Variance	The amount by which the project is ahead or behind the planned delivery date, at a given point in time, expressed as the difference between the earned value and the planned value.	The difference between the work completed to a point in time, usually the data date, and the work planned to be completed to the same point in time.	SV = EV - PV	Positive = Ahead of Schedule Neutral = On schedule Negative = Behind Schedule
VAC	Variance at Completion	A projection of the amount of budget deficit or surplus, expressed as the difference between the budget at completion and the estimate at completion.	The estimated difference in cost at the completion of the project.	VAC = BAC - EAC	Positive = Under planned cost Neutral = On planned cost Negative = Over planned cost
CPI	Cost Performance Index	A measure of the cost efficiency of budgeted resources expressed as the ratio of earned value to actual cost.	A CPI of 1.0 means the project is exactly on budget, that the work actually done so far is exactly the same as the cost so far. Other values show the percentage of how much costs are over or under the budgeted amount for work accomplished.	CPI = EV/AC	Greater than 1.0 = Under planned cost Exactly 1.0 = On planned cost Less than 1.0 = Over planned cost
SPI	Schedule Performance Index	A measure of schedule efficiency expressed as the ratio of earned value to planned value.	An SPI of 1.0 means that the project is exactly on schedule, that the work actually done so far is exactly the same as the work planned to be done so far. Other values show the percentage of how much costs are over or under the budgeted amount for work planned.	SPI = EV/PV	Greater than 1.0 = Ahead of schedule Exactly 1.0 = On schedule Less than 1.0 = Behind schedule
EAC	Estimate At Completion	The expected total cost of completing all work expressed as the sum of the actual cost to date and the estimate to complete.	If the CPI is expected to be the same for the remainder of the project, EAC can be calculated using:	EAC = BAC/CPI	
			If future work will be accomplished at the planned rate, use:	EAC = AC + BAC - EV	
			If the initial plan is no longer valid, use:	EAC = AC + Bottom-up ETC	
			If both the CPI and SPI influence the remaining work, use:	EAC = AC + [(BAC - EV)/ (CPI x SPI)]	
ETC	Estimate to Complete	The expected cost to finish all the remaining project work.	Assuming work is proceeding on plan, the cost of completing the remaining authorized work can be calculated using:	ETC = EAC - AC	
			Reestimate the remaining work from the bottom up.	ETC = Reestimate	
TCPI	To Complete Performance Index	A measure of the cost performance that must be achieved with the remaining resources in order to meet a specified management goal, expressed as the ratio of the cost to finish the outstanding work to the budget available.	The efficiency that must be maintained in order to complete on plan.	TCPI = (BAC - EV)/(BAC - AC)	Greater than 1.0 = Harder to complete Exactly 1.0 = Same to complete Less than 1.0 = Easier to complete
			The efficiency that must be maintained in order to complete the current EAC.	TCPI = (BAC - EV)/(EAC - AC)	Greater than 1.0 = Harder to complete Exactly 1.0 = Same to complete Less than 1.0 = Easier to complete

Table 7-1 (Guide). Earned Value Calculations Summary Table

7.4.2.4 Project Management Information Systems (PMIS)

Three **EVM** dimensions (PV, AV and AC), may be monitored using **Project Management Information Systems (P 268).**

7.4.3 Control Costs: Outputs

7.4.3.1 Work Performance Information

Work Performance Information is comparing how the work is being performed vs. the Cost Baseline. Earned Value Analysis is calculated using CV, SV, CPI, SPI, TCPI and VAC values for WBS components and then logged and communicated to the Stakeholders (P 268).

7.4.3.2 Costs Forecasts

Cost Forecasts are calculated EAC values or, a bottom-up EAC will be recorded and conveyed to stakeholders (P 269).

7.4.3.3 Change Requests

Change Requests may occur if an analysis of the project's performance deems it necessary

7.4.3.4 Project Management Plan Updates

Some Factors of the **Project Management Plan** that might be updated may include (P 269):

- **Cost Management Plan**: Changes to this plan are in direct response to Stakeholders feedback
- **Cost Baseline**: Changes are made in response to changes in scope, schedule performance or cost estimates or variances
- **Performance Measurement Baseline**: Changes are in responses to approved changes in scope, schedule performance or cost estimates

7.4.3.5 Project Documents Updates

Project Documents that might be updated (P 270):

- **Assumption Log**: Cost performance may indicate the need to revise assumptions on resource productivity and other factors influencing cost performance

- **Basis of Estimate**: Cost performance may indicate the need to revisit the actual cost efficiency for the project
- **Cost Estimates**: May need updating to reflect the actual cost efficiency for the project
- **Lessons Learned Register**: Updated with techniques that were effective in maintaining the budget, variance analysis, earned value analysis, forecasting and corrective actions that were used to respond to cost variances
- **Risk Register**: May be updated if the cost variances have crossed, or are likely to cross the Cost threshold

Summary: Answers to Student Learning Outcomes

1. **Project Cost Management** four (4) Process Steps, in sequence, are (P 231):

    1. **Plan Cost Management:** The process of defining how the project costs will be estimated, budgeted, managed, monitored and controlled
    2. **Estimate Costs:** The process of developing an approximation of the monetary resources needed to complete project work
    3. **Determine Budget:** The process of aggregating the estimated costs of individual activities or work packages to establish an authorized cost baseline
    4. **Control Costs:** The process of monitoring the status of the project to update the project costs and manage changes to the cost baseline

    It is very important to know that these processing categories are clearly logical and inter- and intra-dependent. One cannot **manage** costs, unless one knows how to **plan** costs, **estimate** costs, **determine the budget** and **control** the cost expenditures for that project. The accuracy of the earlier descriptions of the work planned in Project Scope Management and Project Schedule Management knowledge areas must be documented before project costs can be accurately assessed. Anything short of precision in the findings and decisions derived in these two (2) knowledge areas will immediately pose a threat associated with cost management.

    Fig. 7-1, P 232, *Project Cost Management Overview*

2. The Project Manager needs to understand the following three (3) key concepts related to Project Cost Management (P 233):

    - **Return on Investment**
    - **Discounted Cash Flow**
    - **Investment Payback Analysis**

3. The Project Manager needs to measure work efficiency. The **Schedule Performance Index** (SPI) using earned value metrics has replaced the schedule variance measurements used in traditional **Earned Value Measurement** (EVM) analysis (P 233).

4. The following are **Cost Tailoring approaches** (P 234):

- **Knowledge Management**
- **Estimating and Budgeting**
- **Earned Value Management**
- **Use of Agile Approach**
- **Governance**

5. The **Cost Baseline** (P 233) is used as a basis of comparison to actual results (P 748), and is important because it is the financial foundation point in time that establishes the overall budget for the project or that phase. This baseline forms the funding level from which money will be withdrawn and used to pay for the project work. This approved money fund is used from the start of the project or phase to the end of the project/phase.

   The three (3) general **Financial Management Techniques** regarding *cost predictions and analysis* are (P 233):

   1. **Return on Investment**
   2. **Discounted Cash Flow**
   3. **Investment Payback Analysis**

6. **Plan Cost Management** (P 235) is a process that needs special attention by the Project Manager (PM) and their team. It is a process of defining how the project costs will be estimated, budgeted, managed, monitored and controlled.

   Fig. 7-2, P 235, *Plan Cost Management: ITTO's*
   Fig. 7-3, P 236, *Plan Cost Management: Data Flow Diagram*

   The **key benefit** of this process is to provide guidance and direction on how the project costs will be managed as the project work evolves and project deliverables/milestones are met throughout the project.

7. **Plan Cost Management,** a component of the Project Management Plan**,** as stated above, is a process using various types of documentation to manage costs/funds throughout the entire duration of the project/phase (P 238-239). The **Cost Management Plan** is the output of Plan Cost Management. The **Cost Management Plan** describes how the project costs will be planned, structured, and controlled and includes documented elements outlined below:

- **Units of Measure**
- **Level of Precision**
- **Level of Accuracy**
- **Organizational Procedure Links**
- **Control Thresholds**
- **Rules of Performance Measurement**
- **Reporting Formats**
- **Additional Detail**

Read and study this very carefully

8. **Estimate Costs** is the process of developing an approximation of the cost of all resources needed to complete project work (P 246). Its **key benefit** is that it determines the monetary resources required to complete the project. ROM is, at best, a **Rough Order of Magnitude** of all project costs. This is completed *before* the project detail costs are determined. *Estimating Costs* is a process of developing an approximation of the cost of resources to complete the project work (P 241). Cost estimates are, at best, a *prediction* of what it will cost to do a project/phase at a given point in time, whether you are at the start, middle, or near the end of the project/phase.

   Fig. 7-4, P 240 *Estimate Costs: Inputs, Tools & Techniques and Outputs*
   Fig. 7-5, P 240, *Estimate Costs: Data Flow Diagram*

9. The **Scope Baseline** is input to the process, Estimating Costs. It is comprised of three (3) components (P 242):

   - **Project Scope Statement:** Reflects funding constraints by period
   - **Work Breakdown Structure:** Shows relationships among all the project deliverables
   - **WBS Dictionary**: Provides an identification of the deliverables and descriptions of the work in each EBS deliverable component

   Study and read these components as detailed on P 242.

10. **Three Point Estimating** is a tool used in **Estimate Costs**. There are three (3) approximate cost range estimates used to determine this based upon a single activity in cost estimates. They are (P 244):

- **Most Likely (cM):** Cost of the activity, based on realistic effort
- **Optimistic (cO):** Cost of activity, based on analysis and best-case scenario
- **Pessimistic Cost (cP):** Cost of activity based on worst-case scenario

In Three Point Estimating, the **Triangular Distribution** and **Beta Distribution Formulas** (P 248-249) are used to clarify the range of uncertainty around expected costs.

Triangular Distribution: $cE = (cO + cM + cP)/3$

Beta Distribution: $cE = (cO + 4cM + cP)/6$

11. **Determine Budget** is a process of summing up (i.e. aggregating or totaling-up) the estimate costs of the project's work packages or individual activities to establish an **authorized cost baseline.** Its **key benefit** is it determines the cost baseline against which **project performance** can be monitored and controlled (P 248).

Fig. 7-6, P 254, *Determine Budget: Inputs, Tools & Techniques and Outputs*
Fig. 7-7, P 255, *Determine Budget: Data Flow Diagram*

12. In **Determine Project Budget**, the following six (6) tools and techniques can be useful (P 252-253):
    - **Expert Judgment**
    - **Cost Aggregation**
    - **Data Analysis (Reserve Analysis)**
    - **Historical Information Review**
    - **Funding Limit Reconciliation**
    - **Financing**

13. There are three **(3) Project Budget Components** in the **Project Cost Baseline.** These components can be used once they are established to make the budget more flexible, as it is often difficult to estimate needed funds to do project work. The three (3) Components are (P 254-255):
    - **Management Reserves**
    - **Contingency Reserves**
    - **Activity Contingency Reserves**

Fig. 7-8, P 254 *Project Budget Components*
Fig. 7-9, P 255 *Cost Baseline, Expenditures and Funding Requirements*

The ***Project Cost Baseline*** is the approved version of the time phased project budged excluding any management reserves. When the ***Cost Baseline Budget*** is exceeded, then the PM may, through Change Control, tap into these applicable funds to shore up needed monies. In the area of Cost Control, the PM must determine if additional money reserves (i.e. contingent or management reserves are still needed (P 254). By freeing up these funds, the PM can consider their use in other projects.

Reserve Analysis is an analytical technique used to determine essential features and relationships of cost components in the Project Management Plan. This analysis is used to establish a reserve for the schedule, duration, budget, estimated costs or funds for a project (P 719)

14. **Control Costs i**s a process of monitoring project status to update project costs and to manage changes to the Cost Baseline. This process requires the PM to monitor the financial status of the project's progress and to manage changes to the project work in order that the work is completed within the agreed upon cost baseline. The **key benefit** of Control Costs is to maintain the cost baseline throughout the project.

    Fig.7-10, P 257 *Control Costs: Inputs, Tools & Techniques and Outputs*
    Fig.7-11, P 258 *Control Costs: Data Flow Diagram*

15. There are **five (5) Control Costs Tools and Techniques** that all PM's should have a deep knowledge. They are (P 260-265):

    1. **Expert Judgment**
    2. **Earned Value analysis (P 261)**
    3. **Variance Analysis (P 262)**
    4. **Trend Analysis (P 263)**
    5. **Reserve Analysis (P 265)**

16. **Earned Value Analysis (EVM)** (P261) is a methodology that encompasses the performance measurement base line to the actual schedule and cost performance. EVM can be used in any industry. The **key costs dimensions** that may be used to develop and monitor the financials of each work package and control account are:

    1. **Planned Value (P** 261)
    2. **Earned Value** (P 261)
    3. **Actual Costs** (P 261)

Four (4) **Variance Analysis** that may be computed to help monitor variations from the approved cost schedule baselines are (P 262-263):

1. **Schedule Variance**
2. **Cost Variance**
3. **Schedule Performance Index**
4. **Cost Performance Index**

17. In **Cost Forecasting**, the three (3) Cost Performance Reviews that are useful when using EVM are (P 264-265):

    1. **EAC (Estimate at Completion) Forecast for ETC (Estimate to Complete)** work performed at the budgeted rate.
       Equation: $EAC = AC + (BAC - EV)$
    2. **EAC (Estimate at Completion) Forecast for ETC (Estimate to Complete)** work performed at the present Cost Performance Index (CPI).
       Equation: $EAC = BAC/CPI$
    3. **EAC (Estimate at Completion) Forecast for ETC (Estimate to Complete)** work performed considered using both SPI (Schedule Performance Index) and CPI (Cost Performance Index) factors.
       Equation: $EAC = AC + [(BAC - EV) / (CPI \times SPI)]$

18. The ***EVA formulas (calculations)*** that need to be understood and memorized are:

    Table 7-1, P 267, *Earned Value Calculations Summary Table*

    This is an arduous task of memorization and a very difficult area to master, and requires your focus and devoted time. There will multiple PMP exam questions using some of these formulas.

    No one passes the PMP exam <u>without knowing and understanding</u> **Estimated Value Analysis** (EVA).

Similar Questions that may be on the PMI Exam related to Chapter 7

1. A contingency allowance is fixed at 9% of a total project cost to cover risks. When the project nears completion, money remaining in the contingency fund is ______.

   A. Spent to ensure that there is no extra money shown in the budget
   B. Reduced to decrease unnecessary extra accounting work
   C. Reduced to reflect the true percentage of work performed
   D. Retained at the balance level

   Correct answer is D: When the project is at completion stage, balance contingency funds are reduced from the planned budget at completion so as to get a true reflection of percentage of work performed or the earned value.

2. The seller delivers a fixed price plus incentive fee project at a cost of $90,000. The terms of the contract are a ceiling price of $120,000, a target cost of $100,000, a target profit of $10,000, and a target price of $110,000. The share ratio is 70/30. The final price (your total reimbursement) would be ______.

   A. $93,000
   B. $96,000
   C. $97,000
   D. $103,000

   Correct answer is D: Target profit is $10,000 and the actual cost is $90,000, which is below the target of $100,000. The saving is $100,000 – $90,000 = $10,000. The share ratio is 70/30, which means 70% for buyer and 30% for seller. It also means that the seller gets 30% of $10,000 or $3,000. The seller will now get $90,000 (actual cost) + $10,000 (target profit) + incentive of $3,000 = $103,000.

3. Your project has received a cost and schedule jolt. The variances that caused the problems are identified as atypical. Assume that the budget is $120,000, EV is $75,000 and CPI is 0.8. What is the ETC?

   A. $47,000

B. $40,000
C. $35,000
D. $45,000

Correct answer is D: Since the variances are atypical, we will use the following formula
ETC = BAC – EV = 120,000 – 75,000 = $45,000

4. You are a project manager in a children's toys manufacturing company. Your project team is in the process of designing a new toy for the Christmas season. The project is progressing well and you are in the process of assessing project performance. The project was estimated to cost $4,000 per month and an additional expense of $4,000. The project is halfway through the five-month project and is progressing as per plan. What is the earned value (EV) of the project?

A. $8,000
B. $12,000
C. There is not enough information
D. $10,000

Correct answer is B:
BAC = (4,000 × 5) + 4,000 = 24,000
Percentage complete = 50%
EV = 24,000 × 50 = 12,000

5. You are a manager of a construction project. You are responsible to install 900 wardrobes in a few new residential towers. You have installed 350 wardrobes so far. As per the schedule, you should have installed 400 planned wardrobes. The project contract states, you shall be paid a fixed price of $75 per wardrobe installation. However, you have already spent $45,000 on the project. Considering your situation, what possible actions could you take as a project manager?

A. Fast tracking
B. Value analysis
C. A and B
D. Revisit the assumptions made for balance jobs

Correct answer is C: Total budget sanctioned = 900 × $75 = $67,500

Actual cost spent = $45,000
EV = 350 ÷ 900 × $67,500 = $26,250
PV = 400 ÷ 900 × $67,500 = $29,970
CPI = EV ÷ AC = $26,250 ÷ $45,000 = 0.583
SPI = EV ÷ PV = $26,250 ÷ $29,970 = 0.876

Considering that the project is running behind the schedule, and over the budget, it would be prudent to fast track and do a value analysis. This would have no reduction in scope and quality and perform at a lesser cost.

6. You are a project manager for the children's toys manufacturer. Your project team is in the process of designing a new children's toy for the Christmas season. The project is progressing well and you are in the process of assessing project performance. If AC is greater than the PV for a project with SPI equal to 1, what does that mean?

   A. The project is under the planned cost
   B. The project is over the planned cost
   C. The project is on the planned cost
   D. Planned Cost cannot be determined

   Correct answer is B: With SPI equal to 1; EV is equal to PV. When AC is greater than EV, then the CPI is less than 1, making the project over the planned cost.

7. You are managing a software engineering project when two team members come to you with a conflict. The lead developer has identified an important project risk: you have a subcontractor that may not deliver on time. The team estimates that there is a 40% chance that the subcontractor will fail to deliver. If that happens, it will cost an additional $15,250 to pay your engineers to rewrite the work, and the delay will cost the company $20,000 in lost business. Another team member points out an opportunity to save money in another area to offset the risk. If an existing component can be adapted, it will save the project $4,500 in engineering costs. There is a 65% probability that the team can take advantage of that opportunity. What is the expected monetary value (EMV) of these two things?

   A. Minus$14,100
   B. $6,100
   C. Minus $11,175

D. $39, 750

Correct answer is C: To calculate the expected monetary value (EMV) of a set of risks and opportunities, multiply each probability by its total cost and add them together. In this question, the cost of the risk is -$15,250 + -$20,000 = -$35,250, so its EMV is 40% x -$35,250 = -$14,100. The value of the opportunity is $4,500 and its probability is 65%, so its EMV is 65% x $4,500 = $2,925. The total EMV for the two is -$14,100 + $2,925 = -$11,175.

8. Stella is working on a project which has a budget at completion (BAC) of $850,000.00 and is 24 months long. As on date her project is 35% complete, while it was supposed to be 40% complete at present. She has also reported that $425,000.00 has already been spent on the project. Her project sponsor wants to know the performance level the remaining work of the project must achieve to meet the budget. Which statement is true?

A. Her sponsor has asked for to-complete performance index (TCPI) which is 0.7
B. Her sponsor has asked for to-complete performance index (TCPI) which is 1.3
C. Her sponsor has asked for estimate at completion (EAC) which is $789,286.00
D. Her sponsor has asked for estimate to complete which is $789,286.00

Correct answer is B: Her sponsor wants to know the To-Complete Performance Index (TCPI) i.e., Projected performance level the remaining work of the project must achieve to meet the Budget at Completion (BAC). TCPI = (BAC-EV) / (BAC-AC) BAC = 850000 EV = 297500 AC = 425000 TCPI = (850000-297500)/(825000-425000) = 552500/425000 = 1.3.

9. Kiran is working on a project as a project manager. Her earned value is less than actual cost. Which statement holds true?

A. Her project is under budget
B. Her project is over budget
C. Her project is behind the schedule
D. Her project is ahead of schedule

Correct answer is B: Based on the information available EV is less than AC which means CPI is less than 1. Project is over budget.

10. You are a project manager for a project which is budgeted at $13,750. As of the date, the project was supposed to be 45% complete, but after a complete review it is revealed that only 40% is complete. The amount already spent is $6,000. What is the current status of the project?

    A. Project is over budget and behind schedule
    B. Project is under budget and ahead of schedule
    C. Project is on budget and on schedule
    D. Project is complete

Correct option is A: To determine if a project is on schedule and on budget, one has to know the CPI (Cost Performance Index) and SPI (Schedule Performance Index). In order to calculate CPI and SPI one has to know the Earned Value (EV) and Present Value (PV) EV = 40% of the Budget = 40% $13,75.00 = $5,500.00 PV = 45% of Budget = 45% $13,750.00 = $6,187.50 CPI = EV/AC = 5500.00/6000.00 = 0.92 SPI = EV/PV = 5500.00/6187.50 = 0.89 Since, CPI is less than 1 it indicates the project is over budget and since SPI is less than 1 it indicates the project is behind schedule.

You may now move on to Chapter Eight: Project Quality Management

Chapter 8: Project Quality Management: Produce Quality – Always

PMI, PMP, CAPM, PMI-ACP, PMI-RMP, PMI-SP and *PMBOK® Guide* are registered marks of the Project Management Institute, 2017 and all references, from this point on, are from the Project Management Institute, (A Guide to the Project Management Body of Knowledge, *(PMBOK® Guide)* – Sixth Edition).

"Quality is not an Act, it is a Habit." Aristotle

Student Learning Outcomes

1. Describe in detail why Project Quality Management is so very important (P 271-272)?
2. There are three (3) process components of Project Quality Management. List the order sequence of the process components of Project Quality Management and the ITTO's (P 271-272).
3. The project team must have a working knowledge of statistical control. What is the difference between the following pairs (P 274)?
    - **Prevention and Inspection**
    - **Attribute Sampling and Variable Sampling**
    - **Tolerances and Control Limits**
4. What is the difference between **Quality and Grade** (P 274)?
5. Wisdom suggests that quality management objectives seek to minimize quality variation, delivery, and defined stakeholder requirements, and seek International Organization for Standardization (ISO) compatibility standards. What are the **four (4) trends and emerging Project Quality Management practices** and approaches (P 275)?
   5a. List four (4) tailoring considerations and how agile/adaptive environments shape quality outcomes (P 276). What is Control Quality (P 298)?
6. **What are the objectives and the key benefits of the process, Plan Quality Management (P 277)?**
7. What are the five (5) elements that may be used as input to develop the Quality Management Plan, Quality Metrics, Project Management Plan Updates and Project Document Updates
   (P 277)?
8. Does the **Risk Register**, an input to Plan Quality Management, report information on threats and opportunities that may affect quality requirements (P 280)?
9. **What is meant by Cost of Quality (COQ) (P 274 and P 282)?**
10. What are the Outputs of Plan Quality Management? See Fig. 8-3 and Fig. 8-4, P 277-278.
11. Which of the Outputs of Plan Quality Management describes how the PM Teams will meet the quality requirements set for the Project (P 241)?
12. **What is Manage Quality and its benefits (P 288)?**
13. **What is meant by Control Quality and its benefits?** In **Control Quality**, there are four (4) basic Quality Control Tools and Techniques used in Data Gathering. What are these four Quality Control tools and Techniques (P 277)?

CHAPTER EIGHT INTRODUCTION: PRODUCE QUALITY – ALWAYS

PROJECT QUALITY MANAGEMENT: CHAPTER 8 OVERVIEW: PMBOK® 6th Edition P 271-306

Project Quality Management requires that the participating company or the organization for which you, as a project manager is assigned, uses a quality policy. This quality policy needs to include activities for planning, managing, controlling the project as well as the product quality requirements. The quality will need to meet stakeholder objectives and standard quality compliances.

The Project Quality Management process includes:

(8.1) **Planned Quality Management** This is the process of identifying quality requirements or standards for the project and its deliverables and documents how the project will demonstrate compliance with quality requirements and standards.

(8.2) **Manage Quality** This is the process of translating the quality management plan into executable quality activities that incorporates the organizational quality policies.

(8.3) **Control Quality** This is the process of monitoring and reporting the results of the project manager executing the quality management activities to assess performance and ensure the projects outputs are complete, correct and meet customer requirements.

See Fig. 8 – 1, P 272, *Project Quality Management Overview*
See Fig. 8 – 2, P 273, *Project Quality Management Process Interrelations*

Key Concepts for Project Quality Management

Quality measures and techniques are specific to the types of deliverables that are being produced by the project. It is important that quality management principles are followed. The project and product quality must meet customer requirements. Be sure not to overwork the project team in achieving quality requirements that are not well specified. Rushing planned quality inspections often results in undetected errors to increase profits and post implementation risk. Two (2) terms that are important in the area of quality management are (P 274):

1. Quality (and)
2. Grade

They are not the same concepts. It is important that the project manager's team understands the difference between quality and grade. Cost of quality (COQ) includes all costs to achieve the highest quality required by the project. Failure costs (called cost of poor quality) may be classified as internal and external (P 274).

Trends and Emerging Practices

Project quality management must include customer satisfaction, continual improvement, management responsibility and mutually beneficial quality partnerships with suppliers.

Tailoring Considerations should include:

1. Policy compliance and auditing to quality standards
2. Standards and regulatory compliance
3. Continuous improvement or stakeholder engagement

Considerations for Agile/Adaptive Environments

In the agile approach, quality and frequent review are common and built into the project life cycle. Additionally, agile methods will focus on small batches of work incorporating many elements of the project. This should aid in uncovering inconsistencies in quality.

Plan Quality Management:

Plan quality management is a process of identifying quality requirements and standards for the project and its deliverables and documenting how the project will comply with quality standards.

Manage Quality process drawn out: 6th Edition of PMBOK (7:44 minutes), by The Crowd Training, at https://www.youtube.com/watch?v=84fpY8b2G10

See chart on next page: **PLAN QUALITY MANAGEMENT (Section 8.1)**

Chapter Eight: Project Quality Management

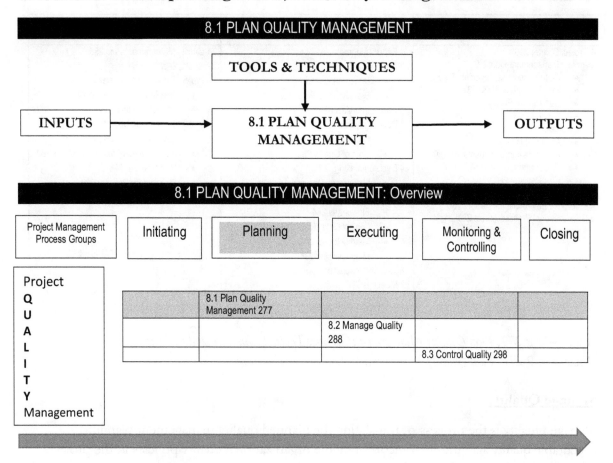

8.1 PLAN QUALITY MANAGEMENT

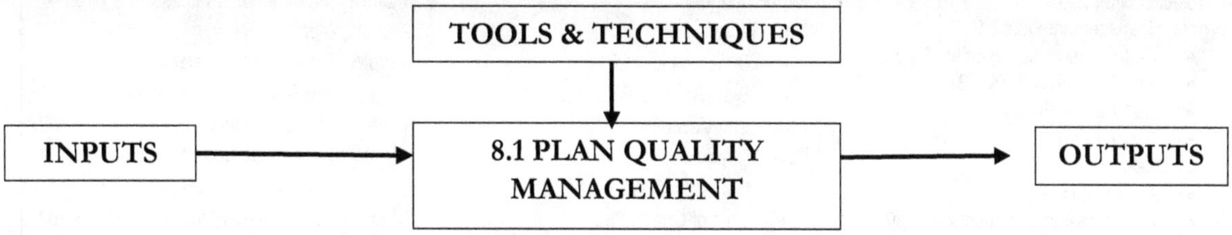

8.1 PLAN QUALITY MANAGEMENT: Overview

Project Management Process Groups	Initiating	Planning	Executing	Monitoring & Controlling	Closing
Project QUALITY Management		8.1 Plan Quality Management 277			
			8.2 Manage Quality 288		
				8.3 Control Quality 298	

8.1 PLAN QUALITY MANAGEMENT: ITTO Processes		
.1 Inputs	.2 Tools and Techniques	.3 Outputs
.1 Project Charter 279 .2 Project Management Plan 279 • Requirements Management Plan 279 • Risk Management Plan 279 • Stakeholder Engagement Plan 279 • Scope Baseline 279 .3 Project Documents 280 • Assumption Log 280 • Requirements Documentation 280 • Requirements Traceability Matrix 280 • Risk Register 280 • Stakeholder Register 280 .4 Enterprise Environmental Factors 280 .5 Organizational Process Assets 281	.1 Expert Judgment 281 .2 Data Gathering 281 • Benchmarking 281 • Brainstorming 281 • Interviews 282 .3 Data Analysis 282 • Cost Benefit Analysis 282 • Cost of Quality 282 .4 Decision Making 283 • Multicriteria Decision Analysis 283 .5 Data Representation 284 • Flowcharts 284 • Logical Data Model 284 • Matrix Models 284 • Mind Mapping 284 .6 Test and Inspection Planning 285 .7 Meetings 286	.1 Quality Management Plan 286 .2 Quality Metrics 267 .3 Project Documents Updates 267 • Risk Management Plan 267 • Scope Baseline 268 .4 Project Documents Updates 268 • Lessons Learned Register 268 • Requirements Traceability Matrix 268 • Risk Register 268 • Stakeholder Register 268

Fig. 8-3, P 277, *Plan Quality Management: Inputs, Tools, Techniques and Outputs*
Fig. 8-4, P 278, *Plan Quality Management: Data Flow Diagram*

Manage Quality:

Manage Quality is the process of translating the planned quality management plan into executable quality activities that incorporate the organizational quality policies in the project. The **key benefit** is that it provides guidance and direction on how quality will be managed and verified throughout the project life cycle. The **key benefit** is that it increases the probability of meeting the quality objectives as well as identifying ineffective processes and causes of poor quality.

See chart on next page: **MANAGE QUALITY (Section 8.2)**

Chapter Eight: Project Quality Management

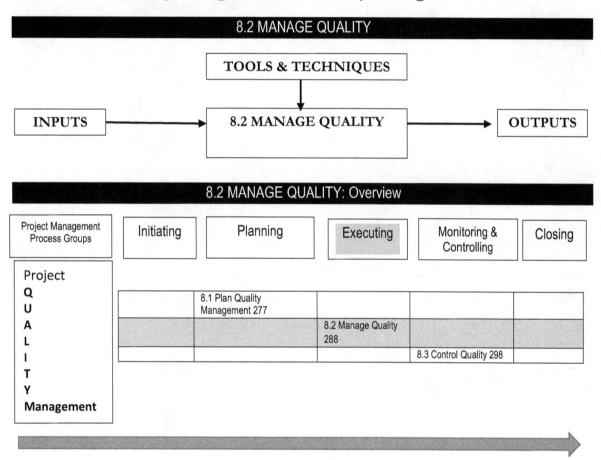

8.2 MANAGE QUALITY

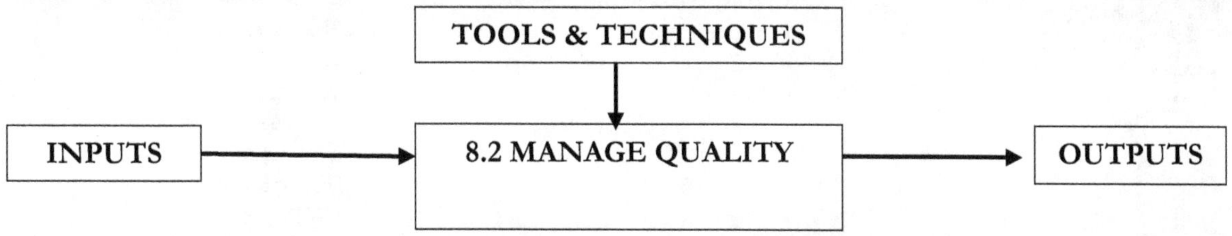

8.2 MANAGE QUALITY: Overview

Project Management Process Groups	Initiating	Planning	Executing	Monitoring & Controlling	Closing
Project **QUALITY Management**		8.1 Plan Quality Management 277			
			8.2 Manage Quality 288		
				8.3 Control Quality 298	

8.2 MANAGE QUALITY: ITTO Processes

.1 Inputs	.2 Tools and Techniques	.3 Outputs
.1 Project Management Plan 290 • Quality Management Plan 290 .2 Project Documents 291 • Lessons Learned Register 291 • Quality Control Measurement 291 • Quality Metrics 291 • Risk Report 291 .3 Organizational Process Assets 291	.1 Data Gathering 292 .2 Data Analysis 292 • Alternative Analysis 292 • Document Analysis 292 • Lessons Learned Register 292 • Process Analysis 292 • Root Cause Analysis 292 .3 Decision Making 293 • Multicriteria Decision Analysis 293 .4 Data Representation 293 • Affinity Diagrams 293 • Cause and Effect Diagrams 293 • Flowcharts 293 • Histograms 293 • Matrix Diagrams 293 • Scatter Diagrams 293 .5 Audits 294 .6 Design for X (DfX) 294 .7 Problem Solving 295 .8 Quality Improvement Methods (296)	.1 Quality Reports 296 .2 Test and Evaluation Documents 296 .3 Change Requests 296 .4 Project Management Plan Updates 297 • Quality Management Plan 297 • Scope Baseline 297 • Schedule Baseline 297 • Cost Baseline 297 .5 Project Documents Updates 297 • Issue Log 297 • Lessons Learned Register 297 • Risk Register 297

Fig. 8-7, P 289, *Manage Quality: Inputs, Tools, Techniques and Outputs*
Fig. 8-8, P 289, *Manage Quality: Inputs, Tools, Techniques and Outputs*

Control Quality:

Control Quality is the process of monitoring and recording results of executing the quality management activities and to assess performance and ensure the project outputs are complete and meet customer expectations. The **key benefit** of this process is to verify that the product deliverables and work meets the key stakeholder requirements for final acceptance.

See chart on next page: **CONTROL QUALITY (Section 8.3)**

Chapter Eight: Project Quality Management

8.3 CONTROL QUALITY

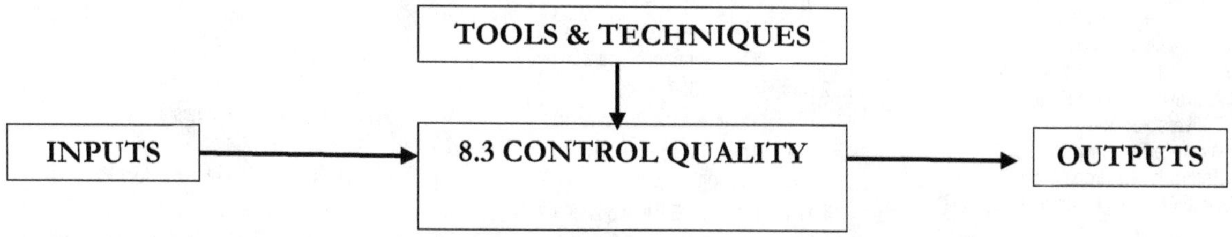

8.3 CONTROL QUALITY: Overview

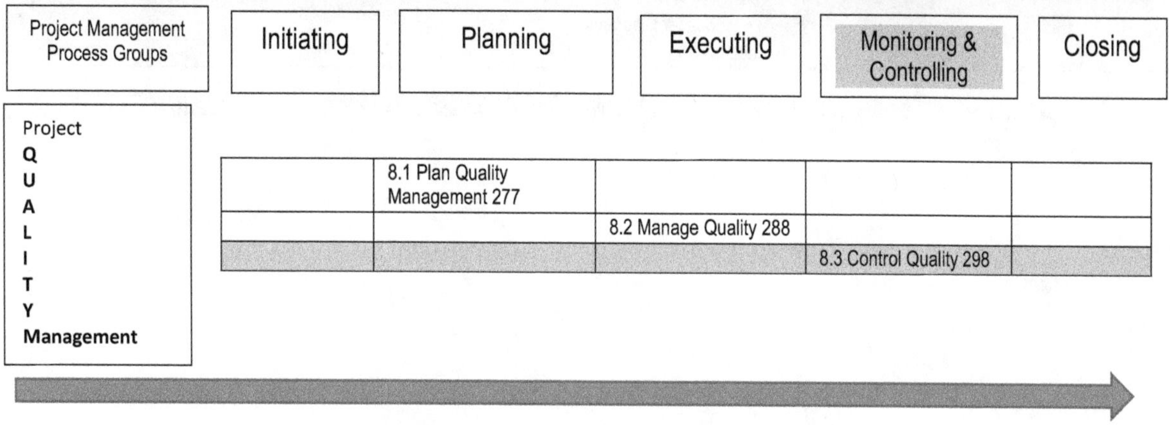

8.3 CONTROL QUALITY: ITTO Processes

.1 Inputs	.2 Tools and Techniques	.3 Outputs
.1 Project Management Plan 300 • Quality Management Plan 300 .2 Project Documents 300 • Lessons Learned Register 300 • Quality Metrics 300 • Task And Evaluation Documents 300 .3 Approved Change Requests 301 .4 Deliverables 300 .5 Work Performance Data 300 .6 Enterprise Environmental Factors 300 .7 Organizational Process Assets 302	.1 Data Gathering 302 • Checklists 302 • Check Sheets 302 • Statistical Sampling 302 • Questionnaires and Surveys 302 .2 Data Analysis 303 • Performance Reviews 303 • Root Cause Analysis 303 .3 Inspection 303 .4 Testing Product Evaluations 303 .5 Data Representation 304 • Cause and Effect Diagrams 282 • Control Charts • Histogram • Scatter Diagrams .6 Meetings 305	.1 Quality Control Measurements 305 .2 Verified Deliverables 305 .3 Work Performance Information 305 .4 Change Requests 306 .5 Project Management Plan Updates306 • Quality Management Plan 306 .6 Project Documents Updates 306 • Issue Log 306 • Lessons Learned Register306 • Risk Register 306 • Test and Evaluation Documents 306

CHAPTER 8 KEY WORDS

- Customer satisfaction
- Continual improvement
- PDCA
- TQM six sigma
- Lean six sigma
- Management responsibility
- Policy compliance and auditing
- Continuous improvement
- Batches of work
- Risk management plan
- Stakeholder engagement plan assumptions log
- Scope baseline
- Benchmarking
- Brainstorming
- Interviews
- Cost-benefit analysis
- Cost of quality
- Prevention cost
- Appraisal cost
- Failure cost
- Decision-making
- Data representation
- Flowcharts
- Logical data model
- Matrix diagram model
- Mind mapping
- Test inspection planning
- Requirements traceability matrix
- Quality control measurements
- Quality metrics
- Risk report
- Alternatives analysis
- Document analysis
- Process analysis
- Root cause analysis RCA
- Data representation
- Affinity diagrams

- Cause-and-effect diagrams
- Ishikawa diagrams
- Fishbone diagrams
- Flowcharts
- Histograms
- Matrix diagrams
- Scatter diagrams
- Audits
- Design for X (DfX)
- Schedule baseline
- Cost baseline
- Issues log
- Level of effort
- Work performance data
- Data Gathering
- Checklist
- Check sheets
- Statistical sampling
- Questionnaires and surveys data analysis
    - Performance reviews
- Root cause analysis
- Data representation
- Cause-and-effect diagrams control charts
- Histograms
- Scatter diagrams
- Meetings
- Retrospective/lessons learned

LEGEND

The following Legend shows how to correctly read the *PMBOK® Guide* references and attributions correctly for Chapter 8: Project Quality Management PMBOK Details.

Legend:

Chapter Section	Chapter Section Title	Page Number

Example from Chapter Six shown below:

6.5.1.4	Enterprise Environmental Factors	(P 209)

All direct quotes are attributed as (A Guide to the Project Management Body of Knowledge, *(PMBOK® Guide)* – Sixth Edition) Project Management Institute Inc., 2017, Page #, after each section and any/all paraphrased or original wording is attributed as (P #), before or after each section. All Graphs, Charts, Tables and Figures are attributed as: (*PMBOK® Guide,* Fig. #-# or #/#, P #, *Title of Graph, Chart, Table or Figure*).

8. PROJECT QUALITY MANAGEMENT

Project Quality Management is the process of incorporating the organization's quality policies regarding planning, managing and controlling the project quality requirements in order to meet stakeholder objectives, and supports continuous process improvement activities (P 271).

8.1 PROJECT QUALITY MANAGEMENT

Project Quality Management is the process of knowing the quality requirements of the project and the product (P 271). The **key benefit** of this process is that it provides guidance and direction on how quality will be managed and verified throughout the project.

The processes involved in Project Quality Management are:

- **Plan Quality Management**
- **Perform Quality Assurance**
- **Control Quality**

Fig. 8-1, P 272, *Project Quality Management Overview*
Fig. 8-2, P 273, *Major Project Quality Management Process Interrelations*

Key Concepts for Project Quality Management:

Project Quality must deal with the management of the project and the deliverables of the project. Quality measures and techniques are specific to the project and to the type of project deliverables being produced. For example: Software deliverables are different than the deliverables of a nuclear power plant. They use different approaches and measurements.

There is a difference between Quality and Grade as shown below. Also, know the difference between prevention and inspection, attribute sampling, tolerances and control limits (P 274):

- **Quality**: The degree to which a set of inherent characteristics fulfill requirements
- **Grade**: A design intent, and a category assigned to deliverables having the same functional use but different technical characteristics

Prevention is preferred over inspection and the following descriptions are important to know (P 274):

- **Prevention**: Keeping errors out of the process

- **Inspection**: Keeping errors out of the hands of the customers
- **Attribute Sampling**: The result either conforms or does not conform
- **Variable Sampling**: The result is rated on a continuous scale that measure the degree of conformity
- **Tolerances**: A specified range of acceptable results
- **Control Limit**: Identifies the boundaries of common variation in a statistically stable process or process performed

The Cost of Quality (COQ) includes all costs incurred over the life of the project.

Shown below are five (5) levels of increasingly effective Quality Management (P 275):

1. The most expensive approach is to let the customer find the defects
2. Detect and correct the defects before the deliverables are sent to the customer
3. Use quality assurance to examine and correct the process itself and not just special defects
4. Incorporate quality into the planning and designing of the project and product
5. Create a culture throughout the organization that is aware and committed to quality in processes and product

Trends and Emerging Practices in Project Quality Management:
Some of the Trends in project Quality Management to minimize variation and deliver quality results to the stakeholders are (P 275):

- **Customer Satisfaction**:
- **Continual improvement**: The **Plan-Do-Check-Act (PDCA)** cycle is the basis for quality improvement
- **Management Responsibility**: Success requires the participation of all members of the Project Team
- **Mutually beneficial partnership with suppliers**: An organization and its suppliers are interdependent, therefore building long-term relationships with suppliers

Tailoring Considerations:

Some Tailoring Considerations to keep in mind are (P 276):

- **Policy Compliance and Auditing**:
  - What Quality Policies and Procedures exist in the Organization?

  - What Quality, Tools, Techniques and Templates are used in the organization?
- **Standard and Regulatory Compliance**:
  - Are there any Quality specific standards in the industry that should be applied?
  - Are there any specific governmental, legal or regulatory constraints that need to be taken into consideration?
- **Continuous Improvement**:
  - How will Quality improvement be managed in the project?
  - Is it managed at the organizational level or at the level of each project?
- **Stakeholder Engagement**:
  - Is there a collaborative environment for Stakeholders and Suppliers?

Consideration for Agile/Adaptive Environments (P 276):

- Agile methods require frequent quality and review steps to be managed throughout the project
- Root causes of issues need to addressed on a regular basis and trials set up to ensure they are working, not working, or need to be continued or discontinued
- Focus is on small increments, incorporating any new methods to weed out any processes that are not to the benefit of the project when project costs are lower

8.1 Plan Quality Management

Plan Quality Management is the process of identifying quality requirements and standards for the project, its deliverables and documentation of how quality requirements and standards will be demonstrated. The **key benefit** of this process is that it provides guidance and direction on how quality will be managed and verified throughout the project (P 277).

Fig. 8-3, P 277, Plan Quality Management: *Inputs, Tools and Techniques and Outputs*
Fig. 8-4, P 278, Plan Quality Management: *Data Flow Diagram*

8.1.1 Plan Quality Management: Inputs

8.1.1.1 Project Charter

The **Project Charter** is essential to managing Stakeholders because it contains data such as (P 279):

- High-Level Project Descriptions
- Product Characteristics
- Project Approval Requirements
- Measurable Project Objectives
- Related Success Criteria

8.1.1.2 Project Management Plan

Some of the factors involved in the **Project Management Plan** are (P 279):

- **Requirements Management Plan**: Provides an approach for identifying, analyzing and managing requirements of the Quality Management Plan
- **Risk Management Plan:** Provides an approach for identifying, analyzing and monitoring risks
- **Stakeholder Management Plan**: Provides the method for documenting the Stakeholders needs and expectations
- **Scope Baseline**: The WBS, deliverables, constraints and assumptions documented in the Scope Baseline are considered when determining quality standards and objectives suitable for the project

8.1.1.3 Project Documents

Some of the **Project Documents** that can be considered as Inputs for the Plan Quality Management Process are shown below (P 280):

- **Assumption Log**: All the Assumptions and Constraints regarding Quality Requirements and Standard Compliance are recorded
- **Requirements Documentation**: Any Requirements the project or product should adhere to regarding Stakeholder needs or expectations are recorded
- **Requirements Traceability Matrix**: Quality requirements are specified and recorded and helps to ensure testing of each requirement, while the matrix provides an overview of the tests required
- **Risk Register**: Contains recorded data regarding threats and opportunities
- **Stakeholder Register**: Identifies Stakeholders with a particular interest or impact on quality

8.1.1.4 Enterprise Environmental Factors

Some of the **Enterprise Environmental Factors** that may affect the Plan Quality Management are (P 280):

- Government Agency Regulations
- Rules, Standards and Guidelines
- Geographic Distribution
- Organizational Structure
- Marketplace Conditions
- Working or Operating Conditions
- Cultural Perceptions

8.1.1.5 Organizational Process Assets

Organizational Process Assets that may affect the Plan Quality Management are (P 281):

- Organizational Quality Management System
- Quality Templates
- Historical Databases
- Lessons Learned Repository

8.1.2 Plan Quality Management: Tools and Techniques

8.1.2.1 Expert Judgment

Expert Judgement is known as expertise in a defined application area, such as a Subject Matter Expert (SME) and this group or person will make appropriate judgments for any activities.

Expertise should be taken into consideration on the following topics concerning Plan Quality Management (P 281):

- Quality Assurance
- Quality Control
- Quality Measurements
- Quality Improvements
- Quality Systems

8.1.2.2 Data Gathering

Some of the **Data Gathering** techniques used in the Plan Quality Management process are (P 281):

- **Benchmarking**: Used when comparing one business model to another of similar origin and deciding which practices are best performed, or to identify needed improvements (P 281).
- **Brainstorming**: The collection of multiple ideas related to project and product requirements
- **Interviews**: **Interviews** can be informal or formal, implicit or explicit, in which a conversation takes place between the interviewer(s) and interviewee(s)

8.1.2.3 Data Analysis

Some of the **Data Analysis** techniques that can be used in the Plan Quality Management process are (P 282):

- **Cost Benefit Analysis**: The purpose of using this tool is to compare the actual cost to the expected benefit
- **Cost of Quality**: Some of the costs of quality are listed below (P 282):
    - Prevention Costs
    - Appraisal Costs
    - Failure Cost

See (PMBOK® Guide, Fig. 8-5, P 283, *Cost of Quality)* for examples.

8.1.2.4 Decision Making

In **Decision Making, Multicriteria Decision Analysis** can be used for this process to identify key issue and any suitable alternatives.

8.1.2.5 Data Representation

Some of the **Data Representation** techniques that can be used in the Plan Quality Management process are (P 284):

- **Flowcharts** (Process Maps): Displays a sequence of steps and branching possibilities to transform one or more Inputs into one or more Outputs

- **Logical Data Model**: Visual representation of an organization's data
- **Matrix Diagrams**: Finds the strengths of relationships among different factors
- **Mind Mapping**: Diagrammatic Method used to visually organize data

See (PMBOK® Guide, Fig. 8-6, P 285, *The SIPOC Model*).

8.1.2.6 Test and Inspection Planning

The PM and the Project Team must determine how to execute all the processes to meet the project requirements through **Test Inspection and Planning** and satisfy the demands of the Stakeholders at the same time (P 285).

8.1.2.7 Meetings

Quality Control **Meetings** are designed for the discussion/development of Plan Quality Management (P 286).

8.1.3 Plan Quality Management: Outputs

8.1.3.1 Quality Management Plan

The **Quality Management Plan** is part of the Project Management Plan, which ensures how quality is monitored and managed within the project. It discusses how applicable policies, procedures and guidelines will be implemented to achieve the quality objectives. It should be reviewed early in the project to avoid quality rework later in the project. This also includes specific details of how the project team will/should meet those requirements. The Quality Management Plan also contains some of the following components, but not all are listed here (P 286):

- Quality Standards
- Quality Objectives
- Quality Roles
- Project Deliverables and Processes
- Quality Control and Management Activities
- Quality Tools
- Major Procedures relevant to the project

8.1.3.2 Quality Metrics

Quality Metrics are the decisions made about a product or the product's attributes and determines how quality is measured and what the value is to the project itself (P 287).

8.1.3.3 Project Management Plan Updates

Some of the components that may require changes or **Updates** to the **Project Management Plan** are (P 287):

- **Risk Management Plan**: Produced as an Output of the Plan Risk Management process
- **Scope Baseline**: Includes the Project Scope Statement, Work Breakdown Structure (WBS) and the WBS Dictionary

8.1.3.4 Project Documents Updates

Some of the **Project Documents** that may be updated are (P 287):

- **Lessons Learned Register**: Lessons Learned from previous projects
- **Requirements Traceability Matrix**: Quality requirements are specified and recorded
- **Risk Register**: New Risks are identified and recorded
- **Stakeholder Register**: New or additional information about Stakeholders are recorded

8.2 MANAGE QUALITY

Manage Quality (Quality Assurance) is the process of translating the quality management plan into executable quality activities that incorporate the organization's project quality policies (P 288).

The **key benefit** is to increase the probability of meeting quality objectives as well as identifying ineffective processes and causes of poor quality (P 288). The **key benefit** of this process is it increases the probability of meeting the quality objectives as well as identifying ineffective processes and causes of poor quality.

Fig. 8-7, P 288, *Manage Quality: Inputs, Tools and Techniques and Outputs*
Fig. 8-8, P 289, *Manage Quality: Data Flow Diagram*

Planned and systematic acts and processes should be designed to help manage quality. They are (P 290):

- Design an optimal and mature produce with specific design guidelines
- Build confidence that a future output will be completed to meet desired requirements
- Confirm the Quality processes are used correctly in order to meet quality objectives
- Improve the efficiency and effectiveness of process and activities to achieve the best results

Quality is considered the work of everyone in the project (P 290).

8.2.1 Manage Quality: Inputs

8.2.1.1 Project Management Plan

The **Project Management Plan** defines an acceptable level for project and product quality. The plan also determines what actions to do in case of nonconformity.

8.2.1.2 Project Documents

Some of the **Project Documents** used in the Quality Control Process are (P 291):

- **Lessons Learned Register**: Lessons Learned from previous projects
- **Quality Control Measurements**: Insures that quality standards are applicable to the specific project/product being developed throughout the project life cycle
- **Quality Metrics:** Decisions made about a product or the product's attributes and determines how quality is measured and what the value is to the project itself
- **Risk Report**: Used in the Manage Quality process to identify sources and drivers of risk to the project that will/may affect quality

8.2.1.3 Organizational Process Assets

Some of the **Organizational Process Assets** used that may affect the Quality Control Process are (P 291):

- Organizational Quality Management System
- Quality Templates
- Previous Audit Results
- Lessons Learned Repository

8.2.2 Manage Quality: Tools and Techniques

8.2.2.1 Data Gathering

One of the **Data Gathering** techniques that may be used at this point is **Checklists**, which is a structured tool containing the acceptance criteria for a project (P 292).

8.2.2.2 Data Analysis

Some of the **Data Analysis** techniques that may be used are (P 292):

- **Alternative Analysis**: A form of deciding on several alternatives and analyzing each one before making a decision
- **Document Analysis**: Used to elicit requirements. This is done by analyzing documentation relevant to requirements
- **Process Analysis**: Process Analysis requires observing a process to find and identify any needed improvements.
- **Root Cause Analysis**: The process of identifying a problem at its core and taking action to prevent or correct the risk

8.2.2.3 Decision Making

One of the tools that may be used at this point is **Multicriteria Decision Making**, which is used to evaluate several criteria before making a choice.

8.2.2.4 Data Representation

Some of the **Data Representation** techniques that may be used in the Manage Quality Process are (P 293):

- **Affinity Diagrams**: Organize potential causes of defects showcasing areas in need of correction
- **Cause and Effect Diagrams (Ishikawa or Fishbone Diagrams)**: Identifies causes and effects
  Fig. 8-9, P 294, *Cause-and-Effect Diagrams*
- **Flowcharts**: Displays sequence of steps, branching loops and possibilities
- **Histograms**: Bar Chart used to describe central tendency, dispersion and shape of a statistical distribution
- **Matrix Diagrams**: Shows strengths of relationships among factor factors, causes and objectives
- **Scatter Diagrams**: Plot ordered pairs used to explain changes

8.2.2.5 Audits

An **Audit** is a structured process which determines if a project complies with all of the policies, process and procedures. Some of the objective for the project will include (P 294):

- Identify all good and best practices being used
- Identify any nonconformity, gaps and shortcomings
- The sharing of good practices form previous similar projects
- Proactively offering assistance in a positive manner
- Highlighting contributions of each audit

8.2.2.6 Design for X (DFX)

Design for X (DfX) is a set of technical guidelines. These guidelines may be used in the product design or a designated part of the design. The X factor in DfX can apply to characteristics of the final product.

8.2.2.7 Problem Solving

Problem Solving methods usually include the following steps (P 295):

1. **Define the Problem**
2. **Identity Root Causes**
3. **Generate Possible Solutions**

4. **Choose the Best Solution**
5. **Implement Solution**
6. **Verify Solution Effectiveness**

8.2.2.8 Quality Improvement Methods

Two of the most common **Quality Improvement Methods** are Six Sigma and Plan-Do-Check-Act (P 296).

8.2.3 Manage Quality: Outputs

8.2.3.1 Quality Reports

The most common forms of Quality Reports (graphical, numerical or qualitative) can be used to determine any needed corrections and perform the necessary actions in order to meet Quality objectives (P 296).

8.2.3.2 Test and Evaluation Documents

Test and Evaluation Documents are Inputs to the Quality Control Process, which may include dedicated checklists and detailed requirements, and are used to determine project quality expectations (P 296).

8.2.3.3 Change Requests

Change Requests are carried out during the Perform Integrated Change Control Process. They are processes used to take action when changes occur during the Manage Quality process (P 296).

8.2.3.4 Project Management Plan Updates

Some of the Project Management Plan Updates are data that may be updated are shown below (P 297):

- **Quality Management Plan**: The process used to control Quality
- **Scope Baseline**: Includes the Project Scope Statement, Work Breakdown Structure (WBS) and the WBS Dictionary
- **Schedule Baseline**: Approved schedule with start and finish dates
- **Cost Baseline**: Accepted time intervals to measure cost performance

8.2.3.5 Project Documents Updates

Some of the Project Documents that may be updated are (P 297):

- **Issue Log**: Documents issues that arise and assigns the responsibility to team members who must resolve a specific issue(s) by agreed upon targeted dates
- **Lessons Learned Register**: History of organizational structures that worked, challenges that were met and risk avoidances in previous projects
- **Risk Register**: Documents Risk characteristics and identifies new risks

8.3 CONTROL QUALITY

Control Quality is the process of monitoring and recording the results of executing the quality management activities in order to assess performance and to ensure that the outputs meet customer requirements. The **key benefit** of **Control Quality** is that it is used to verify project deliverables and work meet the requirements (quality) specified by key stakeholders for final acceptance.

Fig. 8-10, P 298, *Control Quality: Inputs, Tools and Techniques*
Fig. 8-11, P 299, *Control Quality: Data Flow Diagram*

8.3.1 Control Quality: Inputs

8.3.1.1 Project Management Plan

The **Project Management Plan** includes the **Quality Management Plan**, which defines how control quality will be performed (P 300).

8.3.1.2 Project Documents

Some of the **Project Documents** that may be considered Inputs for the Control

Quality process are as follows (P 300):

- **Lessons Learned Register**: History of organizational structures that worked, challenges that were met and risk avoidances in previous projects
- **Quality Metrics**: Describes a Project or Product attribute and how the Control Process will verify compliance
- **Test and Evaluation Documents**: Used to evaluate achievement of quality objectives

8.3.1.3 Approved Change Requests

Approved Change Requests are requests that have been submitted, reviewed and entered into the Change Log, which should be updated as necessary. A review of all Change Requests is made to determine and verify all requests were undertaken and put quality stnadards into practice as described (P 301).

8.3.1.4 Deliverables

A **Deliverable** is a tangible or intangible product with verifiable results produced by an output, ending in a validated quality Deliverable delivered to an external/internal customer (P 301).

8.3.1.5 Work Performance Data

Data that corresponds to work performance is collected, analyzed and organized. This information is then communicated to the stakeholders concerning project status and progress of the project work. The level of detail and presentation content will be adjusted according to the needs of the target audience (P 301).

8.3.1.6 Enterprise Environmental Factors

Some of the **Enterprise Environmental Factors** that may affect the Quality Control process are (P301):

- Project Management Information System (PMIS)
- Governmental Agency Regulations
- Rules, Standards and Guidelines specific to the application area

8.3.2 Control Quality: Tools and Techniques

8.3.2.1 Data Gathering

Some of the Data Gathering techniques used in the Control Quality process are (P 302):

- **Checklists**: Helps to manage Control Quality activities
- **Check Sheets (Tally Sheets)**: Organize facts effectively in order to provide useful information for possible quality problems that may arise
- **Statistical Sampling**: Choosing the correct samples to test, along with the frequency of the tests, in order to ensure the testing samples represent the population of interest.
- **Questionnaires and Surveys**: Techniques for compiling information quickly. A target group is asked explicit questions related to a project's needs and/or requirements (P 116).

See (PMBOK® Guide, Fig. 8-12, P 302, *Check Sheets)*.

8.3.2.2 Data Analysis

Some of the **Data Analysis** techniques used in the Control Quality process are (P 303):

- **Performance Reviews**: Compare, measure and analyze schedule performance
- **Root Cause Analysis (RCA)**: The process of identifying a problem's core source of defects and taking action to prevent or correct the risk

8.3.2.3 Inspection

Inspection is a tool used to evaluate products and decide whether the product meets the desired outcome.

8.3.2.4 Testing/Product Evaluations

Testing/Product Evaluations are used throughout the process of Quality Control to provide objective information on the status of the project (P 303).

8.3.2.5 Data Representation

Some of the **Data Representation** techniques used in the Control Quality process are (P 302):

- **Cause and Effect Diagrams**: Trace a problem's source back to an activity's root cause.

- **Control Charts**: Determines whether or not a process is stable or has predictable performance. Upper and lower specification limits are used to determine out-of-range quality issues.
- **Scatter Diagrams (Correlation Charts)**: Plot ordered pairs (X, Y) shows planned performance on one axis and actual performance on the other axis.

8.3.2.6 Meetings

The types of **Meetings** shown below are commonly implemented in the Quality Control Process (P 305):

- **Approved Change Request Review**: Approved Change Requests should be reviewed to determine if they have been implemented correctly/successfully
- **Retrospective/Lessons Learned**: A meeting held by the Project Team to discuss the following:
    - Successful elements in the Project/Phase
    - What could be improved
    - What to incorporate in the ongoing/future project
    - What to add to the Organizational Process Assets

8.3.3 Control Quality: Outputs

8.3.3.1 Quality Control Measurements

The **Quality Control Measurements**, the outcome of quality control practices, need to be recorded and designed as specified in the Plan Quality Management Process (P 305).

8.3.3.2 Verified deliverables

Verified Deliverables are completed deliverables examined as part of the quality control process. The purpose of quality control is to determine the correctness of the deliverables, and if need be, making use of the defect repair process. Verified Deliverables then become an input to Validate Scope (P 305).

8.3.3.3 Work Performance Information

Work Performance Information includes data for project requirements, causes for rejection, any rework, any corrective actions needed to be taken, etc.

8.3.3.4 Change Requests

Change Requests include, Corrective Action, Preventative Action and Defect Repair. If a change request is required, this appeal should be started and then takes place in the Perform Integrated Change Control process (P 306).

8.3.3.5 Project Management Plan Updates

Project Management Plan Updates could include some of the following (P 253):

- Quality Management Plan
- Process Improvement Plan

8.3.3.6 Project Documents Updates

Some of the Possible **Project Document Updates** may include:

- **Issue Log**: Documents issues that arise and assigns the responsibility to team members who must resolve a specific issue(s) by agreed upon targeted dates
- **Lessons Learned Register**: History of organizational structures that worked, challenges that were met and risk avoidances in previous projects
- **Risk Register**: New Risks are identified and recorded
- **Test and Evaluation Documents:** May be modified as a result of this process for future project use and effectiveness

Summary: Answers to Student Learning Outcomes

1. Project Quality Management is a process that requires the Project Manager (PM) to manage all of the project and product quality issues from the start of the project, throughout the duration of the project to the project's completion. This process includes activities that support quality policies, objectives, and the assignment of personnel to ensure that project and product quality compliance is followed (P 271- 272).

   The task of managing quality is challenging and daunting. The PM needs to know the level of quality and that the work of quality is being budgeted. Quality steps and measurements must be planned, approved, acted upon and completed. Project Quality Management must support continuous process improvement tasks for the performing organization.

   The PM is likely to be involved in all areas of: Planning, managing and controlling quality work. The importance of quality management for the PM and the project team is to know that they are accountable for scheduli8ng project life cycle quality reviews to meet stakeholder requirements for deliverables, etc. The PM needs to create/use an effective framework for quality planning, assurance, and control.

2. The Project Quality Management process components and brief overview of the process descriptions are found in (P 271):

   - **Plan Quality Management**: The identification of quality requirements/standards for the project or its deliverables and how documenting the project demonstrates quality compliance to the standards.

   - **Manage Quality**: The process of translating the quality management plan into executable quality activities that incorporate the organization's quality policies.

   - **Control Quality**: The process of monitoring and recording results of executing the quality management activities resulting in meeting customer expectations. Be sure to study the ITTO's of Fig. 8-1, P 272, *Project Quality Management Overview.*

3. The **Control Process** requires a basic knowledge of pairs of terms used in statistical control. The differences between these pairs are outlined below (P 274):

   - **Prevention**: Making sure errors do not occur in the process
     Inspection: Making sure that the product of project is free of errors before it is delivered to the customer.
   - **Attribute Sampling**: taking a sample of the work product to see if the result conforms or does not conform to specifications.

Variable Sampling: Rating of the sample(s) on a continuous scale that measures the degree of conformity.

- **Tolerances**: To see if the product produced is within the specified range of acceptance.
- **Control Limits**: are determined as low and high. These are boundaries of common variation in a statistically stable process or process performance.

4. In Project Quality Management, two (2) terms are often used (P 274). They are often misinterpreted: They are **Quality** verses **Grade.** They are not the same concepts.

   Quality, according to ISO 9000 [18], states that, "*Quality as a delivered performance or result is 'the degree to which a set of inherent characteristics fulfill requirements.*'"

   Grade, as a design intent is a category assigned to a deliverable having the same functional use, but different technical characteristics.

   A Guide to the Project Management Body of Knowledge, (PMBOK® Guide) – 6th Edition, Project Management Institute Inc., 2017 (P 274).

5. In the context of quality management approaches, quality management promises to meet the following four (4) outcomes (P 275):

   - **Customer Satisfaction**
   - **Continual Improvement**
   - **Management Responsibility**
   - **Mutually beneficial partnership with suppliers**

   Four (4) tailoring considerations are:

   1. **Policy compliance and auditing**
   2. **Standards and regulatory compliance**
   3. **Continuous Improvement**
   4. **Stakeholder Engagement**

   Agile/Adaptive methods stress frequent, incremental delivery, and focus on small batches of quality work incorporating as many project deliverables as possible. Delivering small batches enables quick detection and uncovers quality inconsistencies early on in the project life cycle. Here, the overall costs of change are lower than late detections and correction is a common practice in predictive life cycle approaches (P 274).

6. **Plan Quality Management** is a process (P 279). Its purpose is to identify customer quality requirements and/or standards for the project and its deliverables, etc.

Documenting how the project demonstrates quality compliance to quality requirement and standards is paramount. The key benefit to Plan Quality Management is to provide guidance and direction of how quality will be managed and verified.

7. The **Quality Plan Management** and other outputs are developed by using the following five (5) inputs' information.

    1. Project Charter
    2. Project Management Plan
    3. Project Documents
    4. Enterprise Environmental Factors
    5. Organizational Process Assets

    Fig. 8-3, P 277, *Plan Quality Management: Inputs, Tools and Techniques and Outputs*
    Fig. 8-4, P 278, *Plan Quality Management: Data Flow Diagram*

8. The **Risk Register** is used as an input in updating project documents (P 280). Yes, the Risk Register does record and report on threats and opportunities that may affect quality.

9. In **Plan Quality Management**, one tool/technique in data analysis (See 8.1.2.3) is **Cost of Quality (COQ).** COQ is a method of determining the incurred costs to ensure high quality (® Guide, Glossary, P 703). Some of these cover costs incurred over the life of the product by:
    - **Investment** in preventing non-conformance to requirements;
    - **Appraisal** of the product or service for conformance to requirement and;
    - **Failure** to meet requirements

10. The Outputs (8.1) (P 277) of **Plan Quality Management** are:

    - **Quality Management Plan**: Quality Management Plan is a component of the Project Management Plan. Quality Management Plan identifies quality requirements and documents standards for deliverables, etc.
    - **Quality Metrics**: Describes a project or product attributes and how the quality control process will measure them
    - **Project Management Plan Updates**: Risk Management Plan and Scope Baseline
    - **Project Document Updates**: Lessons Learned Register, Requirements, Traceability Matrix, Risk Register, and Stakeholder Register

11. The project management teams will meet the quality requirements set for the project by using quality metrics. The metrics specifically describes a project or

product attribute and how the quality control process will verify compliance to it.

12. **Manage Quality** is a process of translating the **Quality Management Plan** into executable quality activities (P 288). The **key benefit** is that it is intended to increase the probability of meeting quality objectives and should identify ineffective processes and causes of poor quality.

    The four (4) Basic Quality Control Tools used in data gathering are (P 302-303):

    - **Check Lists**
    - **Check Sheets**
    - **Statistical Sampling**
    - **Questionnaires and Surveys**

13. **Control Quality** is a process of monitoring and recording results of executing quality management activities that assess performance and ensures that the project outputs are complete, correct, and they meet customer requirements (P 298). The **key benefit** of Control Quality is to verify that the project deliverables and work meets stakeholder requirements for final acceptance.

    Fig. 8-10, P 298, *Control Quality: Inputs, Tools and Techniques and Outputs*
    Fig. 8-11, P 299, *Control Quality: Data Flow Diagram*

Similar Questions that may be on the PMI exam related to Chapter 8

1. Linda is asked to do a presentation to key stakeholders on how the new software would work. She has the demo in her laptop but also carries a hard drive in which the demo is installed, just to make sure that in case the demo in her laptop does not work, she can use the one in the hard drive. This is an example of_____.

   A. Corrective Action
   B. Defect Repair
   C. Preventive Action
   D. None of the above

   Correct option is C: Preventive Action is an intentional activity that ensures the future performance of the project work is aligned with the project management plan.

2. Alex is a project manager and working on a critical project which requires a high standard of quality. He is working hard to ensure that his project has few if any defects. All of the following statements are true about defect repairs except_____.

   A. Defect repairing is done when a project component does not meet the requirements or specifications
   B. All the defect repairs must be documented in change log
   C. Defects might be discovered while conducting quality audits
   D. Defect repairs can result due to the scope change at later stages

   Option D is correct: On scope change, the additional work is documented in the WBS as a change request in scope. Since the work is added and not missed, it is not a defect.

3. John is the Project Manager for development of a software for a research-based organization involved in the creation of generic drugs. He has a limited number of developers in his team. The Quality department has identified a large number of defects in the product, which has been shared with the project sponsor. John now wants to minimize any effort and repair processes for as many defects as possible. Which quality-control tool should he use before he directs the efforts of the project team to fix

specific problems?

A. Control Chart
B. Cause and Effect Diagram
C. Pareto Diagram
D. Scatter Diagram

Correct Option is C: Pareto Diagram, which can be used to rank problems based on the frequency of defects caused by them. With this in mind, the Project Manager will make efforts to eliminate those causes at the root of most of the defects.

4. As a project manager, you arrange a team meeting with stakeholders to identify and analyze lessons learned from quality control. What should you do with them?
   A. Document the lessons and make them part of the historical database of the project and the performing organization
   B. Discuss the lessons with management and make sure that they remain otherwise confidential
   C. Publish the lessons in the corporate newsletter
   D. Strategize your decisions, independent from lessons learned. These decisions should be implemented regardless of any outcome

Correct answer is A: Lessons learned during a team meeting with stakeholders should be documented and made part of the historical database of the project and the performing organization.

5. A project manager in Xansa consulting, your latest project entails upgrading an organization's operating system on 215 servers. You are working on this project on contract. Presently you are in the closure process and have reviewed contracting processes to identify lessons learned. Which tool and technique will you use to perform the aforementioned task?

   A. Performance audits
   B. Performance reviews
   C. Procurement audits
   D. Procurement reviews

Correct Answer is C: Procurement Audits help review the procurement process to identify and document lessons learned during the procurement process for future reference.

6. When should you use an inspection and an audit?

   A. When the buyer wants to make sure that the product or service is meeting the standards
   B. When the buyer wants to make sure the seller is performing the agreed quality control
   C. When the buyer wants to make sure that there are not unsettled claims
   D. When the seller moves court because of non-acceptance

   Correct answer is A: Inspections and audits are required by the buyer and supported by the seller, as specified in the procurement contract and can be conducted to verify compliance in the seller's work processes or deliverables.

7. You are leading a project for automation of postal departments in the country. The postal department has smaller/bigger, thousands of offices across the length and breadth of the country. The application programs being developed for them by the programming team have lots of bugs. You are adding extra test cycles and making them more intensive to try to find more problems before they are given to users at one of the central locations for a pilot run. Which process are you performing?

   A. Manage quality
   B. Control quality
   C. Plan quality management
   D. Quality audit

   Correct answer is B: Control quality is about technical function and taking corrective actions.

8. Mark has been running a project for the last six months. This is a complex project which has many stakeholders. Where does comparing actual to baseline schedules, examining the statement of work, understanding cost overruns and assessing risk occur?

A. Stakeholder Meeting
B. Resource Leveling Activity
C. Project Audit
D. Contract Negotiation

Correct answer is C: Project audit is done to check the adherence of the project to the standard procedures and quality management system of the organization. All the key performances of the project parameters and project documentation are reviewed against a standard checklist by an expert auditor.

9. Petal is working as a project manager in an R & D project. This is the first of its kind of project her organization is performing and she is extremely careful of the progress of the project and the quality standards. As the project continues, a technical glitch occurs and she is inclined to find the reason behind the error so that it never arises again. Which tool should she use?

A. Fishbone
B. Statistical Sampling
C. Inspection
D. Rule of seven

Correct answer is A: A Fishbone diagram helps to see all the possible causes in one place so that defects may be prevented in the future.

10. Standard deviation as a measure of random variance can be best improved by ______.

A. Analysis of Control Charts
B. Identifying cause of Variance
C. Improving upon overall production system
D. Increasing the periodicity of inspections

Correct answer is D: Standard Deviation as a measure of random variance can be best improved by increasing the periodicity of inspections.

You may now move on to Chapter Nine: Project Resource Management

Chapter 9: Project Resource Management: Hire the Right Person for the Right Job at the Right Time and the Right Place

"Get the right people. Then no matter what all else you might do wrong after that, the people will save you. That's what management is all about." Tom DeMarco

Student Learning Outcomes

CHAPTER 9 PROJECT RESOURCE MANAGEMENT PMBOK INTRODUCTION OVERVIEW: HIRE THE RIGHT PERSON FOR THE RIGHT JOB AT THE RIGHT TIME AND THE RIGHT PLACE

1. List and describe the six **(6) processes of Project Resource Management** and why Project Resource Management is so very important (P 307-309).
2. List the order **Process Sequence** and importance of the process components of **Project Resource Management.** Identify and describe the Inputs, Tools, Techniques and Outputs (ITTO's) of each of the six (6) processes in the Project Resource Management Overview (P 308).
3. The Project Manager is both a leader and a manager. To lead a high performing team, the Project Manager/Leader must form the team as an effective group. List some of the factors that influence **team formation** (P 309).
4. List **four (4) Trends and Emerging Practices for Project Resource Management** (P 310-311).
5. **Project Resource Management approaches** may need to be tailored by the Project Manager. **List six (6) considerations for tailoring** (P 311).
6. **Collaboration** is useful in agile/adaptive environments. What effect does collaboration accomplish in such environments (P 311)?
7. **What are the objectives and key benefits of the Plan Resource Management process (P 312)?**
8. **The Resource Management Plan** is an output of the **Plan Resource Management** process (P 312). What are the other two (2) Outputs?
9. There are three **(3) types of hierarchal charts** that may be used in **Plan Resource Management data representation** (Tools and Techniques), and in documenting team member roles and responsibilities (P 315). Identify and describe these three (3) types of hierarchal charts (P 316-317).
10. What is a **RACI matrix** and what is its importance? See Fig. 9-4, P 317, *Sample RACI Chart.* What is a text-oriented format?
11. What are the attributes (i.e. role, authority, responsibility and competence of the resource plan management), and why is it important to know them when describing team member roles and responsibilities (P 318)?
12. What are the **nine (9) elements** that may be included in the **Project Resource Management Plan** (P 318-319)?
13. **What does it mean to Estimate Activity Resources and what is the key benefit of this process (P 320)? What are the ITTO's of estimate activity resources?**
14. What are the four (4) **Outputs of Estimate Activity** Resources (P 321)?
15. What are the seven (7) **Tools and Techniques used in Estimate Activity Resources** (P 321)?
16. **What is Acquire Resources and what are the key benefits (P 328)?**
17. What are **virtual teams,** their benefits, and how does this model serve as a communications means for many possibilities (P 333)?
18. **What is meant by Develop Team? What is the key benefit of this process (P 336)? What are the ITTO's?**
19. What is the **Tuckman Ladder** of **team development** and what are the stages (P 338)?

20. What is meant by **colocation** and why is it important (P 340)?
21. What is included in a **team performance assessment**, which is an output of **Develop**

Team (P 343)?

22. **What is meant by Managing Team and what are the benefits (P 345)? What are the ITTO's?**
23. **Conflict Management** is a technique often used in managing team issues. What are some factors that influence the selection/choice of certain conflict resolution techniques, and what are the five **(5) general techniques for resolving conflicts** (P 348-349)?
24. **What are Control Resources (P 352) and the key benefits of this?**
25. **Control Resources: Tools and Techniques** are used in **problem solving**. List the **6 methodical steps** that are in use in problem solving (P 356).

CHAPTER NINE INTRODUCTION: HIRE THE RIGHT PERSON FOR THE RIGHT JOB

PROJECT RESOURCE MANAGEMENT: CHAPTER 9 OVERVIEW: PMBOK® 6th Edition P 307-358

Project Resource Management is a process. It consists of six (6) process steps to identify, acquire and manage the resources that are need for a successful project. It ensures that the right resources will be available on time and in place for the project manager and project team. The project resource management processes are outlined below:

- **Plan Resource Management** This is a process that determines how to estimate, acquire, manage and utilize physical and team resources.
- **Estimate Activity Resources** This is a process of estimating the type and quantities of team resources, material, equipment and supplies that are needful to do project work.
- **Acquire Resources** This process requires that the project manager obtains team members, facilities, equipment, materials, supplies and other resources necessary to complete the project work.
- **Develop Team** This is a process to improve the competencies of team members, team interactions, and to enhance project performance.
- **Manage Team** process tracks team member performance, provides feedback, resolves issues and manages team changes to maximize project performance.
- **Control Resources** process ensures that the physical resources are assigned and allocated to the project that they are available according to the project plan includes a monitoring plan versus actual usage of resources and taking necessary corrective action.

See Fig. 9-1, P 308, *Project Resource Management Overview*

Key Concepts for Project Resource Management

The project manager (PM) should be both a leader and manager of the project team (P 309). The PM should invest effort in acquiring, managing, motivating and empowering the project team. There are various aspects that influence project team productivity and success. They are team environment, geographical locations of team members, stakeholder communications, organizational change management, internal and external politics, cultural issues, organizational uniqueness and numerous other factors affecting project performance.

Trends and Emerging Practices in Project Resource Management

There are four (4) trends and emerging practices in Project Resource Management and others that are not included here (P 310):

1. **Resource management methods**
2. **Emotional Intelligence (EI)**
3. **Self-Organizing Teams**
4. **Virtual Teams/Distributed Teams**

Tailoring Considerations

The project manager is responsible to tailor project resource management processes. They may include: diversity, physical location, industry-specific resources, acquisition of team members, management team and lifecycle approaches (P 311).

Considerations for Agile/Adaptive Environments

Self-organizing teams and collaboration should be extensively used to increase productivity and facilitate innovative problem solving. Collaborative teams are often critical to the success of projects that are characterized by a high degree of variability in rapid changes (P 311).

Plan Resource Management:

The purpose of Plan Resource Management is to define how to estimate, acquire, manage and use team and physical resources.

The **key benefit** is to establish the approach and level of management effort needed to manage resources based upon the complexity and type of project.

See chart on next page: **PLAN RESOURCE MANAGEMENT (Section 9.1)**

Chapter Nine: Project Resource Management

9.1 PLAN RESOURCE MANAGEMENT

TOOLS & TECHNIQUES

INPUTS → 9.1 PLAN RESOURCE MANAGEMENT → OUTPUTS

9.1 PLAN HUMAN RESOURCE MANAGEMENT: Overview

Project Management Process Groups	Initiating	Planning	Executing	Monitoring & Controlling	Closing
Project RESOURCE Management		9.1Plan Resource Management 312			
		9.2 estimate Activity Resources 320			
			9.3 Acquire Resources 328		
			9.4 Develop Project Team 336		
			9.5 Manage Team 345		
				9.6 Control Resources 352	

9.1 PLAN RESOURCE MANAGEMENT: ITTO Processes

.1 Inputs	.2 Tools and Techniques	.3 Outputs
.1 Project Charter 314 .2 Project Management Plan 314 • Quality Management Plan 314 • Scope Baseline 314 .3 Project Documents 314 • Project Schedule 314 • Requirements Documentation 314 • Risk Register 314 • Stakeholder Register 314 .4 Enterprise Environmental Factors 315 .5 Organizational Process Assets 315	.1 Expert Judgment 315 .2 Data Representation 316 • Hierarchal Type Charts 316 • Assignment Matrix 317 • Text Oriented Formats 317 .3 Organizational Theory 318 .4 Meetings 318	.1 Resource Management Plan 318 .2 Team Charter 319 .3 Project Documents Updates 320 • Assumption Log 320 • Risk Register 320

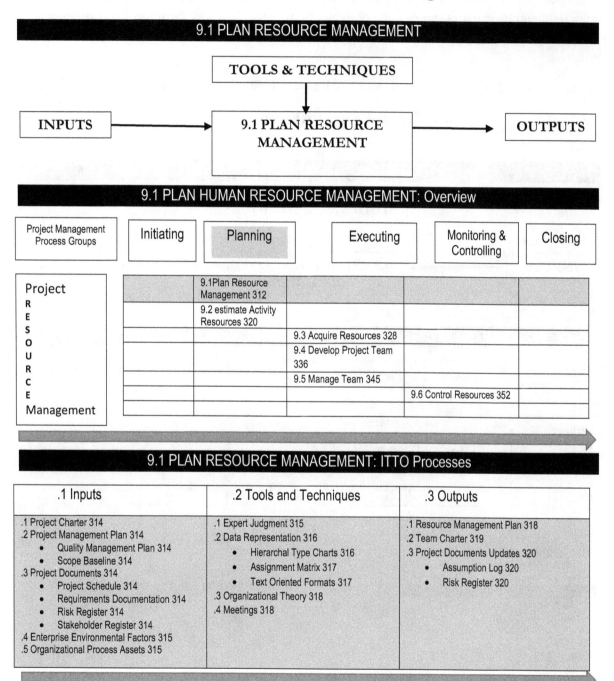

Fig. 9-2, P 312, *Plan Resource Management: Inputs, Tools, Techniques and Outputs*
Fig. 9-3, 313, *Plan Resource Management: Data Flow Diagram*

Estimate Activity Resources:

Estimate Activity Resources is the process of estimating team resource types and quantities of materials, equipment and supplies to complete the project. The **key benefit** of this process is to identify the type, quantity and characteristics of the needed resources to perform the project work.

See chart below: **ESTIMATE ACTIVITY RESOURCES (Section 9.2)**

Chapter Nine: Project Resource Management

9.2 ESTIMATE ACTIVITY RESOURCES

TOOLS & TECHNIQUES

INPUTS → 9.2 ESTIMATE ACTIVITY RESOURCES → OUTPUTS

9.2 ESTIMATE ACTIVITY RESOURCES: Overview

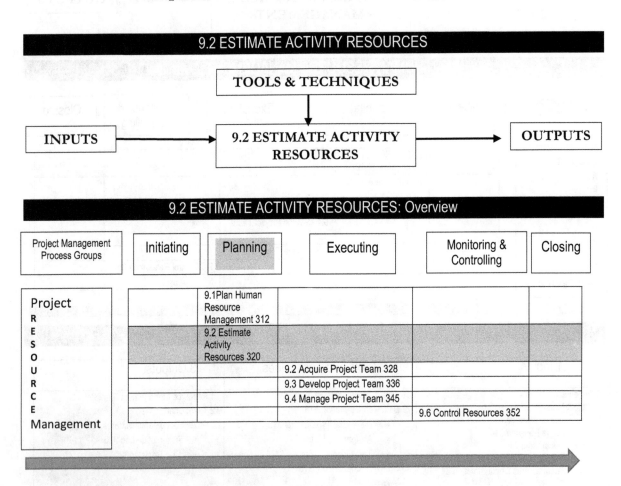

Project Management Process Groups	Initiating	Planning	Executing	Monitoring & Controlling	Closing
Project RESOURCE Management		9.1Plan Human Resource Management 312			
		9.2 Estimate Activity Resources 320			
			9.2 Acquire Project Team 328		
			9.3 Develop Project Team 336		
			9.4 Manage Project Team 345		
				9.6 Control Resources 352	

9.2 ESTIMATE ACTIVITY RESOURCES: ITTO Processes

.1 Inputs	.2 Tools and Techniques	.3 Outputs
.1 Project Management Plan 322 • Resource Management Plan 322 • Scope Baseline 322 .2 Project Documents 322 • Activity Attributes 322 • Activity List 322 • Assumption Log 323 • Cost Estimates 323 • Resource Calendars 323 • Risk Register 323 .3 Enterprise Environmental Factors 323 .4 Organization Process Assets 324	.1 Expert Judgment 324 .2 Bottom Up Estimating 324 .3 Analogous Estimating 324 .4 Parametric Estimating 324 .5 Data Analysis 325 • Alternative Analysis 325 .6 Project Management Information System 325 .7 Meetings 325	.1 Resource Requirements 325 .2 Basis of Estimates 326 .3 Resource Breakdown Structure 326 .4 Project Documents Updates 327 • Activity Attributes 327 • Assumption Log 327 • Lessons Learned Register 327

Fig. 9-5, P 321, *Estimate Activity Resources: Inputs, Tools, Techniques and Outputs*
Fig. 9-6 P 321, *Estimate Activity Resources: Data Flow Diagram*

<u>Acquire Resources:</u>

Acquire resources is the process of obtaining team members facilities, equipment, material, supplies, and other resources to complete project work.

The **key benefit** of Acquire Resources is that it outlines and guarantees selecting resources and assigns them to their respective activities.

Check out the article, *You've been asking the Wrong Interview Questions*, by Carol Quinn, located at https://www.higheredjobs.com/articles/articleDisplay.cfm?ID=1758&utm_source=11_14_2018&utm_medium=email&utm_campaign=InsiderUpdate

See chart on next page: **ACQUIRE RESOURCES (Section 9.3)**

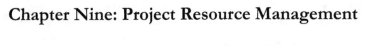

Chapter Nine: Project Resource Management

9.3 ACQUIRE RESOURCES

TOOLS & TECHNIQUES → 9.3 ACQUIRE RESOURCES

INPUTS → 9.3 ACQUIRE RESOURCES → OUTPUTS

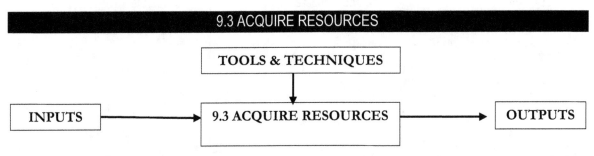

9.3 ACQUIRE RESOURCES: Overview

Project Management Process Groups	Initiating	Planning	Executing	Monitoring & Controlling	Closing
Project RESOURCE Management		9.1Plan Resource Management 312			
		9.2 Estimate Activity Resources 320			
			9.3 Acquire Resources 328		
			9.4 Develop Team 336		
			9.5 Manage Team 345		
				9.6 Control Resources 352	

9.3 ACQUIRE RESOURCES: ITTO Processes

.1 Inputs	.2 Tools and Techniques	.3 Outputs
.1 Project Management Plan 330 • Resource Management Plan 330 • Procurement Management Plan 330 • Cost Baseline 330 .2 Project Documents 331 • Project Schedule 331 • Resource Calendars 331 • Resource Requirements 331 • Stakeholder Register 331 .3 Enterprise Environmental Factors 331 .4 Organization Process Assets 331	.1 Decision Making 332 • Multicriteria Decision Analysis 306 .2 Interpersonal and Team Skills 306 • Negotiation 306 .3 Pre-Assignment 333 .4 Virtual Teams 333	.1 Physical Resource Assignments 333 .2 Project Team Assignments 334 .3 Resource Calendars 308 .4 Change Requests 308 .5 Project Management Plan Updates 308 • Resource Management Plan 308 • Cost Baseline 308 .6 Project Documents Updates 335 • Lessons Learned Register 335 • Project Schedule 335 • Resource Breakdown Schedule 335 • Resource Requirements 335 • Risk Register 335 • Stakeholder Register 335 .7 Enterprise Environmental Factors 335 .8 Organization Process Assets 335

Fig. 9-8, P 328, *Acquire Resources: Inputs, Tools, Techniques and Outputs*
Fig. 9-9, P 329, *Acquire Resources: Data Flow Diagram*

Develop Team:

Develop team is the process of approving competencies, team member interaction, and overall team environments to increase project performance.

The key benefit of Develop Team is to create teamwork, interpersonal skills, highly motivated employees, reduced attrition and improved project performance.

See chart on next page: **DEVELOP TEAM (Section 9.4)**

9.4 DEVELOP TEAM

TOOLS & TECHNIQUES

INPUTS → **9.4 DEVELOP TEAM** → **OUTPUTS**

9.4 DEVELOP TEAM: Overview

Project Management Process Groups	Initiating	Planning	Executing	Monitoring & Controlling	Closing
Project RESOURCE Management		9.1Plan Resource Management 312			
		9.2 Estimate Activity Resources 320			
			9.3 Acquire Resources 328		
			9.4 Develop Team 336		
			9.5 Manage Team 345		
				9.6 Control Resources 352	

9.4 DEVELOP TEAM: ITTO Processes

.1 Inputs	.2 Tools and Techniques	.3 Outputs
.1 Project Management Plan 339 • Resource Management Plan 339 .2 Project Documents 339 • Lessons Learned Register 339 • Project Schedule 339 • Project Team Assignments 339 • Resource Calendars 339 • Resource Requirements 339 • Team Charter 339 .3 Enterprise Environmental Factors 339 .4 Organization Process Assets 340	.1 Colocation 340 .2 Virtual Teams 340 .3 Communication Technology 340 .4 Interpersonal And Team Skills 341 • Conflict management 341 • Influencing 341 • Motivation 341 • Negotiation 341 • Team Building 341 .5 Recognition and Awards 341 .6 Training 342 .7 Individual and Team Assessments 342 .8 Meetings 342	.1 Team Performance Assessments 343 .2 Change Requests 343 .3 Project Management Plan Updates 343 • Resource Management Plan 343 .4 Project Document Updates 344 • Lessons Learned Register 344 • Project Schedule 317 • Project Team Assignments 344 • Resource Calendars 344 • Team Charter 344 .5 Enterprise Environmental Factors 344 .6 Organization Process Assets 344

Fig. 9-10, P 336, *Develop Team: Inputs, Tools, Techniques and Outputs*
Fig. 9-11, P 337, *Develop Team: Data Flow Diagram*

Team development may follow the Tuckman Ladder. This includes five stages that teams go through when working on a project. The five (5) stages are forming; storming; norming, performing, and adjourning.

Manage Team:

Manage team is the process of tracking team member performance, providing people feedback, resolving issues and managing team attitudes/behaviors, manage conflict and resolve issues.

The **key benefit** of this process is that it influences team behavior, manage conflict and resolves issues throughout the project life cycle.

See chart on next page: **MANAGE TEAM (Section 9.5)**

Chapter Nine: Project Resource Management

9.5 MANAGE TEAM

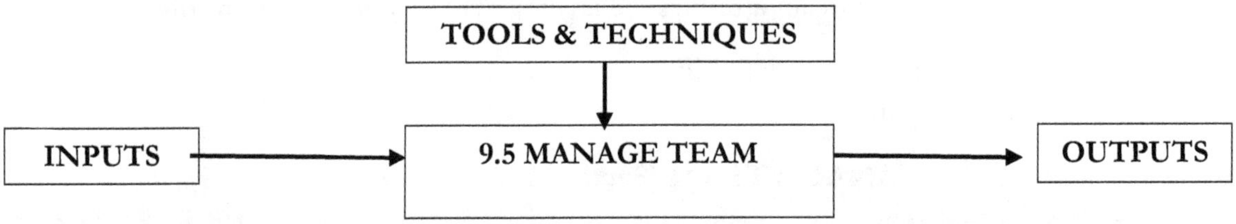

9.5 MANAGE TEAM: Overview

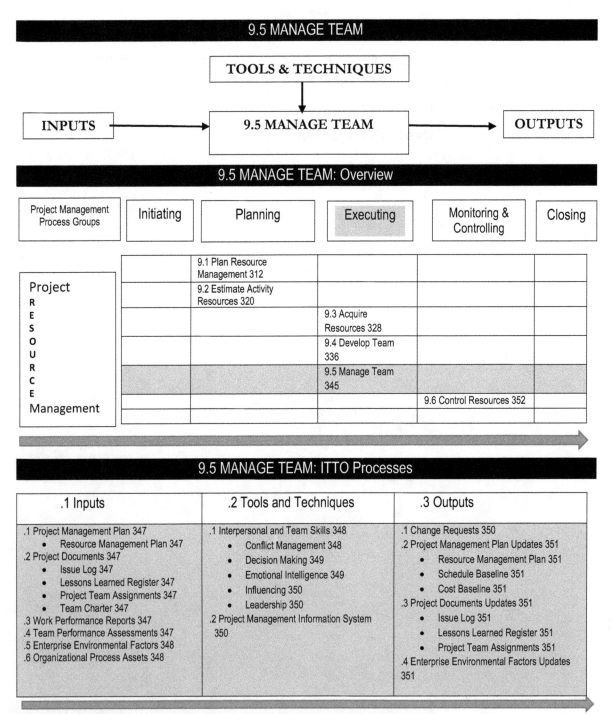

Project Management Process Groups	Initiating	Planning	Executing	Monitoring & Controlling	Closing
Project RESOURCE Management		9.1 Plan Resource Management 312			
		9.2 Estimate Activity Resources 320			
			9.3 Acquire Resources 328		
			9.4 Develop Team 336		
			9.5 Manage Team 345		
				9.6 Control Resources 352	

9.5 MANAGE TEAM: ITTO Processes

.1 Inputs	.2 Tools and Techniques	.3 Outputs
.1 Project Management Plan 347 • Resource Management Plan 347 .2 Project Documents 347 • Issue Log 347 • Lessons Learned Register 347 • Project Team Assignments 347 • Team Charter 347 .3 Work Performance Reports 347 .4 Team Performance Assessments 347 .5 Enterprise Environmental Factors 348 .6 Organizational Process Assets 348	.1 Interpersonal and Team Skills 348 • Conflict Management 348 • Decision Making 349 • Emotional Intelligence 349 • Influencing 350 • Leadership 350 .2 Project Management Information System 350	.1 Change Requests 350 .2 Project Management Plan Updates 351 • Resource Management Plan 351 • Schedule Baseline 351 • Cost Baseline 351 .3 Project Documents Updates 351 • Issue Log 351 • Lessons Learned Register 351 • Project Team Assignments 351 .4 Enterprise Environmental Factors Updates 351

Fig. 9-12, P 345, *Develop Team: Inputs, Tools, Techniques and Outputs*
Fig. 9-13, P 346, *Manage Team: Data Flow Diagram*

Control Resources:

Control Resources is the process of ensuring that the physical resources assigned are allocated to the project as planned. It includes monitoring the plan versus actual utilization of resources and taking corrective action when required.

The **key benefit** of Control Resources is to make certain the assigned resources are available at the right time, right place, and released when no longer needed.

See chart on next page: **CONTROL RESOURCES (Section 9.6)**

Chapter Nine: Project Resource Management

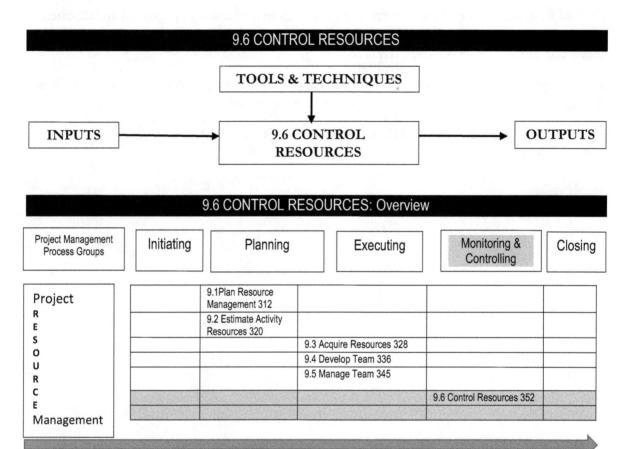

9.6 CONTROL RESOURCES

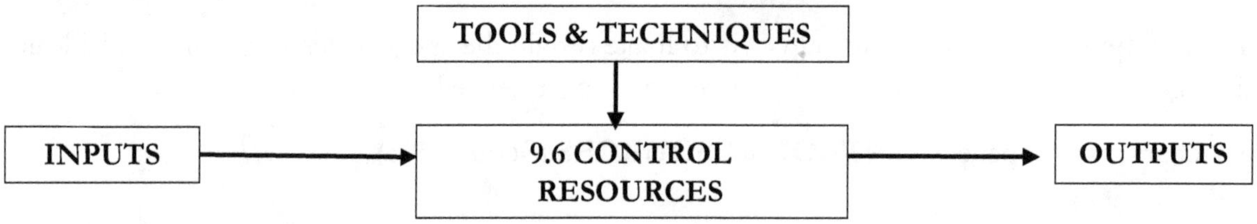

9.6 CONTROL RESOURCES: Overview

Project Management Process Groups	Initiating	Planning	Executing	Monitoring & Controlling	Closing
Project RESOURCE Management		9.1Plan Resource Management 312			
		9.2 Estimate Activity Resources 320			
			9.3 Acquire Resources 328		
			9.4 Develop Team 336		
			9.5 Manage Team 345		
				9.6 Control Resources 352	

9.6 CONTROL RESOURCES: ITTO Processes

.1 Inputs	.2 Tools and Techniques	.3 Outputs
.1 Project Management Plan 354 • Resource Management Plan 354 .2 Project Documents 354 • Issue Log 354 • Lessons Learned Register 354 • Physical Resource Assignments 354 • Project Schedule 355 • Resource Breakdown Structure 355 • Resource Requirements 355 • Risk Register 355 .3 Work Performance Data 355 .4 Agreements 355 .5 Organizational Process Assets 355	.1 Data Analysis 356 • Alternative Analysis 356 • Cost Benefit Analysis 356 • Performance Reviews 356 • Trend Analysis 356 .2 Problem Solving 356 .3 Interpersonal And Team Skills 357 • Negotiation 357 • Influencing 357 .4 Project Management Information System 357	.1 Work Performance Information 357 .2 Change Requests 357 .3 Project Management Plan Updates 357 • Resource Management Plan 357 • Schedule Baseline 357 • Cost Baseline 357 .4 Project Document Updates 358 • Assumption Log 358 • Issue Log 358 • Lessons Learned Register 358 • Physical Resource Breakdown Structure 358 • Risk Register 358

Fig. 9-14, P 352, *Control Resources: Inputs, Tools, Techniques and Outputs*
Fig. 9-15 P 353, *Control Resources: Data Flow Diagram*

KEY WORDS: CHAPTER 9

- Plan resource management
- Estimate Activity Resources
- Acquire Resources
- Develop Team
- Manage Team
- Control Resources
- Lean Management
- Just in Time (JIT) Manufacturing
- Kaizen
- Total Productive Maintenance (TPM)
- Theory of Constraints (TOC)
- Emotional Intelligence (EI)Keep working
- Self-Organizing Teams
- Virtual Teams/Distributive Teams
- Collaborative Teams
- Scope Baseline
- Risk Register
- Stakeholder Register
- Hierarchal Charts
- Assignment Matrix
- RAM
- Responsible, Accountable, Consult, Inform (RACI)
- Authority
- Responsibility
- Competence
- Team Charter
- Activity Attributes
- Activity List
- Assumptions Log
- Risk Register
- Bottom-Up Estimating
- Analogous Estimating
- Parametric Estimating
- Data Analysis
- Resource Breakdown Structure
- Activity Attributes
- Procurement Management Plan
- Cost Baseline
- Resource Calendars
- Functional Managers
- External Organization and Suppliers
- Pre Assignment
- Virtual Teams
- Tuckman Ladder
- Forming
- Storming
- Norming
- Performing
- Adjourning
- Resource Calendars
- Team Charter
- Co-Location
- Shared Portal
- Video Conferencing
- Audio Conferencing
- Email Chat
- Conflict Management
- Withdrawal/Avoid
- Smooth/Accommodate
- Compromise/Reconcile
- Force/Direct
- Collaborate/Problem-Solve
- Influencing
- Conflict Negotiation
- Recognition and Rewards
- Issues Log
- Alternatives Analysis
- Cost Benefit Analysis
- Performance Reviews
- Trend Analysis
- Schedule Baseline

- Cost Baseline
- Physical Resource Assignments
- Resource Breakdown Structure (RBS)
- Risk Register

LEGEND

The following Legend shows how to correctly read the *PMBOK® Guide* references and attributions correctly for Chapter 9: Project Resource Management PMBOK Details.

Legend:

Chapter Section	Chapter Section Title	Page Number

Example from Chapter Six shown below:

6.5.1.4	Enterprise Environmental Factors	(P 209)

All direct quotes are attributed as (A Guide to the Project Management Body of Knowledge, *(PMBOK® Guide)* – Sixth Edition) Project Management Institute Inc., 2017, Page #, after each section and any/all paraphrased or original wording is attributed as (P #), before or after each section. All Graphs, Charts, Tables and Figures are attributed as: (*PMBOK® Guide,* Fig. #-# or #/#, P #, *Title of Graph, Chart, Table or Figure*).

9. PROJECT RESOURCE MANAGEMENT

Project Resource Management is the process of identifying, acquiring and managing the resources needed for the successful competition of the project. Physical resources include equipment, materials, facilities and infrastructure and team resources are humans who have varied skillsets. Personnel may be part-time, full-time, or added and removed as necessary.

(9.1) **Plan Resource Management**: The process of defining how to estimate, acquire, manage and utilize physical and team resources.

(9.2) **Estimate Activity Resources**: The process of estimating team resources and the type and quantities of material, equipment and supplies necessary to perform the project work.

(9.3) **Acquire Resources**: The process of obtaining team members, facilities, equipment, materials, supplies and other resources necessary to complete the project work.

(9.4) **Develop Team**: The process of improving competencies, team member interactions and the overall team environment to enhance project performance.

(9.5) **Manage Team**: The process of tracking team member performance, providing feedback, resolving issues and managing team changes to optimize project performance.

(9.6) **Control Resources**: The process of ensuring that the physical resources assigned and allocated to the project is available as planned, as well as monitoring the planned versus actual use of resources and performing corrective action as necessary

Key Concepts for Project Resource Management:

Some of the different aspects that may affect/influence the team that the PM should be aware of are (P 309):

- **Team Environment**
- **Geographical location of team members**
- **Communications among stakeholders**
- **Organizational change management**
- **Internal/external policies**
- **Cultural issues and organizational uniqueness**
- **Other factors that alter project performance**

Trends and Emerging Practices in Project Resource Management:

No longer are Project Managers (PM)'s seen as members working in a command/control structure, but are participating as learners who work in a more collaborative environment. Some of the emerging practices for Project Resource management are (P 310):

- **Resource Management Methods**: Trends that have become popular are Lean Management, Just-in-Time Manufacturing (JIT), Kaizen, Total Productive Maintenance (TPM), Theory of Constraints (TOC), etc.
- **Emotional Intelligence (EI)**: Improves Inbound self-management and self-awareness and Outbound relationship management
- **Self-Organizing Teams**: Absence of centralized control
- **Virtual Teams/Distributed Teams**: Team members are not located in the same geographic area

Tailoring Considerations:

Considerations for Tailoring means adapting to the uniqueness of each project and using tailoring techniques to apply resource management processes as shown below (P 311):

- **Diversity**:
  - What is the background of the team members?
- **Physical Location**:
  - What is the physical location of the team members?
- **Industry-Specific Resources**:
  - How will resources be acquired?
- **Acquisition of Team Members**:
  - How will team members be acquired?
- **Management of Team**:
  - How is team development managed for the project?
  - Are there organizational tools to manage team development or will new ones need to be established?
  - Are there team members who have special needs?
  - Will the team need special training to manage diversity?
- **Life Cycle Approaches**:
  - What life cycle approach will be used?

Considerations for Agile/Adaptive Environments:

Collaboration is needed in a team environment to maximize focus, boost productivity and facilitate problem solving which serves to improve communication, increase knowledge sharing and provide work assignment flexibility (P 311).

9.1 PLAN RESOURCE MANAGEMENT

The **Human Resource Management Plan** is concerned with charting the assignment of roles, responsibilities, skills and relationships and defines how to estimate, acquire, manage and use team and physical resources. The **key benefit** is that it establishes the approach and level of management effort needed for managing project resources based on the type and complexity of the project.

Fig. 9-2, P 312, *Plan Human Resource Management: Inputs, Tools and Techniques and Outputs*
Fig. 9-3, P 313, *Plan Resource Management: Data Flow Diagram*

9.1.1 Plan Resource Management: Inputs

9.1.1.1 Project Charter

The **Project Charter** contains the high-level descriptive requirements. It contains the key preapproved financial resources that may influence the resource management of the project (P 314). The summary milestone schedule and project approval requirements with high-level project descriptions.

9.1.1.2 Project Management Plan

Some of the **Project Management Plan** components are (P 314):

- **Quality Management Plan**: Helps to define the level of resources that will be required
- **Scope Baseline**: Identifies the Deliverables that drives the types and quantities of resources that will be managed

9.1.1.3 Project Documents

Some of the **Project Documents** that can be Inputs to this process are (P 314):

- **Project Schedule**: Shows the Timeline for needed Resources

- **Requirements Documentation**: Dictates the type and amount of resources needed
- **Risk Register**: Contains information on Threats/Risks/Opportunities that may impact resource planning
- **Stakeholder Register**: Aids in identifying Stakeholders with specific interests or having an impact on needed resources

9.1.1.4 Enterprise Environmental Factors

Some of the **Enterprise Environmental Factors** that may affect the Plan Resource Management are (P 315):

Enterprise Environmental Factors that may affect the Plan Human Resources Processes (P 315):

- Organizational Culture and Structure
- Geographical Distribution of Facilities and Resources
- Existing Resources Competencies and Availability
- Marketplace Conditions

9.1.1.5 Organizational Process Assets

Some of the **Organizational Process Assets** that may affect the Plan Resource Management are (P 315):

- Human Resource Policies and Procedures
- Physical Resource Management and Policies
- Safety Policies
- Security Policies
- Templates for the Resource Management Plan
- Historical Information for similar Projects

9.1.2 Plan Resource Management: Tools and Techniques

9.1.2.1 Expert Judgment

The following list is a guide to obtaining expertise when needed from any person(s) or groups (P 315):

- **Negotiating** for the best resources in the organization
- Talent management and **Personnel Development**
- Determining the **preliminary effort level** needed to meet project objectives
- Determining the **reporting requirements** based on the organizational culture
- **Estimating Lead Times** required for acquisition, based on Lessons Learned and Market Conditions
- **Identifying Risks** associated with resource acquisition, retention and release plans
- Complying with applicable **government and union regulations**
- **Managing Sellers** and the **logistics effort** to ensure material and Suppliers are available when needed

9.1.2.2 Data Representation

Some of the ways **Data** can be represented is through the use of Charts.

A **Hierarchal Chart** can be used to represent high-level roles, while a text-based format would be better for documenting detailed responsibilities. Please see below (P 316):

- **Hierarchal Charts**: Can be used to show positions and relationships in a graphical top-down format:
  - **Work Breakdown Structure (WBS):** Designed to show how project deliverables are broken down into work packages and provide a way of showing high levels of responsibility
  - **Organizational Breakdown Structure (OBS):** Arranged according to an organization's existing departments, units or teams with project activities or work packages listed under each title
  - **Resource Breakdown Structure**: An hierarchal list of each team and physical resources related by category and resource type
- **Assignment Matrix**: Show project resources assigned to each work package, such as (PMBOK® Guide, Fig. 9-4, P 317, *Sample RACI Chart).*
- **Text-Oriented Formats**: These documents provide information to include as, responsibilities, authority, competencies and qualifications

9.1.2.3 Organizational Theory

Organizational Theory relates to how an organization operates. By knowing how an organization operates, the PM can adapt to changes that may occur and have a better understanding of how to handle them when if they do occur (P 318). The organizational structure and culture will affect the project organizational structure.

9.1.2.4 Meetings

Meetings (Planning Meetings) will be held for all project management team member, using various tools and techniques to decide on a mutual course of action (P 318).

9.1.3 Plan Resource Management Plan: Outputs

9.1.3.1 Resource Management Plan

The **Human Resource Plan** may include the following (P 318):

- **Identification of Resources**: Methods for identifying and quantifying team and physical resources needed
- **Acquiring Resources**: Guidance on how to acquire team and physical resources
- **Roles and Responsibilities**:
    - **Roles**: Function assumed or assigned to someone in the project
    - **Authority:** (Hierarchal) Gives one person the ability to:
        - Apply Resources
        - Make Decisions
        - Sign Approvals
        - Accept Deliverables
        - Delegate Responsibilities to others
    - **Responsibility:** Assigned duties and work a team member is expected to perform
    - **Competency**: Skill and capacity needed to complete assignments within project constraints
- **Project Organization Charts**: A graphic display of team member and their reporting relationships
- **Project Team Resource Management:** A component of the Human Resource Management Plan that describes when and how project team member will be acquired and how long they will be needed:
- **Training**: Training strategies for team members
- **Team Development**: Methods for developing project team
- **Resource Control**: Methods for ensuring adequate physical resources are available when needed and optimized for project needs

- **Recognition Plan**: Clear criteria for rewards and planned systems for their use will help and promote the desired behavior

Check out the article, *Become a Better Delegator with these Tech Project Management Tips*, by Forbes Technology Council, located at: https://www.forbes.com/sites/forbestechcouncil/2018/09/27/become-a-better-delegator-with-these-tech-project-management-tips/

9.1.3.2 Team Charter

Some of the elements in a **Team Charter** include (P 319):

- **Team Values**
- **Communications Guidelines**
- **Decision Making Criteria and Process**
- **Conflict Resolution Process**
- **Meeting Guidelines**
- **Team Agreements**

The Team Charter establishes clear expectations regarding acceptable behavior by Project Team Members.

9.1.3.3 Project Documents Updates

Some of the project documents that might be updated include the following (P 320):

- **Assumption Log**: Can be updated with assumptions regarding availability, logistics requirements and location of physical resources as well as skill sets and availability of team resources
- **Risk Register**: Updated with risks associated with team and physical resources availability or other known resource-related risks

9.2 ESTIMATE ACTIVITY RESOURCES

Estimate Activity Resources is the process of estimating team resources and the type and quantities of materials, equipment and supplies needed to perform project work. The **key benefit** of this process is that it identifies the type, quantity and characteristics of each needed resource to complete the project.

Fig. 9-5, P 321, *Estimate Activity Resources: Inputs, Tools and Techniques and Outputs*
Fig. 9-6, P 321, *Estimate Activity Resources: Data Flow Diagram*

9.2.1 Estimate Activity Resources: Inputs

Estimate Activity Resources: Identifies resources needed to complete an activity. It identifies the type, quantity and characteristics of resources required.

9.2.1.1 Project Management Plan

Some of the **Project Management Plan** components are (P 322):

- **Resource Management Plan**: Defines the approach to identify the different resources needed and defines the methods to quantify the resources needed
- **Scope Baseline**: Identifies the Project and Product scope necessary to meet project objectives

9.2.1.2 Project Documents

Some of the **Project Documents** that might be considered as Inputs for this process include (P 322):

- **Activity Attributes**: Provide primary source data for use in estimating team and physical resources required for each activity on the activity list
- **Activity List**: Identifies the activities that need resources
- **Assumption Log**: May contain information regarding availability, logistics requirements and location of physical resources as well as skill sets and availability of team resources
- **Cost Estimates**: A prediction of project costs known at a given point in time and may impact resource selection from a quantity and skill level perspective
- **Resource Calendars**: Identifies the working days, shifts, start and end of normal business hours, weekends and public holidays and when each specific resource is available
- **Risk Register**: Describes individual risks that might affect resource selection and availability

9.2.1.3 Enterprise Environmental Factors

Some of the **Enterprise Environmental Factors** that may affect the Acquire Project Team (P 323):

- Resource Location
- Resource Availability
- Team Resource Skills
- Organizational Culture
- Published Estimating Data
- Marketplace Conditions

9.2.1.4 Organizational Process Assets

Some of the **organizational Process Assets** that may influence the estimate activity resources team are (P 323):

- Policies and Procedures regarding staffing
- Policies and Procedures related to supplies and equipment
- Historical Information regarding types of resources used for similar work on previous projects

9.2.2 Estimate Activity Resources: Tools and Techniques

9.2.2.1 Expert Judgement

Expert Judgement is the process of using experts in a particular field with related experience or training in team and physical resources, planning and estimating. These experts will synthesize the data and suggest possible risks based on their expertise (P 324).

9.2.2.2 Bottom-Up Estimating

Bottom-Up Estimating is a method of summing (aggregating) the estimates at the activity level to estimate resources needed for work packages, central accounts and summary project levels (P 324).

9.2.2.3 Analogous Estimating

Analogous Estimating is a technique in using **historical examples of resources from similar projects.** This analogous data is useful in estimating future project resources.

9.2.2.4 Parametric Estimating

Parametric Estimating is a resource estimate formed by using historical data, combined with other variables, calculating estimates and then applying this information to the entire project, or just parts of a project (P 374).

9.2.2.5 Data Analysis

Alternative Analysis is one of the techniques used in the process of **Data Analysis**.

9.2.2.6 Project Management Information System (PMIS)

Project Management Information Systems (PMIS) may include resource management software that helps plan, organize and manage resource pools and develops resource estimates (P 325).

9.2.2.7 Meetings

Planning **Meetings** are held to discuss and estimate need resources, the level of effort (LOE) for Team Members and the quantity of needed materials, etc. (P 325).

9.2.3 Estimate Activity Resources: Outputs

9.2.3.1 Resource Requirements

Resource Requirements: Types and quantities of resources are identified for each work package.

9.2.3.2 Basis of Estimates

Some of the supporting details used in determining a Basis of Estimates are (P 326):

- Method used to develop Estimate
- Resources used to develop Estimate

- Assumptions associated with Estimate
- Known constraints
- Range of Estimate
- Confidence level for Estimate
- Documentation of Identified Risks influencing the estimate

9.2.3.3 Resource Breakdown Structure

Resource Breakdown Structure: A hierarchal structure representing resources by category and type.

Fig. 9-7, P 327, *Sample Resource Breakdown Structure*

9.2.3.4 Project Documents Updates

Some of the Documents that could be updated in this process are (P 327):

- **Activity Attributes**: Updated with Resource Requirements
- **Assumption Log**: Contains information about assumptions and constraints
- **Lessons Learned Register**: Updated with techniques that were effective and efficient in developing resource estimates

9.3 ACQUIRE RESOURCES

Acquire Resources is the process of obtaining resources needed for the project. The **key benefit** of this process is that it outlines and guides the selection of resources and assigns them to their respective activities.

Fig. 9-8, P 328, *Acquire Resources: Inputs, Tools and Techniques and Outputs*
Fig. 9-9, P 329, *Acquire Resources: Data Flow Diagram*
These resources may be Internal, or External to the organization and the Project Team may/may not have control over resource selection. Some of the factors that must be considered during this process are (P 331):

- The project management or team should negotiate and influence others to acquire needed resources
- Failure to acquire resources will affect project success
- Alternative resources may be required in the event of unforeseen

constraints

How to fill your Tech Talent Gap with Part-Time Workers: 10 Tips for Success, (1:31 minutes) by Alison DeNisco Rayome, located at: https://www.techrepublic.com/article/how-to-fill-your-tech-talent-gap-with-part-time-workers-10-tips-for-success/

9.3.1 Acquire Resources: Inputs

9.3.1.1 Project Management Plan

Some of the **Project Management Plan** components are (P 330):

- **Resource Management Plan**: Provides guidance on how to acquire project resources
- **Procurement Management Plan**: Provides information regarding resources acquired outside the project
- **Cost Baseline**: Provides overall budget for activities

9.3.1.2 Project Documents

Some of the **Project Documents** that may be considered as Inputs to this process are (P 331):

- **Project Schedule**: Charts the assignment of roles, responsibilities, skills and relationships, show activities and planned start and end dates and is used to develop the Human Resource Management Plan
- **Resource Calendars**:
  - Identifies working days and shifts for which each specific resource is available
  - Describes necessary time frames for team members, collectively or individually
  - States when staffing acquisition, such as recruiting should start
- **Resource Requirements**: Identifies which resources need to be obtained
- **Stakeholder Register**: Reveals Stakeholders needs and expectations

9.3.1.3 Enterprise Environmental Factors

Some of the **Enterprise Environmental Factors** that might affect the Acquire Resources process are (P 331):

- Existing Information on Organizational Resources
- Marketplace Conditions
- Organizational Structure
- Geographic Locations

9.3.1.4 Organizational Process Assets

Some of the **Organizational Process Assets** that might affect the Acquire Resources process are (P 331):

- Policies and Procedures for acquiring, allocating and assigning necessary resources
- Historical Information and Lessons Learned

9.3.2 Acquire Resources: Tools and Techniques

9.3.2.1 Decision Making

Decision-Making Techniques that may be used in the **Acquire Resources** process may include **Multicriteria Decision Analysis** and the **Selection Criteria** may include (P 332):

- **Availability**: Verify availability of resources
- **Cost**: Verify cost
- **Ability**: Verify team capability
- **Experience**: Verify relevant experience by team members
- **Knowledge**: Verify team has needed knowledge
- **Skills**: Verify team skills
- **Attitude**: Verify communication skills
- **International Factors**: Consider locations, time zones and communication capabilities of team members

9.3.2.2 Interpersonal and Team Skills

Negotiation among team members may consist of conferring with (P 332):

- **Functional Managers**: Ensure the best resources are used in the required timeframe

- **Other Project Management Teams within the Organization**: Assign or share scarce resources
- **External Organizations and Suppliers**: Provide appropriate resources

9.3.2.3 Pre-Assessment

Pre-Assessment means resources are determined in advance or preassigned to the project (P 333).

9.3.2.4 Virtual Teams

Virtual Teams make it possible to (P 333):

- Form teams form the same organization who live in widespread geographical areas
- Add special expertise to a project team even if the SME is not in the same geographic area
- Use employees who work from home
- Form teams who work different hours, shifts or days
- Include people with mobility libations or disabilities
- Move forward with projects that might be cancelled due to travel expenses
- Save expenses of physical office equipment

9.3.3 Acquire Resources: Outputs

9.3.3.1 Physical Resource Assignments

Physical Resource Assignments are documentation of material, equipment, supplies, locations, etc., to be used during the project.

9.3.3.2 Project Team Assignments

Project Team Assignments records team member assignments and responsibilities.

9.3.3.3 Resource Calendars

Resource Calendars (P 334):

- Identify working days and shifts for which each specific resource is available

- Describes necessary time frames for team members, collectively or individually
- States when staffing acquisition, such as recruiting should start

9.3.3.4 Change Requests

Change Requests include, Corrective Action, Preventative Action and the carrying out of **Acquire Resources.**

9.3.3.5 Project Management Plan Updates

Some of the **Project Management Plan Updates** are (P 334):

- **Resource Management Plan**: May be updated to reflect actual experience in acquiring resources for the project
- **Cost Baseline**: May change as a result of Resource Acquisition

9.3.3.6 Project Documents Updates

Some of the **Project Documents** that can be u**pdated** include (P 335):

- **Lessons Learned Register**: Updated with information on challenges encountered
- **Project Schedule**: Changes may result from resource availability
- **Resource Breakdown Structure**: Resources acquired are recorded in the Resource Breakdown Structure
- **Resource Requirements:** Updated to reflect resources acquired
- **Risk Register**: New identified Risks are recorded
- **Stakeholder Register**: Update with new Stakeholders of information about existing Stakeholders

9.3.3.7 Enterprise Environmental Factors

Some of the **Enterprise Environmental Factors** that may be updated are (P 335):

- Resource availability within organization
- Amount of the organization's consumable resources that have been used

9.3.3.8 Organizational Process Assets

Some of the **Organizational Process Assets** that may be updated are documentation related to acquiring, assigning and allocating resources (P 335).

9.4 DEVELOP TEAM

Develop Team is about improving and developing competencies, team member interactions and the overall team environment, resulting in improved teamwork, enhanced personal skills, motivated employees, etc. The **key benefit** of this process is that it results in improved teamwork, enhanced interpersonal skills and competencies, motivated employees, reduced attrition and improved overall project performance.

Fig. 9-10, P 336, *Develop Team: Inputs, Tools and Techniques and Outputs*
Fig. 9-11, P 337, *Develop Team: Data Flow Diagram*

Check out the article: *More Diversity, less hierarchy; how to build a high-performing team*, by Glenn Leibowitz, located at https://www.linkedin.com/pulse/more-diversity-less-hierarchy-how-build-team-glenn-leibowitz?trk=eml-email_feed_ecosystem_digest_01-recommended_articles-8-Unknown&midToken=AQGXo1YSqn8KPw&fromEmail=fromEmail&ut=20vzFlhtXGz8s1

High-Performance Teams work more effectively when the following behaviors are adopted (P 337):

- Use open and effective communication
- Create team-building opportunities
- Develop trust among team members
- Manage conflicts in constructive manner
- Encourage collaboration among team members
- Encourage collaborative problem solving
- Encourage collaborative decision making skills

The PM should focus on developing an effective project team and promote working together in a positive environment.

Please refer to the following article, *5 Ways Your Company can find and Retain More Tech Talent—TechRepublic*, by Dan Roberts, located at: https://www.techrepublic.com/article/5-ways-your-company-can-find-and-retain-more-tech-talent/

Some of this may be accomplished by (P 338):

- Improving the knowledge and skills of team members
- Improving feelings of trust and encouragement
- Creating a dynamic, cohesive and collaborative team culture
- Empower the team to participate in decision-making

The **Tuckman Ladder** is one example of team development and some of the stages of this process are shown below (P 338):

- **Forming**: Team members meet and learn about the project
- **Storming**: Team members begin to address project work
- **Norming**: Team members work together
- **Performing**: Team members become interdependent
- **Adjourning**: Team members complete project work

The Stages of Teamwork Complexity (article), by Lorenzo Pasqualis, at: https://www.coderhood.com/stages-teamwork-complexity/

9.4.1 Develop Team: Inputs

9.4.1.1 Project Management Plan

The **Project Management Plan** includes the Resource Management Plan. The resource management plan provides guidance in planning team member rewards, feedback, training and disciplinary action where/when warranted (P 339).

9.4.1.2 Project Documents

Project Documents that may be considered as Inputs to this process are (P 339):

- **Lessons Learned Register**: Lessons Learned earlier in the project with regard to developing the team can be applied to later phases
- **Project Schedule**: Defines when and how to provide training for the project team

- **Project Team Assignments**: Identifies Team Member roles and responsibilities
- **Resource Calendars**: Identify times when project members can participate in team development activities
- **Team Charter**: Operating guidelines are documented in the Team Charter

9.4.1.3 Enterprise Environmental Factors

Some of the **Enterprise Environmental Factors** that may affect this process are (P 339):

- Human Resource Management Policies
- Team Member Skills
- Geographic distribution of team members

9.4.1.4 Organizational Process Assets

Organizational Process Assets: Historical Information and the Lessons Learned are two (2) of the process that can influence the develop team process (P 340).

9.4.2 Develop Team: Tools and Techniques

9.4.2.1 Colocation

Colocation can be temporary or span the entire project lifecycle. Strategies for team colocation can include a team meeting room, places to post schedules and a sense of community.

9.4.2.2 Virtual Teams

Some of the **Virtual Team** benefits are more skills, reduced costs, less travel and relocation expenses.

9.4.2.3 Communication Theory

Communication Theory builds a more cohesive environment among team members and some of the ways in which this can be achieved are shown below (P 340):

- **Shared Portal**: Shared Repository for Information Sharing
- **Video Conferencing**: Important for Virtual Teams
- **Audio Conferencing**: A technique capable of building rapport
- **Email/Chat**: Regular communication is an effective technique

9.4.2.4 Interpersonal and Team Skills

Some of **the Interpersonal and Team Skills** used in this process may include (P 341):

- **Conflict Management**: The PM needs to resolve conflicts in constructive and timely fashion
- **Influencing**: Key influencing skills include:
  - Ability to be persuasive by clearly articulating points or positions
  - High levels of active and effective listening skills
  - Awareness of and consideration for various perspectives in a given situation
  - Gathering relevant and critical information to address important issues and reach agreements while maintain mutual trust
- **Motivation**: The PM needs to empower the team in order to motivate the members of the team
- **Negotiation**: Builds trust and harmony and trust to reach a consensus on project needs
- **Team Building**: Conduct social activities to build a collaborative and cooperative working environment

9.4.2.5 Recognition and Rewards

The purpose of **Recognition and Reward**s is to achieve desirable behavior and it motivates people to see that they are valued. Cultural differences must always be honored.

9.4.2.6 Training

Training is performed to achieve the skills necessary to complete the project, which may be Formal or Informal. This enhances project team competency (P 342).

9.4.2.7 Individual and Team Assessments

Individual and Team Assessments provide the PM with knowledge to identify strengths and weaknesses of team members or individuals (P 342).

9.4.2.8 Meetings

Meetings are for addressing and discussing topics that will help develop the team members.

9.4.3 Develop Team: Outputs

9.4.3.1 Team Performance Assessments

Some of a team's effectiveness could include the following (P 343):

- **Improvements in skills** that allow individuals to perform assignments more efficiently and effectively
- **Improvements in competencies** that help team members perform better as a team
- **Reduced staff turnover rate**
- **Increased team cohesiveness** where team members share information and experiences openly and help each other to improve the overall project performance

9.4.3.2 Change Requests

Change Requests document project Adjustments, Actions or Interventions

9.4.3.3 Project Management Plan Updates

Project Management Plan Updates reflect changes to the Resource Management Plan. Changes must go through the Change Control process via a Change Request.

9.4.3.4 Project Documents Updates

Project Document Updates reflect Forecasts, Work Performance Reports and Issue Log changes. Some of the documents that may be updated include:

- **Lessons Learned Register**: Contains what has been experienced and any challenges or recommendations that worked well in developing the team will be files for future use
- **Project Schedule**: Any work activities required in developing the team may result in project schedule changes
- **Project Team Assignments**: These changes are recorded in the project team assignments documentation
- **Resource Calendars**: Specify when and how resources are available during a prescribed activity
- **Team Charter**: May be updated to reflect changes to agreed-upon team operating guidelines that result from team development

9.4.3.5 Enterprise Environmental Factors

Some of the updates to Enterprise Environmental Factors could include (P 343):

- Employee development plan records
- Skill Assessments

9.4.3.6 Organizational Process Assets

Some of the updates to Organizational Process Assets could include (P 343):

- Training Requirements
- Personnel Assessment

9.5 MANAGE TEAM

Manage Team is the process of tracking the performance of team members to optimize team and project performance. The **key benefit** is to influence team behavior, manage conflict and resolve issues.

Fig. 9-12, P 345, *Manage Team: Inputs, Tools and Techniques and Outputs*
Fig. 9-13, P 346, *Manage Team: Data Flow Diagram*

Managing a project team requires management and leadership skills to create a high-performance team. The emphasis should be on communication, conflict management, negotiation and leadership.

9.5.1 Manage Team: Inputs

9.5.1.1 Project Management Plan

The **Project Management Plan** components include the Resource Management Plan (P 347).

9.5.1.2 Project Documents

Project Documents that are considered Inputs to this process include (P 347):

- **Issue Log**: Documents the effects of managing the project team and monitors who is responsible for resolving specific team issues by a target date
- **Lessons Learned Register**:
- **Project Team Assignments**: Identifies Team member roles and responsibilities
- **Team Charter**: Provide guidance for how the team will make

decisions, conduct meetings and resolve conflict

9.5.1.3 Work Performance Reports

Work Performance Reports are a physical or electronic source of information and can help the project management team determine future Team Resource requirements.

9.5.1.4 Team Performance Assessments

Team Performance Assessments are made on a regular basis by using formal or informal assessments (P 347).

9.5.1.5 Enterprise Environmental Factors

The **Enterprise Environmental Factors** that may affect the Manage Team process include Human Resource Management Policies and procedures.

9.5.1.6 Organizational Process Assets

Some of the **Organizational Process Assets** affecting the manage team process could include (P 348):

- Certificates of Appreciation
- Corporate Apparel
- Other Organizational Perquisites

9.5.2 Manage Team: Tools and Techniques

9.5.2.1 Interpersonal and Team Skills

Interpersonal and Team Skills that might be used for this process include (P 349):

- **Conflict Management**: Successful conflict management depends on the ability to resolve conflict and some of those techniques may include (P 348):
    - Importance and Intensity of the conflict
    - Time pressure for resolving the conflict
    - Relative power of the people involved in the conflict
    - Importance of maintaining a good relationship
    - Motivation to resolve conflict on a long-term or short-term basis
    - Five (5) general techniques for resolving conflict are:
        - Withdraw/Avoid: Postponing the issue
        - Smooth/Accommodate: Emphasizing areas of

agreement instead of difference
    - Compromise/Reconcile: A win-win solution for all parties
    - Force/Direct: Push one's viewpoint at the expense of others
    - Collaborate/Problem Solve: Incorporate multiple viewpoints and insights from differing perspectives which may result in a win-win solution

- **Decision Making**: The ability to negotiate and influence the organization and the Project Management Team. Some guidelines for decision-making are shown below:
    - Focus on goals to be served
    - Follow a decision making process
    - Study the environmental factors
    - Analyze available information
    - Stimulate team creativity
    - Account for risk
- **Emotional Intelligence**: The ability to identify, assess and manage the personal emotions of oneself and others as well as collective emotions of groups of people
- **Influencing**: A Project Manager's ability to influence Stakeholders and some of the key skills include:
    - Persuasiveness
    - Clearly articulating points and positions
    - High level of active and effective and listening skills
    - Awareness of and consideration for various perspectives in any situation
- **Leadership**: The ability to lead a team and inspire others. There are multiple leadership theories and styles. See section 3.4.5.1, Leadership styles (P 65).

9.5.2.2 Project Management Information Systems (PMIS)

Project Management Information Systems (PMIS) can include Resource Management or Scheduling Software.

9.5.3 Manage Team: Outputs

9.5.3.1 Change Requests

Change Requests occur as a result of carrying out the manage team process. Staffing needs may change whether by choice or unforeseen events, such as team members who move, quit or are reassigned. All change requests must go through the Perform Integrated Change Control Process.

9.5.3.2 Project Management Plan Updates

Project Management Plan Updates may occur, requiring a Change Request and could include (P 351):

- **Resource Management Plan**: Will be updated to reflect actual experience in managing the project team
- **Schedule Baseline**: Changes to Project Schedule may be required to reflect the way the team is performing
- **Cost Baseline**: Changes to the Project Cost Baseline may be required to reflect the way the team is performing

9.5.3.3 Project Documents Updates

Some of the **Project Documents** that may be updated include (P 351):

- **Issue Log**: New issues raised are recorded in the Issue Log
- **Lessons Learned Register**: Updated with information on challenges encountered
- **Project Team Assignments**: Changes to the team are recorded in the project team assignments documentation

9.5.3.4 Enterprise Environmental Factors

Some of the **Enterprise Environmental Factors** that can be updated as a result of this process are (P 351):

- Input to Organizational Performance Appraisals
- Personnel Skill

9.6 CONTROL RESOURCES

Control Resources is the process of monitoring the planned versus the actual utilization of the resources and take corrective action. The **key benefit** is to ensure that the physical resources assigned and available, at the right place and time, and allocated to the project as planned, then released when they are no longer needed.

Fig. 9-14, P 352, *Control Resources: Inputs, Tools and Techniques and Outputs*
Fig. 9-15, P 353, *Control Resources: Data Flow Diagram*

This process, which is concerned with physical resources, should be performed throughout the project life cycle in all project phases. The Control Resources process is concerned with the following (P 354):

- **Monitoring resource expenditures**
- **Identifying and dealing with resource shortage/surplus** in a timely manner
- Ensuring that **resources are used and released** according to the plan and project needs
- Informing appropriate stakeholders if any issues arise with relevant resources
- Influencing the **factors that can create resources utilization change**
- **Managing the actual changes** as they occur

9.6.1 Control Resources: Inputs

9.6.1.1 Project Management Plan

The **Project Management Plan** contains the Resource Management Plan, which includes guidance on how physical resources should be used, controlled and released (P 354).

9.6.1.2 Project Documents

Some of the **Project Documents** that may be considered as Inputs are (P 354):

- **Issue Log**: Documents issues that arise and assigns the responsibility to team members who must resolve a specific issue(s) by agreed upon targeted dates and they can include lack of resources, delay in supplies, or low-grade material
- **Lessons Learned Register**: Lessons learned earlier in the project can be applied to later phases in the project
- **Physical Resource Assignments**: Documentation of material, equipment, supplies, locations, etc. and whether resources are

internal or outsourced

- **Project Schedule:** Shows the resources that are needed, when they are needed and the location where they are needed
- **Resource Breakdown Structure**: Provides a reference in case any resource needs to be replaced or reacquired during the project
- **Risk Register:** Identifies risks and any pertinent data belonging to a particular risk that can affect equipment, materials or supplies

9.6.1.3 Work Performance Data

Work Performance Data involves data on project status and the number and type of resources used.

9.6.1.4 Agreements

Agreements are an understanding between parties and the duties of each party and are made within the context of the project. Agreements are the basis of all resources external to the organization (P 355).

9.6.1.5 Organizational Process Assets

Some of the **Organizational Process Assets** that may affect the Control Resources are (P 355):

- Policies regarding resource control and assignment
- Escalation procedures
- Lessons Learned Repository

9.6.2 Control Resources: Tools and Techniques

9.6.2.1 Data Analysis

Some of the Data Analysis techniques used in this process are (P 357):

- **Alternative Analysis**: A form of deciding on several alternatives and analyzing each one before making a decision.
- **Cost-Benefit Analysis**: Determines the best corrective action in the event of a deviation in cost
- **Performance Analysis**: Measures, compares and analyzes planned resources utilization to actual utilization

- **Trend Analysis**: Determines resources needed at upcoming stages of the project and examines project performance over time to determine whether performance is improving or deteriorating

9.6.2.2 Problem Solving

Methodical steps need to be taken when **Problem Solving** by using a set of tools which includes those listed below (P 356):

- **Identify/specify** the problem
- **Define and break down the problem** into smaller steps
- **Investigate and collect data**
- **Analyze/find the root cause** of the problem
- **Solve/choose the suitable solution** from a variety of available sources
- **Check/determine if the problem is fixed**

9.6.2.3 Interpersonal and Team skills

Some of the **Interpersonal and Team Skills** used in this process are (P 357):

Negotiation: The need may arise to negotiate for additional physical resources, changes in those resources or costs associated with those resources
Influencing: Helps the PM to solve problems and obtain needed resources in a timely manner

9.6.2.4 Project Management Information Systems (PMIS)

The **Project Management Information Systems** (PMIS) can include resource management or scheduling software to obtain the right resources, to work on the right activities and at the right time and place (P 357).

9.6.3 Control Resources: Outputs

9.6.3.1 Work Performance Information

Work Performance Information is data that is collected, analyzed, correlated and contextualized and provides a foundation for project decisions. This includes using the information to compare resource requirements/allocations to resource utilization levels (P 357).

9.6.3.2 Change Requests

A **Change Request** is a formal request to change/alter a factor(s)/element(s) in a project.

9.6.3.3 Project Management Plan Updates

Some of the **Project Management Plan Updates** include (P 358):

- **Resource Management Plan:** Updated to reflect actual experience in managing resources
- **Schedule Baseline**: The finalized and approved schedule for the project or the phase of the project with start and finish dates and may be modified or changed if it becomes necessary to reflect the way project resources are being managed
- **Cost Baseline**: Accepted time intervals to measure cost performance of project resources and how they are being managed

9.6.3.4 Project Documents Updates

Some of the **Project Document Updates** include (P 358):

- **Assumption Log**: Updated with new assumptions regarding equipment, materials, supplies, etc.
- **Issue Log**: New issues raised are recorded
- **Lessons Learned Register**: Updated with techniques that were effective in managing resource logistics, scrap, utilization variances, etc.
- **Physical Resource Assignments:** Subject to change due to availability, the project, organization, etc.
- **Resource Breakdown Structure**: Changes may be required to reflect the way project resources are being used
- **Risk Register**: Updated with new risks associated with resource availability and utilization, etc.

Summary: Answers to Student Learning Outcomes

1. **Project Resource Management** is a process (P 307). It requires the Project Manager to organize, manage and lead the project team members from the start of the project, throughout the duration of the project to the project's completion. This process includes activities that identify, acquire, and manage the resources needed for project success and support the assignment of team personnel and resources for the development of people and job descriptions so that all team members know who does which tasks in the assigned work package. The right resources need to be available to the project manager and team at the right time and place.

2. **Project Resource Management** consists of the **following process components** (P 307):

    - **Plan Resource Management**: The planning process of defining how to estimate, acquire, manage, and utilize physical and team resources.
    - **Estimate Activity Resources**: A planning process that estimates team resources, the types and quantities of material, equipment and supplies needed to perform project work.
    - **Acquire Resources**: An executing process that deals with obtaining team members, facilities, equipment, materials, supplies and other resources to complete the project work.
    - **Develop Project Team**: An executing process that deals in principally improving competencies, team member interaction and the overall team environment.
    - **Manage Project Team**: This is an executing process. The Project Manager tracks the team performance, provides feedback, resolving issues, and managing team changes to optimize project performance, etc.
    - **Control Resources** The process of monitoring, controlling and ensuring that the physical resources assigned and allocated to the project are available as planned. This requires monitoring the plan verses actual use of resources and performing corrective action as needed.

    Fig. 9-1, P 308, *Project Resource Management Overview*

3. The Project Manager (P 309) is both a leader and a manager. To lead a high performing team, the project manager leader must form the team as an effective group. The following **are factors that influence team formation**:

- **Team Environment**
- **Geographical Location**
- **Stakeholder Communications**
- **Organizational Change Management**
- **Politics (Internal and External)**
- **Cultural/Organizational Issues**
- **Miscellaneous Project Performance Factors**

4. The following **trends and emerging practices should be considered in Project Resource Management** (P 310):

   - **Resource Management** methods, such as Lean Management, JIT Management, Kanban, TPM, Theory of Constraints (TOC), etc.
   - **Emotional Intelligence (EI)**
   - **Self-Organizing Teams**
   - **Virtual/Distributed Teams**

5. The following lists six **(6) Plan Resource Management approaches** that may need the project manager to consider for **tailoring** (P 311):

   - **Diversity**
   - **Physical Location**
   - **Industry Specific Resources**
   - **Acquisition of Team Members**
   - **Management of Team**
   - **Life Cycle Approach**

6. **Collaboration** is useful in agile/adaptive environments and can accomplish the following (P 311):
   - **Boost Productivity**
   - **Facilitate Innovative Problem solving**
   - **Accelerate Work Integration**
   - **Improve Communication**
   - **Increase Knowledge Sharing**
   - **Provide Work Assignment(s) Flexibility**

7. **Plan Resource Management** is just that. It means that the PM needs as outlined in the Project Charter and/or the Project Plan, to have teams of workers available when needed to do the work required to meet the project objectives. It is a process to define how to estimate, acquire, manage and use team and physical resources. Plan Resource Management has the key benefits of establishing the approach and level of management effort required for managing resources based upon the type and complexity of the project (P 312).

   Fig. 9-2, 312, *Plan Resource Management: Inputs, Tools and Techniques and Outputs*
   Fig. 9-3, P 313, *Plan Resource Management: Data Flow Diagram*

   The **Resource Management Plan** is a subsidiary plan of the Project Management Plan and an output of the Plan Resource Management Process. The team charter and project documents updates to include in the assumption log and risk register are the other two (2) inputs of plan resource management.

8. The outputs of the **Plan Resource Management** process are (P 312):

   1. Team Charter See 9.1.3.2, (P 319)
   2. Project Documents Updates (Assumption Log and Risk Register) See 9.1.3.3 (P 320)

9. In **Plan Resource Management Data Representation: Tools and Techniques,** there are three (3) formats shown below that are used in documenting high-level member's roles and responsibilities, etc.

   They are (P 316-317):

   1. **Hierarchal charts**
   2. **Assignment matrix**
   3. **Text-oriented formats**

   Hierarchal-Type Charts show relationships and positions in a graphical, top-down format (P 316).

   - The **Work Breakdown Structure** (WBS) shows how project deliverables are divided into work packages and show high-level responsibilities.
   - The **Organizational Breakdown Structure** (OBS) shows the organization's existing departments, etc.

- The **Resource Breakdown Structure** (RBS) is an hierarchical structure and shows resources by category and type used to facilitate project planning, managing and controlling project work.

10. **Responsibility Assignment Matrix Chart (RAM)**: The responsibility assignment matrix chart shows project resources assigned to work packages. It is used to show the connections to work packages and project team members that are assigned to the work package. An example of a (RAM) is the Responsible, Accountable, Consult and Inform (RACI) Chart. This is important as it can delineate internal and external resources.

    Fig. 9-4, P 317, *Sample RACI Chart*

    Text oriented formats (P 317): This text-oriented format is also known as position descriptions and role responsibility-authority forms. It details the descriptions of each person's responsibility, authority, competency and qualifications.

11. When describing **team member's project roles and responsibilities**, the following attributes should be discussed with the team, so the team can become a high-performance team destined to create project success. These attributes are integral to the **Resource Management Plan**. See section 9.1.3.1 (P 318). The Resource Management Plan, a component of the Project Management Plan, provides guidance on how projects resources should be categorized, allocated, managed and released.

    - **Role**: Describes team function. Ex. Business Analyst, Beta Test Coordinator, Civil Engineer and Testing Coordinator.
    - **Authority**: A given right to apply project resources, make decisions, and sign approvals, etc.
    - **Responsibility**: Assigned work that someone is expected to perform.
    - **Competency**: the skills and capacity to complete assigned work.

12. The **Resource Management Plan** is a subsidiary component of the Project Management Plan. It describes when the project team members will be acquired and how long they will be assigned to the project. **The Resource Management** Plan is continually updated while the project is ongoing. It will consist of at least nine **(9) elements** that will most likely vary by the size and complexity of the project. These nine elements are (P 318-319):

    1. **Identification of resources**
    2. **Acquiring resources**

3. **Roles and responsibilities**
4. **Project organization charts**
5. **Project team resource management**
6. **Training**
7. **Team development**
8. **Resource control**
9. **Recognition plan**

13. **Estimate Activity Resources** is a process of estimating team resources and the type and quantities of material, equipment, and supplies needed to perform project work. The key benefit is that it identifies the type, quantity and resources needed to complete the project (P 320).

Fig. 9-5, P 321, *Estimate Activity Resources: Inputs, Tools and Techniques and Outputs*
Fig. 9-6, P 321, *Estimate Activity Resources: Data Flow Diagram*

14. **Outputs of Estimate Activity Resources.** The four Outputs are listed below (P 321):

1. **Resource requirements**
2. **Basis of estimates**
3. **Resource breakdown structure**
4. **Project documents updates: activity attributes, assumption log and lessons learned register**

15. **Seven (7) Tools and Techniques used in Estimate Activity Resources (P 324-325)** are listed as follows:

1. **Expert Judgment**
2. **Bottom-Up Estimating**
3. **Analogous Estimating**
4. **Parametric Estimating**
5. **Data Analysis**
6. **Project Management Information System (PMIS)**
7. **Meetings**

16. **Acquire Resources** is the process of obtaining team members, facilities, equipment, material, supplies, and other resources needed to complete the project work. The key benefit is that it outlines and guides the selection of resources and assigns them to their respective activities, or work packages (P 328).

Fig. 9-8, 328, *Acquire Resources: Inputs, Tools and Techniques and Outputs*
Fig. 9-9, 329, *Acquire Resources: Data Flow Diagram*

17. **Virtual Teams** are a very popular means of running projects (P 333). Conducting project work with little need for face-to-face meetings is a characteristic of Virtual Teams. Virtual teams can use a variety of communication technologies and the value of virtual teams is many. For example, they provide:

    - Teams from same organizations in **different geographic areas**
    - A common **communication means** (email, audio/video conferencing, cell phone, etc., for members that are geographically dispersed.
    - **Engage employees** from home offices
    - A **means and ease** of acquiring SME's (Subject Matter Experts) who are able to meet on line and provide their expertise
    - The ability to have **people to work in different time zones**, shifts, hours or days, etc.
    - May include stakeholders with **mobility limitations**
    - They provide **project possibilities** where the project was cancelled due to travel expenses
    - **Reduction in office expense** and **physical equipment**

18. **Develop Team** is a process whose purpose is to improve team competencies and interaction so that the overall team's environment increases and enhances project performance. The key benefit of this process is that there should be improved teamwork, interpersonal skills, competencies, more highly motivated employees, reduced attrition and improved project performance (P 336).

    Fig. 9-10, P 336, *Develop Team: Inputs, Tools and Techniques and Outputs*
    Fig. 9-11, P 337, *Develop Team: Data Flow Diagram*

19. **Team Development Activities** are often described by the **Tuckman Ladder** (9.4) (P 338). This model (Ladder) illustrates the stages of team growth, development and participation. It is possible for teams to be stuck in certain stages if they are unable to perform individually or collectively. Some stages can be skipped if the team has worked together in the past. The stages are as follows:

    1. **Forming**: Team meets and learns

2. **Storming**: Team begins to address the project work
3. **Norming**: Team is working together and adjusting their work patterns
4. **Performing**: Team is becoming a high performance team
5. **Adjourning**: Once the project is completed, they move on from the project

20. **Colocation** is called a **Tight Matrix**, as the team members are located in the same physical location (P 340). Collocation can be temporary and may require meetings strategic at certain times or may continue throughout the project life cycle.

    They often hold team meetings in what is called a **War Room**. These locations are great for holding strategy sessions, posting notes, and schedule, using white boards and creating a sense of community (P 340).

21. **Team Performance Assessment** (an output of Develop Team) criteria needs designed into the **Develop Team Process**. The team performance assessment is usually an output document, though it may be in the form of a verbal assessment. The following criteria needs to be considered and measured by evaluating the team's effectiveness (P343):

    - Skill Improvements;
    - Competency Improvements
    - Reduced Staff Turnover, etc.
    - Increase team cohesiveness

    See P 343, for a more complete description.

22. To **Manage Team** means that the Project Manager tracks individual and team performance throughout the project life cycle (P 345). This is an executing process that produces the following key benefits:

    - Influences Overall Team behavior
    - Manages conflicts and issues, etc.

    Fig. 9-12, P 345, *Manage Team: Inputs, Tools and Techniques and Outputs*
    Fig. 9-13, P 346, *Manage Team: Data Flow Diagram*

23. **Conflict Management** is the process of reducing the negative factors of

conflict while increasing positive outcomes (P 348). The purpose is to enhance team learning and group interaction and productivity. Factors that serve as a basis of choosing conflict resolution methods include but are not limited to (P 349):

- **Importance and intensity** of conflict
- Amount of **time needed to deal with the conflict** issue
- **Relative power** of individuals
- **Maintaining good stakeholder relationships**
- **Motivation to resolve conflict** on a long or short term basis

Resolving conflict may require choosing one or more of the following approaches (P 348):

- **Withdraw/Avoid**: Retreat from conflict or postpone issue for a later time
- **Smooth/Accommodate**: Emphasize areas of agreement rather than areas of difference
- **Compromise/Reconcile**: Reaching out to areas that produce some degree of solution or satisfaction.
- **Force/Direct**: Pushing viewpoints that only offer a win-lose solution.
- **Collaborate/Problem Solve**: An approach that leads to a consensus, strengthens commitment, and requires multiple viewpoints, considerations and insights from differing perspectives.

24. **Control Resources** is a process to make certain that resources are available as assigned according to the Plan Schedule. These resources are then allocated and the project manager will monitor resource utilization and compare planned to actual usage. Corrective actions may be needed. The key benefits are resources are available at the right time and place. When resources are not further needed, they are released.

    Fig. 9-14, P 352, *Control Resources: Inputs, Tools and Techniques and Outputs*
    Fig. 9-15, P 353, *Control Resources: Data Flow Diagram*
25. **Control Resources: Tools and Techniques. Problem Solving Steps** are (P 356):

    1. **Identify the problem**
    2. **Define the problem**
    3. **Investigate the issues**
    4. **Analyze the root causes of the problem**
    5. **Solve/select suitable solution options**
    6. **Check the solution**

Similar Questions that may be on the PMI Exam related to Chapter 9

1. A project manager in a leading manufacturer of consumer electronics, personal computers and peripherals. You have been assigned a project to drive growth and profit by integrating an online CRM (customer relationship management) solution. The project is nearing its completion. Which of the following is an output of close project or phase process?

    A. Organizational process asset updates
    B. Project management plan updates
    C. Accepted deliverables
    D. Work performance reports

    Correct answer is A: The project management plan is not updated after project closure. Accepted deliverables are inputs to the Close Project or Phase process. Work Performance reports are outputs of monitors and control project work. Organizational process assets are updated with project files, closure documents, lessons learned, etc.

2. Ground rules are established to set clear expectations regarding acceptable behavior by the project team members. Whose responsibility is it to enforce ground rules?

    A. The project manager
    B. All project team members share the responsibility for enforcing the rules once they are established
    C. The HR team
    D. The project manager and senior team members

    Correct answer is B: All project team members share responsibility for enforcing the rules once they are established.

3. In addition to improving the success rate for goal achievements, team building has many benefits for individuals, but one characteristic that is not a benefit of team building is ______.

    A. Clear organizational structure
    B. Clear aims/goals
    C. Improved individual creativity
    D. Improved monitory rewards

Correct answer is D: Team building activities does not result directly in monetary rewards.

4. Hardy is the project manager at a leading manufacturer of consumer electronics, personal computers and peripherals. He has been assigned a project to drive growth and profit by integrating an online CRM (customer relationship management) solution. The project team is new and it is high visibility project. As a part of team development, which of the following tool would be useful to get insights into team members' strengths and weakness?

   A. Training
   B. Personnel assessment tools
   C. Co-location
   D. Interpersonal Skills

   Correct answer is B: As per the PMBOK, Personnel assessment tools give the project manager and the project team insight into areas of strengths and weaknesses. These tools help project managers assess the team preferences, aspirations, how they process and organize information, how they tend to make decisions and how they prefer to interact with people.

5. John is working hard over weekends to complete project objectives. According to the expectancy theory of motivation _____.

   A. Managers should not expect workers to work extra hours
   B. Motivation to act is linked to an outcome that is expected to have value
   C. Managers should expect that employees who are paid more will work harder
   D. Downsizing companies can expect to have motivation problems

   Correct answer is B: According to the expectancy theory, people are motivated in anticipation of rewards and recognition, if given a goal.

6. Two team members of your team, Philip and Ramie were having a conflict. You used the problem solving conflict resolution technique, which is _____.

   A. A win-win situation
   B. A win-lose situation
   C. A lose-lose situation
   D. Delaying the solution

   Correct answer is A: Problem solving is a win-win resolution technique.

7. Which of the following management styles is appropriate when the project manager wants to encourage the staff to pool its knowledge to make the best decision possible?

   A. Laissez-faire
   B. Antipodal
   C. Directive
   D. Democratic

   Correct answer is D: Democratic style ensures all are given opportunities to share their opinion.

8. Russell is working as a project manager in KWSoft.com. He has faith in his team and occasionally reviews the documents prepared by his team members. What kind of manager is Russell?

   A. Theory X
   B. Theory Y
   C. Theory Z
   D. None of the above

   Correct answer is B: Russell has faith and trust in his team members, which makes him a Theory Y manager.

9. Precise Incorporated, and NYSE listed multinational manufacturing company, has presence in 30 countries worldwide. Your company is selected to implement Enterprise Resource Planning (ERP) system in Precise to streamline their operations. This implementation is expected to improve/enhance company's manufacturing, procurement, sales, supply chain and payment systems. You are the project manager for the same and currently are involved in execution phase. Since, it is a deadline driven, high-visibility project, there is a clear mandate from the senior management to ensure optimal level of coordination and proper teamwork within the project. Which of the following symptoms, typically, does not reflect bad teamwork?

   A. Excessive meetings
   B. Lack of trust or confidence in the project manager
   C. Unhealthy competition
   D. Unproductive meetings

Correct answer is A: Excessive meetings could be a result of certain unique requirements, e.g., likes project complexity, working with virtual teams, geographical spread of the project, etc. This should not be considered a symptom of bad teamwork until and unless it is clear that these excessive meetings are causing a rift within the team. All other signs reflect bad teamwork.

10. When building team confidence, a project manager should _____ with team members and avoid _____.

    A. Set limited times and opportunities for discussions; social contacts
    B. Practice what he/she preaches; social contacts
    C. Encourage frank discussions; making promises
    D. Encourage open conversations; politics

Correct answer is D: By doing this, a project manager can build a sense of trust and confidence among team members toward himself/herself.

You may now move on to Chapter Ten: Project Communications Management

Chapter 10: Project Communications Management: Listen More, Talk Less

"The single biggest problem in communication is the illusion that it has taken place." George Bernard Shaw

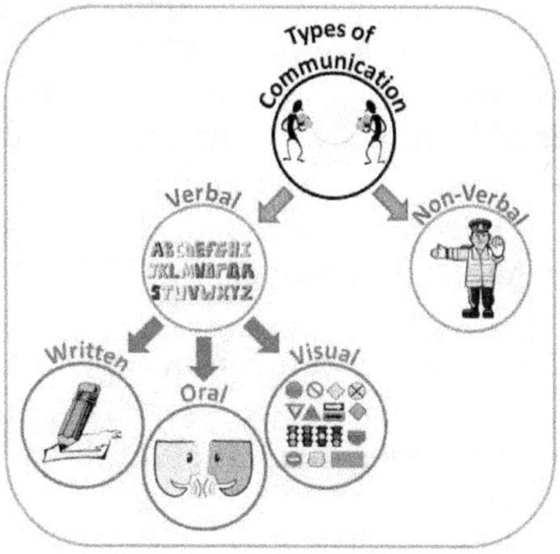

Carmine Gallo, a best-selling Author and Harvard professor, tells a story about the lost art of persuasion and communication, located at: *The Secret to Great Communication: Be like Aristotle*: http://knowledge.wharton.upenn.edu/article/the-secret-to-great-communication-skills/?utm_source=kw_newsletter&utm_medium=email&utm_campaign=2018-09-20

> *"[Lincoln] worked hard to develop a simple compact style of speaking and writing, with short clear sentences that could be 'understood by all…'"*
>
> Doris Kearns Goodwin in reference to Abraham Lincoln

CHAPTER 10 PROJECT COMMUNICATIONS MANAGEMENT INTRODUCTION OVERVIEW: LISTEN MORE, TALK LESS

Student Learning Outcomes

1. List and describe in detail the three (3) **processes for Project Communications Management** (P 359). What are the ITTO's of Communication Management?
2. List and describe the **six (6) mechanisms** used in information exchange (P 360).
3. List **eight (8) Communication Dimensions** that are common to general communications (P 361).
4. What are the **five (5) C's of Written Communication** (P 363-364)?
5. What are the **four (4) major communication skills** needed by a Project Manager (P 363)?
6. There are numerous **Trends and Emerging Project Communications Practices**. Please list them (P 364). Also, list possible **tailoring** communications that may be **considered.**
7. **What is Plan Communications Management and its key benefits (P 366)? What are the ITTO's of Plan Communications Management?**
8. There are five (5) software factors that can affect the product choice of **Communication Technology** in Plan Communications. What are they (P 370)?
9. List five **(5) Sequences of Communications** steps found within a basic sender/receiver/interactive communication model, to include cross-cultural communication. List in Order (P 371).
10. There are two **(2) Communication Models** (P 371-372) used to share information. What are they?
11. List the fourteen **(14) Project Communication Information Content Areas** (sections) that you would see in Communications Management Plan (P 377).
12. **What are the purpose and the key benefit of Manage Communication (P 379)? What are the ITTO's?**
13. List the four (**4) Communication Skills** that are a part of the tools and techniques in the **Manage Communications** process (P 383-384).
14. The **Project Management Information System (PMIS)** is a repository that uses a variety of tools. List all three (3) tools (P 385).
15. What is **Project Reporting** (P 385)?
16. **What is Monitor Communications and its key benefits (P 388)? What are the ITTO's?**
17. Why is it important to use a **Communications Issue Log** to document and monitor issue resolution (P 387)?
18. There are four (4) **Monitor Communications outputs** (P 392-393). List and describe the importance of each.
19. List five (5) methods that the project manager may use to monitor communications (P 389).

CHAPTER TEN INTRODUCTION: LISTEN MORE, TALK LESS

PROJECT COMMUNICATIONS MANAGEMENT: CHAPTER 10 OVERVIEW: PMBOK® 6th Edition P 359-394

Project Communications Management includes processes that are necessary to pass along (i.e. distribute) information about the project to its stakeholders. It includes the use of artifacts (ex.: notice boards, newsletters, press releases, etc.) and the implementation of activities to achieve effective information exchange and mutual understanding. Project Communications Management consists of two (2) parts:

1. **Developing Stakeholder Strategy**
2. **Carrying out the activities necessary to implement the communication strategy**

The Project Communications Management process consists of:

(10.1) **Plan Communications Management:** The process of developing an appropriate approach and plan for project communication activities based on the information needs of each stakeholder or group, available organizational assets and the needs of the project.

(10.2) **Manage Communications:** The process of ensuring timely and appropriate collection, creation, distribution, storage, retrieval, management, monitoring and the ultimate disposition of project information.

(10.3) **Monitor Communications:** The process of ensuring the information needs of the project and its stakeholders are met.

Plan Communications Management

Planned Communications Management requires that an appropriate approach and plan for communications activities that are based upon the needs of each stakeholder or group, available organizational assets and the needs of the project.

Fig. 10-1, P 360, *Project Communications Overview*

Manage Communications

Manage Communications ensures the timely and appropriate collection, creation, distribution storage, retrieval, management, monitoring, and the ultimate disposition of project information.

Monitor Communications

This is a process of ensuring that information needs meet the project and stakeholder's requirements.

Fig. 10-1, P 360, *Project Communications Overview*

Key Concepts for Project Communications Management

There are a number of mechanisms that may be used in exchanging information that are outlined. Communications dimensions are numerous as well. See P 360 and P 361.

To reduce misunderstanding and miscommunication, there are five 'C's' of written communications. They are (P 363):

- 'C' Correct Grammar and Spelling
- 'C' Concise expression and elimination of excess words
- 'C' Clear purpose and expression directed to the needs of the reader
- 'C' Current logical flow of ideas
- 'C' Controlling the flow of words and ideas

Other supporting communications skills listed with the 5 C's are listening actively; awareness of cultural and personal differences; identifying, setting and managing stakeholder expectations, and enhancement of skills.

- Fundamental attributes of communication activities and development of artifacts include (P 363):
    1. Clarity of communication's purpose
    2. Understanding receiver-sender moral
    3. Monitoring and measuring communication effectiveness

To help ensure your communication method is being understood by the right people at the right time, Check out the article, *How to Gain more Confidence in your Writing*, by August Birch, which can be found at https://medium.com/the-book-mechanic/how-to-gain-more-confidence-in-your-writing-2476a9f6394b

Trends and Emerging Practices in Project Communications Management

These are (P 364):

- Inclusion of stakeholders in project reviews
- Inclusion of stakeholders in project meetings
- Increased use of social computing

- Multifaceted approaches to communications

Tailoring Communications consideration must be given to the following (P 365):

- Stakeholders
- Physical location
- Communications technology
- Language
- Knowledge management

Considerations for Agile/Adaptive Environments

There is a significant need to eliminate ambiguity in communications. Agile communications requires on-the-spot team member access to stakeholders and sponsors when developing and using adaptive project management development tools (P 365).

Plan Communications Management:

This process develops the approach and plan for project communications activities. It includes recognizing the needs of stakeholders or groups and the needs of the project sponsors (P 366). The **key benefit** of this process is a documented approach to effectively engage stakeholders by presenting timely and relevant information (P 366).

Please 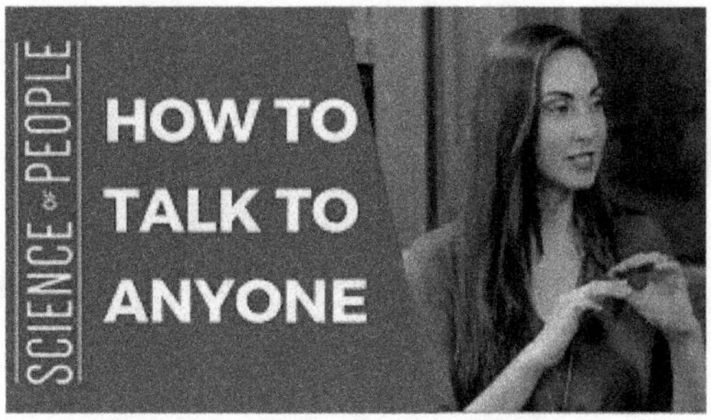

refer to the following YouTube Video, (7:27 minutes) *How to Talk to anyone with Ease and Confidence*, https://youtu.be/PMmnPpjtU7c

See chart on next page: **PLAN COMMUNICATIONS MANAGEMENT (Section 10.1)**

Chapter Ten: Project Communications Management

10.1 PLAN COMMUNICATIONS MANAGEMENT

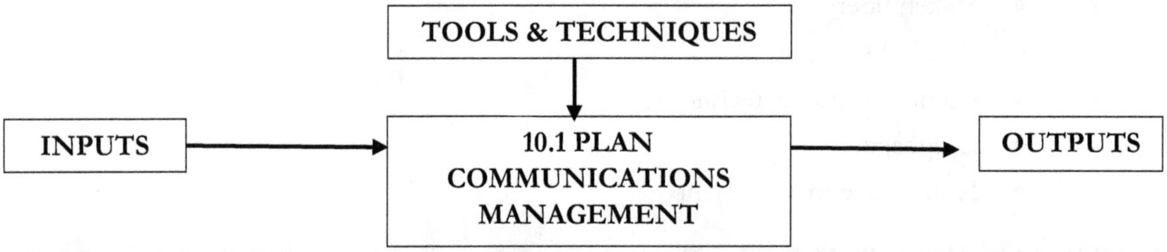

10.1 PLAN COMMUNICATIONS MANAGEMENT: Overview

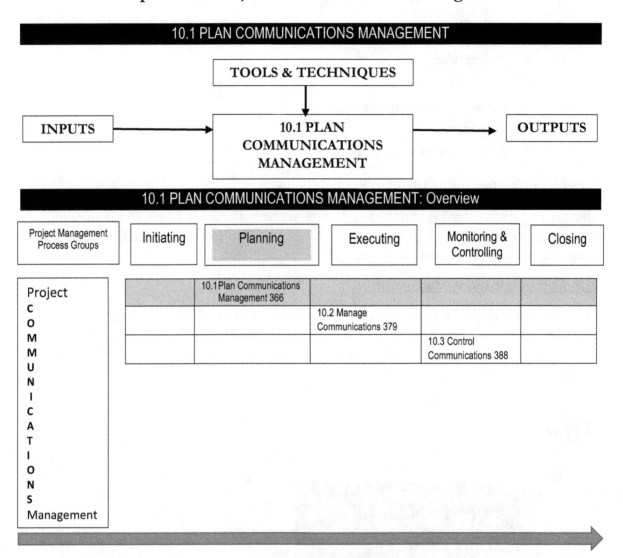

Project Management Process Groups	Initiating	Planning	Executing	Monitoring & Controlling	Closing
Project COMMUNICATIONS Management		10.1 Plan Communications Management 366			
			10.2 Manage Communications 379		
				10.3 Control Communications 388	

10.1 PLAN COMMUNICATIONS MANAGEMENT: ITTO Processes

.1 Inputs	.2 Tools and Techniques	.3 Outputs
.1 Project Charter 368 .2 Project Management Plan 368 • Resource Management Plan 368 • Stakeholder Engagement Plan 368 .3 Project Documents 368 • Requirements Documentation 368 • Stakeholder Register 368 .4 Enterprise Environmental Factors 368 .5 Organizational Process Assets 369	.1 Expert Judgment 369 .2 Communications Requirements Analysis 369 .3 Communications Technology 370 .4 Communication Models 371 .5 Communication Methods 374 .6 Interpersonal and Team Skills 375 • Communication Styles Assessment 375 • Political Awareness 375 • Cultural Awareness 375 .7 Data Representation 376 • Stakeholder Engagement Assessment Matrix 376 .8 Meetings 376	.1 Communications Management Plan 378 .2 Project Management Plan Updates 378 • Stakeholder Engagement Plan 378 .3 Project Documents Updates 379 • Project Schedule 379 • Stakeholder Register 379

Fig. 10-2, P 366, *Plan Communications Management: Inputs, Tools and Techniques and Outputs*
Fig. 10-3, P 367, *Plan Communications Management: Data Flow Diagram*

Communications planning is performed early on in the project when the project manager identifies when the stakeholder and project management plan is being developed. This process is performed throughout the project life cycle (P 379).

Manage Communications:

Manage communications is the process of collecting, creating, distributing, storing, retrieving, monitoring and deciding upon the ultimate disposition of project information in a timely basis. The **key benefit** of this process is to make certain efficient information flow occurs between the project team and the project stakeholders.

See chart on next page: **MANAGE COMMUNICATIONS (Section 10.2)**

Chapter Ten: Project Communications Management

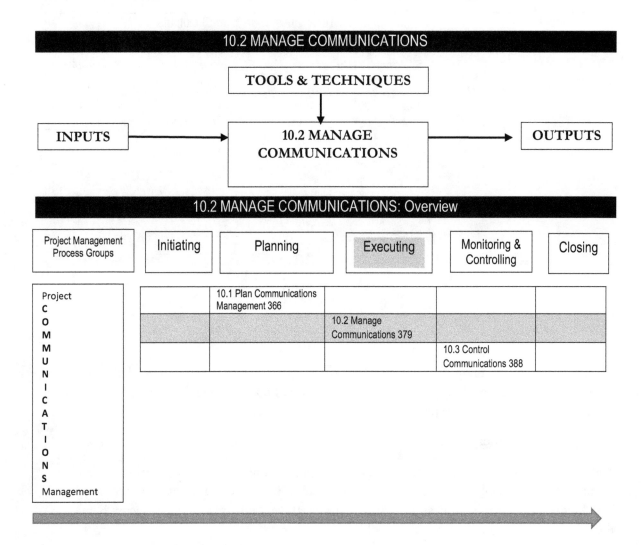

10.2 MANAGE COMMUNICATIONS

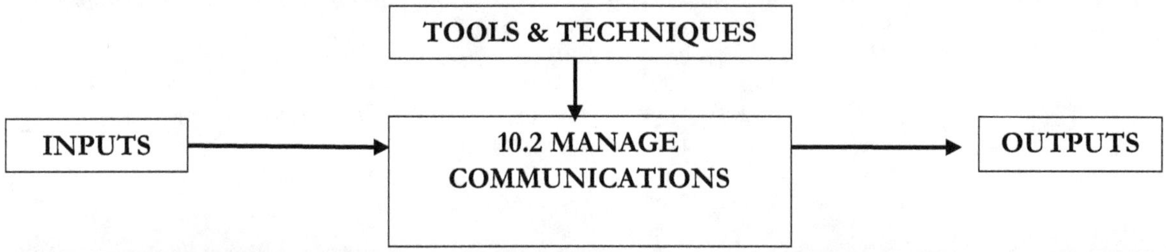

10.2 MANAGE COMMUNICATIONS: Overview

Project Management Process Groups	Initiating	Planning	Executing	Monitoring & Controlling	Closing
Project COMMUNICATIONS Management		10.1 Plan Communications Management 366			
			10.2 Manage Communications 379		
				10.3 Control Communications 388	

10.2 MANAGE COMMUNICATIONS: ITTO Processes

.1 Inputs	.2 Tools and Techniques	.3 Outputs
.1 Project Management Plan 381 • Resource Management Plan 381 • Communications Management Plan 381 • Stakeholder Engagement Plan 381 .2 Project Documents 382 • Change Log 382 • Issue Log 382 • Lessons Learned Register 382 • Quality Report 382 • Risk Report 382 • Stakeholder Register 382 .3 Work Performance Reports 382 .4 Enterprise Environmental Factors 383 .5 Organizational Process Assets 383	.1 Communication Technology 383 .2 Communications Methods 383 .3 Communication Skills 384 • Communication Competence 384 • Feedback 384 • Nonverbal 384 • Presentations 384 .4 Project Management Information Systems 385 .5 Project Reporting 385 .6 Interpersonal and Team Skills 386 • Active Listening 386 • Conflict Management 386 • Cultural Awareness 386 • Meeting Management 386 • Networking 386 • Political Awareness 386 .7 Meetings 386	.1 Project Communications 387 .2 Project Management Plan Updates 387 • Communications Management Plan 387 • Stakeholder Engagement Plan 387 .3 Project Document Updates 387 • Issue Log 387 • Lessons Learned Register 387 • Project Schedule 387 • Risk Register 387 • Stakeholder Register 387 .4 Organizational Process Assets Updates 388

Fig. 10-5, P 379, *Manage Communications: Inputs, Tools and Techniques and Outputs*
Fig. 10-6, P 380, *Manage Communications: Data Flow Diagram*

Monitor Communications:

This is a process to ensure that information needs of the project and stakeholders are met. The **key benefit** of Monitor Communications is the optimal information flow as defined in the Communications Plan and the Stakeholder Engagement Plan (P 388).

See chart on next page: **MONITOR COMMUNICATIONS (Section 10.3)**

Chapter Ten: Project Communications Management

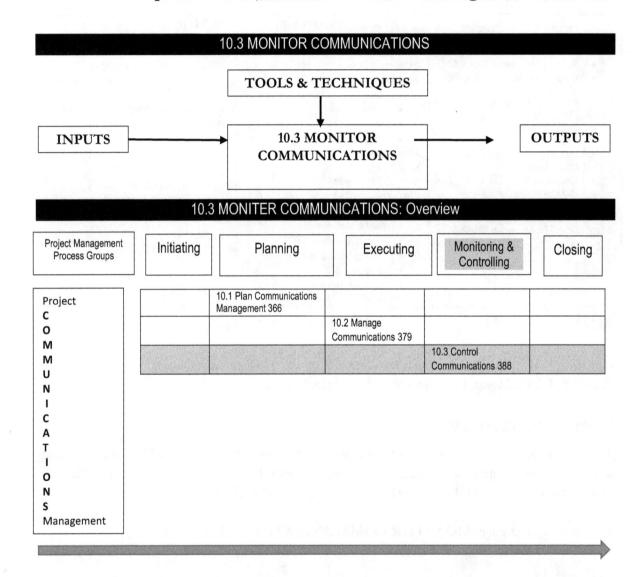

10.3 MONITOR COMMUNICATIONS

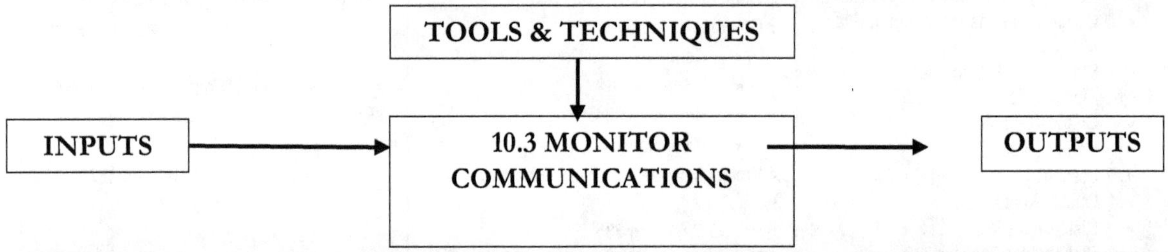

10.3 MONITER COMMUNICATIONS: Overview

Project Management Process Groups	Initiating	Planning	Executing	Monitoring & Controlling	Closing
Project COMMUNICATIONS Management		10.1 Plan Communications Management 366			
			10.2 Manage Communications 379		
				10.3 Control Communications 388	

10.3 MONITOR COMMUNICATIONS: ITTO Processes

.1 Inputs	.2 Tools and Techniques	.3 Outputs
.1 Project Management Plan 390 • Resource Management Plan 390 • Communications Management Plan 390 • Stakeholder Management Plan 390 .2 Project Documents 390 • Issue Log 390 • Lessons Learned Register 390 • Project Communications 390 .3 Work Performance Data 390 .4 Enterprise Environmental Factors 391 .5 Organizational Process Assets 391	.1 Expert Judgment 391 .2 Project Management Information System 392 .3 Data Analysis/Representation 392 • Stakeholder Engagement Assessment Matrix 392 .4 Interpersonal and Team Skills 392 • Observation/Conversation 392 .5 Meetings 392	.1 Work Performance Information 392 .2 Change Requests 393 .3 Project Management Plan Updates 393 • Communications Management Plan 393 • Stakeholder Engagement Plan 393 .4 Project Document Updates 393 • Issue Log 393 • Lessons Learned Register 393 • Stakeholder Register 393

Fig. 10-7, P 388, *Monitor Communications: Inputs, Tools, Techniques and Outputs*
Fig. 10-8, P 389, *Monitor Communications: Data Flow Diagram*

KEY WORDS: CHAPTER 10

- Plan communication management
- Manage communications
- Monitor communications
- Hierarchal focus
- Official/unofficial
- Written versus oral communication
- Logical flow of ideas
- Cultural and personal awareness
- Multi-faceted approaches to communication
- Resource management plan
- Stakeholder engagement plan
- Requirements documentation
- Stakeholder register
- Sensitivity and confidentiality of information
- Current emotional state
- Culture
- Generational
- National
- Professional
- Discipline
- Sender
- Personality biases/assumptions
- Basic sender/receiver communication models
- Encode, transmit message, decode, acknowledge message, feedback message
  feedback/response
- Interactive communications
- Push communications
- Pull communications
- Project schedule
- Stakeholder register
- Resource plan
- Vacations planned
- Stakeholder engagement plan
- Change log
- Issue log
- Lessons learned register
- Risk report
- Stakeholder register
- Nonverbal communications
- Social media management
- Active listing
- Issues log
- Lessons learned register

LEGEND

The following Legend shows how to correctly read the *PMBOK® Guide* references and attributions correctly for Chapter 10: Project Communications Management PMBOK Details.

Legend:

Chapter Section	Chapter Section Title	Page Number

Example from Chapter Six shown below:

6.5.1.4	Enterprise Environmental Factors	(P 209)

All direct quotes are attributed as (A Guide to the Project Management Body of Knowledge, (*PMBOK® Guide)* – Sixth Edition) Project Management Institute Inc., 2017, Page #, after each section and any/all paraphrased or original wording is attributed as (P #), before or after each section. All Graphs, Charts, Tables and Figures are attributed as: (*PMBOK® Guide*, Fig. #-# or #/#, P #, *Title of Graph, Chart, Table or Figure*).

10. PROJECT COMMUNICATIONS MANAGEMENT

Project Communications Management is about how Communications Management principles need to be followed in the project work from the start of the project, throughout the project work, to its completion.

Fig. 10-1, P 360, *Project Communications Overview*.

Key Concepts for Project Communications Management:

Information is exchanged by way of the following mechanisms (P 360):

- **Written Form**: Electronic or Physical
- **Spoken**: Face-to-Face or Remote
- **Formal or Informal**: Paper or Social Media
- **Gestures**: Tone of Voice or Facial Expression
- **Media**: Pictures, Actions, or Choice of Words
- **Choice of Words**: There is more than one way to express an idea and there are subtle variations in words and phrases

Communication Activities have many dimensions to include but not limited to (P 361):

- **Internal**: Focuses on Stakeholders within the project and the organization
- **External**: Customers, vendors, other projects, organizations, government, public and environmental advocates
- **Formal**: Reports, formal meetings, meeting agendas and minutes, stakeholder briefings and presentations
- **Informal**: E-mail, social media, websites and informal ad hoc discussions
- **Hierarchical Focus**: The position of the Stakeholder or group with respect to the project team will affect the format and content of the message in ways that are shown below:
    - Upward: Senior Management Stakeholders
    - Downward: Team and others who contribute to the work of the project
    - Horizontal: Peers of the Project Manager or Team
- **Official**: Annual Reports and Reports to regulators or government bodies
- **Unofficial**: Communications that focus on establishing and maintaining the profile and recognition of the project and building strong

relationships between the project team and its Stakeholders using flexible and often informal means

- **Written and Oral**: Verbal and Nonverbal, social media and webistes, media releases

The project Manager should use the appropriate communication methods to develop stakeholder relationships and prevent misunderstandings.

The 5C's of written communication when composing the traditional written or oral message are (P 363):

- Correct grammar and spelling
- Concise expression and elimination of excess words
- Clear purpose and expressions directed to the needs of the reader
- Coherent logical flow of ideas
- Controlling flow of words and ideas
- Listening actively
- Awareness of cultural and personal differences
- Identifying, setting and managing stakeholder expectations
- Enhancement of skills
    - Persuading a person, team or organization to perform an action
    - Motivating people and providing encouragement or reassurance
    - Coaching to improve performance and achieve desired results
    - Negotiation to achieved mutually acceptable agreements between parties and reduce approval or decision delays
    - Resolving conflict to prevent disruptive impacts

The fundamental attributes of effective communication activities and developing effective communication artifacts are shown below:

- Clarity on the communication's purpose
- Understanding as much as possible about the receiver and meeting their needs and preferences
- Monitoring and measuring the effectiveness of the communication

Trends and Emerging Practices in Project Communications Management:

Some of the Trends and Emerging Practices in Project Communications Management are (P 364):

- Inclusion of Stakeholders in Project Reviews
- Inclusion of Stakeholders in Project Meetings
- Increased use of Social Computing
- Multifaceted Approaches to Communication

Tailoring Considerations (P 365):

Some Tailoring Considerations to take into account are:

- **Stakeholders**:
  - Are the Stakeholders Internal or External to the Organization, or both?
- **Physical Location**:
  - What is the physical location of team members?
  - Is the team co-located?
  - Is the team in the same geographical area?
  - Is the team distributed across multiple time zones?
- **Communication Technology**:
  - What technology is available to develop, record, transmit, retrieve, track and store communication artifacts?
  - What technologies are most appropriate and cost effective for communicating to Stakeholders?
- **Language**: A main factor to consider in communication activities:
  - Is one language used?
  - Are many languages used?
  - Have allowances been made to adjust to the complexity of the team members from diverse language groups?
- **Knowledge Management**:
  - Does the organization have a formal knowledge management repository?
  - Is the repository used?

Considerations for Agile/adaptive Environments (P 365):

Agile/Adaptive environments require the ability to communicate evolving and emerging details quickly and effectively.

10.1 PLAN COMMUNICATIONS MANAGEMENT

Plan Communications Management means to develop an approach and plan for Communication information needed for each stakeholder or group. The **key benefit** is the presentation of information to stakeholders in a clear format, in an appropriate form and within a specified timeframe.

Fig. 10-2, P 366, *Plan Communications Management: Inputs, Tools and Techniques and Outputs*
Fig. 10-3, P 367, *Plan Communications Management: Data Flow Diagram*

The Communications Management Plan should be updated when necessary. This process is performed very early, during the stakeholder identification and Project Management Plan development (P 367).

10.1 Plan Communications Management: Inputs

10.1.1.1 Project Charter

The **Project Charter** lists the key Stakeholders roles and responsibilities.

10.1.1.2 Project Management Plan

Some of the **Project Management Plan** components are (P 368):

- **Resource Management**: Provides guidance on how team resources will be categorized, allocated, managed and released
- **Stakeholder Engagement**: Identifies the management strategies required to effectively engage Stakeholders

10.1.1.4 Enterprise Environmental Factors

Some of the **Enterprise Environmental Factors** that may affect this process are (P 368):

- Organizational culture, political climate and governance framework
- Personnel and administration policies
- Stakeholder risk thresholds
- Established communication channels, tools and systems

- Global, local or regional trends, practices and habits
- Geographic distribution of facilities and resources

10.1.1.3 Project Documents

Some of the **Project Documents** that can be considered as Inputs to this process are (P 368):

- **Requirements documentation**: Can include project stakeholder communications
- **Stakeholder register**: Used to plan communication activities with stakeholders

10.1.1.5 Organizational Process Assets

Some of the **Organizational Process Assets** that may affect Plan Communications Management are (P 369):

- Organizational policies and procedures for social media, ethics and security
- Organizational policies and procedures for issue, risk, change and data management
- Organizational communication requirements
- Standardized guidelines for development, exchange, storage and retrieval of information
- Historical information and lessons learned repository
- Stakeholder and communications data and information from previous projects

10.1.2 Plan Communications Management: Tools and Techniques

10.1.2.1Expert Judgment

Expert Judgment: Groups or Individuals with specialized knowledge or training or extensive knowledge should be consulted in the areas shown below (P 369):

- Politics and power structures in the organization
- Environment and culture of the organization and other customer

organizations
- Organizational change management approach and practices
- Industry or type of project deliverables
- Organizational communications technologies
- Organizational policies and procedures regarding legal requirements of corporate communications
- Organizational policies and procedures regarding security
- Stakeholder, including customers or sponsors

10.1.2.2 Communications Requirements Analysis

Communications Requirements Analysis: Some of the information that is generally used to identify and define Project Communications Management is (P 370):

- **Stakeholder information and communication requirements** from within the stakeholder register and stakeholder engagement plan
- **Number of potential communication channels or paths**
- **Organizational charts**
- Project organization and **stakeholder responsibility, relationships and interdependencies**
- **Development approach**
- **Disciplines,** departments and specialties involved in the project
- **Logistics** of how many persons will be involved with the project and at which locations
- **Internal information needs**
- **External information needs**
- **Legal requirements**

10.1.2.3 Communication Technology

Some of the factors that may affect the choice of Communication Technology are (P 370):

- **Urgency of the need for information**: This may vary from project to project
- **Availability and reliability of technology**: Should be compatible, available and accessible for all stakeholders throughout the

project
- **Ease of use**: Should be suitable for project participants and proper training events should be planned, where appropriate
- **Project environment**: Where the team will meet, virtual or face-to-face, where they will be located, use multiple languages and where there are any other project constraints
- **Sensitivity and confidentiality of the information**: Whether information to be communicated is sensitive or confidential and social media policies for employees to ensure appropriate behavior, security and the protection of proprietary information
-

10.1.2.4 Communication Models

Some possible **Communication Model** choices for a Sender/Receiver process are (P 371):

- **Sample Basic Sender /Receiver Model**: Two parties who are concerned with making sure the message is **delivered, rather than understood** and the sequence of steps for a communication model are (P 371):
  - **Encode**: The message is encoded with symbols
  - **Transmit Message**: Sent via a communication channel
  - **Decode**: Data is translated by the receiver back into a form useful to receiver
- **Sample Interactive Communication Model**: A process between a sender and a receiver consisting of the following steps in an interactive communication model (P 372). Here we want to **ensure message is understood**:
  - **Acknowledge**: On receipt, the receiver signals receipt of message, **not understanding**, but only that it was received
  - **Feedback/Response**: Once the message is **decoded and understood**, the receiver encodes thoughts and ideas and returns the new message to the sender

The sender is responsible for the transmission of the message. The Receiver is responsible for ensuring the information is received in its entirety. Cultural differences can account for messages being incorrectly interpreted due to the sender's emotional state.

Fig. 10-4, P 373, *Communication Model for Cross-Cultural Communication*

Other factors may also affect communications such as, national, professional, discipline, sender, knowledge, background, personality biases, culture and other biases.

10.1.2.5 Communication Methods

There are several **Communication Methods**, which are broadly classified as follows (P 374):

- **Interactive Communication**: Consist of two or more parties, multi-directional, exclusive, etc.
- **Push Communication**: Sent to carefully chosen recipients: Letters, memos, reports, etc.
- **Pull Communication**: Used for large amount of information, large audiences and gives the participants use of access to web portals, intranet sites, e-learning, etc.

Different approaches can be applied such as those that follow (P 374):

- **Interpersonal**: Generally this is a face-to-face information exchange
- **Small Group Communication**: Groups of about three to six persons
- **Public Communication**: Single speaker addressing a group
- **Mass Communication**: Minimal connection between the person or group sending the message and the large, sometimes anonymous groups for whom the information is intended
- **Networks and Social Computing Communication**: Supports emerging communication trends of many-to-many supported by social computing technology and media

Some of the **communications artifacts and methods** used are (P 375):

- Notice Boards
- Newsletters/In-House Magazines/E-Magazines
- Letters to Staff/Volunteers
- Press Releases
- Annual Reports
- E-Mails and Intranets
- Web Portals and other Information Repositories
- Phone Conversations

- Presentations
- Team Briefings/Group Meetings
- Focus Groups
- Face-to-Face Formal or Informal Meetings between Various Stakeholders
- Consultation Groups or Staff Forums
- Social Computing Technology and Media

10.1.2.6 Interpersonal and Team Skills

Some of the **Interpersonal and Team Skills** that might be used for this process are (P 375):

- **Communication Styles Assessment**: Used to assess communication styles and identify the preferred communication method
- **Political Awareness**: Helps the PM to plan communications based on the project and political environment
- **Cultural Awareness**: An understanding of the differences between individuals, groups and adapting the project's communication strategy in the context of these differences

10.1.2.7 Data Representation

Data Representation is a technique not limited to a Stakeholder Engagement Assessment Matrix, which displays gaps between current and desired engagement levels, etc.

Fig. 13-6, P 522, *Stakeholder Engagement Assessment Matrix*

10.1.2.8 Meetings

Meetings can be virtual or face-to-face and supported by collaboration techniques, including e-mail and project websites.

10.1.3 Plan Communications Management: Outputs

10.1.3.1 Communication Management Plan

The **Communication Management Plan** will contain the information shown below, but can also include guidelines and templates for project status meetings, project team meetings, e-meetings and e-mail messages (P 377):

- Stakeholder Communication Requirements
- Information to be communicated
- Escalation processes
- Reason for the distribution of that information
- Timeframe and frequency for the distribution of that information and receipt of acknowledgement or response
- Person responsible for communication the information
- Person responsible for authorizing release of confidential information
- Person or groups who will receive the information
- Methods or technologies used to convey the information
- Resources allocated for communication activities
- Method for updating and refining the communications management plan as the project progresses and develops
- Glossary of common terminology
- Flow charts of the information flow in the project, workflows with possible sequences of information, list of reports, meetings, etc.
- Constraints derived from specific legislation or regulation, technology, organizational policies, etc.

10.1.3.2 Project Management Plan Updates

Project Management Plan Updates: The Stakeholder Plan is a component in this process that will be updated to reflect any processes, procedures, tools or techniques that will affect the Stakeholders (P 378).

10.1.3.3 Project Documents Updates

Some of the **Project Documents** that may be updated include (P 378):

- **Project Schedule**: Updated to reflect communication activities
- **Stakeholder Register**: Updated to reflect communications planned

10.2 MANAGE COMMUNICATIONS

Manage Communications is the process of making sure all project information is collected, created, distributed, stored, etc. and the **key benefit** is to enable an efficient process of information flow between stakeholders and the project team.

Fig. 10-5, P 379, *Manage Communications: Inputs, Tools and Techniques and Outputs*
Fig. 10-6, P 380, *Manage Communications: Data Flow Diagram*

Some of the Techniques and Considerations for Communications Management are (P 381):

- **Sender-Receiver Models**: incorporating feedback loops to provide opportunities for interaction/participation and remove barriers to effective communication
- **Choice of Media**: Decisions about application of communications artifacts to meet specific project needs
- **Writing Style**: Active vs. passive voice, sentence structure and word choice
- **Meeting Management**: preparing an agenda, inviting essential participants and ensuring they attend and dealing with conflicts
- **Presentations**: Awareness of the impact of body language and design of visual aids
- **Facilitation**: Building consensus and overcoming obstacles such as difficult group dynamics and maintaining interest and enthusiasm among group members
- **Active Listening**: Involves acknowledging, clarifying and confirming, understanding and removing barriers that adversely affect comprehension

10.2.1 Manage Communications: Inputs

10.2.1.1 Project Management Plan

Some of the **Project Management Plan Components** are (P 381):

- **Resource Management Plan**: Describes the communications needed for management of the team or physical resources
- **Communications Management Plan**: Describes how project communications will be planned, structured, monitored and controlled
- **Stakeholder Engagement Plan**: Describes how Stakeholders will be engaged through appropriate communication strategies

10.2.1.2 Project Documents

Some **Project Documents** that can be considered as Inputs to this process are (P383):

- **Change Log**: Used to communicate changes and approved, deferred and rejected change requests to the impacted Stakeholders
- **Issue Log**: Information about issues is communicated to impacted Stakeholders
- **Lessons Learned Register**: Lessons learned earlier in the project can be applied to later phases in the project to improve the efficiency and effectiveness of validating deliverables
- **Quality Report**: Includes quality issues, project and product improvements and process improvements
- **Risk Report**: Presents information on sources of overall project risk, with summary information on identified individual project risks
- **Stakeholder Register**: Identifies the individuals, groups or organizations that will need various types of information

10.2.1.3 Work Performance Reports

Work Performance Reports are distributed to Stakeholders as defined in the Communications Management Plan.

10.2.1.4 Enterprise Environmental Factors

Some of the **Enterprise Environmental Factors** that can affect this process are (P 383):

- Organizational culture, political climate and governance framework
- Personnel and administration policies
- Stakeholder risk thresholds
- Established communication channels, tools and systems
- Global, local or regional trends, practices and habits
- Geographic distribution of facilities and resources

10.2.1.5 Organizational Process Assets

Some of the **Organizational Process Assets** that can affect this process are (P 383):

- Corporate policies and procedures for social media, ethics and security
- Corporate policies and procedures for issue, risk, change and data management
- Organizational communications requirements
- Standardized guideline for development, exchange, storage and retrieval of information
- Historical information from previous projects, including the lessons learned repository

10.2.2 Manage Communications: Tools and Techniques

10.2.2.1 Communication Technology

Communication Technology concerns whether the team is collocated, information sensitivity, resources available to team members and how the organizational culture affects the way meetings and discussions are managed (P 383).

10.2.2.3 Communication Skills

Some of the **Communication Skills** that can be used in this process are (P 384):

- **Communication Competence:**
- **Feedback:** Information about reactions to communications, a deliverable or a situation
- **Nonverbal:** How team members express themselves by way of body language
- **Presentations:** Formal delivery of information and/or documentation and clear and effective presentations can include the following (P 384):
    - Progress reports and information updates to stakeholders
    - Background information to support decision making
    - General information about the project and its objectives
    - Specific information aimed at increasing understanding and support of the work and objectives of the project

  Presentations will be successful when the content and delivery consider the following (P 384):
    - Audience expectation and needs
    - Needs and objectives of the project and project team

10.2.2.4 Project Management Information System Services (PMIS)

Project Management Information Systems (PMIS) help to ensure that Stakeholders can retrieve information needed in a timely way, such as (P 385):

- **Electronic Project Management Tools**: Project Management Software, meeting and virtual office support software, web interfaces, specialized project portals and dashboards and collaborative work management tools
- **Electronic Communications Management**: E-mail, fax and voicemail, audio, video and web conferencing and websites and web publishing
- **Social Media Management**: Websites and web publishing, blogs and applications

10.2.2.5 Project Reporting

In **Project Reporting**, the information is distributed and adapted to the Stakeholder's needs and expectations.

10.2.2.6 Interpersonal and Team Skills

Some of the **Interpersonal and Team Skills** used in this process are (P 386):

- **Active Listening**: Involves acknowledging, clarifying and confirming, understanding and removing barriers that adversely affect comprehension
- **Conflict Management**: Preparing an agenda, inviting essential participants and ensuring they attend and dealing with conflicts
- **Cultural Awareness**: An understanding of the differences between individuals, groups and adapting the project's communication strategy in the context of these differences
- **Meeting Management**: Taking steps to ensure meetings meet their intended objectives and the steps shown below should be taken into consideration (P 386):
    - **Prepare and distribute the agenda** stating the objectives of the meeting
    - **Ensure the start and finish** meeting times are met
    - Ensure the **appropriate participants** attend
    - Stay on topic
    - **Manage expectations**, issues an conflicts during the meeting

- **Record** all actions and those who have been allocated the responsibility for completing the action
- **Networking**: Allows informal connections and relations among project Stakeholders
- **Political Awareness**: **Political Awareness**: Helps the PM to plan communications based on the project and political environment
- **Cultural Awareness**: An understanding of the differences between individuals, groups and adapting the project's communication strategy in the context of these differences

10.2.2.7 Meetings

Meetings with key stakeholders are held to refine project objective, establish success criteria, determine key deliverables, agree on high-level requirements and other needed data and support the actions defined in the communication plan strategy (P 386).

10.2.3 Manage Communications: Outputs

10.2.3.1 Project Communications

Some of the communications artifacts in **Project Communications** include (P 387):

- **Performance reports**
- **Deliverable status**
- **Schedule progress**
- **Cost incurred**
- **Presentations, etc.**

10.2.3.2 Project Management Plan Updates

Some components of the **Project Management Plan** that may be **updated** include (P 387):

- **Communications management plan**: When changes are made to this plan they are reflected in the project communications plan
- **Stakeholder engagement plan**: Stakeholder communications requirements and agreed-upon communication strategies are updated as a result of this process

10.2.3.3 Project Documents Updates

Some of the **Project Documents** that may be **updated** as a result of this process include (P 387):

- **Issue Log**: Updated to reflect any communication issues
- **Lessons Learned Register**: Updated with information on challenges
- **Project Schedule:** Updated to reflect status of communication activities
- **Risk Register**: Updated to capture risks associated with managing communications
- **Stakeholder Register**: Updated to include information regarding communications activities with project stakeholders

10.2.3.4 Organizational Process Updates

Some of the **Organizational Process Assets** that may be updated include (P 388):

- Project Records
- Planned and ad hoc project reports and presentations

10.3 MONITOR COMMUNICATIONS

Monitor is the process of making sure the project's information needs and the information needs of the Stakeholders are met. This should show the optimal information flow between and among stakeholders. The **key benefit** is contained in the **Communications Management Plan** and the **Stakeholder Management Plan.**

Fig. 10-7, P 388, *Monitor Communications: Inputs, Tools and Techniques and Outputs*
Fig. 10-8, P 389, *Monitor Communications: Data Flow Diagram*

When communications are monitored, the artifacts and activities will be updated and strengthened to assure compliance and that the information is delivered in time to the right audience with the proper context. In this process, the iterations of the Plan Communications Management and Manage Communications processes improves the effectiveness through the potential likelihood of any amended communications and activities.

10.3.1 Monitor Communications: Inputs

10.3.1.1 Project Management Plan

Some of the **Project Management Plan** components include (391):

- **Resource Management Plan**: Used to understand the actual project organization and any changes
- **Communications Management Plan**: Contains the current plan for collecting, creating and distributing information in a timely manner
- **Stakeholder Engagement Plan**: Identifies communication strategies that are planned to engage Stakeholders

10.3.1.2 Project Documents

Some of the **Project Documents** that may be Inputs for this process are (391):

- **Issue Log**: New issues raised as a result of this process are recorded in the Issue Log
- **Lessons Learned Register**: Effective responses for variances and corrective and preventative actions are recorded in the Lessons Learned Register and used for future reference to improve communication effectiveness
- **Project Communications**: Provides information about communications that have been distributed

10.3.1.3 Work Performance Data

Work Performance Data is the information that has already been distributed to the appropriate audience (P 380).

10.3.1.4 Enterprise Environmental Factors

Some of the **Enterprise Environmental Factors** that may affect this process are (P 391):

- Organizational culture, political climate and governance framework
- Established Communication channels, tools and systems
- Global, Regional or Local Trends
- Geographic distribution of Facilities and Resources

10.3.1.5 Organizational Process Assets

Some of the **Organizational Process Assets** that may affect this process are (P 391):

- **Corporate policies and procedures** for social media, ethics and security
- **Organizational communications requirements**
- **Standardized guideline** for development, exchange, storage and retrieval of information
- **Historical information from previous projects**, including the lessons learned repository
- **Stakeholder and Communications Data and Information from previous projects**

10.3.2 Monitor Communications: Tools and Techniques

10.3.2.1 Expert Judgment

Expert Judgment is guided by **historical information** and can provide environmental insight and information if the PM examines similar projects. Groups or individuals should be considered in the following areas who have specialized training (P 391):

- Communications with the public, community and the media in an international environment, between virtual groups
- Communications and **project management systems**

10.3.2.2 Project Management Information Systems (PMIS)

The **Project Management Information System** contains a set of tools in order to capture, store and distribute information to internal and external stakeholders (P 392).

10.3.2.3 Data Representation

The **Stakeholder Engagement Assessment Matrix** can be included as a part of **Data Representation** and provide information about communication activities and their effectiveness (P 392).

10.3.2.4 Interpersonal and Team Skills

Some of the **Interpersonal and Team Skills** that can be used for this process include (P 392): Observation/conversation which provides information about the best way to update and communicate project performance.

10.3.2.5 Meetings

Meetings with key stakeholders are held to refine project objective, establish success criteria, determine key deliverables, agree on high-level requirements and other needed data. These meetings can be face-to-face or virtual and can take place with suppliers, vendors and other project stakeholders (P 392).

10.3.3 Monitor Communications: Outputs

10.3.3.1 Work Performance Communication

Information on **Work Performance Communication** includes how project communications compares communications that were implemented to those that were planned.

10.3.3.2 Change Requests

Change Requests are processed through the Perform Integrated Change Control Process and these changes may result in the following (P 393):

- Revision of Stakeholder communication requirements and Stakeholder information distribution, content or format and distribution method
- New procedures to eliminate bottlenecks

10.3.3.3 Project Management Plan Updates

Some of the **Project management plan Updates** may include (P 393):

- **Communications Management Plan**: Updated with new information to make communications more effective
- **Stakeholder Engagement Plan**: Updated with revised stakeholder communication requirements

10.3.3.4 Project Documents Updates

Some of the **Project Documents** that can be **updated** are (P 393):

- Issue Log
- Lessons Learned Register
- Stakeholder Register

Summary: Answers to Student Learning Outcomes

1. **Project Communications Management** is a process that requires the Project Manager and their team manager to know how to communicate orally and in writing to stakeholders at all levels of the participating company (P 359-365).

   Communications begin even before the start of the project. Indeed, it continues throughout the project, and through to the project's completion. This process includes activities for the timely creation and distribution of information. It also includes the filtering of project information into some form of electronic storage and includes authorization of information retrieval services. Project Communications Management insures that project and stakeholder information needs are satisfied though the creation of artifacts and activities to achieve successful information exchange. There are two (2) parts of Project Communications Management (P 359):

   - **Developing a Communication Strategy**
   - **Performing the activities of the Communication Strategy**

   Project Communications Management consists of three (3) process groups. They are (P 359):

   - **Plan Communications Management** is a planning process and deals with developing an approach and plan to access each stakeholder's information needs, or group needs and the needs of the project.
   - **Manage Communications** is an executing process. This process deals with creating, collecting and distributing project information. Project information is always managed as there is business, and often regulatory compliance needs to store, distribute and retain project information. Manage communications deals with timely collection, creation, distribution storage, retrieval, management, monitoring and distribution of project information.
   - **Control Communications** is a monitoring and control process to ensure that all the project stakeholder's information needs are met throughout the project life cycle.

   Fig. 10-1, P 360, *Project Communications Overview*

2. There are **six (6) mechanisms** for communicating in the form of ideas, instructions or emotions. They are (P 360):

   1. **Written form**
   2. **Spoken**
   3. **Formal or informal**
   4. **Through gestures**
   5. **Through media**
   6. **Choice of words**

3. **Eight (8) Dimensions** of communications are (P 361):

   1. **Internal**
   2. **External**
   3. **Formal**
   4. **Informal**
   5. **Hierarchal focus (i.e. upward, downward, and horizontal)**
   6. **Official**
   7. **Unofficial**
   8. **Written and Oral**

4. **The Five (5) C's of Communication** are (P 363):

   1. **Correct grammar and spelling**
   2. **Concise expression and elimination of excess words**
   3. **Clear purpose and expression directed to the needs of others**
   4. **Coherent, logical flow**
   5. **Controlling flow of words and ideas**

5. The **four (4) major communications skills** needed by a Project Manager are (P 363):

   1. **Listening actively**
   2. **Awareness of cultural and personal difference**
   3. **Identifying, setting, and managing stakeholder expectations**
   4. **Enhancement of team member skills**

Communication skills always need to be enhanced or improved via persuasion, motivation, coaching, negotiation and resolving conflict management (P 363).

6. **Trends and Emerging Project Communications Practices** include but are not limited to (P 364):
    1. Inclusion of stakeholders in **project reviews**
    2. Inclusion of stakeholders in **project meetings**
    3. Increased use of **social computing** (Media)
    4. **Multifaceted approaches to communications**

Communication often needs to **be tailored** (P 365). Considerations include:

- Stakeholders
- Physical location
- Communication technology
- Language
- Knowledge management

7. **Plan Communication Management** is a process of developing various approaches and plans for communication activities that will identify the needs of stakeholders, groups within the company, and organizational assets (P 359-366). The key benefit is to design and develop a documented approach that aids **engaging stakeholders** to determine their relevant communication needs. This process is performed throughout the project life cycle.

    Fig. 10-2, P 366, *Plan Communications Management: Inputs, Tools and Techniques and Outputs*
    Fig. 10-3, P 367, *Plan Communications Management: Data Flow Diagram*

8. There are many available **software communications technology** products that can be used to assist stakeholders in transferring information among project members. The main (5) factors to make a good communication software selection choice are (P 370):

    1. **Urgency of the need for information**
    2. **Availability and reliability of technology**
    3. **Ease of use**
    4. **Project environment**
    5. **Sensitivity and confidentiality of the information**

9. The basic sender/receiver communications model consists of a sender and receiver and various modes of communication. This model is more about ensuring the message is delivered, rather than understood (P 371-373):

   - **Encode**
   - **Transmit Message**
   - **Decode**
   - **Acknowledge**
   - **Feedback/Response**

   Fig. 10-4, P 373, *Communications Model for Cross-Cultural Communication.*

10. The two (2) Communications Models to share information among stakeholders are (P 371-372):

    - Sample basic sender/receiver communication model
    - Sample interactive communication model

    See P 371-373, for more details.

11. The **Communications Management Plan** (an output of Plan Communication) is considered a subsidiary management plan, and is one of three (3) outputs of Plan Communications, which are:

    - **Communications management plan**
    - **Project management plan updates**
    - **Project documents updates**

    The communications plan will have the following content sections (P 377):

    - Stakeholder communication requirements
    - Information, language, format, context and detail
    - Escalation process
    - Reason for distribution
    - Time frame and frequency of distribution etc.,
    - Person(s) responsible for communications
    - Person authorized to release confidential information
    - Recipients of information
    - Methods/means of communication (i.e. Memos, email, press

releases, social media)
- Resources allocated including time and budget
- Updating methods
- Glossary of terms
- Flowcharts/work flows
- Constraints derived from legislation, regulation, technology, organization, policies, etc.

12. **Manage Communications** is the process of ensuring timely and appropriate collection, creation, distribution, storage, retrieval, management, monitoring, and ultimate disposition of project information. The **key benefit** is to enable an efficient and effective information flow between the project team and the stakeholders (P 379).

    Fig. 10-5, Manage Communications: *Inputs, Tools and Techniques and Outputs*
    Fig. 10-6, Manage Communications: *Data Flow Diagram*

13. **Manage Communications** is a process that may use various tools and techniques. There are four (4) skill considerations for effective communications shown below (P 384):
    - **Communications competence**
    - **Feedback**
    - **Non-Verbal**
    - **Presentation**

14. There are three (3) **Project Management Information Systems (PMIS) Tools** useful in Communications Management. They are (P 385):

    1. **Electronic project management tools**
    2. **Electronic communications management: email, voice, fax, etc.**
    3. **Social media management**

15. **Project Reporting** (P 385) is for the purpose of communication project progress and to report any baseline variances and to forecast or predict results. It is the act of **collecting and distributing** project information and is distributed to many stakeholder groups and may be customized based upon the need of each type of stakeholder. A simple performance report may include:

    - Progress
    - Scope

- Schedule
- Cost
- Quality
- Issues
- Rules, etc.
- Further in-depth reports may include other items

16. **Monitor Communications** is the process of ensuring the project information needs and its stakeholder's needs are met. The key benefit is the optional information flow as defined in the Communication Management Plan and the Stakeholder Engagement Plan is met (P 388).

    Fig. 10-7, P 388, *Manage Communications: Inputs, Tools and Techniques and Outputs*
    Fig. 10-8, P 389, *Manage Communications: Data Flow Diagram*

17. The **Issues Log, is** an output of manage communications, is used to record and maintain a record of project communication issues. The log is a historical record that reports (P 387):

    - Who, by name, is responsible for the communication issue
    - What is the date the issue was detected and reported
    - The date it was closed/resolved

    The issue log is updated to reflect any project communication issues or how they may affect/impact other active issues (P 387).

18. There are four **(4) outputs of Monitor Communications** (P 393):

    - **Work Performance Information**: Compares information differences/from planned to actual and feedback.
    - **Change Requests**: Document project communication adjustments, actions, or interventions.
    - **Project Management Plan Updates**: Reflects changes to communication management plan or changes to the stakeholder engagement plan.
    - **Project Document Updates**: Reflects changes to the issue log, lessons learned register and stakeholder register.

Fig. 10-8, P 388, *Monitor Communications: Inputs, Tools and Techniques and Outputs*
Fig. 10-9, P 389, *Monitor Communications: Data Flow Diagram*

19. Monitor communications determines if the planned communication artifacts are effective in strengthening stakeholder support (P 389).

    Monitor Communications may include (P 389):

    - Distributing customer satisfaction surveys
    - Collecting lessons learned
    - Observations of the team
    - Reviewing data from issue log
    - Evaluating changes in stakeholder engagement assessment matrix (PMBOK, 6th Ed., P 521, Section 13.2.2.5 *Data Representation techniques that may be used in this process …*)

Similar Questions that may be on the PMI Exam related to Chapter 10

1. Communication between a project manager and his/her team member's takes place best through _____.

   A. A Daily Status Report
   B. Approved Forms
   C. Formal Chain of Command
   D. Written and Verbal Communication

   Correct answer is D: A project manager and his/her team should interact both verbally and through written methods to communicate any message.

2. A manager has been appointed to a new project and been granted approval to start the planning requirements. The project manager is new to the organization and has inherited a project team previously selected by the top management. The best method of initiating the communication process with the team and to establish the expectations of the project team is by _____.

   A. Sending a formal memorandum to each team member to outline objectives, requirements, and the time frame for the work
   B. Talking in person to each team member to determine what he/she would like to do on the project and how they can be accommodated
   C. Call a briefing session to set objectives of the management and direct how these objectives will be met
   D. Calling a kickoff meeting to present the objectives and open the floor for discussion on how the objectives will be achieved

   Correct answer is D: the purpose of a kickoff meeting is to bring the performing team together on same page by explaining clearly the project objectives and expectations.

3. Nick has to send progress reports to various stakeholders. He needs to know to whom he should send the progress report. Which documents should he consult?

   A. Stakeholder Register and Communication Plan
   B. Stakeholder Analysis and Stakeholder Register
   C. Communication Plan and Stakeholder Analysis
   D. Reporting Systems and Stakeholder Analysis

   Correct answer is A: The Stakeholder Register helps identify which stakeholders are qualified to receive the information and communication plan, which contains when, what, how, and who should receive the information.

4. Muddy, a manager in an export house, wants to develop in-house software. In developing project team process, which of the following tools is concerned with establishing clear expectations regarding acceptable behavior by project team members?

   A. Ground Rules
   B. Co-Location
   C. Team-Building Activities
   D. Performing

   Correct Answer is A: Ground rules establish clear expectations regarding acceptable behavior by project team members. An early commitment to clear guidelines decreases misunderstandings and increases productivity.

5. For active and effective communication, the listening ability plays an important role. Which of the following is not a way to improve the listening ability?

   A. Listening and giving feedback
   B. Working on another activity while listening
   C. Allowing the speaker to complete his/her message
   D. Focusing on concepts and ideas

   Correct answer is B: Working on another activity while listening will not lead to effective and active communication.

6. A project manager, working in one of the promising start-up is creating a report of the final status of a closed project to the stakeholders. Which of the following is not used in a final project report to communicate the status of a project?

   A. Variance Information
   B. Lessons Learned
   C. Scope Baseline
   D. Status of Deliverables

   Correct answer is C: A baseline is what you use to measure any changes to the project. Whenever there is a change, you want to compare it against the baseline. Once the project is done, the baseline is not necessary any more.

7. You are working as a manager in a computer hardware manufacturing firm. You recently heard the words, War Room from one of your colleague. A War Room is _____.

   A. A place where decisions are made.
   B. A place or room where conflicts are resolved.
   C. A place where the team can sit together and communicate more closely
   D. A power of the manager

   Correct answer is C: Co-location strategies can include a team meeting room, known as the War Room. These are places to post schedules and other conveniences that enhance communication and a sense of community.

8. The Food and Drug Administration or FDA is a federal agency of the United States and conducts careful inspections or audits of regulated facilities to determine a firm's compliance with regulations and the Food, Drug and Cosmetic Act. FDA audit was performed on the company you work a few days ago, and now you need to close a few of the observations. There are many stakeholders who need to be updated every day about how many observations are still open. You have a lot of other work planned and are already short of resources. Which communication model would be most helpful?

   A. Interactive Communication
   B. Push Communication
   C. Pull Communication
   D. Oral Communication

   Correct answer is B: Push communication is sent to specific recipients who need to receive the information. This ensures that the information is distributed. However, this does not mean it actually reached or was understood by the intended audience. Push communication can include the following: letters, memos, reports, e-mails, faxes, voice mails, blogs, press releases, etc.

9. You work for a consulting company and your team has implemented an approved scope change on your project. You need to inform your client that the change has been made. What is the best form of communication to use for this?

   A. Formal Verbal
   B. Formal Written
   C. Informal Written
   D. Informal Verbal

   Correct answer is B: Always use formal written communication when you are communicating with clients about changes in your project.

10. Rahit is a project manager who is conducting a team meeting to discuss a few issues in a project. One team member came late, at the time when you were engaged in delivering context of the meeting. All the members looked at the late arrival and stopped paying attention to you. Who is ultimately responsible to deliver the message in an understandable manner?

    A. Sender
    B. Receiver
    C. Medium
    D. Both Sender and Receiver

    Correct answer is A: Thoughts or ideas are translated (encoded) into the language by the sender. It is the sender's responsibility to encode.

You may now move on to Chapter Eleven: Project Risk Management

Chapter 11: Project Risk Management: Know your Risks

PMI, PMP, CAPM, PMI-ACP, PMI-RMP, PMI-SP and *PMBOK® Guide* are registered marks of the Project Management Institute, 2017 and all references, from this point on, are from the Project Management Institute, (A Guide to the Project Management Body of Knowledge, *(PMBOK® Guide)* – Sixth Edition).

"An Ounce of Prevention is Worth a Pound of Cure."
Benjamin Franklin

Student Learning Outcomes

1. List the seven (7) processes of **Project Risk Management** and explain why Project Risk Management is so very important (P 395-397). What are the key concepts?
2. **What is meant by Plan Risk Management and what are the key benefits? What are the ITTO's (401)? Describe the importance of the process components of Project Risk Management and the ITTO's (P 396-397).**
3. In the pursuit of project goals, the project team needs to know what level of risk exposure is acceptable. What are the two (2) types of **risk exposures** that most organizations and stakeholders hold as views and what is the difference between these two (P 397-P 398)?
4. What are **four (4) Tailoring Considerations in Plan Risk Management** (P 400)?
5. What are the **five (5) Inputs** that may be used to develop the **Risk Management Plan** (P 401)?
6. **Plan Risk Management** is a process and can consist of using three (**3) Tools and Techniques.** What are they (P 401)?
7. List the eleven **(11) elements/sections** found in the **Risk Management Plan**, which is a subsidiary plan of the **Project Management Plan** (P 405-408).
8. What is **RBS** and why is it important (P 405)? What is a **Probability and Impact Matrix** and why is it important (P 407)?
9. **What is meant by Identify Risk (P 409-410)? What is the key benefit of this process? What are the ITTO's?**
10. There are six **(6) inputs to Identify Risk** (P 409). What are they?
11. There are six **(6) different Tools and Techniques** (P 409-P410) that may be used in the process of **Identify Risks**. One of which is that of using **Data Gathering**. What are the other five (5) Tools and Techniques that may be used?
12. What are the **three (3) outputs** of the **Identify Risks Process** (P 409-410)?
13. There are three **(3) Data Gathering Techniques** of **Identify Risks** (P 414). One of these techniques is Brainstorming. Identify the purpose of each (P 414).
14. A **SWOT (Strength, Weakness, Opportunity and Threats) Analysis** (P 415) is a useful technique in helping to detect project risk. How **is SWOT Analysis** useful in detection of project strength, weakness, opportunities and threats?
15. One of the **outputs** of the **Identify Risks Process** is the **Risk Register** (P 417). What context information is included in the **Risk Register**?
16. **Perform Qualitative Risk Analysis is a process (P 419-420). What does perform Qualitative Risk Analysis mean and what are the key benefits? What are the ITTO's, (Inputs, Tools, Techniques, and Outputs) of this process?**
17. **Perform Quantitative Risk Analysis (P 428) is a process. What does Quantitative Risk Analysis mean and what are the key benefits? What are the ITTO's?**
18. In **Perform Quantitative Risk Analysis**, the output is **Project Documents Updates** (**Risk Report**) (P 428-429). What are <u>five (5) types of analysis updates</u> that can be reported in the Project Documents Updates? What are the ITTO's?
19. Plan Risk Responses is a process (P 437). What does this mean and what is the key benefit of Plan Risk Responses? What are the ITTO's?

20. In **Plan Risk Responses**, there are five **(5) Strategies for dealing with Threats** (P 442-443). One strategy is to Avoid Risk. List all strategies.
21. In **Plan Risk Responses**, there are five **(5) Strategies for Opportunities**. One is to **Escalate** and use it as a strategy response. Identify and define all **(5) Strategies For Opportunities in Plan Risk Responses** (P 444).
22. **What does Implement Risk Responses mean and what is the key benefit (P 449)? What are the ITTO's?**
23. What are the two **(2) Outputs of the Implement Risk Response** process (P 449-450)?
24. **Monitor Risk is a process. What does this mean and what are the key benefits of Monitor Risk (P 453-454)? What are the ITTO's?**
25. What is a **Reserve Analysis** (P 456)?
26. One of the **Outputs** of the **Monitor Risk Process** is **Change Requests** (P 457). **Change Requests** may be used to document contingency plans or workarounds which would then be submitted to the **Perform Integrated Change Control Process** (P 113). What are the two **(2) types of recommended change requests** and what is the significance of each?

CHAPTER ELEVEN INTRODUCTION: KNOW YOUR RISKS

PROJECT RISK MANAGEMENT: CHAPTER 11 OVERVIEW: PMBOK® 6th Edition P 395-458

Project Risk Management includes a number of processes that include conducting risk management planning, identification, qualitative and quantitative analysis, response planning, implementation and monitoring risk. The objective of Project Risk Management is to increase the probability of project success, the benefits and the impact of positive risk, and decrease the probability, and impact of negative risks.

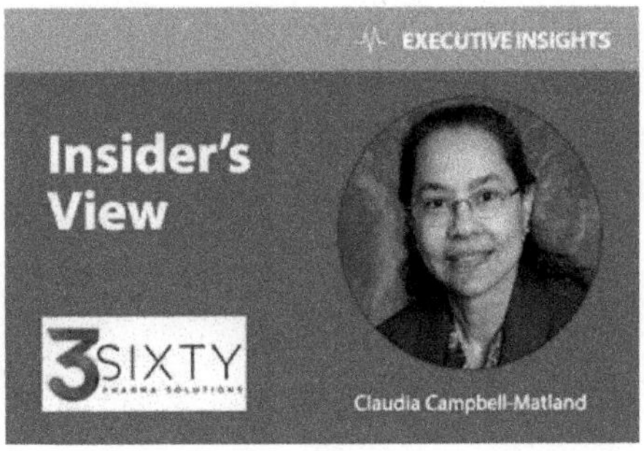

Claudia Campbell Matland, *Managing Risk for Medical Device Clinical Trials*, located at https://www.meddeviceonline.com/doc/managing-risk-for-medical-device-clinical-trials-0001

There are seven (7) processes in Project Risk Management:

(11.1) **Plan Risk Management**: Defines how to conduct risk management work for a project.

(11.2) **Identify Risk**: Identify individual project risk and their sources and document their characteristics.

(11.3) **Perform Qualitative Risk Analysis**: Prioritize individual risks, undertake analysis activities and assess their probability of impact.

(11.4) **Perform Quantitative Risk Analysis**: Numerically analyze the combined effect of individuals, identify sources of uncertainty and overall project objectives.

(11.5) **Plan Risk Responses**: Develop options, select strategy approaches and establish agreement to address overall risk exposure, and treat individual project risks.

(11.6) **Implement Risk Responses**: Implement agreed upon response plans (action steps.)

(11.7) **Monitor Risk**: Monitor and track identified risks and evaluate the overall risk process effectiveness.

Fig. 11-1, P 396, *Project Risk Management Overview*

Key Concepts for Project Risk Management

In terms of key concepts for Project Risk Management, it is important to recognize and address levels of risk. One is the Individual project risk, and the other is at Overall Project Risk. Individual project risk is an uncertain event or condition that, if it occurs, has a positive or negative effect on one or more project objectives. Overall project risk is the effect of the uncertainty of the project as a whole.

The project manager needs to be aware of two (2) elements of managing risk:

1. What is the risk appetite of the organization and its stakeholders, and what level of risk is acceptable to pursue project objectives (P 398)?
2. What is the risk threshold which expresses a degree of acceptable variation or other objective?

Trends and Emerging Practices in Project Risk Management

There are three (3) trends that have been affecting the discussions, research and the application of project risk management. These trends are emerging and they have been developed over time.

The first trend is a **Non-Event Risk** which can be divided into two (2) main types**,** See P 398:

1. **Variability Risk**
2. **Ambiguity Risk**

The second trend is called, **Project Resilience** (P 399): Here, the existence of emergent risk is becoming clear with the growing awareness of so-called **unknowable unknowns**. Risks such as these, are recognized only after they occur.

The last trend is Integrated Risk Management (P 399): Here, project risks that exist in the organizational context may form a part of a program or portfolio. Integrated risk management means that we need to consider the effects of risk upon either the program or the portfolio, or both.

Tailoring Considerations

In order to be effective, the project manager needs to tailor the risk management processes to the organization and to the project. There are four (4) considerations to evaluate, which are (P 400):

1. **Project size**
2. **Project complexity**
3. **Project importance**
4. **Project development approach**

Considerations for Adaptive/Agile Environments:

High variability environments, by definition, tend to increase the probability of more uncertainty and risk. In such a setting, especially in an agile/adaptive approach, there are going to be reviews that are more frequent in incremental work, product risk and cross-functional project team risk (P 400).

Plan Risk Management:

Plan risk management is the process of defining how to conduct risk management activities for a project. The **key benefit** is that the degree, type and visibility of risk management need to be proportional to both the risk and the importance to the organization, as well as to stakeholders (P 401).

Refer to chart on next page: **PLAN RISK MANAGEMENT (Section 11.1)**

Chapter Eleven: Project Risk Management

11.1 PLAN RISK MANAGEMENT

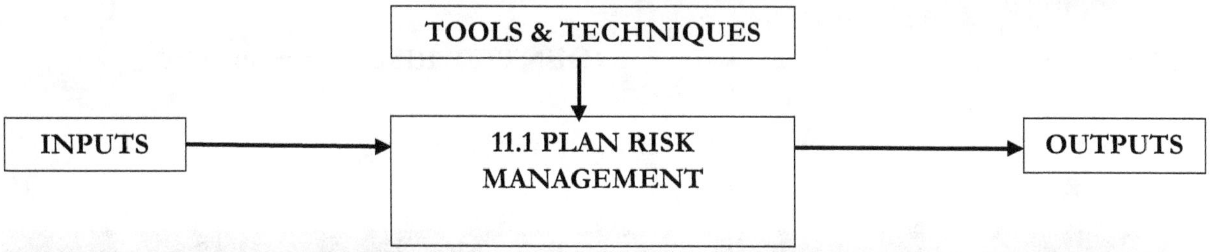

11.1 PLAN RISK MANAGEMENT: Overview

Project Management Process Groups	Initiating	Planning	Executing	Monitoring & Controlling	Closing
Project RISK Management		11.1 Plan Risk Management 401			
		11.2 Identify Risks 409			
		11.3 Perform Qualitative Risk Analysis 419			
		11.4 Perform Quantitative Risk Analysis 428			
		11.5 Plan Risk Responses 437			
			11.6 Implement Risk Response 449		
				11.7 Monitor Risk 453	

11.1 PLAN RISK MANAGEMENT: ITTO Processes

.1 Inputs	.2 Tools and Techniques	.3 Outputs
.1 Project Charter 402 .2 Project Management Plan 403 • All Components 403 .3 Project Documents 403 • Stakeholder Register 403 .4 Enterprise Environmental Factors 403 .5 Organizational Process Assets 403	.1 Expert Judgment 404 .2 Data Analysis 404 • Stakeholder Analysis 404 .3 Meetings 404	.1 Risk Management Plan 405

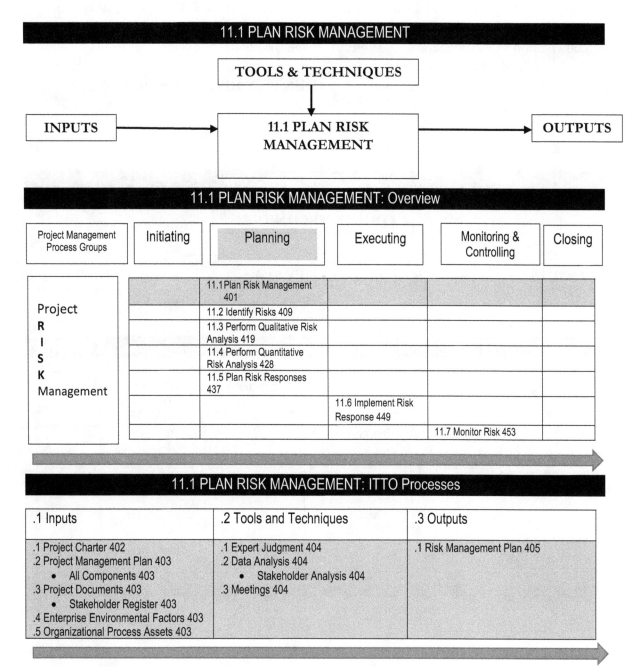

Fig. 11-2, P 401, Plan Risk Management: *Inputs, Tools and Techniques and Outputs*
Fig. 11-3, p 402, Plan Risk Management: *Data Flow Diagram*

Identify Risk:

Identify Risk is the process of identifying individual project risk as well as sources of overall project risk and documenting their characteristics. The **key benefit** of identifying risk is the documentation of existing individual project risk and the source of overall project risk (P 409).

Refer to the chart on the following two pages: **IDENTIFY RISKS (Section 11.2)**

Chapter Eleven: Project Risk Management

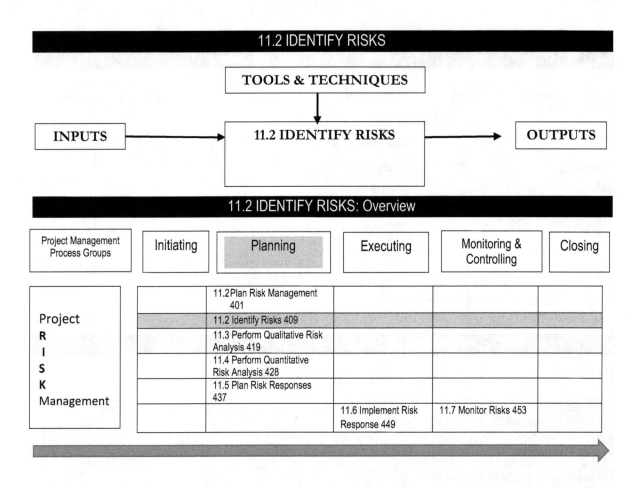

11.2 IDENTIFY RISKS

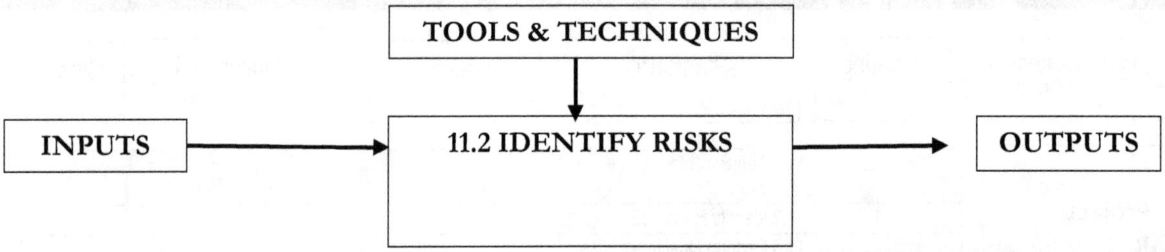

11.2 IDENTIFY RISKS: Overview

Project Management Process Groups	Initiating	Planning	Executing	Monitoring & Controlling	Closing
Project RISK Management		11.2Plan Risk Management 401			
		11.2 Identify Risks 409			
		11.3 Perform Qualitative Risk Analysis 419			
		11.4 Perform Quantitative Risk Analysis 428			
		11.5 Plan Risk Responses 437			
			11.6 Implement Risk Response 449	11.7 Monitor Risks 453	

Cont. on next page….

11.2 IDENTIFY RISKS: ITTO Processes

.1 Inputs	.2 Tools and Techniques	.3 Outputs
.1 Project Management Plan 411 • Requirements Management Plan 411 • Schedule Management Plan 411 • Cost Management Plan 411 • Quality Management Plan 411 • Resource Management Plan 411 • Risk Management Plan 412 • Scope Baseline 412 • Schedule Baseline 412 • Cost Baseline 412 .2 Project Documents 412 • Assumption Log 412 • Cost Estimates 412 • Duration Estimates 412 • Issue Log 412 • Lessons Learned Register 412 • Requirements Documentation 412 • Resource Requirements 413 • Stakeholder Register 413 .3 Agreements 413 .4 Procurement Documentation 413 .5 Enterprise Environmental Factors 413 .6 Organizational Process Assets 413	.1 Expert Judgment 414 .2 Data Gathering 414 • Brainstorming 414 • Checklists 414 • Interviews 414 .3 Data Analysis 415 • Root Cause Analysis 415 • Assumption and Constraint Analysis 415 • SWOT Analysis 415 • Document Analysis 415 .4 Interpersonal and Team Skills 416 • Facilitation 416 .5 Prompts Lists 416 .6 Meetings 416	.1 Risk Register 417 .2 Risk Report 418 .3 Project Documents Updates 418 • Assumption Log 418 • Issue Log 418 • Lessons Learned Register 418

Fig. 11-6, P 409, *Identify Risks: Inputs, Tools and Techniques and Outputs*
Fig. 11-7, P 410, *Identify Risks: Data Flow Diagram*

Perform Qualitative Risk Analysis:

Perform Qualitative Risk Analysis is the process of prioritizing individual project risk for further analysis or action by assessing the probability of occurrence and impact. The **key benefit** of Qualitative Risk Analysis is that it focuses efforts on high-priority risks (P 419).

See chart on next page: **PERFORM QUALITATIVE RISK ANLAYSIS (Section 11.3)**

Chapter Eleven: Project Risk Management

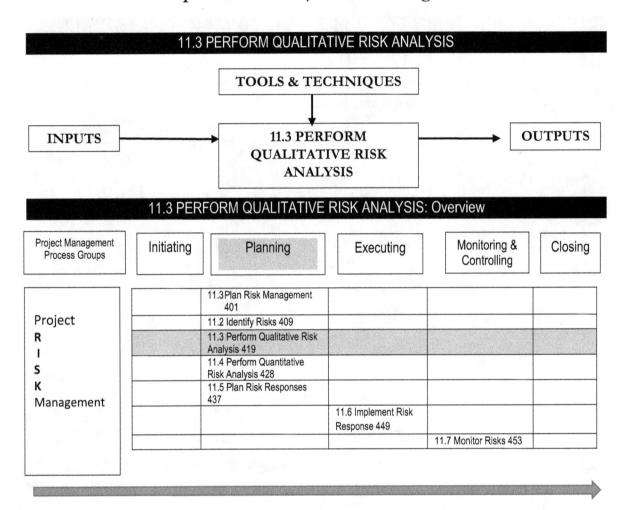

11.3 PERFORM QUALITATIVE RISK ANALYSIS

TOOLS & TECHNIQUES

INPUTS → 11.3 PERFORM QUALITATIVE RISK ANALYSIS → OUTPUTS

11.3 PERFORM QUALITATIVE RISK ANALYSIS: Overview

Project Management Process Groups	Initiating	Planning	Executing	Monitoring & Controlling	Closing
Project RISK Management		11.3Plan Risk Management 401			
		11.2 Identify Risks 409			
		11.3 Perform Qualitative Risk Analysis 419			
		11.4 Perform Quantitative Risk Analysis 428			
		11.5 Plan Risk Responses 437			
			11.6 Implement Risk Response 449		
				11.7 Monitor Risks 453	

11.3 PERFORM QUALITATIVE RISK ANALYSIS: ITTO Processes

.1 Inputs	.2 Tools and Techniques	.3 Outputs
.1 Project Management Plan 421 • Risk Management Plan 421 .2 Project documents 421 • Assumption Log 421 • Risk Register 421 • Stakeholder Register 421 .3 Enterprise Environmental Factors 422 .4 Organizational Process Assets 422	.1 Expert Judgment 422 .2 Data Gathering 422 • Interviews 422 .3 Data Analysis 423 • Risk Data Quality Assessment 423 • Risk Probability and Impact Assessment 423 • Assessment of other Risk Parameters 423 .4 Interpersonal And Team Skills 424 • Facilitation 424 .5 Risk Categorization 425 .6 Data Representation 425 • Probability and Impact Matrix 425 • Hierarchical Charts 425 .7 Meetings 426	.1 Project Document Updates 427 • Assumption Log 427 • Issue Log 427 • Risk Register 427 • Risk Report 427

Fig. 11-11, P 428, *Perform Quantitative Risk Analysis: Inputs, Tools and Techniques and Outputs*

Perform Quantitative Risk Analysis:

Perform Quantitative Risk Analysis is the process of numerically analyzing the combined effort of identified initial project risk and other sources of uncertainty and overall project risk objectives. The **key benefit** of this process is that it quantifies overall project risk exposure and it can provide additional quantitative risk information to support risk response planning (P 428).

See chart on next page: **PEFORM QUANTITAIVE RISK ANALYSIS (Section 11.4)**

Chapter Eleven: Project Risk Management

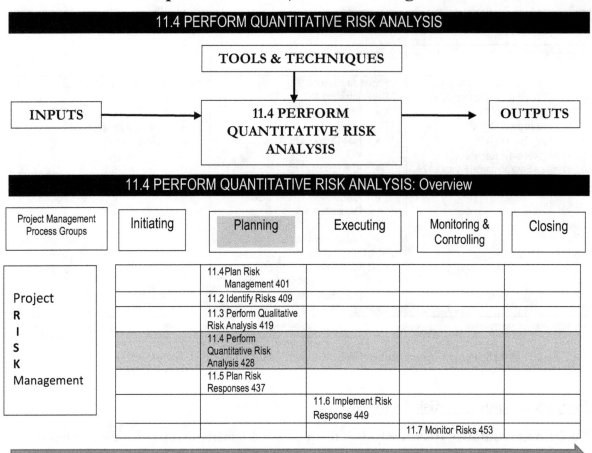

11.4 PERFORM QUANTITATIVE RISK ANALYSIS

TOOLS & TECHNIQUES

INPUTS → **11.4 PERFORM QUANTITATIVE RISK ANALYSIS** → **OUTPUTS**

11.4 PERFORM QUANTITATIVE RISK ANALYSIS: Overview

Project Management Process Groups	Initiating	Planning	Executing	Monitoring & Controlling	Closing
Project RISK Management		11.4Plan Risk Management 401			
		11.2 Identify Risks 409			
		11.3 Perform Qualitative Risk Analysis 419			
		11.4 Perform Quantitative Risk Analysis 428			
		11.5 Plan Risk Responses 437			
			11.6 Implement Risk Response 449		
				11.7 Monitor Risks 453	

.1 Inputs	.2 Tools and Techniques	.3 Outputs
.1 Project Management Plan 430 • Risk Management Plan 430 • Scope Baseline 430 • Schedule Baseline 430 • Cost Baseline 430 .2 Project Documents 430 • Assumption Log 430 • Basis of Estimate 430 • Cost Estimate 430 • Cost Forecasts 430 • Duration Estimates 430 • Milestone List 389 • Resource Requirements 431 • Risk Register 431 • Risk Report 431 • Schedule Forecasts 431 .3 Enterprise Environmental 431 Factors 431 .4 Organizational Process Assets 431	.1 Expert Judgment 431 .2 Data Gathering 432 • Interviews 432 .3 Interpersonal and Team Skills 432 • Facilitation 432 .4 Representations of Uncertainty 432 .5 Data Analysis 433 • Simulations 433 • Sensitivity Analysis 434 • Decision Tree Analysis 435 • Influence Diagrams 436	.1 Project Documents Update • Risk Report

11.4 PERFORM QUANTITATIVE RISK ANALYSIS: ITTO Processes

Fig. 11-12, P 429, *Perform Quantitative Risk Analysis: Data Flow Diagram*

Plan Risk Responses:

Plan Risk Responses is the process of developing options, selecting strategies, and agreeing on actions to address overall project risk exposure as well as to treat individual project risk. The **key benefit** is that it identifies appropriate ways to address overall project risk and individual project risk (P 437).

See chart on next page: **PLAN RISK RESPONSES (Section 11.5)**

Chapter Eleven: Project Risk Management

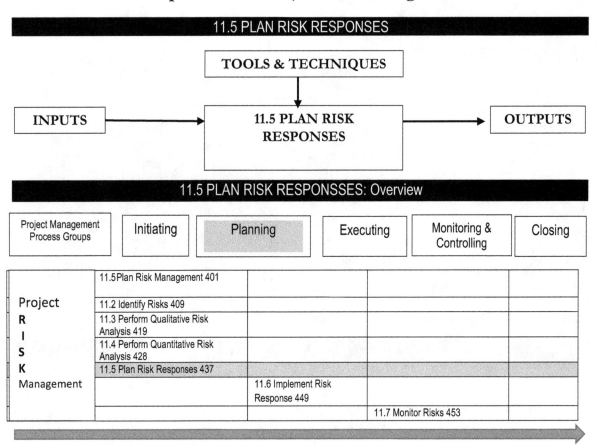

11.5 PLAN RISK RESPONSES

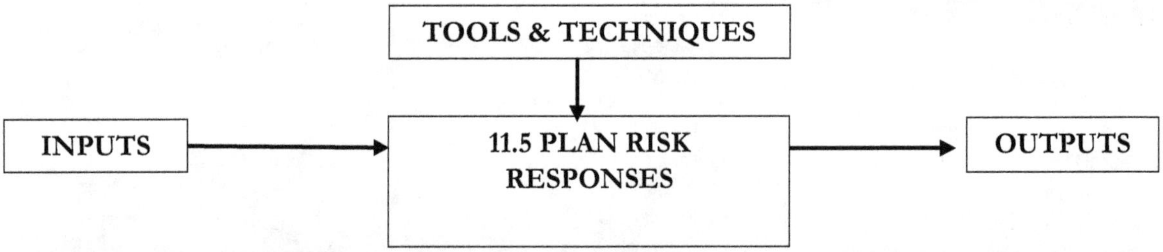

11.5 PLAN RISK RESPONSSES: Overview

Project Management Process Groups	Initiating	Planning	Executing	Monitoring & Controlling	Closing

Project	11.5Plan Risk Management 401			
R	11.2 Identify Risks 409			
I	11.3 Perform Qualitative Risk Analysis 419			
S	11.4 Perform Quantitative Risk Analysis 428			
K	11.5 Plan Risk Responses 437			
Management		11.6 Implement Risk Response 449		
			11.7 Monitor Risks 453	

.1 Inputs	.2 Tools and Techniques	.3 Outputs
.1 Project Management Plan 439 • Resource Management Plan 439 • Risk Management Plan 439 • Cost Baseline 439 .2 Project Documents 440 • Lessons Learned Register 440 • Project Schedule 440 • Project Team Assignments 440 • Resource Calendars 440 • Risk Register 440 • Risk Report 440 • Stakeholder Register 440 .3 Enterprise Environmental Factors 441 .4 Organizational Process Assets 441	.1 Expert Judgment 441 .2 Data Gathering 442 • Interviews 442 .3 Interpersonal And Team Skills 442 • Facilitation 442 .4 Strategies For Threats 442 .5 Strategies For Opportunities 444 .6 Contingent Response Strategies 445 .7 Strategies for overall Project Risk 445 .8 Data Analysis 446 • Alternative Analysis 446 • Cost-Benefit Analysis 446 .9 Decision Making 446 • Multicriteria Decision Analysis 446	.1 Change Requests 447 .2 Project Management Plan Updates 447 • Schedule Management Plan 447 • Cost Management Plan 447 • Quality Management Plan 447 • Resource Management Plan 447 • Procurement Management Plan 447 • Scope Baseline 447 • Schedule Baseline 447 • Cost Baseline 447 .3 Project Document Updates 448 • Assumption Log 448 • Cost Forecasts 448 • Lesson Learned Register 448 • Project Schedule 448 • Project Team Assignments 448 • Risk Register 448 • Risk Report 448

11.5 PLAN RISK RESPONSES: ITTO Processes

Fig. 11-16, P 437, *Plan Risk Responses: Inputs, Tools and Techniques and Outputs*
Fig. 11-17, P 438, *Plan Risk Responses: Data Flow Diagram*

Implement Risk Responses:

Implement Risk Responses is the process of implementing agreed-upon risk response plans. The **key benefit** is that it ensures the agreed upon risk responses were executed and planned in order to address overall project exposure and minimize individual project threats while maximizing individual project opportunities (P 449).

See chart below: **IMPLEMENT RISK RESPONSE (Section 11.6)**

Chapter Eleven: Project Risk Management

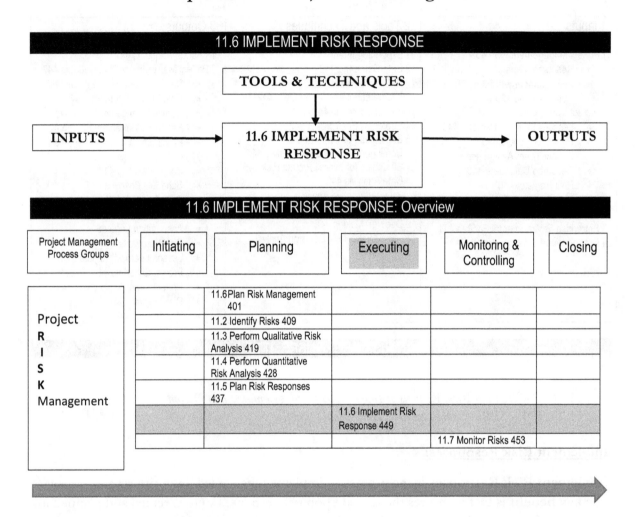

11.6 IMPLEMENT RISK RESPONSE

TOOLS & TECHNIQUES → **11.6 IMPLEMENT RISK RESPONSE**

INPUTS → **11.6 IMPLEMENT RISK RESPONSE** → **OUTPUTS**

11.6 IMPLEMENT RISK RESPONSE: Overview

Project Management Process Groups	Initiating	Planning	Executing	Monitoring & Controlling	Closing
Project RISK Management		11.6Plan Risk Management 401			
		11.2 Identify Risks 409			
		11.3 Perform Qualitative Risk Analysis 419			
		11.4 Perform Quantitative Risk Analysis 428			
		11.5 Plan Risk Responses 437			
			11.6 Implement Risk Response 449		
				11.7 Monitor Risks 453	

11.6 IMPLEMENT RISK RESPONSE: ITTO Processes

.1 Inputs	.2 Tools and Techniques	.3 Outputs
.1 Project Management Plan 450 • Risk Management Plan 450 .2 Project Documents 450 • Lessons Learned Register 450 • Risk Register 450 • Risk Report 450 .3 Organizational Process Assets 450	.1 Expert Judgment 451 .2 Interpersonal and Team Skills 451 • Influencing 451 .3 Project Management Information System 451	.1 Change Requests 451 .2 Project Document Updates 452 • Issue Log 452 • Lessons Learned Register 452 • Project Team Assignment 452 • Risk Register 452 • Risk Report 452

Fig. 11-18, P 449, *Implement Risk Responses: Inputs, Tools and Techniques and Outputs*
Fig. 11-19, P 449, *Implement Risk Responses: Data Flow Diagram*

Monitor Risk:

Monitor Risk is the process of monitoring the implementation of agreed-upon risk response plans, actively identifying risk and analyzing exposure to new risks in individual project risk. The **key benefit** is of this process is that it enables project decisions to be based on current information about overall project risk (453).

See chart on next page: **MONITOR RISK (Section 11.7)**

Chapter Eleven: Project Risk Management

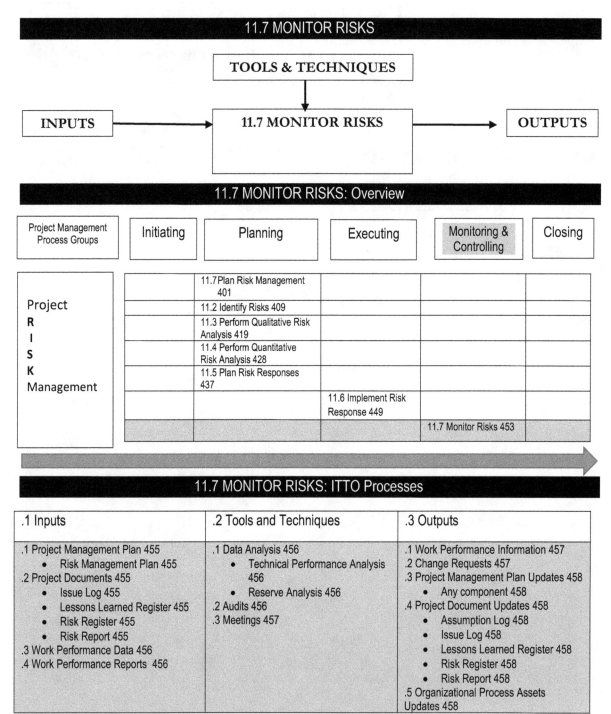

11.7 MONITOR RISKS

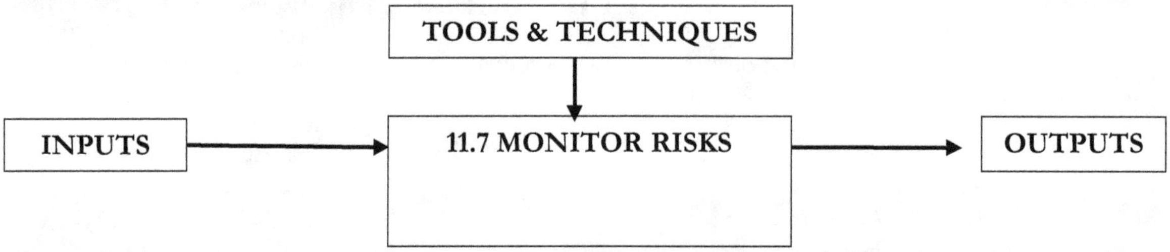

11.7 MONITOR RISKS: Overview

Project Management Process Groups	Initiating	Planning	Executing	Monitoring & Controlling	Closing
Project RISK Management		11.7Plan Risk Management 401			
		11.2 Identify Risks 409			
		11.3 Perform Qualitative Risk Analysis 419			
		11.4 Perform Quantitative Risk Analysis 428			
		11.5 Plan Risk Responses 437			
			11.6 Implement Risk Response 449		
				11.7 Monitor Risks 453	

11.7 MONITOR RISKS: ITTO Processes

.1 Inputs	.2 Tools and Techniques	.3 Outputs
.1 Project Management Plan 455 • Risk Management Plan 455 .2 Project Documents 455 • Issue Log 455 • Lessons Learned Register 455 • Risk Register 455 • Risk Report 455 .3 Work Performance Data 456 .4 Work Performance Reports 456	.1 Data Analysis 456 • Technical Performance Analysis 456 • Reserve Analysis 456 .2 Audits 456 .3 Meetings 457	.1 Work Performance Information 457 .2 Change Requests 457 .3 Project Management Plan Updates 458 • Any component 458 .4 Project Document Updates 458 • Assumption Log 458 • Issue Log 458 • Lessons Learned Register 458 • Risk Register 458 • Risk Report 458 .5 Organizational Process Assets Updates 458

Fig. 11-20, P 453, *Monitor Risk: Inputs, Tools and Techniques and Outputs*
Fig. 11-21, P 454, *Monitor Risk: Data Flow Diagram*

KEY WORDS: CHAPTER 11

- Plan risk management
- Identify risks
- Perform quantitative risk analysis
- Perform qualitative risk analysis
- Plan risk responses
- Implement risk responses
- Monitor risks
- Individual project risk
- Overall project risk
- Non-event risk
    - Variability risk
    - Ambiguity risk
- Project resilience
- Integrated risk management
- Risk strategy
- Risk categories
- Stakeholder risk appetite
- Risk probability and impacts
- Probability and impact matrix
- Tracking
- Swan analysis
- Document analysis
- Prompt list
- Risk register
- Qualitative risk
- Risk categorization
- Data representation
    - Probability and impacts matrix
    - Hierarchal charts
    - Meetings
- Quantitative risk analysis
- Simulation
- Sensitivity analysis
- Decision tree analysis
- Influence diagrams
- Strategies for threats
    - Escalate
    - Avoid
    - Transfer
    - Mitigate
    - Accept
- Strategies for opportunities
    - Escalate
    - Share
    - Exploit
    - Enhance
    - Accept
- Strategies for overall project risk
    - Avoid
    - Exploit
    - Transfer/share
    - Mitigate/enhance
    - Accept
- Technical performance analysis
- Reserve analysis

LEGEND

The following Legend shows how to correctly read the *PMBOK® Guide* references and attributions correctly for Chapter 11: Project Risk Management PMBOK Details.

Legend:

Chapter Section	Chapter Section Title	Page Number

Example from Chapter Six shown below:

6.5.1.4	Enterprise Environmental Factors	(P 209)

All direct quotes are attributed as (A Guide to the Project Management Body of Knowledge, *(PMBOK® Guide)* – Sixth Edition) Project Management Institute Inc., 2017, Page #, after each section and any/all paraphrased or original wording is attributed as (P #), before or after each section. All Graphs, Charts, Tables and Figures are attributed as: (*PMBOK® Guide,* Fig. #-# or #/#, P #, *Title of Graph, Chart, Table or Figure*).

11. PROJECT RISK MANAGEMENT

Project Risk Management for a project is a process of deciding how to conduct risk management planning, identification of analysis response planning, response implementation and monitoring project risks. The **key benefit** is to increase the probability/impact of positive risks and to decrease the probability and/or impact of negative risks in order to optimize the chances of project success.

Fig. 11-1, P 396, *Project Risk Management Overview*

This process should begin when a project is first started and completed early on.

Key Concepts for Project Risk Management:

Every project contains risks, but there are two (2) main risks levels to keep in mind shown below (P 397):

- **Individual Project Risk**: An uncertain event or condition that has a positive/negative effect on one or more project objectives
- **Overall Project Risk**: The effect of uncertainty on a project as a whole

Trends and Emerging Practices in Project Risk Management:

- **Non-Event Risk**: Non-Event risks need to be identified and managed throughout the project life cycle. Shown below are two (2) main types of non-event risks (P 398):

    - **Variability Risk**: Uncertainty exists about some key characteristics of a planned event or activity or decision.
    - **Ambiguity Risk**: Uncertainty exists about what might happen in the future.

- **Project Resilience**: The existence of risk is becoming clear, with a growing awareness of so-called **unknowable unknowns** and every project is required to have the following (P 399):

    - **Right level of budget and schedule contingency** for emergent risks and a specific risk budget for known risks
    - **Flexible project processes** that can cope with emergent risks while maintaining overall direction toward project goals
    - **Empowered project team** that has clear objectives and is trusted to get the job done as agreed
    - **Frequent review of early warning signs** to identify emergent risks as early as possible

- **Clear input from stakeholders** to clarify areas where the project scope or strategy can be adjusted in response to emergent risks.
- **Integrated Risk Management**: Risks should be managed and owned at the appropriate level of program, portfolio or both (P 399)

Tailoring Considerations: Some of the four (4) considerations for tailoring include (P 400):

- **Project Size**:
  - Does the **project size,** in terms of budget, duration, scope or team size require a more detailed approach to risk management, or is it small enough to justify a simplified risk management process?
- **Project Complexity**:
  - Is a **robust risk approach** demanded by high levels of innovation, new technology, commercial arrangements, interfaces or external dependencies that increase project complexity?
  - Is the project simple enough that a reduced risk process will suffice?
- **Project Importance**:
- Is the project **strategically important?**
  - Is the level of risk increased for this project because it aims to produce breakthrough opportunities, addresses significant blocks to the organization's performance or involves major product innovation?
- **Development Approach**:
  - Is this a **waterfall project**, where risk processes can be followed sequentially and iteratively, or does the project follow an **agile approach** where risk is addressed at the start of each iteration as well as during its execution?

Considerations for Agile/Adaptive Environments:

An Agile/Adaptive approach works best in a high-variability environment where the requirements are updated frequently. Here frequent reviews of incremental work products are needed if the potential of risk is identified and discussed. When selecting the content of each iteration, risks will be identified, analyzed and managed during each iteration (P 400).

11.1 PLAN RISK MANAGEMENT

Plan Risk Management is a process of deciding how to conduct and manage project risk activities. The **key benefits** are that will ensure the degree, type and visibility of risk are proportionate to both risks and importance to the project, organization and stakeholders.

Fig. 11-2, P 401, *Plan Risk Management: Inputs, Tools and Techniques and Outputs*
Fig. 11-3, P 402, *Plan Risk Management: Data Flow Diagram*

11.1.1 Plan Risk Management: Inputs

11.1.1.1 Project Charter

The **Project Charter** contains inputs, such as (P 402):

- High-level project descriptions and boundaries
- High-level requirements
- High-level risks

11.1.1.2 Project Management Plan

Methodologies outlined in the **Project Management Plan** may influence the Plan Risk Management process (P 403).

11.1.1.3 Project Documents

One of the **Project Documents** that can be considered for this process includes the Stakeholder Register (P 403).

11.1.1.4 Enterprise Environmental Factors

Enterprise Environmental Factors that may affect the Plan Risk Management process are overall risk thresholds. Such thresholds are set by the organization or key project stakeholders (P 403)

11.1.1.5 Organizational Process Assets

Some of the **Organizational Process Assets** that may affect this process are (P 403):

- Organizational risk policy
- Risk categories
- Common definitions of risk concepts and terms
- Risk statement formats
- Templates for the risk management plan, risk register and risk report
- Roles and responsibilities
- Authority levels for decision making
- Lessons learned repository

11.1.2 Plan Risk Management: Tools and Techniques

11.1.2.1 Expert Judgment

Expert Judgment: Groups or Individuals with specialized knowledge or training or extensive knowledge should be consulted in the areas shown below (P 404):

- Familiarity with the organization's approach to managing risk
- Tailoring risk management to the specific needs of the project
- Types of risks that are likely to be encountered on project in the same area

11.1.2.2 Data Analysis

Data Analysis techniques that can be used for this process are not limited to a Stakeholder Analysis to determine the risk appetite of project stakeholders (P 404).

11.1.2.3 Meetings

The purpose of **Meetings** are to discuss strategies, approaches and the execution process as to how the risk management process will be conducted, monitored and controlled and should include the project manager, sponsor, stakeholders, team members, customers, sellers and regulators (P 404).

11.1.3 Plan Risk Management: Outputs

11.1.3.1 Risk Management Plan

The **Risk Management Plan** describes the structure and how the risks will be addressed. Some of the components in the Risk Management Plan include (P 405):

- **Risk Strategy**: The approach taken to manage risk on a project
- **Methodology**: The specific approach, tools and data sources required to perform risk management on a project
- **Roles and Responsibilities**: Defines the lead, support and risk management team members for each type of activity described in the risk management plan and clarifies each of the responsibilities
- **Funding**: Identifies the funds needed to perform activities related to project risk management and establishes protocols for the application of

contingency and management reserves

- **Timing**: Defines when and how often the project risk management processes will be performed throughout the project lifecycle and establishes risk management activities for inclusion into the project schedule
- **Risk Categories**: Provide a means for grouping individual project risks using a common structure known as RBS, Risk Breakdown Structure.
  Fig. 11-4, P 406, *Extract from Simple Risk Breakdown Structure (RBS)*
- **Stakeholder Risk Appetite**: The level of risk each key Stakeholder deems acceptable
- **Definitions of Risk Probability and Impacts**: Definitions of risk probability and impact are specific to each project.
  Table 11-1, P 407, *Examples of Definitions for Probability and Impact).*
- **Probability and Impact and Matrix***:* Prioritization Rules may be specified by the organization in advance of the project and be included in the Organizational Process Assets or Tailored to specific project needs. Opportunities/Threats are represented in a Probability Matrix.
  Fig. 11-5, 408, *Example Probability and Impact Matrix with Scoring Scheme).*
- **Reporting Formats**: Defines the outcomes of the Project Risk Management Risk process
- **Tracking**: Documents how Risk activities will be recorded and how the Risk Management process will be audited

11.2 Identify Risks

Identify Risks, an iterative process, is the task of identifying each risk separately and the overall sources of project risks. The **key benefit** is obtained by writing down and entering the information for each risk along with the sources so it brings the data together in one location to make retrieval easier.

Fig. 11-6, P 409, *Identify Risks: Inputs, Tools and Techniques and Outputs*
Fig. 11-7, P 410, *Identify Risks: Data Flow Diagram*

In this process, both individual risks and the sources of any overall project risks are considered. A consistent format should be used to make sure the risks are understood clearly.

11.2.1 Identify Risks: Inputs

11.2.1.1 Project Management Plan

Some of the components of the **Project Management Plan** are (P 411):

- **Requirements Management Plan**: May include project objectives that are at risk
- **Schedule Management Plan**: May identify areas that are subject to uncertainty or ambiguity
- **Cost Management Plan**: May identify areas that are subject to uncertainty or ambiguity
- **Quality Management Plan**: May identify areas that are subject to uncertainty or ambiguity
- **Resource Management Plan**: May identify areas that are subject to uncertainty or ambiguity
- **Risk Management**: Provides information on risk-related roles and responsibilities
- **Scope Baseline**: Includes deliverables and criteria for their acceptance, some of which might give rise to risk, and also contains the WBS
- **Schedule Baseline**: May be reviewed to identify milestones and deliverable due dates that are subject to uncertainty or ambiguity
- **Cost Baseline**: May be reviewed to identify costs or funding requirements that are subject to uncertainty or ambiguity

11.2.1.2 Project Documents

Some of the **Project Documents** that may be considered as Inputs to this process are (P 411):

- **Assumption Log**: Assumptions and constraints recorded in the assumption log may give rise to individual project risks and also influence the overall project risks
- **Cost Estimates**: Provide quantitative assessments of project costs and risks
- **Duration Estimates**: Provide quantitative assessments of project duration risk
- **Issue Log**: Issues recorded in this log may give rise to individual project risks
- **Lessons Learned Register**: Updated with information on techniques that were effective in identifying risks to improve performance in later phases or other projects

- **Requirements Documentation**: Lists the project requirements
- **Resource Requirements**: Provide quantitative assessments of project resource requirements and items that may pose as project risks
- **Stakeholder Register**: Contains data about Stakeholders, that might be of use in initiating risk information on requirements and the expectations of those stakeholders are also recorded, along with those who are available to act as risk owners

11.2.1.3Agreements

Agreements are an understanding between parties and the duties of each party and may contain information such as, milestone dates, contract types, acceptance criteria, awards and penalties that may present threats/opportunities (P 413).

11.2.1.4 Procurement Documentation

Procurement Documentation should be reviewed when procuring from outside sources because they may increase/decrease overall project risk factors (P 413).

11.2.1.5 Enterprise Environmental Factors

Some of the Enterprise Environmental Factors that may affect this process are (P 413):

- **Published material**, including commercial risk databases or checklists
- **Academic studies**
- **Benchmarking results**
- **Industry studies** of similar projects

11.2.1.6 Organizational Process Assets

Some of the Organizational Process Assets that may affect this process are (P 413):

- **Project files**, including actual data
- **Organizational and project process controls**
- **Risk statement formats**
- **Checklists** from previous similar projects

11.2.2 Identify Risks: Tools and Techniques

11.2.2.1 Expert Judgment

Expert Judgment: Groups or Individuals with specialized knowledge or training or extensive knowledge should be consulted and identified by the Project Manager (PM) and invited to consider all aspects of project risk, individual as well as overall risk in the areas shown below (P 414):

- Familiarity with the organization's approach to managing risk
- Tailoring risk management to the specific needs of the project
- Types of risks that are likely to be encountered on project in the same area

11.2.2.2 Data Gathering

Some of the **Data Gathering** techniques used in this process are (P 414):

- **Brainstorming**: The collection of multiple ideas related to project and product requirements and to obtain a comprehensive list of overall project risk
- **Checklists**: A list of items, actions or points to be considered
- **Interviews**: Individual project risks and sources of overall project risk can be identified by interviewing experience project participants, stakeholders and subject matter experts (SME)'s

11.2.2.3 Data Analysis

Some of the **Data Analysis** techniques used in this process are (P 415):

- **Root Cause Analysis:** Used to discover underlying causes that lead to a problem and develop preventative actions
- **Assumption and Constraint Analysis:** Explores the validity of assumptions and constraints to discover which ones pose a risk to the project
- **SWOT Analysis**: Examines the project form each of the strengths, weaknesses, opportunities and threats (SWOT) perspectives
- **Document Analysis**: Risks may be identified from a structured review of project documents

11.2.2.4 Interpersonal and Team Skills

Interpersonal and Team Skills include facilitation. A skilled facilitator can help participants remain focused on risk identification (P 416).

11.2.2.5 Prompt Lists

A **Prompt List** is a predetermined **list of risk categories** that may become individual or overall project risks/threats (P 416).

11.2.2.6 Meetings

A specialized **Meeting** (Risk Workshop) may be implemented using brainstorming techniques.

11.2.3 Identify Risks: Outputs

11.2.3.1 Risk Register

Some of the components contained in the **Risk Register** are (P 417):

- **List of Identified Risks**: Identified risks are clearly described in detail
- **Potential Risk Owners**: The risk owner is recorded
- **List of Potential Risk Responses**: When a potential risk has been identified, it is recorded

11.2.3.2 Risk Report

Overall project risk is contained in the **Risk Report** and recorded progressively throughout the Project Risk Management process. The risk report may include some of the following, depending on the reporting requirements specified in the **Risk Management Plan** (P 418):

- **Sources of overall project risk**, indicating which are the most important of drivers of overall project risk
- **Summary information** on identified individual project risks

11.2.3.3 Project Documents Updates

Some of the **Project Documents** that may be updated include (P 418):

- **Assumption Log**: New assumptions can be made, new constraints identified and existing assumptions or constraints may be revisited and changed
- **Issue Log**: Should be updated to capture any new issues that are uncovered or any changes in previously logged issues
- **Lessons Learned Register**: Updated with information on techniques that were effective in identifying risks to improve performance in later phases or other projects

11.3 PERFORM QUALITATIVE RISK ANALYSIS

Perform Qualitative Risk Analysis is the process required to make certain that all project risks are prioritized in terms of levels of importance. This process assesses the priority of identified risks to decide which mitigation action steps need to be taken after assessing their probability of occurrence and impact upon the project and is performed regularly throughout the project. This process also identifies a risk owner for each risk. The **key benefit** is documenting all risks and the sources of those risks to allow the PM to focus on the higher risks associated with the project and reduce levels of uncertainty (P 419).

Fig. 11-8, p 419, *Qualitative Risk Analysis: Inputs, Tools and Techniques and Outputs*
Fig. 11-9, P 420, *Qualitative Risk Analysis: Data Flow Diagram*

11.3.1 Perform Qualitative Risk Analysis: Inputs

11.3.1.1 Project Management Plan

The components of the **Project Management Plan** should include the Risk Management Plan. Here the PM will emphasize (P 421):

- Roles and responsibilities for conducting risk management
- Budgets for risk management
- Schedule activities for risk management
- Risk categories (often defined in the RBS, risk breakdown structure)
- Definitions of probability and impact
- The probability and impact matrix
- Stakeholder risk thresholds

11.3.1.2 Project Documents

Some of the **Project Documents** used in this process may include (P 421):

- **Assumption Log**:
- **Risk Register**:
- **Stakeholder Register**:

11.3.1.3 Enterprise Environmental Factors

Some of the **Enterprise Environmental Factors** that may affect this process may include (P 422):

- Industry studies of similar projects
- Published Information, including commercial risk databases or checklists

11.3.1.4 Organizational Process Assets

Some of the **Organizational Process Assets** used in this process may include information about completed similar projects (P 422):

11.3.2 Perform Qualitative Risk Analysis: Tools and Techniques

11.3.2.1 Expert Judgment

Expert Judgment: Groups or Individuals with specialized knowledge or training or extensive knowledge in the following areas should be consulted and identified (P 422):

- Previous Similar Projects
- Qualitative Risk Analysis

Be careful to look for SME's in risk who may be biased and less objective, as a result than other SME's.

11.3.2.2 Data Gathering

Some of the **Data Gathering Techniques** used in this process may include Interviews (P 422).

11.3.2.3 Data Analysis

Some of the **Data Analysis** techniques used in this process may include (P 423):

- **Risk Data Quality Assessment**: Evaluates the degree to which the data about individual project risks is accurate and reliable as a basis for qualitative risk assessment
- **Risk Probability and Impact Assessment**: Considers the likelihood that a risk will occur
- **Assessment of other Risk Parameters**: May consider other characteristics of risk when prioritizing for further analysis and action and may include the following characteristics (P 423):

    - **Urgency**: The period of time in which a response is needed
    - **Proximity**: The period of time before a risk may impact the project
    - **Dormancy**: The period of time that may elapse after a risk has occurred
    - **Manageability**: The ease with which a PM can manage an occurrence
    - **Controllability**: The degree to which the risk owner is able to control the risk
    - **Detectability**: The ease with which the results of the risk occurring , or being able to occur, can be detected and recognized
    - **Connectivity**: The extent to which the risk is related to other individual project risks
    - **Strategic Impact**: The potential for the risk to have a positive/negative effect on the organization's goals
    - **Propinquity**: The degree to which a risk is perceived to matter by one or more stakeholders

11.3.2.4 Interpersonal and Team Skills

One of the **Interpersonal and Team Skills** used in this process may include Facilitation (P 424).

11.3.2.5 Risk Categorization

Risks can be grouped into **Risk Categorization** areas using the **Risk Breakdown**

Structure (RBS). See the following areas of potential risk(s) and the project area that may be affected Generic risk responses may be helpful when areas of highest risk exposure are identified (P 425):

Fig. 11-4, P 407, *Examples of Definitions for Probability and Impacts*
Fig. 5-12, P 158, *Sample WBS Decomposed Down through Work Packages*
Fig. 5-13, P 159, *Sample WBS Organized by Phase*
Fig. 5-14, P 160, *Sample WBS with Major Deliverables*

11.3.2.6 Data Representation

Some of the **Data Representation** techniques used in this process may include (P 425).

- **Probability and Impact Matrix**: A grid for mapping the probability of each risk occurrence and its impact on the project objectives
- **Hierarchal Charts**: When risks have been categorized, using one or more parameters, the Probability and Impact Matrix cannot be used and other graphical representations will be used, such as a Bubble Chart as shown in (PMBOK® Guide, Fig. 11-10, P 426, *Example Bubble Chart showing Detectability, Proximity and Impact Value).*

11.3.2.7 Meetings

Meetings are a way to undertake Qualitative Risk Analysis by conducting a Risk Workshop, as it may be called (P 426).

11.3.3 Perform Qualitative Risk Analysis: Outputs

11.3.3.1 Project Documents Updates

Some of the **Project Documents** that may be **updated** in this process may include (P 427).

- **Assumption Log**: New assumptions may be made, constraints identified and existing assumptions and constraints may be revisited and changed through updating
- **Issue Log**: Updated to capture new issues as they arise
- **Risk Register**: Updated with new information generated during the Perform Qualitative Risk Analysis process
- **Risk Report**: Updated to reflect the most important individual project risks

11.4 PERFORM QUANTITATIVE RISK ANALYSIS

Perform Quantitative Risk Analysis is the process of numerically analyzing the combined effect of identified risks on overall project objectives and the Output is Project Documents. The **key benefit** is that it quantifies overall risk exposure and aids in supporting risk response planning.

Fig. 11-11, P 428, *Perform Quantitative Risk Analysis: Inputs, Tools and Techniques and Outputs*
Fig. 11-12, P 429, *Perform Quantitative Risk Analysis: Data Flow Diagram*

Although Perform Quantitative Risk Analysis is not required for all projects, it does require specialized software and expertise in the development of and interpretation of risk models.

Perform Quantitative Risk Analysis uses information on individual project risks that have been assessed by the qualitative risk process and outputs from this process may be used as inputs to the Plan Risk Response Process (P 428-429).

11.4.1 Perform Quantitative Risk Analysis: Inputs

11.4.1.1 Project Management Plan

Some of the components in the **Project Management Plan** include (P 430):

- **Risk Management Plan: C**oncerned with the strategies, tools and techniques used in Quantitative
- **Risk Analysis**: A planning process to prioritize (i.e. rank order) the specific risks and analyze and assess their probability of occurrence and impact upon the project
- **Scope Baseline**: A component of the Project Management Plan which describes the starting point from which the effect of individual project risks and other sources of uncertainty can be evaluated
- **Schedule Baseline**: Describes the starting point from which the effect of individual project risks and other sources of uncertainty can be evaluated
- **Cost Baseline**: Describes the starting point from which the effect of individual project risks and other sources of uncertainty can be evaluated

11.4.1.2 Project Documents

Some of the **Project Documents** that can be considered as Inputs for this process include (P 430):

- **Assumption log**: May form Inputs to the quantitative risk analysis if they are assessed as posing a risk to project objectives
- **Basis of estimates**: Used in the planning of the project may be reflected in variability modeled during a risk analysis process, which may include information on the estimate's purpose, classification, assumed accuracy, methodology and source
- **Cost estimates**: Provides the starting point from which cost variability is evaluated
- **Cost forecasts**: The project's estimate to complete (ETC), estimate a completion (EAC), budget at completion (BAC) and to-complete performance index (TCPI) may be compared to the results of a quantitative cost risk analysis to determine the confidence level associated with achieving these targets
- **Duration estimates**: Provide the starting point from which schedule variability is evaluated
- **Milestone list**: significant events in the project define the schedule targets against which the results of a quantitative cost risk analysis to determine the confidence level associated with achieving these targets
- **Resource requirements**: Provides a starting point from which variability is evaluated
- **Risk register**: Contains details of individual project risks
- **Risk report**: Describes sources of overall project risk and current overall risk status
- **Schedule forecasts**: May be compared to the results of a quantitative schedule risk analysis to determine the confidence level associated with achieving these targets

11.4.1.3 Enterprise Environmental Factors

Enterprise Environmental Factors that may help with the Risk Analysis process (P 335):

- **Industry studies** of similar projects by risk specialists
- **Published material**, including commercial risk databases or checklists

11.4.1.4 Organizational Process Assets

Some of the **Organizational Process Assets** used in this process may include data from similar competed projects (P 431).

11.4.2 Perform Quantitative Risk Analysis: Tools and Techniques

11.4.2.1 Expert Judgment

Expert Judgment: Groups or Individuals with specialized knowledge or training or extensive knowledge in the following areas (P 431):

- **Translating information** on individual project risks and other sources of uncertainty into numeric inputs for the quantitative risk analysis model
- **Selecting the most appropriate representation of uncertainty** to model particular risks or other source of uncertainty
- **Modeling techniques** that are appropriate in the context of the project
- **Identifying which tools would be most suitable** for the selected modeling techniques
- **Interpreting the outputs** of quantitative risk models

11.4.2.2 Data Gathering

Data Gathering, such as interviews and facilitated workshops are used to generate Inputs for the Quantitative Risk Analysis (P 432).

11.4.2.3 Interpersonal and Team Skills

Interpersonal and Team Skills for this process include **Facilitation** (P 432).

11.4.2.4 Representations of Uncertainty

Representations of Uncertainty means that a quantitative risk analysis requires Inputs to a quantitative risk analysis model to reflect individual project risks and other sources of uncertainty.

11.4.2.5 Data Analysis

Some of the **Data Analysis** techniques that may be used in this process include (P 436).

- **Simulation:** This model simulates the combined effects of individual project risks and other levels of uncertainty to evaluate the potential impact on achieving project objectives and the Output is a quantitative risk analysis model.

Fig. 11-13, P 433, *Example S-Curve from Quantitative Cost Risk Analysis*

- **Sensitivity Analysis**: Helps to determine which individual project risks or other sources of uncertainty will have the most impact on the project outcomes. See

  Fig. 11-14, P 435, *Example Tornado Diagram*

- **Decision Tree Analysis**: Used to support selection of the best of several alternative courses of action and is evaluated by calculating the expected monetary value of each branch to determine the optimal path.

  Fig. 11-15, P 435, *Example Decision Tree*

- **Influence Diagrams**: Graphical aids to decision making under uncertainty. Outputs from this diagram are similar to other quantitative risk analysis methods, including S-Curves and Tornado Diagrams.

11.4.3 Perform Quantitative Risk Analysis: Outputs

11.4.3.1 Project Documents Updates

Some of the **Project Documents** that can be considered as Outputs for this process include the following and the Risk Report will be updated to reflect the results of the quantitative risk analysis, which will usually include the following components (P 437):

- **Assessment of overall project risk exposure**: This is reflected in the following two (2) key measurements:
  - Chances of project success
  - Degree of inherent variability within the project
- **Detailed Probabilistic analysis of the project**: Key outputs are presented form the quantitative risk analysis, such as S-Curve, Tornado Diagrams and Critical Analysis and the possible detailed results of a quantitative risk analysis may include the following:
  - Amount of contingency reserve needed to provide a specified level of confidence
  - Identity of individual project risks or other sources of uncertainty
  - Major drivers of overall project risks
- **Prioritized list of individual project risks**: Includes those individual project risks that pose the greatest threat or opportunity indicated by the sensitivity analysis

- **Trends in quantitative risk analysis results**: As the analysis is repeated at various times, trends may become apparent
- **Recommended risk responses**: May present suggested risk responses to the level of overall project risk exposure or key individual project risks, based on results of the quantitative risk analysis and these recommendations will form the Inputs to the Plan Risk Responses

11.5 PLAN RISK RESPONSES

Plan Risk Responses is the process of developing options, selecting strategies and actions to enhance opportunities and address overall threats to project objectives. The **key benefit** is to identify appropriate strategies to deal with project risks (P 439).

Fig. 11-16, P 437, *Plan Risk Responses: Inputs, Tools and Techniques and Outputs*
Fig. 11-17, P 438, *Plan Risk Responses: Data Flow Diagram*

By planning risk responses, individual threats can be reduced, opportunities can be maximized and overall project risk is reduced. Usually a mix of strategies works well and is the more effective way to address risk and risk exposure. Specific actions can be developed to develop the agreed-upon task response strategy, including backup strategies. A contingency plan (fallback plan), can be developed for implementation where needed (P 439).

11.5.1 Plan Risk Responses: Inputs

11.5.1.1 Project Management Plan

Some of the **Project Management Plan** components are (P 439):

- **Resource Management Plan**: Used to help determine how resources allocated to agreed-upon risks responses will be coordinated with other project resources
- **Risk Management Plan**: Risk Management roles and responsibilities are risk thresholds are used in this process
- **Cost Baseline**: Contains information on the contingency fund that is allocated to respond to risks

11.5.1.2 Project Documents

Some of the **Project Documents** used in this process are (P 440):

- **Lessons Learned Register**: Effective risk responses used in the past are reviewed to determine if they might be useful in the current project
- **Project Schedule**: Used to determine how agreed-upon risk responses will be scheduled alongside other project activities
- **Project Team Assignments**: Shows the resources that can be allocated to agreed-upon risk responses
- **Resource Calendar**: Identify when potential resources are available to be allocated to agreed-upon risk responses
- **Risk Register**: Includes detail of individual identified risks, which have been prioritized and for which responses need to be addressed
- **Risk Report**: Shows the current level of overall risk exposure and the selection of risk response strategies and the prioritization of risk levels
- **Stakeholder Register**: Identifies potential owners for risk responses

11.5.1.3 Enterprise Environmental Factors

Some of the **Enterprise Environmental Factors** that can affect this process are the risk appetite and risk thresholds of the stakeholders (P 441).

11.5.1.4 Organizational Process Assets

Some of the **Organizational Process Assets** used in this process are (P 441):

- Templates for the risk management plan, risk register and risk report
- Historical databases
- Lessons learned repositories from similar projects

11.5.2 Plan Risk Responses: Tools and Techniques

11.5.2.1 Expert Judgment

Expert Judgment: Groups or Individuals with specialized knowledge or training or extensive knowledge should be consulted in the areas shown below (P 441):

- Threat Response Strategies
- Opportunity Response Strategies
- Contingent Response Strategies
- Overall Project Risk Response Strategies

11.5.2.2 Data Gathering

Some of the **Data Gathering** techniques that can affect this process are interviews (P 442).

11.5.2.3 Interpersonal and Team Skills

One of the **Interpersonal and Team Skills** used in this process is Facilitation (P 442).

11.5.2.4 Strategies for Threats

Five (5) Alternative **Strategies for Threats** are shown below (P 442):

- **Escalate**: Threats are escalated to the level that matches the objectives, but no action is taken unless the threat occurs
- **Avoid**: Avoid the risk entirely
- **Transfer**: Transfer the impact of risk to another party through ownership
- **Mitigate**: Reduce the probability of occurrence or impact of the risk, to within acceptable limits
- **Accept**: Reduce the probability of occurrence or impact of the risk, to within acceptable limits

Be sure to read and study this section (P 442-443). This section is extremely important.

11.5.2.5 Strategies for Opportunities

Five 95) Alternative **Strategies for Opportunities** are shown below (P 444):

- **Escalate**: Opportunities are escalated to the level that matches the objectives, but no action is taken unless the opportunity occurs
- **Exploit**: To eliminate uncertainty, by making sure the opportunity occurs
- **Share**: Allocating some or all of the ownership to a third party
- **Enhance**: Increase the probability and/or positive impact of an opportunity
- **Accept**: Increase the probability and/or positive impact of an opportunity

Be sure to read and study this section (P 444). This section is extremely important.

11.5.2.6 Contingent Response Strategies

Contingent Response Strategies are **used only in specific pre-defined situations.** If such a condition occurs, the **contingency plan**, will be put into action and should be defined and tracked.

11.5.2.7 Strategies for Overall Project Risks

Some of the **Strategies for Overall Project Risks** are shown below (P 445):

- **Avoid**: Avoid the risk entirely
- **Exploit**: To eliminate uncertainty, by making sure the opportunity occurs
- **Transfer/Share**: When the overall risk is negative a third party may be called in to manage the risk and a transfer strategy is required
- **Mitigate/Enhance**: Changing the level of overall project risk
- **Accept**: Taking advantage of an opportunity if it arises, but not actively pursuing it

Be sure to **read and study this section** (P 445-446). This section is extremely important.

11.5.2.8 Data Analysis

Data Analysis: Some of the Strategies for a preferred risk response are shown below (P 446):

- **Alternative Analysis**: Comparison of risk response strategies to determine the best option
- **Cost Benefit Analysis**: The ratio of (change in impact level) ÷ (implementation cost) gives the cost effectiveness of the response strategy

11.5.2.9 Decision Making

One of the techniques in **Decision Making** to select a risk response strategy may include a **Multicriteria Decision Analysis** that uses a **decision matrix** to provide a systematic approach for establishing key decision criteria (P 446).

Be sure to **read and study this section** (P **446).**

11.5.3 Plan Risk Responses: Outputs

11.5.3.1 Change Requests

Change Requests to the cost or schedule baselines or other components of the Project Management Plan may be the result of a planned risk response (P 447).

11.5.3.2 Project Management Plan Updates

Some of the **Project Management Plan Updates** are shown below (P 447):

- **Schedule management plan**: Changes to the schedule management plan are updated **as necessary**
- **Cost management plan**: Changes to the cost management plan are updated when **necessary**
- **Quality management plan**: Changes to the quality management plan are updated as **needed**
- **Resource management plan**: Changes to the resource management plan are updated when needed
- **Procurement management plan**: Changes to the procurement management plan are updated when necessary
- **Scope baseline**: Changes in the scope baseline are incorporated in response to approved changes in scope that may arise from agreed-upon risks
- **Schedule baseline:** Changes in the schedule baseline are incorporated in response to approved changes in schedule estimates that may arise from agreed-upon risks
- **Cost baseline**: Changes in the cost baseline are incorporated in response to approved changes in cost estimates that may arise from agreed-upon risks

11.5.3.3 Project Documents Updates

Some of the **Project Documents Updates** are shown below (P 447):

- **Assumption Log**: Contains a record of all the risks assumptions and constraints and may be updated or closed out
- **Cost Forecasts:** May change as a result of planned risk responses
- **Lessons Learned Register**: Lessons Learned will be finalized updated with information about risk responses

- **Project Schedule**: Activities relating to agreed-upon risk responses may be added to the project schedule
- **Project Team Assignments**: Once the responses are confirmed, the necessary resources should be allocated to each action associated with a risk response plan
- **Risk Register**: Provides information on all chosen and agreed upon risk responses. This updated risk register may include:
    - Agreed upon risk strategies
    - Specific actions to implement the chosen risk response strategy, etc.
- **Risk Report**: Provides current information on identified Project Risks and the sources of overall project risk along with the selection of risk response strategies

Study **and** read (P 448).

11.6 IMPLEMENT RISK RESPONSES

Implement Risk Responses are the process of implementing agreed-upon risk response plan and the key benefit is to ensure these responses are executed as planned to minimize risk threats and maximize risk opportunities. The **key benefit** of this process is that it ensures that agreed-upon risk responses are executed as planned in order to address overall project risk exposure, minimize individual project threats and maximize individual project opportunities.

Fig. 11-18, P 449, *Implement Risk Responses: Inputs, Tools and Techniques and Outputs*
Fig. 11-19, P 449, *Implement Risk Responses: Data Flow Diagram*

11.6.1 Implement Risk Responses: Inputs

11.6.1.1 Project Management Plan

The **Project Management Plan** stipulates the conditions necessary for monitoring and controlling risk (P 450).

11.6.1.2 Project Documents

Some of the **Project Documents** that can be considered as Inputs to this process include (P 451):

- **Lessons Learned**: Effective risk responses used in the past are reviewed to determine if they might be useful in the current project
- **Risk Register**: Contains the agreed-upon risk responses, each **individual risk** and the nominated owners

- **Risk Report**: Includes an assessment of the **current overall project risk exposure,** as well as the risk response strategy

11.6.1.3 Organizational Process Assets

One of **Data Gathering** techniques that can affect this process is the Lessons Learned Repository (P 450).

11.6.2 Implement Risk Responses: Tools and Techniques

11.6.2.1 Expert Judgment

Expert Judgment: Groups or Individuals with specialized knowledge or training or extensive knowledge will be necessary to validate or modify risk responses if needed and decide how to implement them in an efficient manner (P 451).

11.6.2.2 Interpersonal and Team Skills

One of the **Interpersonal and Team Skills** that can be used for this process includes using individuals or, groups with **Subject Matter Experts** (SME) have to validate/modify risk responses if needed (P 451).

11.6.2.3 Project Management Information Systems (PMIS)

The **Project Management Information System** contains a set of tools in order to capture, store and distribute information to internal and external stakeholders (P 451).

11.6.3 Implement Risk Responses: Outputs

11.6.3.1 Change Requests

Change Requests concerning risks may be made to the cost and schedule baseline are a result of implementation of risk responses. This is accomplished through the **Perform Integrated Change Control** process.

11.6.3.2 Project Documents Updates

Some of the Project Documents Updates as a result of this process are (P 452):

- **Issue Log**: Information about issues is communicated to impacted Stakeholders
- **Lessons Learned Register**: : May contain information on effective responses for variances and corrective and preventative actions and how they could have been avoided
- **Project Team Assignments:** Once the risk responses are confirmed, the necessary resources should be allocated to each action associated with a risk response plan
- **Risk Register**: Provides information on threats and opportunities
- **Risk Report**: Provides information on the overall Project risk exposure made as a result of the implement risk response process

11.7 MONITOR RISKS

Monitor Risk is the process of monitoring the implementation of agreed-upon risk response plans, tracking risks, analyzing new risks and evaluating the risk process and the **key benefit** is to enable project decisions to be based on current information concerning overall project risk exposure and individual project risks.

Fig. 11-20, P 453, *Monitor Risks: Inputs, Tools and Techniques and Outputs*
Fig. 11-21, P 454, *Monitor Risks: Data Flow Diagram*

Project work should be monitored at all times and use performance information to determine if (P 454):

- Implemented risk responses are effective
- Level of overall project risk has changed
- Status of identified individual project risk has changed
- New individual risks have arisen
- Risk management approach is still effective
- Project assumptions are still valid
- Risk management policies and procedures are being followed
- Contingency reserves for cost or schedule require modification
- Project strategy is still valid

11.7.1 Monitor Risks: Inputs

11.7.1.1 Project Management Plan

One of the **Project Management Plan** components is the Risk Management Plan (P 455):

11.7.1.2 Project Documents

Some of the **Project Documents** that can be considered as Inputs to this process include (P 455):

- **Issue Log**: Used to see if any of the open risk issues have been updated and necessitate an update
- **Lessons Learned Register**: Updated with information on techniques that were effective in identifying risks to improve performance in later phases or other projects
- **Risk Register**: May contain information on effective responses for variances and corrective and preventative actions
- **Risk Report**: Provides information on the overall Project risk as well as individual risks

11.7.1.3 Work Performance Data

Work Performance Data contains information on project risk status.

11.7.1.4 Work Performance Reports

Work Performance Reports are a necessity for performance information measurements that can be analyzed regarding availability, schedule and cost data, earned value reports: such as, burndown or burnup charts, along with variance analysis, earned value data and forecasting data.

11.7.2 Monitor Risks: Tools and Techniques

11.7.2.1 Data Analysis

Some of the **Data Analysis** techniques that may be used for this process include (P 456):

- **Technical Performance Analysis**: Compares technical accomplishments during project execution to the schedule of technical achievements
- **Reserve Analysis**: The process of assembling specific contingency reserves into the project schedule and the communications transmitted using graphical representations, such as a burndown chart

11.7.2.2 Audits

Risk audits means to reduce or minimize the effects of risks, using qualitative risk analysis, on a project thereby deciding whether or not a risk is more or less likely to occur. Risks are ranked by high and low probability on the **Risk Audit**. The Risk Audit is an output of the Risk Register. Risk audits may be included during routine project review meetings or special risk review meetings (P 456).

Read and study this section.

11.7.2.3 Meetings

One of the types of **Meetings** used in this process is known as a Risk Review.

11.7.3 Monitor Risks: Outputs

11.7.3.1 Work Performance Information

Work Performance Information is compared to risk occurrences and risk expectations. It will reveal the success of the effectiveness of the response planning and response implementation process. This information will determine if corrective or preventative action is necessary (P 459).

11.7.3.2 Change Requests

Change Requests are unaccepted deliverables needing a defect repair process, which requires reason(s) for the change(s) and includes any/all corrective action, preventative action and defect repair associated with the cost and schedule baselines of the components of the project management plan. Change Requests to the cost and schedule baseline are a result of the implementation of risk responses and are processed for review though the Perform Integrated Change Control Process**.** Change requests can include recommended corrective and preventative actions (P 457).

11.7.3.3 Project Management Plan Updates

Any change(s) to the Project Management Plan may affect any component included in the plan.

11.7.3.4 Project Documents Updates

Some of the **Project Document Updates** may include (P 458):

- **Assumption Log**: Contains a record of all the assumptions and constraints, new and old
- **Issue Log**: Should be updated as needs change during the project
- **Lessons Learned Register**: what has been experienced and process improvement recommendations should be filed for future use
- **Risk Register**: May contain information on effective responses for variances and corrective and preventative actions
- **Risk Report**: Provides information on the overall Project risk as well as individual risks

Study and read this section.

11.7.3.5 Organizational Process Updates

Some of the Organizational Process **Updates** may include (P 458):

- **Templates** for the risk management plan, risk register and risk report
- **Risk breakdown structure (RBS)**

Summary: Answers to Student Learning Outcomes

The seven (7) **Plan Risk Management** processes are:

1. (11.1) **Plan Risk Management**: Defines how to conduct risk management work for a project.
2. (11.2) **Identify Risk**: Identify individual project risk and their sources and document their characteristics.
3. (11.3) **Perform Qualitative Risk Analysis**: Prioritize individual risks, undertake analysis activities and assess their probability of impact.
4. (11.4) **Perform Quantitative Risk Analysis**: Numerically analyze the combined effect of individuals, identify sources of uncertainty and overall project objectives.
5. (11.5) **Plan Risk Responses**: Develop options, select strategy approaches and establish agreement to address overall risk exposure, and treat individual project risks.
6. (11.6) **Implement Risk Responses**: Implement agreed upon response plans (action steps.)
7. (11.7) **Monitor Risk**: Monitor and track identified risks and evaluate the overall risk process effectiveness.

Plan Risk Management is a process. It requires that the Project Manager and their team knows how to conduct project risk management work (P 395).

Project Risk Management begins even before the start of the project. Plan Risk Management is a **part of the Needs Assessment, Business Case and Benefits Management Plan** (P 29-32). Project Risk Management is included in the Project Charter and the Project Management Plan. Risk Management processes need to proceed well. If risk is not anticipated, responded to and acted upon, the project will be in great jeopardy from start to finish (P 397).

Risk Management is the process of **defining how** to conduct risk management activities for a project (P 401). The objective is to increase the probability and/or impact of positive risks and to decrease the probability and impact of negative risks and to optimize the chances of project success.

1. The objective of **Project Risk Management,** see #1 above, is to increase project success and consists of the following process components in the following order (P 395):

    1. **Plan Risk Management**
    2. **Identify Risks**
    3. **Perform Qualitative Risk Analysis**
    4. **Perform Quantitative Risk Analysis**
    5. **Plan Risk Responses**
    6. **Implement Risk Responses**
    7. **Monitor Risks**

    Fig. 11-1, P 396, *Plan Risk Management: Overview*

    The above chart and overview needs to be studied. This chart depicts each of the ITTO's Concepts. The importance of the ITTO's are to show how each of the (7) process components (i.e. Plan Risk Management, Identify Risks, Perform Qualitative risk Analysis, Perform Quantitative Risk Analysis, Plan Risk Responses, Implement Risk Responses, and Monitor Risks) use various Tools and Techniques to transform the Input sources into Outputs (P 396).

2. Organizations and stakeholders perceive risks differently. The project team needs to know what level of **risk exposure** is acceptable (P 398). Risks are reflected by:

    - **Risk Appetite**: The degree of uncertainty an entity is willing to take on an anticipation of a reward.
    - **Risk Threshold**: The level of uncertainty or risk toleration at which a specific stakeholder may have a specific interest.

3. The Project Manager may need to **tailor** the Project Risk Process (P 400). This depends upon the uniqueness of the project. The **Tailoring Techniques** include consideration of:

    - **Project Size**
    - **Project Complexity**
    - **Project Importance**
    - **Development Approach**

4. The **Risk Management Plan** is the only **Output of Plan Risk Management** and has **five (5) inputs** that may be used (via **Tools and Techniques**) to develop the **Risk Management Plan**, which is considered a subsidiary plan:

   Fig. 11-2, P 401 *Risk Management Plan: ITTO's*
   Fig. 11-3, P 402 Risk *Management Plan: Data Flow Diagram*

   The **five (5) Inputs to develop Risk Management Plan:**

   - **Project Charter**
   - **Project Management Plan** and all subsidiary components as appropriate and study their value in specific types of projects (PMBOK, 6th ED., P 87)
   - **Project Documents (Stakeholder Register)**
   - **Enterprise Environmental Factors**
   - **Organizational Process Assets**

5. The Process of **Plan Risk Management** may use either or all three (3) **ITTO's** (Inputs, Tools , Techniques or Outputs) (P 401):

   - **Expert Judgment**
   - **Data Analysis (Stakeholder Analysis)**
   - **Meetings**

6. The Project Manager develops the **Risk Management Plan** to include the following **11 elements** or sections (P 405-408):

   1. **Risk Strategy**
   2. **Methodology**
   3. **Roles and Responsibilities**
   4. **Funding**
   5. **Timing**
   6. **Risk Categories**
   7. **Stakeholder Risk Appetite**
   8. **Definitions of Risk Probability and Impact**
   9. **Probability and Impact Matrix**
   10. **Reporting Formats**
   11. **Tracking**

7. An **RBS (Risk Breakdown Structure)** is a **hierarchical representation** of **potential sources of risks** according to their risk level and is important because it provides a means for grouping potential causes of risks. **Study RBS levels, one (1) and two (2).**

   Fig. 11-4, P 406, *Extract from Sample Risk Breakdown Structure*

   A **Probability and Impact Matrix** is specific to the project context and reflects the risk appetite and the organization's key stakeholder thresholds (P 407).

   Table 11-1, P 407, *Example of Definitions for Probability and Impact*

8. **Identify Risk** is a process of **identifying individual project risks** and **sources of overall risks**, and **documenting** their characteristics. The key benefit of this process is to **identify and document sources of overall risks** associated with the project. This allows the Project Manager to foresee any and all dangers to the project if and when they occur (P 409).

   Fig. 11-6, 409, *Identify Risks: Inputs, Tools and Techniques and Outputs*
   Fig. 11-7, 410, *Identify Risks: Data Flow Diagram*

9. There are six (**6) Inputs to Identify Risks** (P 409):

   1. **Project Management Plan**
   2. **Project Documents**
   3. **Agreements**
   4. **Procurement Documentation**
   5. **Enterprise Environmental Factors**
   6. **Organizational Process Assets**

   Fig. 11-6, 409, *Identify Risks: Inputs, Tools and Techniques and Outputs*
   Fig. 11-7, 410, *Identify Risks: Data Flow Diagram*

10. **Identifying Risks,** consists of six **(6) Tools and Techniques,** one is Data Gathering. The other five (5) are listed below (P 409-410):

    1. **Expert Judgment**
    2. **Data Analysis**
    3. **Interpersonal and Team Skills**
    4. **Prompt Lists**
    5. **Meetings**

    See Fig. 11-6, P 409, *Identifying Risks: Inputs, Tools and Techniques and Outputs*
    See Fig. 11-7, P 410, *Identifying Risks: Data Flow Diagram*

11. The **Risk Register; Risk Report; and Project Documents Updates (Assumption Log, Issue Log and Lessons Learned Register)** are **the three (3) Outputs of the Identify Risks Process** (P 409).

12. Listed below are three (3) **Data Gathering Tools and Techniques** of **Identify Risks** and a short explanation of each (P 414):

    - **Brainstorming:** A comprehensive listing of individual project risks and sources of overall project risks.
    - **Checklists:** A list of items, actions or points to be considered.
    - **Interviews**: are used to interview experienced project participants, stakeholders and SME's.

13. A **SWOT analysis (Strength, Weakness, Opportunities and Threats)** can be useful in Risk Identification. The SWOT may be used to increase the breadth of identified risks by including internally generated risks. These risks may be in the form of opportunities or threat perceptions (P 415).

    Note: A SWOT Analysis is also useful for evaluating external company opportunities/threats.

14. **A Risk Register** is an output of identify risks and may contain the following content information (P 417):

    - **List of Identified Risks**
    - **Potential Risk Owners**
    - **List of Potential Risk Responses**

15. **Perform Qualitative Risk Analysis** is a process of prioritizing individual project risk for further analysis or action to assess their **probability of occurrence and impact** as well as other characteristics. The **key benefit** of this process is that it **focuses effort on high-priority risks** (P 419-420).
    The ITTO's for this process are shown below

INPUTS:

- **Project Management Plan** (Risk Management Plan)
- **Project Documents** (Assumption Log, Risk Register, Stakeholder Register)
- **Enterprise Environmental Factors**
- **Organizational Process Assets**

TOOLS and TECHNIQUES

- **Expert Judgment**
- **Data Gathering** (Interviews)
- **Data Analysis**
- **Interpersonal and Team Skills**
- **Risk Categorization**
- **Data Representation**
- **Meetings**

OUTPUTS

- **Project Documents Updates** (Assumption Log, Issue Log, Risk Register, Risk Report)

Fig.11-8, P 409, *Perform Qualitative Risk Analysis: Inputs, Tools and Techniques and Outputs*
Fig.11-9, P 410, *Perform Qualitative Risk Analysis: Data Flow Diagram*

16. The process P**erform Quantitative Risk Analysis (P 428-436)** means to **numerically analyze** the combined effect of identified individual project risks and other sources of uncertainty on overall project objectives. The **key benefit** of this process is it **quantifies overall project risk exposure** and can provide additional quantitative risk information to support risk response planning. This process is **not required** by every project, but is performed throughout the project life cycle.

INPUTS:

- **Project Management Plan**
- **Project Documents**
- **Enterprise Environmental Factors**
- **Organizational Process Assets**

TOOLS and TECHNIQUES

- **Expert Judgment**
- **Data Gathering**
- **Interpersonal and Team Skills**
- **Representations of Uncertainty**
- **Data Analysis**

OUTPUTS

- **Project Documents Updates**

Fig. 11-11, P 428, *Perform Quantitative Risk Analysis: Inputs, Tools and Techniques and Outputs*
Fig. 11-12, P 429, *Perform Quantitative Risk Analysis: Data Flow Diagram*

17. There are five (5) Types of **Project Documents Updates** (i.e. risk analysis) in the **Perform Quantitative Risk Analysis Process**. They are (P 428-429):

- **Assessment of overall project risk exposure**
- **Detailed probabilistic analysis of the project**
- **Prioritized lists of individual project risks**
- **Trends in quantitative risk analysis results**
- **Recommended risk responses**

Study and read section 11.4.3.1, P 436.

18. The **Plan Risk Response's** purpose is a process of **developing options, selecting strategies, and agreeing on actions** to address overall project risk exposure and to treat individual project risks. The **key benefit** is that the process identifies appropriate ways to mitigate overall risks as well as individual project risks (P 437)

The key benefit is that the process identifies ways to mitigate overall risks, allocates resources and activities into the project management plan and project documents.

INPUTS:

- **Project Management Plan**
- **Project documents**
- **Enterprise Environmental Factors**
- **Organizational Process Assets**

TOOLS and TECHNIQUES

- **Expert Judgment**
- **Data Gathering**
- **Interpersonal and Team Skills**
- **Strategies for Threats**
- **Strategies for Opportunities**
- **Contingent Response Strategies**
- **Strategies for Overall Project Risk**
- **Data Analysis**
- **Decision Making**

OUTPUTS

- **Change Requests**
- **Project Management Plan Updates**
- **Project Documents Updates**

Fig. 11-16, P 437, *Plan Risk Responses: Inputs, Tools and Techniques and Outputs*
Fig. 11-17, P 438, *Plan Risk Responses: Data Flow Diagram*

19. There are five (5) **Strategies** for dealing with **Threats** in plan risk responses. They are (P 442-443):

    1. **Escalate**: Used to deal with threats outside the project
    2. **Avoid**: Eliminate the threat or protect the project from the impact
    3. **Transfer**: Ownership of the threat and response to the threat shifts to a third party
    4. **Mitigate:** A way to reduce the probability of occurrence or risk of a threat.
    5. **Accept**: Risk is acknowledged and no pro-action is taken unless the risk occurs

    Study and carefully read (P 442-443).

20. There are five (5) **Strategies for** dealing with **Opportunities** (P 445-446):

    1. **Escalate**: Used when opportunities are outside project scope.
    2. **Exploit**: Opportunities are realized when uncertainties are eliminated
    3. **Enhance**: Increase the probability or impact of an opportunity
    4. **Share:** Some of the ownership is transferred to a third party, who is able to capture the opportunity so that all parties benefit from any actions taken
    5. **Accept**: Taking advantage of the opportunity, but not actively pursuing the opportunity

    Study and carefully read (P 445-446).

21. **Implement Risk Responses** is the process of **implementing agreed-upon risk response plans.** Its **key benefit** is to insure that *agreed upon risk responses* are executed as planned to **reduce risk exposure, minimize individual project threats, and maximize individual project opportunities** (P 449).

    Fig. 11-18, P 449, *Plan Risk Responses: Inputs, Tools and Techniques and Outputs*
    Fig. 11-19, P 450, *Plan Risk Responses: Data Flow Diagram*

22. **Implement Risk Responses** has two **(2) Outputs** (P 449-450):

    1. **Change Requests**
    2. **Project Documents Updates**

23. **Monitor Risk** is a process of **monitoring** the implementation of agreed-upon risk response plans, **tracking** identified risks, **identifying and analyzing** new risks, and **evaluating** risk process effectiveness for the duration of the project. The benefits are to insure reduction in project risk exposure, minimize individual project threats and maximize individual project opportunities (P 453).

Monitor Risk ITTO's (P 453)

INPUTS:

- **Project Management Plan** (Risk Management Plan)
- **Project Documents**
- **Work Performance Data**
- **Work Performance Reports**

TOOLS and TECHNIQUES

- **Data Analysis**
- **Audits**
- **Meetings**

OUTPUTS

- **Work Performance Information**
- **Change Requests**
- **Project Management Plan Updates**
- **Project Documents Updates**
- **Organizational Process Assets Updates**

Fig. 11-20, P 453, *Monitor Risk: Inputs, Tools and Techniques and Outputs*
Fig. 11-21, P 454, *Monitor Risk: Data Flow Diagram*

24. **Reserve Analysis** compares the amount of contingency reserves to budget and schedule, and to the amount of risk remaining to determine if reserves will last the duration of the project. It is a Data Analysis Tool and Technique (P 456).

25. The two (2) types of **Change Requests** (an output of monitor risks) are (P 457):

    1. **Recommended Corrective Actions**: Activities that realign the performance of the project work with the Project Management Plan (Definitions P 703).
    2. **Recommended Preventative Actions**: Activities that ensure future performance of project work is aligned with the Project Management Plan (Definitions P 714).

Similar Questions that may be on the PMI Exam related to Chapter 11

1. Mark is working as project manager in a leading medical device company which has a strong focus on risk management. While preparing the risk responses, Mark has identified additional risks. What should he do next?

    A. Increase the contingency fund to accommodate new risks
    B. Ignore, as the process to identify risks is already complete
    C. Notify new risks to the sponsor
    D. Record the risks and estimate probability of their occurrence and impact. Also, estimate the EVM if felt appropriate

    Correct Answer is D: Any time when risks are identified, they should be qualified and then a plan should be put in place after analyzing the risk and responses.

2. Which of the following is not involved in monitor risk process?

    A. Looking for the occurrence of Risk Triggers
    B. Monitoring Residual Risks
    C. Evaluating the effectiveness of the Risk Management Plan
    D. Planning Risk Responses

    Correct Answer is D: Looking for triggers, monitoring residual risks, and evaluating risk management processes is part of Monitor Risk process.

3. Risk monitoring and control process does not involve _____.

    A. Tracking identified risks
    B. Monitoring trigger conditions for contingency plan
    C. Re-analyzing existing risks
    D. Assessing the probability of achieving project objectives

    Correct answer is A: Monitoring and controlling risks is about keeping a track of new risks/changing risk priorities/triggers and workarounds. It is not about re-assessing the probability of achieving project objectives.

4. Jacob is a project manager who has been asked to provide an entire computerized system and internet connectivity in an old resort renovation project. Around 100 workstations will be installed, 200 network connections, 10 servers and 22 printers. They will be networked through a LAN. All the risks have been identified and have gone

through quantitative analysis and a contingency reserve has been created. One of the risks identified was that the building owner would inspect the work causing additional delays or rework. This probability is 0.55 and the impact $3, 00.000.00. The other risk identified was the network printers need to be centrally located, but the cables should not be visible, with a probability of 50% and impact of $7, 50,000.00. Jacob has identified that the cabling risk will actually cost $9, 00,000.00. What is the impact if both of the risks happen?

A. Schedule delays that can also grow if the risk is not solved quickly
B. The contingency reserve will be reduced by $12,00,000.00
C. There will be no schedule delays only the reduction in contingency reserve
D. The contingency reserve will be also reduced apart from schedule delays

Correct option is D: The contingency reserve will be also reduced apart from schedule delays ($3, 00,000 plus $9, 00,000).

5. Phil has been assigned a new marketing project in BCL Marketing Pvt. Ltd. You are currently identifying any risks. Which of the following people should be part of identifying risk process?

A. Project Manager
B. Stakeholders
C. Team Member(s)
D. All Project Personnel

Correct Answer is D: Identification of risks is done along with the Project team, Experts, Sponsors, and all concerned stakeholders.

6. A project manager discovers that a project problem has occurred. The problem was never discussed during risk planning activities or added to the risk register, and it will now cost the project money. What is the best response?

A. Do not take action, just accept the problem
B. Stop all project activity and approach senior management for advice
C. Add the risk to the risk register and gather information about its probability and impact
D. Use the management reserve to cover the costs of the problem

Correct answer is D: This is a tough situation for any project manager. You have a problem that is going to cost you money. After all, you are the project manager and it is your job to figure out what to do. There is no point risk planning, because you already know the probability (100%) and affect, the cost of fixing the problem.

7. As you are executing your project, you are constantly checking your risk register to be sure that you have planned responses for all of your risks. At one team status meeting, you find that a lower-priority risk has suddenly become more likely. Where do you keep information about low-priority risks?

    A. Triggers
    B. Watch List
    C. Risk Management Plan
    D. Qualitative Analysis Documents

Correct answer is B: Some risks have low probability and impact, so you will not put them in the register. Instead, you can add them to a watch list, which is a list of risks that you do not want to forget about, but you do not need to track closely. You need to check your watch list from time to time to keep an eye on things.

8. You are conducting a status meeting and monitoring your risk register when you discover a risk that remains even after you implement all of your response strategies. What kind of risk is this and what should you do about it?

    A. It is a secondary risk; you don't need to worry about it
    B. It is a residual risk; you need to plan a response strategy for it
    C. It is a residual risk; you do not need to plan a response strategy for it because you have already implemented all of the risk responses
    D. It is a contingency reserve; You should only use it if the first risk occurs

Correct Answer is C: Residual risks are risks that remain even after you have planned for and implemented all of your risk response strategies. They do not need any further analysis because you have already planned the most complete response strategy you know in dealing with the risk that came before them.

9. Your team has identified a risk with some of the chemicals you are using on your highway construction project. It is really difficult to mix them just right and, based on past projects, you have figured out that there is a high probability that about 14% of the chemical supply will be lost in mixing problems. You decide to buy an extra 15% of the chemicals up front so that you will be prepared for those losses and your project will not be delayed. Which response strategy are you using?

    A. Avoid
    B. Accept
    C. Mitigate
    D. Transfer

    Correct Answer is C: By buying the extra chemical stock, you are mitigating the risk.

10. Mike is a project manager for an IT technology implementation project. He is using an Ishikawa diagram to figure out what could cause potential risks on his project. Which process is he doing?

    A. Identify Risks
    B. Perform Qualitative Risk Analysis
    C. Perform Quality Control
    D. Plan Risk Responses

    Correct Answer is A: Diagramming Techniques (including Ishikawa diagrams and flowcharts) are a tool of the Identify Risks process. You use them to find the root cause of defects in Quality Management processes but they can also be useful in finding the risks that can lead to trouble in Risk Management.

You may now move on to Chapter Twelve: Project Procurement Management

Chapter 12: Project Procurement Management: Decide How, When and Where you Spend your Money

"What gets measured, gets managed." Peter Drucker

Student Learning Outcomes

1. List and describe the three (3**) processes of Plan Procurement Management**. Why is Project Procurement Management so important (P 459)?
2. Only an authorized person (P 460-462), and likely not the Project Manager, is able to sign a legal agreement **binding** the buyer (participating company) to the seller. List the **key concepts** for Project Procurement Management regarding contracts and contractual relationships.
3. There are **six (6) Major Trends/Practices** that are occurring in **Procurement Managemen**t. Please List them (P 463-464). List four (4) tailoring considerations. What is a MSA, Master Service Agreement (P 465)?
4. List the order sequence and importance of the process components of **Plan Procurement Management** and the ITTO's (P 466-467).
5. The **Procurement Management Plan** is one (1) of ten (10) outputs of **the Plan Procurement Management Process.** What are the **10 Outputs of Plan Procurement Management** (P 466-P 467)?
6. **What is Plan Procurement Management and its key benefits? Plan Procurement Management is a process, and can consist of using (4) Tools and Techniques. What are they (P 466-P 467)?**
7. What are the six (6) **Inputs to Plan Procurement Management** (P 466-P 467)?
8. List the four (4) Components found in the **Project Management Plan** (P 469).
9. There are three **(3) types of general contracts.** What are they called (P 471-472)?
10. What is a **Fixed Price Contract** (P 471)?
11. What are the three **(3) types of Fixed Price Contracts** (P 471)?
12. What is **a Cost Reimbursable Contract** (P 472)?
13. What are the three **(3) types of Cost Reimbursable Contracts** (P 472)?
14. What is **a Time and Material Contract** (P 472)?
15. **Make-or-Buy Analysis** is a general management technique used in **Plan Procurement Management: Tools and Techniques** (P 473). Please explain.
16. How are **Bid Documents** used? What is **RFI, RFP, RFQ, IFB** and their importance (P 477)? What is a TOR, Terms of Reference (P 478).
17. What is the **Procurement Statement of Work (SOW)** and what can it include (P 477)?
18. What is the meaning of **Source Selection Criteria**, and what are some of the criteria (P 478)?
19. **What is meant by Conduct Procurement and what is its key benefit (P 482)? What are the ITTO's?**
20. What is a **Short List** (P 468)?
21. There are six (6) **Inputs to Conduct Requirements** (P 482-483). What are the six inputs?
22. There are five (5) different **Tools and Techniques** that may be used in the process of **Conduct Procurements**, one of which is using **Bidder Conferences**. What are the five (5) tools and techniques that may be used (P 482-483)?
23. What is **Procurement Negotiations** and what may it include (P 488)?

24. List the major components of an **Agreement Document** (P 489).
25. **Control Procurements is a process of managing procurement buyer/seller relationships, monitoring compliance and performance and making contract changes as appropriate and closing out contracts (P 492-493). What is the key benefit of Control Procurements and what are the ITTO's of Control Procurements?**
26. What is meant by **Claims Administration** (P 498)?
27. What are the **Components of the Project Management Plan** which is an input to **Control Procurements** (P 495)?
28. What are the **Organizational Process Assets Updates** that are the outputs of Control Procurements (P 501)?

CHAPTER TWELVE INTRODUCTION: DECIDE HOW, WHEN AND WHERE YOU SPEND YOUR MONEY

PROJECT PROCUREMENT MANAGEMENT: CHAPTER 12 OVERVIEW: PMBOK® 6th Edition P 459-502

Project Procurement Management includes necessary processes to purchase or acquire products, services, or results needed from outside the project team. It includes the management and control processes to develop and administer agreements, such as: contracts, purchase orders, memoranda of agreements (MOA's) or internal service level agreements (SLA's).

Project Procurement Management processes include See P 459:

(12.1) **Plan Procurement Management:** This process reflects project procurement decisions, and also the approach in identifying potential sellers.

(12.2) **Conduct Procurements:** This process obtains seller responses, selects a seller and then awards a contract.

(12.3) **Control Procurements**: This process deals with procurements relationships, monitoring contract performance, and making changes and/or corrections as needed in closing out the contract.

Fig. 12-1, P 460, *Project Procurement Management Overview*

Key Concepts for Project Procurement Management

The Project Procurement Management process involves written agreements to accomplish the following (P 460-461):

1. The **need to describe the relationship between the buyer and the seller**
2. The **contract** should clearly state the deliverables and the results expected
3. A **purchasing contract includes terms and conditions**, and may incorporate buyer specifics as to what the seller is going to perform or provide
4. **Organizations document policies and procedures** specifically defining procurement rules and specifying who has the authority to sign and administer agreements
5. **Project documents** may be subject to some form of review and approval, oftentimes involving the legal department
6. **Multiple contracts** may occur simultaneously or in sequence based upon the complexity of the project
7. Depending on the application area, **the seller may be identified** as a contractor, vendor, **service provider or supplier. The buyer is considered the owner of the final product, a subcontractor, requiring organization, a service requestor or the purchaser**

Trends and Emerging Practices in Project Procurement Management

There are numerous major trends taking place across different industries related to the use of software tools, risks, logistics and technology. The following are some of the trends and emerging practices (P 463):

- **Advances in tools**
- **More advanced risk management**
- **Changing contracting processes**
- **Logistics and supply chain management**
- **Technology stakeholder relations**
- **Trial engagements**

Study and read (P 463-464).

Tailoring organizations

The project manager may need to tailor the Project Procurement Management process. Four considerations may be used (P 465):

1. Complexity of procurement
2. Physical location
3. Governance and regulatory environment
4. Availability of contractors

Considerations for Agile/Adaptive Environments

In an Agile environment, the buyer and seller may share the risk and rewards that are associated in a project. In large projects that use adaptive approaches, a governing agreement called a Master Service Agreement (MSA) may be used. This allows changes to occur without affecting the overall contract.

Plan Procurement Management:

Plan Procurement Management is the process of documenting project procurement decisions and specifying the approach and identifying potential sellers. The **key benefit** of this process is that it determines whether to acquire goods and services from outside the project, what to acquire, as well as how and when to acquire it (P 466).

See chart on next page: **PROJECT PROCUREMENT MANAGEMENT (Section 12.1)**

Chapter Twelve: Project Procurement Management

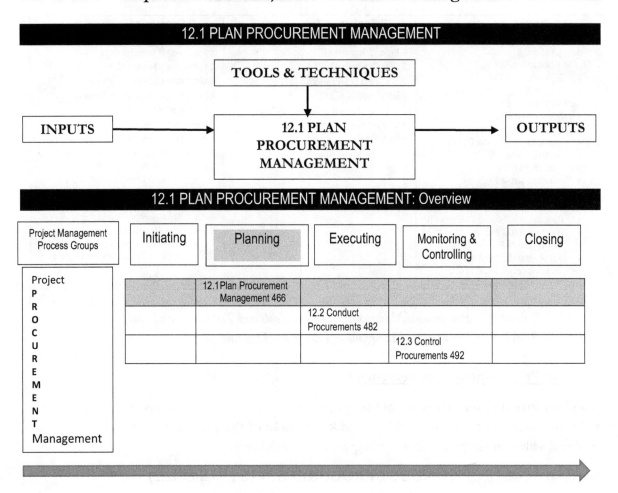

12.1 PLAN PROCUREMENT MANAGEMENT

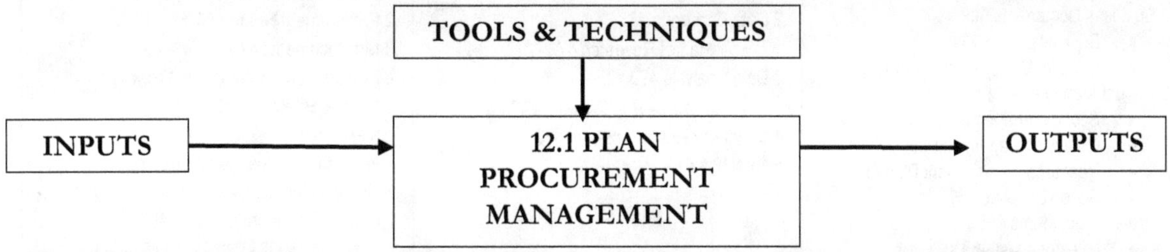

12.1 PLAN PROCUREMENT MANAGEMENT: Overview

Project Management Process Groups	Initiating	Planning	Executing	Monitoring & Controlling	Closing
Project PROCUREMENT Management		12.1 Plan Procurement Management 466			
			12.2 Conduct Procurements 482		
				12.3 Control Procurements 492	

12.1 PLAN PROCUREMENT MANAGEMENT: ITTO Processes

.1 Inputs	.2 Tools and Techniques	.3 Outputs
.1 Project Charter 468 .2 Business Documents 469 • Business Case 469 • Benefits Management Plan 469 .3 Project Management Plan 469 • Scope Management Plan 469 • Quality Management Plan 469 • Resource Management Plan 469 • Scope Baseline 469 .4 Project Documents 469 • Milestone List 469 • Project Team Assignments 469 • Requirements Documentation 470 • Requirements Traceability Matrix 470 • Resource Requirements 470 • Risk Register 470 • Stakeholder Register 470 .5 Enterprise Environmental Factors 470 .6 Organizational Process Assets 471	.1 Expert Judgment 472 .2 Data Gathering 473 • Market Research 473 .3 Data Analysis 473 • Make-or-Buy Decisions 473 .4 Source Selection Analysis 473 .5 Meetings 474	.1 Procurement Management Plan 475 .2 Procurement Strategy 476 .3 Bid Documents 476 .4 Procurement Statement of Work 477 .5 Source Selection Criteria 478 .6 Make-or-Buy Decisions 479 .7 Independent Cost Estimates 479 .8 Change Requests 479 .9 Project Document Updates 480 • Lessons Learned Register 480 • Milestone List 480 • Requirements Documentation 480 • Requirements Traceability Matrix 480 • Risk Register 480 • Stakeholder Register 480 10. Organizational Process Assets Updates 481

Fig. 12-2, P 466, *Plan Procurement Management: Inputs, Tools and Techniques and Outputs*
Fig. 12-3, P 467, *Plan Procurement Management: Data Flow Diagram*

Conduct Procurement Requirements:

Conduct Procurement Requirements is a process of obtaining seller responses, selecting a seller and awarding a contract (P 482). The **key benefit** of this process is that it selects a qualified seller, and implements a legal agreement for delivery.

See chart on next page: **CONDUCT PROCUREMENTS (Section 12.2)**

Chapter Twelve: Project Procurement Management

12.2 CONDUCT PROCUREMENTS

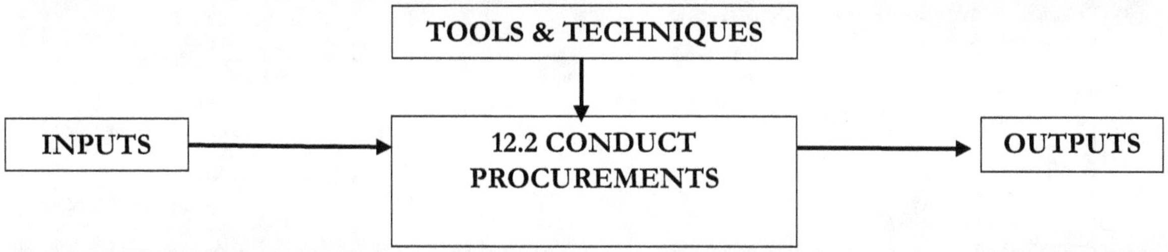

12.2 CONDUCT PROCUREMENTS: Overview

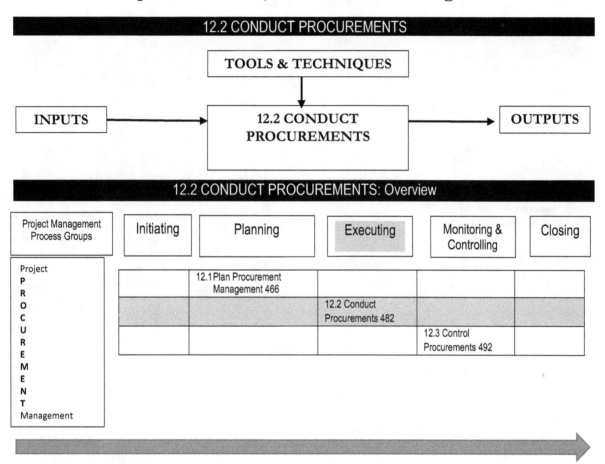

Project Management Process Groups	Initiating	Planning	Executing	Monitoring & Controlling	Closing
Project PROCUREMENT Management		12.1 Plan Procurement Management 466			
			12.2 Conduct Procurements 482		
				12.3 Control Procurements 492	

12.2 CONDUCT PROCUREMENS: ITTO Processes

.1 Inputs	.2 Tools and Techniques	.3 Outputs
.1 Project Management Plan 484 • Scope Management Plan 484 • Requirements Management Plan 484 • Communications Management Plan 484 • Risk Management Plan 484 • Procurement Management Plan 484 • Configuration Management Plan 484 • Cost Baseline 484 .2 Project Documents 484 • Lessons Learned Register 484 • Project Schedule 484 • Requirements Documentation 485 • Risk Register 485 • Stakeholder Register 485 .3 Procurement Documentation 485 .4 Seller Proposals 486 .5 Enterprise Environmental Factors 486 .6 Organizational Process Assets 486	.1 Expert Judgment 487 .2 Advertising 487 .3 Bidder Conferences 487 .4 Data Analysis 487 • Proposal Evaluation 487 .5 Interpersonal And Team Skills 488 • Negotiation 488	.1 Selected Sellers 488 .2 Agreements 489 .3 Change Requests 489 .4 Project Management Updates 490 • Requirements Management Plan 490 • Quality Management Plan 490 • Communications Management Plan 490 • Risk Management Plan 490 • Procurement Management Plan 490 • Scope Baseline 490 • Schedule Baseline 490 • Cost Baseline 490 .5 Project Document Updates 491 • Lessons Learned Register 491 • Requirements Documentation 491 • Requirements Traceability Matrix 491 • Resource Calendars 491 • Risk Register 491 • Stakeholder Register 491 .6 Organizational Process Assets 491

Fig. 12-4, P 482, *Conduct Procurements: Inputs, Tools and Techniques and Outputs*
Fig. 12-5, P 483, *Conduct Procurements: Data Flow Diagram*

Control Procurements:

Control Procurements is a process of conducting procurement relationships and monitoring contract performance and making changes as appropriate in closing out the contracts. The **key benefit** of this process is that it assures the buyers and sellers' performance meets the requirements according to the legal agreement (P 492).

See chart on next page: **CONTROL PROCUREMENTS (Section 12.3)**

Fig. 12-6, P 492, *Control Procurements: Inputs, Tools and Techniques and Outputs*
Fig. 12-7, P 493, *Control Procurements: Data Flow Diagram*

Chapter Twelve: Project Procurement Management

12.3 CONTROL PROCUREMENTS

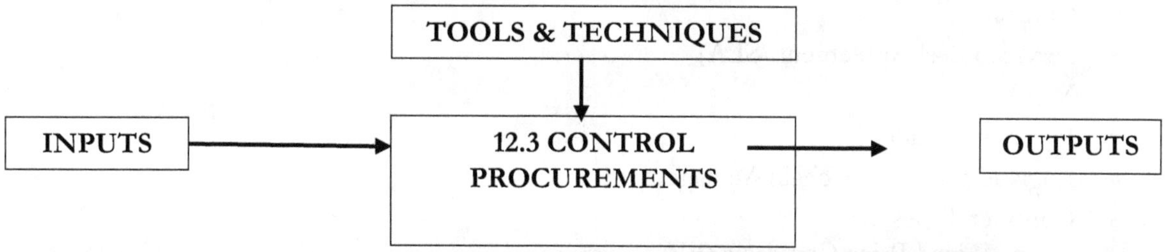

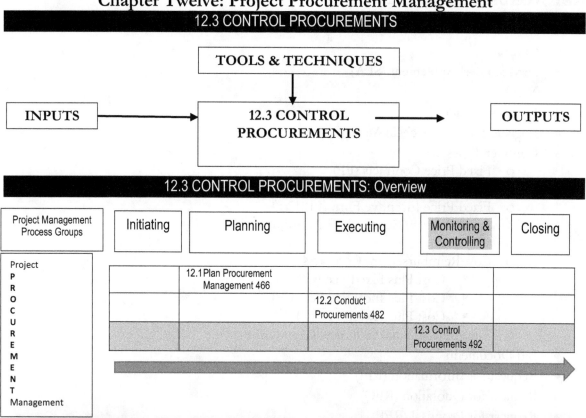

12.3 CONTROL PROCUREMENTS: Overview

Project Management Process Groups	Initiating	Planning	Executing	Monitoring & Controlling	Closing
Project PROCUREMENT Management		12.1 Plan Procurement Management 466			
			12.2 Conduct Procurements 482		
				12.3 Control Procurements 492	

12.3 CONTROL PROCUREMENTS: ITTO Processes

.1 Inputs	.2 Tools and Techniques	.3 Outputs
.1 Project Management Plan 495 • Requirements Management Plan 495 • Risk Management Plan 495 • Procurement Management Plan 495 • Change Management Plan 495 • Schedule Baseline 495 .2 Project Documents 495 • Assumption Log 495 • Lessons Learned Register 495 • Milestone List 495 • Quality Reports 495 • Requirements Documentation 495 • Requirements Traceability Matrix 496 • Risk Register 496 • Stakeholder Register 496 .3 Agreements 496 .4 Procurement Documentation 496 .5 Approved Change Requests 496 .6 Work Performance Data 496 .7 Enterprise Environmental Factors 497 .8 Organizational Process Assets 497	.1 Expert Judgment 497 .2 Claims Administration 498 .3 Data Analysis 498 • Performance Reviews 498 • Earned Value Analysis 498 • Trend Analysis 498 .4 Inspection 498 .5 Audits 498	.1 Closed Procurements 499 .2 Work Performance Information 499 .3 Procurement Documentation Updates 499 .4 Change Requests 499 .5 Project Management Updates 500 • Risk Management Plan 500 • Procurement Management Plan 500 • Schedule Baseline 500 • Cost Baseline 500 .6 Project Document Updates 500 • Lessons Learned Register 500 • Resource Requirements 500 • Requirements Traceability Matrix 501 • Risk Register 501 • Stakeholder Register 501 .7 Organizational Process Assets Updates 501

KEY WORDS: CHAPTER 12

- Contract
- Service Level Agreement (SLA)
- MOA
- Purchase Order
- Logistic and Supply chain Management
- Contract Types
  - Fixed Price Contracts (FP)
  - Firm Fixed Price Contracts (FFP)
  - Fixed Price Incentive Firm (FPIF)
  - Fixed Price w/Economic Price Adjustments
  - (FPEPA)
  - Cost Reimbursement Contracts
    - Cost Plus Fixed Fee (CPFF)
    - Cost Plus Incentive Fee (CPIF)
    - Cost Plus Award Fee (CPAF)
  - Time and Material Contracts (T and M)
- Bid Documents
- Request for Information (RFI)
- Request for Quotation (RFQ)
- Request for Proposal (RFP)
- Procurement Statement of Work
  - Statement of Work (SOW)
  - Make or Buy Decisions
- Procurement Management Plan
- Configuration Management Plan
- Bidder Conferences
- Approve Change Request
- Procurement documentation
- Claims Administration
- Data Analysis
  - Earned Value Analysis (EVA)
  - Performance Reviews
  - Trend Analysis (TA)

LEGEND

The following Legend shows how to correctly read the *PMBOK® Guide* references and attributions correctly for Chapter 12: Project Procurement Management PMBOK Details.

Legend:

Chapter Section	Chapter Section Title	Page Number

Example from Chapter Six shown below:

6.5.1.4	Enterprise Environmental Factors	(P 209)

All direct quotes are attributed as (A Guide to the Project Management Body of Knowledge, *(PMBOK® Guide)* – Sixth Edition) Project Management Institute Inc., 2017, Page #, after each section and any/all paraphrased or original wording is attributed as (P #), before or after each section. All Graphs, Charts, Tables and Figures are attributed as: *(PMBOK® Guide,* Fig. #-# or #/#, P #, *Title of Graph, Chart, Table or Figure*).

12.1 PLAN PROCUREMENT MANAGEMENT

The importance of **Project Procurement Management** is to establish a mechanism to produce or acquire products, services and results from an outside source and documents the approach used to identify the sellers of products, services or result of a project. The **key benefit** is that it determines whether to acquire good and services from outside the project, and if so, what to acquire as well as how and when to acquire it.

Fig. 12-1, P 460, *Project Procurement Management: Overview*

In this process, there are legal obligations and penalties tied to the procurement of products and services. This procurement process involves the agreements that describe any relationship of the buyer to the seller and the contract should clearly state the obligations of each party involved.

The Project Manager is not usually the one to sign any binding agreements associated with the organization's procurement processes. However, it is the Project Management Team's responsibility to make sure all procurement processes are met in accordance with the contract terms and conditions.

The Seller may be identified as **contractor, vendor, service provider or supplier** and the buyer could be a service requestor or a purchase.

The **winning bidder** for a project may manage the work as a project and in these cases (P 462):

- **The buyer becomes the customer to any subcontractors, suppliers and service providers and is a key stakeholder from the seller perspective**
- **The seller's project management team may be concerned with any processes involved in performing the work or services**
- **Terms and conditions of the contract and the procurement statement of work (SOSW) become key inputs to many of the seller management processes**
- **The seller may become a buyer of low-tiered products, services and materials from subcontractors and suppliers**

The **Seller is generally from outside the organization**, but the PM may assume purchasing authority in a smaller organization.

The following are **Trends and Emerging Practices in Procurement Management** (P 463):

- **Advances in Tools:** Online tools are now available and the use of information bidding models (BIM) are becoming popular

- **More Advanced Risk Management**: Contracts can now be written to accurately allocate specific risks to the entities most capable of managing them
- **Changing Contracting Processes**: Megaprojects may involve international contracts with multiple contractors and are more risk-prone, therefore, the use of internationally recognized standards contract forms is increasingly being used
- **Logistics and Supply Chain Management**: Long lead times require the manufacturer of the items and their transportation to the project site become schedule-driven
- **Technology and Stakeholder Relations**: Web cameras are now being used to improve Stakeholder and communication and relations
- **Trial Engagements**: Some projects will engage several candidates for initial deliverables and work products on a paid basis before making the full commitment to a larger portion of the project's scope

Tailoring Considerations include (P 465):

Complexity of Procurement: There may be one main procurement or multiple procurements at different times and with different sellers
Physical Location: Buyers and Sellers may be in the same location, reasonably close, or in different time zones, countries or continents
Governance and Regulatory Environment: Local laws and ordinances regarding procurement policies may be integrated with the organization's procurement policies and could affect contracting auditing requirements
Availability of Contractors: Available contractors may be capable of providing the work or services needed

Considerations for Agile/Adaptive Environments:

Larger organizations will use an **Adaptive Approach** for some deliverables and in these situations; a **Master Service Agreement** (MSA) may be utilized for the overall engagement and put into an appendix or supplement, which allows changes on the adaptive scope without affecting the overall contract (P 465).

12.1 Plan Procurement Management

The **Plan Procurement Management** process documents project procurement decisions and planning for contract sand legal discussions between the buyer and potential sellers, as what to acquire, when to acquire and how to acquire the needed resources. The **key benefit** is that it determines whether to acquire resources from outside the project.

Fig. 12-2, P 466, *Plan Procurement Management: Inputs, Tools and Techniques and Outputs*
Fig. 12-3, P 467, *Plan Procurement: Data Flow Diagram*

When defining the roles and responsibilities related to Procurement, these responsibilities should be established in the Project Procurement Plan and some of the ten (10) steps may involve (P 468):

1. Preparing The **Procurement Statement Of Work (Sow),** Or Terms Of Refinance
2. Preparing A **High-Level Cost Estimate** To Determine Budget
3. **Advertising** The Opportunity
4. Identifying A **Short List Of Qualified Sellers**
5. Preparing And Issuing **Bid Documents**
6. Preparing And Submitting **Proposals** By The Seller
7. Conducting A **Technical Evaluation** Of The Proposals, Including Quality
8. Performing A **Cost Evaluation** Of The Proposals
9. Preparing The **Final Combined Quality And Cost Evaluation** To Select The **Winning Proposal**
10. **Finalizing Negotiations And Signing Contracts** Between The Buyer And The Seller

Read and Study P 468, 10 Steps of Plan Procurement Management.

12.1.1 Plan Procurement Management: Inputs

12.1.1.1 Project Charter

The **Project Charter** will include the following (P 468):

- **Objectives**
- **Project Descriptions**
- **Summary Milestones**
- **Preapproved Financial Resources**

12.1.1.2 Business Documents

The Business Documents will include the following (P 469):

- **Business Case**: The Business Case and Procurement Strategy need to be aligned to ensure the Business Case remains valid
- **Benefits Management Plan**: Describes when specific benefits are available for use

12.1.1.3 Project Management Plan

Some of the **Project Management Plan** components are (P 469):

- **Scope Management Plan**: Describes how the scope of work by the contractors will be managed through the execution phase of the project
- **Quality Management Plan**: Contains applicable industry standards and codes the project is required to follow
- **Resource Management Plan**: Has information on which resources will be purchased or leased, along with assumptions or constraints that would influence the procurement
- **Scope Baseline**: Contains the Scope Statement, WBS and WBS Dictionary

12.1.1.4 Project Documents

Some of the **Project Documents** involved in this process are (P 469):

- **Milestone List**: Shows when Sellers are required to deliver results
- **Project Team Assignments**: Contains information on the skills and abilities of the project team and their availability to support procurement activities
- **Requirements Documentation**: This may include:
  - Technical requirements the Seller is required to satisfy
  - Requirements with contractual and legal implications that may include health, safety, security, performance, environmental, insurance, intellectual property rights, equal employment opportunity, licenses, permits and other non-technical requirements
- **Requirements Traceability Matrix**: Links product requirement from their origin to the deliverables that satisfy them
- **Resource Requirements**: Contain information on specific needs such as team and physical resources that may need to be acquired
- **Risk Register**: Provides a list of risks, along with the results of risk analysis and risk response planning
- **Stakeholder Register**: Provides details on the project participants and their interest in the project, includes regulatory agencies, contracting personnel and legal personnel

12.1.1.5 Enterprise Environmental Factors

Some of the **Enterprise Environmental Factors** involved in this process are (P 470):

- **Marketplace conditions**
- **Products, services and results** that are available in the marketplace
- **Seller,** including their past performance or reputation
- **Typical terms and conditions** for products, service and results, or for the specific industry
- **Unique local requirements**, such as regulatory requirements for local labor or sellers
- **Legal advice** regarding procurements
- **Contract management systems**, including procedures for contract change control
- **Established multi-tier supplier system** of prequalified sellers based on prior experience
- **Financial accounting** and contract **payments systems**

12.1.1.6 Organizational Process Assets

Some of the **Organizational Process Assets** involved in this process are (P 471):

- **Preapproved Seller Lists**: Lists of Sellers that have been vetted
- **Formal Procurement Policies, Procedures or Guidelines**: Most organizations have formal procurement policies and buying organizations
- **Contract Types**: All legal contracts fall into one of two categories, but can be hybrids of both as shown below:
    - **Fixed Price Contracts (FFP):** A total fixed price for a defined product, service or result to be acquired and are shown below:
        - **Firm Fixed Price (FPIP):** Favored by most buying organizations because the price is set at the beginning and not subject to change unless the scope of work changes
        - **Fixed Price Incentive Fee (FPIF):** Gives the buyer and seller more flexibility because it allows for deviation in performance, with financial incentives tied to achieving agreed-upon metrics
        - **Fixed Price with Economic Price Adjustments (FPEPA):** A fixed price contract, but with special provisions that allow for predefined final adjustment to the contract price due to changed conditions, such as inflation or cost increase/decrease for specific commodities. Used when the seller's performance period spans a considerable period of years, or if the payment is made in a different

currency

- **Cost Reimbursable Contracts:** The seller is reimbursed for all legitimate costs for completed work, plus a fee representing seller profit. Three common types of cost-reimbursable contracts are (P 477):
    - **Cost Plus Fixed Fee (CPFF):** Seller is reimbursed for all allowable costs for performing the project work and receives a fixed fee payment calculated as a percentage of initial estimated project costs, fee is paid only for completed work.
    - **Cost Plus Incentive Fee (CPIF):** Seller is reimbursed for all allowable costs for performing the project work and receives a predetermined incentive fee payment, based upon finishing performance objectives.
    - **Cost Plus Award (CPAF):** Seller is reimbursed for all legitimate costs, dependent on the subjective determination of seller performance by the buyer of work performed and generally not subject to appeals.
    - **Time and Materials Contract** (T and M): A Time and Material Contract that contains both cost-reimbursable and fixed price contracts (P 472).
- **Time and Material Contract (T and M)**: A Time and Material Contract contains both cost-reimbursable and fixed price contracts.

Master your PMP exam procurement questions - then Master PMP! (45 minutes), by Dave Litten, at https://www.youtube.com/watch?v=Rd7JEPJvu5A

12.1.2 Plan Procurement Management: Tools and Techniques

12.1.2.1 Expert Judgment

The **Expert Judgment** technique is used to research inputs and outputs, and may be used to develop or modify the criteria used to evaluate seller proposals and expertise or training in the following topics should be considered (P 472):

- Procurement and Purchasing
- Contract Types and Contract Documents
- Regulations and Compliance Topics

12.1.2.2 Data Gathering

One of the **Data Gathering** techniques used in this process is Market Research, which includes an examination of industry and seller capabilities (P 473).

12.1.2.3 Data Analysis

One of the **Data Analysis** techniques involved in this process is the (P 473):

Make-or-Buy Analysis: Used to determine whether work deliverables should/should not be obtained from outside sources. This technique uses:

- **Payback period**
- **Return on investment (ROI)**
- **Internal rate of return (IRR)**
- **Discounted cash flow**
- **Net present value (NPV)**
- **Benefit/cost analysis (BCA), etc.**

12.1.2.4 Source Selection Analysis

Some of the **Source Selection Analysis** methods involved in this process are (P 473):

- **Least Cost**: May be appropriate for procurements of a standard or routine nature where well-established practices and standards exist and from which a specific and will-defined outcome is expected
- **Qualifications Only**: Applies when the time and cost of a full selection process would not make sense because the value of the procurement is relatively small. Here the buyer creates a short list and selects the bidder with the best credentials, qualifications, experience, quality-based record, specialization, etc.
- **Quality Based/Highest Technical Proposal Score**: The seller who submitted the highest-ranked technical proposal is selected if their financial proposal can be negotiated and accepted
- **Sole Source**: Only accepted when there is no other alternative and properly justified, but must be viewed as an exception
- **Fixed Budget**: The available is disclosed to available sellers and they will in return adapt their services and products to meet that budget, however, the budget must be compatible with the SOW and be the highest-ranking proposal within the budget by the buyer

12.1.2.5 Meetings

Meetings can be used to determine the strategy for managing and monitoring the procurement process.

12.1.3 Plan Procurement Management: Outputs

12.1.3.1 Procurement Management Plan

Contains the activities to be undertaken during this process and should document whether international, national or local competitive bidding should be done. The **Procurement Management Plan** can be formal or informal, highly detailed and/or broadly framed and based on the needs of the project can provide guidance for the following (P 475):

- How procurement will be coordinated with other project aspects
- Timetable of key procurement activities
- Procurement metrics to be used to manage contracts
- Stakeholder roles and responsibilities related to procurement
- Constraints and assumptions that could impact the planned procurements
- The legal jurisdiction and the currency in which payments will be made
- Determination of whether independent estimates will be used and whether they are needed as evaluation criteria
- Risk management issues including identifying requirement for performance bonds or insurance contracts to mitigate some form of project risks
- Prequalified sellers, if any to be used

12.1.3.2 Procurement Strategy

Once the make-or-buy decision is made**, a Procurement Strategy** should be identified. A procurement strategy contains various contract areas or stipulations and is meant to determine the project delivery method, the type of legally binding agreements, and how the procurement process will advance through the procurement phase. See the following (P 476):

- **Delivery Methods**: May vary according to professional service vs. construction projects (P 476):
    - Professional Services, delivery methods include:
        - Buyer/Services provider with subcontracting allowed
        - joint venture between buyer and services provider
        - Buyer/Services provider acts as the representative

- Industrial or Commercial Construction, delivery methods include:
  - Turnkey
  - Design Build (DB)
  - Design Bid Build (DBB)
  - Design Build Operate (DBO)
  - Build Own Operate Transfer (BOOT)
  - Etc.

- **Contract Payment Types**: Separate from the project delivery methods and coordinated with the buying organization's internal financial systems and include the following:
  - Fixed Price Contracts
  - Cost Plus Contracts
  - Incentives and Awards

- **Procurement Phases**: Can include information on procurement phases, which may include the following:
  - Sequencing or phasing of the procurement, a description of each phase and the specific objectives of each phase
  - Procurement performance indicators and milestones to be used in monitoring
  - Criteria for moving from phase to phase
  - Monitoring and evaluation plan for tracking progress
  - Process for knowledge transfer for use in subsequent phases

12.1.3.3 Bid Documents

Bid Documents, such as a **Request for Information** (RFI), **Request for Quotation** (RFQ), **Request for Proposal** (RFP) or other appropriate documents are considered **Bid Documents**. Conditions involving their use are shown below (P 477):

Request for Information (RFI): Used when more information on the goods and services to be acquired is needed from the sellers, and will be typically be followed by and RFQ or RFP
Request for Quotation (RFQ): Used when more information is needed on how vendors would satisfy the requirements and/or how much it will cost
Request for Proposal (RFP): The most formal of the 'request for' documents and is used when there is a problem in the project and no easy solution has been determined

All the above documents should contain sufficiently detailed information to ensure consistent and appropriate responses, but with flexibility.

12.1.3.4 Procurement Statement of Work

The **Procurement Statement of Work (SOW)** work is developed from the **project scope baseline**. It is what is **In-Scope**, regarding procurements. If properly and clearly written, the SOW specifically outlines the following (P 477):

- **Tasks** the contractor is required to perform
- **Standards** the contractor will fulfill that are applicable to the project
- **Data** that needs to be submitted for approval
- **Detailed list of all data and services** that will be provided to the contractor by the buyer for use in performing the contract, if applicable
- **Definition of the schedule** for initial submission and the **review/approval time required**

12.1.3.5 Source Selection Criteria

Source Selection Criteria is a process used to identify the **best provider** to help provide or offer solution options when using the Project Procurement Management process (P 478).

Some of the **Source Selection Criteria** factors that may be used in Source Selection are:

- **Capability and capacity**
- **Product cost and life cycle cost**
- **Delivery dates**
- **Technical expertise and approach**
- **Specific relevant experience**
- **Adequacy of the proposed approach and work plan in response to the SOW**
- **Key staff's qualifications, availability and competence**
- **Financial stability of the firm**
- **Management experience**
- **Suitability of the knowledge transfer program, including training**

12.1.3.6 Make-or-Buy Decisions

Management decides the **Make-or-Buy Decisions**, in other words, whether the work should be done in-house or contracted out (P 479).

12.1.3.7 Independent Cost Estimates

The procuring organization may decide to draw up **Independent Cost Estimates**, or have the estimate drawn up by on an outside estimator, which will then become a benchmark on any proposed responses (P 479).

12.1.3.8 Change Requests

All **Change Requests** are processed through the Perform Integrated Change Control process and are the result of any decision that involves procuring goods, services or resources that require alterations to the Project Management Plan, subsidiary plans and other components.

12.1.3.9 Project Documents Updates

Some of the **Project Documents** that may be **updated** as a result of this process could include (P 480):

- **Lessons Learned Register**: Updated with any relevant lessons regarding regulations and compliance, data gathering, data analysis and source selection analysis
- **Milestone List**: Show when sellers are expected to deliver results
- **Requirements Documentation**: May include the following:
    - Technical requirements the seller is required to satisfy
    - Requirements with contractual and legal implications that may include health, safety, security, performance, environmental, insurance, intellectual property rights, equal employment opportunity, licenses, permits and other nontechnical requirements.
- **Requirements Traceability Matrix**: Links product requirements from their origin to the deliverables that satisfy them
- **Risk Register**: Each approved seller come with its own unique set of risks, depending on the seller's organization, the duration of the contract, the external environment, the project delivery method, the type of contracting vehicle chosen and the final agree-upon price
- **Stakeholder Register**: Updated with any additional information on stakeholders, particularly regulatory agencies, contracting personnel and legal personnel

12.1.3.10 Organizational Process Assets Updates

Some of the **Organizational Process Assets** that may be updated as a result of this process will include information on qualified sellers.

Table 12-1, P 481, *Comparison of Procurement Documentation*

12.2 CONDUCT PROCUREMENTS

Conduct Procurements is the process of **obtaining seller proposals**, **deciding on a particular seller(s)** (based on project needs and previously defined selection criteria) and **choosing (awarding) the contract** to the desired seller(s). The **key benefit** is that it selects a qualified seller and implements the legal agreement for delivery.

Fig. 12-4, P 482, *Conduct Procurements: Inputs, Tools and Techniques and Outputs*
Fig. 12-5, P 483, *Conduct Procurements: Data Flow Diagram*

12.2.1 Conduct Procurements: Inputs

12.2.1.1 Project Management Plan

Some of the **Project Management Plan components** are (P 484):

- **Scope Management Plan**: Contains information on how the Scope Management Plan will be defined and developed**,** including the scope performed by sellers
- **Requirements Management Plan:** Contains information on how project requirements will be collected, analyzed and documented
- **Communications Management Plan**: Describes how project communications will be planned, structured, monitored and controlled between buyers and sellers
- **Risk Management Plan**: A component of the Project Management Plan which describes how risk management activities are composed and executed
- **Procurement Management Plan**: Contains the activities to be undertaken during the Conduct Procurements process
- **Configuration Management Plan**: Defines those items that are configurable, those that require formal change control and the process for controlling changes to these items
- **Cost Baseline**: Includes the budget for the procurement as well as costs associated with managing the procurement process and sellers

12.2.1.2 Project Documents

Some of the **Project Documents that may be** considered as Inputs to this process are (P 484):

- **Lessons Learned Register**: Identifies where to set rules or guidelines
- **Project Schedule**: Identifies the start and end dates of project activities, including procurement activities and defines when contractor deliverables are due
- **Requirements Documentation**: New requirements may be identified during this process and may include the following:
    - **Technical requirements** the seller is required to satisfy
    - **Requirements with legal and contractual implications** that may include health, safety, security, performance, environmental, insurance, intellectual property rights, equal employment opportunity, licenses, permits and other non-technical requirements
- **Risk Register**: Provides information on all known Threats and Opportunities
- **Stakeholder Register**: Additional information on new or existing Stakeholders are gathered and recorded

12.2.1.3 Procurement Documentation

Some of the **Procurement Documentation** that may be required for this process includes (P 485):

- **Bid Documents**: These documents include the RFI, RFP, RFQ, or other documents sent to sellers so they can develop a bid response
- **Procurement Statement of Work**: Provides sellers with a clearly stated set of goals, requirements and outcomes from which they can provide a quantifiable response
- **Independent Cost Estimates:** Developed either internally or by using external resources and provide a reasonableness check against the proposals submitted by sellers
- **Source Selection Criteria:** Describes how bidder proposals will be evaluated, including evaluation criteria and weights

12.2.1.4 Seller Proposals

Seller Proposals are prepared from the basic information used by an evaluation body to select one or more successful bidders.

12.2.1.5 Enterprise Environmental Factors

Some of the **Enterprise Environmental Factors** that may influence this process includes (P 486):

- **Local laws and regulations** regarding procurements
- **Local laws and regulations** ensuring that the major procurements involve local sellers
- **External economic environment** constraining procurement processes
- Marketplace conditions
- **Information on relevant past experience with sellers**, both good and bad
- **Prior agreements** already in place
- **Contract management systems**

12.2.1.6 Organizational Process Assets Updates

Some of the **Organizational Process Assets Updates** that may influence the Conduct Procurements process includes (P 486):

- **List of preferred sellers** that have been prequalified
- **Organizational policies** that influence the selection of a seller
- **Specific organizational templates or guidelines** that will determine the way agreements are drafted and built
- **Financial policies and procedures** regarding invoicing and payment processes

12.2.2 Conduct Procurements: Tools and Techniques

12.2.2.1 Expert Judgment

Expert Judgment: Groups or Individuals with **specialized knowledge, training** or **extensive knowledge** should be consulted in the areas shown below (P 487):

- **Proposal evaluation**
- **Technical or subject matter**
- **Relevant functional areas** such as, finance, engineering, design, development, supply chain management, etc.
- **Industry regulatory environment**
- **Law, regulations and compliance requirements**
- **Negotiation**

12.2.2.2 Advertising

Advertising is a means of communication with users or potential users of a product, service or result (P 487).

12.2.2.3 Bidder Conferences

Meetings between the buyer and prospective seller are known as **Bidder Conferences.**

12.2.2.4 Data Analysis

One of the **Data Analysis** techniques that can be used for this process is Proposal Evaluation (P 487).

12.2.2.5 Interpersonal and Team Skills

One of the **Interpersonal and Team Skills** that can be used for this process is Negotiation. Study and read (P 488).

12.2.3 Conduct Procurements: Outputs

12.2.3.1 Selected Sellers

When choosing **Selected Sellers,** the final approval will generally require organizational senior management decisions prior to any complex, high-value, high-risk procurement award (P 488).

12.2.3.2 Agreements

Some of the components of an **Agreement** will include (P 489):

- **Procurement Statement of Work (SOW)** or major deliverables
- **Schedule, milestones or date** by which a schedule is required
- **Performance reporting**
- **Pricing and payment terms**
- **Inspection, quality and acceptance criteria**
- **Warranty and future product support**

- **Incentives and penalties**
- **Insurance and performance bonds**
- **Subordinate contractor approvals**
- **General terms and conditions**
- **Change request handling**
- **Termination clause and alternative dispute resolutions mechanisms**

Read and Study P 489.

12.2.3.3 Change Requests

Any **Change Requests** are processed through the **Perform Integrated Change Control Process.**
There are three (3) types of change, which are:

1. **Corrective Change**
2. **Preventative Action**
3. **Defect Repair**

12.2.3.4 Project Management Plan Updates

Some of the Project Management Plan Updates will include (P 490):

- **Requirements Management Plan:** Changes to project requirements may occur due to changes identified by sellers
- **Quality Management Plan**: Sellers may offer alternative quality approaches
- **Communications Management Plan**: The communications plan is updated when new sellers are hired
- **Risk Management Plan**: Each seller has their own specific set of risks that may be encountered requiring updates to the Risk Register
- **Procurement Management Plan**: Updates may be required depending on the results of the contracting and negotiation process
- **Scope Baseline**: The project WBS and deliverables documented in the scope baseline are considered when performing procurement activities
- **Schedule Baseline**: If there are delivery changes created by sellers that impact overall project schedule performance, the baseline schedule may need to be updated
- **Cost Baseline**: Contractor and material prices can change frequently during a project

12.2.3.5 Project Documents Updates

Some of the **Project Documents** that will be u**pdated** include (P 491):

- **Lessons Learned Register**: Identifies where to set rules or guidelines and updated when challenges encountered while conducting procurements are necessary
- **Requirements Documentation**: New requirements may be identified during this process and may include the following:
    - **Technical requirements** the seller is required to satisfy
    - **Requirements with legal and contractual implications** that may include health, safety, security, performance, environmental, insurance, intellectual property rights, equal employment opportunity, licenses, permits and other non-technical requirements
- **Requirements Traceability Matrix:** Links Product requirements to the Deliverables and as sellers are incorporated into the project's plan, the requirements register and the traceability matrix may change depending on the capabilities of the specific seller
- **Resource Calendars:** May need to be updated depending on the availability of the sellers
- **Risk Register**: Provides information on all known threats and opportunities and each seller comes with a specific set of risks
- **Stakeholder Register**: Additional information on new or existing Stakeholders are gathered and recorded and as agreements are made

12.2.3.6 Organizational Process Assets Updates

Some of the **Organizational Process Assets** that can be **updated** include (P 491):

- **List of prospective and prequalified sellers**
- Information on **relevant past experience with sellers**, both good and bad

12.3 CONTROL PROCUREMENTS

Control Procurements is a process. Here, the designated person(s) manages the relationship(s) and changers and makes corrections as appropriate and also monitors how the contract specifications are completed, or how the contractor performs and closes out the contract. The **key benefit** of this process is that it ensures both the seller's and buyer's performance meet the project's requirements according to the terms of the legal agreement (P 492).

Its **key benefit** is to ensure that the Buyers and Sellers are performing the contracted work as specified by the contract and application of the appropriate project management process.

Fig. 12-6, P 492, *Control Procurements: Inputs, Tools and Techniques and Outputs*
Fig. 12-7, P 493, *Control Procurements: Data Flow Diagram*

This process also includes some of the **administration activities** shown below (P 494):

- **Collection of data and managing project records**, including maintenance of detailed records of physical and financial performance and establishment of measureable procurement performance indicators.
- **Refinement of procurement plans and schedules**
- **Set up for gathering, analyzing and reporting procurement-related data** and preparation of reports to the organization
- **Monitoring the procurement environment** so that implementation can be facilitated or adjustments made
- **Payment of invoices**

The organization's code of ethics, legal counsel and external legal advisory arrangement, etc., can contribute to proper procurement controls. Contracts must be linked by payments made (outputs and deliverables) to the work accomplished.

12.3.1 Control Procurements: Inputs

12.3.1.1 Project Management Plan

Some of the components in the **Project Management Plan** include (P 495):

- **Requirements Management Plan:** Contains information on how contractor requirements will be analyzed, documented and managed
- **Risk Management Plan:** Describes how risk activities created by sellers will be structured and performed
- **Procurement Management Plan**: Contains the activities to be performed during the control procurement process
- **Change Management Plan**: Contains information about how seller-created changes will be processed
- **Schedule Baseline**: Provides any updates created by sellers that may impact the overall process

12.3.1.2 Project Documents

Some of the **Project Documents** that may be considered Inputs to this process include (P 495):

- **Assumption Log:** Contains a record of all the assumptions and constraints that have been made during the procurement process and may be updated or closed out
- **Lessons Learned Register:** Lessons learned earlier in the project can be applied to later phases in the project to improve the efficiency and effectiveness of validating deliverables and will be finalized before being entered into the Repository and updates will occur as needed to improve future performance
- **Milestone List**: Shows scheduled dates for specific milestones that sellers have agreed to deliver
- **Quality Reports:** May include all quality assurance issues managed or escalated by the team, recommendations for improvement and the summary of findings from the Quality Control process and identify seller processes, procedures or products that are out of compliance
- **Requirements Documentation**: New requirements may be identified during this process and those requirements are compared to the actual results to determine if a change, corrective action or preventative action is deemed necessary and may include the following (P 495):
  - Technical requirements the Seller is required to satisfy
  - Requirements with contractual and legal implications that may include health, safety, security, performance, environmental, insurance, intellectual property rights, equal employment opportunity, licenses, permits and other non-technical requirements
- **Requirements Traceability Matrix**: Links product requirements from their origin to the deliverables that satisfy them and contains information about those requirements, including how they will be validated
- **Risk Register**: Provides information on all known risks and each seller comes with a specific set of risks
- **Stakeholder Register**: Additional information on new or existing stakeholders are gathered and recorded, including contracted team members, selected sellers, contracting officers and other stakeholders who are involved in procurements

12.3.1.3 Agreements

Agreements are understandings between sellers and buyers (P 496).

12.3.1.4 Project Documentation

Project Documentation is any supporting records for carrying out the procurement process.

12.3.1.5 Approved Change Requests

Approved Change Requests are requests that have been submitted, reviewed and entered into the Change Log, which should be updated as necessary. Change Requests can include modifications to the terms and conditions of the contract, including the procurement statement of work (SOW), pricing and description of the products, services or results to be provided.

12.3.1.6 Work Performance Data

Some of the **Work Performance Data** includes seller data on project status, such as (P 496):

- **Technical performance**
- **Activities that have started**
- **Activities in progress**
- **Activities that have been completed**
- **Costs that have been incurred or committed**
- **Seller invoices that have been paid**

12.3.1.7 Enterprise Environmental Factors

Some of the **Enterprise Environmental Factors** used in this process include (P 497):

- **Contract change control system**
- **Marketplace conditions**
- **Financial management and accounts payable systems**
- **Buying organizations code of ethics**

12.3.1.8 Organizational Process Assets

One of **Organizational Process Assets** used in this process includes Procurement Policies (P 497):

12.3.2 Control Procurements: Tools and Techniques

12.3.2.1 Expert Judgment

Expert Judgment: Groups or Individuals with specialized knowledge or training or extensive knowledge should be consulted in the areas shown below (P 497):

- Relevant functional areas such as, finance, engineering, design, development, supply chain management, etc.
- Laws, regulations and compliance requirements
- Claims administration

12.3.2.2 Claims Administration

Claims Administration is undertaken when the buyer and seller do not agree on a change, or that a change has occurred. In this case, if the claim is not resolved by both parties, an **Alternate Dispute Resolution** (ADR) will generally follow (P 498). **Study and read** this section.

12.3.2.3 Data Analysis

Some of the **Data Analysis** that can be used in this process is (P 498):

- **Performance Reviews**: Compares, measures quality, resource and schedule performance against the agreement
- **Earned Value Analysis (EVA)**: Compares performance measurement baselines to the actual schedule or cost performance against the degree of variance from the target
- **Trend Analysis**: Examines project performance over time as a way of determining improvement or deterioration using one of the Trend Analysis Techniques known as Forecasting and may use an estimate at completion (EAC) for cost performance to see if project performance improves or deteriorates

12.3.2.4 Inspection

Inspection is a structured review used to evaluate products and decide whether the product meets the desired outcome (P 498). Study and read this section.

12.3.2.5 Audits

Audits are a structured review containing rights and obligations described in the procurement process. Adjustments may become necessary if observations change. Study and read this section.

12.3.3 Control Procurements: Outputs

12.3.3.1 Closed Procurements

Closed Procurements are those deliverables that have been delivered on time and meet all requirements. Study and read this section.

12.3.3.2 Work Performance Information

Work Performance Information includes data for project requirements, causes for rejection, any rework, any corrective actions needed to be taken, etc. Also includes data about how a seller is performing by comparing deliverables received, technical performance achieved and cost incurred and accepted against the SOW budget (P 499).

12.3.3.3 Procurement Documentation Updates

Some of the **Procurement Documentation Updates** in this process are (P 499):

- **Contract with all supporting schedules**
- **Requested unapproved contract changes**
- **Approved change requests**
- **Seller-developed technical documentation**
- **Deliverables associated with work performance**
- **Seller performance reports and warranties**
- **Financial documents, including invoices and payment records**
- **Contract-related inspection results**

12.3.3.4 Change Requests

Change Requests are processed through the Perform Integrated Change Control Process (P 499).

12.3.3.5 Project Management Plan Updates

Some of the **Project Management Plan Updates** will include (P 501):

- **Risk Management Plan:** Each approved seller come with its own unique set of risks that may require updates

- **Procurement Management Plan**: Contains the activities to be undertaken during the Conduct Procurements process
- **Schedule Baseline**: Significant schedule changes by sellers will require updates
- **Cost Baseline**: Contractor and material prices can change frequently during a project requiring updates

12.3.3.6 Project Documents Updates

Some of the **Project Documents Updates** will include (P 500):

- **Lessons Learned**: What information should be collected? How will Historical and Lessons Learned be archived?
- **Resource Requirements**: Resource leveling can impact preliminary estimates for the type and quantities of resources required
- **Requirements Traceability Matrix**: Updated with new information on requirements that have been satisfied
- **Risk Register**: Each approved seller come with its own unique set of risks that may require updates
- **Stakeholder Register**: Contractors and suppliers may change throughout the course of the project and updates will be required

12.3.3.7 Organizational Process Assets Updates

Some of the Organizational Process Assets Updates will include (P 500):

- **Payment Schedules and Requests**: All payments should be made in accordance with her procurement contract terms and conditions
- **Seller Performance Evaluation Documents**: Prepared by the buyer and documents the seller's ability to continue to perform work on the current contract, indicates whether the seller can be allowed to perform work on future projects, or rates how well the seller is performing the project work, or has performed in the past
- **Prequalified Seller Lists Updates**: Lists of potential sellers who have been approved
- **Lessons Learned Repository**: Contains information from previous projects that have been experienced and any process improvement recommendations will be filed for future use
- **Procurement File**: A complete set of indexed contract documentation, including the closed contract, is prepared for inclusion with the final project files

Summary: Answers to Student Learning Outcomes

1. The importance of **Project Procurement Management** is to establish a mechanism to purchase or acquire products, services and/or results from an outside source/project team or outside the project. it includes the management and central processes to develop and administer agreements, such as contracts, purchase orders, memorandum of agreements (MOA)'s, or internal service level agreements (SLA)'s (P 459).

   The Project **Procurement Management Process** has three (3) major process areas as follows (P 459):

   1. **Plan Procurement Management**: The process to document project procurement decisions, specifying the approach and identifying potential sellers.
   2. **Conduct Procurements:** The process is to obtain seller response from **Request for Information (RFI), Request for Quotes (RFQ), Request for Proposal (RFP),** etc., and select a seller. Afterwards, a contract is awarded.
   3. **Control Procurements**: This process is to manage the buyer-seller procurement relationships, monitoring the performance of the contract and making changes as appropriate, and closing out contracts.

   Fig. 12-1, P *460 Project Procurement Management Overview*

2. The key concepts of Project Procurement are as follows: (P 460-P 461):

   1. **Contracts** may be **simple or complex** in terms of the agreement narrative and the deliverables or effort required. Contracts must conform to local, national, and international laws.
   2. A **contract** should state clearly the **deliverables; knowledge transfers required, and reflect culture and local law and enforceability**.
   3. An **Agreement** can be a **contract**, a **Service Level Agreement (SLA), a Memorandum of Understanding (MOU), or a Purchase Order** (PO), depending on the application area.
   4. **Policies and procedures** should identify the contracting parties, rules, and who has the authority to sign and administer the agreement.
   5. Often the participating company will involve the **legal department** to contract, review, and approve all agreements.

6. A **complex project** may include **multiple contracts** and the seller is normally considered the contractor, vendor, service provider, or supplier based on the specifics of the application area. During the procurement process, the seller can be viewed first as a **bidder**, then as the **selected source**, and finally, as the **contracted supplier** or **vendor**.

Study and read P 461-462.

3. The six (6) major **Trends and Emerging Practices** in Procurement Management are (P 463-464):

    1. **Advances** in tool usage
    2. **More advanced risk management** (such as the buyer who is required to accept risks that a contractor has no control over.)
    3. **Changing contractor processes**, (to include megaprojects, multi-billion dollar projects and/or international contracts with multiple contractors, etc.)
    4. **Logistics** and **supply chain management**
    5. **Technology and stakeholder relations**
    6. **Trial engagements**

The four (4) tailoring considerations of **Procurement Management** are (P 465):

1. **Complexity of procurement**
2. **Physical location**
3. **Governance and regulatory environment**
4. **Availability of contractors**

A **Master Service Agreement** (MSA) may be used for the overall engagement within an agile/adaptive environment (P 465).

4. **Plan Procurement Management** is a process that records (documents) project procurement and specifies the approach used to identify the potential sellers. The **key benefit** of this process is whether to acquire goods/services, and/or identify what services will be obtained, how (i.e. outside the project or even from other parts of the participating organization, or from external sources), and when the goods/services will be acquired (P 466).

    Fig. 12-1, P 466 *Plan Procurement Management: Inputs, Tools and Techniques and Outputs*
    Fig. 12-2, P 467 *Plan Procurement Management: Data Flow Diagram*

5. The ten **(10) Outputs of Plan Procurement Management** are (P 466-467):

1. **Procurement Management Plan**
2. **Procurement Strategy**
3. **Bid Documents**
4. **Procurement Statement of Work (SOW)**
5. **Source Selection Criteria**
6. **Make vs. Buy Analysis**
7. **Independent Cost Estimates**
8. **Change Requests**
9. **Project Documents Updates**
10. **Organizational Process Assets Updates**

6. **Plan Procurement Management** is the process of documenting project procurements decisions, specifying the approach and identifying potential sellers. The **key benefit** is that it determines whether to acquire goods and services from outside the project and if so, what to acquire as well as how and when to acquire it. **Plan Procurement Management** can consist of using all four (4) tools and techniques shown below (P 466-467):

    1. **Expert Judgment**
    2. **Data Gathering (Market Research)**
    3. **Data Analysis (Make-or-Buy Analysis)**
    4. **Meetings**

7. **Six (6) Inputs to Plan Procurement Management** are (P 466-467):

    1. **Project Charter**
    2. **Business Documents (Business Case, Business Management Plan)**
    3. **Project Management Plan**
    4. **Project Documents**
    5. **Enterprise Environmental Factors**
    6. **Organizational Process Assets**

    See Fig.12-2, P 466 *Plan Procurement Management: ITTO's*
    See Fig. 12-3, P 467 *Plan Procurement Management: Data Flow Diagram*

8. **The four (4) Components** found in the **Project Management Plan** that establish project boundaries to meet justification and requirement needs are (P 469):

1. **Scope Management Plan**
2. **Quality Management Plan**
3. **Resource Management Plan**
4. **Scope Baseline**

9. The **three (3) types of General Contracts** are (P 471-472):

    1. **Fixed Price Contracts** (P 471)
    2. **Cost Reimbursable Contracts** (P 472)
    3. **Time and Material Contracts** (T & M) hybrid type (P 472)

10. A **Fixed Price Contract** involves setting a fixed total price for specifically defined product, service or results to be provided to the participating company and will be **used when requirements are well defined and there are no significant changes** expected to the scope (P 471).

11. The three **(3) types of Fixed Price Contracts** are (P 471):

    1. **Firm Fixed Price (FFP)**
    2. **Fixed Price Incentive Fee (FPIF)**
    3. **Fixed Price with Economic Price Adjustment (FP – EPA)**

12. A **Cost Reimbursable Contract** offers project flexibility when high risks may exist. It includes the **cost reimbursements (payments) to the seller for all legitimate actual costs, plus a seller's fee** for the seller's profits. This contract type should be used if the scope of work for completed work is expected to change significantly during contract execution (P 472).

13. The **three (3) types of Cost Reimbursable Contracts** are (P 472):

    1. **Cost Plus Fixed Fee (CPFF)**
    2. **Cost Plus Incentive Fee (CPIF)**
    3. **Cost Plus Award Fee (CPAF)**

Read and study **each Type** (P 472).

14. A **Time and Material Contract** (P 472) (Also called Time and Materials) is a hybrid contract that contains features of both cost-reimbursable and fixed price contracts. They are often used for small augmentation, acquisition of experts,

etc., and used when a precise statement of work (SOW) cannot be quickly prescribed.

15. **Make-or-Buy Analysis** is a general management technique that **results in a decision** to determine whether the work should be accomplished within the participating company's project team, or should be purchased using outside sources. This is used in **Plan Procurement Management Tools and Techniques**. Make-or-Buy Analysis may use (P 473):

- **Payback period;**
- **Return on investment (ROI)**
- **Internal rate of return (IRR)**
- **Discounted cash flow**
- **Net project value (NPV)**
- **Benefit/cost analysis (BEA)**

16. **Bid Documents** are used to (P 477):

- **Solicit proposals** from selected sellers or providers.
- **Facilitate an accurate and complete response** from prospective sellers.
- **Promote easy evaluations** of sellers and their responses.
- **Include response flexibility**
- **Aid in publication of the request**, say in newspapers, trade journals, on-line, etc.

Bid Documents (P 477) can include the following:

- **Request for Information (RFI)** is used to gather information and data about the prospective seller and the company. It is typically followed by the **RFQ** or **RFP**.
- **Request for Quote (RFQ)** is a standard business process whose purpose is to invite suppliers into a bidding process to bid on specific products or services and documents how vendors would satisfy the requirements or determine the cost. It is sometimes called an **Invitation for Bid (IFB)**.
- **Request for Proposal (RFP)** is a solicitation made through a bidding process by a company interested in procurement of product, service, or result. It is sent out to suppliers to submit business proposal in response to the RFP or when there is a

problem in the project and the solution is not easy to determine.

- **Invitation for Bid (IFB)** is an invitation to contractors, through a bidding process, to submit a proposal on a project, product or service.

17. The **Procurement Statement of Work (SOW)** is a document used for early procurement, developed from the **Project Scope Baseline** and defines only the portion of project scope to be included within the related contract that should be clear, complete and concise. It describes the procurement items in detail to help the sellers determine their capability to provide the products, services or results to the buyer. The phrase, Terms of Reference (TOR), is sometimes used when contracting for services (P 478). The **SOW** can include (P 477):

    1. **Specifications**
    2. **Quantity Desired**
    3. **Quality Levels**
    4. **Performance Data**
    5. **Performance Schedule (Period of work to be performed)**
    6. **Work Location**
    7. **Other Requirements, etc.**

18. **Source Selection Criteria** is the process of identifying and choosing the best supplier/vendor that will provide the product/service/result that is required by the participating company. Source Selection Criteria may use a weighting system depicted by (P 478):

    The most **common source selection criteria** are:

    1. **Capability and Capacity**
    2. **Product and Life Cycle Cost**
    3. **Delivery Dates**
    4. **Technical Expertise and Approach**
    5. **Specific Sellers Relevant Experience**
    6. **Proposed Approach and Work Plan Adequacy in Responding to SOW**
    7. **Sellers Staff Qualifications Availability and Competence**
    8. **Sellers Financial Stability**
    9. **Sellers Management Experience**

    The specific criteria may include:

    - **The numerical score**
    - **Color code**

- **Written description of the sellers capability to meet the buyers needs (P 479)**

19. **Conduct Procurements** is a process, which includes (P 482):

    - **Obtaining Seller Responses**
    - **Selecting a Seller**
    - **Awarding a Contract**

    Its **key benefit** is that it selects a qualified seller and implements the legal agreement for delivery.

    Fig. 12-4, P 482, *Conduct Procurements: Inputs, Tools and Techniques and Outputs*
    Fig. 12-5, P 483, *Conduct Procurements: Data Flow Diagram*

20. A **Short List** is a list of qualified sellers that appears to be the best candidates providing contractual services as required (P 468).

21. There are six (6) **Inputs to Conduct Requirements** (P 482-483):

    1. **Project Management Plan**
    2. **Project Documents**
    3. **Procurement Documentation**
    4. **Seller Proposals**
    5. **Enterprise Environmental Factors**
    6. **Organizational Process Assets**

22. The **Bidder Conference** is a meeting between buyer or seller, prior to the seller submitting a bid. The **Conduct Procurement Process** may use the following **Tools and Techniques** (P 482-483):

    - **Expert Judgment**
    - **Advertising**
    - **Bidder Conferences**
    - **Data Analysis (Proposal Evaluation)** Here you may have a short list of top sellers
    - **Interpersonal and Team Skills (Negotiation)**

23. **Negotiation** (a process in interpersonal and team skills) takes place before the signing of a procurement contract. It is a discussion between the buyer(s) and seller(s) designed to reach an agreement. It includes (P 488):

    - **Contract structure clarification**
    - **Rights of Buyer and Seller(s)**
    - **Obligation of the parties**
    - **Purchase Terms, etc.**

    Negotiation concludes with a signed contract document or other formal agreements.

24. The **Agreement** (P 489) (document) may include some of the following **components** (P 489)

    - **Procurement Statement of Work or deliverables.**
    - **Schedule, Milestone or date by which a schedule is required.**
    - **Performance Reporting**
    - **Pricing and payment terms**
    - **Inspection, quality and acceptance criteria**
    - **Warranty and future product support**
    - **Incentives and penalties**
    - **Insurance and performance bands**
    - **Subordinate subcontractor approvals**
    - **General terms and conditions**
    - **Change request handling**
    - **Termination clause and alternative dispute resolution mechanisms**

25. The **key benefit** of **Control Procurements** (P 482) is to be certain that both the seller(s) and buyer(s) performance meet the project's requirements according to the terms of the legal document. There are five (5) different **Tools and Techniques** that may be used in the process of **Control Procurements**, one of which is using expert judgment. Listed below are **the tools and techniques** that may be used in **Control Procurements:**

1. **Expert Judgment**
2. **Claims Administration**
3. **Data Analysis (Performance Reviews, Earned Value Analysis (EVA), Trend Analysis)**
4. **Inspection**
5. **Audits**

Fig. 12-6, P 492, *Control Procurements: Inputs, Tools and Techniques and Outputs*
Fig. 12-7, P 493, *Control Procurements: Inputs, Data Flow Diagram*

26. **Claims Administration** deals with claims, disputes, or appeals (P 498).
Read and study P 498.

27. The **components** of the **Project Management Plan**, which is an input to Control Procurements, include but are not limited to (P 495):

- **Requirements Management Plan**
- **Risk Management Plan**
- **Procurement Management Plan**
- **Change Management Plan**
- **Schedule Baseline**

28. **Organizational Process Assets** that can be updated as a result of the control Procurements Process include, but are not limited to (P 501):

- **Payment Schedule Requests**
- **Seller Performance Evaluation Documentation**
- **Prequalified Seller Lists Updates**
- **Lesson Learned Repository**
- **Procurement File**

Read and study P 50.

Similar Questions that may be on the PMI Exam related to Chapter 12

1. You are talking to experts and gathering independent estimates for your contract. Which of the following best describes what you are doing?

   A. Plan Procurements
   B. Conduct Procurements
   C. Administer Procurements
   D. Control Procurements

   Correct Answer is B: When you are working with procurements, Independent Estimates is one of the tools and techniques of the Conduct Procurements process. It certainly sounds a lot like something you would do while planning out your procurements. Do not forget that the Conduct Procurements process involves finding sellers as well as carrying out the work to complete the contract. That would be why you use things like Bidder Conferences and Qualified Seller Lists in Conduct Procurements.

2. Metro Railways has invited a bid to construct an underground tunnel for 2 kms on a fixed price contract. Targeted cost, as per independent estimates is $100mn. The bids received from five (5) of the major contractors is in the range of $190mn-$200mn. What is the most likely reason?

   A. Cartelization
   B. Lack of clarity of scope
   C. Costs have skyrocketed between the times, when bids' preparation was started and bids were released
   D. An extremely specialized job with lots of risk

   Correct option is B: Metro Railways was expecting bids near to their independent estimates, which takes care of all things including some potential risks expected to be faced by contractors. The most likely reason the estimate is nearly double the independent estimates suggest that all the contractors did not have complete clarity on the scope and everyone has assumed some context of the scope differently.

3. A seller completes work as specified in the contract and signs off. However, the buyer is not happy with the results. What is the status of the contract?

   A. Null and Void
   B. Waived
   C. Incomplete
   D. Complete

   Correct answer is D: The work would stand complete if the appropriate sign offs are in place against the SOW.

4. Two members of a team in client organization are documenting and validating the product. Other team members are updating records, performing audit, and archiving lessons learned. What activity are the team members engaged in?

   A. Close Project/Phase
   B. Control Procurements
   C. Manage Quality
   D. Quality Control

   Correct answer is B: Procurement audits are part of control procurements.

5. There is a cost-reimbursable contract between an organization and a vendor. The organization now wants to expand the scope of services by changing to a fixed price contract. Which of the following is not a vendor's option?

   A. The vendor should complete original work on a cost-reimbursable contract and then negotiate a fixed price for any additional work
   B. The vendor should complete original work and reject the additional work
   C. The vendor should negotiate a fixed price contract that includes the work
   D. The vendor should start over with a new contract

   Correct Answer is D: Since the organization wants to expand scope to a fixed price contract, the vendor/seller should start over with a new contract.

6. Jackson Technologies decides to purchase certain components required for an ongoing project from a vendor. The company negotiates with the vendor and agrees on a fixed price plus incentive-free contract. The target cost $800,000; share ratio 80/20; target incentive fee $100,000; actual cost $9, 00,000; ceiling price: $1000, 000. What amount shall Jackson technologies pay to the vendor?

    A. In this case ceiling price is higher than total cost of procurement, so Jackson technologies will be paying the procurement cost
    B. In this case ceiling price is higher than total cost of procurement, so Jackson technologies will be paying the ceiling price
    C. In this case ceiling price is lesser than total cost of procurement, so Jackson technologies will be paying the ceiling price
    D. In this case ceiling price is lesser than total cost of procurement, so Jackson technologies will be paying the total cost of procurement

    Correct answer is A: Incentive = (Target Cost - Actual Cost). Seller's percent of Cost Savings Incentive = ($800,000 - $900,000) 20/100 = $20,000. Final Contract Cost or Fee or Overhead (given to seller) = Target Fee + Incentive = $100,000 + ($20,000). Final Contract Cost or Fee or Overhead (given to seller) = $80000. Total Cost or Cost of Procurement = Actual Cost + Final Contract Cost = $900,000 + $80,000 = $980,000. In this case ceiling price is higher than total cost of procurement. Therefore, Jackson Technologies will pay the procurement cost.

7. Petal has outsourced a work package of her project to a vendor. What should be her next step?

    A. Conduct Procurement
    B. Plan Procurement
    C. Control
    D. None of these

    Correct Answer is C: Petal has already done the outsourcing agreement. It is now time to manage the vendor.

8. Which of the following alternatives represents the most appropriate reason to conduct post contract evaluation?

    A. Final payment depends on the ultimate contract performance
    B. Act as a reference point for making legal procurements
    C. Contractual requirement
    D. It makes a historical base for future contractor selection

    Correct answer is D: The present performance of a contractor becomes a part of the historical information and the basis for their selection in future projects.

9. Which of the following least likely describes a weighting system used in the select seller(s) process?

    A. Select a single seller that will be asked to sign the contract
    B. Ensure that the prospective sellers have a clear understanding of the requirements
    C. Rank sellers based on the sellers past performance and quality
    D. Rank all proposals by weighed evaluation scores

    Correct answer is B: Ensure that prospective sellers have a clear understanding of the requirements, is not in select seller process, because this step was already completed before you entered the select seller process.

10. A records management system is used by the project manager to manage contract and procurement documentation and records. Which among the following is not typically included in the records management system?

    A. Procurement Statement of Work
    B. Contract Negotiation
    C. Terms and Conditions
    D. Vendor Performance Reports

    Correct answer is B: Contract negotiation is a process and not a document. A document is stored in the records management system.

You may now move on to Chapter Thirteen: Project Stakeholder Engagement

Chapter 13: Project Stakeholder Engagement: Stakeholders are anyone affected by a Project

"...Take a diverse number of stakeholders, extract needs, concerns, and dreams, then create a beautiful yet tangible solution that is loved by the users and the community at large..." Cameron Sinclair

Student Learning Outcomes

1. List and describe the **four (4) processes of Project Stakeholder Management** and its importance (P 503) and review and list the ITTO's in the Project Stakeholder Management Overview (P 503- 504).
2. Every Project can **be impacted** either negatively or positively by its **stakeholders** (P 504). Describe the process of **identifying, prioritizing** and **engaging stakeholders** for the benefit of the project.
3. There are numerous **Trends and Emerging Practices in Project Stakeholder Engagement.** List five (5) reasons that stakeholder engagement will vary from project to project (P 505).
4. List three **(3) Tailoring Considerations** when **modifying Project Stakeholder Management Processes** (P 506).
5. **What is meant by Identify Stakeholders and what is its key benefit? What are the ITTO's (P 507)?**
6. What two (2) documents are used as **sources** of project information in **the first Iteration of Identify Stakeholders** (P 509)?
7. List the five **(5) Tools and Techniques** that may be used in **Identify Stakeholders** (P 511).
8. **Brain Storming** is a **Data Gathering Technique** used in **Identify Stakeholders** (P 511). This data gathering technique includes **Brain Storming** and **Brain Writing.** What is the difference between these two terms?
9. What is meant by **Stakeholder Analysis** (P 512)?
10. What is the meaning of **Stakeholder's Stake** (P 512)?
11. List the seven **(7) common methods** used to **categorize stakeholders** (P 512-513).
12. Describe the **characteristics** of the following **Grid/Model** (P 512).
    1) The Power/Interest Grid
    2) The Power/Influence Grid
    3) Influence/Impact Grid
    4) The Salience Model
13. What is a **Stakeholder Register**, why is this vital to the project, and what type of information does it contain (P 514)?
14. **What is Plan Stakeholder Management and what are the key benefits (P 516)? Identify and explain the tools and techniques that may be used in Plan Stakeholder Management (P 516)?**
15. **What is meant by Manage Stakeholder Engagement and its key benefit (P 523)?**
16. What are the Inputs, Tools, Techniques and Outputs **(ITTO's)** for **Manage Stakeholder Engagement** (P 516-P 517)?
17. What is the purpose or importance of an **Issue Log** in Project Stakeholder Management (P 525)?
18. **What does Monitor Stakeholder Engagement mean, and what key**

benefit does it provide (P 530)?

19. What are the Inputs, Tools, Techniques and Outputs **(ITTO's)** for **Monitor Stakeholder Engagement** (P 530-P 531)?
20. List some of the updates that may be included in the **Project Management Plan Updates** (P 535).
21. What are some of the updates that may affect the **Project Documents Updates** (P 536)?

CHAPTER THIRTEEN INTRODUCTION: STAKEHOLDERS ARE ANYONE AFFECTED BY A PROJECT

PROJECT STAKEHOLDER MANAGEMENT: CHAPTER 13 OVERVIEW:

PMBOK® 6th Edition P 503-536

Project Stakeholder Management includes the processes required to identify management tools and processes required to identify people, groups or organizations that could impact or be impacted by the project as well as (P 503):

- Analyze Stakeholder expectations and their impact upon the project;
- Develop appropriate management strategies for engaging stakeholders.

The **Project Stakeholder Management** processes are as follows:

(13.1) **Identify Stakeholders:** The process of identifying project stakeholders, analyzing and documenting stakeholder interest or involvement, etc.

(13.2) **Plan Stakeholder Engagement**: The process of developing approaches (i.e. strategy) to involve project stakeholders based upon their needs and expectations, etc.

(13.3) **Manage Stakeholder Engagement:** The process of communicating and working with stakeholders to meet their needs and expectations, etc.

(13.4) **Monitor Stakeholder Engagement**: The process of monitoring stakeholder relationships and tailoring stakeholder strategies through modification of engagement plans.

The Project Management Professional (PMP)® The Next Step in your Career, (7:03 minutes), located at https://www.youtube.com/watch?v=bLIW_ChhMK4

Fig. 13-1, P 504, *Project Stakeholder Management Overview*

Key Concepts for Project Stakeholder Management

Every project stakeholder is either for or against the project, or somewhere in between (neutral position). A structured approach needs to take place to identify, prioritize and figure out the level of enthusiasm and engagement of all stakeholders. Stakeholder identification and engagement should commence as soon as possible after the Project Charter has been approved. The process of identifying and engaging stakeholders is iterative (P 504).

Trends and Emerging Practices in Project Stakeholder Management

The following trends and emerging practices (P 505) may include:

1. Identify all stakeholders as soon as or before starting the project
2. Make sure all team members are involved in activities of stakeholder engagement
3. Review the stakeholder community environment regularly
4. Consult with stakeholders
5. Capture the value affecting stakeholder engagement for both positive and negative viewpoints

Tailoring Considerations

The project manager may need to tailor the way project stakeholders' management processes are applied. Such considerations (P 506) include:

1. Stakeholder Diversity
2. Complexity of Stakeholder Relationships
3. Communication Technology

Considerations for Agile/Adaptive Environments

Projects that experience a high degree of change require active engagement and participation with stakeholders (P 506). Oftentimes, the client, user and developer will exchange information in a dynamic co-creative manner. Regular interactions with stakeholders will help mitigate project risks, build trust and support early adjustments to the project.

Identify Stakeholders:

Identify stakeholders is the process of identifying project stakeholders regularly throughout the entire project, analyzing, and documenting relevant information regarding their interests and involvement, etc. The **key benefit** of this process is that it enables the project teams to identify the appropriate focus, serious or casual, for engagement of certain stakeholders or groups of stakeholders. This process is performed periodically throughout the project.

See chart on next page: **IDENTIFY STAKEHOLDERS (Section 13.1)**

Chapter Thirteen: Project Stakeholder Management

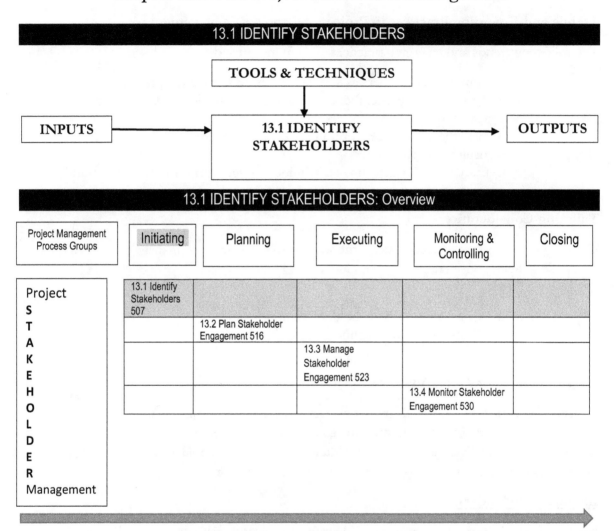

13.1 IDENTIFY STAKEHOLDERS

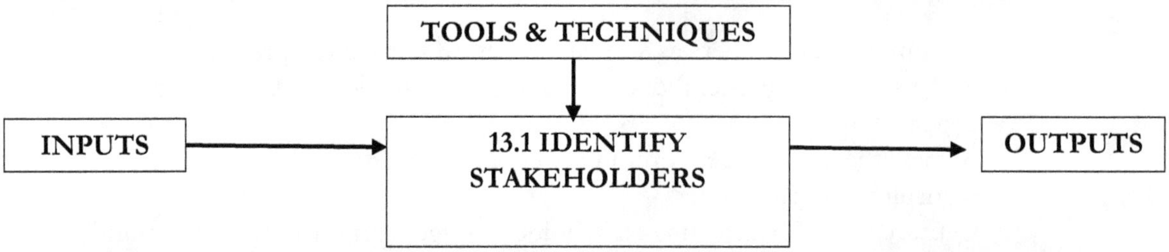

13.1 IDENTIFY STAKEHOLDERS: Overview

Project Management Process Groups	Initiating	Planning	Executing	Monitoring & Controlling	Closing
Project STAKEHOLDER Management	13.1 Identify Stakeholders 507				
		13.2 Plan Stakeholder Engagement 516			
			13.3 Manage Stakeholder Engagement 523		
				13.4 Monitor Stakeholder Engagement 530	

13.1 IDENTIFY STAKEHOLDERS: ITTO Processes

.1 Inputs	.2 Tools and Techniques	.3 Outputs
.1 Project Charter 509 .2 Business Documents 509 • Business Case 509 • Benefits Management Plan 509 .3 Project Management Plan 509 • Communications Management Plan 509 • Stakeholder Engagement Plan 509 .4 Project Documents 510 • Change Log 510 • Issue Log 510 • Requirements Documentation 510 .5 Agreements 510 .6 Enterprise Environmental Factors 510 .7 Organizational Process Assets 510	.1 Expert Judgment 511 .2 Data Gathering 511 • Questionnaires and Surveys 511 • Brainstorming 511 .3 Data Analysis 512 • Stakeholder Analysis 512 • Document Analysis 511 .4 Data Representation 512 • Stakeholder Mapping/Representation 512 .5 Meetings 514	.1 Stakeholder Register 514 .2 Change Requests 514 .3 Project Management Plan Updates 515 • Requirements Management Plan 515 • Communications Management Plan 515 • Risk Management Plan 515 • Stakeholder Engagement Plan 515 .4 Project Documents Updates 515 • Assumption Log 515 • Issue Log 515 • Risk Register 515

Fig. 13-2, P 507, *Identify Stakeholders: Inputs, Tools and Techniques and Outputs*
Fig. 13-3, P 508, *Identify Stakeholders: Data Flow Diagram*

<u>Plan Stakeholder Engagement:</u>

Plan Stakeholder Engagement is the process of developing various approaches when engaging project stakeholders. Considerations are based on stakeholder needs, expectations, interest, and potential impact upon the project. The **key benefit** is that it provides an actionable plan to interact effectively with stakeholders. An effective plan will recognize the diverse information needs of various project stakeholder groups and who should be identified early in the project lifecycle, and updates that should be regularly made as the stakeholder community changes.

See chart on next page: **PLAN STAKEHOLDER ENGAGENT (Section 13.2)**

Chapter Thirteen: Project Stakeholder Management

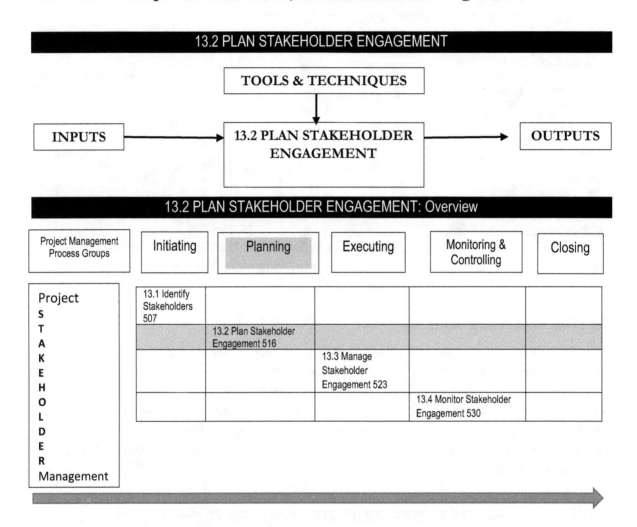

13.2 PLAN STAKEHOLDER ENGAGEMENT

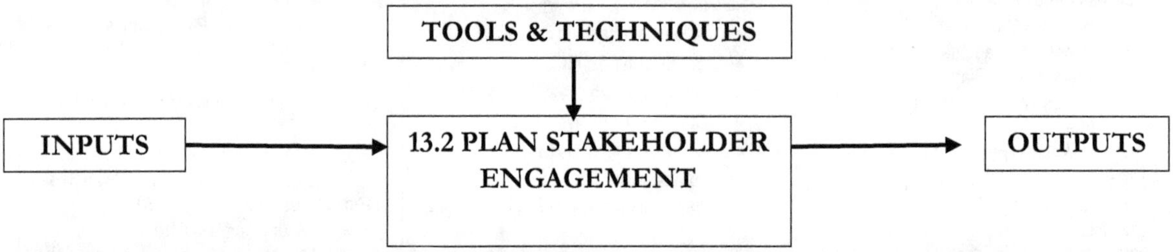

13.2 PLAN STAKEHOLDER ENGAGEMENT: Overview

Project Management Process Groups	Initiating	Planning	Executing	Monitoring & Controlling	Closing
Project STAKEHOLDER Management	13.1 Identify Stakeholders 507				
		13.2 Plan Stakeholder Engagement 516			
			13.3 Manage Stakeholder Engagement 523		
				13.4 Monitor Stakeholder Engagement 530	

13.2 PLAN STAKEHOLDER ENGAGEMENT: ITTO Processes

.1 Inputs	.2 Tools and Techniques	.3 Outputs
.1 Project Charter 518 .2 Project Management Plan 518 • Resource Management Plan 518 • Communications Management Plan 518 • Risk Management Plan 518 .3 Project Documents 519 • Assumption Log 519 • Change Log 519 • Issue Log 519 • Project Schedule 519 • Risk Register 519 • Stakeholder Register 519 .4 Agreements 519 .5 Enterprise Environmental Factors 519 .6 Organizational Process Assets 520	.1 Expert Judgment 520 .2 Data Gathering 520 • Benchmarking .3 Data Analysis 521 • Assumptions And Constraint Analysis 521 • Root Cause Analysis 521 .4 Decision Making 521 • Prioritization/Ranking 521 .5 Data Representation 521 • Mind Mapping 521 • Stakeholder Engagement Assessment Matrix 521 .6 Meetings 522	.1 Stakeholder Engagement Plan 522

Fig. 13-4, 516, *Plan Stakeholder Engagement: Inputs, Tools and Techniques and Outputs*
Fig. 13-5, 517, *Plan Stakeholder Engagement: Data Flow diagram*

Manage Stakeholder Engagement:

Manage Stakeholder Engagement is the process of communicating and working with stakeholders to meet their needs and expectations, address issues and foster stakeholder involvement. The **key benefit** of this process is that it allows the project manager to increase, fortify, support and minimize resistance from stakeholders.

See chart on next page: **MANAGE STAKEHOLDER ENGAGENT (Section 13.3)**

Chapter Thirteen: Project Stakeholder Management

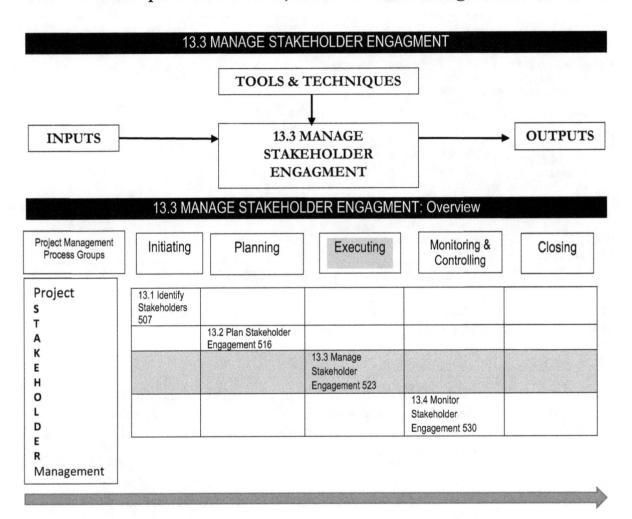

13.3 MANAGE STAKEHOLDER ENGAGMENT

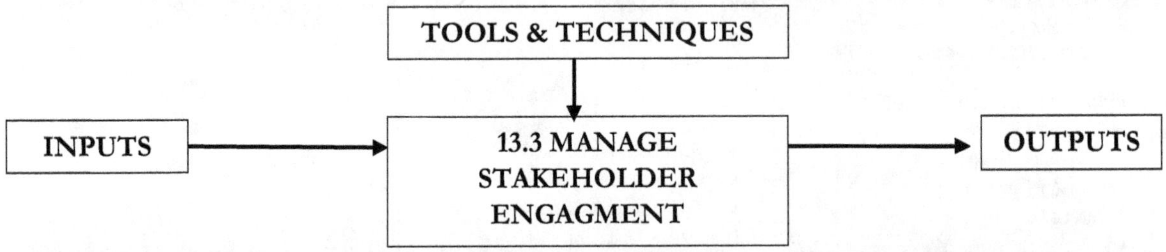

13.3 MANAGE STAKEHOLDER ENGAGMENT: Overview

Project Management Process Groups	Initiating	Planning	Executing	Monitoring & Controlling	Closing
Project STAKEHOLDER Management	13.1 Identify Stakeholders 507				
		13.2 Plan Stakeholder Engagement 516			
			13.3 Manage Stakeholder Engagement 523		
				13.4 Monitor Stakeholder Engagement 530	

13.3 MANAGE STAKEHOLDER ENGAGMENT: ITTO Processes

.1 Inputs	.2 Tools and Techniques	.3 Outputs
.1 Project Management Plan 525 • Communications Management Plan 525 • Risk Management Plan 525 • Stakeholder Engagement Plan 525 • Change Management Plan 525 .2 Project Documents 525 • Change Log 525 • Issue Log 525 • Lessons Learned Register 525 • Stakeholder Register 525 .3 Enterprise Environmental Factors 526 .4 Organizational Process Assets 526	.1 Expert Judgment 526 .2 Communication Skills 527 • Feedback 527 .3 Interpersonal And Team Skills 527 • Conflict Management 527 • Cultural Awareness 527 • Negotiation 527 • Observation/Conversation 527 • Political Awareness 527 .4 Ground Rules 528 .5 Meetings 528	.1 Change Requests 528 .2 Project Management Plan Updates 529 • Communications Management Plan 529 • Stakeholder Engagement Plan 529 .4 Project Documents Updates 529 • Change Log 529 • Issue Log 529 • Lessons Learned Register 529 • Stakeholder Register 529

Fig. 13-7, P 523, *Manage Stakeholder Engagement: Inputs, Tools and Techniques and Outputs*
Fig. 13-8, P 524, *Manage Stakeholder Engagement: Data Flow Diagram*

Monitor Stakeholder Engagement:

Monitor Stakeholder Engagement is the process of monitoring project stakeholder relationships and tailoring strategies for engaging stakeholders through modification of engagement strategies and plans. The **key benefit** of this process is that it maintains or increases the efficiency and effectiveness of stakeholder engagement activities as the project evolves.

See chart on next page: **MONITOR STAKEHOLDER ENGAGENT (Section 13.4)**

Chapter Thirteen: Project Stakeholder Management

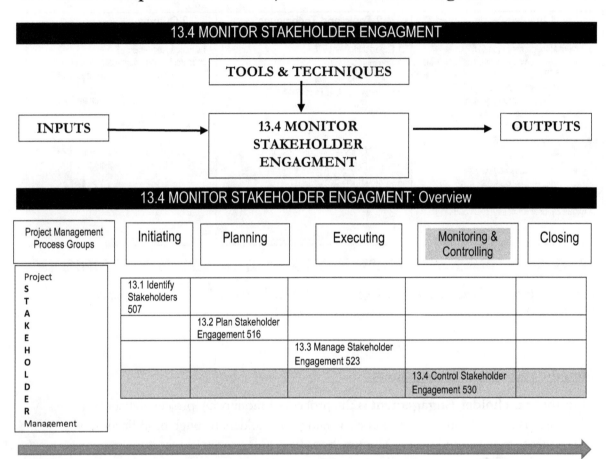

13.4 MONITOR STAKEHOLDER ENGAGMENT

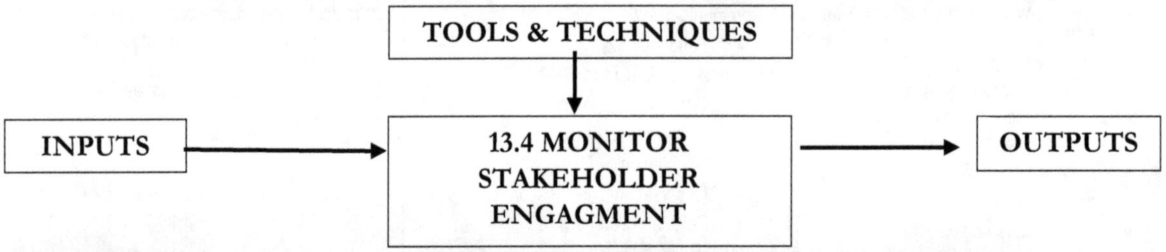

13.4 MONITOR STAKEHOLDER ENGAGMENT: Overview

Project Management Process Groups	Initiating	Planning	Executing	Monitoring & Controlling	Closing
Project STAKEHOLDER Management	13.1 Identify Stakeholders 507				
		13.2 Plan Stakeholder Engagement 516			
			13.3 Manage Stakeholder Engagement 523		
				13.4 Control Stakeholder Engagement 530	

13.4 MONITOROL STAKEHOLDER ENGAGMENT: ITTO Processes

.1 Inputs	.2 Tools and Techniques	.3 Outputs
.1 Project Management Plan 532 • Resource Management Plan 532 • Communications Management Plan 532 • Stakeholder Engagement Plan 532 .2 Project Document Updates 532 • Issue Log 532 • Lessons Learned Register 532 • Project Communications 532 • Risk Register 532 • Stakeholder Register 532 .3 Work Performance Data 532 .4 Enterprise Environmental Factors 533 .5 Organizational Process Assets 533	.1 Data Analysis 533 • Alternative Analysis 533 • Root Cause Analysis 533 • Stakeholder Analysis 533 .2 Decision Making 534 • Multicriteria Decision Analysis 534 • Voting 534 .3 Data Representation 534 • Stakeholder Engagement 534 • Assessment Matrix 534 .4 Communication Skills 534 • Feedback 534 • Presentations 534 .5 Interpersonal and Team Skills 534 • Active Listening 534 • Cultural Awareness 534 • Leadership 534 • Networking 534 • Political Awareness 534 .6 Meetings 535	.1 Work Performance Information 535 .2 Change Requests 535 .3 Project Management Plan Updates 536 • Resource Management Plan • Communications Management Plan • Stakeholder Engagement Plan .4 Project Documents Updates 536 • Issue Log 536 • Lessons Learned Register 536 • Risk Register 536 • Stakeholder Register 536

Fig. 13-9, P 530, *Monitor Stakeholder Engagement: Inputs, Tools and Techniques and Outputs*
Fig. 13-10, P 531, *Monitor Stakeholder Engagement: Data Flow Diagram*

KEY WORDS: CHAPTER 13

- Stakeholder Diversity
- Complexity of Stakeholder Relationships
- Communications Technology
- Questionnaires
- Surveys
- Brainstorming
- Stakeholder Analysis
- Power/Interest Grid
- Power/Influence Grid
- Impact/Influence Grid
- Stakeholder Cube
- Salience Model
- Directions of Influence
    - Upward
    - Downward
    - Sideward
    - Prioritization
- Stakeholder Engagement Assessment Matrix
    - Unaware
    - Resistant
    - Neutral
    - Leading
- Cultural Awareness
- Negotiation
- Political Awareness
- Root Cause Analysis
- Stakeholder Analysis
- Multi-Criteria Decision Analysis
- Voting

LEGEND

The following Legend shows how to correctly read the *PMBOK® Guide* references and attributions correctly for Chapter 13: Project Stakeholder Management PMBOK Details.

Legend:

Chapter Section	Chapter Section Title	Page Number

Example from Chapter Six shown below:

6.5.1.4	Enterprise Environmental Factors	(P 209)

All direct quotes are attributed as (A Guide to the Project Management Body of Knowledge, *(PMBOK® Guide)* – Sixth Edition) Project Management Institute Inc., 2017, Page #, after each section and any/all paraphrased or original wording is attributed as (P #), before or after each section. All Graphs, Charts, Tables and Figures are attributed as: (*PMBOK® Guide*, Fig. #-# or #/#, P #, *Title of Graph, Chart, Table or Figure*).

13. PROJECT STAKEHOLDER MANAGEMENT

Project Stakeholder Management are the processes required to identify how Project Stakeholder Management principles must be followed for all project work from the start of the project, during the project, and through the project's completion. This is accomplished by determining who has a stake in the outcome of the project. The first step in this process is identifying any organization, people or groups of people who can/could be impacted by a decision, activity or outcome of the project. Stakeholder expectations must be analyzed to develop appropriate management strategies needed to make wise project decisions and executions. The involvement of any of these groups or individuals needs to be considered, as stakeholders will have various degrees of interest and will focus on different projects.

Fig. 13-1, P 504, *Project Stakeholder Management: Overview*).

Also refer to, *The Project Management Professional, PMP® The Next Step in your Career* (7:03 minutes), at https://www.youtube.com/watch?v=bLIW_ChhMK4

Key Concepts for Project Stakeholder Management (P 505):

- The ability of the PM to effectively manage and appropriately engage Stakeholders can mean the difference between success and failure of the project. To help ensure success, identifying the Stakeholders as soon as possible after the Project Charter is approved, is of the utmost importance. Stakeholder satisfactions should be measured as a the project's objective are being achieved and should be reviewed and updated on a continuing basis during the following times:
  - When the project moves through different phases in the life cycle
  - Current stakeholders are no longer involved in the project or when new stakeholders become involved
  - When significant changes in the organization take place, or when a wider stakeholder community becomes involved in the project

Trends and Emerging Practices in Project Stakeholder Management:

- Some of the **Trends and Emerging Practices** in Stakeholder Management are:

- Identifying all stakeholders, not just a limited set, as soon as possible
- Ensuring all team members are involved in stakeholder engagement activities
- Review of the stakeholder community regularly, often in review of parallel of individual project risks
- Consulting with stakeholders who are most affected/influenced by the work or the outcomes of the project through the concept of co-creation
- Capturing the value of (both positive and negative) effective stakeholder engagement, attitudes and actions, both positive or negative

Tailoring Considerations:

The PM may need to tailor the way Project Stakeholder processes are managed and some of the considerations for this follow (P 506):

- **Stakeholder Diversity**:
    - How many Stakeholders are there?
    - How diverse is the stakeholder culture within the community?
- **Complexity of Stakeholder Relationships**:
    - How complex are the people/business relationships within the Stakeholder community?
- **Communicating Technology**:
    - What communication technology is available?
    - What support mechanisms are in place to ensure that the best value is achieved from the technology?

Considerations for Agile/Adaptive Environments:

Projects with a high degree of change require an Agile/Adaptive approach, with active engagement and continued participation with vested stakeholders. In this way, project risk is mitigated, trust is built and support adjustments earlier in the project cycle will help to reduce costs and increase the likelihood of project success (P 506).

The New Frontier: Agile Automation at Scale, by Federico Berruti, Geet Chandratre and Zaid Rab, located at: https://www.mckinsey.com/business-functions/operations/our-insights/the-new-frontier-agile-automation-at-scale

13.1 IDENTIFY STAKEHOLDERS

Identify Stakeholders is the process of identifying project stakeholders on a regular basis and analyzing and documenting relevant information about their needs, level of interest, etc. and potential impact on project success. The success of a project may/will depend on the people/groups/organizations (external) involved, but may also be internal, anyone within the performing organization, such as team members, groups and departments. The **key benefit** of this process is that it enables the project team to identify the appropriate focus for engagement of each stakeholder or group of stakeholders (P 50).

Fig. 13-2, P 507, *Identify Stakeholders: Inputs, Tools and Techniques and Outputs*
Fig. 13-3, P 508, *Identify Stakeholders: Data Flow Diagram*

13.1.1 Identify Stakeholders: Inputs

13.1.1.1 Project Charter

The **Project Charter** provides information about the key stakeholders and their responsibilities. It can reflect stakeholder characteristics, whose involvement can affect the success of the project outcome (P 509).

13.1.1.2 Business Documents

In the first iteration in the Identify Stakeholders process, two (2) very important **Business Documents** are (P 509):

- **Business Case**: Identifies the project objective and provides an initial list of Stakeholders
- **Benefits Management Plan**: Describes the expected plan for realizing the benefits claimed in the business case and may identify stakeholder groups and/or individuals that will benefit from the delivery of the project outcome

13.1.1.3 Project Management Plan

Some of the components involved in the **Project Management Plan** are (P 509):

- **Communications Management Plan**: Information in this plan is a source of knowledge about the project's stakeholders
- **Stakeholder Engagement Plan**: Identifies the management strategies and actions required to effectively engage stakeholders

13.1.1.4 Project Documents

Some of the Project Documents in this plan will include (P 510):

- **Change Log**: May introduce a new stakeholder or change the nature of an existing stakeholder's relationship to the project
- **Issue Log**: May introduce new stakeholders to the project or changes the type of project participation of existing stakeholders needs and project requirements
- **Requirements Documentation**: Provides information on potential stakeholders

13.1.1.5 Agreements

Agreements: A procurement agreement is a document that outlines the terms and conditions of buyer and seller decisions as to what each will provide the other in terms of products and/or what services will be performed. These agreements can contain references to future stakeholders or their participating roles in the project (P 516).

13.1.1.6 Enterprise Environmental Factors

Some of the **Enterprise Environmental Factors** involved in the **Identify Stakeholder** process are (P 510):

- Organizational culture, political climate and governance framework
- Government or industry standards
- Global, regional or local trends and practices or habits
- Geographic distribution of facilities and resources

13.1.1.7 Organizational Process Assets

Some of the components of the **Organizational Process Assets** in this process are (P 510):

- **Stakeholder templates**, registration and instructions
- **Stakeholder registers** from previous projects
- **Lessons learned repository** with information about the preferences, actions and involvement of stakeholders

13.1.2 Identify Stakeholders: Tools and Techniques

13.1.2.1 Expert Judgment

Expert Judgment: Groups or Individuals with specialized knowledge or training or extensive knowledge should be consulted in the areas shown below (P 511):

- **Understanding the politics and power structures** in the organization
- **Knowledge of the environment and culture of the organization** and other affected organizations, including customers and the wider environment
- **Knowledge of the industry or type of project deliverables**
- **Knowledge of individual team member** contributions and expertise

13.1.2.2 Data Gathering

Some of the **Data Gathering** techniques used in this process are (P 511):

- **Questionnaires and Surveys**: Can include one-on-one stakeholder reviews, focus group sessions or other mass information collection techniques
- **Brainstorming**: Used to identify stakeholders and can include both brainstorming and brain writing
    - **Brainstorming**: Elicits inputs from groups such as team members or subject matter experts
    - **Brain Writing**: Allows participants to consider the questions individually before the group creativity session is held

13.1.2.3 Data Analysis

Some of the **Data Analysis** techniques used in this process are (P 512):

- **Stakeholder Analysis**: Provides essential information on stakeholders, such as their positions in the organization, roles on the project, expectations, attitudes: level of support, their interest in information about the project and a list of the following:
    - **Interest:** A person or group may be affected by a decision related to the project or the outcome of the project

    - **Rights (legal or moral):** Legal rights may be defined in the legislation framework of a country and moral rights may involve concepts of protection of historical sites or environmental sustainability
    - **Ownership:** A person or group has a legal title to an asset or property
    - **Knowledge**: Specialist knowledge which can benefit the project through more efficient delivery of project objectives
    - **Contribution:** Provision of funds or other resources, including human resources, or providing support for the project in more tangible ways
- **Document Analysis**: Assessing the available project documentation and lessons learned from previous projects to identify stakeholders and other supporting information

13.1.2.4 Data Representation

One of the **Data Representation** techniques that may be used in this process is stakeholder analysis. This method of categorizing Stakeholder Analysis will help the team in building relationships and some of the methods of doing this include (P 512):

- **Power/Interest Grid, Power/Influence Grid, Impact/Influence Grid**: A grouping of Stakeholders according to their level of authority, level of concern, ability to influences the project's outcomes, or ability to cause changes to the project's planning or execution.
- **Stakeholder Cube**: A refinement of grid models previously mentioned, combining the grid elements into a 3-D model.
- **Salience Model**: Describes classes of Stakeholders based on assessments of power, authority to ability to influence the project's outcome.
- **Directions of Influence**: Classifies Stakeholders according to their influence levels and can be classified by the following:
    - Upward: Senior Management, etc.
    - Downward: Team or specialists
    - Outward: Stakeholder groups and their representatives
    - Sideward: Peers, etc.
- **Prioritization**: May be necessary for projects with a large number of stakeholders, when the project is complex or the stakeholder community is changing frequently, etc.

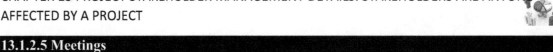

13.1.2.5 Meetings

Meetings are undertaken to create a more complete understanding of stakeholders who hold more power and influence on the project's outcome and their stakeholders.

13.1.3 Identify Stakeholders: Outputs

13.1.3.1 Stakeholder Register

The **Stakeholder Register** contains information about stakeholders and includes data, such as (P 514):

- **Identification Information**: Name, organizational position, location, contact details, role on/in the project
- **Assessment Information**: Major requirements, expectations, potential for influencing project outcome, phase of the project life cycle where the Stakeholder has the most influence or impact
- **Stakeholder Classification**: Internal/External, Impact/Influence/Power/Interest, Upward/Downward/Outward, or any other classification model chosen by the PM

13.1.3.2 Change Requests

Change Requests do not take place during the first iteration of identifying stakeholders, but later on, they are processed for review and disposition through the **Integrated Change Control** process.
Read and study this section.

13.1.3.3 Project Management Plan Updates

Some of the **Project Management Plan Updates** include (P 515):

- **Requirements Management Plan**: Newly identified Stakeholders can impact how requirement activities will be planned, tracked and reported
- **Communications Management Plan**: Stakeholder communication requirements and agreed-upon communication strategies are recorded in the Communications Management plan
- **Risk Management Plan**: Stakeholder communication requirements are recorded in the Risk Management Plan

- **Stakeholder Engagement Plan**: Agreed-upon communication strategies for identified Stakeholders are recorded in the Stakeholder Engagement Plan

13.1.3.4 Project Documents Updates

Some of the **Project Documents** Updates include (P 515):

- **Assumption Log**: Much of the information about Stakeholders is based on assumptions and entered into the Assumption Log, along with any constraints
- **Issue log**: New issues raised as a result of this process are recorded
- **Risk register**: New risks identified are recorded and managed using the risk management process

13.2 PLAN STAKEHOLDER ENGAGEMENT

Plan Stakeholder Engagement is concerned with the ongoing process of creating ways to engage stakeholders, based on prior analysis of their particular needs, concerns and their possible future impact on the project's success. The **key benefit** is that this process provides an actionable plan to effectively interact with stakeholders. This process is performed throughout the project life cycle.

Fig. 13-4, P 516, *Plan Stakeholder Engagement: Inputs, Tools and Techniques and Outputs*
Fig. 13-5, P 517, *Plan Stakeholder Engagement: Data Flow Diagram*

Some **trigger situations** requiring updates to the Stakeholder Engagement Plan include those shown below (P 518):

- When a new phase of the project begins
- When there are changes to the organizational structure or within the industry
- When new individuals or groups become stakeholders, current stakeholders may not be a part of the stakeholder community, or the importance of particular stakeholders to the success of the project changes
- When outputs of other process areas, such as change management, risk management, or issue management requires a review of stakeholder engagement levels and activities

13.2.1 Plan Stakeholder Engagement: Inputs

13.2.1.1 Project Charter

The **Project Charter** which contains, project scope, objectives and success criteria, is essential in managing Stakeholders, which also provides data concerning stakeholders (internal/external). One way of determining a Key Stakeholder(s) is to identify anyone or any group who has a reason for being involved in the project and will be affected by executing the project work. The Project Charter contains criteria that can be used when planning how to engage Stakeholders (P 518).

13.2.1.2 Project Management Plan

The **Project Management Plan** is an input to the **plan stakeholder engagement** and data needed for this process may include (P 518):

- **Resource Management Plan**: may contain information regarding roles and responsibilities of the team and other Stakeholders listed in the Stakeholder Register
- **Communications Management Plan**: Stakeholder communication strategies for Stakeholder management and their implementation plans are both Inputs to, and recipients of, information from processes in Project Stakeholder Management
- **Risk Management Plan**: May contain risk thresholds or risk attitudes that can assist in the selection of the optimal stakeholder engagement strategy mix

13.2.1.3 Project Documents

Some of the **Project Documents** that can be considered as Inputs to this process are (P 519):

- **Assumption Log**: Contains information about assumptions and constraints and may be linked to specific Stakeholders
- **Change Log**: Contains changes to the original scope of the project
- **Issue Log**: Managing and resolving issues contained in the Issue Log will require additional communications with the Stakeholders who are affected
- **Project Schedule**: Contains activities that may be linked to specific Stakeholders as owners or executors

- **Risk Register**: Contains the identified risks of the project and generally links them to specific Stakeholders as either risk owners or as subject to risk impact
- **Stakeholder Register**: Provides the list of project Stakeholders including additional classification data and other information

13.2.1.4 Agreements

Agreements ensure contractors and suppliers are effectively managed within their procurement/contacting group.

13.2.1.5 Enterprise Environmental Factors

Some of the **Enterprise Environmental Factors** that may influence this process are (P 519):

- Organizational culture, political climate and governance framework
- Personnel administration policies
- Stakeholder risk appetites
- Established communication channels
- Global regional or local trends, practices or habits
- Geographic distribution of facilities and resources

13.2.1.6 Organizational Process Assets

Some of the Organizational Process Assets that may influence this process are (P 520):

- Corporate policies and procedures for social media, ethics and security
- Corporate policies and procedures for issue, risk, change and data management
- Organizational communication requirements
- Standardized guidelines for development, exchange, storage and retrieval of information
- Lessons learned repository with information about the preferences, actions and involvement of stakeholders
- Software tools needed to support effective Stakeholder engagement

13.2.2 Plan Stakeholder Engagement: Tools and Techniques

13.2.2.1 Expert Judgment

Expert Judgment: Groups or Individuals with specialized knowledge or training or extensive knowledge should be consulted in the areas shown below (P 520):

- **Politics and power structures** in and out of the organization
- **Environment and culture** of the organization
- **Analytical and assessment techniques** to be used for stakeholder engagement processes
- **Communication means and strategies**
- **Knowledge from previous projects** of the characteristics of stakeholders and Stakeholder groups and organizations involved in the current project that may have been involved in similar projects

13.2.2.2 Data Gathering

One of the **Data Gathering** techniques that can affect this process is **Benchmarking**. **Read and study** section 8.1.2.2 (P 281). See glossary definitions of benchmarking (P 699), 6th Ed.

13.2.2.3 Data Analysis

Some of the **Data Analysis** techniques that can be used in this process are (521):

- **Assumption and Constraint Analysis**: Explores the validity of assumptions and constraints to discover which ones pose a risk to the project and the tailoring of appropriate strategies to use
- **Root Cause Analysis**: Used to discover underlying causes that lead to a problem

13.2.2.4 Decision Making

One of the **Decision Making** techniques that can affect this process is Prioritization/Ranking.

13.2.2.5 Data Representation

Some of the **Data Representation** techniques that can be used in this process are (521):

- **Mind Mapping**: Used to visually organize information about Stakeholders and their relationships to each other and the organization

- **Stakeholder Engagement Assessment Matrix**: Support comparisons between the current engagement levels of Stakeholders and the desired engagement level of Stakeholders.

Fig. 13-6, P 522, *Stakeholder Engagement Assessment Matrix*

Engagement levels of stakeholders are classified as follows (P 521):

- **Unaware:** Unaware of the project and the potential impacts
- **Resistant:** Aware of the project and the potential impacts, but resistant to any changes that may occur as a result of the work or outcomes of the project
- **Neutral:** Aware, but neither supportive or unsupportive
- **Supportive:** Aware of the project and the potential impacts and supportive of the work and the outcomes
- **Leading:** Aware of the project and any potential impacts and actively engaged in ensuring that the project is a success

13.2.2.6 Meetings

The purpose of **meetings,** are to discuss strategies and approaches as to how stakeholder engagement will be conducted and to develop a sound **Stakeholder Engagement Plan** (P 522).

13.2.3 Plan Stakeholder Engagement: Outputs

13.2.3.1 Stakeholder Engagement Plan

The **Stakeholder Engagement Plan is u**sed to understand Stakeholder communication requirements and the level of Stakeholder engagement in order to assess and adapt to the level of Stakeholder participation in requirements activities. The stakeholder engagement plan is part of the Project Management Plan (P 522).

13.3 MANAGE STAKEHOLDER ENGAGEMENT

Manage Stakeholder Engagement is the process of communication and working with stakeholders to meet their needs, expectations, address issues and foster appropriate stakeholder involvement. Establishing communication and engaging with stakeholders should take place throughout the project life cycle. The **key benefit** is that it will allow the PM to increase support and reduce resistance from Stakeholders.

Fig. 13-7, P 523, *Manage Stakeholder Engagement: Tools and Techniques and Outputs*
Fig. 13-8, P 524, *Manage Stakeholder Engagement: Data Flow Diagram*

Some of the activities involved in **Manage Stakeholder Engagement** are shown below (P 524):

- **Engaging stakeholders at appropriate project stages** to obtain or confirm their continued commitment to the success of the project
- **Managing Stakeholders expectations** through negotiation and communication
- **Addressing any risks or potential concerns** that have not yet become issues and anticipating future problems that may be raised by stakeholders which must be identified and discussed as soon as possible
- **Clarifying and resolving issues** that have been identified

By performing the above actions, the Stakeholders should clearly understand the benefits of the project as well as their contribution to its success.

13.3.1 Manage Stakeholder Engagement: Inputs

13.3.1.1 Project Management Plan

Some of the **Project Management Plan** components that are considered subsidiary project management plans can be used in this process are (P 525):

- **Communications Management Plan**: Describes methods, formats and technologies used in Stakeholder communication
- **Risk Management Plan**: Describes risk categories, risk appetites and reporting formats that can be used to manage Stakeholder engagement
- **Stakeholder Engagement Plan**: Provides guidance and information on managing Stakeholder expectations
- **Change Management Plan:** Describes the process for submitting, evaluation and implementing change to the project

13.3.1.2 Project Documents

Some of the **Project Documents** considered as Inputs to this process and can be used in this process are (P 525):

- **Change Log:** May introduce a new stakeholder or change the nature of an existing stakeholder's relationship to the project

- **Issue Log**: May introduce new stakeholders to the project or change the type of participation of existing stakeholders
- **Lessons Learned Register:** Created to register categories and descriptions of any impacts, recommendations and proposed actions that are connected with a particular situation affecting the project.
- **Stakeholder Register:** Provides a list of project Stakeholders and any information needed to execute the Stakeholder Engagement Plan

13.3.1.3 Enterprise Environmental Factors

Some of the **Enterprise Environmental Factors** that may affect this process are (P 526):

- **Organizational culture, political climate and governance framework**
- **Personnel Administration Policies**
- **Stakeholder Risk Thresholds**
- **Established Communication channels**
- **Global, Regional or Local Trends, Practices or Habits**
- **Geographic distribution of Facilities and Resources**

13.3.1.4 Organizational Process Assets

Some of the **Organizational Process Assets** that may affect this process are (P 526):

- **Corporate policies and procedures for social media, ethics and security**
- **Corporate policies and procedures for issue, risk, change and data management**
- **Organizational communications requirements**
- **Standardized guideline for development, exchange, storage and retrieval of information**
- **Historical information from previous projects**

13.3.2 Manage Stakeholder Engagement: Tools and Techniques

13.3.2.1 Expert Judgment

Expert Judgment: Groups or Individuals with specialized knowledge or training or extensive knowledge should be consulted in the areas shown below (P 526):

- Politics and power structures in or outside the organization
- Environment and culture of the organization and outside the organization
- Analytical and assessment techniques to be used for the stakeholder engagement process
- Communication methods and strategies
- Characteristics of Stakeholders and Stakeholder groups and organizations involved in the current project that may have been involved in similar projects

13.3.2.2 Communication Skills

In **Communication Skills**, some of the feedback that is used in this process may be obtained in the following ways (P 527):

- Conversations, both Formal And Informal
- Issue Identification and Discussion
- Meetings
- Progress Reporting
- Surveys

13.3.2.3 Interpersonal and Team Skills

Some of the **Interpersonal and Team Skills** that can be used in this process are (P 527):

- **Conflict Management**: The PM should ensure that conflicts are resolved in a timely manner
- **Cultural Awareness**: Used to help the PM and team to communicate effectively by considering cultural differences and the requirements of the Stakeholders
- **Negotiation**: Used to achieve support or agreements that supports the work of the project team members and other Stakeholders
- **Observation/Conversation**: Used to stay in touch with the work or attitudes of project team members and other Stakeholders
- **Political Awareness**: Achieved through understanding the power relationships within and around the project

13.3.2.4 Ground Rules

Ground Rules: **Defined in the Team Charter** for expected behavior of the Team Members and the Stakeholders.

13.3.2.5 Meetings

The types of **Meetings** used in this process may be as follows (P 528):

- Decision Making
- Issue Resolution
- Lessons Learned And Retrospectives
- Project Kickoff
- Sprint Planning
- Status Updates

13.3.3 Manage Stakeholder Engagement: Outputs

13.3.3.1 Change Requests

Change Requests means changes to the project scope or product scope may crop up and are processes for review or disposition thorough the **Perform Integrated Change Control** process (P 528).

13.3.3.2 Project Management Plan Updates

Some of the **Project Management Plan Updates** used in this process may be as follows (P 529):

- **Communications Management Plan**: Updated to reflect new or changed Stakeholder requirements
- **Stakeholder Engagement Plan**: Updated to reflect new or changed management strategies required to effectively engage Stakeholders

Study and review section 4.3.2.1, **Subsidiary Management Plans** (P 87).

13.3.3.3 Project Documents Updates

Some of the **Project Document Updates** used in this process may be as follows (P 529):

- **Change Log**: Updated based on any change requests
- **Issue Log**: Updated to reflect an update to, or the development of, and issue log entry
- **Lessons Learned Register**: Updated with effective/ineffective approaches to managing Stakeholder engagement to be used in future projects
- **Stakeholder Register**: Updated based on new information provided to Stakeholders about resolved issues, approved changes and general project status

13.4 MONITOR STAKEHOLDER ENGAGEMENT

Monitor Stakeholder Engagement is an ongoing system for monitoring stakeholder relationships and tailoring strategies and plans for engaging stakeholders. The **key benefit** of this process is to maintain or increase the effectiveness and efficiency of Stakeholder engagement activities as the project environment changes.

Fig. 13-9, P 530, *Monitor Stakeholder Engagement: Inputs, Tools and Techniques and Outputs*
Fig. 13-10, P 531, *Monitor Stakeholder Engagement: Data Flow Diagram*

13.4.1 Monitor Stakeholder Engagement: Inputs

13.4.1.2 Project Documents

Some of the **Project Documents** which may be considered as Inputs to this process are (P 532):

- **Issue Log**: Documents all known issues related to the project and Stakeholders
- **Lessons Learned Register**: Lessons learned earlier can be applied to later phases of the project
- **Project Communications**: Any communications that have been distributed to the Stakeholders
- **Risk Register**: Contains the identified risks for the project
- **Stakeholder Register**: Contains Stakeholder information, including Stakeholder identification, assessment and classification

13.4.1.1 Project Management Plan

Some of the **Project Management Plan** (Input to the Stakeholder Management Plan) components include the following (P 532):

- **Resource Management Plan**: Identifies the methods for team member management
- **Communications Management Plan**: Describes the plans and strategies for communication to the project's Stakeholders
- **Stakeholder Engagement Plan**: Defines the plans for managing Stakeholder needs and expectations

Study and review: Subsidiary plans, section 4.3.2.1, P 87.

13.4.1.3 Work Performance Data

Work Performance Data contains data on project status performance as to which stakeholders are supporting and their level and type of support (P 535).

13.4.1.4 Enterprise Environmental Factors

Some of the **Enterprise Environmental Factors** which may influence this process are (P 533):

- **Organizational Culture, Political Climate and Governance Framework**
- **Personnel Administration Policies**
- **Stakeholder Risk Thresholds**
- **Established Communication Channels**
- **Global, regional or local trends, practices or habits**
- **Geographic distribution of facilities and resources**

13.4.1.5 Organizational Process Assets

Some of the **Organizational Process Assets** which may influence this process are (P 533):

- **Corporate policies and procedures** for social media, ethics and security
- **Corporate policies and procedures** for issue, risk, change and data management
- **Organizational communications requirements**
- **Standardized guidelines** for development, exchange, storage and retrieval of information
- **Historical information** from previous projects, including the lessons learned repository

13.4.2 Monitor Stakeholder Engagement: Tools and Techniques

13.4.2.1 Data Analysis

Some of the **Data Analysis** techniques that can be used in this process include (P 533):

- **Alternative Analysis:** A form of deciding on several alternatives and analyzing each one before making a decision
- **Root Cause Analysis**: The process of identifying a problem at its core and taking action to prevent or correct the risk
- **Stakeholder analysis**: Provides essential information on Stakeholders, such as their positions in the organization, roles on the project, expectations, attitudes: level of support and their interest in information about the project

13.4.2.2 Decision Making

Some of the **Decision Making** techniques used in this process are (P 534):

- **Multicriteria Decision Analysis**: Criteria for successful Stakeholder engagement are prioritized and weighted to identify the most appropriate choice
- **Voting**: Used to select the best response for a variance in Stakeholder engagement

13.4.2.3 Data Representation

One of the **Data Representation** techniques used in this process includes the Stakeholder Engagement Assessment Matrix.

13.4.2.4 Communication Skills

Some of the **Communication Skill** techniques used in this process include (P 534):

- **Feedback**: Used to ensure the information given to Stakeholders is received and understood
- **Presentations**: Provide a means for communication in a clear manner to Stakeholders

13.4.2.5 Interpersonal and Team Skills

Some of the **Interpersonal and Team Skills** used in this process include (P 534):

- **Active Listening**: Used to reduce stakeholder misunderstandings and miscommunication
- **Cultural Awareness**: Cultural awareness and cultural sensitivity help the PM to plan communications based on the cultural differences and requirements of Stakeholders and team members
- **Leadership**: Strong leadership skills are required to communicate the vision and inspire Stakeholders to support the work and the outcomes of the project
- **Networking**: Ensures access to information about levels of engagement of Stakeholders
- **Political Awareness**: Used to understand the strategies of the organization, understand who wields power and influence in this arena and to develop an ability to communicate with these Stakeholders

13.4.2.6 Meetings

Some types of **Meetings** in this process may include (P 534):

- Status meetings
- Standup meetings
- Retrospective Meetings

Study and read about the many types of meetings (P 535).

13.4.3 Manage Stakeholder Engagement: Outputs:

13.4.3.1 Work Performance Information

Work Performance Information Includes the status of Stakeholder engagement.

13.4.3.2 Change Requests

Change Requests include corrective and preventative actions to improve the engagement levels of stakeholder's engagement and can be initiated from inside or outside the project. Change requests are processed for review and disposition through the **Perform Integrated Change Control** process.

13.4.3.3 Project Management Plan updates

Some of the **Project Management Plan Updates** can include the following (P 535):

- **Resource Management Plan**: Identifies the methods for team member management and responsibilities for Stakeholder engagement activities
- **Communications Management Plan**: Describes updates to the plans and strategies for communicating to the project's Stakeholders
- **Stakeholder Engagement Plan**: Defines the plans for managing stakeholder communication needs and expectations

13.4.3.4 Project Documents Updates

Some of the **Project Document Updates** can include the following (P 536):

- **Issue Log**: Indicates Stakeholder attitudes and necessary updates as needed
- **Lessons Learned Register**: Updated with information on challenges and how they could have been avoided and approaches that worked well and did not work well
- **Risk Register**: Responses to Stakeholder risks updates
- **Stakeholder Register**: Updated with information as a result of monitoring Stakeholder engagement

Summary: Answers to Student Learning Outcomes

1. There are four processes in **Project Stakeholder Management** (P 503). ITTO's found in the Project Management Overview are found in your PMBOK study guide.

   Fig. 13-1, P 504, *Project Stakeholder Management Overview*

   This process requires:

   1. **Identifying Stakeholders**:
      a. **Identification of stakeholder engagement** is done on a regular basis and analyzing and documenting relevant information about their interests, involvement, interdependencies, and determine their potential impact on project success
   2. **Plan Stakeholder Engagement:** The process of developing approaches to involve project stakeholders, based on their needs, expectations, interests and potential project impact
   3. **Managing Stakeholder Engagement:** The process of communicating and working with stakeholders to meet their needs and expectations, address issues and foster appropriate stakeholder engagement
   4. **Monitor Stakeholder Engagement**: A process of monitoring project stakeholder relationships and tailoring strategies for engaging stakeholders through the modification of engagement strategies and plans

2. **Identifying and engaging the stakeholders** takes place **throughout** the project life cycle. It is an **iterative** process as stakeholders come and go from the project. Because the project moves through different phases, some stakeholders start, but might not always remain directly involved at certain times (P 505). The Project Manager must always be alert and aware of the transitory roles of different stakeholders. Identification and engagement should start as soon as possible after the project charter has been approved, the project manager has been assigned and the teams have been formed (P 504).

3. The **Project Manager** needs to recognize that stakeholder engagements are reflective of **Trends and Emerging Practices**, that include (P 505):

    1. **Identify all stakeholders** from the start to the end of the project
    2. **Encourage all team members** to be involved in stakeholder engagement activities
    3. **Review the roles of stakeholders** and their representative community, especially for individual project risks
    4. **Consult with stakeholders** by emphasizing their importance as team partners.
    5. **Capture the value of negative and positive stakeholder** impact upon project success.

4. There are three (**3) Tailoring considerations** when the Project Manager wishes to **modify project stakeholder** processes. They are (P 506):

    1. **Stakeholder Diversity**
    2. **Complexity of stakeholder relationships**
    3. **Communication technology**

5. **Identify Stakeholders** requires that the Project Manager and team **identify project stakeholders** on a regular basis and **analyze** and **document** their potential impact upon the project (P 507). This includes recognizing their interests, level of involvement, interdependencies and influence. The **key benefit** is that this knowledge will enable the project team to identify courses of action and focus on each stakeholder's requirements that are necessary for project success. This process is performed throughout the project.

    Fig. 13-2, P 507 *Identify Stakeholders: Inputs, Tools and Techniques and Outputs*
    Fig. 13-3, P 507 *Identify Stakeholders: Data Flow Diagram*

6. The **Business Case** and the **Benefits Management Plan** (P 509) are the two (2) documents that initially list the stakeholders that are involved or to be involved in the specific project. These **Source Documents** are used in the first iteration of the **Identify Stakeholder Process (P 509).**

7. The following are **Tools and Techniques** may be used in the process called: **Identify Stakeholders** (P 511):

    - **Expert Judgment**
    - **Data Gathering (Questionnaires, Surveys and Brainstorming)**

- **Data Analysis (Stakeholder Analysis and Document Analysis)**
- **Data Representation (Stakeholder Mapping and Representation)**
- **Meetings**

See P 511-513, for a deep dive into the specifics of the tools and techniques.

8. **Brainstorming** is a general data gathering and creativity technique that elicits input from team members or **Subject Matter Experts (SME)**'s (P 511).

   Brain Writing is a **refinement of brainstorming** that allows individual participants **time** to answer questions before group creativity sessions begin (P 511).

9. **Stakeholder Analysis** is a system of gathering and analyzing quantitative and qualitative data to help identify key stakeholders who will be affected by the project. It results in a list of stakeholders and relevant information as to (P 512):

   - **Positions in the organization**
   - **Project roles**
   - **Stakes**
   - **Expectations**
   - **Attitudes**
   - **Interest in the project**

   Read and study, **Stakeholder Stakes**: to include interests, rights, ownership, knowledge and contribution (P 512).

10. **Stakeholder's Stake** can include but are not limited to a combination of the following (P 512):

    - **Interests**
    - **Rights (legal or moral)**
    - **Ownership**
    - **Knowledge**
    - **Contributions**

11. The seven (7) common methods to **categorize stakeholders** are (P 512-513):
    - Power/Interest Grid
    - Power/Influence Grid
    - Impact/Influence Grid
    - Stakeholder Cube
    - Salience Model
    - Directions of Influence (Upward, downward, outward, sideward)
    - Prioritization

    Carefully **Read and Study** the above-mentioned categories (P 512-513).

12. The following **classification models** that might be used in a **Stakeholder Analysis Process** are (P 512) :

    - **Power/Interest Grid**: Stakeholder grouping by level of authority (power), interest and concern about project outcomes.
    - **Power/Influence Grid**: Stakeholder grouping based upon action, involvement and influence in the project.
    - **Impact/Influence Grid**: Stakeholder grouping based upon action, involvement, influence and the stakeholder's ability to effect/impact changes to the project.
    - **Salience Model**: Stakeholder grouping based upon power, urgency and legitimacy.
    - **Other**: See stakeholder cube, direction of influence and prioritization P 512-513).

13. **The Stakeholder Register** is an **Output** of **Identify Stakeholders**, and contains information about identified stakeholders (P 514):

    - **Identification information:** Name, organization, position, etc.
    - **Assessment information:** Major requirements, etc.
    - **Stakeholder classification:** Internal/external, impact/influence, etc.

    The purpose of a **Stakeholder Register** is to provide data needed to engage stakeholders and must be updated on a regular basis, as stakeholders may or may not play an instrumental role throughout the entire project life cycle or its phases.

14. **Plan Stakeholder Management** is the process of **developing approaches** to **involve stakeholders** based upon their needs, expectations, interests and potential overall project impact (P 516-517). The **Tools and Techniques** that may be considered for usage are:

    Expert Judgment: Judgment and expertise should be solicited and consulted from groups such as:

    1. Senior Management
        - Project Team Members
        - Identified Key Stakeholder
        - Other Units or Individuals within Organization
        - Project Managers who have worked on a project in the same area
        - Subject Matter Experts (SME's)
        - Industry Groups and consultants
        - Professional and Technical Associations
        - Regulatory Bodies
    2. Non-Governmental Organizations (NGO's)
        - Data Gathering
        - Benchmarking
    3. Data Analysis
        - Assumptions, constraints and analysis
        - Root cause analysis
    4. Decision Making
        - Prioritization and ranking
    5. Data Representation
        - Mind mapping, stakeholder analysis
    6. Meetings: Project team members and experts should meet to decide how to engage the stakeholders and how best to satisfy their requirements. This information can be useful in preparing the Stakeholder Management Plan.

    The **key benefit** of **Plan Stakeholder Management** (P 516) is to provide an actionable plan to **interact** effectively with stakeholders.

    Fig. 13-4, P 516, *Plan Stakeholder Engagement: Inputs, Tools and Techniques and Outputs*
    Fig. 13-5, P 517*, Plan Stakeholder Engagement: Data Flow Diagram*

7. **Manage Stakeholder Engagement** (P 523) is the process of **communicating** and **working** with stakeholders to meet their needs and expectations, address issues, and foster appropriate stakeholder involvement. The **key benefit** is to

allow the project manager to **increase support** and **minimize stakeholder resistance.**

Fig. 13-7, P 523 *Manage Stakeholder Engagement: Inputs, Tools and Techniques and Outputs*
Fig. 13-8, P 524 *Manage Stakeholder Engagement: Data Flow Diagram*

8. The **Inputs, Tools, Techniques, and Outputs** (ITTO's) **for Manage Stakeholder Engagement** are (P 523-524):

Inputs:

Project Management Plan
Project Documents
Enterprise Environmental Factors
Organizational Process Assets Updates

Tools and Techniques:

Expert Judgment
Communication Skills
Interpersonal and Team Skills
Ground Rules
Meetings

Outputs:

Change Requests
Project Management Plan Updates
Project Documents Updates

Fig. 13-7, P 523 *Manage Stakeholder Engagement: Inputs, Tools and Techniques and Outputs*
Fig. 13-8, P 524 *Manage Stakeholder Engagement: Data Flow Diagram*

9. **Managing Stakeholder Engagement** could result in an **issue log**, which is used for **managing stakeholder's issues and concerns** and can include any assigned action items associated with managing the issue (P 525). The issue log should be updated regularly so that new issues are addressed and old and current issues are dealt with accordingly. Note: The issues log is also updated in Monitor Stakeholder Engagement (P 536). Here, the stakeholder's attitude about the project may be recorded in the Issue Log.

10. **Monitor Stakeholder Engagement** is the process of **monitoring overall**

project stakeholder relationships and tailoring strategies for engaging stakeholders through modification of engagement strategies and plans (P 539). The **key benefit** of this process is that it maintains or increases the efficiency and effectiveness of stakeholder engagement activities as the project evolves and the environment changes.

Fig. 13-9, P 530, *Monitor Stakeholder Engagement: Inputs, Tools and Techniques and Outputs*
Fig. 13-10, P 531, *Monitor Stakeholder Engagement: Data Flow Diagram*

The **Inputs, Tools, Techniques, and Outputs** (ITTO's) for **Monitor Stakeholder Engagement** are (P 530-P 531):

Inputs:

Project Management Plan
Project Documents
Work Performance Data
Enterprise Environmental Factors
Organizational Process Assets

Tools and Techniques:

Data Analysis
Decision Making
Data Representation
Communication Skills
Interpersonal and Team Skills
Meetings

Outputs:

Work Performance Information
Change Requests
Project Management Plan Updates
Project Documents Updates

Fig. 13-9, P 530 *Monitor Stakeholder Engagement: Inputs, Tools and Techniques and Outputs*
Fig. 13-10, P 531 *Monitor Stakeholder Engagement: Data Flow Diagram*

11. Some of the updates in **Monitor Stakeholder Engagement** that may be included in the **Project Management Plan Updates** are shown below (P 535):
    - Resource Management Plan
    - Communication Management Plan
    - Stakeholder Engagement Plan

Please note: All of the updates shown above are considered subsidiary components of the **Project Management Plan.** Also, review section (4.2.3.1) Project Management Plan (P 86) and the list of other subsidiary management plans on P 87.

12. Some of the updates in **Monitor Stakeholder Engagement** that may be included in the **project documents updates** (P 536) are:

- **Issue Log**

a. **Lessons Learned Register**
b. **Risk Register**
c. **Stakeholder Register**

Similar Questions that may be on the PMI Exam related to Chapter 13

1. Monika is one of the most experienced project managers in the company, Aion Airways. The company has recently been facing a few challenges on managing the lead to revenue process. There have been huge revenue leakages due to issues in this process. The CIO authorized Monika to look into the process and come up with a plan to decrease revenue losses by 10% in the next six months, so Monika categorized the stakeholders into categories. Some of the stakeholders are very negative about the outcome of the project. Which category these particular stakeholders fall under?

   A. Resistant
   B. Neutral
   C. Supportive
   D. Leading

   Correct Option is A: Resistant Stakeholders are those who are aware of the project and the potential impacts. They are resistant to change.

2. Stakeholder Management Strategy includes the following except _____.

   A. Level of participation in the project desired for each identified stakeholder
   B. Key stakeholders who can significantly impact the project
   C. Name, organizational position, location of stakeholders
   D. Stakeholder groups and their management

   Correct option is C: Name, organizational position and the location of stakeholders is documented in the Stakeholder register. Stakeholders are analyzed and a management strategy is devised to deal with them effectively.

3. A project manager of a construction company is trying to track team member performance and identify whether recruitment of new resources is required. Which of the following tools would be of the least help?

   A. Resource calendars
   B. Work performance reports
   C. Team performance assessments
   D. Project staff assignments

   Correct answer is A: Resource calendars help in tracking resource usage not performance.

4. Nate, a manager in an export house is responsible for automating manual processes. He recruits a few software developers, designers and testers on a contract basis to work on project deliverables as per the scope. The new team members were stationed at different parts of the building. However, rather than enhanced output, there was more of a misunderstanding and repetitive explanation of the context. What can be done in this situation to improve team efficiency?

    A. Implement ground rules
    B. Co-locate the team
    C. Deploy project management software
    D. This is normal and will pass gradually

    Correct answer is B: Co-location, also referred to as a tight matrix, involves placing many or most active members of the project in the same physical location to enhance their ability to communicate and thus perform as a team. Co-location can be temporary, such as at strategically important times during the project, or for the entire project. Co-location strategies can include a team meeting room, sometimes called the war room, places to post schedules, and other conveniences that enhance communication and a sense of community.

5. Jack is working in a start-up company which is focusing emerging 3D Printing technologies, especially for Aerospace and Medical manufacturers. He is working on a project to establish relationships with external partners to provide cost effective solutions to his customers. There are many stakeholders involved in the project and he is always in contact with Sponsors to manage stakeholders. Who is responsible for managing stakeholder engagement?

    A. Project manager, because actively managing stakeholder engagement will reduce project risk and help unresolved issues get resolved quickly
    B. Project sponsor, because the overall success or failure of the project rests on this individual
    C. All stakeholders have responsibility to make sure their expectations are managed and they receive the proper information at the right time
    D. Project manager and the project team members together have the responsibility because the project manager alone cannot manage all the stakeholders on a large, complex project

Correct answer is A: The project manager alone is responsible for managing stakeholder engagement. The project manager may work with sponsors and others to manage them.

6. You are a project manager working in a large bank based out of New York. You are conducting a project meeting with the project stakeholders in your company to access their engagement levels in the project. You heard that Patrick, Vice President of Quality, has not been on good terms with your manager. You manager is not comfortable with in-depth details and always likes to keep the short content. You have had a few conversations with Patrick in the past and felt that he is very detailed-oriented and always needs data before he makes any decision. You have prepared well for your meeting with proper data for all the project matrices. In your meeting, Patrick took lots of interest in the project and appreciated the presentation. What is Patrick's current engagement level in the project?

    A. Unaware
    B. Supportive
    C. Resistant
    D. Neutral

Correct answer is B: This is a tricky question. Patrick may have had conflicts with your supervisor in the past, but analyzed his current requirements and understand them well. He is supportive, because he took an interest in your detailed content. Unaware and Neutral options are ruled out. If you have chosen Resistant then you are wrong, as Patrick may have resisted in the past which may be a different scenario which is not in your control.

7. You are a project manager in a telecom company. Your project's schedule is already finalized when your client's management told you that due to some pressure, the project needs to be finished two months earlier than scheduled. You have already reviewed the scope and the schedule and you know that nothing can be cut. What would be the most appropriate thing to do in this situation?

    A. Initiate change control processes, explain that the new project schedule needs to stand, and review the risks involved
    B. Meet with the team and evaluate if each activity can be cut by 10 percent to accomplish the goal
    C. Think to do more critical path activities in parallel
    D. Meet with management to review the original project management plan and discuss scope changes that would reduce project timeline

    Correct answer is C: PM should not cut duration on critical path activities by a percentage without doing an analysis, because it might affect the project scope/quality, or increase cost. He should consider fast tracking and try doing more critical path activities in parallel.

8. Ronaldo has just finished a project and has been assigned another project. This is a new technology, which has never been used by the company before for any of the earlier projects. He is currently collecting the detailed requirements. He is using the interview technique. Which of the following is true about interview technique?

    A. Interviews are conducted when the target audience is huge in number
    B. Interviews can be conducted via e-mails, phone calls, letters, etc.
    C. Interviews are conducted when the target audience is huge in number and Interviews can be conducted via e-mails, phone calls, letters, etc.
    D. Interviews are conducted to find the detailed requirements from stakeholders

    Correct answer is D: Interviews are a formal or an informal approach to elicit information from stakeholders by talking to them directly.

9. As part of the stakeholder analysis, you have prepared an influence/impact grid on a scale of one being the lowest and five being the highest rating on each coordinate. Which of the following will be the most appropriate rating of the project sponsor on the grid?

   A. Influence = 1.8: Impact = 4.8
   B. Influence = 4.2: Impact = 2.2
   C. Influence = 4.8: Impact = 4.4
   D. Influence = 4.6: Impact = 6.2

   Correct answer is C: The project sponsor is a stakeholder who would have high ratings on the parameters, vis-à-vis influence and impact. (A) And (B) do not fit these criteria, and (C) has a value outside the defined limit.

10. Jim is the new project manager for the implementation of ERP and CRM modules for an MNC conglomerate. The CEO of the company sends an e-mail to Jim. He also explains the contents in person, listing project objectives, timelines, tentative budget, major deliverables and risks perceived by them. He asks Jim to meet stakeholders. What is the **Identify Stakeholder Process** about?

    A. It is the process of making relevant information available to stakeholders as planned
    B. It is the process of defining the project stakeholder information needs and defining a communication approach
    C. It is the process of identifying all people or organizations impacted by the project, and documenting relevant information regarding their interests, involvement, and impact on project success
    D. It is the process of communicating and working with stakeholders to meet their needs and addressing issues as they occur

    Correct answer is C: Identify Stakeholder is the process of identifying people, groups or organizations, that can impact, or are influenced by your project and are then classified on the basis of their power, level of interests, and expected involvements.

You may now move on to Part Two: The Standard for Project Management

PART TWO: The Standard for Project Management

LEARNING OUTCOMES: THE STANDARD FOR PROJECT MANAGEMENT

Overview questions for Chapter 1-6 follow:

CHAPTER 1 INTRODUCTION (P 541)

1. What is a **Standard** (P 541)?
2. What is a **Project,** and its **Project Constraints** (P 542)?
3. What is **Project Success** and **Benefits Management** (P 546)?
4. What is the **Project Life Cycle** (P 547-548)?
5. What are **Project Stakeholders** (P 550)?
6. What is the role of the **Project Manager** (P 552)?
7. What are the **Project Management Knowledge Areas** (P 553)?
8. What are the five (5) **Project Management Process Groups** (P 554-555)?
   Fig. 1-5, P 555, *Example of Process Group Interactions within a Project or Phase*
   Table 1-1, P 556, *Project Management Process Group and Knowledge Area Mapping*
9. What are the two (2) **major categories** that can **favorably** or **unfavorably affect** the project (P 557)?
10. The Project Manager and the project management team can **select** and **adapt** their **approach** to the appropriate artifacts for use in the project. What is this called (P 558)?

CHAPTERS 2 INITIATING PROCESS GROUP (P 561)

11. What are the **Inputs and Outputs** of the **Initiating Process Group** (P 561-564)?

See the following pages for these sections in this manual:

- 2.1 Develop Project Charter (P 563)
- 2.2 Identify Stakeholders in the following pages (P 563)

CHAPTER 3 PLANNING PROCESS GROUP (P 565)

12. What are the **Inputs and Outputs** of the **Planning Process Group** (P 565-594)?

See the following pages for these sections:

CHAPTER 4 EXECUTING PROCESS GROUP (P 595)

13. What are the processes **Inputs and Outputs** of the **Executing Process Group** (P 595-611)?

See the following pages for these sections in this manual:

CHAPTER 5 MONITORING AND CONTROLLING PROCESS GROUP (P 613)

14. What are the processes **Inputs and Outputs** of the **Monitoring and Controlling Process Group** (P 613-632)?

See the following pages for these sections in this manual:

CHAPTER 6 CLOSING PROCESS GROUP

15. What are the **Inputs and Outputs** of **Close Project or Phase** (P 634)?

See the following pages for this section in this manual:

CHAPTER ONE INTRODUCTION

ANSWER

A **Standard** is a document used in Project Management considered to be good practice and are organized by process groups, which are then broken down into smaller segments. These segments consists of key project management concepts, and also covers information on project life cycles, project stakeholders and the role of the project Manager (PM). This **Standard** is the foundation and framework of *A Guide to Project Management Body of Knowledge* (*PMBOK®* Guide).

Section 1: Discusses key concepts and provides contextual information about project management.

Section 2 – 6: Provides definitions for each of the **five (5) process groups** and describes the processes within those process groups. These sections also describe the key benefits, inputs and outputs for each project management process.

1.1 Projects and Project Management

"A Project is a temporary endeavor undertaken to create a unique product, service or result" *A Guide to the Project Management Body of Knowledge, (PMBOK® Guide)* – Sixth Edition, Project Management Institute Inc., 2017 (P 4). Project constraints should be balanced.

Keep in mind, temporary can mean a very short, very long or any range in-between length of time. Any size project will most likely include the following (P542):

- Identifying project requirements
- Addressing the various needs, concerns and expectations of Stakeholders
- Establishing and m maintaining active communication with Stakeholders
- Managing resources
- **Balancing competing project constraints**
    - Scope
    - Schedule
    - Cost
    - Quality
    - Resources
    - Risk

1.2 Relationships among Portfolios, Programs and Projects

ANSWER

"A **Project** is a temporary endeavor undertaken to create a unique product, service or result" *A Guide to the Project Management Body of Knowledge, (PMBOK® Guide)* – Sixth Edition, Project Management Institute Inc., 2017 (P 4).

- Project Management is concerned with achieving certain scope objectives, and lastly, Organizational Project Management takes all the above processes and connects them with organizational enablers.

A **Portfolio** is a collection/gathering of project and operations, along with related documents. Portfolio Management is the process of managing programs, operations and sub-portfolios as a group.

- Portfolio Management is the process of deciding what programs or projects will be included in the portfolio, what order they will be completed and what resources are necessary to finish the project.

A **Program** is a subset of Portfolios, but may also contain work that is operational in nature. Program Management is concerned with the realization of special benefits by way of controlling projects and programs.

- Program Management is the management of all programs within the project, meaning one or multiple portfolios, with groupings by common outcomes or related associations, managed by the PM and supports the organizational strategies by authorizing, changing or terminating projects and managing interdependencies, which may involve the following (P 543):
  - Resolving resource constraints and/or conflicts affecting program components
  - Aligning with the organization's strategies affecting program goals and objectives
  - Managing issues and employing change management within a shared government structure
  - Addressing project and program risks that can impact one or more components
  - Managing program benefits realization by effectively analyzing, sequencing and monitoring component interdependencies

The management of a Program and the management of a Portfolio may draw from the same resource pool and may involve the same Stakeholders, which means there may be conflicts. This is the purpose for managing the relationships among them to obtain a satisfactory balance and a successful project outcome.

A Project may be managed in three different (3) scenarios shown below:

- Stand-Alone Project (outside a Program or Portfolio)
- Within a Program
- Within a Portfolio

Portfolios, Programs and Projects are all motivated by organizational strategies.

Fig. 1-1, P 544, *Example of Portfolio, Programs and Project Management Interface*

Organizational Project Management (OPM) utilizes Portfolios, Programs and Project Management.

1.3 Linking Organizational Governance and Project Governance

ANSWER

Organizational governance principles, decisions and processes may affect the governance of Portfolios, programs and Projects as shown below (P 545):

- The enforcement of legal, regulatory, standards and compliance requirements
- The definition of ethical, social and environmental responsibilities
- The specification of operational, legal and risk policies

Project Governance is the framework, functions and processes that guide Project Management activities and this governance includes:

- Guiding and overseeing the management of project work
- Ensuring adherence to policies, standards and guidelines
- Establishing governance roles, responsibilities and authorities
- Decision-making regarding risk escalations, changes and resources
- Ensuring appropriate stakeholder engagement
- Monitoring performance

Project Governance elements may include the following (P 545):

- Stage Gate or Phase Reviews
- Identifying, escalating and resolving risk issues
- Defining roles, responsibilities and authorities
- Process for project knowledge management and capturing lessons

learned
- Decision making, problem solving and escalating topics that are beyond the PM's authority
- Reviewing and approving changes to the project, and product changes that are beyond the PM's authority

1.4 Project Success and Benefits Management

ANSWER

Project success results in achieving project objectives that are aligned with organizational strategies. Projects are usually initiated because of the following (P 546):

- Market demand
- Strategic opportunity/business need
- Social need
- Environmental consideration
- Customer request
- Technological advancement
- Legal or regulatory requirement
- Existing or forecasted problem

A **Benefits Management** program may include the following:

- **Target Benefits**: The expected tangible and intangible business value to be gained by the implementation of the product, service or result
- **Strategic Alignment**: How the Project Benefits support and align with the business strategies of the organization
- **Timeframe for realizing Benefits**: Benefits by Phase: Short term, Long Term, Ongoing
- **Benefits Owner**: The accountable person or group that monitors, record and reports realized benefits throughout the timeframe established in the plan
- **Metrics**: The Direct and Indirect measurements used to show the benefits realized
- **Risks**: The Risks associated with achieving Target Benefits

1.5 The Project Life Cycle

ANSWER

The **Project Life Cycle** is a series of phases and a phase is a collection of related project activities. Phases can be sequential, iterative or overlapping and are time-bound with a start and end date.

The Life Cycle provides a framework for managing the project and although a project can vary greatly in size and complexity, most project can be mapped to the following Life Cycle structure (P 548):

- Starting the project
- Organizing and preparing
- Carrying out the work
- Closing the project

Fig. 1-2, P 548, *Generic Depiction of a Project Life Cycle.*

A Generic Life Cycle structure may display the following characteristics (P 549):

- Costs and staffing are low at the start and increase as the work is carried out and drop as the project comes to a close.
- Risk is greatest at the start as shown in Fig. 1-3, P 549, *Impact of Variables over Time.*
- The ability of stakeholders to influence the final characteristics of the project's product, without significantly affecting the cost and schedule is highest at the start and decreases as the project progresses. Once again, refer back to Fig. 1-3, P 549, *Impact of Variables over Time.*

1.6 Project Stakeholders

ANSWER

Project Stakeholder examples (P 550):

- Internal:
    - Sponsor
    - Resource Manager
    - Project Management Office (PMO)
    - Portfolio Steering Committee
    - Program Manager
    - Project Managers of other Projects
    - Team Members

- External:
    - Customers
    - End Users
    - Suppliers
    - Shareholders
    - Regulatory Bodies
    - Competitors

Fig. 1-4, P 551, *Examples of Project Stakeholders.*

The Stakeholder's involvement may change over time, the type of involvement and the level of involvement during the course of a project's life cycle.

1.7 Role of the Project Manager

ANSWER

The **Role of the Project Manager** is the person acting as the leader for the team and must have the particular skill sets shown below (P 552):

- Knowledge about Project Management, Business Environment and Technical Aspects
- Skills to lead the team, coordinate the needed work, collaborate with stakeholders, solve problems and make decisions
- Ability to develop and manage scope, schedule, budget, resources, risks, plans, presentations and reports
- Other attributes required to successfully manage the project, such as personality, attitude, ethics and leadership

Project Managers (PM's) must also have the following interpersonal skills:

- Leadership
- Team Building
- Motivating
- Communicating
- Influencing
- Decision-making
- Political and Cultural Awareness
- Negotiation
- Facilitating
- Managing Conflict
- Coaching

1.8 Project Management Knowledge Areas

ANSWER

Project Management Knowledge Areas are fields or areas of specialization and are a set of processes associated with particular topics and are employed on most projects, most of the time. Although there may be more knowledge areas, the most commonly used are the ten (10) areas shown below (P 553):

1. **Project Integration Management**: Identifies, defines, combines, unifies and coordinates the processes and Project management activities within the Project Management Process groups
2. **Project Scope Management**: Includes the processes required to ensure that the project includes all the work required, and only the work required
3. **Project Schedule Management**: Includes the processes required to manage the timely completion of a project
4. **Project Cost Management**: Includes the processes required in planning, estimating, budgeting, financing, funding, managing and controlling costs so that the project can be completed within the approved budget
5. **Project Quality Management**: Includes the processes for incorporating the organization's quality policy regarding planning, managing and controlling project and product quality requirements
6. **Project Resource Management**: Includes the processes used to identify, acquire and manage the resources the resources needed for the project's completion
7. **Project Communications Management**: Includes the processes required to ensure timely and appropriate planning, collection, distribution, storage, retrieval, management, control, monitoring and ultimate disposition of project information
8. **Project Risk Management**: Includes the processes of conducting risk management planning, identification, analysis, response planning, response implementation and monitoring risk on a project
9. **Project Procurement Management**: Includes the processes necessary to purchase or acquire products, services or results needed from outside the project team
10. **Project Stakeholder Management**: Includes the processes required to identify the people, groups, or organizations that could affect or be affected by the project, to analyze stakeholder expectations and their influence on the project and to develop appropriate management strategies for effectively engaging stakeholders in project decisions and executions

1.9 Project Management Process Groups

ANSWER

There are five (5) **Project Management Process Groups** shown below (P 554):

Table 1-4, P25, *Process Management Process Group and Knowledge Area Mapping*

- **Initiating Process Group**: The processes used to define a new project or a new phase of an existing project by obtaining authorization to start the project or new phase
- **Planning Process Group**: The processes required to establish the scope of the project, refine the objectives and define the course of action required to attain the objectives of the project
- **Executing Process Group**: The processes performed to complete the work defined in the Project Management Plan to satisfy the project objectives
- **Monitoring and Controlling Process Group**: The processes required to track, review and regulate the progress and performance of the project; identify any areas in which changes to the plan are required and initiate the corresponding changes
- **Closing Process Group**: The processes performed to formally complete or close a project, phase or contract

These five (5) Process Groups are independent of the application areas, or industry focus and the individual process in these groups are often iterated prior to the completion of a project or phase. These processes usually fall into one of three (3) categories shown below (P 554):

- Processes used once or at predefined points in the project
- Processes that are performed periodically
  Processes that are performed continuously throughout the project

The Output of one process most likely will become an Input to another process or a deliverable of the project or phase.

Fig. 1-5, P 555, *Example of Process Group Interactions within a Project or Phase*

A Process Group is <u>not</u> a Project Phase.

1.10 Enterprise Environmental Factors and Organizational Process Assets

ANSWER

Enterprise Environmental Factors and Organizational Process Assets are two (2) categories that can influence a project favorably/unfavorably. See below (P 557):

EEF's (Outside the environment): These factors are also outside of the enterprise. Conditions not under control of the project team impacts the project, enterprise, program or portfolio levels.

OPA's (Internal to the enterprise): These are within the enterprise, a program, portfolio, another project or combination of any or all. They may be plans, processes, policies, procedures and knowledge bases.

1.11 Tailoring the Project Artifacts

ANSWER

Tailoring the Project Artifacts: The term **Artifact** refers to Project Management processes, inputs, tools, techniques, outputs, EEF's and OPA's. The PM decides which Artifact to use and/or adapt for a specific project's use, also known as **Tailoring**. The most prevalent Artifact is the Project Management Plan. Part of the Tailoring process is deciding which components will be needed for a particular project and then selecting and adapting the tailoring approach. .

Other documents used will consist of **Business Documents**, depending on the project's needs and identified by the PM. Business Documents usually originate outside the project and are used as Inputs. Any EEF's and OPA's that may influence the project will depend on the project and project environment.

Table 1-2, P 559, *Project Management Plan and Project Documents*

This Table provides a list of Project Management Plan components and Project Documents, but it not comprehensive. It does however, list some of the possibilities used to manage a project.

2. INITIATING PROCESS GROUP

Initiating Process Group: Authorization must be obtained before starting a project or phase. The purpose is to make sure the Stakeholders expectations and the project's purpose are aligned with one another. At the start, the initial scope is defined and financial resources are committed. The PM is assigned, key Stakeholders are identified and all the information is put into the Stakeholder Register and the Project Charter. Once the project is authorized, the PM will apply organizational resources to project activities.

The **key benefit** is to align the project with the organization's strategic objectives and see to it they are authorized and the Business Case, Benefits and Stakeholders are considered from the start of the project's initiation. This Standard assumes the project has been approved by the sponsor or another governing agency (P 561).

Business Documents usually originate outside the project and are used as Inputs to the Project and may include the **Business Case** and **Benefits Management Plan.**

In order to keep a project aligned with the goals it was undertaken to address, the first phase or initiation (start) must be re-examined to determine if the previous information is still valid. All components of the project charter and business documents are reviewed and Stakeholder expectations of success are examined to increase success factors for everyone involved.

Fig. 2-2, P 562, *Initiating Process Group*

2.1 Develop Project Charter

In order to **Develop the Project Charter**, authorization must be obtained. This process will provide the PM the ability to apply organizational resources to any/all project activities. The **key benefit** is to provide a direct link between the objectives and the project, to create a formal record and shows a commitment to the project itself. This process is performed at predefined points during the life cycle of the project.

Fig. 2-3, P 563, *Develop Project Charter: Inputs and Outputs*

ANSWER: List of Inputs and Outputs Shown Below

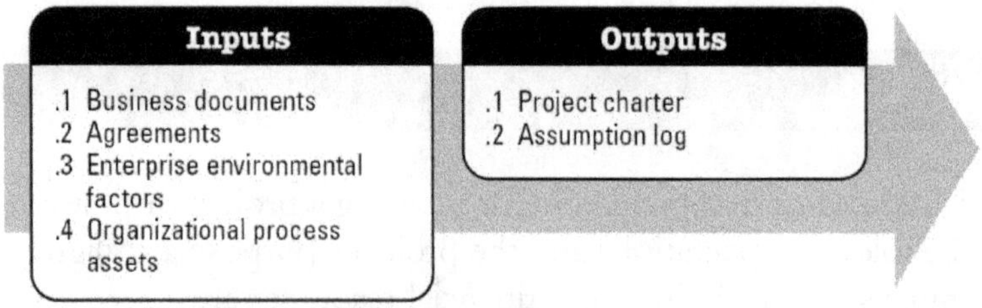

Figure 2-3 (Standard). Develop Project Charter: Inputs and Outputs

2.2 Identify Stakeholders

The process used to **Identify Stakeholders** means identifying new Stakeholders on a regular basis and then analyzing and documenting all relevant information. The **key benefit** is the focus on Stakeholder needs, appropriate engagement processes and communication methods, depending on the target audience.

Fig. 2-4, P 563, *Identify Stakeholders: Inputs and Outputs*

ANSWER: List of Inputs and Outputs Shown Below

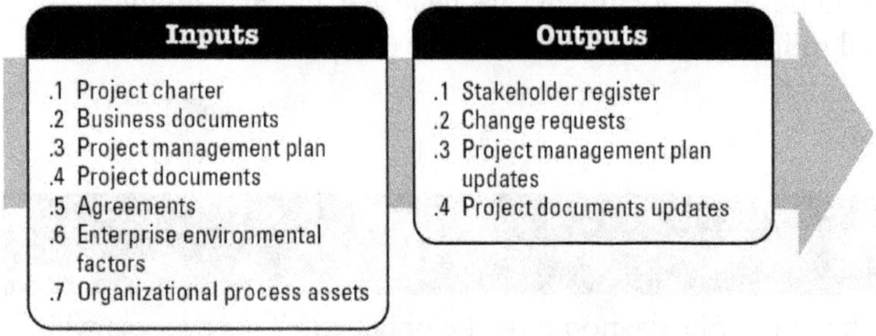

Figure 2-4 (Standard). Identify Stakeholders: Inputs and Outputs

2.2.1 Project Management Plan Components

Some **Project Management Plan Components** examples are shown below (P 564):

- Communications Management Plan
- Stakeholder Engagement Plan

2.2.2 Project Documents Examples

Some **Project Document Examples** are shown below (P 564):

- Change Log
- Issue Log
- Requirements Documentation

2.2.3 Project Management Plan Updates

Some **Project Management Plan Update** examples are shown below (P 564):

- Requirements Management Plan
- Communications Management Plan
- Risk Management Plan
- Stakeholder Engagement Plan

2.2.4 Project Documents Updates

Some **Project Documents Updates** examples are shown below (P 564):

- Assumption Log
- Issue Log
- Risk Register

3. PLANNING PROCESS GROUP

The **Planning Process Group** establishes the scope, defines the objectives, develops a course of action, develops the components of the Project Management Plan and any project documents that are used in the project. In this process, additional analysis may be used or changes are required, which necessitates the ongoing refinement of **Progressive Elaboration** (aka: Iterative activities). The **key benefit** of this process is the defining of the actions needed to carry out the objectives.

3.1 Develop Project Management Plan

Defining, preparing and coordinating the plan components are the outcome of the **Develop Project Management Plan** processes. The key benefit is a document that stipulates what will be performed and how it will be carried out.

Fig. 3-2, P 567, *Develop Project Management Plan: Inputs and Outputs*

ANSWER: List of Inputs and Outputs Shown Below

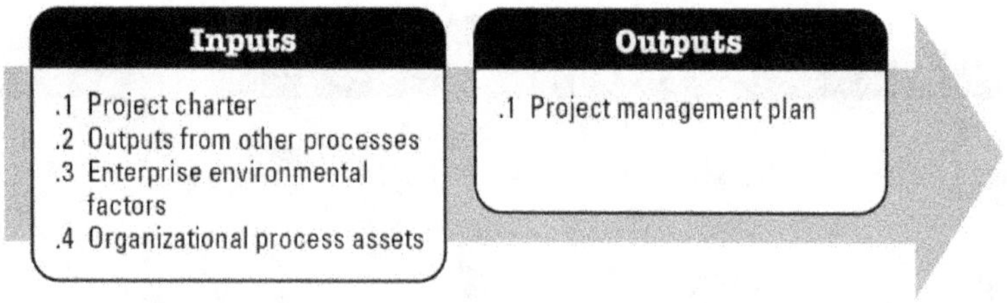

Inputs
.1 Project charter
.2 Outputs from other processes
.3 Enterprise environmental factors
.4 Organizational process assets
Outputs
.1 Project management plan

Figure 3-2 (Standard). Develop Project Management Plan: Inputs and Outputs

3.2 Plan Scope Management

How the project is defined, controlled and validated is the outcome of **Plan Scope Management**. The key benefit is to provide guidance and direction on how the scope is managed.

Fig. 3-3, P 567, *Plan Scope Management: Inputs and Outputs*

ANSWER: List of Inputs and Outputs Shown Below

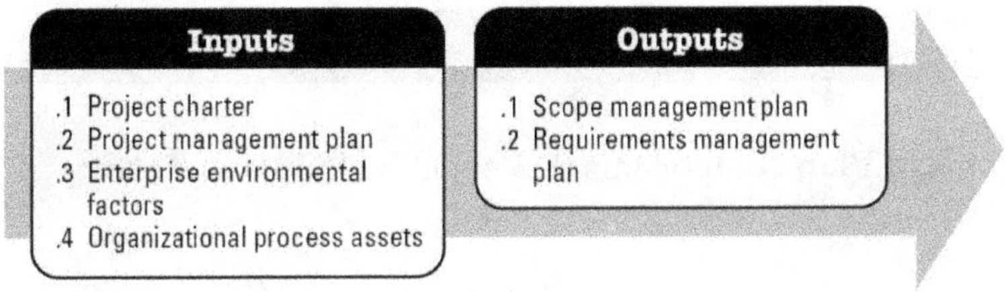

Figure 3-3 (Standard). Plan Scope Management: Inputs and Outputs

3.2.1 Project Management Plan Components

Some examples of **Project Management Plan** components for Plan Scope Management are (P 568):

- Quality Management Plan
- Project Life Cycle Description
- Development Approach

3.3 Collect Requirements

Determining, documenting and managing stakeholder needs and requirements is the outcome of **Collect Requirements**. The key benefit of this process is that is clarifies the project scope and product scope.

Fig. 3-4, P 568, *Collect Requirements: Inputs and Outputs*

ANSWER: List of Inputs and Outputs Shown Below

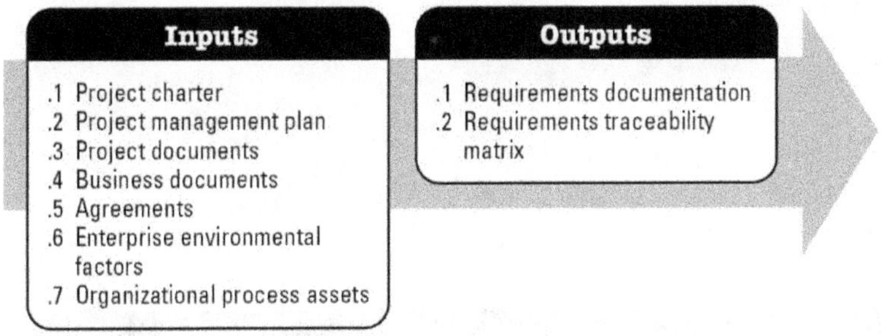

Figure 3-4 (Standard). Collect Requirements: Inputs and Outputs

3.3.1 Project Management Plan Components

Some examples of **Project Management Plan** components that could be Inputs to Collect Requirements are (P 568):

- Scope Management Plan
- Requirements Management Plan
- Stakeholder Engagement Plan

3.3.2 Project Documents Examples

Some examples of **Project Documents** are (P 569):

- Assumption Log
- Lessons Learned Register
- Stakeholder Register

3.4 Define Scope

Define Scope is means to develop the project and product in great detail and they key benefit is that this process will set the boundaries and acceptance criteria limits.

Fig. 3-5, P 569, *Define Scope: Inputs and Outputs*

ANSWER: List of Inputs and Outputs Shown Below

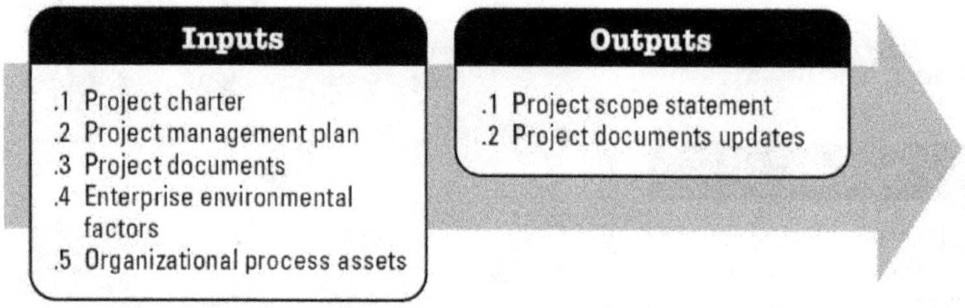

Figure 3-5 (Standard). Define Scope: Inputs and Outputs

3.4.1 Project Management Plan Components

One example of a **Project Management Plan Component** that could be an Input for this process is the Scope Management Plan.

3.4.2 Project Documents Examples

Some examples of **Project Documents** are (P 569):

- Assumption Log
- Requirements Documentation
- Risk Register

3.4.3 Project Documents Updates

Some examples of **Project Documents** that may be **updated** are (P 570):

- Assumption Log
- Requirements Documentation
- Requirements Traceability Matrix
- Stakeholder Register

3.5 Create WBS

In order to **Create** the **WBS** (Work Breakdown Structure), the dismantling of project deliverables and project work into smaller components, it will become easier to perform the objectives. The key benefit of this process is that it provides a framework for the deliverables and will be performed at predefined points when carrying out the project work.

Fig. 3-6, P 570, *Create WBS: Inputs and Outputs*

ANSWER: List of Inputs and Outputs Shown Below

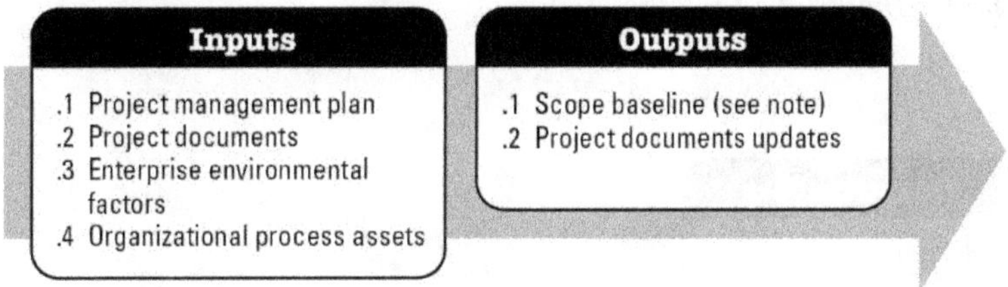

Note: The scope baseline is the approved version of a scope statement, WBS, and its associated WBS dictionary.

Figure 3-6 (Standard). Create WBS: Inputs and Outputs

3.5.1 Project Management Plan Components

One example of a **Project Management Plan Component** that could be an Input for this process is the Scope Management Plan.

3.5.2 Project Documents Examples

Some examples of **Project Documents** that might be Inputs for this process are (P 571):

- Project Scope Statement
- Requirements Documentation

3.5.3 Project Documents Updates

Some examples of **Project Documents** that may be **updated** are (P 570):

- Assumption Log
- Requirements Documentation

3.6 Plan Schedule Management

Plan Schedule Management is the establishment of policies, procedures and documentation for planning, developing, managing, executing and controlling the project schedule. The key benefit is to provide information on how the project will be managed and this process will be performed at set points during the course of the project life cycle.

Fig. 3-7, P 571, *Plan Schedule Management: Inputs and Outputs*

ANSWER: List of Inputs and Outputs Shown Below

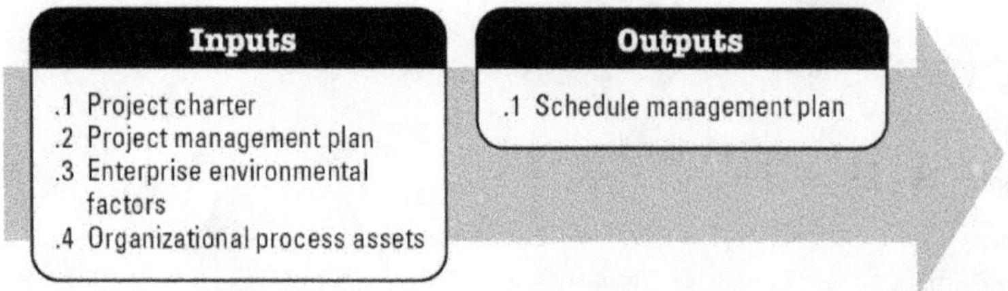

Figure 3-7 (Standard). Plan Schedule Management: Inputs and Outputs

3.6.1 Project Management Plan Components

Some examples of **Project Management Plan Components** that might be Inputs for this process are (P 572):

- Scope Management Plan
- Development Approach

3.7 Define Activities

Define Activities is the process of identifying and documenting particular actions needed to produce project deliverables. The key benefit is that the actions decompose into work packages into schedule activities. In this way, a basis can be provided to estimate, schedule, execute, monitor and control the project work and is performed for the duration of the project.

Fig. 3-8, P 572, *Define Activities: Inputs and Outputs*

ANSWER: List of Inputs and Outputs Shown on next page

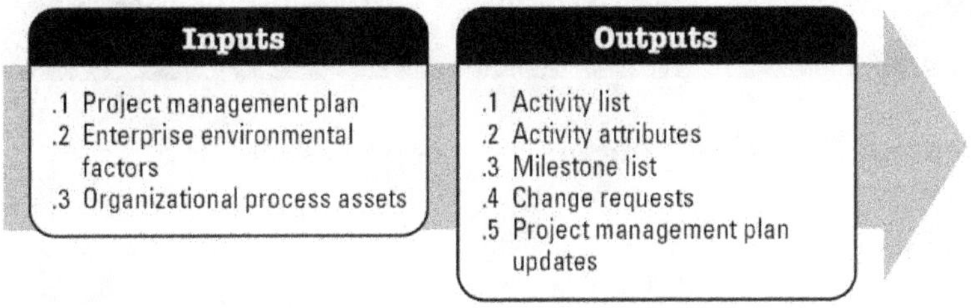

Figure 3-8 (Standard). Define Activities: Inputs and Out

A Guide to the Project Management Body of Knowledge (PMBOK® Guide) – Sixth Edition.

3.7.1 Project Management Plan Components

Some examples of **Project Management Plan Components** that might be Inputs for this process are (P 572):

- Schedule Management Plan
- Scope Baseline

3.7.2 Project Management Plan Updates

Some examples of **Project Management Plan Updates** that might be updated as a result of this process are (P 572):

- Schedule Baseline
- Cost Baseline

Sequence Activities is the process of identifying and documenting the relationships among project activities. The key benefit is that the logical sequence of work is determined and this process is ongoing throughout the project.

Fig. 3-9, P 573, *Sequence Activities: Inputs and Outputs*

ANSWER: List of Inputs and Outputs Shown Below

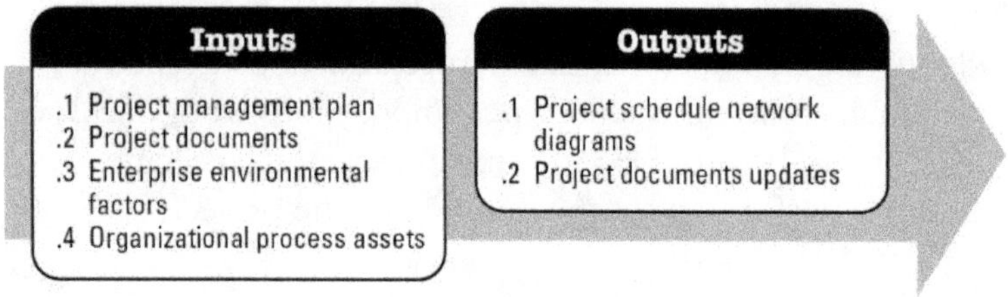

Figure 3-9 (Standard). Sequence Activities: Inputs and Outputs

A Guide to the Project Management Body of Knowledge (PMBOK® Guide) – Sixth Edition.

3.8.1 Project Management Plan Components

Some examples of **Project Management Plan Components** for this process are (P 573):

- Schedule Management Plan
- Scope Baseline

3.8.2 Project Documents Examples

Some **Project Documents Examples** are (P 573):

- Activity Attributes
- Activity List
- Assumption Log
- Milestone List

3.8.3 Project Documents Updates

Some **Project Documents Updates e**xamples as a result of this process are (P 573):

- Activity Attributes
- Activity List
- Assumption Log
- Milestone List

3.9 Estimate Activity Durations

Estimate Activity Durations is the process of determining the work periods needed and comparing them to the estimated resources available. The key benefit is providing an estimated time schedule to complete each activity.

Fig. 3-10, P 574, *Estimate Activity Durations: Inputs and Outputs*

ANSWER: List of Inputs and Outputs Shown Below

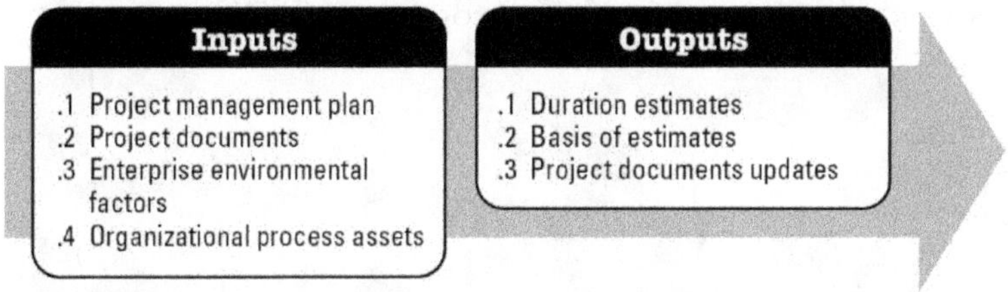
Inputs
.1 Project management plan
.2 Project documents
.3 Enterprise environmental factors
.4 Organizational process assets
Outputs
.1 Duration estimates
.2 Basis of estimates
.3 Project documents updates

Figure 3-10 (Standard). Estimate Activity Durations: Inputs and Outputs

3.9.1 Project Management Plan Components

Some examples of **Project Management Plan Components** are (P 574):

- Schedule Management Plan
- Scope Baseline

3.9.2 Project Documents Examples

Some **Project Documents Examples** that may be Inputs to this process are (P 574):

- Activity Attributes
- Activity List
- Assumption Log
- Lessons Learned
- Milestone List
- Project Team Assignments
- Resource Breakdown Structure
- Resource Calendars
- Resource Requirements
- Risk Register

3.9.3 Project Documents Updates

Some **Project Documents Updates e**xamples as a result of this process are (P 575):

- Activity Attributes
- Assumption Log
- Lessons Learned

3.10 Develop Schedule

Develop Schedule is the process of determining activity resource requirements, activity durations, activity sequences and the ability to produce a schedule model. The key benefit is providing a schedule plan with start and end dates for the completion of project activities.

Fig. 3-11, P 575, *Develop Schedule: Inputs and Outputs*

ANSWER: List of Inputs and Outputs Shown on next page

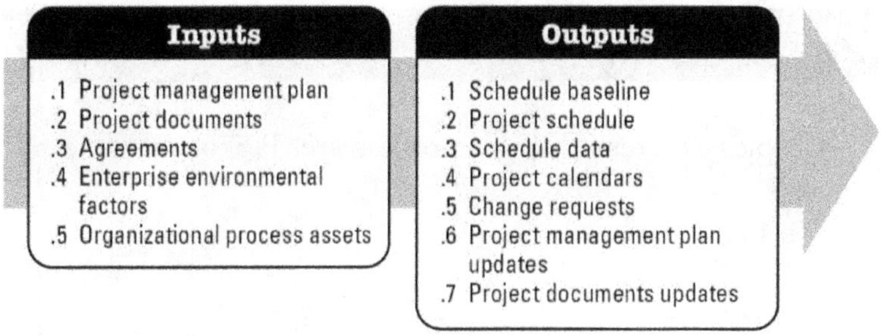

Inputs
.1 Project management plan
.2 Project documents
.3 Agreements
.4 Enterprise environmental factors
.5 Organizational process assets
Outputs
.1 Schedule baseline
.2 Project schedule
.3 Schedule data
.4 Project calendars
.5 Change requests
.6 Project management plan updates
.7 Project documents updates

Figure 3-11 (Standard). Develop Schedule: Inputs and Outputs

A Guide to the Project Management Body of Knowledge (PMBOK®Guide) – Sixth Edition.

3.10.1 Project Management Plan Components

Some examples of **Project Management Plan Components** are (P 575):

- Schedule Management Plan
- Scope Baseline

3.10.2 Project Documents Examples

Some **Project Documents Examples** that may be Inputs to this process are (P 576):

- Activity Attributes
- Activity List
- Assumption Log
- Basis of Estimates
- Duration Estimates
- Lessons Learned
- Milestone List
- Project Schedule Network Diagram
- Project Team Assignments
- Resource Calendars
- Resource Requirements
- Risk Register

3.10.3 Project Management Plan Updates

Some **Project Documents Update e**xamples as a result of this process are (P 576):

- Schedule Management Plan
- Cost Baseline

3.10.4 Project Documents Updates

Some **Project Documents Update e**xamples as a result of this process are (P 576):

- Activity Attributes
- Assumption Log
- Duration Estimates
- Lessons Learned
- Resource Requirements
- Risk Register

3.11 Plan Cost Management

Plan Cost Management is the process of determining how the costs will be calculated, budgeted for and managed, monitored and controlled. The key benefit is providing guidance and direction on the management of costs associated with the project.

Fig. 3-12, P 577, *Plan Cost Management: Inputs and Outputs*

ANSWER: List of Inputs and Outputs Shown Below

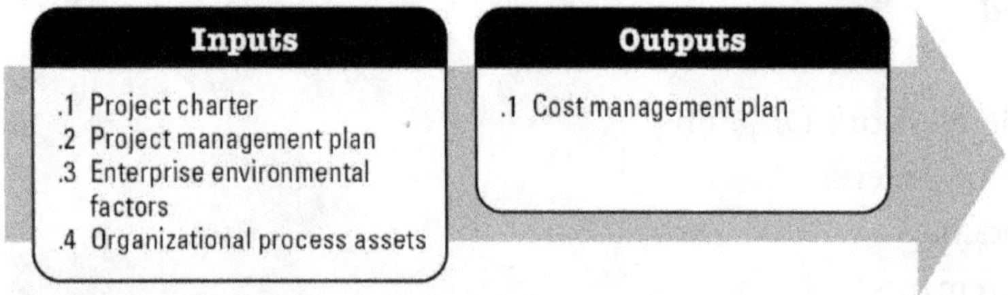

Figure 3-12 (Standard). Plan Cost Management: Inputs and Outputs

3.11.1 Project Management Plan Components

Some examples of **Project Management Plan Components** may be (P 575):

- Schedule Management Plan
- Risk Management Plan

3.12 Estimate Costs

Estimate Costs is the process of approximating the money needed to complete the project. The key benefit is to provide the monies associated for completion of the project.

Fig. 3-13, P 577, *Estimate Costs: Inputs and Outputs*

ANSWER: List of Inputs and Outputs Shown Below

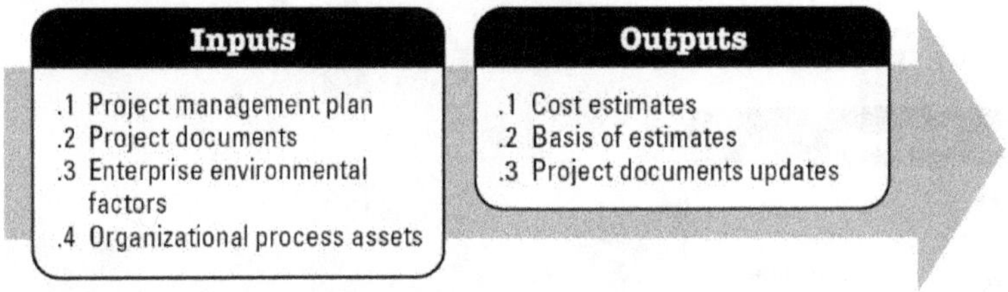
Inputs
.1 Project management plan
.2 Project documents
.3 Enterprise environmental factors
.4 Organizational process assets
Outputs
.1 Cost estimates
.2 Basis of estimates
.3 Project documents updates

Figure 3-13 (Standard). Estimate Costs: Inputs and Outputs

3.12.1 Project Management Plan Components

Some examples of **Project Management Plan Components** are (P 578):

- Cost Management Plan
- Quality Management Plan
- Scope Baseline

3.12.2 Project Documents Examples

Some **Project Documents Update e**xamples as a result of this process are (P 578):

- Assumption Log
- Lessons Learned
- Risk Register

3.12.3 Project Documents Updates

Some **Project Documents Update e**xamples as a result of this process are (P 578):

- Assumption Log
- Lessons Learned
- Risk Register

3.13 Determine Budget

Determine Budget is the process of establishing an authorized cost baseline by aggregating estimated costs of work packages and individual work activities. The key benefit is providing a cost baseline.

Fig. 3-14, P 579, *Determine Budget: Inputs and Outputs*

ANSWER: List of Inputs and Outputs Shown Below

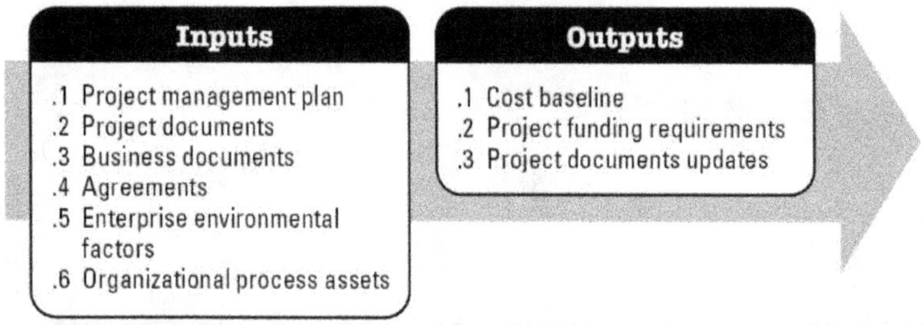

Figure 3-14 (Standard). Determine Budget: Inputs and Outputs

3.13.1 Project Management Plan Components

Some examples of **Project Management Plan Components** are (P 579):

- Cost Management Plan
- Resource Management Plan
- Scope Baseline

3.13.2 Project Documents Examples

Some **Project Documents Examples** that could be Inputs to this process are (P 579):

- Basis of Estimates
- Costs Estimates
- Project Schedule
- Risk Register

3.13.3 Project Documents Updates

Some **Project Documents Update e**xamples as a result of this process are (P 579):

- Cost Estimates
- Project Schedule
- Risk Register

3.14 Plan Quality Management

Plan Quality Management is the process of establishing quality requirements and standards, and how the organization will comply with those requirements and standards. The key benefit is providing guidance and direction on how quality will be managed.

Fig. 3-15, P 580, *Plan Quality Management: Inputs and Outputs*

ANSWER: List of Inputs and Outputs Shown Below

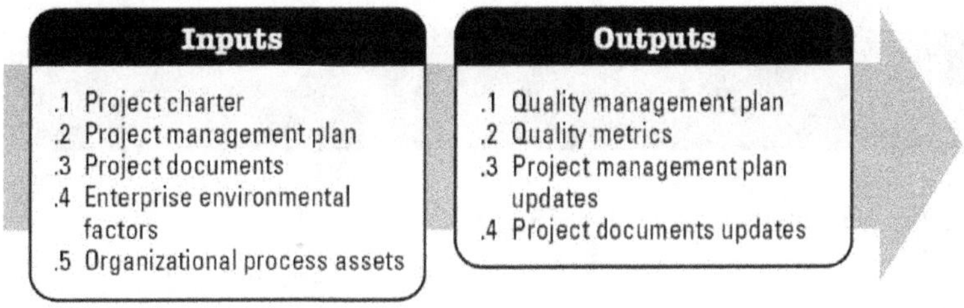

Figure 3-15 (Standard). Plan Quality Management: Inputs and Outputs

3.14.1 Project Management Plan Components

Some examples of **Project Management Plan Components** are (P 580):

- Requirements Management Plan
- Risk Management Plan
- Stakeholder Engagement Plan
- Scope Baseline

3.14.2 Project Documents Examples

Some **Project Documents Update e**xamples as a result of this process are (P 580):

- Assumption Log
- Requirements Documentation
- Requirements Traceability Matrix
- Risk Register
- Stakeholder Register

3.14.3 Project Management Plan Updates

Some examples of **Project Management Plan Updates** are (P 581):

- Risk Management Plan
- Scope Baseline

3.14.4 Project Documents Updates

Some **Project Documents Update** examples as a result of this process are (P 581):

- Lessons Learned Register
- Requirements Traceability Matrix
- Risk Register
- Stakeholder Register

3.15 Plan Resource Management

Plan Resource Management is the process of estimating, acquiring, managing and using team and physical resources. The key benefit is providing the type of approach and management levels needed to manage specific resources.

Fig. 3-16, P 581, *Plan Resource Management: Inputs and Outputs*

ANSWER: List of Inputs and Outputs Shown Below

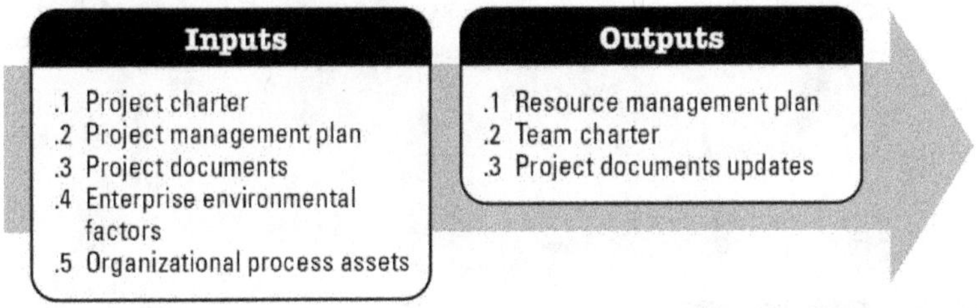

Figure 3-16 (Standard). Plan Resource Management: Inputs and Outputs

3.15.1 Project Management Plan Components

Some examples of **Project Management Plan Components** are (P 582):

- Quality Management Plan
- Scope Baseline

3.15.2 Project Documents

Some **Project Documents** examples as a result of this process are (P 582):

- Project Schedule
- Requirements Documentation
- Risk Register
- Stakeholder Register

3.15.3 Project Documents Updates

Some of the possible **Project Documents Updates** that could be Inputs to this process are (P 582):

- Assumption Log
- Risk Register

3.16 Estimate Activity Resources

Estimate Activity Resources is the process of estimating the necessary team resources. The key benefit is to identify the type, quantity and characteristics of those resources.

Fig. 3-17, P 583, *Estimate Activity Resources: Inputs and Outputs*

ANSWER: List of Inputs and Outputs Shown Below

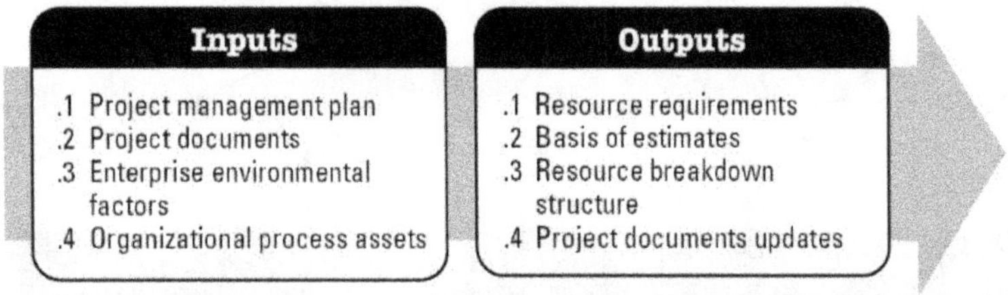

Figure 3-17 (Standard). Estimate Activity Resources: Inputs and Outputs

3.16.1 Project Management Plan Components

Some examples of **Project Management Plan Components** are (P 583):

- Resource Management Plan
- Scope Baseline

3.16.2 Project Documents Examples

Some **Project Documents Examples** that could be Inputs to this process are (P 583):

- Activity Attributes
- Activity List
- Assumption Log
- Cost Estimates
- Resource Calendar
- Risk Register

3.16.3 Project Documents Updates

Some of the possible **Project Documents Updates** that could be Inputs to this process are (P 583):

- Activity Attributes
- Assumption Log
- Lessons Learned

3.17 Plan Communications Management

Plan Communications Management is the process of establishing the correct approach to the target audience. The key benefit is to provide a documented approach to engage stakeholders by presenting the appropriate information in a specified timeframe. This process is performed throughout the project to keep the stakeholders up-to-date on all aspects of the project at all times.
Fig. 3-18, P 584, *Plan Communications Management: Inputs and Outputs*

ANSWER: List of Inputs and Outputs Shown Below

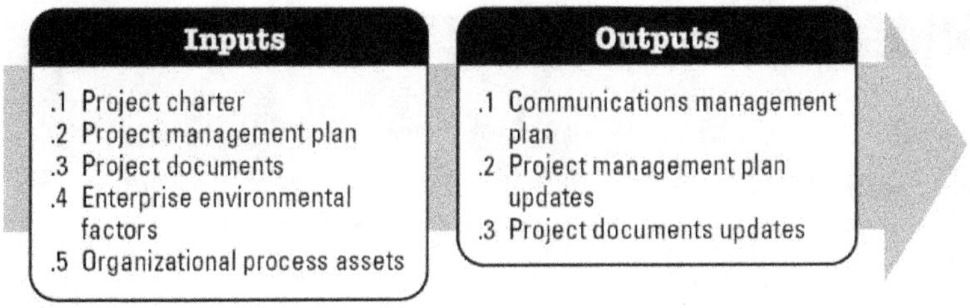
Inputs
.1 Project charter
.2 Project management plan
.3 Project documents
.4 Enterprise environmental factors
.5 Organizational process assets
Outputs
.1 Communications management plan
.2 Project management plan updates
.3 Project documents updates

Figure 3-18 (Standard). Plan Communications Management: Inputs and Outputs

A Guide to the Project Management Body of Knowledge (PMBOK® Guide) – Sixth Edition.

3.17.1 Project Management Plan Components

Some examples of **Project Management Plan Components** are (P 584):

- Resource Management Plan
- Stakeholder Engagement Plan

3.17.2 Project Documents Examples

Some **Project Documents Examples** that could be Inputs to this process are (P 584):

- Requirements Documentation
- Stakeholder Register

3.17.3 Project Management Plan Updates

One example of **Project Management Plan Updates** as a result of this process is the Stakeholder Engagement Plan (P 584).

3.17.4 Project Documents Updates

Some of the possible **Project Documents Updates** that could be Inputs to this process are (P 585):

- Project Schedule
- Stakeholder Register

3.18 Plan Risk Management

Plan Risk Management is the process of conducting risk management activities for the project. The key benefit is to provide a documented approach to ensure the type, degree and visibility of risk management activities are appropriate to the risks of the project.

Fig. 3-19, P 585, *Plan Risk Management: Inputs and Outputs*

ANSWER: List of Inputs and Outputs Shown Below

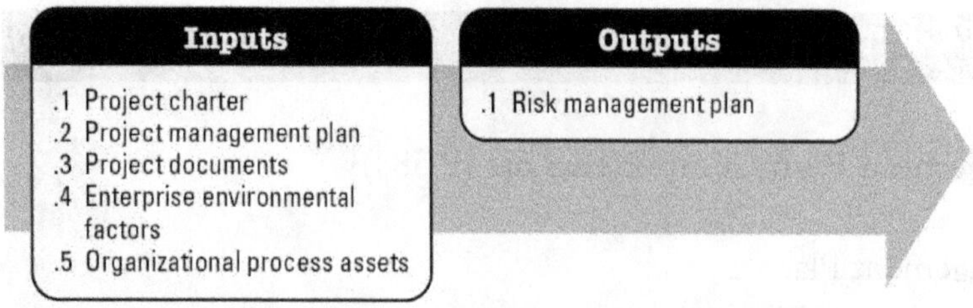

Figure 3-19 (Standard). Plan Risk Management: Inputs and Outputs

3.18.1 Project Management Plan Components

When planning Risk Management, all **Project Management Plan Components** need to be considered (P 585).

3.18.2 Project Documents Examples

One **Project Documents Example** that can be considered an Input to this process is the Stakeholder Register (P 585).

3.19 Identify Risks

Identify Risks is the process of conducting risk assessment for all sources of individual as well as overall risks. The key benefit is to provide a documented approach for all risks and their sources so that appropriate actions can be taken and is performed throughout the project.

Fig. 3-20, P 586, *Identify Risks: Inputs and Outputs*

ANSWER: List of Inputs and Outputs Shown Below

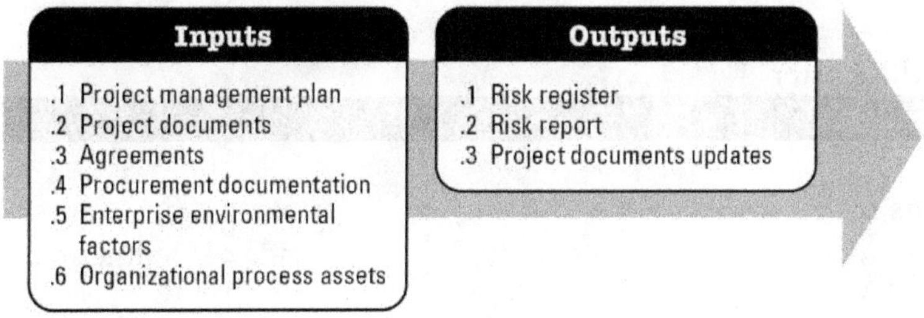

Inputs
.1 Project management plan
.2 Project documents
.3 Agreements
.4 Procurement documentation
.5 Enterprise environmental factors
.6 Organizational process assets
Outputs
.1 Risk register
.2 Risk report
.3 Project documents updates

Figure 3-20 (Standard). Identify Risks: Inputs and Outputs

3.19.1 Project Management Plan Components

Some examples of **Project Management Plan Components** are (P 586):

- Requirements Management Plan
- Schedule Management Plan
- Cost Management Plan
- Quality Management Plan
- Resource Management Plan
- Risk Management Plan
- Scope Baseline
- Schedule Baseline
- Cost Baseline

3.19.2 Project Documents Examples

Some **Project Documents Examples** that could be Inputs to this process are (P 587):

- Assumption Log
- Cost Estimates
- Duration Estimates
- Issue Log
- Lessons Learned Register
- Requirements Documentation
- Resource Requirements
- Stakeholder Register

3.19.3 Project Documents Updates

Some of the possible **Project Documents Updates** that could be Inputs to this process are (P 587):

- Assumption Log
- Issue Log
- Lessons Learned Register

3.20 Perform Qualitative Risk Analysis

Perform Qualitative Risk Analysis is the process of conducting and prioritizing a risk analysis of all risks and the probability of their occurrence. The key benefit is to provide a documented and focused approach for all high priority risks.

Fig. 3-21, P 588, *Perform Qualitative Risk Analysis: Inputs and Outputs*

ANSWER: List of Inputs and Outputs Shown Below

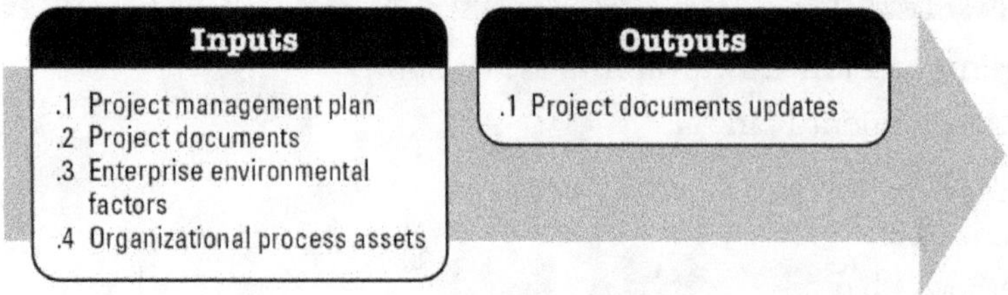

Figure 3-21 (Standard). Perform Qualitative Risk Analysis: Inputs and Outputs

A Guide to the Project Management Body of Knowledge (PMBOK®Guide) – Sixth Edition.

3.20.1 Project Management Plan Components

One of the possible **Project Management Plan Components** that may be an Input to this process is the Risk Management Plan (P 588).

3.20.2 Project Documents Examples

Some **Project Documents Examples** that could be Inputs to this process are (P 588):

- Assumption Log
- Risk Register
- Stakeholder Register

3.20.3 Project Documents Updates

Some of the possible **Project Documents Updates** that could be Inputs to this process are (P 589):

- Assumption Log
- Issue Log
- Risk Register
- Risk Report

3.2.1 Perform Quantitative Risk Analysis

Perform Quantitative Risk Analysis is numerically analyzing the effect of project risks. The key benefit is to quantify overall risk exposure and information so that risks can be effectively documented and a focused approach taken for all risks. S

Fig. 3-22, P 589, *Perform Quantitative Risk Analysis: Inputs and Outputs*

ANSWER: List of Inputs and Outputs Shown Below

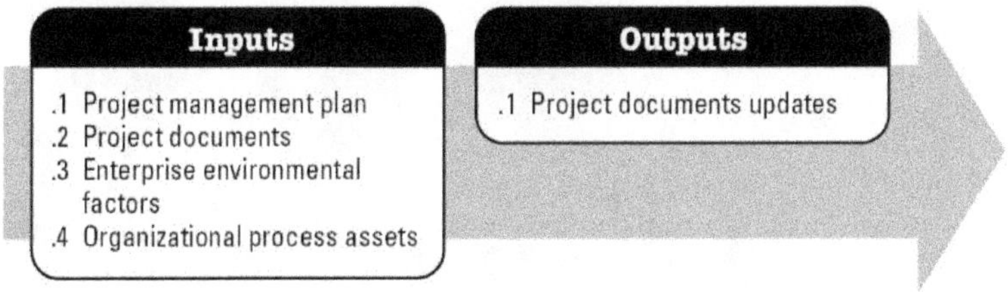

Figure 3-22 (Standard). Perform Quantitative Risk Analysis: Inputs and Outputs

3.21.1 Project Management Plan Components

Some examples of **Project Management Plan Components** are (P 589):

- Risk Management Plan
- Scope Baseline
- Schedule Baseline
- Cost Baseline

3.21.2 Project Documents Examples

Some **Project Documents Examples** that could be Inputs to this process are (P 590):

- Assumption Log
- Basis of Estimate
- Cost Estimate
- Cost Forecast
- Duration Estimates
- Milestone List
- Resource Requirements
- Risk Register
- Risk Report
- Schedule Forecasts

3.21.3 Project Documents Updates

One of the possible **Project Documents Updates** as a result of this process is the Risk Report (P 590).

3.22 Plan Risk Responses

Plan Risk Responses is developing options, selecting strategies and agreeing on actions to address overall as well as individual project risks. The key benefit is to identify the means to address overall and individual project risks.

Fig. 3-23, P 590, *Plan Risk Responses: Inputs and Outputs*

ANSWER: List of Inputs and Outputs Shown Below

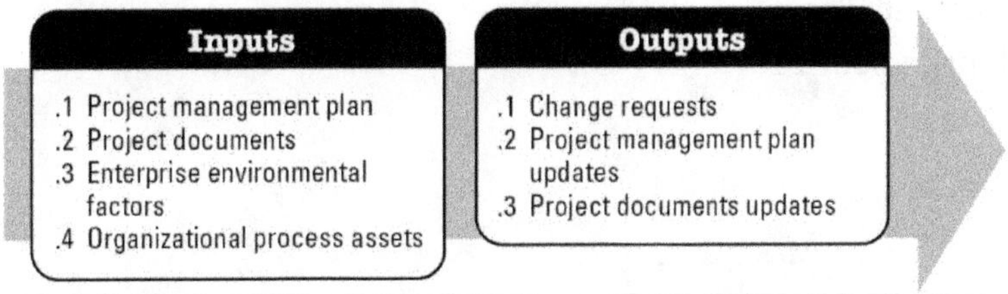

Inputs
.1 Project management plan
.2 Project documents
.3 Enterprise environmental factors
.4 Organizational process assets
Outputs
.1 Change requests
.2 Project management plan updates
.3 Project documents updates

Figure 3-23 (Standard). Plan Risk Responses: Inputs and Outputs

3.22.1 Project Management Plan Components

Some examples of **Project Management Plan Components** are (P 591):

- Resource Management Plan
- Risk Management Plan
- Cost Baseline

3.22.2 Project Documents Examples

Some **Project Documents Examples** that could be Inputs to this process are (P 591):

- Lessons Learned Register
- Project Schedule
- Project Team Assignments
- Resource Calendars
- Risk Register
- Risk Report
- Stakeholder Register

3.22.3 Project Management Plan Updates

Some of the possible **Project Management Plan Updates** as a result of this process are (P 591):

- Schedule Management Plan
- Cost Management Plan
- Quality Management Plan
- Resource Management Plan
- Procurement Management Plan
- Scope Baseline
- Schedule Baseline
- Cost Baseline

3.22.4 Project Documents Updates

Some of the possible **Project Documents Updates** that could be Inputs to this process are (P 592):

- Assumption Log
- Cost Forecasts
- Lessons Learned Register
- Project Schedule
- Project Team Assignments
- Risk Register
- Risk Report

3.23 Plan Procurement Management

Plan Procurement Management is the documentation of decisions and specifying the approach and the identification of sellers. The key benefit is to identify whether or not to procure services or goods from outside sources.

Fig. 3-24, P 592, *Plan Procurement Management: Inputs and Outputs*

ANSWER: List of Inputs and Outputs Shown on next page

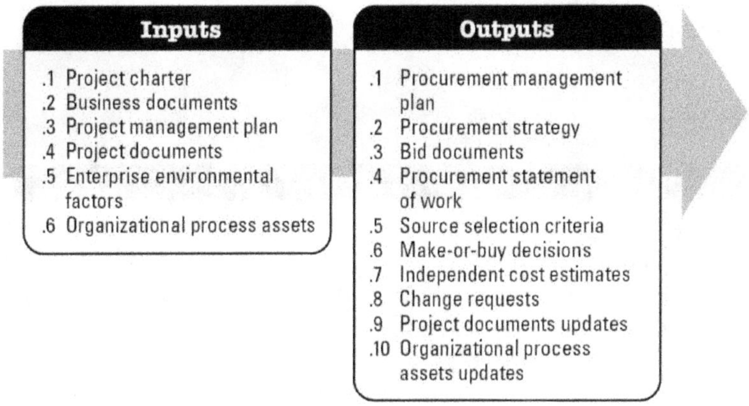

Inputs
.1 Project charter
.2 Business documents
.3 Project management plan
.4 Project documents
.5 Enterprise environmental factors
.6 Organizational process assets
Outputs
.1 Procurement management plan
.2 Procurement strategy
.3 Bid documents
.4 Procurement statement of work
.5 Source selection criteria
.6 Make-or-buy decisions
.7 Independent cost estimates
.8 Change requests
.9 Project documents updates
.10 Organizational process assets updates

Figure 3-24 (Standard). Plan Procurement Management: Inputs and Outputs

Some examples of **Project Management Plan Components** are (P 593):

- Scope Management Plan
- Quality Management Plan
- Resource Management Plan
- Scope Baseline

3.23.2 Project Documents Examples

Some **Project Documents Examples** that could be Inputs to this process are (P 593):

- Milestone List
- Project Team Assignments
- Requirements Documentation
- Requirements Traceability Matrix
- Resource Requirements
- Risk Register
- Stakeholder Register

3.23.3 Project Documents Updates

Some of the possible **Project Documents Updates** that could be Inputs to this process are (P 593):

- Lessons Learned Register
- Milestone List
- Requirements Documentation

- Requirements Traceability Matrix
- Risk Register
- Stakeholder Register

3.24 Plan Stakeholder Engagement

Plan Stakeholder Engagement is developing the approaches to engaging stakeholders in the project, depending on their needs, expectations and their potential impact on the project. The key benefit is provide a plan to engage stakeholders effectively.

Fig. 3-25, P 594, *Plan Stakeholder Engagement: Inputs and Outputs*

ANSWER: List of Inputs and Outputs Shown Below

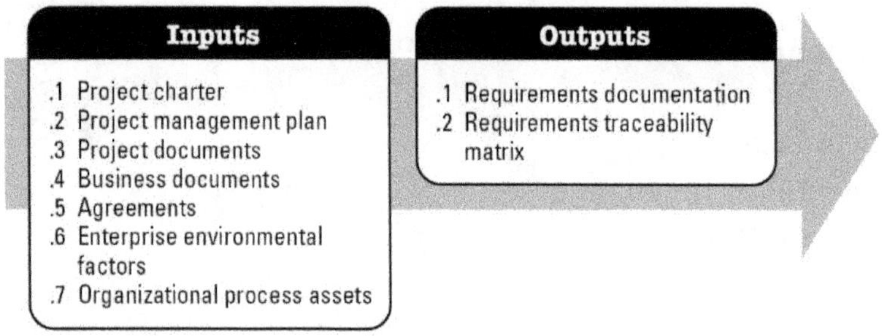

Figure 3-4 (Standard). Collect Requirements: Inputs and Outputs

A Guide to the Project Management Body of Knowledge (PMBOK® Guide) – Sixth Edition.

3.24.1 Project Management Plan Components

Some examples of **Project Management Plan Components** are (P 594):

- Resource Management Plan
- Communications Management Plan
- Risk Management Plan

3.24.2 Project Documents Examples

Some of the possible **Project Documents Updates** that could be Inputs to this process are (P 594):

- Assumption Log
- Change Log
- Issue Log
- Project Schedule
- Risk Register
- Stakeholder Register

4. EXECUTING PROCESS GROUP

The **Executing Process Group** indicates the tasks needed to perform the work, as outlined in the Project Management Plan. It includes managing the stakeholders, project team, scope, cost, risks, quality, time and other knowledge areas etc. The key benefit is knowing the work needed will be performed according to the Project Management Plan. This process may generate Change Requests and if approved, may also result in a modified Project Management Plan, Project Documents and new baselines. See Fig. 4-1, p 596, *Executing Process Group.*

4.1 Direct and Manage Project Work

Direct and Manage Project Work is the process of leading and defining the project work an implementing any required changes. The key benefit is to provide overall management for the project work and deliverables.

Fig.4-2, P 597, *Direct and Manage Project Work: Inputs and Outputs*

ANSWER: List of Inputs and Outputs Shown Below

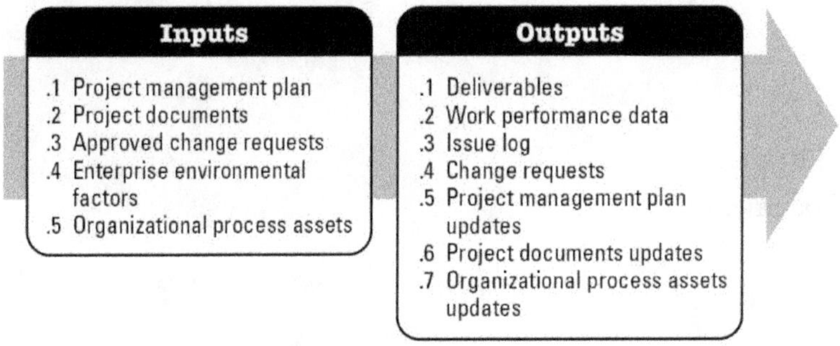

Inputs
.1 Project management plan
.2 Project documents
.3 Approved change requests
.4 Enterprise environmental factors
.5 Organizational process assets
Outputs
.1 Deliverables
.2 Work performance data
.3 Issue log
.4 Change requests
.5 Project management plan updates
.6 Project documents updates
.7 Organizational process assets updates

Figure 4-2 (Standard). Direct and Manage Project Work: Inputs and Outputs

4.1.1 Project Management Plan Components

Any component in the Project Management Plan can be considered as an Input for the **Project Documents Updates** in this process (P 597).

4.1.2 Project Documents Examples

Some of the possible **Project Documents Updates** that could be Inputs to this process are (P 597):

- Change Log
- Lessons Learned Register
- Milestone List
- Project Communications
- Project Schedule
- Requirements Traceability Matrix
- Risk Register
- Risk Report

4.1.3 Project Management Plan Updates

Any component in the **Project Management Plan** can be **updated** as a result for this process (P 598).

4.1.4 Project Documents Updates

Some of the possible **Project Documents Updates** that could be Inputs to this process are (P 598):

- Activity List
- Assumption Log
- Lessons Learned Register
- Requirements Documentation
- Risk Register
- Stakeholder Register

4.2 Manage Project Knowledge

Manage Project Knowledge is the process of using current knowledge, while adding to that knowledge to improve the efficiency of organizational learning. The key benefit is by using existing knowledge the project runs efficiently and the use of new knowledge gathered on the current project helps to support future projects. This process is performed throughout the project.

Fig. 4-3, P 598, *Manage Project Knowledge: Inputs and Outputs*

ANSWER: List of Inputs and Outputs Shown on the next page

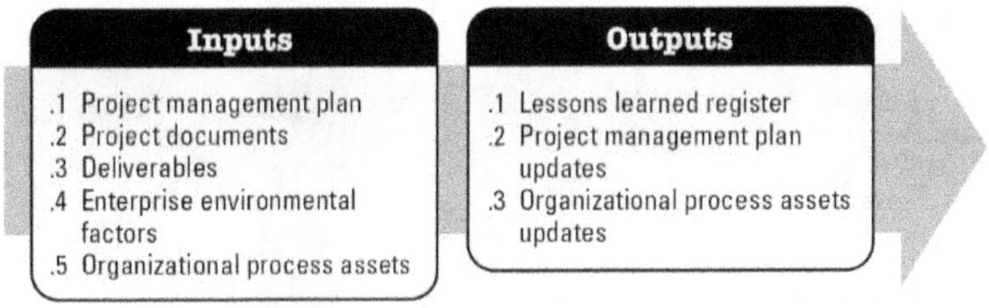

Inputs
.1 Project management plan
.2 Project documents
.3 Deliverables
.4 Enterprise environmental factors
.5 Organizational process assets
Outputs
.1 Lessons learned register
.2 Project management plan updates
.3 Organizational process assets updates

Figure 4-3 (Standard). Manage Project Knowledge: Inputs and Outputs

4.2.1 Project Management Plan Components

Any component in the Project Management Plan can be considered as an Input for the **Project Documents Updates** in this process (P 599).

4.2.2 Project Documents

Some of the possible **Project Documents Updates** that could be Inputs to this process are (P 599):

- Lessons Learned Register
- Project Team Assignments
- Resource Breakdown Structure
- Source Selection Criteria
- Stakeholder Register

4.2.3 Project Management Plan Updates

Any component in the **Project Management Plan** can be **updated** as a result for this process (P 599).

4.3 Manage Quality

Manage Quality is the process of carrying out the Quality Management Plan components decided on originally and turning them into quality policy activities. The key benefit is by using this process the chances of meeting the quality objectives are increased. This process is performed throughout the project.

Fig. 4-4, P 599, *Manage Quality: Inputs and Outputs*

ANSWER: List of Inputs and Outputs Shown on the next page

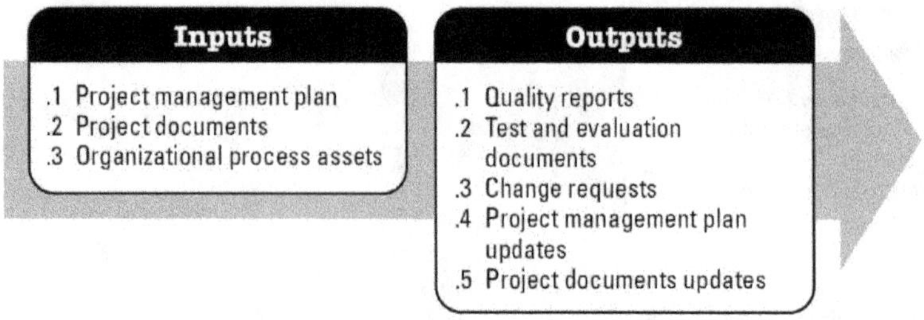

Inputs
.1 Project management plan
.2 Project documents
.3 Organizational process assets
Outputs
.1 Quality reports
.2 Test and evaluation documents
.3 Change requests
.4 Project management plan updates
.5 Project documents updates

Figure 4-4 (Standard). Manage Quality: Inputs and Outputs

4.3.1 Project Management Plan Components

One of the possible **Project Management Plan Components** that may be an Input for this process is the Quality Management Plan (P 600).

4.3.2 Project Documents Examples

Some of the possible **Project Documents Examples** that could be Inputs to this process are (P 600):

- Lessons Learned Register
- Quality Control Measures
- Quality Metric
- Risk Report

4.3.3 Project Management Plan Updates

Some of the possible **Project Management Plan Updates** as a result of this process are (P 600):

- Quality Management Plan
- Scope Baseline
- Schedule Baseline
- Cost Baseline

4.3.4 Project Documents Updates

Some of the possible **Project Documents Updates** as a result of this process are (P 600):

- Issue Log
- Lessons Learned Register
- Risk Register

4.4 Acquire Resources

Acquire Resources is the process of obtaining the resources needed for the project, such as team members, facilities, equipment, materials, supplies, etc. The **key benefit** is by using this process the resources needed are outlined and the selection of resources is guided and assigned to their respective activities. This process is performed throughout the project.

Fig. 4-5, P 601, *Acquire Resources: Inputs and Outputs*

ANSWER: List of Inputs and Outputs Shown on next page

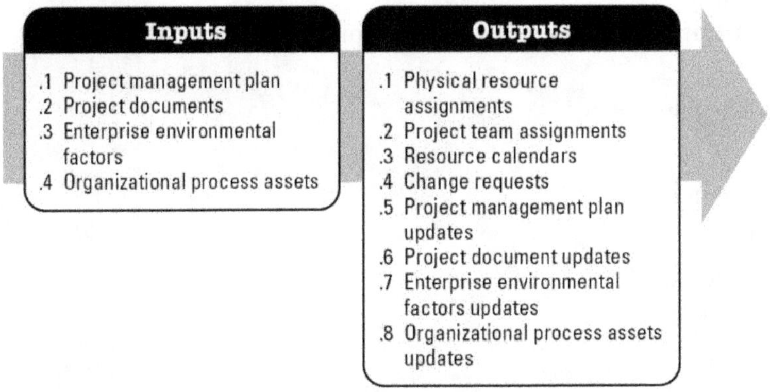
Inputs
.1 Project management plan
.2 Project documents
.3 Enterprise environmental factors
.4 Organizational process assets
Outputs
.1 Physical resource assignments
.2 Project team assignments
.3 Resource calendars
.4 Change requests
.5 Project management plan updates
.6 Project document updates
.7 Enterprise environmental factors updates
.8 Organizational process assets updates

Figure 4-5 (Standard). Acquire Resources: Inputs and Outputs

A Guide to the Project Management Body of Knowledge (PMBOK® Guide) – Sixth Edition.

4.4.1 Project Management Plan Components

Some examples of **Project Management Plan Components** in this process are (P 601):

- Resource Management Plan
- Procurement Management Plan
- Cost Baseline

4.4.2 Project Documents Examples

Some of the possible **Project Documents Examples** that could be Inputs to this process are (P 601):

- Project Schedule
- Resource Calendars
- Resource Requirements
- Stakeholder Register

4.4.3 Project Management Plan Updates

Some of the possible **Project Management Plan Updates** as a result of this process are (P 602):

- Resource Management Plan
- Cost Baseline

4.4.4 Project Documents Updates

Some of the possible **Project Documents Updates** as a result of this process are (P 600):

- Lessons Learned Register
- Project Schedule
- Resource Breakdown Structure
- Resource Calendars
- Resource Requirements
- Risk Register
- Stakeholder Register

4.5 Develop Team

Develop Team is the process of improving competencies, refining the interactions between team members and improving the overall the overall team environment. The **key benefit** is better teamwork relationships, enhanced performance, more motivated employees, etc. This process is performed throughout the project.

Fig. 4-6, P 602, *Develop Team: Inputs and Outputs*

ANSWER: List of Inputs and Outputs Shown Below

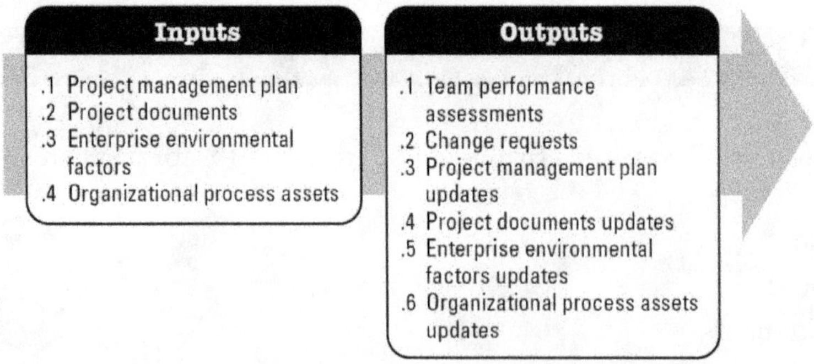

Figure 4-6 (Standard). Develop Team: Inputs and Outputs

A Guide to the Project Management Body of Knowledge (PMBOK® Guide) – Sixth Edition.

4.5.1 Project Management Plan Components

One of the possible **Project Management Plan Components** that could be used as an Input to this process is the Resource Management Plan (P 603).

4.5.2 Project Documents Examples

Some of the possible **Project Documents Examples** that can Inputs to this process are (P 603):

- Lessons Learned Register
- Project Schedule
- Project Team Assignments
- Resource Calendars
- Team Charter

4.5.3 Project Management Plan Updates

One of the possible **Project Management Plan** components that could be **Updated** as a result of this process is the Resource Management Plan (P 603).

4.5.4 Project Documents Updates

Some of the possible **Project Documents Updates** as a result of this process are (P 603):

- Lessons Learned Register
- Project Schedule
- Project Team Assignments
- Resource Calendars
- Team Charter

4.6 Manage Team

Manage Team is the process of tracking team member performance, providing feedback, resolving issues and managing team performance. The **key benefit** of this process is to influence team behavior, manage conflict and resolve issues.

Fig. 4-7, P 604, *Manage Team: Inputs and Outputs*

ANSWER: List of Inputs and Outputs Shown on the next page

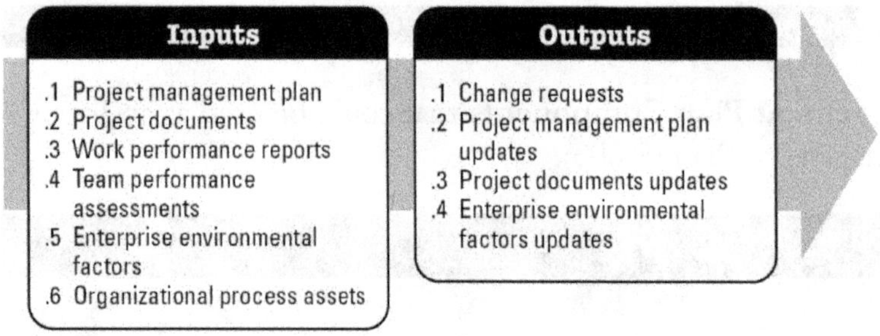
Inputs
.1 Project management plan
.2 Project documents
.3 Work performance reports
.4 Team performance assessments
.5 Enterprise environmental factors
.6 Organizational process assets
Outputs
.1 Change requests
.2 Project management plan updates
.3 Project documents updates
.4 Enterprise environmental factors updates

Figure 4-7 (Standard). Manage Team: Inputs and Outputs

4.6.1 Project Management Plan Components

One of the possible **Project Management Plan Components** that could be used as an Input to this process is the Resource Management Plan (P 604).

4.6.2 Project Documents Examples

Some of the possible **Project Documents Examples** that could be Inputs to this process are (P 604):

- Issue Log
- Lessons Learned
- Project Team Assignments
- Team Charter

4.6.3 Project Management Plan Updates

Some of the possible **Project Management Plan Updates** as a result of this process are (P 605):

- Resource Management Plan
- Schedule Baseline
- Cost Baseline

4.6.4 Project Documents Updates

Some of the possible **Project Documents Updates** as a result of this process are (P 605):

- Issue Log
- Lessons Learned Register
- Project Team Assignments

4.7 Manage Communications

Manage Communications is the process is to ensure timely communication of project information by collecting, creating, distributing, storing, retrieving, managing and the dispersion of that communication. The **key benefit** is to improve the flow of information between the project team and the stakeholders. This process is performed throughout the project.

Fig. 4-8, P 605, *Manage Communications: Inputs and Outputs*

ANSWER: List of Inputs and Outputs Shown Below

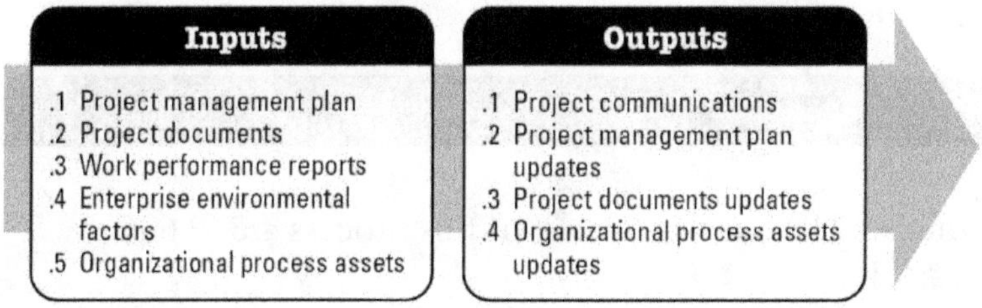

Figure 4-8 (Standard). Manage Communications: Inputs and Outputs

4.7.1 Project Management Plan Components

Some examples of **Project Management Plan Components** in this process are (P 606):

- Resource Management Plan
- Communications Management Plan
- Stakeholder Engagement Plan

4.7.2 Project Documents Examples

Some of the possible **Project Documents Examples** that could be Inputs to this process are (P 606):

- Change Log
- Issue Log
- Lessons Learned Register
- Quality Report
- Risk Report
- Stakeholder Register

4.7.3 Project Management Plan Updates

Some of the possible **Project Management Plan Updates** as a result of this process are (P 605):

- Communications Management Plan
- Stakeholder Engagement Plan

4.7.4 Project Documents Updates

Some of the possible **Project Documents Updates** as a result of this process are (P 606):

- Issue Log
- Lessons Learned Register
- Project Schedule
- Risk Register
- Stakeholder Register

4.8 Implement Risk Responses

Implement Risk Responses is the process of implementing agreed upon risk response plans. The **key benefit** is to ensure the risk responses are acted upon as planned. This process is performed throughout the project.

Fig. 4-9, P 607, *Implement Risk Responses: Inputs and Outputs*

ANSWER: List of Inputs and Outputs Shown on the next page

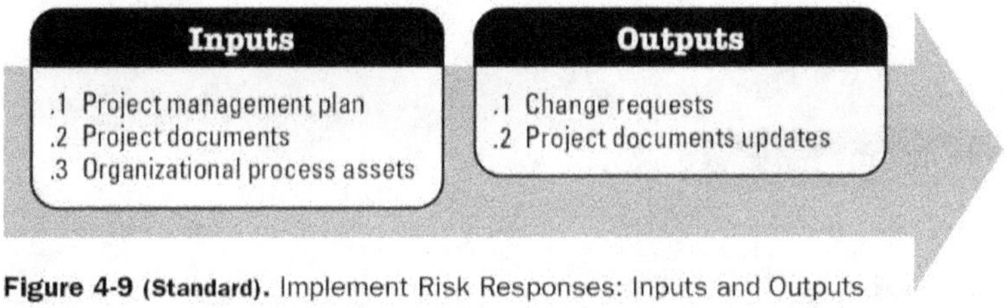

Inputs
.1 Project management plan
.2 Project documents
.3 Organizational process assets
Outputs
.1 Change requests
.2 Project documents updates

Figure 4-9 (Standard). Implement Risk Responses: Inputs and Outputs

4.8.1 Project Management Plan Components

One of the possible **Project Management Plan Components** that could be used as an Input to this process is the Risk Management Plan (P 607).

4.8.2 Project Documents Examples

Some of the possible **Project Documents Examples** that could be Inputs to this process are (P 607):

- Lessons Learned Register
- Risk Register
- Risk Report

4.8.3 Project Documents Updates

Some of the possible **Project Documents Updates** as a result of this process are (P 607):

- Issue Log
- Lessons Learned Register
- Project Team Assignments
- Risk Register
- Risk Report

4.9 Conduct Procurements

Conduct Procurements is the process of Acquiring seller responses, selecting the seller and awarding a contract. The **key benefit** is the selection of a seller and the legal right to ensure delivery. This process is performed throughout the project as needed.

Fig. 4-10, P 608, *Conduct Procurements: Inputs and Outputs*

ANSWER: List of Inputs and Outputs Shown Below

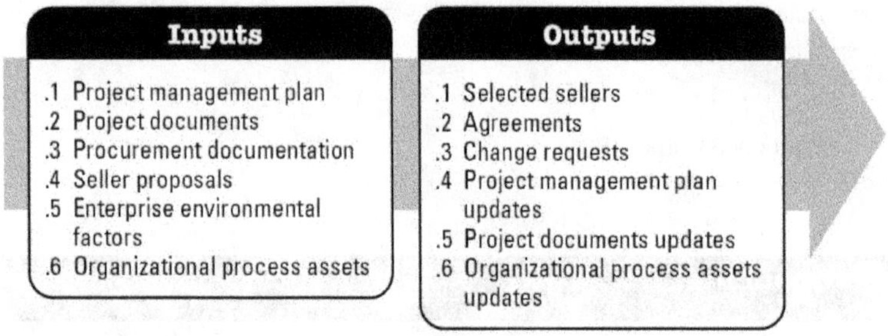

Inputs
.1 Project management plan
.2 Project documents
.3 Procurement documentation
.4 Seller proposals
.5 Enterprise environmental factors
.6 Organizational process assets
Outputs
.1 Selected sellers
.2 Agreements
.3 Change requests
.4 Project management plan updates
.5 Project documents updates
.6 Organizational process assets updates

Figure 4-10 (Standard). Conduct Procurements: Inputs and Outputs

A Guide to the Project Management Body of Knowledge (PMBOK® Guide) – Sixth Edition.

4.9.1 Project Management Plan Components

Some examples of **Project Management Plan Components** in this process are (P 608):

- Scope Management Plan
- Requirements Management Plan
- Communications Management Plan
- Risk Management Plan
- Procurement Management Plan
- Configuration Management Plan
- Cost Baseline

4.9.2 Project Documents Examples

Some of the possible **Project Documents Examples** that could be Inputs to this process are (P 609):

- Lessons Learned Register
- Project Schedule
- Requirements Documentation
- Risk Register
- Stakeholder Register

4.9.3 Project Management Plan Updates

Some of the possible **Project Management Plan Updates** as a result of this process are (P 609):

- Requirements Management Plan
- Quality Management Plan
- Communications Management Plan
- Risk Management Plan
- Procurement Management Plan
- Scope Baseline
- Schedule Baseline
- Cost Baseline

4.9.4 Project Documents Updates

Some of the possible **Project Documents Updates** as a result of this process are (P 607):

- Lessons Learned Register
- Requirements Documentation
- Requirements Traceability Matrix
- Resource Calendar
- Risk Register
- Stakeholder Register

4.10 Manage Stakeholder Engagement

Manage Stakeholder Engagement is the process of communicating with stakeholders to meet their needs and expectations, address issues and encourage engagement. The **key benefit** is to support stakeholder's needs, but also to minimize resistance. This process is performed throughout the project as needed.
Fig., 4-11, P 610, *Manage Stakeholder Engagement: Inputs and Outputs*

ANSWER: List of Inputs and Outputs Shown Below

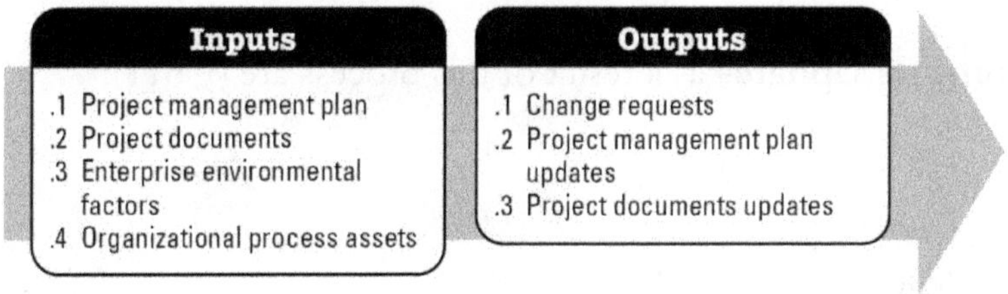

Figure 4-11 (Standard). Manage Stakeholder Engagement: Inputs and Outputs

4.10.1 Project Management Plan Components

Some examples of **Project Management Plan Components** in this process are (P 608):

- Communications Management Plan
- Risk Management Plan
- Stakeholder Engagement Plan
- Change Management Plan

4.10.2 Project Documents Examples

Some of the possible **Project Documents Examples** that could be Inputs to this process are (P 609):

- Change Log
- Issue Log
- Lessons Learned Register
- Stakeholder Register

4.10.3 Project Management Plan Updates

Some of the possible **Project Management Plan Updates** as a result of this process are (P 611):

- Communications Management Plan
- Stakeholder Engagement Plan

4.10.4 Project Documents Updates

Some of the possible **Project Documents Updates** as a result of this process are (P 611):

- Change Log
- Issue Log
- Lessons Learned Register
- Stakeholder Register

5. MONTORING AND CONTROLLING PROCESS GROUP

This group consists of the processes needed to track, review and regulate the project's performance and progress and identify and initiate any needed changes. Monitoring is collecting data, creating performance measures and reporting performance information. Controlling is the comparison of actual performance vs. planned performance. The **Process Group** is considered a background process group, linked by incremental deliverables that are produced as either an output of a specific process group or will serve as an input to another process group. The **key benefit** is that the project's performance is measured at specific intervals, events or when conditions occur and corrections are needed. This group also involves the following (P 613):

- Evaluating change requests and deciding on the appropriate response
- Recommending corrective or preventative action
- Monitoring the ongoing project activities against the project management plan and project baselines
- Influencing the factors that could circumvent the change control process so only approved changes are implemented

By continuously monitoring the project, the project team and stakeholders can identify any areas that may require attention. This group controls the work being done within each knowledge are, process group, life cycle phase and the project as a whole. See Fig. 5-1, P 614, *Monitoring and Controlling Process Group.*

5.1 Monitor and Control Project Work

Monitor and Control Project Work is the process of tracking, reviewing and reporting the overall progress on the project to meet the performance objectives. The **key benefit** is to allow stakeholders to understand the project more thoroughly at given points. This process is performed throughout the project.

Fig. 5-1, P 614, *Monitoring and Controlling Process Group*
Fig. 5-2, P 615, *Monitor and Control Project Work: Inputs and Outputs*

5.1.1 Project Management Plan Components

Any component in the **Project Management Plan** can be an Input for this process (P 615).

5.1.2 Project Documents Examples

Some of the possible **Project Documents Examples** that could be Inputs to this process are (P 615):

- Assumption Log
- Basis of Estimates
- Cost Forecasts
- Change Log
- Issue Log
- Lessons Learned Register
- Milestone List
- Quality Reports
- Risk Register
- Risk Report
- Schedule Forecasts

5.1.3 Project Management Plan Updates

Any component in the **Project Management Plan** can be **Updated** as a result of this process (P 616).

5.1.4 Project Documents Updates

Some of the possible **Project Documents Updates** as a result of this process are (P 616):

- Costs Forecasts
- Issue Log
- Lessons Learned Register
- Risk Register
- Schedule Forecasts

5.2 Perform Integrated Change Control

Perform Integrated Change Control is the process of reviewing, approving and managing all Change Requests to deliverables, organizational process assets, project documents and the Project Management Plan. Communicating the decisions and the resolutions is also included in this process. The **key benefit** is to allow for documented changes to be considered. This process is performed throughout the project.

Fig. 5-3, P 616, *Perform Integrated Change Control: Inputs and Outputs*

ANSWER: List of Inputs and Outputs Shown Below

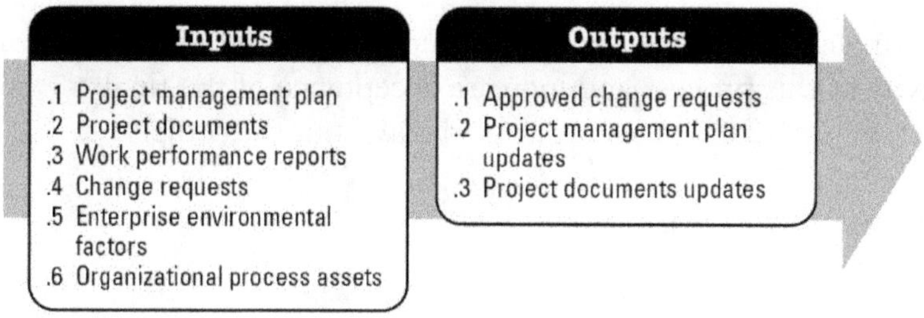

Figure 5-3 (Standard). Perform Integrated Change Control: Inputs and Outputs

A Guide to the Project Management Body of Knowledge (PMBOK® Guide) – Sixth Edition.

5.2.1 Project Management Plan Components

Some examples of **Project Management Plan Components** in this process are (P 617):

- Change Management Plan
- Configuration Management Plan
- Scope Baseline
- Schedule Baseline
- Cost Baseline

5.2.2 Project Documents Examples

Some of the possible **Project Documents Examples** that could be Inputs to this process are (P 617):

- Basis of Estimates
- Requirements Traceability Matrix
- Risk Report

5.2.3 Project Management Plan Updates

Any component in the **Project Management Plan** can be **Updated** as a result of this process (P 617).

5.2.4 Project Documents Updates

Any formally controlled document can be changed in this process. One possibility is the Change Log, used to track changes during a project (P 617).

5.3 Validate Scope

Validate Scope is the process of formalizing the acceptance of completed project deliverables. The **key benefit** is to bring objectivity to this process and increase acceptance of the final product, service or result. This process is performed periodically throughout the project.

Fig. 5-4a, P 618, *Validate Scope: Inputs and Outputs*

ANSWER: List of Inputs and Outputs Shown Below

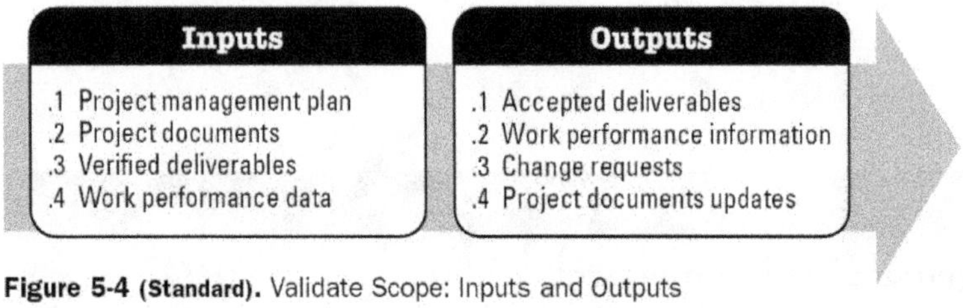

Inputs
.1 Project management plan
.2 Project documents
.3 Verified deliverables
.4 Work performance data
Outputs
.1 Accepted deliverables
.2 Work performance information
.3 Change requests
.4 Project documents updates

Figure 5-4 (Standard). Validate Scope: Inputs and Outputs

5.3.1 Project Management Plan Components

Some examples of **Project Management Plan Components** in this process are (P 618):

- Scope Management Plan
- Requirements Management Plan
- Scope Baseline

5.3.2 Project Documents Examples

Some of the possible **Project Documents Examples** that could be Inputs to this process are (P 618):

- Lessons Learned
- Quality Reports
- Requirements Documentation
- Requirements Traceability Matrix

5.3.3 Project Documents Updates

Some of the possible **Project Documents Updates** as a result of this process are (P 619):

- Lessons Learned
- Quality Reports
- Requirements Documentation
- Requirements Traceability Matrix

5.4 Control Scope

Control Scope is the process of monitoring the progress of the product and the product scope and monitoring changes to the Scope Baseline. The **key benefit** is the Scope Baseline is maintained during the project. This process is performed throughout the project.

Fig. 5-5, P 619, *Control Scope: Inputs and Outputs*

ANSWER: List of Inputs and Outputs Shown Below

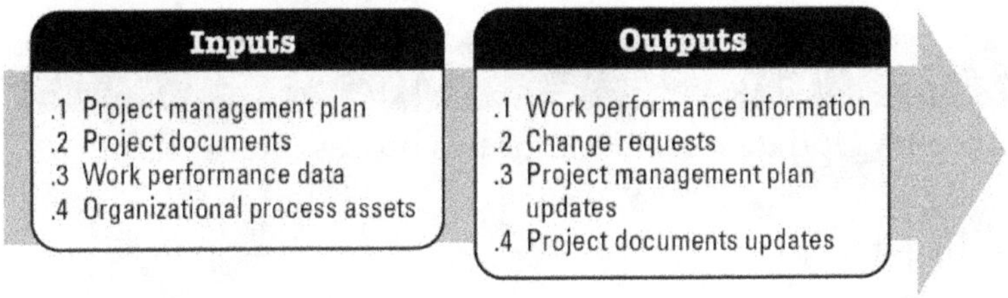

Inputs
.1 Project management plan
.2 Project documents
.3 Work performance data
.4 Organizational process assets
Outputs
.1 Work performance information
.2 Change requests
.3 Project management plan updates
.4 Project documents updates

Figure 5-5 (Standard). Control Scope: Inputs and Outputs

5.4.1 Project Management Plan Components

Some examples of **Project Management Plan Components** in this process are (P 619):

- Scope Management Plan
- Requirements Management Plan
- Change Management Plan
- Configurations Management Plan
- Scope Baseline
- Performance Measurement Baseline

5.4.2 Project Documents Examples

Some of the possible **Project Documents Examples** that could be Inputs to this process are (P 620):

- Lessons Learned Register
- Requirements Documentation
- Requirements Traceability Matrix

5.4.3 Project Management Plan Updates

Some of the possible **Project Management Plan Updates** as a result of this process are (P 620):

- Scope Management Plan
- Scope Baseline
- Schedule Baseline
- Cost Baseline
- Performance Measurement Baseline

5.4.4 Project Documents Updates

Some of the possible **Project Documents Updates** as a result of this process are (P 620):

- Lessons Learned Register
- Requirements Documentation
- Requirements Traceability Matrix

5.5 Control Schedule

Control Schedule is the process of monitoring the status of the project, update the project schedule and manage changes to the Schedule Baseline. The **key benefit** is to allow for documented changes to be considered. This process is the Schedule Baseline is maintained. This process is performed throughout the project.

Fig. 5-6, P 621, *Control Schedule: Inputs and Outputs*

ANSWER: List of Inputs and Outputs Shown Below

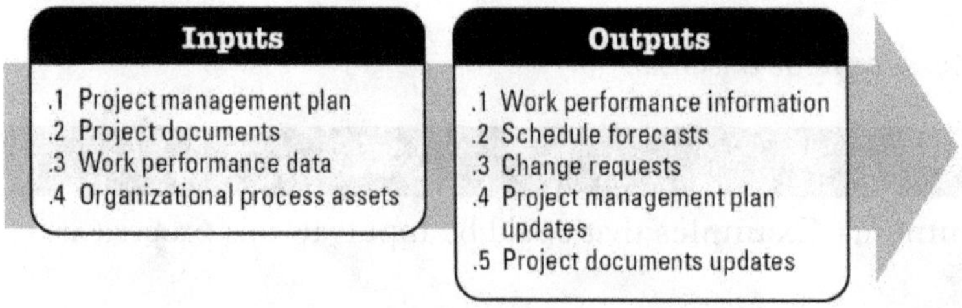

Figure 5-6 (Standard). Control Schedule: Inputs and Outputs

A Guide to the Project Management Body of Knowledge (PMBOK® Guide) – Sixth Edition.

5.5.1 Project Management Plan Components

Some examples of **Project Management Plan Components** in this process are (P 621):

- Schedule Management Plan
- Schedule Baseline
- Scope Baseline
- Performance Measurement Baseline

5.5.2 Project Documents Examples

Some of the possible **Project Documents Examples** that could be Inputs to this process are (P 621):

- Lessons Learned Register
- Project Calendars
- Project Schedule
- Resource Calendars
- Schedule Data

5.5.3 Project Management Plan Updates

Some of the possible **Project Management Plan Updates** as a result of this process are (P 622):

- Schedule Management Plan
- Schedule Baseline
- Cost Baseline
- Performance Measurement Baseline

5.5.4 Project Documents Updates

Some of the possible **Project Documents Updates** as a result of this process are (P 622):

- Assumption Log
- Basis of Estimates
- Lessons Learned Register
- Project schedule
- Resource calendars
- Risk Register
- Schedule Data

5.6 Control Costs

Control Costs is the process of monitoring the status of the project to update the project costs and manage change. The **key benefit** is the Cost Baseline is maintained. This process is performed throughout the project.

Fig. 5-7, P 622, *Control Costs: Inputs and Outputs*

ANSWER: List of Inputs and Outputs Shown Below

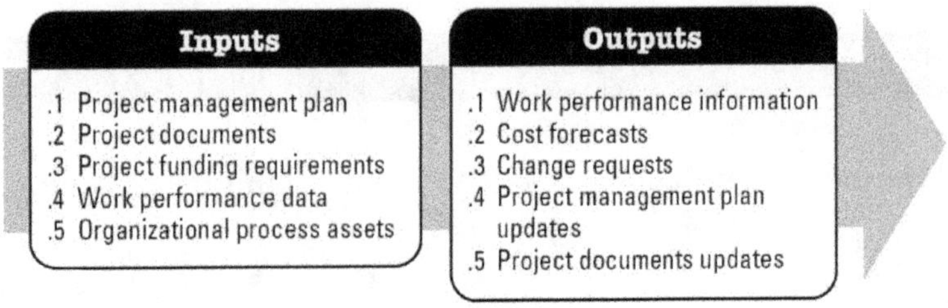

Inputs
.1 Project management plan
.2 Project documents
.3 Project funding requirements
.4 Work performance data
.5 Organizational process assets
Outputs
.1 Work performance information
.2 Cost forecasts
.3 Change requests
.4 Project management plan updates
.5 Project documents updates

Figure 5-7 (Standard). Control Costs: Inputs and Outputs

A Guide to the Project Management Body of Knowledge (PMBOK® Guide) – Sixth Edition.

5.6.1 Project Management Plan Components

Some examples of **Project Management Plan Components** in this process are (P 623):

- Cost Management Plan
- Cost Baseline
- Performance Measurement Baseline

5.6.2 Project Documents Examples

A **Project Documents Example** is the Lessons Learned Register (P 623).

5.6.3 Project Management Plan Updates

Some of the possible **Project Management Plan Updates** as a result of this process are (P 623):

- Cost Management Plan
- Cost Baseline
- Performance Measurement Baseline

5.6.4 Project Documents Updates

Some of the possible **Project Documents Updates** as a result of this process are (P 623):

- Assumption Log
- Basis of Estimates
- Cost Estimates
- Lessons Learned Register
- Risk Register

5.7 Control Quality

Control Costs is the process of recording the results of the Quality Management activities to ensure they meet the customer's satisfaction. The **key benefit** is to verify the project deliverables and work performed meet the expected requirements by key stakeholders. This process is performed throughout the project. S

Fig. 5-8, P 624, *Control Quality: Inputs and Outputs*

ANSWER: List of Inputs and Outputs Shown Below

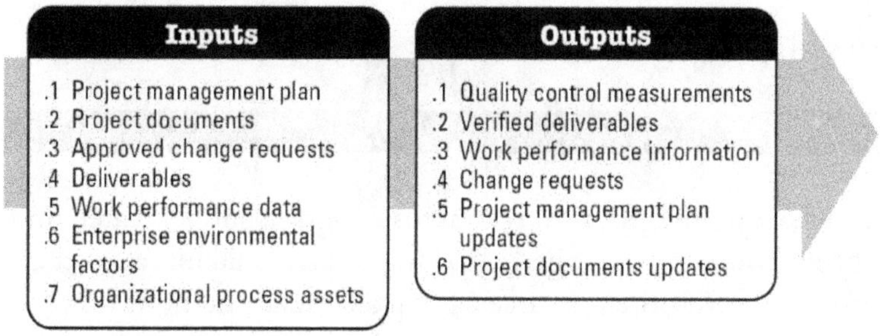
Inputs
.1 Project management plan
.2 Project documents
.3 Approved change requests
.4 Deliverables
.5 Work performance data
.6 Enterprise environmental factors
.7 Organizational process assets
Outputs
.1 Quality control measurements
.2 Verified deliverables
.3 Work performance information
.4 Change requests
.5 Project management plan updates
.6 Project documents updates

Figure 5-8 (Standard). Control Quality: Inputs and Outputs

A Guide to the Project Management Body of Knowledge (PMBOK® Guide) – Sixth Edition.

5.7.1 Project Management Plan Components

One example of a **Project Management Plan** component is the Quality Management Plan (P 624).

5.7.2 Project Documents Examples

Some of the possible **Project Documents Examples** that could be Inputs to this process are (P 624):

- Lessons Learned Register
- Quality Metrics
- Test and Evaluation

5.7.3 Project Management Plan Updates

One example of the **Project Management Plan Updates** is the Quality Management Plan (P 625).

5.7.4 Project Documents Updates

Some of the possible **Project Documents Updates** as a result of this process are (P 625):

- Issue Log
- Lessons Learned Register
- Risk Register
- Test and Evaluation Documents

5.8 Control Resources

Control Resources is the process of ensuring the physical resources assigned and allocated are available as planned. Monitoring those resources as planned vs. actual means making corrects, if and when needed. The **key benefit** is to verify the resources are available at the right time and the right place, and all resources are released when no longer needed. This process is performed throughout the project.

Fig. 5-9, P 625, C*ontrol Resources: Inputs and Outputs*

ANSWER: List of Inputs and Outputs Shown on the next page

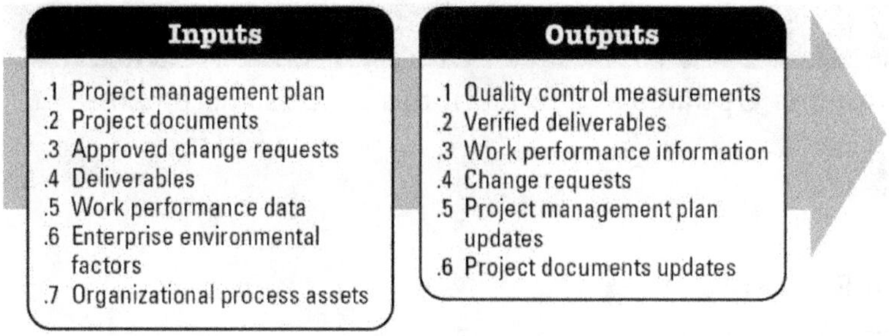

Figure 5-8 (Standard). Control Quality: Inputs and Outputs

5.8.1 Project Management Plan Components

One example of a **Project Management Plan** component is the Resource Management Plan (P 626).

5.8.2 Project Documents Examples

Some of the possible **Project Documents Examples** that could be Inputs to this process are (P 626):

- Issue Log
- Lessons Learned Register
- Physical Resource Assignments
- Project Schedule
- Resource Breakdown Structure
- Resource Requirements
- Risk Register

5.8.3 Project Management Plan Updates

Some of the possible **Project Management Plan Updates** as a result of this process are (P 626):

- Resource Management Plan
- Schedule Baseline
- Cost Baseline

5.8.4 Project Documents Updates

Some of the possible **Project Documents Updates** as a result of this process are (P 626):

- Assumption Log
- Issue Log
- Lessons Learned Register
- Physical Resource Assignments
- Resource Breakdown Structure
- Risk Register

5.9 Monitor Communications

Monitor Communications is the process of ensuring the information needs of the project and the stakeholders are met. The **key benefit** is to provide the smooth flow of information as defined in the Communications Management Plan and the Stakeholder Engagement Plan. This process is performed throughout the project.

Fig. 5-10, P 627, *Monitor Communications: Inputs and Outputs*

ANSWER: List of Inputs and Outputs Shown Below

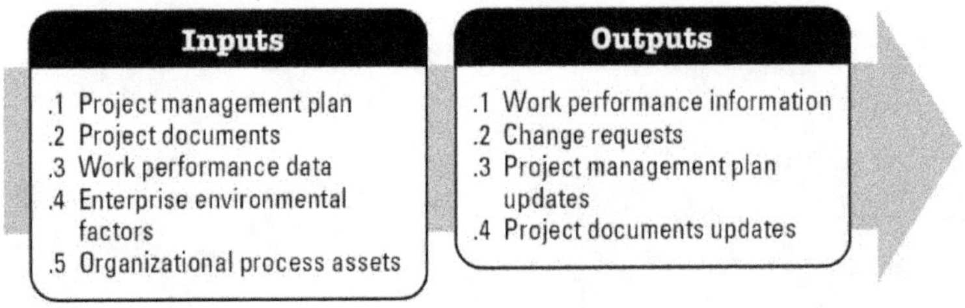

Figure 5-10 (Standard). Monitor Communications: Inputs and Outputs

5.9.1 Project Management Plan Components

Some examples of **Project Management Plan Components** in this process are (P 627):

- Resource Management Plan
- Communications Management Plan
- Stakeholder Engagement Plan
-

5.9.2 Project Documents Examples

Some of the possible **Project Documents Examples** that could be Inputs to this process are (P 627):

- Issue Log
- Lessons Learned Register
- Project Communications

5.9.3 Project Management Plan Updates

Some of the possible **Project Management Plan Updates** as a result of this process are (P 628):

- Communications Management Plan
- Stakeholder Engagement Plan

5.9.4 Project Documents Updates

Some of the possible **Project Documents Updates** as a result of this process are (P 628):

- Issue Log
- Lessons Learned Register
- Stakeholder Register

5.10 Monitor Risks

Monitor Risks is the process of monitoring the implementation of agreed–upon risk response plans, tracking and identifying risks and analyzing new risks and evaluating risk process effectiveness. The **key benefit** is to make decisions on current information regarding overall and individual project risks. This process is performed throughout the project.

Fig. 5-11, P 628, *Monitor Risks: Inputs and Outputs*

ANSWER: List of Inputs and Outputs Shown on the next page

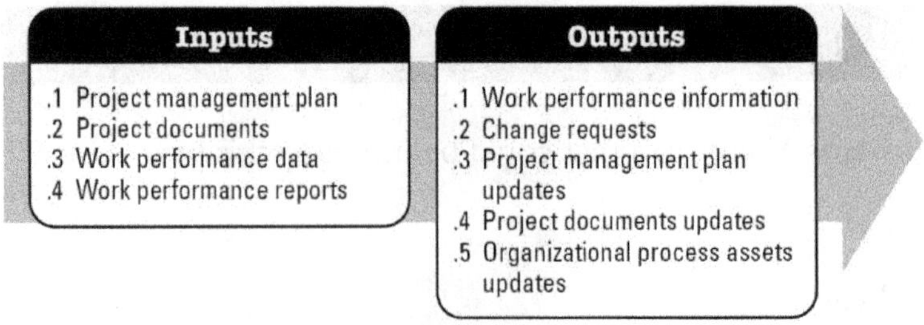

Inputs
.1 Project management plan
.2 Project documents
.3 Work performance data
.4 Work performance reports
Outputs
.1 Work performance information
.2 Change requests
.3 Project management plan updates
.4 Project documents updates
.5 Organizational process assets updates

Figure 5-11 (Standard). Monitor Risks: Inputs and Outputs

5.10.1 Project Management Plan Components

One example of a **Project Management Plan** component is the Risk Management Plan (P 629).

5.10.2 Project Documents Examples

Some of the possible **Project Documents Examples** that could be Inputs to this process are (P 629):

- Issue Log
- Lessons Learned Register
- Risk Register
- Risk Report

5.10.3 Project Management Plan Updates

Any component in the Project Management Plan can be considered as an Input for the **Project Management Plan Updates** in this process (P 629).

5.10.4 Project Documents Updates

Some of the possible **Project Documents Updates** as a result of this process are (P 629):

- Assumption Log
- Issue Log
- Lessons Learned Register
- Risk Register
- Risk Report

5.11 Control Procurements

Monitor Risks is the process of managing procurement relationships, monitoring contract performance, implementing any needed corrections and closing of contracts. The **key benefit** is that it ensures both seller and buyer meet the project specifications according to the legal contracts both parties agreed to be bound by. This process is performed throughout the project when procurements are active. S

Fig. 5-12, P 630, *Control Procurements: Inputs and Outputs*

ANSWER: List of Inputs and Outputs Shown Below

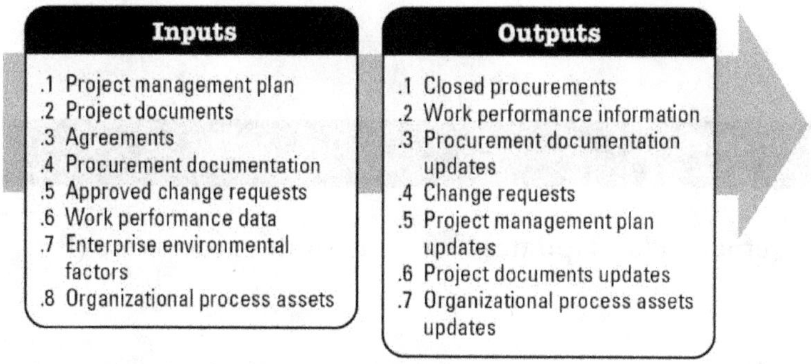
Inputs
.1 Project management plan
.2 Project documents
.3 Agreements
.4 Procurement documentation
.5 Approved change requests
.6 Work performance data
.7 Enterprise environmental factors
.8 Organizational process assets
Outputs
.1 Closed procurements
.2 Work performance information
.3 Procurement documentation updates
.4 Change requests
.5 Project management plan updates
.6 Project documents updates
.7 Organizational process assets updates

Figure 5-12 (Standard). Control Procurements: Inputs and Outputs

A Guide to the Project Management Body of Knowledge (PMBOK® Guide) – Sixth Edition.

5.11.1 Project Management Plan Components

Some examples of **Project Management Plan Components** in this process are (P 630):

- Requirements Management Plan
- Risk Management Plan
- Procurement Management Plan
- Change Management Plan
- Schedule Baseline

5.11.2 Project Documents Examples

Some of the possible **Project Documents Examples** that could be Inputs to this process are (P 630):

- Assumption Log
- Lessons Learned Register
- Milestone List
- Quality Reports
- Requirements Documentation
- Requirements Traceability matrix
- Risk Register
- Stakeholder Register

5.11.3 Project Management Plan Updates

Some of the possible **Project Management Plan Updates** as a result of this process are (P 631):

- Risk Management Plan
- Procurement Management Plan
- Schedule baseline
- Cost baseline

5.11.4 Project Documents Updates

Some of the possible **Project Documents Updates** as a result of this process are (P 631):

- Lessons Learned Register
- Resource Requirements
- Requirements Traceability Matrix
- Risk Register
- Stakeholder Register

5.12 Monitor Stakeholder Engagement

Monitor Stakeholder Engagement is the process of managing stakeholder relationships and tailoring strategies. The **key benefit** is that it maintains or increases stakeholder engagement. This process is performed throughout the project. S

Fig. 5-13, P 631, *Monitor Stakeholder Engagement: Inputs and Outputs*
ANSWER: List of Inputs and Outputs Shown Below

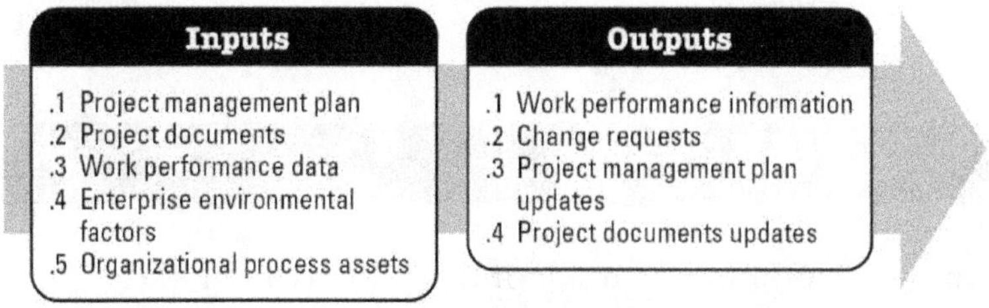
Inputs
.1 Project management plan
.2 Project documents
.3 Work performance data
.4 Enterprise environmental factors
.5 Organizational process assets
Outputs
.1 Work performance information
.2 Change requests
.3 Project management plan updates
.4 Project documents updates

Figure 5-13 (Standard). Monitor Stakeholder Engagement: Inputs and Outputs
A Guide to the Project Management Body of Knowledge (PMBOK® Guide) – Sixth Edition.

5.12.1 Project Management Plan Components

Some examples of **Project Management Plan Components** in this process are (P 632):

- Resource Management Plan
- Communications Management Plan
- Stakeholder engagement Plan

5.12.2 Project Documents Examples

Some of the possible **Project Documents Examples** that could be Inputs to this process are (P 632):

- Issue Log
- Lessons Learned Register
- Project Communications
- Risk Register
- Stakeholder Register

5.12.3 Project Management Plan Updates

Some of the possible **Project Management Plan Updates** as a result of this process are (P 632):

- Resource Management Plan
- Communications Management Plan
- Stakeholder Engagement Plan

5.12.4 Project Documents Updates

Some of the possible **Project Documents Updates** as a result of this process are (P 632):

- Issue Log
- Lessons Learned Register
- Risk Register
- Stakeholder Register

6. CLOSING PROCESS GROUP

The Closing Process Group is the final process in closing down the project work. This process results in officially completing the project, phase or contractual obligations incurred in the project. These administrative, financial, lessons learned, and legal steps closed, assure the stakeholders the project work is complete and meets the expectations and deliverables required by the sponsors and stakeholders. There is only one process in this group, but it may also address early closure projects, aborted projects, or cancelled projects. See Fig. 6-1, P 633, *Closing Process Group*.

6.1. Close Project or Phase

Close Project or Phase is the process of finalizing all activities. The **key benefit** is the project or phase information is archived, the planned work complete and organizational resources are released. This process is performed once, or at predefined points throughout the project.

Fig. 6-2, P 634 *Close Project or Phase: Inputs and Outputs*

ANSWER: List of Inputs and Outputs Shown Below

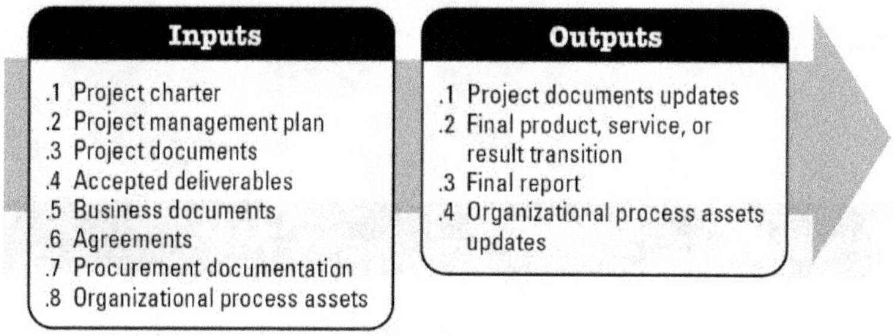
Inputs
.1 Project charter
.2 Project management plan
.3 Project documents
.4 Accepted deliverables
.5 Business documents
.6 Agreements
.7 Procurement documentation
.8 Organizational process assets
Outputs
.1 Project documents updates
.2 Final product, service, or result transition
.3 Final report
.4 Organizational process assets updates

Figure 6-2 (Standard). Close Project or Phase: Inputs and Outputs

6.1.1 Project Management Plan Components

Project Management Plan Components may be comprised of any component in the Project Management Plan and become Inputs to this process (P 634).

6.1.2 Project Documents Examples

Some of the possible **Project Documents Examples** that could be Inputs to this process are (P 634):

- Assumption Log
- Basis of Estimates
- Change Log
- Issue Log
- Lessons Learned Register
- Milestone List
- Project Communications
- Quality Control Measurements
- Quality Reports
- Requirements Documentation
- Risk Register
- Risk Report

6.1.3 Project Documents Updates

Any **Project Documents Updates** in this process could include the Lessons Learned Register.